Oracle Press™

Effective Oracle Database 10*g* Security by Design

David Knox

McGraw-Hill/Osborne

New York Chicago San Francisco
Lisbon London Madrid Mexico City Milan
New Delhi San Juan Seoul Singapore Sydney Toronto

The McGraw-Hill Companies

McGraw-Hill/Osborne
2100 Powell Street, 10th Floor
Emeryville, California 94608
U.S.A.

To arrange bulk purchase discounts for sales promotions, premiums, or fund-raisers, please contact **McGraw-Hill**/Osborne at the above address. For information on translations or book distributors outside the U.S.A., please see the International Contact Information page immediately following the index of this book.

Effective Oracle Database 10*g* Security by Design

1234567890 CUS CUS 01987654

ISBN 0-07-223130-0

Publisher
Brandon A. Nordin

Vice President & Associate Publisher
Scott Rogers

Editorial Director
Wendy Rinaldi

Acquisitions Editor
Lisa McClain

Project Editor
Jenn Tust

Acquisitions Coordinator
Athena Honore

Technical Editors
Wendy Delmolino,
Thomas Kyte

Copy Editor
Sally Engelfried

Proofreader
Marian Selig

Indexer
Valerie Perry

Composition
John Patrus,
Kelly Stanton-Scott

Illustrators
Kathleen Edwards,
Melinda Lytle

Series Design
Jani Beckwith,
Peter F. Hancik

Cover Series Design
Damore Johann Design, Inc.

This book was composed with Corel VENTURA™ Publisher.

This book is dedicated to my parents, Larry and Maggie Knox, whose unconditional love and support have made me possible.

About the Author

David Knox began working at Oracle in early 1995. It wasn't long after his first day that he was asked to work on a security-related project for one of Oracle's government customers. He has been working with Oracle security ever since. David has had the opportunity to work on security issues with many interesting people in the United States Department of Defense and the intelligence community as well as in financial services, healthcare, and higher education. All of the exposure to database security inspired him to obtain his graduate degree in computer science. David's security expertise derives not only from graduate work but also from years of experience in hands-on practice with Oracle.

Through the years, David has worked with Oracle's development teams, sales organizations, and consultants in almost all areas of security. He has the opportunity to review and understand many of Oracle's customer's requirements as well as to help architect and implement solutions for those requirements. The solutions range from applying the current technologies in new and innovative ways to creating pre-packaged consulting solutions and ultimately providing input for product requirements for future enhancements to the Oracle Database. David has created and delivered countless security classes for Oracle Consulting and technical sales support, Oracle's partner companies, and Oracle customers.

David also has authored white papers as well as contributed to books, such as *Expert One on One Oracle* by Thomas Kyte (Wrox Press, 2001) and *Mastering Oracle PL/SQL: Practical Solutions* (Apress, December 2003).

These days you can find David working as the chief engineer in Oracle's Information Assurance Center (IAC). The IAC is a center of expertise that works with Oracle's customers, partners, development, and consulting to design and develop security and high-availability solutions. His work is concentrated on the computer security areas, but his tasks vary widely: delivering presentations, participating in panel discussions, working with consultants, teaching classes, meeting with customers, and answering general security questions on Oracle's internal security lists.

About the Tech Editors

Wendy Delmolino is a master principal sales consultant for Oracle Corporation with over 12 years experience supporting the United States federal government. Wendy specializes in Oracle's Information Assurance technologies and architectures, with an emphasis on Oracle Database security. She leads the Oracle Federal group in recommending security architectures and teaches Oracle Database security courses. In support of her customers, Wendy devises solutions and provides oversight for many of the intelligence community's past, current, and future requirements within Oracle Corporation. Wendy and her husband, Dominic, live outside Washington, DC, and have two children, Peter and Francesca.

Thomas Kyte is a vice president in the Oracle Government, Education, and Healthcare group and is recognized as one of the world's leading Oracle experts. Tom has been working with Oracle technology since version 5.1.5c (a $99 single-user version for DOS that came on 360K floppy disks) and joined Oracle Corporation in 1993. Before starting at Oracle, Tom worked for over six years as a systems integrator building large-scale, heterogeneous databases and applications, mostly for military and government customers. He is the "Tom" behind the "Ask Tom" column in *Oracle Magazine*, where he answers questions about the Oracle Database and its tools. Tom is also the author of *Expert One on One Oracle* (Wrox Press, 2001) and *Effective Oracle by Design* (McGraw-Hill/Osborne, 2003).

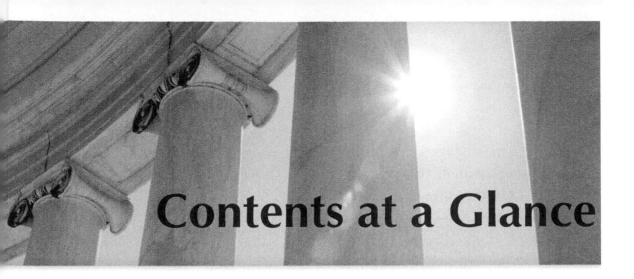

Contents at a Glance

PART V
Appendixes

Contents

PART II

Identification and Authentication

PART III
Authorizations and Auditing

PART IV

Fine-Grained Access Control

PART V

Appendixes

Foreword

Experience is often the best teacher. That's true for life in general and certainly true for cybersecurity. In my experience in the security world, including 32 years at the Central Intelligence Agency, I've not found anyone with more experience in the theory and practice of protecting data than David Knox. David's expertise in this field is born of both his academic training and especially his more than eight years of hands-on experience with Oracle Corporation. In my view, the real value of this book is centered in David's ability to treat technical issues in depth as well as his ability to discuss these issues in terms that the less technically inclined of us can understand. That's especially important today because cybersecurity is as much a responsibility of the CEO and the Board of Directors as it is of the organization's information technology provider. This book may not replace your favorite mystery novel on your bedside table, but I guarantee it will become dog-eared with use. Mine has.

—David W. Carey
former Executive Director
of the Central Intelligence Agency

Acknowledgments

This book represents a lot of hard work and dedication from many people. First, I would like to acknowledge my mentors within Oracle. Tim Hoechst and Dave Carey have been especially supportive in helping me allocate the necessary time to complete this work. My colleagues have also been supportive in many ways, from agreeing to review the work to providing technical information and ideas. I would like to thank all those who have done so. I would especially like to thank Matt Piermarini and Patrick Sack, who have both been invaluable in helping me understand and articulate the security message as it relates to application development. Daniel Wong, Kristy Edwards, and Sudha Iyer in Oracle development were also very helpful and supportive in reviewing the material for accuracy and congruence with Oracle's product intentions and directions; thank you for helping out.

The staff at McGraw-Hill/Osborne has been great to work with. Lisa McClain, Athena Honore, Jenn Tust, and Sally Engelfried have been supportive and understanding in all matters related to the construction of the book, and I cannot thank you enough for your patience and direction. I'd also like to thank the Illustration and Production departments for making the book look so great.

The technical reviewers, Wendy Delmolino and Thomas Kyte, are two important people to ensuring the book's success. Wendy's technical contributions to the editing process have been insightful and valuable. Thank you for taking the time to review and comment on the material. It has been a pleasure working with you on security through the years.

Thomas Kyte has done the most for me in influencing the technical material in this book. Not only did he inspire me to write the book by showing leadership in technical authoring, he helped make the examples more practical. I have learned a tremendous amount from working with Tom over the years in both how the database works and how to write about it. Thank you, Tom, for your candid comments, suggestions, leadership, and friendship. Without your input, this would not be the same book.

Finally, and most importantly, I would like to thank my wife, Sandy, and sons Garrett and Trevor. Sandy's support in writing this book is unparalleled. There have been countless late nights, lost weekends, and impeded vacations that were necessary to complete this work. The hardest part in writing this book has been depriving my family of quality focus and time. Sandy, your understanding and support for this, especially in handling Garrett and Trevor, has been incredible. I love you for it and hope you feel an accomplishment has been reached for you, too. This book could not have been written without your love, support, and dedication. I will never forget it.

Introduction

The database has two important roles: 1. Serve the data—databases are commonly referred to as data servers; 2. Protect the data. Yes that's right, the database is there to serve and protect. Database security features are vast and complex. While the complexity can afford us many ways to provide a robust database application, it also can be very confusing. Users need to know what is available, when to use it, when not to use it, and how it can be leveraged with other complementary technologies. Knowledge is power. Not utilizing these features is analogous to the blinking 12:00 on the VCR—you are not getting your money's worth.

Effective Oracle Database 10g Security by Design provides solutions for the Oracle security puzzle and includes the new Oracle Database 10*g* features. Recommendations, best practices, and code examples lead the reader through examples that illustrate how to build secure applications. This book shows how to effectively utilize, in a complementary manner, the most common Oracle product features: proxy authentication, secure application roles, Enterprise Users, Virtual Private Database, Oracle Label Security, database encryption, and standard and fine-grained auditing. Web applications and client-server applications are addressed as well as PL/SQL programming security best practices. The explanations allow a non-security expert to grasp the relevance of the technology, and the countless examples comprehensively show the different nuances associated with each technology. All of the information will allow you to effectively design, develop, and deploy secure database applications.

This book is targeted to Oracle Database application developers, Oracle DBAs, and anyone whose role is to ensure that proper procedures and due diligence have been followed in building applications (CIO's, CISO's, etc.). This book is about designing, building, and deploying secure applications running against an Oracle Database. The challenge faced for people wishing to do this today is that there are few, if any, best practice documents, technical blueprints (architectures), or other reference guidelines showing how to link together varying technologies to build secure database applications.

Chapter 1 explores security in a broad sense, which is important in understanding the role security plays. Chapter 2 highlights certain fundamental aspects of Oracle Database security. Next, you are led through a natural sequence of security technologies, beginning with Identification and Authentication—the first step to implementing security! This section includes discussions and deep examples of proxy authentication, connection pools, and Enterprise Users.

"Authorizations and Auditing" reviews how privileges can be assigned, enforced, managed, and audited. You will see the best practices for handling privileges for applications as well as view effective auditing techniques. The last section explains the implementation of Oracle's fine-grained access control features, which include column-level security, row-level security with views, VPD, OLS, and the new DBMS_CRYPTO encryption package. The new Oracle Database 10*g* features aren't alluded to or quickly summarized but rather are presented in comprehensive yet easy-to-understand detail.

Throughout the book, careful attention has been paid to provide enough information to describe a technology without being redundant with Oracle Corporation's existing documentation. Since it's useful to be pointed to the place in the official documentation that describes a technology, you'll see references to other documents throughout the book. Unless otherwise noted, the documents are part of Oracle Corporation's product documentation, which can be retrieved from the Oracle Technology Network web site at http://otn.oracle.com.

The examples given in this book are generally run by the SEC_MGR. See Appendix A for how this schema is created and how privileges are granted. Many of the examples are drawn from or use the SCOTT schema and the EMP and DEPT tables, because the tables are simple and most Oracle DBAs are familiar with this schema. The script to install SCOTT is located in the $ORACLE_HOME/rdbms/admin/scott.sql file. A BLAKE user was also created for some of the examples. You can create this user as follows:

```
CREATE USER blake IDENTIFIED BY blake;
GRANT CREATE SESSION TO blake;
```

Almost all the code samples are displayed as the output from a SQL*Plus session. There are three reasons for this. First, it shows and validates that the example works. Second, line numbers are automatically displayed, which helps in the readability of the code. Third, the SQL*Plus prompt has been set up with the user's name and database instance. This was performed by adding the following code to the login.sql file in the $ORACLE_HOME/sqlplus/admin directory.

```
COLUMN global_name new_value gname
SET termout off
SELECT    LOWER (USER) =
       || '@'
       || DECODE (GLOBAL_NAME,
                  'KNOX10G', 'KNOX10g',
                  GLOBAL_NAME) GLOBAL_NAME
  FROM GLOBAL_NAME;
SET sqlprompt '&gname> '
SET termout on
```

This step is helpful because it shows who was executing the code and on which database. I find it is too easy to get confused without these hints.

While product documentation covers the features and functions of a specific product or technology, it often omits how to piece together these various technologies to create effective layers of security. For example, Oracle documentation may describe how to set up Enterprise Users, but it doesn't give any examples of how to link Enterprise Users with proxy authentication, auditing, and its row-level security products. It's rational that the documentation remains autonomous; however, it's then incumbent upon the developer, architect, or DBA to figure out how to link these eclectic pieces together to form some basis of security. They also, then, have to decide when *it is* and *is not* appropriate to use a technology. This book offers not only brief functional descriptions, but also instructions on how to use these technologies as tools to build a high assurance technology platform.

PART I

Quick Start

CHAPTER 1

General Security Best Practices

ecuring the database may be the single biggest action an organization can take in proactively defending itself against the myriad of unforeseen hostile intruders. Databases are the vaults that hold an organization's most valuable digital assets. Compromise of these assets can lead to negative publicity, litigation, lost revenue, loss of customer trust, and many other negative results.

Securing your databases may sound like a simple task, but there are many things you have to understand to do this effectively; and many of the actions and much of the knowledge doesn't even involve technology! Unlike the following chapters, which focus on Oracle database security with lots of sample code, the discussion in this chapter is high level (without any code) and meant to explain the principles and concepts that the examples in the following chapters will adhere to.

This chapter outlines my philosophy on cyber security and fundamental security best practices. These concepts are important as they serve as the guiding principles for understanding and employing effective security. This chapter will paint the security landscape by outlining the processes and defining the concepts, principles, and challenges for implementing effective security. While not meant to be a complete guide to all the security issues, material presented here can serve either as a security primer or as a reminder of the things that should be considered.

Security Policies

Good security implementations are based on good security policies. Security begins not with encryption algorithms, firewalls, or advanced authentication techniques; it begins with a clear and well-defined security policy. The policies define the rules by which everyone should abide. They provide the guidance necessary for effective implementations. Put another way, how can you know if someone is breaking the rules if no one has clearly defined what the rules are?

TIP
Security begins with a clear and comprehensive security policy.

Most people will argue that the Information Technology (IT) security policies are self-evident: users shouldn't do what they're not supposed to do. This isn't good enough. Without a clearly defined policy, there is nothing to implement, nothing to enforce, and no way of knowing if you are secure because there is no reference for comparison.

There must be specific policies about authentication, access control, and auditing. Confidentiality and privacy concerns have to be addressed as well. However, there is no "one-size-fits-all" security policy. Determining *how* to protect is based on *what* you are trying to protect.

An important part to ensuring the policies are effective is by making sure they are supported by the senior management within an organization. Security is a shared responsibility. It is not just your responsibility; it's also your CEO's. However, the CEO may or may not realize this. The senior management should support the security culture through means such as funding, the creation and support of dedicated security personnel, and above all, endorsements that stress the importance of adhering to the company policy.

TIP
Security is a shared responsibility between IT and the organization's CEO.

Different Policies for Different Needs

There is a direct correlation between the security policies, the security implementations, and the data. Security policies range from general and generic to extremely specific. From an IT perspective, they initially apply to all applications throughout an enterprise. For example, a policy might dictate that auditing will be conducted for user accountability. The general policy may not specify how, when, or to what level of detail the auditing needs to take place. As applications are developed and fielded, the security policies associated with the applications can become more specific to the applications.

An application that handles company financial data may further augment the auditing requirement by specifying that auditing will occur within the database and operating systems and will capture all user actions for all transactions of a specific type. The policy might also specify how and for how long the audit records will be managed. A separate application, in contrast, may only audit users as they log on and log off, with no audit retention period specified.

As discussed, the policies can vary in level of detail and level of enforcement. These variations are based on the data sensitivity and the application's intended use. For sensitive data, such as proprietary data, the policies are strict and may cover everything from the physical protection to availability and recoverability to the personnel operating the system. For applications that deal with less sensitive data, such as an intraoffice equipment checkout application, the policies are generally less comprehensive and less strict.

Policies for Compliance

Establishing sound security policies is a good idea without exception. However, sometimes security policies are motivated by external influences. Some policies are created for compliance purposes. Regulations are often written to ensure that companies are properly and responsibly handling data. This is generally based on an analysis of the type and use of the data within an industry, agency, or community. Companies respond by creating a policy that ensures compliance with the statutory regulation(s).

Many times, the challenging part to policy creation is interpreting the loosely defined regulation to which the policy is directed. For example, privacy is an ever-growing concern in many industries and thus for many organizations. There have been many laws passed regarding the handling of privacy data. In essence, the laws say to protect privacy information and disclose it only to appropriate parties. It is left to the organizations affected by the regulations to interpret what this means and then to define a policy that meets and maintains compliance with their interpretation of the regulation.

For example, a company policy may dictate the use of encryption as a guard against the inadvertent disclosure of privacy-related data. The genesis of the policy was compliance with an applicable statutory regulation.

Effective security for meeting and maintaining compliance issues is based on the ability to accurately interpret and understand the intent of the regulation. Does encrypting the data meet compliance? Perhaps it does not. To find the answer, the relevant questions to ask are who is an appropriate party, and how could inadvertent disclosure occur? Compliance may be better met through something other than encryption (for example, controlled physical access to the data coupled with strong authentication). For this reason, it's important that the parties involved in implementing the security are aware of why the security is there and what it is guarding against. Otherwise, it is possible that the wrong tool will be used to solve the problem, a false sense of security will be created, and compliance will not be met.

Understanding Security Requirements

Security is in many ways a defensive art. You have to understand your attackers, what their motivations are, what they are targeting, and how they will try to achieve their goal. For the bank robbery scenario, the motivations and target are obvious. Making a bank secure involves an understanding of who the potential robbers are (employees or nonemployees) and how they will try to steal the money.

If you don't understand why you are protecting something and what you are protecting it from, you might apply a security solution to a problem that either doesn't exist or can't be solved with the tactic you are considering. Many of the techniques used to prevent bank employees from stealing money are different than those used to prevent nonemployees from stealing money.

Similarly, trying to protect the database data from DBAs is different from trying to protect the data from a compromised application server, which in turn is different from meeting a compliance concern. In Chapter 13, you will see that database encryption can be used to help ensure privacy, but it may not be an effective tool for protecting the data from the DBAs. If someone asks, "How do I effectively do database encryption?" You should reply, "Why do you think you need database encryption? What data are you protecting, and from whom?" The answers to these questions will guide you toward the correct security solution and will help you ensure that you are using the appropriate tools and techniques.

Policy Creation

The saying "why reinvent the wheel?" is applicable to policy creation. Policies can and should be reused or based on existing policies whenever possible.

Creating policy templates is a technique practiced often within organizations. The templates represent the basic types of applications and data used within the organization. You create a template by categorizing the different types of information the organization will be working with, such as proprietary, personally identifiable information, publicly accessible, or partner sharable. Policy templates are created with varying levels of specificity, depending on the sensitivity of the information and how it will be used. The templates can then be used as a jumpstart for new data, and applications with specific exceptions or changes can be incorporated as needed.

Many organizations use the security best practices offered by independent organizations and regulating bodies as starting points for their original templates. The National Institutes of Standards and Technologies (NIST) Special Publications for Security (SP800), the International Standards Organization (ISO) 17799, and the Health Insurance Portability and Accountability Act (HIPAA) are three great references for security policies. They are high level, broad, and comprehensive. A Google search will point you to the plethora of Internet resources available describing the different aspects of these policies and regulations.

Practical Policies

Creating policies can be difficult as you can be tempted to define a robust and comprehensive policy. This by itself is not bad, but there is a potentially bad side effect. Before you embark on creating a rigorous and overzealous security policy, be aware: maintaining the correct level of detail and right level of enforcement is important, because too much security can be self-defeating. This is because security often competes with usability. A perfect example of this principle is password policies. Often, companies will create very strict password policies in an effort to increase security. The policy might indicate that the password must be at least 12 characters in length, contain mixed upper- and lowercase characters and at least one number, expire every 21 days, and not be reused for five years. It's easy to get carried away.

The problem in this is it exceeds most people's cognitive abilities. People generally cannot create passwords with that level of sophistication that frequently, and users resort to creative ways of solving this challenge, such as writing the password down. They then leave the documented passwords in plain view so that security overall is not increased, but diminished. In this example, the net result of employing a sophisticated password policy is a less secure environment.

NOTE
Effective security has to incorporate practicality and usability issues to ensure that the overall security of the system will be increased.

The challenging part is keeping the policies practical while still meeting rational security requirements. To do this, it is advisable to have the policies written by and agreed on by not only the security team, but also employee representatives or members from the usability group. This buy-in is essential to ensuring a successful security implementation.

Balancing Security

It's not possible to build systems that are 100 percent secure. Too often I see people trying to do precisely this. As illustrated in the password policy example, what they end up with is something that is impractical, unusable, and often not much more secure than a practical policy. Deciding how to implement effective security is difficult for several reasons.

One of the biggest challenges to employing effective security is recognizing the adequacy of the security measures. Security is sometimes difficult to evaluate because you can't prove that your security is 100 percent effective; you can only prove that it's not effective (or rather someone else can prove it to you).

Related to this is the fact that it is difficult to determine the level and robustness of the security simply from using the application. A lot of security and a little security can look similar. For example, I can log on to my bank over an Internet-served web application to check my account balances, pay bills, and transfer money between accounts. I often wonder how the security is being done and how robust it is. The act of authenticating to the application does not imply that effective security is being employed to guard the data. I can also log on to my Yahoo account, where the information isn't as sensitive as in my bank, but from my perspective the security appears identical.

Effective security requires a thorough understanding of not only how security works from a technical perspective, but also how the user community may try to defeat the security in efforts to make their job easier.

The security teams within organizations tend to be unpopular because they recommend things that tighten security, which is often inconvenient to the users. Security competes with other real-world desirable objectives besides usability such as performance, cost, and administration. Typically, as security increases, usability and performance decrease, and costs and administration increase. Overall, you must keep in mind that there are going to be trade-offs (probably not what you expected to read in a book dedicated to security).

Figure 1-1 represents the competing requirements. You can mark an "X" somewhere on the pyramid to represent your goal, or perhaps the reality, of where you have balanced the competing factors.

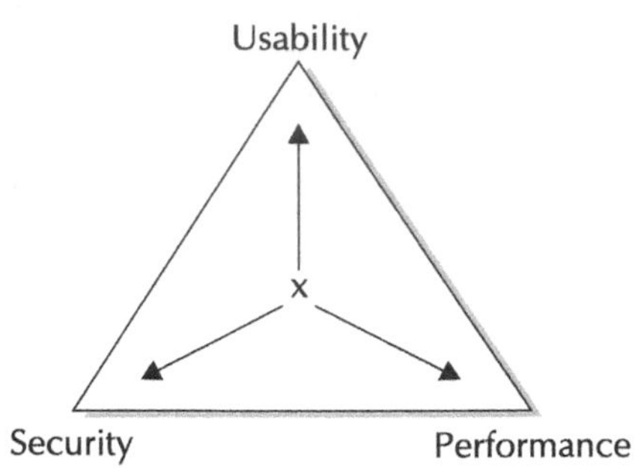

FIGURE 1-1. *Balancing requirements*

There are times when you'll want to be flexible in your ability to move through the triangle. Perhaps in a time of crisis you might need to move from more secure to more usable, or from more performance to more secure. Ultimately, the goal is to shrink the triangle—that is, to achieve security *and* usability *and* performance. We will explore examples of this throughout the book.

The Tenets of Security

Good security practices help to create good security implementations. Within the security community, there are a few tenets that come up time and again. Many or all of the implementation best practices can be traced back to these principles, which are explored in the next few sections. I have found that these tenets, when carefully followed, help to ensure effective security.

An important observation is that these tenets are proactive and persistent. They must be analyzed and discussed *before* any coding, and certainly before anything goes into production. They should also remain constant both in time and in applicability. They should apply to all applications, databases, and digital and nondigital processes.

Security by Design

When asked, "When does security begin?" many will answer when the user authenticates. It's a trick question. Security begins when the application is designed. The first tenet is this: *Security has to be built into the system, not bolted on afterward.* This is also the overall message of this book. A proper security design helps to ensure that an application will be secure.

By applying this principle to an every-day example—automobiles—a powerful analogy becomes apparent. In today's world, automobiles are built with security features incorporated by design. Door locks are probably the most obvious example. For the sake of argument, assume the opposite. Pretend that automobiles don't come with door locks. (In fact, at one time, this was true.) Assume when the car is built, it has a door that is easily opened all the time. Door locks and other security measures were considered, but they interfered with the usability of the automobile and drove production costs up. Substitute the word "application" for "automobile" in the previous sentence and you may recognize a familiar argument.

To ensure my analogy is consistent, consider security only after the car has been built. Assume the car is now delivered, and you, the owner (user), immediately recognize the security shortcomings. Because the car has no locks, what can you do to secure it? Perhaps you are envisioning a car with a big chain and a padlock around it. Perhaps you are thinking of a way to retrofit something on the side of the car that would be used to attach a rope around the door handle.

Whatever security solution you think of, it's probably not elegant. The same applies to database applications when security is not part of the design. In many cases, performance and practical implementation issues may prevent the security "feature" from actually being used at all.

The lesson is simple: make security a first-class citizen. Spend some time thinking about the application from the security angle before you start building. In the end, you will have a much more functional and secure application.

Defense in Depth

The second tenet for effective security says that *security should be a multilayered composition.* This is commonly known as "defense in depth," and it implies there will be no single point of failure from within the security domain. By creating multiple layers or rings of security, you can generate a system with higher security assurance. If one layer of defense is defeated, another will hold. And you don't need to be limited to just two; you want as many layers as practical. Defense in depth is successfully employed in many areas of technology, and it's also applicable to database applications.

Automobile designers today practice the defense in depth principle. To prevent automobile theft, cars are secured by more than just door locks. Breaking the window to unlock the car doors is easy. Many cars come equipped with sophisticated alarm systems that not only sound an alarm but also disable the ignition system of the car. If that's not enough, the car can be further protected by placing a metal bar across the steering wheel, preventing a would-be thief from successfully steering the car even if they were able to start it. Each layer incrementally adds more security.

A bank also represents a wonderful example of defense in depth in action. The first layer of security lies in the robust construction of the bank. The bank walls are fortified. Inside the bank, bullet-proof glass and physical barriers separating the bank customers from bank employees provides additional layers of security. Perhaps even a security guard is employed as another security measure. Valuables in banks are secured by a huge, nearly impenetrable, time-operated safe. There is no single point of security failure within the bank. If the security guard calls in sick, it does not imply that the valuables in the safe are immediately accessible.

Within an enterprise IT infrastructure, defense in depth is just as important. You use firewalls to separate the outsiders from the insiders. You may also use network encryption to protect data as it travels within the walls of an organization's intranet.

To further protect insiders from other insiders, you can utilize operating system security and application security. If the data is what you are trying to protect, then you also have to apply security where the data lives. This means you have to add the layer of database security. The databases act as the impenetrable safe or data vault. The job of the database, like the job of the police, is to both serve (the data) and to protect (the data).

By using the appropriate security tools, designed and deployed in layers, you can set the groundwork for a truly secure environment.

Least Privileges

The third tenet of effective security is to *maintain least privileges.* "Least privileges" means you give people only the permissions they need to do their job and nothing more: you give them the least amount of privileges. One of the easiest ways to compromise a system is to exploit accounts that have been granted too much privilege.

The least privilege principle is probably practiced in many parts of your life already. For example, an employee usually does not have the privileges to grant themselves a salary increase. Most employees can't approve their expense reports either. Why? Even though employers generally trust their employees, there is too high a risk that the privileges could be easily abused.

The process of abiding by least privileges is simple: start by granting no privileges and then give only the minimum privileges needed. Not following the least privilege principle can result in serious consequences. Why isn't this principle followed regularly? One primary reason the least privilege principle is not practiced is laziness. (I hate to use that word but I believe it to be accurate.)

Consider a database example. For administrators who are unfamiliar with database security, it generally takes work to ascertain precisely what privilege(s) are needed to perform a set of tasks. Documentation has to be referenced, and even then the answer may not be obvious. The shortcut is to grant all privileges. This is bad.

I see examples like the following all the time. Assume a database application developer needs the privileges to create a database table and a database procedure. Instead of granting the two simple privileges to perform these tasks, the user is granted the database administrator (DBA) role, which provides the user with unrestricted access to the entire database. This makes life easy for the developer because she can now create tables and procedures. It makes life easy for the administrator because he doesn't have to know what privileges were needed, nor will he be bothered with any more privilege requests since the developer now has every privilege in the database. This creates a huge risk because the developer can now do anything—read any table, update any data, execute any procedure in any schema, and so much more.

Database security is based on privileges. Privilege abuse cannot occur if the privileges haven't been granted in the first place. While it requires some effort to determine what privileges are needed, it's essential for maintaining least privileges and least privileges are essential for effective security.

Risk Analysis

One of the first and most essential things to do is to conduct an analysis of the security landscape and think about the security universe at it pertains to your organization. For each application you have to determine how it can be exploited, what would happen if something were to happen, and how to mitigate such occurrences. The term "application" in the previous sentence is meant to apply to all facets of applications—not only the user interface but also the servers and databases. This is often referred to as risk analysis, and it must be done. It can be very tedious, but it's a necessary and valuable exercise.

In a simplified view of risk analysis, the first step is to determine the assets being protected and their associated value. The value can be determined either qualitatively or quantitatively. Referring back to the car example, your car has both a quantitative value and a qualitative value. Its quantitative value can be defined by a monetary amount. Its qualitative value may be in its reliability and possibly any nostalgic memories associated with places the car has taken you. Companies, company assets such as computer servers, and even data have similar values. Sometimes a concrete value can be determined quantitatively. For example, the company lost $6,000 due to the theft of a computer server. Qualitative values can be more difficult to calculate. For example, if the stolen server contained a database, there would also be a loss associated with the data that was stored within that database. A security breach that was made public could damage a company's reputation.

The next step is to consider all possible threats to the assets. These threats aren't just external or from outsiders, they also include insiders who may be privileged and authorized to access parts of or all of the application. Threats also include nonhuman or natural causes such as fire, floods, earthquakes, power loss, tornadoes, and so on.

The last step it to predict a rate of occurrence, or the overall likelihood that the threats will happen. Because there can be an infinite number of threats, it's important to focus on the threats that have higher probability of happening. Power loss has a higher rate of occurrence than does a tornado or earthquake, so ensuring your site has backup power may be a higher priority than building a tornado- or earthquake-proof structure.

Returning to the car example, assume your car cost $10,000. If you live, work, and drive in a safe part of town, you may conclude that the likelihood of car theft is very small. Buying and installing an alarm system that costs $30,000 may be unreasonable. However, if the rate of occurrence of auto theft is sufficiently high, then the extra expense and inconvenience of the alarm system is well worth it.

For your IT assets, the threats also can be external and internal. Firewalls may be used to address the external threat, but the internal threat will still exist.

The risk analysis process has to evolve over time. You have to remain vigilant about your security. Your security posture should always reflect the new insights and perspectives you have about your data, applications, users, operating systems, and policies.

Risk analysis is important and valuable. The lists of assets, their value, and the threats associated with those assets helps to guide and influence prudent security decisions.

Document Your Risk Analysis

The results of the risk analysis should be documented. The documentation should explain the decisions that were made and why they were made and list all the identified threats and vulnerabilities.

The benefits to documentation are many. First, the results of the analysis can be used as a reference or checklist for audits. The documentation can also serve as a template for other, future systems. The risk analysis results may also be useful in proving due diligence in the event that something bad happens. It's not unreasonable to assume a civil suit may occur as the result of what appears to be negligence on your organization's behalf. The documented analysis should help to prove that security was taken seriously and that the occurrence was an anomaly and not the result of gross negligence.

Expect the Unexpected

Many successful system attacks are executed by unconventional means. Make sure to consider the unexpected when you are gathering information for your risk analysis. What you expect to happen to your system may not actually be what's going to happen to your system. For example, for better home security, you might install a new steel-reinforced front door with an industrial-strength dead bolt. It is unwise to assume a burglar can only gain entry to your house through the front door just because that's the way people normally enter and leave the house. An unlocked ground floor window can provide an easy alternative and unsecured entry path for a burglar. Similarly, you should assume that hackers and attackers can get to your data in ways other than through the normal access paths that you use. Consider the following two examples.

You may believe the only way to access your database data is via an application since that's the way your users access the database. A great amount of effort may then be focused on securing the application; however, the assumption that all access to the data is by way of application is wrong. There are many ways to connect to the database, and your application only represents one of them. There may be nothing preventing a user from bypassing the application and all the application's security by connecting directly to the database. Applying security in the database, like locking the ground floor windows, is a good solution for this.

Assume you have now secured your database and your application(s). There is still a risk. The unexpected attack now shifts to the possible theft of the database's backup tapes. Theft of the backup tapes can be easy if the tapes are left on someone's desk in an unprotected area, or worse, left in a box in the mail room.

This last threat leads to another point. There are a lot of known technology-based attacks: network eavesdropping, IP spoofing, password cracking, and so on. However, there are many more unconventional methods that are just as effective, if not more so. For example, a social engineering technique would be to impersonate someone from the help desk. The attacker simply asks for a user's password to fix a problem or asks the user to set their password to "admin" to allow them in. Proper education for your user community is helpful in thwarting these attacks. But note that many methods are not technological in nature, so using technology as a solution may prove ineffective.

Expecting the unexpected means that you anticipate the use of unconventional tactics. You must assume that there is no single way to do anything. People are creative, ingenious, and curious, and they'll prove this to you by testing your designs and implementations.

Contingency Planning and Incident Response

With all the risks properly identified, the next step is to decide how to properly respond when incidents occur. This is called contingency planning and incident response, and I can't stress enough how important this is. For example, you know what to do in the event of a fire: get out of the building as fast and safely as you can. Leave your valuables in the building to burn. This has probably been drilled into you since elementary school, if not before that. But what do you do about your databases in the case of a fire? Yes, you leave those to burn too, but once the fire is out, then what?

Contingency planning outlines what you will do in the event that fire destroys the computer room. It also states what to do if you are under cyber attack. These guidelines are essential because they may be the only pillar of stability in a time of crisis. For example, in case of a data center outage, you need to direct your applications to a failover site, which may simply require an update to the internal domain name servers (DNS). In the case of cyber attack, you need to disconnect the servers from the network, alert the response team, and make sure you do *not* reboot the servers. Rebooting can delete potential evidence or clues about how the attack occurred and whether anything was compromised.

For the same reasons you conduct fire drills, it's important to rehearse your incident responses, too. People tend to not think clearly when overwhelmed by anxiety. Having a plan gives you a sane reference point in the midst of insanity. Don't forget to keep the plans in a safe place so that they are also not destroyed in the fire!

Snapshots and Situational Awareness

A phrase often used in military circles, *situational awareness* refers to the ability to understand what is happening at any time, all the time. It's a comprehensive understanding of where the good guys are, where the bad guys are, who is doing what, and why they are doing it.

The same concept proves valuable within the IT community. You should know all the interrelationships among your networks, servers, applications, and databases. Furthermore, within the database, you should know what schemas, applications, and users exist and what privileges they each should and should not have. Also important is understanding what applications are being accessed by what community of users for what data.

A simple snapshot of the baseline configuration combined with ongoing and vigilant monitoring is practice you will find very valuable. The resulting snapshot should be documented. The document does not have to be fancy; SQL output may prove sufficient. This snapshot will allow you to more easily identify anomalies and react to them. Often, a security compromise will occur over long periods of time. How can they go on for so long without anyone noticing? It's because there was no awareness of what was going on when it was going on. For example, if someone were robbing you one penny at a time, you might never realize it was even happening if you never balanced your checkbooks.

Another benefit of snapshots is that they help you understand what damage has occurred if something does happen. If a schema is compromised, ask yourself simple questions like, "What privileges did the schema have? What data was there? What procedures were in place? What data did those procedures act on?" You can extend this concept into one of threat assessments (actually part of risk analysis) to predict the results of bad things that might happen.

This overall awareness of the system is important to understanding how to design a secure system and how to respond logically, quickly, and accurately to security incidents.

Cover All the Areas

The concept of security transcends database security, and even computer security. Overall, an organization is concerned with all facets of security. There is, in a sense, a security ecosystem. One area of security complements and relates to other areas. A challenge to implementing computer security is in understanding the complex inter-relationships. Here is a list of some of the other security areas that should be considered when addressing security:

- **Physical security** Protect the assets from physical abuse, including theft. As mentioned previously, theft of a server is not only theft of the hardware but also theft of the data. Booting a server to a "startup" level, changing the super-user password, and exploiting the rest of the system is easy to do if the physical access to the server is compromised.
- **Personnel security** Ensure people are honest and ethical. This one may be the hardest, because you have to trust people. Generally, you should marry the access a person is given with the amount of trust you have for that person. For people who actually run the systems, some background checks may be necessary and desirable. Keep track of personnel status. A disgruntled employee can cause an enormous amount of IT damage.

- **Training** Teach people the good behavior required to provide a secure environment. A simple course or document that explains the company policies and describes good security behavior is invaluable to an organization. Include instructions such as
  - Lock the door to your office
  - Don't leave confidential material laying around
  - Use "strong" passwords
  - Lock unattended computers
- **Contingency plans** Plan for power failures, security compromises, and disasters. If you don't have a plan, make one. It will provide a framework for you and guidance to those who are involved in the disaster. Your plan may indicate that there is no contingency for a certain event, but that is okay. It shows you have thought about it and decided to do nothing. It can be a "placeholder" for when you do have a strategy.
- **Information access management** Access to IT systems should be diligently governed in accordance with the least-privilege principle. This means that application owners, DBAs, and security officers should agree on who has access to what kind of data. This agreement should be documented and audited for compliance.
- **Information security** Provide confidentiality, privacy, and integrity of your data. Information may take various forms; digital is only one. Digital security will not prevent someone from stealing a confidential printout from an unsecured printer or overhearing a phone conversation about confidential information. Note that theft of a printout is not the same as physical security, which could be used to prevent a person from getting access to the printer altogether. Instructing employees on proper behaviors is critical to ensuring the security ecosystem is functioning well.

To implement security effectively, you need a heterogeneous collection of mandatory controls that cannot be bypassed, such as encryption for confidentiality. You also need discretionary controls that you must hope are not misused by users. All of the areas are equally important to providing a secure ecosystem.

Hardening the Infrastructure

When applications and databases are installed today, they start in a state that is often configured to help the user become productive as quickly as possible. As such, one of the first things you should do to protect yourself is to tighten your configurations against attacks—also referred to as *hardening*. An important aspect of this process is that *everything* needs to be hardened. For example, paying attention to just the network security while forsaking the operating system security is not a good idea. Security extends from the infrastructure components to the applications themselves. The old saying is true: a chain is as strong as its weakest link.

The following sections suggest ways to harden your systems. It's important to understand the hardening process for the operating system, the network, and application server because the database ultimately depends on and interacts with all three of these components.

The Operating System

Operating systems vary in practically every aspect. They not only serve different roles within an organization, they also have different design targets from their respective manufacturers. Depending on the operating system, the version, and the role of the server in which the operating system resides, the actions you must take to harden it will change. The following list is suggestive, not comprehensive, but should nevertheless serve as a guide to some of the most useful practices for hardening an operating system:

- **Physically protect the servers** Real "incidents" have occurred when someone put the server on a cart and wheeled it off. They got not only the hardware, but all applications and data within. Database servers are often prime targets because they hold the information jewels and generally run on the more expensive hardware. Once the server falls into the possession of someone else, it's very difficult to ensure that the data within it is still secure.
- **Turn off un-needed daemons and services** You should disable traditional services such as Telnet, ftp, finger, and print services, unless there's a good reason not to do so. On Windows machines, there shouldn't be any open shares. A good practice is to disable everything and then enable only the things that are needed to get the server into its operational state.
- **Check file and directory permissions** Before plugging the machine into the network, the system files should be correctly secured. Setting the correct permissions on files and directories prevents unauthorized people from accessing things they should not. It's a good idea to check the files' settings periodically to ensure that nothing has changed. A lot of valuable information can be leaked from a system where the simple directory and file permissions haven't been set and maintained properly.
- **Remove or disable unused accounts** Many operating systems come with default accounts. Some of the accounts are tied to services. When the services are no longer in operation, it's advisable to disable or remove the account to prevent it from being used as a foothold into your system.
- **Remove unused and unneeded software** This can be a challenging, though necessary, task. Removing unneeded programs limits the possibility that someone will exploit a bug and compromise the system. This especially pertains to default programs that may be out of date, unpatched, and configured in an insecure manner. In addition, any accounts automatically provisioned in support of the application should be removed or, at minimum, disabled.
- **Lock inactive computers** One of the most common times information is stolen is when an employee goes to lunch and leaves an unlocked, unattended computer. Setting the computer to lock itself upon inactivity helps with this problem, as does training the employees to lock computers before leaving them. Typical timeout values vary from one minute of inactivity in highly secure, high-traffic areas, to ten minutes in more controlled areas. Locking prematurely inhibits the usability of the computer, so the timeouts have to be weighed against how the user interacts with the computer. A company policy should establish proper values and be rigorously enforced.

- **Use an Intrusion Detection System (IDS)** An IDS can automate some of the processes needed to detect someone tampering with your system, which is helpful in ensuring everything is as it should be. Create a procedure for handling incidents that arise. For example, if the system administrator sees someone or something changing directory and file permissions, they should know how to respond immediately to the event.
- **Turn off banners to prevent fingerprinting** *Fingerprinting*, or *profiling*, is the act of interrogating a system, either actively or passively, to determine the make and model of the server. Fingerprinting allows someone to tailor their attacks for the known vulnerabilities of that specific system. Welcome banners are a favorite target. Simply issuing a Telnet or ftp to a server with banners will generally give the OS and version release. Therefore, banners and anything else that identifies key aspects of the server should be disabled or turned off. While there are many ways to determine information about a system, turning off banners is a simple way to make the job of system fingerprinting a little more challenging for hackers.
- **Run virus protection software** This is a must and should be enforced via a company policy. Infections spread through contact. One infected client computer can cause major disruption throughout an entire organization. Regular and frequent updates to the software's virus definitions are mandatory for virus protection to work effectively.
- **Keep it patched** Software is imperfect. Application of patches, and in particular, security patches, is a key ingredient in maintaining a secure infrastructure. Delaying patch application can result in a compromised system or systems. However, there are prudent reasons why patch application may be deferred; see the upcoming bullet "Apply Patches" for more details.
- **Monitor the OS logs and keep them secure** Log files may be your best hope in determining suspicious activity. For this reason, it is important to check these files regularly for irregularities. Also, be sure the log files are secured from nonadministrative users. This helps to prevent an attacker from deleting the log files and thus covering their tracks.
- **Restrict the number of super-users** Ensure that the super-user privilege is given only to a certain group of administrators who are willing to be accountable for anything bad that happens to the system. Also ensure that the shared password is strong and not written on a sticky note underneath the keyboard of the server!
- **Read, read, read** Several books have been written discussing the hardening process for specific operating systems. Some of the titles to consider are McGraw-Hill/Osborne's *Hardening Linux* by John H. Terpstra, *Hardening Windows Systems* by Roberta Bragg, and *Hardening Network Infrastructure* by Wesley J. Noonan. These books are invaluable tools that cover the nuances of each particular operating system. While the suggestions given here are generally applicable to all operating systems, these books often spell out particular idiosyncrasies of various operating systems.

The Network

In some ways, the network poses the biggest security challenge. It is the connective tissue linking together the various clients, servers, corporations, partners, and quite frankly everything and everyone. The usefulness of your IT systems is generally based on these vast and varied interconnections, but the connections also introduce risks.

Network security can be simply described as providing data confidentiality and data integrity and preventing data disruption for data in transit. The problem is simple: you are trying to pass sensitive data over an unprotected medium. As data moves through the "ether," it is susceptible to everything in the great unknown.

Another concern is manifested by what a network is. The network provides a connection path, not just for the authorized people, but the unauthorized as well. Think of networks as the hallways that interconnect the rooms in a big apartment building. Almost anyone can walk the halls. Similarly, almost anyone can traverse the network. The halls lead to the offices. The networks lead to the computers. The offices have valuables. The computers store valuable data. Just as the hallways can allow a thief to gain access to an office, a network can allow hackers to attack your servers from afar. Protecting the network means you are protecting everything that touches the network.

Network security distills into encrypting the data streams, providing data integrity checks, and limiting access into certain networks and servers to authorized people. There are many things that can be done to provide network security. Here are some of the most popular:

- **Use a good network topology** A good network topology and design can mitigate risks and help secure the infrastructure. The topology includes placement of hubs, routers, firewalls, wireless access points, and modems. Designing a network also involves making decisions such as whether to utilize shared networks, bus architectures, or switched networks. Think carefully about the design from a security perspective as well as the normal bandwidth and hardware cost perspectives. This is not a one-time process. Every new piece of network hardware added to the network should trigger someone to rethink and re-evaluate the network topology.
- **Use Virtual Private Networks (VPNs)** VPNs are good for securing all traffic, regardless of protocol, across unprotected network domains. VPNs are also attractive solutions for linking field offices to the main office when using public (shared) networks.
- **Use IPSec or Secure Socket Layer (SSL) for strong encryption and authentication** SSL was originally developed by Netscape for use in their browsers. It has become the de facto standard for securing http traffic. SSL is also a key technology in allowing e-commerce to prosper.
- **Firewalls, firewalls, firewalls** Probably the most exciting part about network security, other than cryptography, is the firewall. Firewall technology has grown exponentially since it was started. Today, there are many types and many to choose from, and they have vast and varying capabilities. The challenge of firewalls lies in properly configuring them to secure your enterprise networks while still making things accessible and usable. Basic designs often incorporate a demilitarized zone (DMZ), a technique for isolating Internet traffic from intranet traffic. Consider mixing vendor products because vulnerabilities found in one vendor's product are unlikely to be found in another vendor's product.
- **Check configurations regularly** Security is a perpetual process. Your network device configurations may have to be tweaked on regular intervals. Plan for this. The configurations should start with the most restrictive policy and then relax to accommodate the needed ports and protocols.

- **Use Network Address Translations (NAT)** This technique hides the real IP addresses of your computers from the outsiders. When done correctly, NAT can be a useful security technique because it shields your network topology from hackers.
- **Apply patches** Patch the routers, switches, firewalls, and computer networking software as often as possible. It usually isn't long from the time an exploit is discovered until it is made public, and someone has posted a script on the Internet to be used by anyone and everyone to exercise this new vulnerability. Quickly applying patches may be your only defense.
- **Use Network Intrusion Detection Systems (IDS)** Network IDS provide another layer of defense. They typically monitor the network and can detect things such as denial-of-service attacks, IP spoofing, and other signs of malicious activity.
- **Stay abreast of technology developments** Research and development in the area of network security continues at a rapid pace. Interesting developments include the use of personal firewalls, IDS capabilities, and application filtering. Stay current and knowledgeable on what's available and how to use it properly to secure your enterprise. Hackers are always on the bleeding edge of technology, and you should be too.

The Application Server

Application servers are a critical part of your infrastructure. Here, I am not only referring to the Oracle Application Server, but also to anyone's application server. Because application servers provide an environment for applications, they are particularly attractive targets. They typically provide access to databases that hold key information and may contain encryption keys, passwords, and other valuable pieces of information. Many of the actions needed to secure application servers are similar to the actions discussed for securing the OS and network.

- **Turn off banners** Just as with operating systems, you want to keep your application server's cards close to your chest. Identifying information can be a hacker's ally.
- **Remove ports and services that are not in use** Many application servers include a broad array of network services. Turn everything off, and then selectively turn on the features that are needed. In some cases, this may not be easy because there can be a lot of infrastructure ports that are needed by the server.
- **Consider nonstandard ports for services** Everyone knows the ports for http, LDAP, and so on. While switching ports is somewhat remedial, an attacker has to guess which one of the 65,000 other ports you might have chosen. If you have removed banners and turned off everything except what you need, this step can help solidify your security even more.
- **Use virtual hosting to conceal the host name** Similar in concept to using NAT, it is beneficial to hide the actual hostname from hackers.

Summary

Best practices for computer security have many dimensions. In this chapter, you looked at some of the most important. Security starts with well-defined policies that need to be supported by everyone in the organization—especially the senior management. The policies and procedures form the structure by which the technical security measures will be implemented. Without defined and unambiguous policies, it's impossible to implement effective security.

The security policies will vary in specificity and details based on the sensitivity of the data they protect. Ensuring the right level of strictness in developing the policies is important to a successful implementation. Policies that are too restrictive can inadvertently cause insecure behaviors to be practiced. The policies have to be practical and should be based on the tenets of security.

I proposed three critical tenets of security—design security into your applications before you begin development, abide by least privileges, and build defense in-depth. These form the guiding principles for employing effective security.

With the security policies and security guidelines in mind, it's then time to determine what your environment looks like from a security perspective. Security is about managing risks. Risk assessments and risk analysis are important in determining the current state of security as well as what should be developed to increase security in the future. Asset identification and valuation coupled with risk assessments help you determine how much and what type of security measures you should employ. Without a careful analysis, you won't have properly identified the problems and therefore will not be able to provide effective security solutions.

The only way to ascertain your security posture is to understand the security inter-relationships that exist within your organization. Knowing who is accessing what and how, coupled with other operational information, creates an awareness of the overall security ecosystem. This is criticial in deploying effective security because it provides the knowledge necessary for designing security across applications, application servers, and databases. Taking snapshots of your system allows you to respond logically, quickly, and accurately to security incidents if and when they arise.

A key and fundamental element of security involves ensuring your IT systems are properly configured. Secure configurations apply to all entities in the security ecosystem—the operating systems, the networks, the application servers, the database servers, and the applications. Hardening the servers and networks ensures a solid foundation upon which to build.

In the next chapters, we'll dive into the Oracle database and explore the various technologies and techniques that can be used to build secure database applications. All of that will be done under the assumptions and principles presented in this chapter.

CHAPTER 2

Securing the Database

This chapter focuses on the steps you'll use to help secure your OracleDatabases. You'll see how applying the best practice principles (explored in Chapter 1) to an Oracle database will help to further secure it.

This chapter looks at securing database schemas by limiting their privileges, providing good password support, restricting access using multiple defenses, and securing the network channels to and from the database. These steps represent many of the best practices used by organizations today. *These are the actions you should also be taking to configure and operate a secure Oracle Database.*

The remaining chapters of this book discuss how to effectively apply technology features and capabilities to the task of building secure database applications. For this to happen successfully, you'll first have to apply the lessons taught in this chapter. You'll need to take certain actions and practice certain behaviors to ensure a good security foundation.

Securing (Default) User Accounts

A new Oracle database typically comes installed with over 20 default database schemas (the actual number will vary because some of these schemas are optionally installed during the database creation).

As a Google search on "Default Oracle Users" illustrates, the names, passwords, and privileges of these accounts are anything but secret. These accounts are often used to store metadata and procedures for specific database options, such as the Text Option and the Spatial Option. Consequently, many of these accounts have very significant privileges. They may also have well-known passwords listed both in the Oracle product documentation and on the Internet. This combination creates a risk that an unauthorized person will connect to one of these privileged accounts and access, or manipulate, your sensitive data.

During database creation, you can use the Database Configuration Assistant (DBCA) to choose which default accounts (directly associated with database options) to install. It's important to be selective in your decision about the options you need for your database. Installing options that you'll not be using creates an unnecessary risk.

Keep in mind that commercial applications, as well as Oracle applications, will also have associated and well-known schemas. They all represent targets of opportunity for a hacker. These accounts should also be closely guarded.

While the number of accounts and the associated privileges vary from release to release, it's important to ensure these accounts are secured to limit the risk stated above. This section offers suggestions on how to ensure these accounts are secure. Whether you are securing an Oracle created account, or one that you have created, the process for securing these accounts is the same.

Securing Access and Logon

The following suggestions offer ways of controlling access to database accounts. The actions range from restricting logins to the account to removing the account entirely. Combining several of these suggestions together is good practice as it supports a defense in depth approach.

- *Change the default passwords and create a strong password.* The DBCA provides a shortcut for creating the initial passwords during the database creation. It allows you to use the same password for all the accounts. *Do not choose this option.* Create a strong and different password for each schema!

- *Create an impossible password.* After installation, this little trick, which is covered in the upcoming "Oracle Passwords" section, maintains the account objects and privileges but prevents anyone from directly logging in because the password can't be supplied.
- *Create a database log-on trigger to check for specific users that you don't want to log in, and fail the trigger if one tries.* A failed log-on trigger prevents a user from logging in. This technique doesn't work for certain privileged users, such as SYS (SYSDBA) and users with the ADMINISTER DATABASE TRIGGER system privilege. Nevertheless, it may be advantageous to only allow these privileged users into the database. As such, this is an excellent little trick for locking out all other users.
- *Revoke CREATE SESSION and/or the CONNECT role.* Removing the privilege to log in to the database is an obvious way to prevent someone from logging in to an account. Note this will prevent both hackers *and* legitimate users and applications from logging in to the account. It doesn't matter if they know the password; the privilege to log on has been removed.
- *Lock the account.* This is a preferred option because it keeps all the data objects and associated procedures while preventing people from logging in. The effect to this is similar to revoking the privilege to log on to the database but no privileges have to be revoked. This capability was introduced with the Oracle9*i* Database.
- *Revoke all privileges and roles.* Revoking the schema's privileges allows you to maintain all the existing data while helping to ensure that if the account is compromised, the hacker will not be able to use privileges to access or manipulate data in other schemas. This suggestion is applicable to the schemas that you believe are no longer being used but are reluctant to remove completely. It's particularly useful for the very privileged default schemas installed with the database. Note that revoking privileges could break procedures that are defined within the schema. It's a good idea to capture all the privileges and role grants before revoking them in case you later need to undo this action.
- *Drop the schema.* You can drop the schemas that you don't need. However, there is significant risk to doing this. Dropping schemas is very destructive. Not only can the user no longer connect, but all of the tables, data, and procedures are gone, too.

For certain database options, such as the Oracle Label Security, there's an officially supported process for removing the option and schema. The Oracle Universal Installer is the best tool for removing already installed database options. Before dropping any Oracle installed schemas, consult the Oracle product documentation to ensure that your removal of the schema is done correctly. Although dropping schemas is the most certain measure you can take to guarantee the account will not be compromised (because it no longer exists), it should be used with caution.

Lock Down Example

This example illustrates how you might accomplish the task of securing a default account. The following code snippet shows this process as done for the MDSYS schema. MDSYS is the schema that supports the Oracle Spatial technology and as such has been granted access (by way of role privileges) to many powerful procedures and data.

Securing Access to Default Accounts

In the default installation, the MDSYS account is locked and the password is expired. This means that the account is made accessible by unlocking the schema and providing the initial password that just happens to be "mdsys." A user with the ALTER USER system privilege only has to unlock the MDSYS account to gain access. Since you may never actually need to log in to this account, there are a couple things you can do to further secure it.

First, revoke the CREATE SESSION privilege *and* the CONNECT role from MDSYS. You do this because the CONNECT role has been granted the CREATE SESSION privilege, too, so the MDSYS has the privilege twice—once as a direct grant, and once as an indirect grant received via the CONNECT role. Revoking only the role or only the privilege will not prevent someone from logging in as this user.

After you revoke the privileges, modify the password. The default password is *mdsys,* which could be easily guessed. In the following example, the privileges are revoked from MDSYS and the password is altered.

```
sec_mgr@KNOX10g> REVOKE CONNECT, CREATE SESSION FROM MDSYS;

Revoke succeeded.

sec_mgr@KNOX10g> ALTER USER MDSYS IDENTIFIED BY ti1hp2r4m;

User altered.
```

This process helps to secure the account while still making it usable. That is, the spatial data features can still be used.

Securing Access to Application Schemas

For an example of a schema that represents one you have created, let's look at securing the SCOTT schema. Prior to Oracle Database 10*g*, the SCOTT schema was often created and available through the well-known password *tiger,* and the account was not locked.

Assume your requirement is to maintain the schema's data while preventing someone from logging into the account. In Oracle9*i* Database and beyond, you can lock the account. Our approach is to augment this with a few additional measures. First, build a database log-on trigger to prevent someone from logging into the SCOTT schema.

```
sec_mgr@KNOX10g> CREATE OR REPLACE TRIGGER logon_check
     AFTER LOGON ON DATABASE
   BEGIN
     IF (SYS_CONTEXT ('USERENV', 'SESSION_USER') = 'SCOTT')
     THEN
       raise_application_error (-20001,
                                'Unauthorized Login');
     END IF;
   END;
   /

Trigger created.
```

An attempt to connect as SCOTT results in the following:

```
sec_mgr@KNOX10g> conn scott/tiger
ERROR:
ORA-00604: error occurred at recursive SQL level 1
ORA-20001: Unauthorized Login
ORA-06512: at line 4

Warning: You are no longer connected to ORACLE.
```

Two words of caution with the log-on trigger approach. First, while log-on triggers can be a security ally, they will fire for every user log on and can subsequently degrade the database connection time. In the previous example, the time would be unperceivable. However, if your trigger code queries tables or makes an external call, the degradation could become very noticeable and make this an unviable alternative.

When database log-on triggers were initially released with Oracle8*i* Database, an exception thrown in the trigger would prevent the user from logging in. Often the exceptions were neither intentional nor handled gracefully. The result was that *all* users were unable to log on to the database. The only way to get back in to the database was to connect as SYSDBA (internal) and drop or disable the log-on trigger.

To prevent this inadvertent lock out, the Oracle9*i* Database was altered to not expel users with the ADMINISTER DATABASE TRIGGER system privilege if the log-on trigger throws an exception. This privilege has been granted to the DBA role, so any user with the DBA role will also bypass the previous log-on trigger technique. You can determine who will be exempt from the log-on trigger exceptions with the following query, which lists users and roles that have been granted the privilege.

```
SELECT grantee
  FROM dba_sys_privs
 WHERE PRIVILEGE = 'ADMINISTER DATABASE TRIGGER';
```

Removing Privileges

Another technique for securing an account is to revoke all privileges and roles that have been granted to the schema. To do this efficiently, use the following procedure, which accepts the username as a parameter and removes system privileges, object privileges, and roles. The procedure also prints the undo statements that can be used to recreate the privileges on the schema.

```
CREATE OR REPLACE PROCEDURE deactivate_user (
  p_username   IN   VARCHAR2)
AS
  TYPE l_role_list_type IS TABLE OF VARCHAR2 (30)
    INDEX BY BINARY_INTEGER;

  l_role_list     l_role_list_type;
  l_role_index    BINARY_INTEGER   := 1;
  l_role_string   VARCHAR2 (32767);
  l_username      VARCHAR2 (30)    := upper(p_username);
BEGIN
```

```
-- revoke System priviliges granted directly to the user
FOR rec IN (SELECT PRIVILEGE, admin_option
              FROM dba_sys_privs
             WHERE grantee = l_username)
LOOP
  IF (rec.admin_option = 'NO')
  THEN
    DBMS_OUTPUT.put_line (    'grant '
                          || rec.PRIVILEGE
                          || ' to '
                          || l_username
                          || ';');
  ELSE
    DBMS_OUTPUT.put_line (    'grant '
                          || rec.PRIVILEGE
                          || ' to '
                          || l_username
                          || ' WITH ADMIN OPTION;');
  END IF;

  EXECUTE IMMEDIATE    'REVOKE '
                    || rec.PRIVILEGE
                    || ' FROM '
                    || l_username;
END LOOP;

-- revoke Object priviliges granted directly to the user
FOR rec IN (SELECT owner,
                   table_name,
                   PRIVILEGE,
                   grantable
              FROM dba_tab_privs
             WHERE grantee = l_username)
LOOP
  IF (rec.grantable = 'NO')
  THEN
    DBMS_OUTPUT.put_line (    'grant '
                          || rec.PRIVILEGE
                          || ' ON '
                          || rec.owner
                          || '.'
                          || rec.table_name
                          || ' to '
                          || l_username
                          || ';');
  ELSE
    DBMS_OUTPUT.put_line (    'grant '
                          || rec.PRIVILEGE
                          || ' ON '
                          || rec.owner
```

```
                              || '.'
                              || rec.table_name
                              || ' to '
                              || l_username
                              || ' WITH ADMIN OPTION;');
  END IF;

  EXECUTE IMMEDIATE    'REVOKE '
                    || rec.PRIVILEGE
                    || ' ON '
                    || rec.owner
                    || '.'
                    || rec.table_name
                    || ' FROM '
                    || l_username;
END LOOP;

-- revoke roles granted directly to the user
FOR rec IN (SELECT *
              FROM dba_role_privs
             WHERE grantee = l_username)
LOOP
  IF (rec.admin_option = 'NO')
  THEN

    DBMS_OUTPUT.put_line (    'grant '
                          || rec.granted_role
                          || ' to '
                          || l_username
                          || ';');
  ELSE
    DBMS_OUTPUT.put_line (    'grant '
                          || rec.granted_role
                          || ' to '
                          || l_username
                          || ' WITH ADMIN OPTION;');
  END IF;

  IF (rec.default_role = 'YES')
  THEN
    l_role_list (l_role_index) := rec.granted_role;
    l_role_index := l_role_index + 1;
  END IF;

  EXECUTE IMMEDIATE    'REVOKE '
                    || rec.granted_role
                    || ' FROM '
                    || l_username;
END LOOP;
```

```
  IF l_role_index > 1
  THEN
    l_role_string :=
         'alter user ' || l_username ||' default roles '
      || l_role_list (1);

    FOR i IN 2 .. l_role_index - 1
    LOOP
      l_role_string :=
               l_role_string || ', ' || l_role_list (i);
    END LOOP;

    DBMS_OUTPUT.put_line (l_role_string || ';');
  END IF;
END;
/
```

Executing the procedure for SCOTT results in the following output:

```
sec_mgr@KNOX10g> SET serveroutput on
sec_mgr@KNOX10g> SPOOL scottPrivs.sql
sec_mgr@KNOX10g> EXEC deactivate_user('scott')
grant UNLIMITED TABLESPACE to SCOTT;
grant CONNECT to scott;
grant RESOURCE to scott;
alter user SCOTT default roles CONNECT, RESOURCE;

PL/SQL procedure successfully completed.

sec_mgr@KNOX10g> spool off
```

Locking the account will add another layer of defense:

```
system@KNOX10g> ALTER USER scott ACCOUNT LOCK;

User altered.

system@KNOX10g> conn scott/tiger
ERROR:
ORA-28000: the account is locked

Warning: You are no longer connected to ORACLE.
```

Combining several different techniques as shown here is a good idea. This approach is consistent with defense in depth. A hacker now has several hurdles to overcome before an account can be accessed. First, the account has to be unlocked. Next, the privilege to create a session has to be restored. Then the trigger has to be disabled, dropped, or altered. Finally, the password has to be altered or guessed.

You can vary the actual steps used in securing your accounts as relevant to your particular use of the schema. However, you should consider some action(s) for every schema in your database. Even a single schema, left unsecured, could create a foothold for an unauthorized user. Using a combination of techniques will help to harden the database and prevent unauthorized access to it.

Throw Out Anything Stale

Over time, it often happens that users and applications no longer require access to the database. Perhaps the user got a new job and will no longer be logging in to your database—at least, not through legitimate means!

A security best practice for operating systems, networks, and databases is to *remove unused or unneeded accounts*. This is a simple concept that can be simply accomplished, yet it represents one of the most common and serious security risks and bad practices. Stale accounts should be locked at the very least, and preferably dropped. I've seen many instances when former employees still had active accounts on production systems years after their termination. Whether this is due to laziness or simply a lack of a good process, it's a huge security risk!

To remove unused and unneeded accounts successfully, it's important to know who *is* and who *should be* accessing the database. The schemas may not belong to just end users. A previously installed application, used and then abandoned on your database, also creates a security risk.

CAUTION
Be careful dropping schemas even if no one has logged in to them in months. These schemas may hold data and procedures needed by an application.

This again emphasizes the importance of knowing which schemas are doing what. If you're not sure whether an account still has relevant information, at the very least, export the data and procedures first!

How do you know if the account is being accessed? Auditing. You can audit connections to user schemas and access to objects within the schemas. You can even run a batch job to query the audit trail to look for unauthorized accesses and notify an administrator immediately upon detection. For more ideas and auditing examples, see Chapter 8.

Oracle Passwords

The Oracle Database stores user passwords in the data dictionary. For database authenticated users, the values stored aren't actually the plaintext passwords themselves but the password verifiers. *Password verifiers* are hashed (see Chapter 13 for more details on hashing) representations of plaintext passwords. The value is stored in a hexadecimal representation (numbers 0–9 and letters A–F).

The authentication process is performed by computing a password verifier for the plaintext password a user has submitted for authentication and comparing the resulting value with the one stored in the data dictionary. If they match, the user has supplied the same password and is authenticated.

Application Password Authentication Using Oracle's Native Password Store

Application user authentication is an important step to ensuring security for database applications. There are times when the application requires authentication but a default mechanism isn't provided. There are three possible methods for implementing your own user authentication for your application. First, you could build, maintain, and/or synchronize your own password repository and authentication scheme. You'll see an example of how to implement a password authentication solution in Chapter 13, which discusses the use of the new DBMS_CRYPTO package.

Second, assuming the application users are also database users, the application could authenticate users by trying to connect to the database as the respective user(s). This is a bad alternative because it can be costly—from a time and performance perspective—to create and destroy database connections just to authenticate.

The final method, which also assumes the application users are database users, utilizes the database's internal password store. Unfortunately, Oracle supplies no password verifier program for developers to use, so you must build your own interface.

You can do this with a simple trick, commonly referred to as *identified by values*, that uses a syntactical variation of the ALTER USER DDL. The algorithm is similar to the one the database uses to authenticate its users. You simply need to compute a password verifier for the plaintext password a user submits and compare that value to the one stored in the database.

The following function is based on a program originally written by Tom Kyte. To start the function, obtain the user's current password verifier from the data dictionary:

```
sec_mgr@KNOX10g> CREATE OR REPLACE FUNCTION is_auth_password
    p_username  IN  VARCHAR2,
    p_password  IN  VARCHAR2)
    RETURN BOOLEAN
  AS
    l_orig_password_verifier  dba_users.PASSWORD%TYPE;
    l_new_password_verifier   dba_users.PASSWORD%TYPE;
  BEGIN
    SELECT PASSWORD
      INTO l_orig_password_verifier
      FROM dba_users
     WHERE username = UPPER (p_username);
```

Next, alter the user's password and set it to the password you want to verify. When you do this, the database recomputes the password verifier based on this password. The result is stored in the database dictionary:

```
    EXECUTE IMMEDIATE    'alter user '
                      || p_username
                      || ' identified by '
                      || p_password;
```

Select this second verifier out and compare it to the original that you've stored. If they match, the passwords must have been the same.

```
    SELECT PASSWORD
      INTO l_new_password_verifier
```

```
      FROM dba_users
     WHERE username = UPPER (p_username);
```

This works well when the passwords are identical. However, the problem is that if the passwords don't match, you've changed the user's password (perhaps to one that they don't know). To resolve this, set the password back to its original value. Since you don't have the original plaintext password, you can't use the traditional ALTER USER syntax. Instead, reset the password by issuing an ALTER USER <username> IDENTIFIED BY **VALUES** '<original password verifier>'. Passing the original password verifier in single quotes after the values clause resets the password back to the user's original password. The database sees the word "values" and doesn't recompute the password verifier, but it stores the value specified in the quotes directly in the password column for the user.

```
    EXECUTE IMMEDIATE    'alter user '
                      || p_username
                      || ' identified by values '''
                      || l_orig_password_verifier
                      || '''';
    RETURN l_orig_password_verifier =
                              l_new_password_verifier;
  END;
  /

Function created.
```

To test the program, check the Boolean return value of the function:

```
sec_mgr@KNOX10g> BEGIN
    IF (is_auth_password ('scott', 'tiger') = TRUE)
    THEN
      DBMS_OUTPUT.put_line ('scott/tiger is valid');
    ELSE
      DBMS_OUTPUT.put_line
                          ('scott/tiger is NOT valid');
    END IF;

    IF (is_auth_password ('scott', 'lion') = TRUE)
    THEN
      DBMS_OUTPUT.put_line ('scott/lion is valid');
    ELSE
      DBMS_OUTPUT.put_line
                           ('scott/lion is NOT valid');
    END IF;
  END;
  /
scott/tiger is valid
scott/lion is NOT valid
```

This function allows you to authenticate users against the database password store without having to know or manage the user's actual password.

Checking for Weak or Default Passwords

Passwords are often the weak link in the security chain. A poorly chosen password, or well-known default password that has not been changed, is one of the greatest security risks to a database. To help manage this risk use the following program, which compares a list of known usernames and password verifiers to the users and verifiers actually being used in the database. The list is created by a helper program.

To start, a table is created that stores usernames, their plaintext passwords, and the respective computed password verifiers:

```
sec_mgr@KNOX10g> CREATE TABLE passwords
    (
    username VARCHAR2(30),
    passwd   VARCHAR2(30),
    verifier VARCHAR2(30)
    )
  /

Table created.

sec_mgr@KNOX10g> ALTER TABLE PASSWORDS ADD (
    CONSTRAINT PWD_PK PRIMARY KEY (PASSWD, USERNAME));

Table altered.

sec_mgr@KNOX10g> CREATE INDEX VERIFIER ON PASSWORDS
  (USERNAME, VERIFIER);

Index created.
```

To populate the table, a procedure is created that utilizes the identified by values clause introduced in the IS_AUTH_PASSWORD function shown earlier. The procedure takes a password parameter. The program iterates through the DBA_USERS view and sets the passwords for all the users to the value passed as the parameter. The program then inserts the resulting password verifier into the PASSWORDS table. When the parameter is null, the password is set to the username. This has the benefit of allowing you to check for passwords that are the same as the username.

```
sec_mgr@KNOX10g> CREATE OR REPLACE PROCEDURE populate_passwords_tab (
    p_password  IN  VARCHAR2 DEFAULT NULL)
  AS
    l_new_password_verifier  dba_users.PASSWORD%TYPE;
    l_password               dba_users.PASSWORD%TYPE
                               := UPPER (p_password);
  BEGIN
    FOR rec IN (SELECT username, password
                  FROM dba_users)
    LOOP
      IF (p_password IS NULL)
      THEN
        -- password is either passed as parameter
```

```
      -- or set to user's name
      l_password := rec.username;
    END IF;

    -- create new password verifier
    EXECUTE IMMEDIATE    'alter user '
                      || rec.username
                      || ' identified by '
                      || l_password;
    -- retrieve new verifier
    SELECT password
      INTO l_new_password_verifier
      FROM dba_users
     WHERE username = rec.username;
    -- insert value into passwords table
    INSERT INTO passwords
         VALUES (rec.username,
                 l_password,
                 l_new_password_verifier);
    -- set password back to its original value
    EXECUTE IMMEDIATE    'alter user '
                      || rec.username
                      || ' identified by values '''
                      || rec.password
                      || '''';
  END LOOP;
END;
/

Procedure created.
```

Next, execute the above procedure to seed the table first with usernames equal to passwords. Since the procedure modifies user passowords, you should consider running this on a non-production database so this process doesn't interfere with your production applications. Then try some common passwords associated with the default Oracle accounts (there may be additional common and default usernames within your organization). Any standard applications you've installed on Oracle may also carry default schemas and well-known default passwords, so you should consider all default schemas and their passwords, too. Oracle Metalink (http://metalink.oracle.com) lists some of the default usernames and passwords in Note:160861.1.

```
sec_mgr@KNOX10g> -- sets all passwords to that of user's name
sec_mgr@KNOX10g> EXEC populate_passwords_tab

PL/SQL procedure successfully completed.

sec_mgr@KNOX10g> -- check for manager, a common password for DBA accounts
sec_mgr@KNOX10g> EXEC populate_passwords_tab ('manager')

PL/SQL procedure successfully completed.

sec_mgr@KNOX10g> -- check for your company's name here
sec_mgr@KNOX10g> EXEC populate_passwords_tab ('oracle')
```

```
PL/SQL procedure successfully completed.

sec_mgr@KNOX10g> -- SCOTT's default password
sec_mgr@KNOX10g> EXEC populate_passwords_tab ('tiger')

PL/SQL procedure successfully completed.

sec_mgr@KNOX10g> -- SYS' default password
sec_mgr@KNOX10g> EXEC populate_passwords_tab ('change_on_install')

PL/SQL procedure successfully completed.

sec_mgr@KNOX10g> -- common password people use
sec_mgr@KNOX10g> EXEC populate_passwords_tab ('password')

PL/SQL procedure successfully completed.

sec_mgr@KNOX10g> COMMIT ;

Commit complete.
```

Now that you have a data set of precomputed password verifiers, you're ready to run checks against your production database.

NOTE
Once the password table has been created, the same data can be used against any Oracle Database because the password verifiers for the usernames are always the same in every Oracle Database.

For the procedure that actually performs the checking, simply iterate through the database users comparing the password verifier computed there with the one actually stored in the PASSWORDS table. When you find a match, print the matched value and the account's status:

```
sec_mgr@KNOX10g> CREATE OR REPLACE PROCEDURE check_passwords
AS
BEGIN
  FOR rec IN (SELECT username,
                     PASSWORD,
                     account_status
                FROM dba_users)
  LOOP
    FOR irec IN (SELECT *
                   FROM passwords
                  WHERE username = rec.username
                    AND verifier = rec.PASSWORD)
    LOOP
      DBMS_OUTPUT.put_line
                ('------------------------------');
      DBMS_OUTPUT.put_line (    'Password for '
                            || rec.username
```

```
                                  || ' is '
                                  || irec.passwd);
        DBMS_OUTPUT.put_line
                                 (    'Account Status is '
                                  || rec.account_status);
      END LOOP;
    END LOOP;
  END;
  /

Procedure created.

sec_mgr@KNOX10g> set timing on
sec_mgr@KNOX10g> SET serveroutput on
sec_mgr@KNOX10g> EXEC check_passwords
------------------------------
Password for CTXSYS is CHANGE_ON_INSTALL
Account Status is LOCKED
------------------------------
Password for DIP is DIP
Account Status is LOCKED
------------------------------
Password for OLAPSYS is MANAGER
Account Status is LOCKED

PL/SQL procedure successfully completed.

Elapsed: 00:00:00.03
```

The output from the procedure's execution was truncated in the previous output. It simply shows that the procedure was successful in finding passwords (not all successful findings are printed). Because changing default passwords is a best practice, this program can assist you in ensuring your Oracle Databases are compliant with best practices and are thus better secured.

Impossible Passwords

The Oracle database user's password verifier is stored as a 16-character hexadecimal string. If you query the DBA_USERS view, you'll see some passwords that aren't hexadecimals. For example, there's a database user named ANONYMOUS with a password of *anonymous*. How can that be? If you created a user by the name of ANONYMOUS with a password of *anonymous*, the password verifier wouldn't say *anonymous*; it would be a hexadecimal representation of a hash of the password, not a plaintext string. You can check the passwords table previously created to verify this:

```
sec_mgr@KNOX10g> select * from passwords
      where username = 'ANONYMOUS'
        and pwd = 'ANONYMOUS';

USERNAME   PWD                            VERIFIER
---------- ------------------------------ ----------------
ANONYMOUS  ANONYMOUS                      FE0E8CE7C92504E9
```

The reason the string *anonymous* is present, as opposed to the verifier you see above, is that the user wasn't created with the standard CREATE USER syntax but with the identified by values clause, as shown here:

```
SQL> CREATE USER anonymous IDENTIFIED BY VALUES 'anonymous';

User created.

SQL> select username, password
  2  from dba_users
  3  where username = 'ANONYMOUS'
  4  /

USERNAME                       PASSWORD
------------------------------ ------------------------------
ANONYMOUS                      anonymous
```

This is a simple trick you can use to ensure users don't log in to an account. It's similar to creating a very strong password, but it's better because you can't log in to the account with *anonymous* or any other string in the universe!

The reason that no password is possible is because Oracle, on authentication, will compute the password verifier, which will be some 16-character hexadecimal string. This is compared with the one stored for the user. Because you know the password verifiers are stored in hexadecimal format, any values outside of the hexadecimal set (0–9, A–F) will not match the one computed. The result: there is no password the user can provide that will allow them to log in.

Anytime you are creating a database schema to which no one should connect, you should use an impossible password. The account also should be locked and privileges to connect to the database *should not* be given.

Managing and Ensuring Good Passwords

Passwords are the most prevalent form of authentication to Oracle Databases. Oracle provides the ability to enforce the choice of good, strong passwords through the use of password complexity routines. Oracle also provides a way to ensure good password management practices are also being followed through password profile enforcement.

Password Complexity

Oracle supports user-defined password complexity routines that allow you to validate the strength of passwords when they are set. Password complexity routines are critical to ensuring that password best practices are obeyed. The complexity routine technically implements the official password policy in your organization (assuming you have such a policy, and you should). You can check for many things within the routine. The biggest exception is case-sensitivity. Database authenticated user passwords are case insensitive. Here are a few common best practice checks you can administer within the complexity routine:

- Password isn't the same as the username
- Password contains at least one digit
- Password is greater than some specified length

- Password isn't the same as the old password
- Password isn't an easy to guess word, such as manager, oracle, or your company's name

The function that administers the password check has to be implemented in the SYS schema. The password complexity function returns a Boolean value. The value TRUE means the password is okay. However, a good trick is to raise an exception in the function to notify the user of exactly what condition failed during their password change. Otherwise, they will get a generic error. A sample function that implements some of the above checks would look as follows:

```
sys@KNOX10g> CREATE OR REPLACE FUNCTION is_password_strong (
    p_username      VARCHAR2,
    p_new_password  VARCHAR2,
    p_old_password  VARCHAR2)
    -- return TRUE if password is strong enough
  RETURN BOOLEAN
  AS
    l_return_val  BOOLEAN := TRUE;
  BEGIN
    -- Check to be sure password is not the same as username
    IF UPPER (p_new_password) = UPPER (p_username)
    THEN
      l_return_val := FALSE;
      raise_application_error
                      (-20001,
                       'Password same as user name');
    END IF;

    -- force user to change password to something new
    IF UPPER (p_new_password) =
                              UPPER (p_old_password)
    THEN
      l_return_val := FALSE;
      raise_application_error
        (-20004,
         'Password has to be different than old password');
    END IF;

    -- Check for list of predictable passwords
    IF LOWER (p_new_password) IN
         ('manager',
          'change_on_install',
          'oracle',
          'password')
    THEN
      l_return_val := FALSE;
      raise_application_error
                      (-20002,
                       'Password is too predictable');
    END IF;

```

```
   -- make sure password contains at least one digit
   IF (regexp_like (p_new_password, '[0123456789]') =
                                                FALSE)
   THEN
     l_return_val := FALSE;
     raise_application_error
              (-20003,
               'Password needs at least one digit');
   END IF;

   -- make sure password is at least six characters
   IF LENGTH (p_new_password) <= 6
   THEN
     l_return_val := FALSE;
     raise_application_error
                          (-20005,
                           'Password is too short');
   END IF;

   RETURN l_return_val;
 END;
 /

Function created.
```

To enforce the password complexity routine, assign it to a Password Profile and then assign the profile to the user(s). Examples are shown in the following section.

Password Profiles

Oracle allows you to create Password Profiles that govern the behavior of the database with respect to passwords and authentication. To do this, create a profile with values set for the attributes you wish to use. The profile then can be enforced on your users. Oracle supports the following attributes for password profiles:

- **Password lifetime** Allows a password to exist for a specific period of time
- **Grace period** Time at which Database begins to warn users to change their password
- **Reuse time/max** Supports password history and forces users to use new passwords
- **Failed login attempts** Locks the account if the incorrect password is given after specified number of times
- **Account lockout** Disables the account (combined with failed attempts to help prevent brute force attempts into user accounts)
- **Password Verify Function** Defines the password complexity function that will be called when the user changes the password

Chapter 7 of the *Oracle Database Security Guide* gives more detailed explanations of these attributes. A sample profile that sets values for these attributes and assigns the complexity function defined previously would look as follows:

```
sec_mgr@KNOX10g> CREATE PROFILE strong_pwd LIMIT
      PASSWORD_LIFE_TIME 90
      PASSWORD_GRACE_TIME 15
      PASSWORD_REUSE_TIME 180
      PASSWORD_REUSE_MAX UNLIMITED
      FAILED_LOGIN_ATTEMPTS 5
      PASSWORD_LOCK_TIME .5
      PASSWORD_VERIFY_FUNCTION is_password_strong;

Profile created.
```

Now assign this profile to your users. Testing this on the user SCOTT yields the following results:

```
sec_mgr@KNOX10g> -- assign profile
sec_mgr@KNOX10g> ALTER USER scott PROFILE strong_pwd;

User altered.

sec_mgr@KNOX10g> -- test profile
sec_mgr@KNOX10g> -- reset scott's password
sec_mgr@KNOX10g> ALTER USER scott IDENTIFIED BY scott;
ALTER USER scott IDENTIFIED BY scott
*
ERROR at line 1:
ORA-28003: password verification for the specified password failed
ORA-20001: Password same as user name


sec_mgr@KNOX10g> ALTER USER scott IDENTIFIED BY manager;
ALTER USER scott IDENTIFIED BY manager
*
ERROR at line 1:
ORA-28003: password verification for the specified password failed
ORA-20002: Password is too predictable


sec_mgr@KNOX10g> ALTER USER scott IDENTIFIED BY nodigit;
ALTER USER scott IDENTIFIED BY nodigit
*
ERROR at line 1:
ORA-28003: password verification for the specified password failed
ORA-20003: Password needs at least one digit
```

```
sec_mgr@KNOX10g> -- since this is not SCOTT, old password is null
sec_mgr@KNOX10g> ALTER USER scott IDENTIFIED BY tiger;
ALTER USER scott IDENTIFIED BY tiger
*
ERROR at line 1:
ORA-28003: password verification for the specified password failed
ORA-20003: Password needs at least one digit


sec_mgr@KNOX10g> ALTER USER scott IDENTIFIED BY short1;
ALTER USER scott IDENTIFIED BY short1
*
ERROR at line 1:
ORA-28003: password verification for the specified password failed
ORA-20005: Password is too short
```

Normally, after creating a password profile, you'll force your users to change their passwords to ensure all passwords being used comply with the profile. To do this, you expire their existing password. Upon their next login, the database prompts them to reset their password. The new password is checked against the complexity routine and the other password profile values will also be enforced.

When administering this for SCOTT, set the new password to *tiger,* which you can't see when looking at the output below. You may have noticed in the previous example that the complexity function didn't indicate that the new *tiger* password matched the old password. The following output shows a different behavior when SCOTT changes his password. The complexity routine now informs him that the new password is the same as the old password. Note that this is done for security. If a user other than SCOTT received this message, then the database would have divulged the user's password.

```
sec_mgr@KNOX10g> ALTER  USER scott PASSWORD EXPIRE;

User altered.

sec_mgr@KNOX10g> conn scott/tiger
ERROR:
ORA-28001: the password has expired


Changing password for scott
New password:
Retype new password:
ERROR:
ORA-28003: password verification for the specified password failed
ORA-20004: Password has to be different than old password


Password unchanged
Warning: You are no longer connected to ORACLE.
```

Keep the Password Policies Practical

A password profile is a great way to ensure that good password management practices are being used. Once again, however, you have to balance security with usability. While using password profiles is generally a good idea, it can backfire. For example, forcing users to choose a new password each week (that is, expiring passwords too frequently) may in fact force the user to use easy passwords or worse, write down their passwords.

As another example, you may decide after three failed logins, you'll lock the user account for a day. There are unintended consequences to this. The failed login and account locking can aid someone launching a denial of service (DoS) attack. The attack is made easy because a malicious person can intentionally lock *all* the database accounts by simply providing an incorrect password for each database user.

Limiting Database Resources

Whether intentional or malicious, a computer's resources can be monopolized without much effort. Generally, when this is done maliciously, it is known as a *denial of service (DoS) attack.*

DoS attacks are easy to implement and hard to defend against. The defense challenge arises from the fact that there are numerous ways to trigger such attacks. The result is simple: exhaust computing resources to the point that the database can no longer provide adequate service. Fortunately, there are some actions you can take in the database to mitigate the risk of DoS attacks.

Resource Limits

In addition to the password profile capabilities, Oracle supports the use of resource profiles to limit the use of precious database resources. Resource limits help ensure that the application or user doesn't intentionally, or inadvertently, take over the database and system's resources. You can view the various resources that can be managed as well as their values by querying the DBA_PROFILES view:

```
sec_mgr@KNOX10g> SELECT resource_name, LIMIT
  2     FROM dba_profiles
  3    WHERE PROFILE = 'DEFAULT'
  4      AND resource_type = 'KERNEL';

RESOURCE_NAME                     LIMIT
--------------------------------  ------------
COMPOSITE_LIMIT                   UNLIMITED
SESSIONS_PER_USER                 UNLIMITED
CPU_PER_SESSION                   UNLIMITED
CPU_PER_CALL                      UNLIMITED
LOGICAL_READS_PER_SESSION         UNLIMITED
LOGICAL_READS_PER_CALL            UNLIMITED
IDLE_TIME                         UNLIMITED
CONNECT_TIME                      UNLIMITED
PRIVATE_SGA                       UNLIMITED

9 rows selected.
```

Notice that the default values are all set to unlimited. A best practice is to actually define as many of these values as possible. Some general guidelines on the parameters are as follows:

- Set the SESSIONS_PER_USER to the size of your application server connection pool. If you aren't using a connection pool (or have no idea what that means), then set the value to something reasonable. You should consider that an application may lock or a computer may freeze with the connection open, so a value of one may be too restrictive.

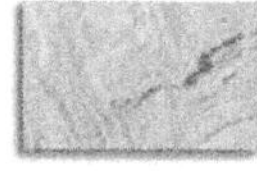

TIP
It's possible to create a denial-of-service attack by utilizing the CREATE SESSION privilege and connecting to the database over and over until the database server exhausts all memory. Setting this parameter helps to ensure this will not happen.

- IDLE_TIME can be set to help ensure that users don't leave a connected terminal in the database while they step out for a lunch break. If their machine is left unlocked, then someone can simply walk up and start accessing the user's data without having to worry about breaking passwords or subverting privileges. This value is more applicable to client-server applications than to web applications; if the latter is using a connection pool, the server shouldn't disconnect the pooled connections.
- CPU_PER_CALL is a hard parameter to guess, but it helps to ensure the availability of the database. Often CPU monopolization occurs not by a malicious user, but by a bad programmer who inadvertently sends the database into a recursive loop (I'm speaking from experience here)!

Refer to the "Create Profile" section in the *Oracle Database SQL Reference 10g* document for specific definitions on all the settings. Setting the profile parameters to the logical and correct values may take a few tries before the best values are selected. Start with a least privilege mentality by setting the values very conservatively. If you find that you need to relax a few privileges for legitimate reasons, do so only after you have determined the values need to be relaxed.

A best practice is to create a profile for each application or class of users in the database. This includes administrators at all levels.

Default Roles

Just as the Oracle Database comes with default schemas, it also comes with several default roles. These roles exist mostly for legacy reasons and according to the Oracle documentation will one day be removed. This section discusses these roles and how to securely interact with them.

CONNECT

The first default role you should understand is the CONNECT role. This is one of the most misused roles probably because its name implies that it's a necessary privilege. Many DBAs grant users CONNECT thinking that it's only the simple privilege to log on to the database. It's not! The actual privilege required to log on to the database is the CREATE SESSION privilege. As you can see from the following code, the CONNECT role has more than this single privilege:

```
sec_mgr@KNOX10g> SELECT PRIVILEGE
  2    FROM dba_sys_privs
  3   WHERE grantee = 'CONNECT';

PRIVILEGE
----------------------------------------
CREATE VIEW
CREATE TABLE
ALTER SESSION
CREATE CLUSTER
CREATE SESSION
CREATE SYNONYM
CREATE SEQUENCE
CREATE DATABASE LINK

8 rows selected.
```

Some of these privileges, such as CREATE VIEW, CREATE TABLE, and CREATE DATABASE LINK, are probably more powerful privileges than you want your users to have. Therefore, in the spirit of least privileges, you shouldn't be granting the CONNECT role to your users as the means by which they are privileged to log on to the database.

RESOURCE

The next default role is RESOURCE. This role has also been in existence for many years and its use should be limited for the same reasons cited above. You can see this role, like the CONNECT role, also has many privileges granted to it:

```
sec_mgr@KNOX10g> SELECT PRIVILEGE
  2    FROM dba_sys_privs
  3   WHERE grantee = 'RESOURCE';

PRIVILEGE
----------------------------------------
CREATE TYPE
CREATE TABLE
CREATE CLUSTER
CREATE TRIGGER
CREATE OPERATOR
CREATE SEQUENCE
CREATE INDEXTYPE
CREATE PROCEDURE

8 rows selected.
```

There is also a hidden system privilege that is granted to users with the RESOURCE role: UNLIMITED TABLESPACE. This can be dangerous because users with this privilege have no effective quota and can use up all available disk space (see how to curtail such use in the previous section, "Limiting Database Resources").

In the following example, a user is created and granted the RESOURCE role, and by checking the user's privileges, you'll notice that the user has an unrestricted quota.

```
sec_mgr@KNOX10g> CREATE USER unlim IDENTIFIED BY VALUES 'noPassword';

User created.

sec_mgr@KNOX10g> -- user has no privileges
sec_mgr@KNOX10g> SELECT *
  2    FROM dba_sys_privs
  3   WHERE grantee = 'UNLIM';

no rows selected

sec_mgr@KNOX10g> -- grant resource role to user
sec_mgr@KNOX10g> GRANT RESOURCE TO unlim;

Grant succeeded.

sec_mgr@KNOX10g> -- note the user now has unlimited quota
sec_mgr@KNOX10g> SELECT PRIVILEGE
  2    FROM dba_sys_privs
  3   WHERE grantee = 'UNLIM';

PRIVILEGE
----------------------------------------
UNLIMITED TABLESPACE
```

It's common to see grants to both the CONNECT and the RESOURCE roles within Oracle example code as well as actual deployed commercial applications. Don't assume that this is a best practice.

NOTE
Complying with the least privilege principle is a best practice and relying on the CONNECT and RESOURCE roles as an easy way to grant privileges to your users is a bad practice.

DBA

Another important role that is commonly granted is the DBA role, which has every system privilege known to the database either directly granted or inherited through another role. It's not unusual for this role to be granted to the data or procedural schemas used for an application. *This is a gross misuse of privileges.*

Granting the DBA role abides by the most privilege principle, rather than the preferred least privilege principle. Chapter 7 shows how to effectively manage privileges and roles. When it comes to ensuring the default roles aren't abused, there are three actions you can take. However, I suggest you only do the last:

- Revoke all privileges assigned to default roles. This can be useful in an application where you are checking to see if a user is a member of a role, but you don't want there to be associated privileges with that role, such as with the DBA role.
- Drop the default roles. Check with support first, because this may have negative effects on your default applications. Be sure to make a sound backup of the database and test it on your development system first!
- *Don't grant the DBA, CONNECT, or RESOURCE roles to users.*

PUBLIC Privileges

One of the principle techniques for securing an Oracle Database involves the careful analysis of the use of the user group PUBLIC. The user group PUBLIC, as the name implies, represents every user in the database; therefore, *a grant to PUBLIC is a grant to everyone in the database.* This shorthand way of granting and revoking privileges can be a very useful feature. It also can create huge security risks especially when trying to ensure the database is operating in a least privileges manner.

When to Grant Privileges to PUBLIC

There are many occasions when grants to PUBLIC are sensible and don't create security risks. For example, most Oracle database application developers recognize that the DUAL table is both very useful and contains absolutely no sensitive information. This is true of other procedures and functions as well—the SYSDATE function is a good example of a useful function that doesn't have security risks associated with it. Therefore, PUBLIC access to the DUAL table and the SYSDATE function don't represent a security risk.

Unfortunately, it's difficult to know whether a grant to PUBLIC is really a security risk. As you develop your applications, you should carefully decide what, if anything, is granted to PUBLIC.

You also should consider what may not appear to be a risk today, could be a risk tomorrow. For example, suppose you have a table that stores user preferences for a web application. Initially, you allow users to save their preferences for the foreground and background colors as well as the font style that will be used in creating a personalized web page for them. Since none of this information is sensitive, you decide that it can be viewed by anyone.

```
scott@KNOX10g> CREATE TABLE user_prefs
  2  (background_color VARCHAR2(6),
  3  foreground_color VARCHAR2(6),
  4  font_style VARCHAR2(20));

Table created.

scott@KNOX10g> GRANT SELECT ON user_prefs TO PUBLIC;

Grant succeeded.
```

Later, you might add a sensitive attribute. For example, you may want to allow the user to store hyperlinks to their favorite web sites and applications.

```
scott@KNOX10g> ALTER TABLE user_prefs ADD favorite_links VARCHAR2(250);

Table altered.
```

The addition of this attribute changes the overall sensitivity of the table. The grant to PUBLIC should now be removed. The security rule for governing PUBLIC privileges is: *when in doubt, do not grant access to PUBLIC.*

Oracle Supplied Objects

In efforts to secure the Oracle database, you also have to consider the privileges that already have been granted to PUBLIC by both the applications you develop, or purchase, and the Oracle-supplied database objects.

There are two areas you should be concerned with respecting default grants to PUBLIC on Oracle objects:

- **Access to data dictionary views** There are several data dictionary views that will give a user information that could be used to aid in a database attack.
- **Execute on procedures** This includes PL/SQL functions and procedures and packages, as well as any Java procedures. These procedures perform many useful functions—such as opening network connections, reading files from the operating system, and setting identifier information about the user or application—all of which might be used in subsequent security processes, such as access control and auditing.

PUBLIC Access to Dictionary Views

The Oracle database already provides some security to the database dictionary metadata by restricting access to the sensitive data. Over time, the definition of "sensitive data" has evolved. Originally, sensitive data referred to items such as the encrypted user passwords. Today, even the list of all usernames in the database is considered sensitive. However, some of this data is still available to PUBLIC.

As an example, the ALL_USERS view is accessible to PUBLIC and it lists the username of every database schema. A technique often used by hackers is to obtain and use a list of valid user accounts to try to access those accounts. Privileged database option schemas (such as MDYS), default application accounts, and user accounts will be listed by the ALL_USERS view as valid targets to a nefarious user. The list of valid database users then becomes a list of valid database targets. A malicious user could easily say, "Oh look, the <insert option name or your application here> is installed. Let me use the default password and try to access this privileged account."

Therefore, you should consider revoking PUBLIC access to certain database metadata. Looking at SYS objects that start with ALL is a good place to start:

```
SELECT table_name
  FROM dba_tab_privs
 WHERE grantee = 'PUBLIC'
   AND owner = 'SYS'
```

```
   AND PRIVILEGE = 'SELECT'
   AND table_name LIKE 'ALL%';
```

Broken Objects

Before revoking PUBLIC access to default database objects, you should know that the revocation may break existing programs or applications. The following example shows 20 database objects that become invalid after the PUBLIC privileges have been removed from the ALL_USERS view.

```
sys@KNOX10g> SELECT count(*) FROM all_objects
  2   WHERE status = 'INVALID';

  COUNT(*)
----------
         0

1 row selected.

sys@KNOX10g> REVOKE SELECT ON all_users FROM PUBLIC;

Revoke succeeded.

sys@KNOX10g> SELECT count(*) FROM all_objects
  2   WHERE status = 'INVALID';

  COUNT(*)
----------
        20

1 row selected.
```

The damage isn't unrepairable. If an application relies on a revoked privilege that was once granted to PUBLIC, it can be fixed by granting the privilege directly to the application. To do this for the data dictionary views, simply list the schemas that require the direct grant.

```
sys@KNOX10g> -- Show whose objects are broken.
sys@KNOX10g> SELECT distinct owner
  2    FROM all_objects
  3   WHERE status = 'INVALID';

OWNER
--------------------
DMSYS
EXFSYS
LBACSYS
SYS
SYSMAN
XDB

6 rows selected.
```

Of these schemas, some have the system privilege SELECT ANY DICTIONARY, which already provides access to the ALL_USERS view. The objects in those schemas will recompile without requiring any grants; however, the other schemas will require a direct grant on the ALL_USERS view. You can display the list of remaining schemas that require the direct grant by using the SQL minus function bolded in the following code. This code wraps the result set in the DDL you'll use to issue the grants:

```
sys@KNOX10g> -- create list of users who require
sys@KNOX10g> -- direct select privileges on ALL_USERS
sys@KNOX10g> SELECT DISTINCT    'grant select on all_users to '
                     || owner
                     || ';' sql_command
               FROM (SELECT DISTINCT owner
                                FROM all_objects
                               WHERE status =
                                             'INVALID'
                                 AND owner != 'SYS'
                     MINUS
                     SELECT grantee
                       FROM dba_sys_privs
                      WHERE PRIVILEGE =
                               'SELECT ANY DICTIONARY');

SQL_COMMAND
------------------------------------------------------------
grant select on all_users to DMSYS;
grant select on all_users to EXFSYS;
grant select on all_users to LBACSYS;
grant select on all_users to XDB;

4 rows selected.
```

Using copy and paste technology for the values in the SQL_COMMAND, issue the direct grant to the users that require it. After the grant has been made, the invalid objects in those schemas will recompile.

Unfortunately, the consequences of the revocation are nearly impossible to predict. This is why Oracle hasn't already removed PUBLIC privileges to the database metadata views. The *Oracle Database Security Guide* also warns that revoking DML privileges from PUBLIC can be nontrivial:

> Revoking a privilege from PUBLIC can cause significant cascading effects. If any privilege related to a DML operation is revoked from PUBLIC, all procedures in the database, including functions and packages, must be reauthorized before they can be used again. Therefore, exercise caution when granting and revoking DML-related privileges to PUBLIC.

PUBLIC Privileges on Programs

Next, analyze the execute privileges on programs granted to PUBLIC. Again, there are too many specific programs to list and the programs will constantly be changing. The same principle applies to securing these programs as to the preceding views. That is, knowing what the programs do is important to understanding what risks, if any, are present.

The programs you should be most concerned with are the ones that start with DBMS% and UTL%:

```
SELECT   table_name
    FROM dba_tab_privs
   WHERE     grantee = 'PUBLIC'
         AND owner = 'SYS'
         AND PRIVILEGE = 'EXECUTE'
         AND table_name LIKE 'DBMS%'
      OR table_name LIKE 'UTL%'
ORDER BY 1;
```

CAUTION
Don't limit your evaluation to just these programs or SYS-owned objects. All options and applications in your database should be evaluated.

The Oracle Database Security Guide suggests revoking execute privileges on UTL_SMTP, UTL_TCP, UTL_HTTP, and UTL_FILE from PUBLIC. You should not only do this, but also remember the point of this exercise is to restrict access to procedures to only those applications, users, *and* objects requiring access.

Just as in the metadata example, there are often application dependencies created upon the PUBLIC grants to these programs. To successfully revoke privileges, you need to understand the dependencies and be able to rectify any problems that are created by the revocation process. Chapter 6 provides an example of this process to revoking the execute privileges on the DBMS_SESSION package.

Securing the Network

For most databases, security begins even before the users gain access to the database. The network that links together the users, applications, and databases is critical in the security chain. There are a few actions you should take to strengthen this link.

Encryption

Today, some believe that network encryption isn't necessary. After all, antivirus software and firewalls are already in place.

This is wrong. While there is some level of security afforded by these technologies, the assumption that network traffic is totally secure is false. Anyone can place a network packet sniffer (readily available on the Internet) on the application server that connects to the database. Both are behind the firewall. With the sniffer they can easily capture all the traffic to and from the application server. Packets can be spooled to a file. Later, after the important data has been collected, the spool file can be sent via e-mail to an "anonymous" Internet account. This is *not* fiction; it really happens. Why bother breaking into the database with all its security when you can easily capture all the important data as it enters and leaves the database? This scenario illustrates the need for network encryption.

NOTE
When deploying applications that communicate with an Oracle Database, the Oracle network encryption capabilities provide seamless and transparent encryption of all your database data as it moves through the network. While it may not be needed in all situations, it should always be considered and is strongly recommended.

There are three benefits to implementing Oracle's network encryption capabilities:

- The algorithm negotiation feature supports the concurrent use of different encryption algorithms with different key sizes for various clients. This flexibility means that security and performance can be accomplished simultaneously.
- The encryption remains transparent to the applications that utilize it.
- Independent lab tests show little overhead costs, which makes it an acceptable trade-off in most cases.

Configuring the network for encryption is simple. Either edit the SQLNET.ORA file with a text editor or use the Oracle Net Manager. A view into the file shows how easy it is to instruct the Oracle network software to secure the channel:

```
SQLNET.CRYPTO_CHECKSUM_TYPES_CLIENT= (SHA1)
SQLNET.CRYPTO_CHECKSUM_TYPES_SERVER= (SHA1)
SQLNET.CRYPTO_SEED =
  thisistheencryptionseed(S)DLKDk0(*)(*#IUI%$,k9r80dsa0__11k098 09cxf-08
SQLNET.ENCRYPTION_SERVER = requested
SQLNET.ENCRYPTION_CLIENT = requested
SQLNET.ENCRYPTION_TYPES_CLIENT= (AES256)
SQLNET.ENCRYPTION_TYPES_SERVER= (AES256)
```

Using these settings, the network software will employ the SHA-1 algorithm to ensure data integrity and also will encrypt all data using the AES algorithm with 256-bit key sizes.

Database Listener

The *database listener* is the process that handles connections over the network destined for the database. Two important points about the listener:

- It is a critical program and needs to be run much of the time.
- It is the forward application, which means that it stands the biggest risk of attack. User programs can interact with the listener directly even if they don't have database accounts.

As with most network processes, there are numerous attacks that can occur against the database listener. Securing the database listener is a top priority. The first task is to password protect the listener process. Limiting status information is critical to securing the listener since the listener will happily explain everything it knows when prompted. This information is useful to both DBAs and to hackers.

The database listener also comes defaulted to a well-known network port or two. While it's by no stretch of the imagination a "robust" security maneuver, changing the default port is nevertheless a good idea. If the listener is on a different port, someone who is scanning the network for open ports will detect a process listening on that port but may not know what it is. Some hackers only probe for well-known ports because the full port scans are obvious and can set off the intrusion detection alarms.

TIP
Changing the listening ports (and not only from 1521 to 1522) is a best practice.

To configure the listener, either edit the LISTENER.ORA file with a text editor or use the Oracle Net Manager.

External Calls

The database supports a useful capability whereby PL/SQL programs running inside the database can make external calls to a program running on the operating system. The benefit is that the OS programs will either execute faster (because they are C programs optimized to perform a specific task) or pass information about the operating system back into the database (such as uptime, currently executing processes, and logged in users).

However, the external procedure call capability is a high security risk; the process runs with the privileges of the database listener. If the external procedure is successfully compromised, the hacker may find themselves sitting in a privileged shell.

If you're using, or need to use, this capability be sure to keep it in check; otherwise, disable it. To do this, modify the Oracle network configuration files (the PLSExtProc service). Removing the binary that allows this, extproc.exe, is also a good idea.

If you need to support external procedures, it's best to configure the extproc listener to run as an unprivileged user; for example, the "nobody" user on UNIX. By default, the process runs with the privileges of the database listener. By following this configuration suggestion, the risks associated with a compromised external procedure are significantly diminished.

IP Validation

IP addresses are the network method for naming entities. While the actual network protocols function at a lower layer (based on the MAC address), IP addresses remain a valuable identification asset. The main drawback with IP-based security is that it's not too difficult, relative to other tricks such as trying to break encryption, to impersonate another computer's IP Address (spoofing). The ability to successfully spoof depends on the network topology and the abilities of the network administrators to enforce strict IP addresses. Many network intrusion detection systems will alert administrators to duplicate IP addresses on their networks.

Assuming the IP address can be used to accurately identify the client, the IP address can then be incorporated into the database security implementations.

The Oracle database listener can be configured to allow or disallow access based on the client's IP address. This is an easy way to begin shielding your database from unwanted users.

The configuration can again be completed using the Oracle Net Manager. The settings are placed in the SQLNET.ORA file (prior to Oracle9*i* Database, this was the PROTOCOL.ORA file). For example, the following configuration will only allow a network connection from a single computer with the IP address of 192.168.1.21:

```
TCP.VALIDNODE_CHECKING = YES
TCP.INVITED_NODES= (192.168.1.21)
```

If your security policy dictates that the database only should be accessed from the application server, which has the previous IP address, these two lines can be added to your SQLNET.ORA file to ensure the database listener process will not accept any other connection requests. You can alternatively specify which specific nodes you want to exclude by setting the TCP.EXCLUDED_NODES value.

Using the valid node checking capability is a good practice because it helps ensure that the only connections coming in over the network are from computers that are authorized.

Summary

Building secure database applications is done on the assumption that the database is already operating securely. To ensure this happens, you often have to perform certain tasks to create a tighter security implementation. There are many important lessons in this chapter.

Securing database schemas means ensuring not only new schemas are created and managed properly but also that the default schemas are secured. The default schemas and their passwords are well known. There are several ways to prevent unwanted and unauthorized users from connecting to these well known and highly privileged accounts. Several techniques were shown for applying the defense in depth principle.

An understanding of Oracle's use of passwords is necessary because password authentication represents the most common authentication mechanism to the database. The database supports both password complexity routines and password profiles to support the secure and proper use of passwords.

Oracle's default roles exist today for legacy reasons and should rarely be used, and revoking existing privileges and limiting grants to the user group PUBLIC is essential for securing the database.

A final necessary piece of the security puzzle is network security. The entire security of an application and database can be subverted through poor network security. The database provides several ways to prevent this from happening. Applying security at the network tier ensures all the links in the security chain are strong.

PART II

Identification and Authentication

CHAPTER 3

Understanding Identification and Authentication

efore you begin to code your database applications, you should have a clear understanding of the security design. This is critical because the design decisions you make before you begin to build determine how effective your security implementation will be once you have built it.

In this chapter, we will review the first steps in the security process known as identification and authentication (I&A). I&A is the necessary base step upon which the database security depends. Therefore, your I&A design decisions are very important. The material presented here will provide supporting information that you can use in determining which methods are appropriate for your organization.

In today's world, a lot of the identification and authentication occurs at the application or application server. In Chapter 4, you will see how to connect the users at the application tier through to the database. Chapter 5 shows another design you may use to provide an efficient way to centrally manage the database users. This chapter provides an overview of the I&A concepts that is necessary for making the correct decisions on material presented in later chapters.

Importance of Identification and Authentication

The database security process flow can be summarized by the following three steps:

1. First, a user presents an identity to the database. For example, they enter their username.
2. The user proves that the identity just presented is valid. For example, they provide a password. The password is checked by the database to determine if it's the correct password for the username presented.
3. Assuming the password is correct, the database assumes the identity can be trusted. The database will then determine, based on the identity, what privileges and authorizations the user has. Data access is regulated by the user's privileges and authorizations.

Typically, people spend the majority of their time and security efforts implementing the processes needed for the third step. The first two steps are important because they form the foundation of security; you need them to get to step three. Step one is identification. Step two is authentication.

TIP
There is an often overlooked fact about designing and implementing security solutions: security cannot be based on anonymity.

You must first identify yourself. To do this securely requires authentication or proof that you are in fact who you say you are. If an application or database doesn't know who you are, it can't grant you the proper authorizations, apply the necessary access controls, and audit your actions. This seems obvious, but in countless database application designs, this point is lost. Most, if not all, database security is based on knowing who the user is.

As a validation of this principle, consider an e-mail application where all the e-mail is stored in a single database. The security policy for e-mail is simply that users can only access their personal e-mail. How would the security be implemented if the user's identity is unknown? It couldn't. Clearly, identifying the user has to be done.

The authentication has to be provided as well to ensure that users aren't trying to impersonate other users. If the authentication is not provided, or is provided weakly, the entire security processes in the application and database will be negated. The application and database will not prevent the nefarious user from carrying out their actions (meaning accessing someone else's e-mail) because the application and database think it is the authorized user.

Let's explore the various ways identification can be implemented to determine how to do it best.

Identification Methods

Identification is the process of specifically and distinctly recognizing an individual. Identification is a part of every day life. You identify yourself at work, on the telephone, through e-mail; you identify yourself so much that you probably don't even realize when you are doing it. Identification comes in many forms: you, photos of you, your fingerprints, your employee number, your bank account or credit card number, your frequent flyer number, your social security number, and of course, your username, all of which can represent you in the identification process.

Today, there are many forms of identification and many ways to identify yourself. Why you need to identify yourself and what or who you're identifying to helps to determine what you use as the identification method. The methods for identification fall into two categories: user-supplied identity and technological identification.

User-Supplied Identification

Asking the user to supply their identity is the most prevalent method for identification today. In most computer applications, identification is based on the username. Your bank probably likes to identify you by your account number(s), and your favorite airline has transformed you into a series of alphanumeric characters. All of these names and numbers serve the single purpose of identifying who you are.

In all cases, the user is responsible for providing the correct identifying information. This is important because knowledge of a valid identity provides some security. For example, you can't withdraw money from a bank account that doesn't exist. You are unlikely to log on to the database if you cannot provide a valid database username. For hackers trying to penetrate a system, a good starting point is to obtain a list of valid users on the system.

Obfuscating the user's name or choosing identifiers that don't indicate the privileges of the person is valuable, too. The username "Administrator" connotes high privileges and thus a more valuable attack target for a hacker than does a more neutral name such as "User125."

However, designing a security implementation exclusively based on the knowledge of the identifier—for example, a username or account number—is a risky proposition because it may be relatively easy to guess, predict, or obtain a valid identity from another source. This was discussed in Chapter 2 with regard to Default User Accounts.

The benefit to using user-provided identification is that the identifier (for example, username) is generally flexible. This allows administrators to create intuitive identifiers that are easy for the users to remember. For example, a username may be created based on the person's first initial and last name (dknox for me). As discussed in the previous paragraph, the benefit is also the weakness. Identifiers that can be easily guessed or predicted may weaken the overall security.

In the upcoming "Authentication" section, you'll see how verifying the identity provides the ability to maintain the security while simultaneously allowing flexibility in the choice of identifiers.

Technological Identification

Technology also offers a choice of ways to identify ourselves including biometrics, computer identities, and digital identities.

Biometric

A quickly growing and exciting technology for supporting user identification is biometric technology. *Biometrics* refers to the biological characteristics of people that can be measured to distinguish the differences among them. You use biometrics constantly to identify people. Your brain uses facial recognition when you see familiar people and voice recognition when you answer a phone call from someone you know.

A mass of companies are currently trying to mature various biometric technologies. Facial recognition, iris scanners, hand geometry, and fingerprint readers are among the most popular.

Biometrics are ideal in many ways. Users can't forget them, and they can be nearly impossible to guess. Theft of the biometric part is unlikely, but there is a risk associated with having the digital biometric representation stolen. If this occurs, there's a chance that someone could pretend to be someone else by copying and replaying the biometric signature or altering the metadata that indicates whose biometric it is.

Confusion around how biometrics are used is common. This is because the same biometric can be used for both the identification and the authentication processes. With biometric identification, the biometric information is considered unique and can be used to accurately identify the person presenting the biometric. This differs from user provided identification because the user is not telling the system who they are; the system identifies them automatically. Note this is not authentication, this is only identification; biometric authentication is the process of comparing the biometric signature with a reference to prove or disprove an identity (i.e., the identity is already known).

Computer Identities

In the computing environment, identity may be based on other nonstandard elements such as the computer's name, physical network address (i.e., MAC address—the unique identifier on the network card for the computer), logical network address (IP address), or some other device that may be affixed to a computer.

IP addresses and IP domains are used within security architectures quite frequently. The address or domain is either allowed access or not. Firewalls and various secure routing technologies are heavily dependent on MAC addresses and IP addresses. Application servers and the database security can also use IP addresses to help provide additional layers of security. You saw in Chapter 2 how the database listener can be configured to allow or disallow database connections based on the incoming IP address.

Digital Identities

Another prevalent form of identification is by way of digital representation or digital identities. An example seen today is the digital certificate used as part of Public Key Infrastructures (PKI). PKI provides many security capabilities, including identification, authentication, encryption, and nonrepudiation.

For identification, PKI uses digital certificates based on a standard format known as X.509. Entities, typically users or computer servers, are given unique digital certificates that represent their identity. The certificates include descriptive information about the entity such as their name, employee number, organization, and location. Think of a certificate as a digitized passport. The digital identities are well defined both structurally and semantically, and are consistent across all applications and platforms that support the certificate standards. This last point is critical to providing interoperability between applications and products provided by different vendors.

Digital certificates are popular not only because the certificates are standards based, but also because the certificates contain additional information that can be used in implementing effective security controls. For example, access to data can be based on both the user's name and the user's organizational affiliation and location.

For user identification, digital certificates are usually installed in the user's Web browsers. They can also be embedded into physical devices such as smart cards. To secure the digital identity, the user may be forced to supply a PIN or password to unlock the certificate.

Many single sign-on technologies, including the Oracle database and the Oracle Application Server Single Sign-On, support digital certificates as an I&A method for users.

Identity Crisis

One of the challenges to implementing effective security involves securing the identities. If security relies on proper identification, then it is natural to conclude that this linchpin in the security process is a high-risk area. Compromise the identity process, and you have compromised the security integrity of the application, the database, or both.

Spoofing

One particularly successful way to defeat good security is to play along with the security. Instead of trying to overcome the access controls and bypass the auditing, one can merely pretend to be someone else. *Masquerading* as another user, or *spoofing,* is the digital equivalent of identity theft that is discussed in the next section. This "someone else" can either be a privileged user or just another user. In both cases, spoofing can lead to disastrous results.

With spoofing, the security of the system can become an ally for the attacker. It may even help protect the information being stolen, manipulated, or copied by the spoofing hacker from other hackers! For example, it may not be difficult to copy or steal a digital certificate that is not properly secured. Digital certificates, which can act as digital identities, are small (roughly 10KB) and can be easily stored on many devices such as floppy disks, USB pen drives, and so on. If the certificate is stolen, it can then be used to falsely identify and authenticate a user. The security architecture of the network can include firewalls, network encryption, and intrusion detection systems, none of which can detect the spoofing actions being conducted.

This generally only happens if the certificate is not secured by some other factor such as a strong password or PIN. Certificate revocation, which exists in practically all applications that support digital certificates, resolves the illicit use of digital certificates but only when the user or administrator becomes aware that the theft has occurred.

There are countless ways to masquerade as someone else, but my main point is that user identity is critical to the security process. Ensuring the identity is secure by proper authentication, implementation, and monitoring is critical to ensuring effective overall security.

Identity Theft

Identity theft is a growing problem plaguing today's world. This term simply describes the misuse and misrepresentation of information associated with one individual for the benefit of another. This unfortunate circumstance has escalated in recent years for numerous reasons. Your job is to ensure that you are not adding to the problem.

Protecting user identities can be just as important as protecting the data the identities get access to. Knowing as little as a person's social security number and their date of birth, someone may be able to steal an identity to open a new bank account, apply for loans, buy expensive toys, or do countless other illegal activities under the guise of being someone else.

Why all this talk about identity theft in this book? Because a lot of the information that can be used to create false identities is siphoned from databases and poorly designed applications. The improper choice of an identifier could be a catalyst for identity theft.

Let's look at a possible table structure to see what risks exist.

```
CREATE TABLE customers
(last_name VARCHAR2(50),
first_name VARCHAR2(50),
ssn VARCHAR2(11),
date_of_birth DATE);
```

The data in this table is clearly sensitive. Protecting access to the data in this table is an obvious security requirement. There is also a not-so-obvious security risk.

It wouldn't be unusual for the application designer to use the SSN as the user's identifier. This is very risky and considered to be a very bad decision. The reason is that user identifiers are sometimes required by application developers for testing or debugging, the DBAs for verifying database access, as well as the intended application users/end users that interact with the application on a daily basis.

As such, there is a significant risk that the SSN and the user's name or date of birth would be handled inappropriately—written on paper and left on someone's desk, or e-mailed in an insecure manner. This could lead to the inadvertent disclosure of this sensitive information. It is this type of practice that can lead to identity theft. You should carefully evaluate the identifiers you use to ensure that sensitive and privacy-related information is not being used to represent the user's identity.

Authentication

Presenting an identity to a system is technically all that is needed for the system to apply authorizations, enforce access control, and audit. Unfortunately, the world isn't comprised of honest people. Therefore, an identity generally has to be accompanied by something else that proves the person's identity is legitimate.

For identification to work successfully, there has to be a process for proving that a person is who they claim to be: authentication is that process.

Methods

Authentication methods fall into the following three categories:

- *Something you know, such as a password or Personal Identification Number (PIN).* Passwords are the most common authentication method for computer systems because they are generally cheap to implement and maintain.
- *Something you possess such as a token card, X.509 certificate, a smart card, a car key, a credit card, or a software license key.* These last examples vary on their ability to support an individual's identity. Sometimes the authentication is just to prove that you are a legitimate entity, such as a building access card that proves you are an employee or a license key that proves you are a paying software subscriber.
- *Something you are, or biometrics.* Fingerprints, facial recognition, iris scans, and maybe someday DNA will be used to authenticate people to their computer applications.

Strong and Weak Authentication

Strong authentication usually implies that the authentication cannot be easily guessed or faked. Authentication technologies have varying abilities to perform their authenticating task. One of the metrics for determining the authentication strength is how hard it is to forge the authentication method.

Something you are and *something you have* are considered stronger forms of authentication than *something you know*. Passwords can be guessed and therefore are considered weak authentication. Forging an X.509 certificate (something you have) or duplicating a biometric (something you are) is not as easy. Consequently, digital certificates, token, and biometric authentications are considered strong authentication.

This isn't meant to imply that passwords shouldn't be used for authentication. You learned in Chapter 2 that there are strong passwords and weak passwords. Strong passwords consist of enough characters and difficulty that they can't be easily guessed; weak passwords are easy to predict or guess—for example, they are the same as the username, or they are a well-known string such as "password." Weak passwords shouldn't be used. Refer back to Chapter 2 for information on how you can ensure that your database users are using strong passwords by implementing a password complexity routine and a password profile.

Multifactor Authentication

Have you ever been asked to present three forms of identification? It's inconvenient, but it provides more security. This is because it's easier to fake or forge single things than it is to fake or forge multiple things. Consequently, combining authentication methods has a similar effect and is generally considered a very good authentication practice. For example, the possession of an object combined with a password or PIN is considered strong authentication. Most bank customers can withdraw cash with possession of an ATM card and the associated PIN. In this example, the card acts as both the identifier (it contains your bank account numbers) as well as one of the factors for authentication. Simple possession of the card wouldn't be sufficient because the card could be lost or stolen.

Generally speaking, the more methods you use for authentication, the higher assurance you have in the authentication. Two forms, or *two-factor authentication*, is better than a single-authenticating item, and three forms, or *multifactor authentication*, is better than two, and so on.

Best Practices for Secure Authentication

Just as it is important to protect sensitive user identifiers, it's very important to protect user authenticators. Protecting the authenticators implies protection not only for the storage of the authenticator, but also security for the authenticator while it's in transit.

You could employ strong authentication and lose a security battle to a hacker because the authentication channel you use or the manner in which the authentication credentials are stored isn't secured. For example, biometric authentication is considered robust, strong authentication; however, compromising biometric authentication is more easily done not by plastic surgery, but by copying and replaying a biometric signature or altering the metadata that indicates whose biometric data is whose.

Encrypt Authenticators

Encryption is an important tool for securing authenticators. For example, let's assume a user is authenticating with a fingerprint. If the fingerprint is passed over an unencrypted network channel, a hacker with a network sniffer could record the user's identity and fingerprint. Later, the hacker could replay or submit the captured identity and fingerprint, thereby successfully spoofing the original user. With network encryption, a new key is used for each communication session. The key used in the first captured session can't be re-used later. Replaying a captured encrypted biometric will not work using standard network encryption such as SSL.

Authenticators are at high risk because they are often traversing the computer networks. Encrypting network traffic is a good defense against authenticator copying and replaying. Encrypting the entire network stream provides optimal security. The encryption protects not only the authenticators, but also the identities of the users, the queries they submit, and the results returned. In Chapter 2 you saw that enabling Oracle's network encryption will guard against these network risks for data going to and from the database. You should also be aware that Oracle doesn't pass plaintext passwords over the network even when you aren't using the network encryption.

Providing security for the authenticator storage is equally as important. Often, authenticators will be stored in an encrypted format to preserve the confidentiality of the authenticator.

Hashed Authenticators

When passwords are used for authentication, the passwords shouldn't be stored in plaintext. Encryption seems to be the natural solution, but it's not. *Encryption*, which is the process of converting plaintext into undecipherable text, implies *decryption*, which is the process of converting the undecipherable text back into plaintext. The golden rule of passwords is that they are never disclosed to anyone at anytime. Encrypting passwords, which allows for potential decryption, could allow this disclosure to occur.

To solve this, you use a technology called hashing. *Hashing* takes plaintext and converts it to undecipherable text. Unlike encryption, however, there is no way to unhash something. That is, there is no way to take a hashed value and determine what created that value. Hashing is called a *one-way function* because of this property. Another important property of hashing is that the same input to the hash will always generate the same output.

Password authentication occurs by hashing the password and storing the resulting hashed value. When the user enters a password to authenticate, you hash the user-supplied authentication value (their password) and compare this hashed result with the stored hashed value. If the hashed values match, then the inputs must also have matched, and therefore the passwords are the same.

The hashing process can be used for other authenticators in the same manner. Since the authenticators are never used for activities such as sorts, aggregate computations, and so on, hashing is a good solution for storing the authentication data.

Keyed hashing, which involves encrypting a hashed value, is often a better alternative than basic hashing as long as the key can be protected. You can see an example of how to build your own password-based authentication that uses these concepts in Chapter 13, which illustrates the uses of the DBMS_CRYPTO package.

Single Sign-On

Single sign-on is both a security solution and a usability solution. It was conceived because in today's world of computer applications, people tend to have too many identifiers (usernames) and too many authenticators (passwords) for too many applications.

Why Single Sign-On Exists

There is no technical security reason for single sign-on to exist; it exists because people's behavior forces it to exist. If the identities are different and the passwords are different for every application or database, the users have to have excellent memories to be able to use them all. The security risk arose because people felt the only way to maintain all the usernames and passwords was to write the usernames and passwords on a piece of paper that would be conveniently placed by their computer.

One solution to the problem would be to make all the usernames and/or passwords the same. While this alleviates the problem of having to remember many usernames and passwords, it leaves the computing environment less usable. Typing in a username and password over and over can be a bothersome task especially when done for strong passwords that consist of many characters combining symbols, numbers, and letters.

Thus, single sign-on, as the name implies, was created to make the computing environment more usable because users only need to authenticate themselves once regardless of the number of applications they want to access. Security can also be maintained because the users have a single username and password. Password administration is also easier because the password only has to be changed once regardless of the number of applications.

There are many implementations for single sign-on, and they vary in the way the user's identity is represented as well as how they accomplish the task of single sign-on. Kerberos, DCE, and PKI-based solutions are among the most popular in use today. The essence of single sign-on is consistent regardless of how it's implemented. The goal is to securely propagate the user's identity from application to application without bothering the user each time. *When used correctly, single sign-on is both a usability and a security solution.*

Challenges to Single Sign-On

Single sign-on is not without its challenges. The challenge to implementing practical single sign-on arises when you try to mix products and platforms by different vendors. Using de-facto or industry standards, such as Kerberos and PKI, helps to mitigate the interoperability issues.

A single sign-on security risk is created when a user logs on to their single sign-on environment and then walks away leaving an open and authenticated terminal. This can be disastrous if a malicious person, or even a curious co-worker, decide to exploit this open, authenticated terminal. This person will not only be authenticated to a single application, they will be authenticated to all applications.

This problem can be solved several ways. First, users should consciously lock their computers before leaving them unattended. Additionally, the computer should be set to lock itself automatically when idle for some period of time. Finally, the single sign-on server can timeout inactive sessions. Using all three of these measures provides a defense in depth approach to ensuring that this security risk doesn't create an actual security incident.

Just as important to authenticating users is the ability to de-authenticate them. Giving the user the capability to log out of the system is important to ensuring that another user will not be able to walk up to the unattended computer and reuse the authenticated sessions. Instructing users to log out of the single sign-on environment is an easy and effective way to ensure that a deployed single sign-on solution doesn't facilitate unauthorized access, theft, or destruction of data.

A centralized single sign-on server will also be a high priority target for data theft. If this server is stolen or otherwise compromised, then a hacker may get a lot of sensitive and valuable information about the users. Protecting access to this server and within this server as well as deploying it to meet high-availability requirements are the critical factors in ensuring an effective and successful single sign-on deployment.

Database I&A

The database's primary I&A mechanism is username and password. The authentication is critical because usernames can be predicted and in some cases are well known. For users identified in the database you have the following authentication choices:

- **Passwords** Passwords can be either authenticated by the database or by the Oracle LDAP directory as shown in Chapter 5.
- **External/Strong** Oracle supports operating system authentication and strong authentication that includes PKI certificates, Kerberos, DCE, and RADIUS. The RADIUS standard extends the authentication capabilities to include token cards, biometrics, and smart cards. Details on how to setup and configure Oracle for strong authentication are given in the *Oracle Database Advanced Security Administrator's Guide 10*g.
- **Proxy** This is covered in detail in Chapter 4.

Oracle supports single sign-on both directly to the database and for Web applications deployed to the Oracle Application Server. The database's support for strong authentication also includes support for single sign-on technologies such as Kerberos, DCE, and PKI certificates.

The Oracle Application Server single sign-on capability is deployed on an Oracle database, which provides the scalability, security, and high-availability requirements needed for an effective implementation. The server supports passwords, PKI certificates, Microsoft Windows (Kerberos on Windows 2000) authentication, and an extensible framework for plugging in third-party authentication such as token cards and biometrics. Refer to the *Oracle Application Server 10*g *Security Guide* for further details.

Associating Users with Database Schemas

Now that you have a good understanding of the various I&A techniques, you have to decide how to represent your end users (applications users) to the database. The overall security of your application and the data it touches is largely affected by how this process is done.

When it comes to building applications, there are typically three models that can be used for mapping actual end users to database accounts. There are different benefits and risks within each model, so it's important to understand each. This understanding is crucial, because the model often restricts what you do and how you do it.

- **1:1** This one-to-one mapping occurs primarily in client-server programs. This means that every end user has a distinct database account, or schema.
- **N:M** This all-to-several mapping occasionally happens in Web applications. It means that all the end users are mapped to several different schemas. Each account is created based on the shared end-user privileges. All users with the same privileges are connected to the same schema.
- **N:1** This all-to-one mapping is a typical Web application. The application connects all end users to the same database schema. The schema has the union of all privileges for all users connected to it.

The mappings are listed in order of easiest to hardest to build database security. There are many factors influencing the model choice. Scalability, performance, and administration ease-of-use often get most of the attention. Security, however, must also be part of the consideration. In some cases, the security requirements may supersede other requirements, such as the administration.

User Privileges for Unique Database Accounts

Depending on how your database will be accessed and the role of your application(s), you may or may not have a lot of actual end-user accounts, that is, the 1:1 mapping model. For example, it's typical for client-server programs to run in this manner and less common for Web applications to do so.

The 1:1 mapping can occur several ways, but the bottom line is that there is a direct mapping of each user to an identity in the database (that is, the database account). In its simplest mode, the user supplies a username and password that are the actual database user account names and account passwords. Alternatively, the application could provide its own mapping. The point is not necessarily *how* it's done, but *that* it's done.

When creating the 1:1 database accounts, it's important to apply the same least-privilege lessons and process used in managing accounts on operating systems. That is, you should create users with no privileges and then selectively grant them the privileges they need to get their job done.

This mapping is especially critical for database administrators and other privileged users. *Sharing a privileged account among a group of users is a bad practice.* In many organizations, sharing user accounts is prohibited by policy, but is nonetheless still often practiced. If something goes wrong in that case, you'll not be able to tell which user was connected as the database user when that something happened. Therefore, there is no user accountability.

The 1:1 mapping makes the database security easy because the user's identity is always available to the database; therefore, the user is accountable. In addition, many of the database security capabilities operate at the individual schema level. If every user has a unique schema, then the database can easily apply appropriate security to the appropriate users based on the schemas. The database can, with high assurance, distinguish between each end user, and in doing so it can employ all of its security capabilities.

Shared Database Accounts

Least privileges are important even if the users are not connecting directly to the database. It's most common for users to have a unique application account and share a database schema. There are two mappings for this.

The first mapping, N:M, partitions users into various schemas. This is generally done by organizing the users by role—all users with the same role connect to the same schema. The important part to this is ensuring that the least-privilege principle is still upheld. You can effectively do this if all users that attach to the shared database schema are supposed to have the exact same database privileges. That is, the users are homogeneous from a privilege perspective. Conveying the user's identity is important in this design, too, since the database may be unable to distinguish between users connected to the same schema. Chapter 6 explores how to do this using Client Identifiers.

The last mapping model, N:1, connects all end users to the same database schema. This mapping is always the most questionable with regard to security. The problem with the design is that it's difficult for the database to separate the security privileges for the different users since they are all connected to the same schema. Ensuring that only the right privileges are available to the user is left mostly to the application. From an auditing perspective, unless you are using Oracle Enterprise Users (discussed in Chapter 5), the user's identity is not natively supported with this design, so their individual actions may be untraceable as well as unregulated.

Consider the scenario of users requiring different privileges sharing the same database schema. Figure 3-1 represents the N:1 mapping. Suppose you have three user groups—one with read-only access, another with read and write access, and an administrator group that can create and drop objects as well as read and write. If all three user groups are mapped to the same database schema, then the application *must* regulate what privileges to enable and disable based on what it knows about the user.

From the database's perspective, all users have the same privileges. This violates least privilege and defense in depth. If the application security fails, or the user circumvents the application, then the security can be compromised.

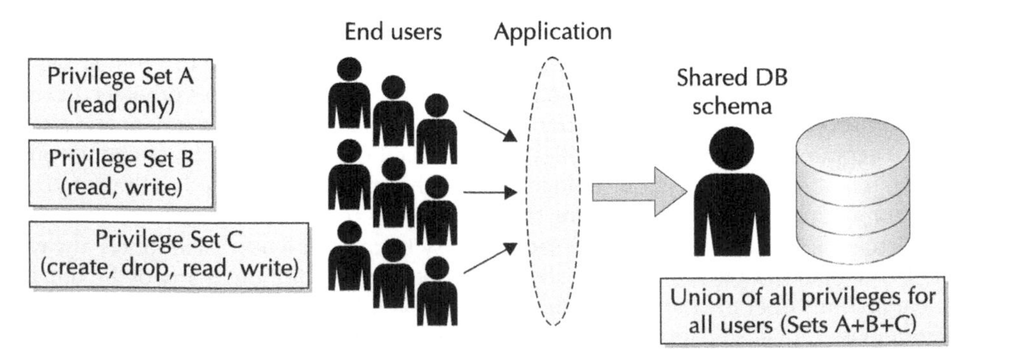

FIGURE 3-1. *End users with different privilege sets shouldn't be mapped to a single schema that has all the privileges of all the users.*

When you are designing and building an application, you should ensure that the least-privilege principle is upheld. Isolating schemas to shared users with the same privileges is one way to do this. Alternatively, using other features of the database such as Enterprise Users, Secure Application Roles, and identity preservations techniques (all covered in later chapters) will allow you to securely share database schemas among the end users.

Separate Users and Data

A critical part to ensuring a successful application is to ensure you have a separation of user database accounts and data/application database accounts. The data owner has all privileges on the data. If the users connect to this schema, even if by way of your application, you run a significant risk of a security incident. That is, if a user can break the application, or the application breaks itself, the user will have complete control on every part of the data. This includes not only access but also destructive capabilities such as truncating tables and dropping objects.

For this reason, a security best practice is to ensure the application users don't connect directly to the data account. You may also consider disabling all user log on to the data schema using one of the techniques discussed in Chapter 2, such as locking the account, revoking privileges to connect, or creating an impossible password.

In the safest design, you have one schema that holds the data, one schema that holds any PL/SQL programs that work on the data, and at least one other schema to which the users attach.

TIP
Never allow your end users to connect to the data schemas.

Identity Preservation

An important aspect of the identification process is identity preservation and propagation. You must ensure that user identities are available everywhere security requires them. The minute the identity stops, security stops. From a secure database perspective, this is a particularly acute problem. It often occurs that the user authenticates to an application, and the application connects to the database not as the actual user but anonymously or pseudo-anonymously. When designing database applications, the more information you can provide about the user's identity, the finer levels of security you can apply. Or as some like to say, "The more the identity, the better the security."

Although many applications (or databases) are designed around user-level access control and auditing, not all require it. This doesn't imply the application or its data is not secure. Almost all applications are based on the users identifying themselves as themselves or as a member of a role or group.

Determining the Appropriate Level of I&A

After all the possible ways of doing I&A, you may be left feeling a little overwhelmed. You shouldn't. There is a practical and sensible approach to determining what tactics and techniques you should be using. Your I&A should be determined by considering the sensitivity of the data and the privileges and access rights of the user as well as by balancing other competing factors.

Your first guiding directive is based on what you are protecting. Stronger I&A is usually required as the sensitivity of the data increases. If an application allows users access to their favorite stock list, then simple passwords with no password restrictions may suffice. If the access granted to the person allows them to obtain the nuclear launch codes, then obviously strong authentication, probably multifactor authentication, is a good choice.

The second factor for determining appropriate I&A is based on what it is the user can see and do. Remember that the greater the privileges and the greater the access, the stronger the authentication. For general users whose access is controlled, strong passwords are generally a good practice. For users with more privileges, such as DBAs, stronger authentication is desirable.

You're probably wondering, "Why not just use strong authentication all the time?" Before you invest in this approach, you have to consider that there are other tradeoffs. Practical security has to be balanced with usability, performance, implementation costs, and administration. Generally, weak authentication, such as passwords, are inexpensive to maintain and easy to manage. Strong authentication, such as biometric or smart cards, involve higher initial and operational costs. In addition, the usability or the intrusive nature of the authentication may be a barrier to its effectiveness. Refer back to the discussion in Chapter 2 which highlights how a password policy that is too strong can be self-defeating. Therefore, the correct authentication method must consider all aspects, not only the security. Note that this doesn't imply that strong I&A is bad; you have to do the cost-benefit comparison that compares the cost of implementation to the cost of a security breech.

Summary

Identification and authentication form the foundation of security processes. They must be implemented first, and they must be done right. It doesn't matter what clever access control and auditing capabilities are in place if the user is not really who you think they are, then everything else is a waste of time, code, and resources.

Other design decisions that are related to I&A also impact security. Preserving user identity to the database enables the use of database security that is consistent with the defense in depth principle. You have to design this security into your applications ahead of time.

The user-to-database modeling is important to forecast what database capabilities you'll be able to use. At the very least you should separate user schemas and data schemas. Administrators shouldn't share accounts. Sharing schemas should only be done when end-user identity can be preserved and the database privileges are identical for all users connected to the same schema.

Understanding the identification and authentication landscape is important to the way you formulate your security policies. You should carefully balance the security requirements—value and sensitivity of data—with the usability, administration, and costs associated with the various authentication technologies.

CHAPTER 4

Connection Pools and Proxy Authentication

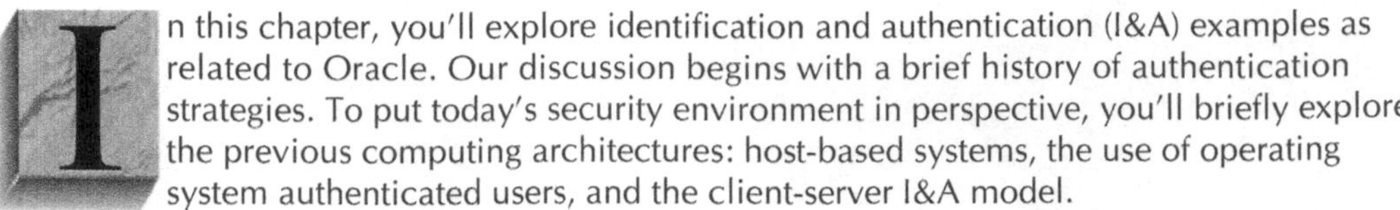

In this chapter, you'll explore identification and authentication (I&A) examples as related to Oracle. Our discussion begins with a brief history of authentication strategies. To put today's security environment in perspective, you'll briefly explore the previous computing architectures: host-based systems, the use of operating system authenticated users, and the client-server I&A model.

Web applications have their own special set of security challenges and requirements. Among them is how to effectively connect application users to the database in a way that meets the high-throughput demands of the Web and preserves end-to-end security. The predominant connection technique used today relies on database connection pools. This chapter will introduce you to the concepts of connection pools and their wide uses today. You'll see how two different types of Oracle connection pools can be used to achieve performance. However, if they're not used correctly—if you don't preserve the user's identity—they can short circuit the database security.

The last half of the chapter shows the best technique for providing identity preservation with the connection pools. Preserving a user's identity is a necessary step to enabling database security.

Heritage

To more fully understand identification and authentication as it is used today, it's helpful to understand not only what challenges exist today, but also how they have come about. Evolutions in computing architectures over the years have changed the ways users identify and authenticate themselves to Oracle Databases. Let's roll back (pun intended) a few years to get a better understanding of how this process has developed.

Host-Based Identification and Authentication

Back in the late 1970's, when Oracle first began producing commercial databases, mainframes were the predominant computing platform within most organizations. Many users didn't do their work from PCs or desktops mainly because PC computers weren't as prolific as they are today. They conducted their work by logging in, usually via a dumb-terminal or "green screen," to mainframes.

To gain access to an Oracle Database, it was quite common for users to first log on to the servers on which the database resided, and then to connect to the database. Instead of connecting directly to the database from a PC, which is common today, they first connected to the mainframe operating system (OS) and then connected to the database. In this environment, sometimes referred to as a *host-based model*, a user had to have an account on the OS *and* the database.

This configuration was sensible and secure. Security occurred in several layers: the user had to have an OS account; the user had to have the privileges to execute the program on the OS that would connect them to the database; and the user optionally had to also authenticate to the database.

In many cases, the database accounts could be directly associated with the OS accounts. This allowed the database to defer user authentication to the OS. Today, you still see support of this capability with Oracle's OS authenticated users.

OS Authenticated Database Users

A DBA can create a user to be authenticated externally. For this discussion, *external authentication* means authentication will be done by the operating system. The database uses a parameter called OS_AUTHENT_PREFIX to translate the actual OS username to a corresponding database username.

The default for this parameter is OPS$. The following example, executed from a Linux OS, illustrates how convenient and easy it is to create an OS authenticated user. To ensure that you create the account name correctly, check the value of the OS_AUTHENT_PREFIX (which has not been modified from the default):

```
system@DAGGER> SHOW parameter os_authent_prefix

NAME                                 TYPE        VALUE
------------------------------------ ----------- ------
os_authent_prefix                    string      ops$
```

Next, create your database user. The username is the prefix value concatenated with the OS username. For an OS user with the name of dknox, the database user account has to be "OPS$dknox":

```
system@DAGGER> CREATE USER ops$dknox IDENTIFIED EXTERNALLY;

User created.

system@DAGGER> GRANT CREATE SESSION TO ops$dknox;

Grant succeeded.
```

From the OS account, you can now connect without issuing a username or password. The database trusts the OS to correctly authenticate the user. Once this authentication occurs, the user is permitted access to the corresponding database account.

```
[dknox@dagger dknox]$ sqlplus /

SQL*Plus: Release 10.1.0.2.0 - Production on Sun Mar 28 15:42:47 2004

Copyright (c) 1982, 2004, Oracle.  All rights reserved.


Connected to:
Oracle Database 10g Enterprise Edition Release 10.1.0.2.0 - Production
With the Partitioning, Oracle Label Security, OLAP and Data Mining options

SQL> sho user
USER is "OPS$DKNOX"
```

With OS authenticated users, each database account is directly linked to an OS account. OS authenticated users was (and still is for some) popular because it allows users to sign on to the database without requiring them to provide another username and password.

Today, the support for OS authentication is a popular method for supporting batch processes that need to be run from the OS. The jobs can be queued and run independently without requiring scripts to store usernames and passwords, which is a security risk in itself.

REMOTE_OS_AUTHENT

As time went on, computer networking proliferated, and applications became more distributed. Support for distributed computing was also embraced by Oracle. The REMOTE_OS_AUTHENT initialization parameter extended the trusted authentication model to the network. This technology allowed the users to have OS accounts on machines other than the server where the database resided. This capability gained popularity as the computing industry moved from mostly mainframes to a mix of large and midsize computing servers, many of which ran UNIX.

Remote authentication was popular because it added flexibility into the operational environment. Users could still enjoy the convenience of single sign-on, and the database server was not required to maintain OS accounts for all the database users.

However, remote authentication, while useful, created a lot of risk. The following example illustrates why.

CAUTION
This is for demonstration—do not do this *on your production servers!*

I modify my database to support remote authentication. By default, the REMOTE_OS_AUTHENT is set to false. Setting it to true allows users on other servers to log in to my database without specifying a username or password.

```
system@DAGGER> ALTER SYSTEM SET remote_os_authent=TRUE SCOPE=SPFILE;

System altered.
```

The new value for the REMOTE_OS_AUTHENT parameter will not take effect until the database is restarted. After restarting the database, I can connect to the OPS$DKNOX database user from an OS user called dknox located on a separate server. To illustrate this, I'll create the dknox OS user on a server called SABRE and connect to my database, which is running on a server called DAGGER. My connect string requires no username and password; it requires only a TNS alias. After connecting, I query my environment to show the name of the user, the host they are authenticated from, and the name of the database:

```
[dknox@sabre dknox]$ sqlplus /@dagger

SQL*Plus: Release 10.1.0.2.0 - Production on Sun Mar 28 15:52:00 2004

Copyright (c) 1982, 2004, Oracle.  All rights reserved.


Connected to:
Oracle Database 10g Enterprise Edition Release 10.1.0.2.0 - Production
With the Partitioning, Oracle Label Security, OLAP and Data Mining options

SQL> COL user              format a10
SQL> COL "User's Server"   format a15
SQL> COL "DB Server"       format a15
SQL> SELECT USER,
```

```
        SYS_CONTEXT ('userenv', 'host')
                                   "User's Server",
        SYS_CONTEXT ('userenv', 'db_name')
                                       "DB Server"
   FROM DUAL;

USER       User's Server   DB Server
---------- --------------- ---------------
OPS$DKNOX  sabre           dagger
```

The risk associated with allowing remote authentication lies in the fact that any administrator or knowledgeable person can create a user with any username and be connected to the database account corresponding to that username. The administrator for the database on DAGGER may not trust the actions occurring on the SABRE (OS) server or any other server. For many, distributing trust in this manner is considered too risky for production servers. Subsequently, this implementation is seldom used today, and the default for REMOTE_OS_AUTHENT is false. *Leave it set to false!*

Security for Host-Based Architecture

From the database's perspective, security for the host-based architecture was uncomplicated. Regardless of how a user authenticated, every user had a separate and distinct database account (the 1:1 user-database mapping discussed in Chapter 3). Oracle subsequently invested great resources in ensuring that the database could support proper security at the user level. These capabilities included various mechanisms for user authentication, role-based access control, object privileges, system privileges, and auditing. All of these capabilities form the core security mechanisms provided by the Oracle Database today.

Client-Server Identification and Authentication

With the proliferation of the personal computer, the computing industry evolved from a host-based model for applications to the client-server architecture. This architecture evolved from a single entity, the host, to two entities, the client (on which the users resided) and the server (on which the database resided). Software companies, including Oracle, rapidly adopted support for secure client-server capabilities.

In this architecture, users always have two accounts, one for the OS and one for the database. It's typical for the database server and the user's personal computer to be running different operating systems. This heterogeneity provides a more user-friendly desktop computing environment and allows the users flexibility in choosing a computer that best meets their personal needs.

Many of the client-server applications are also graphical in nature and are much easier to use than the applications in the host-based model. This helps to extend the reach of the Oracle Database to users who no longer have to understand SQL. Reports can be easily run in which simple questions such as "What are the latest YTD numbers, and how do they compare to last years numbers?" are transparently turned into SQL queries with the results formatted and graphically displayed to give the users the latest, up-to-date information.

Security for Client-Server Architecture

With client-server architecture, like host-based architecture, database access controls and auditing are based on the uncomplicated principle that each user has a separate and distinct database account. For client-server architecture I&A, the database (as opposed to the OS) usually performs the user authentication. While passwords were initially the predominant authentication technique, the computing industry soon began to develop standard ways to allow users to conduct single sign-on. Kerberos and DCE are two popular examples of single sign-on technologies developed to support the single sign-on requirement.

In a client-server connection, the user has a direct link to the server (or database) and vice-versa, much like a phone call, where two people are directly connected to each other and each knows who is on the other end. For client-server database applications, the user authenticates once and stays connected. This is important because the user's identity is established once and is available to the database for the entire session (just as it is in a phone conversation). The database connections aren't shared, and database security is based on the ability to easily distinguish between users.

With client-server computing, securing the network communications from the client to the server is essential to ensuring data is not maliciously copied or altered while in transit. Soon after Oracle began supporting the client-server architecture, they realized the need to secure those communication channels. Oracle subsequently enhanced its networking software and introduced Secure Network Services (SNS) to ensure that data would be protected not only while at rest in the database, but also while in motion to and from the database. SNS, was renamed several times until it finally ended up as the Oracle Advanced Security option, provided for SQL and data encryption. To operate in a secure client-server configuration, applications utilized the SNS capabilities.

NOTE
The client-server architecture also puts an emphasis on network security.

As the value of client-server applications was realized, practically all the major application development companies, most of which ran against database-derived data, built and deployed client-server applications. The client-server architecture was popular for many years and today still plays a significant role for many Oracle customers.

Web Applications

Unfortunately, the client-server architecture arguably presents a few management and administration challenges. Just about when people started realizing the challenges of client-server, the Internet and its promise of connecting everyone everywhere to everything became the next paradigm. More specifically, HTML pages were being strung together in a web of information. HTML offered a platform-agnostic, common, and simple way for users to interact with data and applications. Application development companies began to investigate the Internet as the next medium for information delivery.

When HTML first reached the mainstream, practically all of the content was static. It wasn't long before users requested nonstatic HTML pages containing the most up-to-date information. Internet development began to eclipse the client-server architecture.

To build dynamic content containing the latest information, HTML pages had to be constructed from the results of the database queries submitted by an application. This was not an easy task.

There were some technology issues to overcome, and many clever solutions were developed to overcome these challenges, particularly those concerning performance and security.

The Stateless Environment

Fast forward to today and the universal client application: the Web browser. In today's world, you use the http protocol to connect users to application servers rather than directly to databases. This has important implications on application security, as you shall soon see.

Unfortunately, http, while useful for its original purpose, is stateless and in many cases is not optimal for many of today's current demands. *Stateless* means that there is a new connection established for every request. As such, the state of individual and recurring connections can't be supported by the protocol.

The stateless nature of http forces you to consider new ways of securing recurring communications. Recall that in the client-server analogy, you had a connection that lasted the duration of the application's use (which was similar to the duration of a phone call). With the stateless http environment, every mouse click is a new network call—it's like having to place a new phone call for every sentence in a conversation. The problem is exacerbated by the fact that the web server is conducting many conversations simultaneously. The challenge is not only to string together sentences among all the users, but also making sure the users don't get mixed up. It would be considered a flaw if Bob asked the server for the latest sports scores, and it handed back the latest YTD figures from accounting.

The stateless aspect of http was solved by the application servers for client to application server communications. The solution utilizes browser cookies and the ability of the application server to create and maintain transparent "sessions" and thus state for each client. However, this represents only half of the architecture. The connection from the application server to the database still remains a challenge.

Web Databases

As database use and the value databases provided to organizations increased, so too, increased the user community. Assuming that a preponderance of HTML pages are actually dynamic pages created from a database, I can now focus on the heart of the problem.

Unlike host-based and client-server computing, web users no longer connect directly to the database. There is a middleman involved: the application servers. The application servers connect to the database on the user's behalf. How this is done makes all the difference for two critical reasons: security and performance.

Connection Challenges

Web applications connect to databases to build dynamic and often personalized web pages. To do this securely, you would ultimately like to connect your users to the database using the 1:1 mapping model. That is, you connect each application user to a distinct database account. This is secure because the database knows who is connected and can employ its security capabilities—specifically access control and auditing.

In the host-based and client-server models, the user is always directly connected to the database. In a web environment, the user is rarely, if ever, directly connected to the database; the user is connected to the application, and the application is connected to the database. You might therefore conclude the application should connect each application user to a distinct database account.

Many security administrators dislike this connection model design. One important reason is password security. This design could require the application to know the user's database password and there may be no secure way to manage these passwords. Most application servers today have built-in authentication services that obviate the need for the applications to perform the user authentication. Moreover, for security reasons, the applications are prevented from acquiring the user's password.

Resource limitations are another key factor limiting the effectiveness of this design. Web applications typically support many end users. To connect each user to a private database account, you'll have to establish a dedicated database connection for each user. If you have many users, you could exhaust memory and computing resources on your application server, database, or both by simply trying to create and maintain all the open database connections. For applications with a small number of connections, dedicated and individual connections may be possible.

Also, for web applications, there's no guarantee a user will access the application on any given day, or once they have started accessing it, that they'll continue to use it. I create web expense reports all the time and quite often decide, after logging in and looking at an enormous pile of receipts, that I don't really feel like doing my expense report after all. So I click on the "home" icon in my browser. The expense report application has no idea that I have done this and expects me to submit an expense report. If you are building a web application, then you have to be concerned with these situations. In such cases, an application may be wasting resources on open, dedicated database connections for users that are not and will not be making use of the connections. In Chapter 6, you'll see how to utilize the web session's timeout period to close the database connections for the user.

Alternatively, you may decide to close the database connections between user requests. When a user makes a request, the application logs on to the database as that user, issues the query, and then disconnects. You will now see why this is generally not practical for performance reasons.

Performance

Suppose SCOTT wants to run a report. He connects to the application server from his browser and says, "Application, give me the YTD figures." The application server (or application) translates this question—typically represented via a hyperlink or form button—into SQL queries for the database. Note SCOTT is not connected to the database; the application is connected to the database *for* SCOTT. To retrieve SCOTT's report, the application has to connect to the database and issue the query or queries needed to satisfy the report.

In a web application environment, you need to support many simultaneous user requests. You assume that SCOTT is one of many users asking for a different database report. As such, you need to connect to the database, issue your queries to build your web pages, and return the results as quickly as possible.

The stateless environment is not optimal for application server to database communications. The reason is that database connections add significant time to the overall request. In some cases, the database connection time limits the overall ability of the application to scale to meet the requirements placed upon it.

The connection to the database is similar to placing a phone call. First, you dial the phone number, some switching happens, the phone rings on the other end, someone answers, and you say who you are. All this has to happen before your conversation can begin. For a database connection, you first have to figure out who you want to log in as, then you call the database over a network connection; the database answers, asks who you are, and sets up the context of the database session. At this point, the database is ready for discourse. This process of setting up a new database connection for each user request consumes precious time.

Connection Performance Example

A quick Java program can illustrate this point. The program will measure the time required to connect and then disconnect from a database. No queries will be made yet because the objective is to measure the time associated with creating and deleting a database connection:

```
package OSBD;
import java.sql.*;
import oracle.jdbc.pool.OracleDataSource;
public class ConnectionTest {
  public static void main(String[] args) {
    long connectTime=0, connectionStart=0, connectionStop=0;
    try {
      OracleDataSource ods = new OracleDataSource();
      ods.setURL("jdbc:oracle:thin:scott/tiger@DKNOX:1521:KNOX10G");
      // Start Timer
      connectionStart = System.currentTimeMillis();
      Connection conn = ods.getConnection();
      conn.close();
      // Stop Timer
      connectionStop = System.currentTimeMillis();
      ods.close();
    } catch (Exception e) { System.out.println(e.toString()); }
    // print connection time
    connectTime = (connectionStop - connectionStart);
    System.out.println("Database connection time: " +
                        connectTime + " ms.");
  }
}
```

After running this several times, the average time was just over half a second to open and close a database connection.

```
Database connection time: 531 ms.
```

This is important because 500 ms may be too long for the high-throughput demands of some web applications. It may take more time to connect to the database than it does to query the database. The following code times a simple query that validates this point:

```
package OSBD;
import java.sql.*;
import oracle.jdbc.pool.OracleDataSource;
public class QueryTest {
  public static void main(String[] args) {
    long queryTime=0, queryStart=0, queryStop=0;
    try {
      OracleDataSource ods = new OracleDataSource();
```

```
      ods.setURL("jdbc:oracle:thin:scott/tiger@DKNOX:1521:KNOX10G");
      Connection conn = ods.getConnection();
      Statement stmt = conn.createStatement();
      // Start SQL Timer
      queryStart = System.currentTimeMillis();
      ResultSet rset = stmt.executeQuery(
                          "select object_name from all_objects");
    // Stop SQL Timer
      queryStop = System.currentTimeMillis();
      rset.close();
      stmt.close();
      conn.close();
      ods.close();
    } catch (Exception e) { System.out.println(e.toString()); }
    queryTime = (queryStop - queryStart);
    System.out.println("Database query time: " + queryTime + " ms.");
  }
}
```

The results from this program prove the theory—the time to execute the query was significantly less than the time to connect to the database:

```
Database query time: 60 ms.
```

In this example, you are only considering one user; the problem is exacerbated as the number of users simultaneously accessing the database increases. Therefore, this design—connecting to the database, issuing a query, and then disconnecting—*is not* scalable.

Connection Pools

The performance shortcomings just described were recognized soon after web-database applications came into existence. Today, the problem is commonly solved through the use of connection pools. The *connection pool*, a pool of preestablished database connections, links the application to a database schema. The application opens, and keeps open, several physical database connections. When an incoming request is made, the application will grab a connection from the pool, issue a query (or queries), and then return the connection back to the pool. A connection pool is similar to having the database predial all of the phone numbers it'll need to talk to the database. If someone needs to ask the database a question, the application simply hands them the equivalent of the telephone receiver and lets them talk (or query, as the case may be).

Connection pools are used to enhance performance in a multiuser environment. Concurrent requests can be handled simultaneously by granting each request one of the preestablished connections from the connection pool. Once the user's request has been satisfied, the connection is returned to the pool so it can be used by the next request. In this manner, the connection overhead is minimized and you increase the performance and scalability of your application.

Connection pool implementations vary widely. In the beginning, the pools had to be created and managed by the application. Today, it's more common for the application server to provide the capabilities to make the connection pool management a transparent process (or almost transparent) to the applications themselves. You'll now look at two variations of JDBC connection pooling supported by Oracle: implicit connection cache and the OCI connection pool. OCI stands for Oracle Call Interface and will be discussed in more details in the upcoming "OCI Connection Pool" section.

Choosing Connection's Database Account

Connection pools are ideal for web applications that support many end users. If you have an application that has 20 distinct users, you should consider creating dedicated connections for each user. As the number of application users increases, there comes a point at which the application server and database resources are consumed by open and potentially unused connections. The pool allows the database connections to occur in a manner that doesn't require an open, dedicated connection for each user.

Oracle Implicit Connection Cache

In the first examples, an Oracle JDBC connection pool known as the *implicit connection cache* will be used. JDBC stands for Java Database Connectivity and represents the industry standard way of connecting Java client programs to database servers. To use JDBC, a Java program must incorporate the use of a specific JDBC driver; the *driver* is a vendor provided implementation of the JDBC specification. All JDBC drivers support the same syntax and APIs. For more information on JDBC, refer to the *Oracle Database JDBC Developer's Guide and Reference 10g*.

A connection cache implies a caching of *physical* database connections. For our discussions, the phrases "connection cache" and "connection pool" are synonymous. A physical database connection (in the implicit connection cache) includes both the dedicated client-to-server network connection and the database session. In the OCI Connection Pool section, you'll see that the physical connection and the database session can be separated.

The value in using the implicit connection cache is that the application doesn't have to manage the connection pool. The implicit connection cache does this by creating a logical mapping of the actual physical database connections. This simplifies the application development process as the implicit connection cache has the intelligence to know how to perform the caching in the most effective manner. In the past, the application developer was responsible for the intelligent management of the connection pool.

The driver (program) for the implicit connection cache is provided with the Oracle Database 10*g* JDBC libraries in the file $ORACLE_HOME/jdbc/lib/classes12.jar. The following examples represent the code that would be used by a Java application connecting to the database.

Connection Cache Example

The examples in this chapter are simplified so that you can focus on the connection pooling concepts. Since connection pools were built to solve the performance problems associated with establishing database connections, the first objective is to measure the time required to establish database connections.

This example has been decomposed into sections that should help in making the code more understandable. In the first section, the requisite libraries are imported, variables are defined, and the data source is created.

```
package OSBD;
import java.sql.*;
import oracle.jdbc.pool.OracleDataSource;
public class ConnectionCacheTest {
```

```
public static void main(String[] args)  {
  long connectTime=0, connectionStart=0, connectionStop=0;
  long connectTime2=0, connectionStart2=0, connectionStop2=0;
  long connectTime3=0, connectionStart3=0, connectionStop3=0;
  try {
    OracleDataSource ods = new OracleDataSource();
    ods.setURL("jdbc:oracle:thin:@DKNOX:1521:KNOX10G");
```

The setURL method will be used when you establish database connections. It defines a JDBC type and the required details needed to connect to the database listener. In this example, the thin JDBC driver is used. The thin JDBC driver program is completely written in Java. Its name is derived from the fact that no additional software is required for the database connection to occur. You also can use the OCI JDBC driver that has a Java interface but relies on the Oracle Call Interface APIs (which are written in C) to actually fulfill the connections. The implicit connection cache supports both.

Next, the database username and password are set. This defines the database account (schema) to which the initial connections will be established.

```
    ods.setUser("scott");
    ods.setPassword("tiger");
```

For the connection pool, you have to explicitly tell the data source that you want to enable the connection caching. If you fail to do this, the connections will not get cached. To enable this, execute the following:

```
    ods.setConnectionCachingEnabled(true); // be sure set to true
```

Next, define the bounds in which the connection pool will operate. The InitialLimit property indicates the number of initial physical connections that will be established. The MinLimit sets the minimum number of connections the pool can shrink to. The MaxLimit specifies the maximum number of physical connections ever to be created within the pool.

```
    java.util.Properties prop = new java.util.Properties();
    prop.setProperty("InitialLimit", "3");
    prop.setProperty("MinLimit", "3");
    prop.setProperty("MaxLimit", "20");
    ods.setConnectionCacheProperties (prop);
```

The initial limit of three means that the first time a connection request is made, the connection pool will establish three physical connections (all to the SCOTT user as set in the previous setUser method). The minimum and maximum limits are the bounds in which the connection pool will operate. You can't exceed the maximum number of connections. For the example, requesting the twenty-first connection would return a null object. Being able to limit the pool size is critical because it helps to ensure your application doesn't saturate the database with connections.

For this example, three database connections are made and the time to make the connections is calculated. While not obvious from the code, the first connection request transparently initializes the connection pool. The second connection is to the same user defined in the first connection. And, the third connection will connect to a separate user. Before the program exits, the database connections are closed. The connection times are then printed.

```
        connectionStart = System.currentTimeMillis();
        Connection conn = ods.getConnection("scott", "tiger");
        connectionStop = System.currentTimeMillis();

        connectionStart2 = System.currentTimeMillis();
        Connection conn2 = ods.getConnection("scott", "tiger");
        connectionStop2 = System.currentTimeMillis();
        connectionStart3 = System.currentTimeMillis();
        Connection conn3 = ods.getConnection("blake", "madd0g");
        connectionStop3 = System.currentTimeMillis();

        conn.close();
        conn2.close();
        conn3.close();
        ods.close();
      } catch (Exception e)     { System.out.println(e.toString()); }
      connectTime = (connectionStop - connectionStart);
      System.out.println("Initial connection time for pool: " +
                          connectTime + " ms.");
      connectTime2 = (connectionStop2 - connectionStart2);
      System.out.println("Connection 2 to cached Scott user: " +
                          connectTime2 + " ms.");
      connectTime3 = (connectionStop3 - connectionStart3);
      System.out.println("Connection 3 to Blake user: " +
                          connectTime3 + " ms.");
    }
  }
```

Analyzing the Results

When I executed the code, I got the following results:

```
Initial connection time for pool: 791 ms.
Connection 2 to cached Scott user: 0 ms.
Connection 3 to Blake user: 140 ms.
```

The first connection request (done by invoking the getConnection method) initializes the connection pool. The initialization process in the implicit connection cache creates three physical database connections and returns one of them to the application program. In the previous example, this took 791 milliseconds (ms). All three connections were made to the SCOTT user.

The initialization process and connection time for the initial request increases in proportion to the number of physical connections. Recall that the initial number of connections was set in the InitialLimit property value of the connection pool prior to connecting. Naturally, the higher the number specified in the initial limit, the longer the pool will take to fill. For a web application, you might consider accessing the application if the application server has rebooted so that none of your end users will be personally subject to the time required to populate the initial pool.

The second connection time shows the true benefit of this implementation. The connection was again to the SCOTT user. The connection pool was previously initialized to the SCOTT user. Only one of those three connections is currently in use. Therefore, the implicit connection cache actually returned a preestablished connection from the pool that took no measurable time.

The third connection request shows the time required to start a new physical connection. In the example, the connection is made to the BLAKE user. (This shows that the pool doesn't have to consist of connections to the same database account.) A new connection had to be created because all the connections in the pool were to the SCOTT user. The time to create a new physical connection was 140 milliseconds.

An important point is that any new connection will require roughly the same amount of time. For example, if there was a fourth connection request to the SCOTT user (the cache only has three connections established to SCOTT), a new physical connection would also have to be created. This would have taken about the same amount of time as BLAKE's connection.

If your objective is to completely eliminate the connection time, then you should set your initial limit and minimum limit equal to the maximum limit and always connect to the same database schema. The first connection will take a long time, but all subsequent connections will take very little time (zero milliseconds in my tests). This is how many web applications are designed today. The application creates a connection pool that opens multiple physical connections to the database, and all the connections in the pool are to the same database schema. Performance is the design goal, and it can be achieved using the connection cache.

Security Risks

If all the connections are made to the same database schema, the database has no way of knowing the real identity of the application user. Security can't be done on anonymity; therefore, more work is required to be able to use the database security features along with the connection pool. Chapter 6 offers solutions for the implicit connection cache. The upcoming section, "Proxy Authentication," shows an alternative pooling mechanism that preserves the user's identity.

Closing a connection for a connection pool doesn't close the physical database connection. Rather, the logical connection is returned to the pool where it's available for the next request. In the previous example, if you closed the third connection to the BLAKE user, then later requested a connection to the BLAKE user, you'd get the previously established connection (assuming that no one else had taken it first).

The following code snippet illustrates this:

```
connectionStart3 = System.currentTimeMillis();
Connection conn3 = ods.getConnection("blake", "madd0g");
conn3.close();
connectionStop3 = System.currentTimeMillis();
connectionStart4 = System.currentTimeMillis();
Connection conn4 = ods.getConnection("blake", "madd0g");
connectionStop4 = System.currentTimeMillis();
```

The implicit connection cache knows the fourth connection (conn4) is to a database user to which a connection has already been established. This preestablished connection is consequently returned. By capturing the timing as before, you'll see the preceding code returns a 0 ms connect time for the fourth connection:

```
Initial connection time for pool: 791 ms.
Connection 2 to cached Scott user: 0 ms.
Connection 3 to Blake user: 150 ms.
Connection 4 to cached Blake user: 0 ms.
```

The security risk with caching connections is that the database session is never reset. Database roles that were enabled, PL/SQL programs that were invoked, and application context (see Chapter 9) values that have been set are still in the same state as when the last person used the connection. Therefore, to use this connection cache, you have to reset the database session between end-user requests. Chapter 6 explores how to do this.

Role Schemas

One excellent use of the implicit connection cache is to support role schema designs. This is the N:M mapping model discussed in Chapter 3, where multiple end users share security privileges based on the role or function they perform in the application. That is, all the accountants' connect to the ACCOUNTANT schema, all the clerks connect to the CLERK schema, and so on.

You can create multiple connection caches, one for each role schema. You can either start all connection caches when the application starts, or create the connection caches on demand—that is, create the pool for each role schema the first time a user for that role schema makes a request. The Oracle software automatically grabs the correct connection from the corresponding cache based on the username and password supplied in the getConnection request. If you use this design, you must also use Client Identifiers and application contexts to achieve true end-user security. See Chapter 6 for more details.

Viewing the Connections

It's a good idea to validate your application connection schemes. To do this, run the program again and query the V$SESSION view while the program is executing. This is a good method for verifying the connections your application is making. An artificial stall has been inserted to make the program sleep for ten seconds because the program executes too quickly to be able to issue the query (at least for me). To accomplish this, place the following line of code just above the first conn.close() statement:

```
// previous code
      Thread.sleep(10000);
      conn.close();
      conn2.close();
// remaining code
```

Execute the program again, and within the ten second window, query the V$SESSION table:

```
sec_mgr@KNOX10g> COL module format a20
sec_mgr@KNOX10g> SELECT   username, server, module
  2       FROM v$session
  3      WHERE TYPE != 'BACKGROUND'
  4        AND username IS NOT NULL
  5   ORDER BY username;

USERNAME                       SERVER    MODULE
------------------------------ --------- ----------
BLAKE                          DEDICATED
SCOTT                          DEDICATED
SCOTT                          DEDICATED
SCOTT                          DEDICATED
SEC_MGR                        DEDICATED SQL*Plus
```

This verifies the pool configuration. The three dedicated connections from SCOTT were created when the connection pool was created. The last connection was created for the single connection to the BLAKE user. The record for the SEC_MGR user was for the query itself, which was issued from SQL*Plus.

Session Pools and the Oracle OCI Connection Pool

The implicit connection cache works very well, but there are two considerations worth further investigation. The first is that the cache isn't optimized for end-user authentication. In the event that you want to log in as a different user, say the BLAKE user in the preceding example, you suffer the costs of starting a new physical connection. The second area of interest is that the connections are all physical connections. In most cases, you typically associate a physical database connection with a database session. However, this isn't always true.

Oracle supports fine-grained management of database connections and database sessions. The physical connection and the database session can be decoupled. The OCI layer exploits this by allowing developers to multiplex database sessions over the same physical connection. Because physical connections are more costly to establish, this ability is very desirable. OCI will therefore allow you to create multiple database sessions over a single physical connection, thereby offering a more efficient way to handle resources.

Oracle supports session multiplexing in JDBC with the Oracle OCI connection pool. In a similar manner to the implicit connection cache, the Oracle OCI connection pool allows you to create multiple physical connections to the database. The OCI layer will then multiplex database sessions over all the available physical connections in the pool. The OCI layer transparently manages all the session multiplexing and physical pool allocation, thereby hiding the complexities from the application developer.

NOTE
The OCI connection pool is only available to the thick JDBC drivers, and these thick drivers require the installation of the Oracle Client Network libraries.

OCI Connection Pool Example

The preceding example has been ported to use the OCI connection pool. The setup is quite similar to the implicit connection cache. The OCI Connection Pool library has been imported, the data source has changed object types, and a variable was created to hold the database TNS connection information.

```
package OSBD;
import java.sql.*;
import oracle.jdbc.*;
import oracle.jdbc.pool.OracleOCIConnectionPool;
import oracle.jdbc.oci.OracleOCIConnection;
public class ConnectionPoolTest {
  public static void main(String[] args)  {
```

```
long connectTime=0, connectionStart=0, connectionStop=0;
long connectTime2=0, connectionStart2=0, connectionStop2=0;
long connectTime3=0, connectionStart3=0, connectionStop3=0;
String tnsAlias = "(DESCRIPTION = (ADDRESS_LIST = (ADDRESS = " +
                  "  (PROTOCOL = TCP)(HOST = DKNOX)(PORT = 1521)) )" +
                  "  (CONNECT_DATA = (SERVICE_NAME = knox10g) ) )";
try {
  OracleOCIConnectionPool ods = new OracleOCIConnectionPool();
  ods.setURL("jdbc:oracle:oci:@"+tnsAlias);
  ods.setUser("scott");
  ods.setPassword("tiger");
```

The OCI connection pool also allows you to configure the pool parameters. The OCI connection pool size is set to be the same as the implicit connection cache so you can compare connection performance. Because the OCI connection pool will be multiplexing sessions over your physical connections, in implementation you may not need as many physical connections as you would using the implicit connection cache.

```
  java.util.Properties prop = new java.util.Properties();
  prop.setProperty(OracleOCIConnectionPool.CONNPOOL_MIN_LIMIT, "3");
  prop.setProperty(OracleOCIConnectionPool.CONNPOOL_MAX_LIMIT, "20");
  prop.setProperty(OracleOCIConnectionPool.CONNPOOL_INCREMENT, "1");
  ods.setPoolConfig(prop);
```

Timings are performed for the same three connections that were created in the connection cache test. The first connection establishes the pool. The second connection is to the same user that was used to create the connection pool. The third connection is to a user outside of the pool. Once completed, the connections are closed and the result times are printed.

```
  connectionStart = System.currentTimeMillis();
  Connection conn = ods.getConnection("scott", "tiger");
  connectionStop = System.currentTimeMillis();

  connectionStart2 = System.currentTimeMillis();
  Connection conn2 = ods.getConnection("scott", "tiger");
  connectionStop2 = System.currentTimeMillis();

  connectionStart3 = System.currentTimeMillis();
  Connection conn3 = ods.getConnection("blake", "madd0g");
  connectionStop3 = System.currentTimeMillis();
  conn.close();
  conn2.close();
  conn3.close();
  ods.close();
} catch (Exception e)   { System.out.println(e.toString()); }

// print connection time
connectTime = (connectionStop - connectionStart);
System.out.println("Initial connection time for pool: " +
                   connectTime + " ms.");
```

```
        connectTime2 = (connectionStop2 - connectionStart2);
        System.out.println("Connection 2 to Scott user: " +
                           connectTime2 + " ms.");
        connectTime3 = (connectionStop3 - connectionStart3);
        System.out.println("Connection 3 to Blake user: " +
                           connectTime3 + " ms.");
    }
}
```

Analyzing the Results

The results are significantly different from those received from the implicit connection cache test:

```
Initial connection time for pool: 170 ms.
Connection 2 to Scott user: 20 ms.
Connection 3 to Blake user: 20 ms.
```

The initial connection pool created three physical connections. This initial value is significantly less than the approximately 800 ms required to create a pool of three connections for the implicit connection cache. The difference has nothing to do with the JDBC driver type either. Testing with the thick driver for the implicit connection cache yields connect times greater than 800 ms.

The drastic difference in connect times may be attributed to the OCI implementation. Remember that the OCI layer is written in C and will most likely execute faster than the same program written in Java.

Another interesting result is seen with the two identical connection times for the SCOTT user and the BLAKE user. In the implicit connection cache example, SCOTT's second connection took 0 ms. SCOTT's subsequent connection using the OCI connection pool took 20 ms longer. However, the BLAKE user required 150 ms with the implicit connection cache because a new physical database connection had to be established *and* a database session created. With the OCI connection pool, the time required to get a new connection is only 20 ms because a new database session is created using an already established physical connection.

Viewing the Connections

You can use the same thread.sleep() call that was shown in the implicit connection cache to view the database sessions. While the program is sleeping, query the V$SESSION view:

```
sec_mgr@KNOX10g> SELECT   username, server, module
  2       FROM v$session
  3      WHERE TYPE != 'BACKGROUND'
  4        AND username IS NOT NULL
  5   ORDER BY username;

USERNAME                       SERVER    MODULE
------------------------------ --------- -------------
BLAKE                          PSEUDO    javaw.exe
SCOTT                          DEDICATED javaw.exe
SCOTT                          DEDICATED javaw.exe
SCOTT                          DEDICATED javaw.exe
SCOTT                          PSEUDO    javaw.exe
```

```
SCOTT                           PSEUDO    javaw.exe
SEC_MGR                         DEDICATED SQL*Plus

7 rows selected.
```

The records with the SERVER column value of DEDICATED are for the three dedicated sessions that were configured in the initialization value for the connection pool. Recall that this connection pool connected to the SCOTT user. The SEC_MGR query is from the SQL*Plus connection.

The records with the SERVER column value of PSUEDO are "lightweight" database sessions. The sessions are what is returned from the connection request. When the connection request is made, the OCI layer creates a new database session for the user utilizing one of the existing physical connections in the pool. Once the session is established, the physical connection is free and can be used to spawn new database sessions. The OCI Connection Pool will multiplex the creation of all the database sessions over the pool of physical connections that are available.

Starting a session over a preestablished database connection is faster than starting a brand new database connection and session. This explains why the creation of a new session (even to a new user) took 20 ms, and the creation of a new connection using the implicit connection cache took 150 ms.

Points of Note

The OCI connection pool uses resources from the database's large pool. As the number of concurrent users grows, you may find that you need to increase the large_pool_size to accommodate the additional memory required to handle the concurrent requests.

Another important point to note is the OCI connection pool doesn't support transparent application failover (TAF). *TAF* allows you to transparently reconnect your application to a clustered database instance in case the instance you are already connected to fail. TAF is only relevant in failing over database connections when using Oracle's Real Application Clusters.

By comparing the test results, you might conclude that an application that always connects to the same database schema would perform best with the implicit connection cache, and an application that needs to connect to different database schemas would perform better with the OCI connection pool. Connecting to the same database schema is useful in some situations, but it may be the wrong design when your application users require different database authorizations.

Let's explore connecting to separate database schemas in more detail because there is still an unresolved issue lurking.

Password Management Risk

If you need to support separate authentications for separate users, the application will need some way of obtaining the user's database password. There are three solutions. First, the application could prompt the user for the password. This will work and could be secure, but it's seldom done in practice. With the proliferation of single sign-on solutions, many applications can't gain access to the user's password. The application knows only the user's identity and that the user has successfully authenticated to the single sign-on server.

Second, the application could securely store the user's password. The preferred method for secure password storage is to compute a one-way hash of the password. Unfortunately, you can't use the hashed password as the authenticator for the user; you need the plaintext password for database authentication.

Storing the password in each application also creates a password maintenance challenge. When the user changes their password, the password will have to be changed in all the applications that store a copy of the user's password. There are several other challenges presented by allowing applications to handle passwords, all of which helped drive the industry to using single sign-on solutions and organizational wide master directory services.

NOTE
In a single sign-on environment, the application typically doesn't have access to the user's password.

Proxy Authentication

Your third alternative is proxy authentication. Proxy authentication uses the OCI connection pool and offers a new connection method called getProxyConnection. This connection call doesn't require the user's password. In spite of this fact, proxy authentication is still secure because the authentication requires special privileges.

NOTE
Proxy authentication doesn't require the user's password.

Proxy Example

The proxy authentication process is simple. The application first establishes the connection pool to the database via the proxy account. The *proxy account* is the account configured simply to allow the physical database connections (the connection pool) to be established. Figure 4-1 depicts this happening for a connection pool to a database schema APP_USER.

The following example illustrates how to use proxy authentication, and it's derived from the connection pool examples used above. The first few lines are identical to the OCI Connection Pool code. The first change will be to connect your pool to a new database user called APP_USER. This is done to more accurately portray how you will use proxy authentication for your real applications. You'll see how to set up and secure this database account in the upcoming "Proxy Authentication Database Setup" section. If you're following along by executing this code, you'll need to jump to the user creation steps in the database setup section.

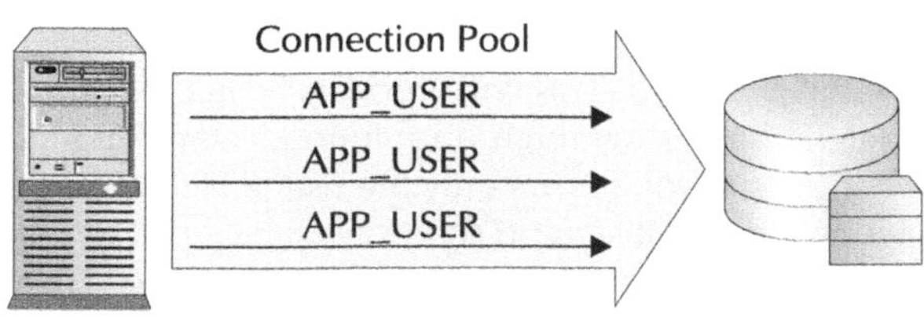

FIGURE 4-1. *A connection pool is established to the proxy account prior to any web requests*

```
package OSBD;
import java.sql.*;
import oracle.jdbc.*;
import oracle.jdbc.pool.OracleOCIConnectionPool;
import oracle.jdbc.oci.OracleOCIConnection;
public class ProxyAuthenticationTest  {
  public static void main(String[] args)  {
    long connectTime=0, connectionStart=0, connectionStop=0;
    long connectTime2=0, connectionStart2=0, connectionStop2=0;
    long connectTime3=0, connectionStart3=0, connectionStop3=0;
    String tnsAlias = "(DESCRIPTION = (ADDRESS_LIST = (ADDRESS = " +
                      "  (PROTOCOL = TCP)(HOST = DKNOX)(PORT = 1521)) )" +
                      "  (CONNECT_DATA = (SERVICE_NAME = knox10g) ) )";
    try {
      OracleOCIConnectionPool ods = new OracleOCIConnectionPool();
      ods.setURL("jdbc:oracle:oci:@" + tnsAlias);
      ods.setUser("app_user");
      ods.setPassword("qej4k91D");
      java.util.Properties prop = new java.util.Properties();
      prop.setProperty(OracleOCIConnectionPool.CONNPOOL_MIN_LIMIT, "3");
      prop.setProperty(OracleOCIConnectionPool.CONNPOOL_MAX_LIMIT, "20");
      prop.setProperty(OracleOCIConnectionPool.CONNPOOL_INCREMENT, "1");
      ods.setPoolConfig(prop);
```

The proxy authentication call uses a property value to determine which user to create a proxy database session for. You'll first establish your connection to SCOTT:

```
      java.util.Properties userNameProp = new java.util.Properties();
      userNameProp.setProperty(OracleOCIConnectionPool.PROXY_USER_NAME,
                               "scott");
```

To obtain a proxy connection, you have to invoke the getProxyConnection method. The first parameter indicates how you will be authenticating. The upcoming "Proxy Authentication Modes" section discusses the possibilities. This example will record the proxy connection time and uses the username for the proxy authentication mode:

```
      connectionStart = System.currentTimeMillis();
      Connection conn = ods.getProxyConnection(
                          OracleOCIConnectionPool.PROXYTYPE_USER_NAME,
                          userNameProp);
      connectionStop = System.currentTimeMillis();
```

For the remainder of the program, the only changes from the OCI connection pool examples are the replacements of getConnection with getProxyConnection and one extra call to change the user's name in the property object to BLAKE:

```
      connectionStart2 = System.currentTimeMillis();
      Connection conn2 = ods.getProxyConnection(
                          OracleOCIConnectionPool.PROXYTYPE_USER_NAME,
                          userNameProp);
```

```
        connectionStop2 = System.currentTimeMillis();
        connectionStart3 = System.currentTimeMillis();
        userNameProp.setProperty(OracleOCIConnectionPool.PROXY_USER_NAME,
                                 "blake");
        Connection conn3 = ods.getProxyConnection(
                             OracleOCIConnectionPool.PROXYTYPE_USER_NAME,
                             userNameProp);
        connectionStop3 = System.currentTimeMillis();
        conn.close();
        conn2.close();
        conn3.close();
        ods.close();
      } catch (Exception e)     { System.out.println(e.toString()); }
      // print connection times
      connectTime = (connectionStop - connectionStart);
      System.out.println("Initial connection time for pool: " +
                         connectTime + " ms.");
      connectTime2 = (connectionStop2 - connectionStart2);
      System.out.println("Connection 2 to Scott user: " +
                         connectTime2 + " ms.");
      connectTime3 = (connectionStop3 - connectionStart3);
      System.out.println("Connection 3 to Blake user: " +
                         connectTime3 + " ms.");
  }
}
```

Analyzing the Results

The results from this test are consistent with those in the OCI connection pool using the standard getConnection call:

```
Initial connection time for pool: 180 ms.
Connection 2 to Scott user: 20 ms.
Connection 3 to Blake user: 20 ms.
```

Viewing the Connections

Once again, you can insert a sleep call in your Java code and query the database prior to closing the connections:

```
sec_mgr@KNOX10g> SELECT   username, server, module
  2        FROM v$session
  3       WHERE TYPE != 'BACKGROUND'
  4         AND username IS NOT NULL
  5    ORDER BY username;

USERNAME   SERVER    MODULE
---------- --------- -----------
APP_USER   DEDICATED javaw.exe
APP_USER   DEDICATED javaw.exe
APP_USER   DEDICATED javaw.exe
```

```
BLAKE        PSEUDO    javaw.exe
SCOTT        PSEUDO    javaw.exe
SCOTT        PSEUDO    javaw.exe
SYSTEM       DEDICATED SQL*Plus

7 rows selected.
```

The records where the server value is PSEUDO are the proxy sessions. To help you visualize an OCI connection pool, Figure 4-2 depicts a single physical connection with three sessions multiplexed. The top session is for the user BLAKE, and the bottom two are for the user SCOTT. The dedicated physical connection is to the APP_USER schema.

Proxy Authentication Database Setup

The APP_USER schema requires only one privilege: the CREATE SESSION privilege. *No other privileges are needed nor should be given to this account.* This is in contrast to the way most connection pool database accounts are configured today where that account generally has all privileges. The proxy account should only have the ability to connect to the database; it shouldn't have the superset of all privileges of all users! This configuration conforms to the least-privilege principle.

Creating the Proxy User

Creating the proxy user is a simple task:

```
sec_mgr@KNOX10g> CREATE USER app_user IDENTIFIED BY qej4k91d;

User created.

sec_mgr@KNOX10g> GRANT CREATE SESSION TO app_user;

Grant succeeded.
```

Next, you must allow APP_USER to connect as the end users that will be using your application. In the preceding example code, the APP_USER could proxy to SCOTT and BLAKE. Intuitively, you might think that you have to issue something like "Grant proxy authenticate to APP_USER for

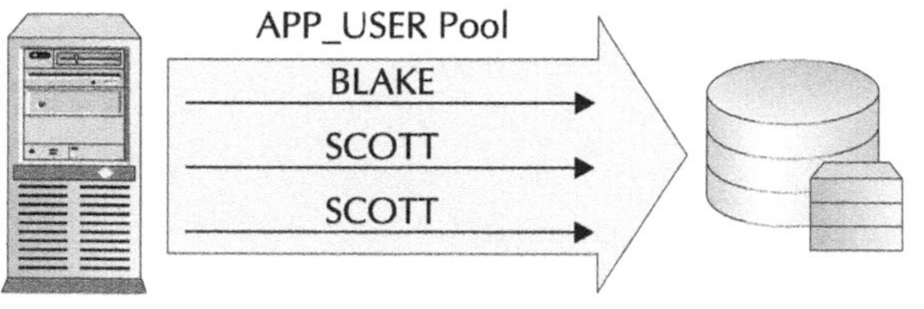

FIGURE 4-2. *A dedicated physical connection to the APP_USER schema with three sessions multiplexed via the OCI connection pool*

SCOTT", but as you can see this syntax doesn't flow well. Instead, the syntax isn't granting a privilege to APP_USER, but rather altering the user to allow someone to proxy to him:

```
sec_mgr@KNOX10g> ALTER USER scott GRANT CONNECT THROUGH app_user;

User altered.

sec_mgr@KNOX10g> ALTER USER blake GRANT CONNECT THROUGH app_user;

User altered.
```

This syntax shows the least restrictive way to issue this privilege. You can, and should, further restrict what roles the user can enable, and explore whether the proxy authentication request needs additional authenticating credentials.

Securing the Proxy Account

The proxy account, APP_USER in the previous example, should be protected either by strong password or some form of strong authentication. Even though APP_USER has the least amount of privileges possible (the CREATE SESSION privilege), you don't want people to be able to easily guess the password. Another reason to avoid this is that if the user has privileges they could also issue proxy authentication calls to other user accounts.

Because the proxy authentication calls have to be done over Oracle's OCI layer, which can use the Advanced Security features, the network encryption and integrity capabilities can and should be leveraged. When configured, all connections are secured from the application server to the database. If this isn't done, there's a risk of network eavesdropping, and this may prove to be the weakest link in the chain. It's much easier to snoop packets than to hack the database authentication, access control, and auditing mechanisms. Refer to Chapter 2 or the *Oracle Database Advanced Security Administrator's Guide 10*g for information on how to set up the secure network connection.

Restricting Access to Roles

You can restrict the authorizations that occur through your proxy connection by specifying the roles that can be enabled when you grant the privileges within the database. Assuming the application needs only the APP_A_ROLE, you can prevent the application from enabling other database roles. This is especially important for the DBA role and roles for other applications and most importantly supports the concept of least-privileges. For more detailed information on database roles, see Chapter 7.

```
sec_mgr@KNOX10g> -- create database role
sec_mgr@KNOX10g> CREATE ROLE app_a_role;

Role created.

sec_mgr@KNOX10g> -- grant role to user
sec_mgr@KNOX10g> GRANT  app_a_role TO scott;

Grant succeeded.

sec_mgr@KNOX10g> -- disable role by default
sec_mgr@KNOX10g> ALTER USER scott DEFAULT ROLE ALL EXCEPT app_a_role;
```

```
User altered.

sec_mgr@KNOX10g> -- grant proxy privileges along with
sec_mgr@KNOX10g> -- ability to enable the app_a_role
sec_mgr@KNOX10g> ALTER  USER scott GRANT CONNECT THROUGH app_user
  2               WITH ROLE app_a_role;

User altered.
```

The preceding configuration restricts SCOTT to the APP_A_ROLE when proxied from the APP_USER account. *All other roles, including default enabled roles, can't be enabled.*

This is very practical because privileges for an application can be grouped into roles specific for that application.

TIP
To enforce a good security design, the proxy authentication grants should be made to allow only the roles needed by the application.

The preceding syntax does just that for the APP_A_ROLE. Note also the following examples:

```
-- this disallows any roles to be set
ALTER USER scott GRANT CONNECT THROUGH app_user
  WITH NO ROLES;

--this allows all roles but DBA
ALTER USER scott GRANT CONNECT THROUGH app_user
  WITH ROLE ALL EXCEPT DBA;
```

To illustrate the role restrictions, we'll look at an example that restricts users to specific roles when proxy authenticating. The SCOTT user, by default, is granted the CONNECT and RESOURCE roles. Both are default roles that are automatically enabled upon logon. This is illustrated by the following query issued after logon as the SCOTT user:

```
scott@KNOX10g> SELECT ROLE FROM session_roles;

ROLE
------------------------------
CONNECT
RESOURCE
```

Assume you want to disable the RESOURCE role when the user connects via proxy authentication. The CONNECT role will remain enabled for proxy authentication because it contains the CREATE SESSION privilege needed to establish his database session. The RESOURCE role is disabled for proxy authentication because the user requires no privileges from this role when accessing the database via your application.

```
sec_mgr@KNOX10g> ALTER USER scott
  2      GRANT CONNECT THROUGH app_user
  3      WITH ROLE ALL EXCEPT RESOURCE;

User altered.
```

The following program is used to illustrate the role restrictions. The program will proxy authenticate to SCOTT and check the currently enabled roles. This first section of code shows the connection pool creation and the proxy authentication call.

```
package OSBD;
import java.sql.*;
import oracle.jdbc.*;
import oracle.jdbc.pool.OracleOCIConnectionPool;
import oracle.jdbc.oci.OracleOCIConnection;
public class ProxyRoles  {
  public static void main(String[] args)  {
    String tnsAlias = "(DESCRIPTION = (ADDRESS_LIST = (ADDRESS = " +
                      "   (PROTOCOL = TCP)(HOST = DKNOX)(PORT = 1521)) )" +
                      "   (CONNECT_DATA = (SERVICE_NAME = knox10g) ) )";
    OracleOCIConnectionPool ods = null;
    try {
      ods = new OracleOCIConnectionPool();
      ods.setURL("jdbc:oracle:oci:@" + tnsAlias);
      ods.setUser("app_user");
      ods.setPassword("qej4k91D");
      java.util.Properties userNameProp = new java.util.Properties();
      userNameProp.setProperty(OracleOCIConnectionPool.PROXY_USER_NAME,
                               "scott");
      Connection conn = ods.getProxyConnection(
                          OracleOCIConnectionPool.PROXYTYPE_USER_NAME,
                          userNameProp);
```

At this point, the program retrieves the user's enabled roles:

```
      Statement stmt = conn.createStatement();
      ResultSet rset = stmt.executeQuery("select role from session_roles");
      while (rset.next()) {
        System.out.println(rset.getString(1));
      }
```

Next, the program will attempt to enable the RESOURCE role. Afterward, the roles are printed to verify whether this succeeded.

```
      CallableStatement cstmt = conn.prepareCall(
                               "{CALL DBMS_SESSION.SET_ROLE('RESOURCE')}");
      cstmt.executeUpdate();
      rset = stmt.executeQuery("select role from session_roles");
      while (rset.next()) {
        System.out.println(rset.getString(1));
      }
```

The remaining code closes the connections. There is also one very important thing to do now: catch any thrown exceptions and close your data source in the exception handler. This is a good practice. Exceptions are thrown all the time for many reasons. If you don't close your connections in the exception handler, the connections may be left open to consume precious resources on the server:

```
      cstmt.close();
      rset.close();
```

```
        stmt.close();
        conn.close();
        ods.close();
      } catch (Exception e) {
        System.out.println(e.toString());
        try {
          ods.close();
        } catch (Exception e2) {}
      }
    }
  }
```

The output from this program validates your security configuration:

```
CONNECT
java.sql.SQLException: ORA-28157: Proxy user 'APP_USER' forbidden to set role
'RESOURCE' for client 'SCOTT'
ORA-06512: at "SYS.DBMS_SESSION", line 124
ORA-06512: at line 1
```

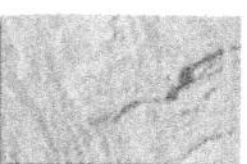

NOTE
The RESOURCE role in the previous code, which is actually a default role when the user logs in directly, isn't a default role for the proxy session.

Figure 4-3 illustrates the fact that the user is able to enable different roles and thus different privileges depending on how they are connected. The database supports a distinct set of privileges for the proxy authentication. This is important because the RESOURCE role might instead be the DBA role. You don't want the user to have DBA privileges when accessing the database through your application. Oracle can enforce this security policy for you.

This feature allows you to support least privileges when you have a user accessing the same database through multiple applications. Each application may have its own security policy. When the user accesses the database via one application, they should have only the privileges required for that application. For example, application "A" would have a connection pool to the APP_USER_A schema and would be allowed to proxy authenticate SCOTT with APP_A_ROLE. Application "B" would have a connection pool to the APP_USER_B schema and would be allowed to proxy authenticate SCOTT with APP_B_ROLE. Restricting roles via proxy authentication ensures that you are running in a least-privilege environment.

While this prevents users who are proxy authenticated from enabling certain roles, it doesn't prevent directly authenticated users from enabling roles. To prevent directly authenticated users from enabling roles, see Chapter 7.

NOTE
Database global roles and secure application roles can't be restricted in proxy authentication, and any roles granted to PUBLIC can't be restricted either.

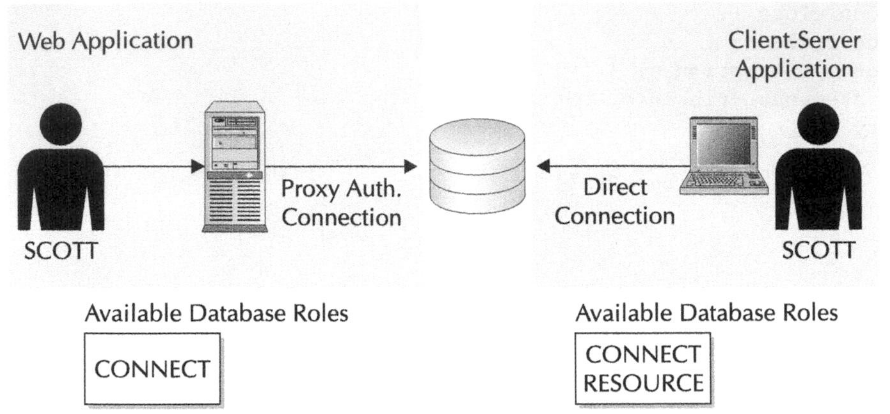

FIGURE 4-3. *Users' roles can be disabled when accessing the database via proxy authentication.*

The database privileges can be verified by querying the PROXY_USERS view, as shown in the following example:

```
sec_mgr@KNOX10g> COL proxy format a10
sec_mgr@KNOX10g> COL client format a10
sec_mgr@KNOX10g> SELECT * FROM proxy_users;

PROXY      CLIENT     AUT FLAGS
---------- ---------- --- -----------------------------------
APP_USER   BLAKE      NO  PROXY MAY ACTIVATE ALL CLIENT ROLES
APP_USER   SCOTT      YES PROXY MAY ACTIVATE ROLE
```

Proxy Authentication Modes

The preceding example shows how privileges are granted and how roles can be restricted using proxy authentication. You have seen how the user can be proxy authenticated by username. There are four modes supported for proxy authentication requests:

- Proxy by providing only the username
- Proxy by providing the username and password
- Proxy by providing the user's distinguished name
- Proxy by providing the user's X.509 certificate

Simple Username Proxy

In the first mode, which you have already seen in the examples, the proxy call simply passes the name of the user to which you want to connect. No other credentials are required. The benefit of this mode is in its simplicity. The application merely needs to determine what user to proxy to, and the proxy connection will occur.

From the security perspective, the database privileges have to exist for this to succeed, meaning that there is no significant security risk in doing this even though no other credentials are being passed to the database.

Username and Password

In the second mode, the user is proxied by supplying both the username and the user's (database) password. This is identical to obtaining a standard connection from the OCI connection pool except for one big difference: the proxy authentication allows you to restrict the roles the application can enable. Therefore, if there is a way to obtain the user's database password in a secure manner, proxy authentication is a better method than using a standard OCI connection because it supports role restrictions.

For all modes of proxy authentication, you can specify which mode you plan to use when you grant the privileges in the database. This provides additional security because it ensures a proxy authentication call can't occur unless you have the user's database password. The following example illustrates how to enforce the password authentication to the SCOTT user when proxied from APP_USER.

```
ALTER USER scott
    GRANT CONNECT THROUGH app_user
    AUTHENTICATED USING PASSWORD;
```

When you try to connect from your Java application used in the preceding example, which does not provide the user's password, you get the following error:

```
java.sql.SQLException: ORA-28183: proper authentication not provided by proxy
```

Proxy by Distinguished Name

A third option is to proxy by distinguished name (DN). The DNs are the primary key equivalents to an LDAP directory and are used to uniquely identify objects located within the directory—users, in this case.

This proxy mode is attractive because many applications and application servers use LDAP for their authentication mechanisms. The Oracle Application Server in conjunction with Oracle Single Sign-on uses LDAP for authentication. Consequently, you have easy access to the user's DN by simply making a request to the application container. An example of how to do this is given in Chapter 6.

Proxy by Certificate

The fourth mode is the ability to proxy via X.509 certificate. The X.509 certificate can be used in a secure, strongly authenticated http with SSL session from the client browser to the application server. The application server can take this public certificate and use it as the authentication mode to the database. A benefit to this is that it allows the database to interrogate the certificate for other access control measures it may wish to enforce.

Forcing Proxy Authentication

Applying what you've learned about proxy authentication, associated privileges, and Oracle passwords, you can create a design that allows a user to be authenticated only via proxy authentication.

The security requirement is to only allow user access to the database when access is done via the application(s). If you wish to restrict access to the database through a specific application, you can't lock the account or revoke the CREATE SESSION privilege because these are needed for proxy authentication. You could potentially write a log-on trigger to do this, but there is a more effective way.

Set the database user's password to be an impossible password (see Chapter 2 for more details). This ensures that the user can't log on directly using a password (although SSL authentication would still be possible). The only way for a user to get a database session will be to use proxy authentication.

Summary

In this chapter, you learned how the identification and authentication process evolved with computing architectures. When Oracle began producing databases, the host-based model was popular. The security was centralized on the host server. OS authentication allowed users to enjoy single sign-on between their OS and the database. Most importantly, the database users had unique accounts that formed the basis of the database security support you see today.

The client-server era ushered in new capabilities and new requirements. While the model still supported individual database users, identification and authentication were no longer centralized on the server that ran the database. Network security became increasingly important. Oracle's support for security in the client-server architecture evolved to support these new requirements.

Today, web-developed applications have a major impact on identification and authentication of users to the database. The Web is based on a stateless protocol, making it difficult to support (stateful) database sessions. The popularity of the Web has placed an extraordinary demand for performance and scalability on web-based applications.

Supporting scalability and performance while leveraging the user-level security capabilities of the database inspired the creation of Oracle's support for connection pools and proxy authentication. The overhead of connecting and disconnecting from the database prevents many web applications from scaling. Connection pools allow applications to issue database queries without requiring new database connections for every request.

When an application connects to the database, user-level security can be easily achieved by connecting as the actual user making the request. Once the database knows the user's identity, the proper access controls and auditing can occur. However, it's a security risk and often inefficient for applications to store the users' passwords. Proxy authentication allows applications to connect to the database as the end user without the security risks and challenges associated with password management. Proxy authentication also allows you to restrict the roles that can be enabled. This helps to enforce the least-privilege principle when connecting your users through web applications.

The basis of much of the security discussion in this chapter is identity preservation. You should identify and authenticate the users to the database because the database natively supports user-level security. However, managing users can create its own set of problems. In the next chapter, you'll see how the users can securely share database accounts, which will allow you to easily manage many users across many databases within an organization.

CHAPTER 5

Identity Management and Enterprise Users

hapter 4 discussed ways to connect application users to the database. The discussion was based on the fact that the application user population is large and continues to grow, which places an emphasis on scalability and security. The important security principle was identity preservation which, when adhered to, allows the database to exercise all of its security capabilities. Proxy authentication allows the identity to be preserved, and it has one important requirement: each application user has to be a database user.

This chapter explores Oracle's Enterprise User Security (EUS) feature, which allows the Oracle database users to be authenticated by an LDAP-compliant directory. The goal with EUS is simple: centralize the administration of database users thereby facilitating single sign-on, single usernames and passwords, and increased security by more efficient user management. You'll see how EUS supports each of these objectives.

Enterprise Users fits into a broader security area known as identity management. The chapter begins with an overview of identity management and then positions Oracle EUS into this broader concept.

Identity Management

With the proliferation of applications and application users, the computing industry has recognized the need for a way to manage the user-application relationship. Creating user accounts, resetting passwords, and assigning application privileges consumes an enormous amount of administrative cycles. With so many applications and users, the job of managing all the accounts can be onerous.

To relieve this challenge, identity management solutions are being developed and deployed. *Identity management* (*IM*) provides complete services for the administration of users within an organization. IM offers the ability to create users, manage their authentication credentials (passwords and digital certificates), assign privileges and authorizations, and suspend or delete user accounts. IM is the complete ability to do *everything* that is needed with regard to managing user accounts.

IM is becoming increasingly important today because many organizations are feeling the stress of implementing numerous applications for numerous users. IM allows centralized administration for user management tasks and provides the single source of truth for the enterprise applications that need access to user authorizations and other credentials.

Centralization is the critical factor to providing the benefits. When the user credentials are *centralized*, the user only has to be created once. Any modifications, including account deletions, will be handled once. All applications will be referencing the same user, which alleviates any inconsistencies that typically are associated with redundant user information. For example, the user password is stored once and will be the same authenticator for every application that participates in the IM implementation. Because users can generally remember a single password better than multiple passwords, they're less likely to write their passwords on paper and leave it by their computer. If the user's password has to be reset or changed, it can be done once for all applications. Authorizations and other data about the user will also be consistent across the enterprise.

IM reduces administration tasks, increases overall usability, and provides better security.

Directory Services

In efforts to solve the IM challenges, the industry has gravitated to the use of directories as the single point of storage and access for information about their employees and application users. The first digital directories were built to handle the management of e-mail addresses. The value of a digital directory was quickly realized and a standard—ISO X.500—was developed to allow any application access to the directory. The ISO X.500 standard represents a standard protocol and hierarchical categorization of data that is needed to allow applications a consistent and well-defined method for accessing information. ISO X.500 was comprehensive but it also was considered too complex to be practical for many implementations.

The LDAP (Lightweight Directory Access Protocol) standard was subsequently developed by the University of Michigan as a practical alternative to X.500. LDAP provides much of the same functionality as X.500 but without all the complexity and overhead. LDAP Version 3 is the current industry-wide directory standard.

The concept of a directory is congruent with the role it serves in IM. That is, it provides the common user information that is needed by applications throughout the enterprise. It's common to use directories as the information providers for many of an organization's entities. Physical devices and available services such as locations of servers, network routers, and printers can also be stored in a directory. Applications and users then have a single place to reference when they need this information.

A common use of LDAP directories today is to provide publicly available user information, such as office phone numbers and e-mail addresses. Many commercially available e-mail programs allow you to configure an LDAP server to look up other users' e-mail addresses. The e-mail program can log on to the LDAP directory anonymously and conduct searches. Most of this happens transparently to the e-mail user. This works because the directory is built on a standard protocol.

From a security perspective, directories are becoming the de-facto authentication engines for the enterprise applications. User passwords are centrally stored in the directory, along with the other user information, which provides a single place and process for authenticating application users.

IM Components

The directory is one piece of the identity management infrastructure. Other components, which provide the services or capabilities needed to actually manage the identity information, are also required. The Oracle IM infrastructure consists of these components:

- **Oracle Internet Directory** This is an LDAP-compliant directory that allows storage and retrieval of information about the various entities (users, applications, groups, privileges, and so on) that wish to participate in IM. This is discussed in more detail in the section "Oracle Internet Directory (OiD)" later in this chapter.
- **Oracle Delegated Administration Services** These are the services needed to support IM functions, such as creating users, assigning privileges to users, and deleting users. The administration duties can be distributed, or delegated, to multiple administrators within an organization. A self-service capability is also provided, which allows users to change their passwords and update other personal information.
- **OracleAS Single Sign-On** This is a single sign-on solution for web applications.
- **OracleAS Certificate Authority** This offers the services required for creating, distributing, and revoking user and server Public Key Infrastructure credentials (digital certificates).
- **Oracle Directory Integration Service** This provides infrastructure and APIs for integrating and synchronizing information in the Oracle Internet Directory with other sources, such as HR applications and other directories. These services are generally integrated into the user management features so that changes to user accounts are automatically synchronized.

Discussing all the IM components in detail is beyond the scope of this book. They are referenced because it's helpful in understanding how Oracle EUS works with respect to the other Oracle products and technologies. Further information on each of these components can be found in the *Oracle Application Server 10g Security Guide.*

Oracle's IM is primarily constructed to support the Oracle Application Server 10*g*. The database, however, is also an indirect participant in the IM scheme. You'll see how this relationship exists and why it's important in deploying effective security as you read the upcoming sections.

Oracle Internet Directory (OiD)

Oracle, recognizing the value of centralizing information as well as the value of the LDAP standard, built its own LDAP server, the Oracle Internet Directory (OiD), which is at the heart of Oracle's IM solution.

The IM components—an administration service, a digital certificate authority, a single sign-on server, and an integration service—all use OiD as the reference and storage engine. OiD also allows Oracle databases to operate in a similar manner to that of other LDAP clients. That is, the database supports LDAP as a mechanism for centralizing user authentication and authorization functions.

OiD is an implementation of the LDAP Version 3 standard that uses an Oracle database for storage and retrieval of the directory data. To fulfill its LDAP duties, OiD utilizes several operating system processes to translate client requests from the standard LDAP format to SQL queries in the database. This translation is hidden; applications interact with the directory only via the standard LDAP protocols. OiD includes software development kits (SDK) for Java, C, and PL/SQL programs. The database structure is proprietary, and direct access is unsupported.

Oracle chose to build its LDAP implementation on the database so it could leverage the already proven benefits that accompany an Oracle database such as portability, high availability, and scalability—all of which are requirements for a centralized directory server.

Enterprise Users

Oracle Enterprise User Security (EUS) is the centralized user administration capability for Oracle databases. User authentication and authorization data, along with other user attributes, are stored centrally in the directory server. The IM benefits provided to applications and application users are precisely the same benefits that EUS provides to Oracle database administrators and database users.

For database administrators, the directory becomes a centralized place for creating, updating, and deleting users, assigning their database roles, and defining schema mappings. You will see in the upcoming "User-Schema Mappings" section how different mappings allow you to create unique or shared schemas for the users.

For database users, the directory stores their identification and authentication (I&A) credentials allowing them consistent access to all Oracle databases. EUS supports users authenticated by passwords, Kerberos, and X.509 certificates.

History

When EUS was first introduced in Oracle 8.1.5 Database, Enterprise Users had to be authenticated via an X.509 certificate using the SSL protocol; the users had to have a digital certificate installed on their computers. The certificate was used for the identification and authentication process.

The major inhibitor to its wide-scale use was in setting up the PKI infrastructure. Creating and distributing PKI credentials to every user was not something many organizations were prepared for. The configuration tasks were tedious and prone to error. While very secure, this proved somewhat impractical for many organizations that wanted the user centralization but not the management issues associated with deploying a PKI infrastructure.

With Oracle 9.0.X Database and later, EUS users can utilize a username and password for I&A. One of the most significant advantages of this support is that it's backward compatible, allowing practically all client programs that use usernames and passwords for I&A to be supported—the only requirement is that the database version is 9.0.X or newer.

Setting Up EUS

In this section, you'll learn how to configure your Oracle databases to use EUS. Note that the actual steps for this setup vary depending on database and LDAP versions. This description is for the Oracle Database 10*g*. See the *Oracle Advanced Security Administrator's Guide* for details on setup for Oracle9*i* Database.

NOTE
The steps for EUS setup depend on the database and LDAP version that you are using.

LDAP Setup

The first step required for EUS is to install the LDAP directory. The most desirable architecture isolates the directory from other enterprise applications. This will ensure that the database providing the centralized directory services isn't overwhelmed because, for example, it also has to support the company's accounting application. When using OiD, the server requires enough capacity to support the OiD database and the throughput requirements necessary for all the users in your enterprise. A more powerful machine will be needed if you have a large user population with many applications and if you require high throughput.

These are the two basic requirements for the directory setup:

- *Create the IM infrastructure in the directory.* This is done by default if you're using OiD as part of the IM capability to the Oracle Application Server. If you don't have the infrastructure installed, the database registration process, detailed in the upcoming "Database Setup" section, will allow you to install the needed directory schema.
- *Modify the default properties to accommodate any differences in your desired configuration and the default.* You can change the attribute for the user's log-on name (the default is cn for common name) and modify where searches begin within the directory tree.

Database Setup

Given an existing directory with the IM infrastructure installed, you're now ready to configure the database(s). For clients wishing to use the username and password I&A to EUS, there is no configuration required. You'll be using the username and password I&A for the examples in this chapter.

For the database, there are two things that have to be done to complete the setup. First, you need to tell the database where the directory server is. This can be done by either registering the directory in the corporate Domain Name System (DNS) or by creating an ldap.ora file. For this setup, you'll use the ldap.ora file. More information on using DNS for directory discovery can be found in the *Oracle Internet Directory Administrator's Guide.* The second step for database setup is to register the database with the directory.

Creating ldap.ora

To create the directory configuration file, you'll need to run the Network Configuration Assistant tool. This is invoked by running netca on the command line.

When the Network Configuration Assistant (netca) starts, select the Directory Usage Configuration button. The next screen prompts you for a directory type. The two directory types supported are Oracle Internet Directory and Active Directory. If you select Active Directory, netca will ask you if the directory already has the necessary IM infrastructure or if you want it to be created. If you don't have the infrastructure installed, netca can create one for you. You'll not be able to proceed without the IM LDAP schema installed in your directory.

The third screen asks for the hostname, port, and SSL port of the directory. The final screen asks you to choose the security context in which the user information will be placed. A default context is created when the infrastructure is installed, and you can add contexts later to support delegated administration.

The preceding steps serve as an easy way to create an ldap.ora file. This file, which resides in your $ORACLE_HOME/network/admin directory, tells your database where the directory is and where in the directory to look when authenticating users. An example file will look as follows:

```
# Generated by Oracle configuration tools.

DIRECTORY_SERVERS= (sabre.us.oracle.com:389:636)
DEFAULT_ADMIN_CONTEXT = "dc=iac,dc=oracle,dc=com"
DIRECTORY_SERVER_TYPE = OID
```

This file is critical because the next step relies on its existence.

Registering the Database

The second task required to complete the database setup is to register the database with the directory and set the database authentication mode. The Database Configuration Assistant performs these tasks for you.

To run the database configuration assistant program, type **dbca** on the command line. Once the ldap.ora file has been created, the Database Configuration Assistant (dbca) will allow you to register the database.

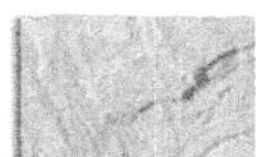

NOTE
If the ldap.ora file doesn't exist, the option to register the database in a directory will not be available to you.

In the first step of the dbca wizard, select the Configure Database Options radio button. On the next screen, the wizard asks for the database instance you want to configure and a user with the DBA role for that instance. What it's really asking for is a user with the *SYSDBA* role. If you supply a user without the SYSDBA role, you'll get an error indicating insufficient privileges.

Providing the database instance and a privileged user leads you to step 3, which asks if you want to register the database. When you select the Yes, register the database radio button, you'll also have to supply the administrator user and password for your directory. In the default Oracle installation, the administrator user has the username orcladmin. However, you can't enter **orcladmin** in the username field; you have to enter the username as **cn=orcladmin**. Access to this directory account is required because the dbca has to insert records that will be used to identify the database for the directory.

This screen also requires you to enter an Oracle wallet password. Oracle uses the wallet as a metaphor for how an entity stores its security credentials. This is the technological equivalent of a person's wallet. Just as you would keep your security credentials—driver's license and credit cards—in your wallet for identification purposes, the Oracle wallet stores the credentials needed by users or the database. The dbca generates a random strong password and stores it securely in the wallet. This enables the database to authenticate to the directory when it needs to perform user authentication. The actual password the database uses to authenticate to the directory is not the same as the one you provide for the wallet. (Note that prior to Oracle Database 10*g*, the wallet was used only to hold PKI credentials.)

ldap_directory_access

The last part in the process is the modification of an init.ora parameter called ldap_directory_access. The ldap_directory_access initialization parameter is new to Oracle Database 10*g*. It replaces the rdbms_server_dn parameter used in Oracle8*i* Database and Oracle9*i* Database. The rdbms_server_dn served three purposes.

First, rdbms_server_dn defined the database's identity within the directory. The value stored was the database's distinguished name (DN), which was used to uniquely identify the database in the central directory. Unfortunately, you had to manually set the value and many people set it incorrectly because the correct value wasn't obviously defined. In Oracle Database 10*g*, the database's identity is created automatically and securely stored in the database's wallet.

The second purpose of the rdbms_server_dn parameter was to act as a directory lookup indicator for the database. The database would use this value to determine whether it should consult the directory for user authorizations and mappings. In Oracle8*i* Database and Oracle9*i* Database, an SSL-authenticated user could either be a directory user (an Enterprise User) or a nondirectory user. If the rdbms_server_dn parameter was set, then the database used the directory for user authorizations and mappings; otherwise, the user was self-contained in the database. Thus, the database supported SSL-authenticated users without requiring the use of the directory.

A third use of this parameter was as a shutoff switch for directory access. It allowed DBAs to easily disable directory access for either performance or security reasons by simply setting the value to null.

In Oracle Database 10*g*, the ldap_directory_access still serves as an indicator of directory access. It supports the use of nondirectory-based SSL-authenticated users and can be used to quickly disable directory use. To disable directory access, a DBA simply issues the following:

```
ALTER SYSTEM SET ldap_directory_access = NONE SCOPE=MEMORY;
```

The possible values for this parameter are NONE, SSL, and PASSWORD with NONE set as the default during database creation. The dbca changes this value to PASSWORD and then reboots the database during this part of the EUS configuration. The other use for this parameter, as the parameter's name implies, is to instruct the database on the I&A method it'll use to connect to the directory.

Verifying the Database Setup

You can do three things to verify the database setup. After the database has rebooted, you can check the value of the ldap_directory_access parameter. It should now be set to PASSWORD:

```
sec_mgr@KNOX10g> show parameter ldap

NAME                                 TYPE        VALUE
------------------------------------ ----------- ---------
ldap_directory_access                string      PASSWORD
```

The next item to validate is the existence of the database wallet. This wallet will securely hold the database's distinguished name and its directory password. The actual values are inaccessible from the wallet manager. The wallet will be located in a subdirectory called wallet in the same directory where the database dump files are written. On UNIX, the default directory is in $ORACLE_HOME/admin/<SID>/wallet.

Figure 5-1 illustrates what the wallet looks like when you open it with the Oracle Wallet Manager, which is invoked by typing **owm** from the command line on UNIX or running the Wallet Manager program from Windows. You can see the Secret Store contains the database identity and password.

The database is now registered in the directory, and that too can be viewed and verified. The best way to see this is to launch the Oracle Enterprise Security Manager program by typing **esm** from the command line.

NOTE
The Enterprise Security Manager is installed with the Oracle Client Software, not with the Oracle Database software.

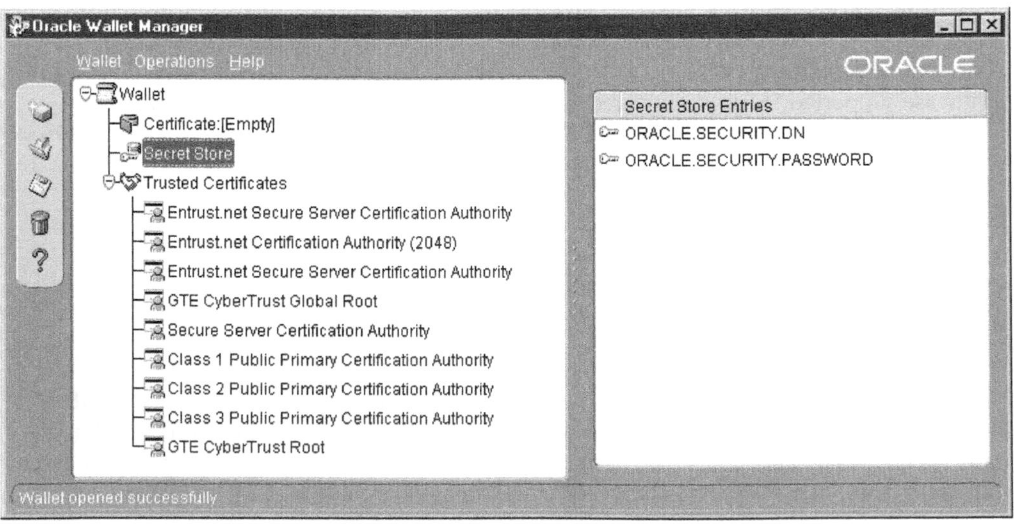

FIGURE 5-1. *The Oracle Wallet securely stores sensitive information for users and databases.*

You must log on as the directory administrator. After expanding the directory tree, you should see the database you just registered. Figure 5-2 shows the results of registering your database instance KNOX10G.

SSL I&A

The database can be configured to authenticate to the directory with SSL. This provides not only strong encryption but also strong I&A for both the database and the directory.

This was the default I&A prior to Oracle Database 10*g*. It's no longer the default because it's much more difficult to set up the PKI infrastructure, and it potentially operates more slowly. The performance is due to the PKI processes and network encryption that occur. For some, the database and the directory may reside on a switched network or private network and the addition of SSL is not necessary. For unprotected networks, Oracle recommends using SSL for database-to-directory I&A.

Configuring SSL is unnecessary for the examples required in this chapter, and you should consider using password authentication first; it's trivial to configure and it'll allow you to begin using and understanding EUS. After you're comfortable with the EUS abilities, switch the database authentication to SSL. You should strongly consider using SSL on your production systems unless the network can be protected through some other mechanism. SSL also provides strong database and directory authentication. Details for configuring your networks for SSL are given in the *Oracle Advanced Security Administrator's Guide 10*g.

Applying EUS

From an application-building perspective, EUS is attractive. Nothing special has to be done. Enterprise Users are transparent to the application's client connection. That is, the application connects using a username and password, and the application doesn't specify, hint, or in any way control whether it's connected to a "regular" database user or an Enterprise User. It doesn't matter whether the user is connected directly to the database or whether the application connects to the database on the user's behalf (proxy or otherwise). This is a wonderful feature because it's the basis for backward compatibility.

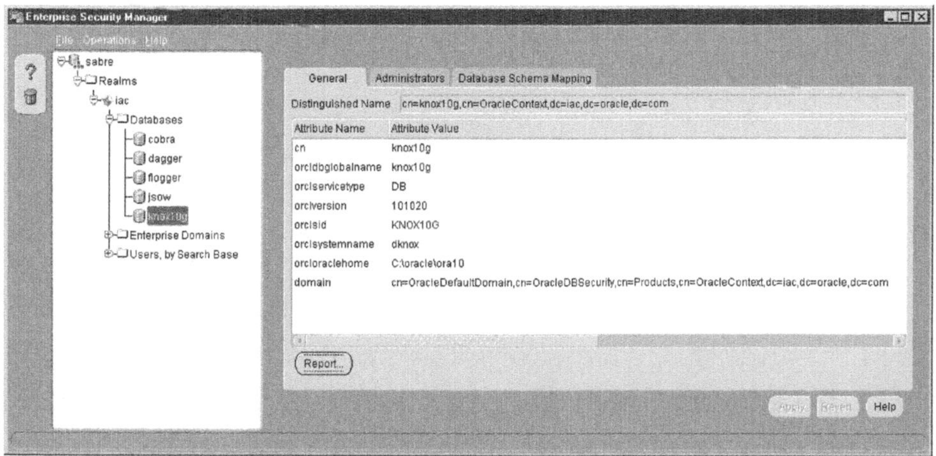

FIGURE 5-2. *The Enterprise Security Manager shows five registered databases participating in EUS for the iac security realm.*

Creating the Enterprise User

There are two ways to create your Enterprise Users. Chapter 6 shows how you can use the Delegated Administration Services web interface known as OiDDAS. Your second choice is to use the Enterprise Security Manager web console. In Oracle Database 10*g*, the Enterprise Security Manager (ESM) program is a client-server program that allows you only to view users and add/revoke authorizations; in previous releases, you could add, modify, and delete users from this tool. To create new users or delete existing ones, the Enterprise Security Manager web console can be used. The web console can be found by selecting the ESM Console URL from the File menu of the ESM (client-server) program.

To create users, you have to log on to the directory as an administrator. By default, the directory administrator is the orcladmin user. By selecting the Users and Groups tab, you'll see two subtabs, User and Group. Select the User subtab and click the Create button to see the administration screen for creating a new user. Figure 5-3 shows the Create User screen that can be used to add new directory users.

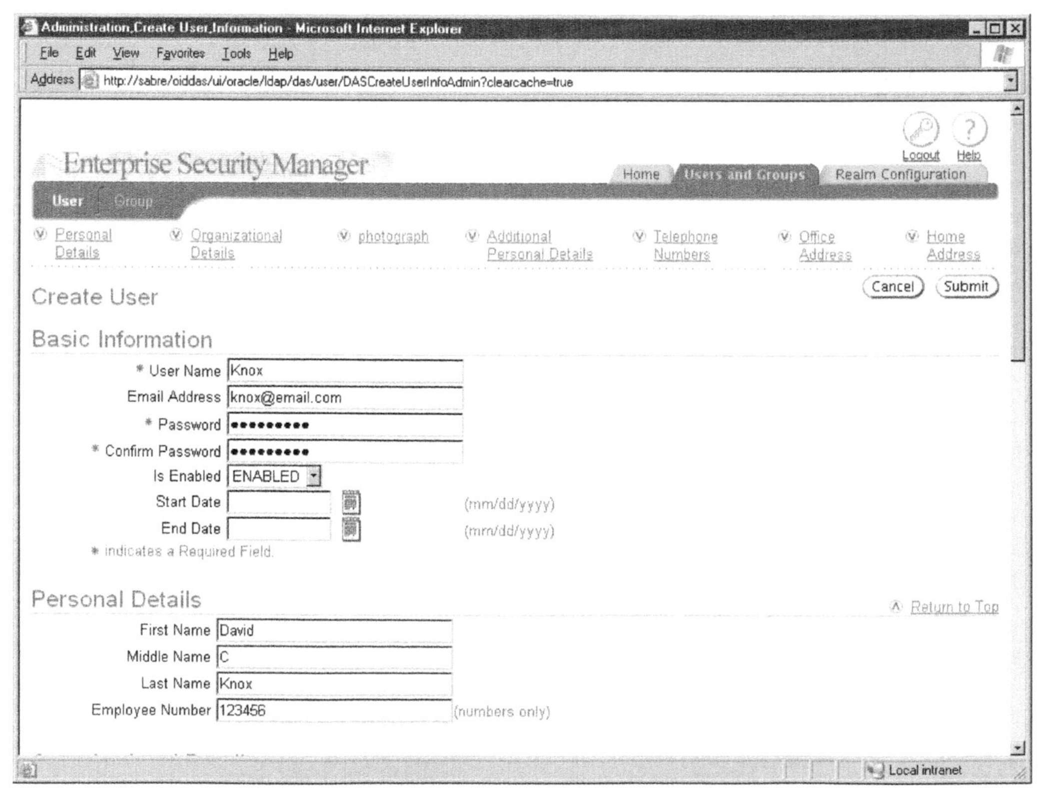

FIGURE 5-3. *The Enterprise Security Manager web console can be used to manage the creation and deletion of Enterprise Users.*

Unfortunately, the web console doesn't allow you to administer anything else in the database-directory relationship. For example, you can't see the databases that are registered, or any mapping or authorization information for the users. To access those elements, you have to use the ESM client-server program.

The Connection Process

When an Enterprise User logs on to the database, the database doesn't immediately know if the user is a directory-authenticated user or a database-authenticated user. On login, the database first searches for a database user account that matches the username presented. Assuming the password is correct, if no username entry is found, the database checks the value of the ldap_directory_access parameter. If it's set to NONE, then the database returns an ORA-1017: invalid username/password message:

```
system@KNOX10g> -- disable directory access
system@KNOX10g> ALTER SYSTEM SET ldap_directory_access=NONE SCOPE=MEMORY;

System altered.

system@KNOX10g> -- connect as an Enterprise User
system@KNOX10g> CONN knox/oracle10g
ERROR:
ORA-01017: invalid username/password; logon denied
```

TIP
By setting the ldap_directory_access to NONE you can quickly disable directory access if there is a security risk.

If the ldap_directory_access parameter is set to either PASSWORD or SSL, the database assumes this is a directory-authenticated user and queries the directory for the user entry matching this user's name. The user's name is a specific subcomponent of the distinguished name and is referred to as the *nickname*. The default nickname is the common name, or cn, and this is one of the configurable components you can manage during the initial directory setup. If the user isn't a database user or a directory user, a different error is raised:

```
system@KNOX10g> -- enable directory access
system@KNOX10g> ALTER SYSTEM
  2    SET ldap_directory_access=PASSWORD SCOPE=MEMORY;

System altered.

system@KNOX10g> -- connect as a user that does not exist in DB or directory
system@KNOX10g> CONN aldfjaslkjd/aslkd
ERROR:
ORA-28273: No mapping for user nickname to LDAP distinguished name exists.
```

When the appropriate entry is found, the password presented will be authenticated against the password stored in the LDAP server:

```
C:\>sqlplus knox/oracle10g

SQL*Plus: Release 10.1.0.2.0 - Production on Fri Apr 2 21:44:56 2004

Copyright (c) 1982, 2004, Oracle.  All rights reserved.


Connected to:
Oracle Database 10g Enterprise Edition Release 10.1.0.2.0 - Production
With the Partitioning, Oracle Label Security, OLAP and Data Mining options

app_public@KNOX10g>
```

The user was able to log on, but it looks as if the database has put them into the wrong schema! Actually, it hasn't because there is no KNOX database schema. If there were a KNOX schema, the initial log in would have worked (assuming the password was correct).

When you create an Enterprise User, you have to define a database schema for them. This mapping determines the schema to which the user will be attached. In the above example, there is a mapping for the KNOX Enterprise User to the APP_PUBLIC database schema. Setting up the user-schema mapping is a two-step process. The first step is to create the database schema; the second step is to define the mapping within the directory.

User-Schema Mappings

The directory maintains the mapping for the Enterprise Users to specific database schemas. Before EUS, if you wanted to create database users that had separate usernames, passwords, and privileges, you had to create individual database schemas for each user. With EUS, this 1:1 mapping model is still supported, but so are the shared schema designs.

The separation of user from schema allows administrators to provision the user once in the directory and then create a mapping or mappings to the databases that participate in the EUS. The user will then be able to log on to any of the databases within the domain as long as a mapping for the user exists.

Creating the Shared Schemas

The most common use of mapping is a shared schema in which multiple Enterprise Users share the same schema (N:M mapping). The first step is to create a container schema that will be shared by the users. For the KNOX Enterprise User example, we had to first create a shared schema and grant the privileges to connect:

```
sec_mgr@KNOX10g> CREATE USER app_public IDENTIFIED GLOBALLY AS '';

User created.
```

```
sec_mgr@KNOX10g> GRANT CREATE SESSION TO app_public;

Grant succeeded.
```

The syntax used to create this schema is what makes it sharable. There is no password, and the empty single quotes indicate that the account is anonymous from the database's view. The directory will be able to map users to this schema (sometimes referred to as the shared schema). Notice that there is no way to log on directly to the schema because there is no password. If you check the password value stored in the database for the APP_PUBLIC schema, you'll see that there's a non-null value:

```
sec_mgr@KNOX10g> SELECT username, password
  2     FROM dba_users
  3    WHERE username = 'APP_PUBLIC';

USERNAME                       PASSWORD
------------------------------ --------------------
APP_PUBLIC                     GLOBAL
```

It appears as though the database schema APP_PUBLIC was created with the "Identified by values 'GLOBAL'" syntax you learned in Chapter 2. These two creation statements are identical. In the following example, the APP_PUBLIC user is dropped and then re-created using the identified by values clause. The Enterprise User is then able to connect to this schema. *Note that this is done for illustrative purposes and isn't the officially supported way to create shared schemas*:

```
sec_mgr@KNOX10g> DROP USER app_public;

User dropped.

sec_mgr@KNOX10g> -- create user with password of GLOBAL
sec_mgr@KNOX10g> -- Note this is NOT the officially supported
sec_mgr@KNOX10g> -- way to create shared schemas
sec_mgr@KNOX10g> CREATE USER app_public IDENTIFIED BY VALUES 'GLOBAL';

User created.

sec_mgr@KNOX10g> GRANT CREATE SESSION TO app_public;

Grant succeeded.

sec_mgr@KNOX10g> CONN knox/oracle10g
Connected.
app_public@KNOX10g>
```

You can't map an Enterprise User to a schema that doesn't have 'GLOBAL' as the password value. If you map an Enterprise User to a database-authenticated schema, for example SCOTT, the Enterprise User will receive an ORA-01017: invalid username/password error when they try to log on. When you create the database schema for the Enterprise User, use the *identified globally as ''* syntax.

Directory Mappings

Now that the database has a schema to which the Enterprise User can attach, you need to define the mappings. The user mappings can be done at both the domain level and the individual database level. The first choice is to allow a domain-level mapping that defines the user-schema relationship across all databases in a domain. When you set up EUS, you register your databases in specific domains. The domain-level mapping is convenient because you only have to create one mapping for all of your databases. From a management perspective, it provides the consistency that the user(s) defined in the directory server are always mapped to the same schema(s) everywhere in your enterprise. This also assumes that every database has the same shared schemas.

The second mapping choice you have is to provide a mapping for each individual database. This adds the flexibility of allowing the same user to attach to different schemas for different databases. This would be used in designs where an application account already exists for the user but differs across databases. For example, a user might already have an account of DKNOX in one database, and DKNOX_US in a different database. These accounts (schemas) can be preserved by supplying a specific mapping for each database. The benefit? The user can now log in to both databases using the same username and password.

There is another dimension to the mapping that must be understood before the process can occur.

Directory Entry Mappings and Subtree Mappings

There are two more ways to define the user-schema relationship for both domain-level mapping and individual database mapping. First and most specifically, the mapping is from the individual directory user to a database schema. This is called an *entry mapping* because it maps a specific user entry to a specific database schema.

Second and more generally, the mapping can be defined for a group of directory users. That is, all the users located in a certain part of the directory tree will share a mapping to a database schema. This is called a *subtree mapping*.

Mapping Permutations Example

For an Enterprise User, there are four possible ways the user can be mapped. The database will follow a specific path of most specific to least specific in trying to determine in which schema a user should reside. The following example illustrates the various mappings as well as how the user's schema is resolved.

Creating the Schemas

For this example, four database schemas are used. Each schema will be used as a container for the Enterprise User.

```
CREATE USER domain_entry IDENTIFIED GLOBALLY AS '';
GRANT CREATE SESSION TO domain_entry;
CREATE USER domain_subtree IDENTIFIED GLOBALLY AS '';
GRANT CREATE SESSION TO domain_subtree;
CREATE USER db_entry IDENTIFIED GLOBALLY AS '';
GRANT CREATE SESSION TO db_entry;
CREATE USER db_subtree IDENTIFIED GLOBALLY AS '';
GRANT CREATE SESSION TO db_subtree;
```

The Enterprise User requires the CREATE SESSION privilege to log on to the database. You can either grant the privilege to the Enterprise User using Enterprise Roles (see Chapter 7), or grant the privilege to the database schema to which they will attach. You may find it easier to grant the privilege once to the database schema rather than grant it many times to all the Enterprise Users that will be sharing the schema.

NOTE
There is no security concern in granting the privilege to the shared database schema because a user can't log on directly to the shared schema, and the CREATE SESSION privilege will be required by all users (if you want them to actually attach to your database); therefore, you're not violating the least-privilege principle.

NOTE
You should only grant database object and system privileges to shared database schemas when all users sharing the schema require those privileges.

Creating the Mappings

To create the user-schema mappings, you'll use the ESM client-server program. For this example, we'll create four user mappings, one to each database schema. We'll log on as the KNOX user to show which mapping was used.

For clarity, the schema names created above describe the level of mapping that will occur. For example, the DOMAIN_SUBTREE schema will apply to all users in the directory subtree across all databases within the enterprise domain. Figure 5-4 shows a domain mapping with one entry mapping and one subtree mapping. The first entry shows that all users that exist in the subtree defined by the Directory Entry field will be mapped to the DOMAIN_SUBTREE schema. The second entry shows the Knox user will be mapped to the DOMAIN_ENTRY schema. There are five databases defined in this domain, which means these two mappings will exist across all five databases.

The directory doesn't verify that the database schema does or doesn't exist. This will be done at the time the user logs on. If the user(s) is mapped to a schema that doesn't exist, an ORA-01017: invalid username/password error will be raised. This is a great technique for allowing all but one user into the database. That is, provide a mapping to a schema that doesn't exist, and the user will not be able to log on.

TIP
To prevent a user from accessing your database while at the same time allowing general user access, create a user-schema mapping to a schema that doesn't exist.

The same types of mappings are defined at the individual database levels; for each database in a domain, you can specify entry or subtree mappings. In Figure 5-5, you'll see two analogous entries for the knox10g database. The first entry maps all users in the directory subtree to the DB_SUBTREE schema. The second entry maps the Knox directory user to the DB_ENTRY schema. The database-level mappings supersede the domain-level mappings.

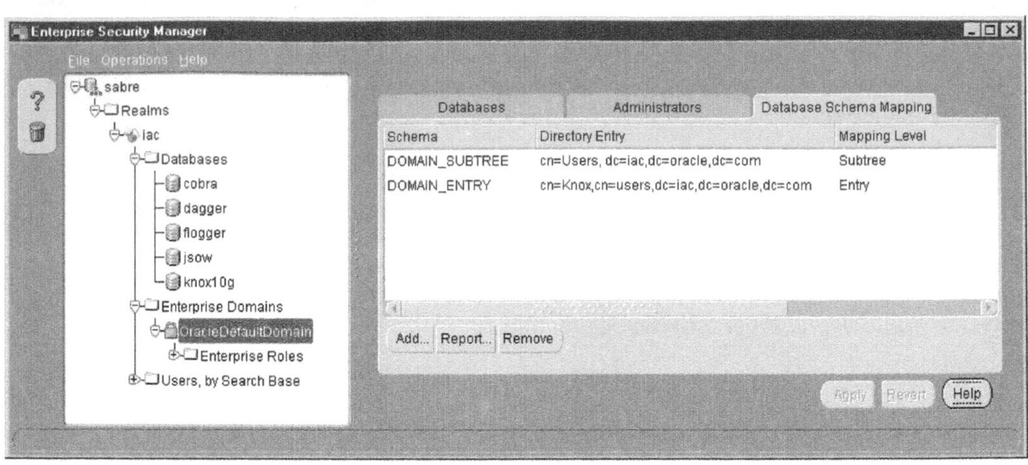

FIGURE 5-4. *Domain mappings apply to all databases registered in the domain.*

Testing the Mappings

Using the four previously defined mappings, you'll see how the actual user-schema resolution occurs. This is crucial because it ultimately determines which schema the user will be attached to, which is important for ensuring your users have the correct database privileges.

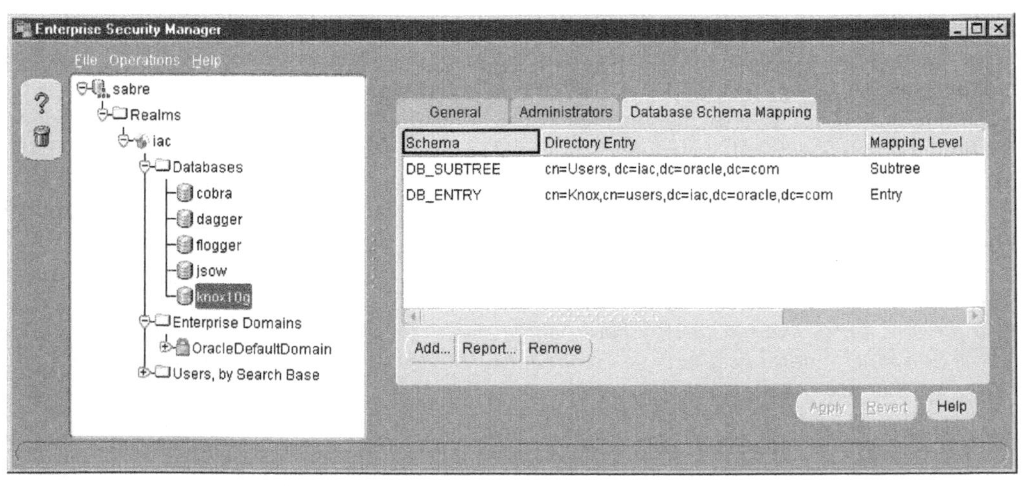

FIGURE 5-5. *Database mappings are specific to the database and supersede domain mappings.*

The resolution process starts from the most specific mapping definition to the least specific. The directory will search in the following order:

1. Specific user entry for the specific database
2. Directory subtree entry for the specific database
3. Specific user entry for the domain
4. Directory subtree entry for the domain

For the database knox10g, a database-specific mapping for the Knox user exists for the DB_ENTRY schema. When the user connects to the Dagger database, there's no database-specific mapping, but there's an entry-level mapping for the Knox user to the DOMAIN_ENTRY schema.

To illustrate the identity preservation, the following SQL connects as the Knox user and then displays the database schema and the database name, which are also viewed in the SQL prompt, and the directory user's identity. This last item shows how the Enterprise User's identity is preserved even when connected to a shared database schema.

```
SQL> -- test DB specific mappings
SQL> -- conn to Knox10g database which has database specific entry
SQL> CONN Knox/oracle10g@knox10g
Connected.
db_entry@KNOX10g> COL "Directory User" format a40
db_entry@KNOX10g> COL schema format a15
db_entry@KNOX10g> COL database format a10
db_entry@KNOX10g> SELECT SYS_CONTEXT ('userenv', 'external_name')
  2                                      "Directory User",
  3          USER SCHEMA,
  4          SYS_CONTEXT ('userenv', 'db_name')
  5                                                      DATABASE
  6     FROM DUAL;

Directory User                           SCHEMA          DATABASE
---------------------------------------- --------------- ----------
cn=Knox,cn=users,dc=iac,dc=oracle,dc=com DB_ENTRY        knox10g

db_entry@KNOX10g> -- test domain mapping by connecting to different database
db_entry@KNOX10g> -- Note, must create database schemas on target database
db_entry@KNOX10g> -- for this to work
db_entry@KNOX10g> CONN Knox/oracle10g@dagger
Connected.
domain_entry@DAGGER> SELECT SYS_CONTEXT ('userenv', 'external_name')
  2                                      "Directory User",
  3          USER SCHEMA,
  4          SYS_CONTEXT ('userenv', 'db_name')
  5                                                      DATABASE
  6     FROM DUAL;
```

```
Directory User                           SCHEMA          DATABASE
---------------------------------------- --------------- ----------
cn=Knox,cn=users,dc=iac,dc=oracle,dc=com DOMAIN_ENTRY    dagger
```

Removing the user-specific entries for the Knox user at both the database and the domain levels forces the mapping to resolve to the subtree entries. Running the connection test again validates the resolution order:

```
SQL> -- conn to Knox10g database which has database specific entry
SQL> CONN Knox/oracle10g@knox10g
Connected.
db_subtree@KNOX10g> SELECT SYS_CONTEXT ('userenv', 'external_name')
  2                                 "Directory User",
  3          USER SCHEMA,
  4          SYS_CONTEXT ('userenv', 'db_name')
  5                                         DATABASE
  6     FROM DUAL;

Directory User                           SCHEMA          DATABASE
---------------------------------------- --------------- ----------
cn=Knox,cn=users,dc=iac,dc=oracle,dc=com DB_SUBTREE      knox10g

db_subtree@KNOX10g> -- test mapping by connecting to different database
db_subtree@KNOX10g> -- Note, must create database schemas on target database
db_subtree@KNOX10g> -- for this to work
db_subtree@KNOX10g> CONN Knox/oracle10g@dagger
Connected.
domain_subtree@DAGGER> SELECT SYS_CONTEXT ('userenv', 'external_name')
  2                                 "Directory User",
  3          USER SCHEMA,
  4          SYS_CONTEXT ('userenv', 'db_name')
  5                                         DATABASE
  6     FROM DUAL;

Directory User                           SCHEMA          DATABASE
---------------------------------------- --------------- ----------
cn=Knox,cn=users,dc=iac,dc=oracle,dc=com DOMAIN_SUBTREE  dagger
```

Security for Shared Schemas

A majority of the EUS configurations utilize the shared schema capability. As the name implies, the users share a database schema; however, this differs from the anonymous connections where the application connects to the same schema because anonymous connections are handled by applications so the user's identity *may not* be preserved.

As shown in the previous example, the EUS shared schema design preserves the user's identity. The identity is automatically stored in a USERENV attribute called external_name. Not only is this value accessible to your database programs—triggers, secure application roles, VPD policies, and so on, the value is also audited when auditing is enabled. This allows you to use database security with the assurance that the security controls are being accurately applied to the real end users.

For database object and system privileges, you can use Enterprise Roles, which are discussed in Chapter 7.

Exclusive Schemas

The Enterprise Users don't have to share database schemas. You can create distinct user-schema (1:1) mappings. The benefit to using exclusive schemas is that the database security processes can be based on the database schema. It's often desirable to have exclusive mappings for privileged users because the security assurance is higher. Because the schema isn't shared, security access controls and auditing that operates at a schema level can be easily and intuitively implemented. (For two users sharing a database schema, there is no way to audit one of the users and not the other.) The obvious administration drawback with 1:1 mappings is that there's potentially a database schema and an LDAP entry for every end user.

There are two ways to implement exclusive schemas. First, you can use ESM to create an entry-level mapping for the directory user to a database schema. The exclusivity is provided when you don't assign any other directory users to the database schema. The important point: there is no way to enforce the exclusive mapping in the directory.

The alternative implementation is to have the database do the user-schema mapping. This ensures that the exclusivity is upheld. You create the mapping at the same time you create the database schema by providing the user's DN in the CREATE USER DDL. For example, to create an exclusive schema mapping for the KNOX directory user to the KNOX_DB database schema, you would issue the following:

```
sec_mgr@KNOX10g> -- Create a database mapped Enterprise User
sec_mgr@KNOX10g> CREATE USER knox_db IDENTIFIED
  2    GLOBALLY AS 'cn=Knox,cn=users,dc=iac,dc=oracle,dc=com';

User created.

sec_mgr@KNOX10g> GRANT CREATE SESSION TO knox_db;

Grant succeeded.

sec_mgr@KNOX10g> CONN knox/oracle10g
Connected.
knox_db@KNOX10g> COL "Directory User" format a40
knox_db@KNOX10g> SELECT SYS_CONTEXT ('userenv', 'external_name')
  2                                 "Directory User"
  3    FROM DUAL;

Directory User
----------------------------------------
cn=Knox,cn=users,dc=iac,dc=oracle,dc=com
```

Note that the user provides KNOX as the username during database log on. The directory is performing the authentication, however the database is providing the schema mapping. A database schema mapping supersedes any directory mapping for the user. Unlike operating system authenticated users, there is no dependency on the database schema name and the directory username; the database schema in the previous example could have been named anything.

When you view the exclusive schema in the DBA_USERS view, you can identify the directory user that is mapped by looking at the EXTERNAL_NAME column. Note that both the exclusive schema KNOX_DB and the shared schema APP_PUBLIC have the password 'GLOBAL', but the KNOX_DB also has an EXTERNAL_NAME value. This shows that both database schemas are used for EUS; the APP_PUBLIC mappings are created by the directory, and the KNOX_DB mapping is provided locally by the database.

```
sec_mgr@KNOX10g> COL password format a20
sec_mgr@KNOX10g> COL username format a10
sec_mgr@KNOX10g> COL external_name format a40
sec_mgr@KNOX10g> SELECT username, password, external_name
  2    FROM dba_users
  3   WHERE username IN ('KNOX_DB', 'APP_PUBLIC');

USERNAME   PASSWORD             EXTERNAL_NAME
---------- -------------------- ----------------------------------------
APP_PUBLIC GLOBAL
KNOX_DB    GLOBAL               cn=Knox,cn=users,dc=iac,dc=oracle,dc=com
```

Converting Existing Database Users to Directory Users

The exclusive schema design is often the first step in introducing EUS to existing applications. The 1:1 security model is consistent with the existing security. Assuming you have already configured your database for EUS, you can change currently defined database users to Enterprise Users in three easy steps. The following example shows how this can be done for the SCOTT user. First, alter the user by changing their database authentication to be directory-based. Note that this doesn't alter any of the schema objects or privileges.

```
sec_mgr@KNOX10g> ALTER USER scott IDENTIFIED GLOBALLY AS '';

User altered.
```

Next, create the user in the directory. The Enterprise Security Manager will allow you to create the SCOTT user in the directory. The final step is to create the exclusive mapping for the Scott directory user to the database schema SCOTT. When you now connect to the database with a username of SCOTT, the password is authenticated with the directory. All of the original schema privileges and objects are still enabled and available. The transparency of making these changes makes them applicable to existing applications. The user or application will not know that the user is now being authenticated by the directory.

```
sec_mgr@KNOX10g> CONN scott
Enter password:
Connected.
scott@KNOX10g>
```

If you later decide you want to revert back from the directory-authenticated user to the database-authenticated user, you simply alter the user again:

```
sec_mgr@KNOX10g> ALTER USER scott IDENTIFIED BY tiger;

User altered.

sec_mgr@KNOX10g> conn scott/tiger
Connected.
scott@KNOX10g>
```

In "The Connection Process" section, earlier in the chapter, you learned that the database first checks for the user's password locally. It's only if the password has the value of GLOBAL that the database refers to the directory for user authentication. This allows you to switch database users from locally authenticated to directory authenticated by simply using the ALTER USER command as just illustrated.

Another attractive alternative for moving all your database users to Enterprise Users is to employ the User Migration Utility. This is a program that you can configure for bulk migration of your existing database users to directory users. Exclusive schemas and shared schemas are supported. See Appendix G of the *Oracle Advanced Administrator's Guide 10g* for more information.

Considerations

The EUS capability is impressive. Many organizations have standardized on the concept for their best practices level. Before you begin converting, be aware of a couple of caveats.

Single Credentials and Performance

Single sign-on is motivated by ease of administration, which is generally accomplished via centralization of user data, and ease of use, meaning that the user doesn't have to remember or supply multiple identifiers and authenticators for the different applications or databases.

The primary goal with EUS is to support these two requirements for database users. The user information is centrally stored in a directory. The Oracle databases are also registered with the directory. When the user wants to access a database, the database defers authentication to the directory. The directory also provides authorization information by way of role mappings (see Chapter 7 for more information).

While often promoted as a single sign-on capability, the EUS implementation is actually a single-credential capability. The authentication occurs every time a user requests a connection to an Oracle database. The username and password just happen to be the same for all Oracle databases participating in EUS. When using a certificate for logon, the user simply connects to a database by supplying the connection alias—no username or passwords are required. It subsequently gives the user a single sign-on experience. This is an important distinction to recognize when deciding on overall system performance, because every login will require an authentication call to OiD.

A potential issue for deploying EUS centers on performance. For every Enterprise User, the database has to look up the user's authentication, find their schema mapping, and determine which authorizations they should have. (See Chapter 7 for more on enterprise authorizations.) As such, the connection process can take substantially more time than if the user is database authenticated. It's not that the process is necessarily slow, but it's slower than if the database was performing authentication itself. In addition, using SSL between the database and LDAP server will invariably slow performance (while giving you a secure connection).

This slow down in the authentication process may not be an issue. It's generally only an issue when the application scalability or performance characteristics are high. My internal tests show different times ranging from a couple hundred milliseconds to a couple of seconds. Location of servers, network utilization, processor speed, number of users, and about a dozen other things affect these results. Your mileage will vary.

In general, the authentication process is almost always acceptable, but it'll definitely take longer than database authentication. If there is a need to have the authentication process occur as quickly as possible, EUS will have to be thoughtfully compared.

Dependencies

With the implementation of a single authentication source also comes the risk that the single source will become a single point of failure. Oracle builds its LDAP server on the Oracle database to help ensure reliability and availability. However, if you don't prepare for and utilize these Oracle features, such as Real Application Clusters, you won't have a high availability solution.

Other bad things can happen, too. Network failures or other hardware failures can make the LDAP server unreachable or unavailable. It's important to consider this when deciding on how and when to use EUS. Network redundancy and data mirroring are two critical elements for ensuring the enterprise directory is always available and accessible.

Summary

EUS is an excellent solution for managing many users with many databases. It simplifies the administration tasks and adds security to an environment by allowing identity preservation. Centralizing the user accounts also ensures that user modifications—especially those done for security reasons—occur quickly, easily, and consistently.

EUS is also ideal when you want to integrate your applications, database authentication, and authorization architectures. Good security policies typically and correctly dictate a consistent and well-defined security model, which EUS can provide. Many applications and application servers will use LDAP for their authentication and authorization directories. Adding enterprise databases to this makes for a consistent and congruent security environment.

However, EUS may not be ideal in every situation. The "E" is for enterprise, and the connotation is that scalability and value are generally realized only when the size of the system has grown to a significant level. The number of databases, users, and applications required to achieve the value is subjective. There may not be a need to centralize users if they only access two databases. Beyond that, the administration and user experience are enhanced by the centralization.

The EUS capability complements other Oracle security technologies such as Oracle Label Security, Virtual Private Database, Secure Application Roles, and auditing. When used in combination, these technologies provide rings of security that help to protect your data.

CHAPTER 6

Identification and Authentication for Web Applications

In this chapter, you'll look at two ways of enabling database security through identity propagation. This chapter outlines the necessary steps for linking application security to database security. In the first half of the chapter, you'll analyze a J2EE application that uses the Oracle Application Server 10*g*, single sign-on, proxy authentication, and database Enterprise Users. In the second half of the chapter, you'll look at setting up database security when proxy authentication isn't used.

Passing information about the user to the database is the most important process in designing and deploying secure database applications. If handled correctly, the result is a well-defined, easily managed environment for users, applications, and data. If done incorrectly, database security will likely be forfeited, resulting in a disconnected architecture and fragmented security. My focus here is on the intersection points necessary for connecting the application securely to the database. In this chapter, security and performance battle head-to-head, and you'll look at ways to ensure that both can be maintained.

Application Processes for Identification and Authentication

In most web-based applications, users have to authenticate to the application before they can do anything. The application will typically use this information to differentiate what the different end users can see and mediate the actions they can perform within the application. Application security is necessary, and applications should always provide some security. However, it shouldn't be the only layer of security. Data security should exist in the database; application security should exist within the application.

The application must work in concert with the database. You must ensure that the user's identity doesn't stop at the application tier. The preferred method for accomplishing this task is by using proxy authentication. In instances where proxy authentication can't be used, you can rely on another technique utilizing PL/SQL packages and/or Client Identifiers, which are discussed later in the chapter. This basic principle of identity propagation is necessary for effective database security.

The first step in this process is application authentication. In many cases, the application *server* has been configured to perform the actual user authentication. That is, there is no code in the application that checks to see if the user has already authenticated. That job is left to the application server, and it does it quite well. The application is then configured to only allow authenticated and authorized users access.

There are many ways a user can authenticate to the application and/or application server. For this discussion, you really don't care *how* the user authenticated as much as you care *that* they authenticated.

Integrated Authentication

For your first case study, you'll analyze an application that authenticates to Oracle's Application Server. The Oracle Application Server installs a single sign-on (SSO) server to provide application-wide authentication for users. The Oracle SSO is flexible and supports standard authentication technologies such as SSL and the Java Authentication and Authorization Service (JAAS) specification.

By default, the Oracle SSO utilizes the Oracle Internet Directory (OiD) for its user repository. When a new user is created, several entries are automatically made into OiD. Authentication and authorization information for each user is stored in OiD.

Creating the Application User

The first step in this process will be to create a new user. For the database, you will be using Enterprise Users. All users will be mapped to the same database schema. Therefore, you don't have to create a new database schema for the users; you only have to map them to a database schema. You will do this later in the "Database Account Setup" section.

The users will access the database via an application deployed to the Oracle Application Server, so an application account is needed. You'll create the user utilizing Oracle's OiD Delegated Administration Services (OiDDAS). OiDDAS is the web-based tool deployed with the Oracle Application Server that is used to manage web-based user accounts. The "delegated" part of OiDDAS refers to the ability to distribute responsibility for managing users to separate security administrators within an organization.

When OiDDAS creates the user, it creates a new entry in the LDAP server for the user. This account is the same account the database uses when referencing the Enterprise User. To create the user, you login to OiDDAS as the administrator for the realm (the security domain) in which you wish to create the user. Navigating to the Directory tab, you can create a user by clicking the Create button when the User subtab is selected. Figure 6-1 shows the resulting screen used to create the Knox user.

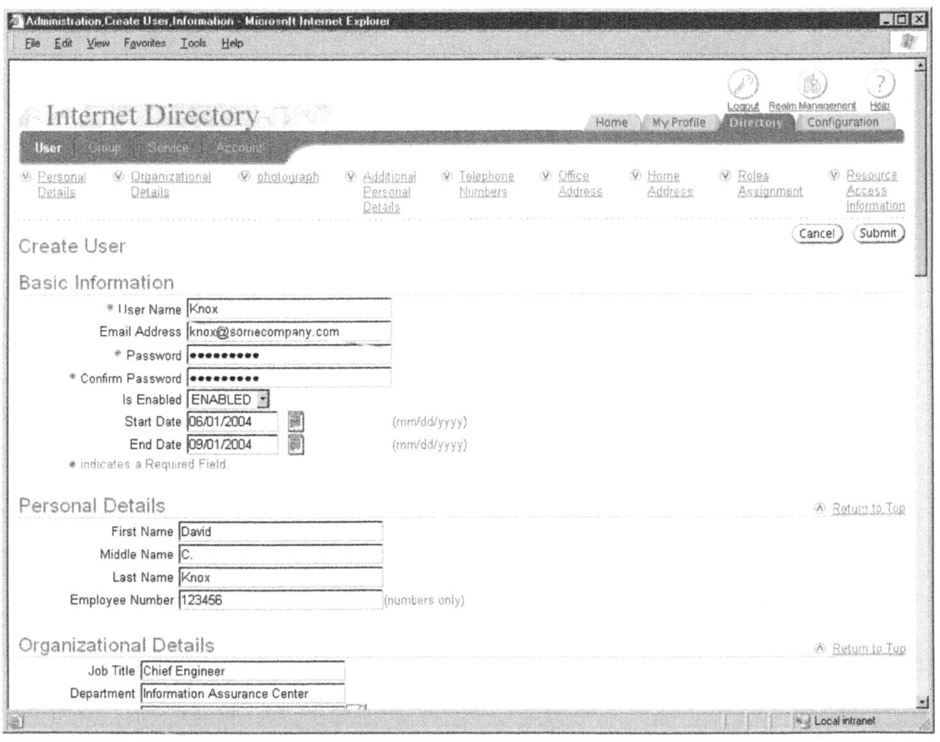

FIGURE 6-1. *OiDDAS allows delegated administration of user accounts for different security realms within an organization.*

As part of the user creation, appropriate privileges and roles are assigned to the users. This step is also supported through OiDDAS. These privileges and roles control access to the applications. As illustrated in Figure 6-2, you can use the Oracle Enterprise Manager to restrict access to your application to users who have the appropriate privileges. Application privileges, like database privileges, can be either directly granted to users or indirectly granted via roles. Privileges to access a J2EE application are managed by configuration settings, not by code.

Once the user is created, they can log in to the application by authenticating to the SSO server. After authentication, the user's authorizations are automatically retrieved. If the user possesses the correct privileges or roles, the application server will allow them to execute the application.

The important point is that all of this happens transparently (and almost magically) to the application itself. The application doesn't have to perform any authentication or authorization checks. This greatly simplifies your application code.

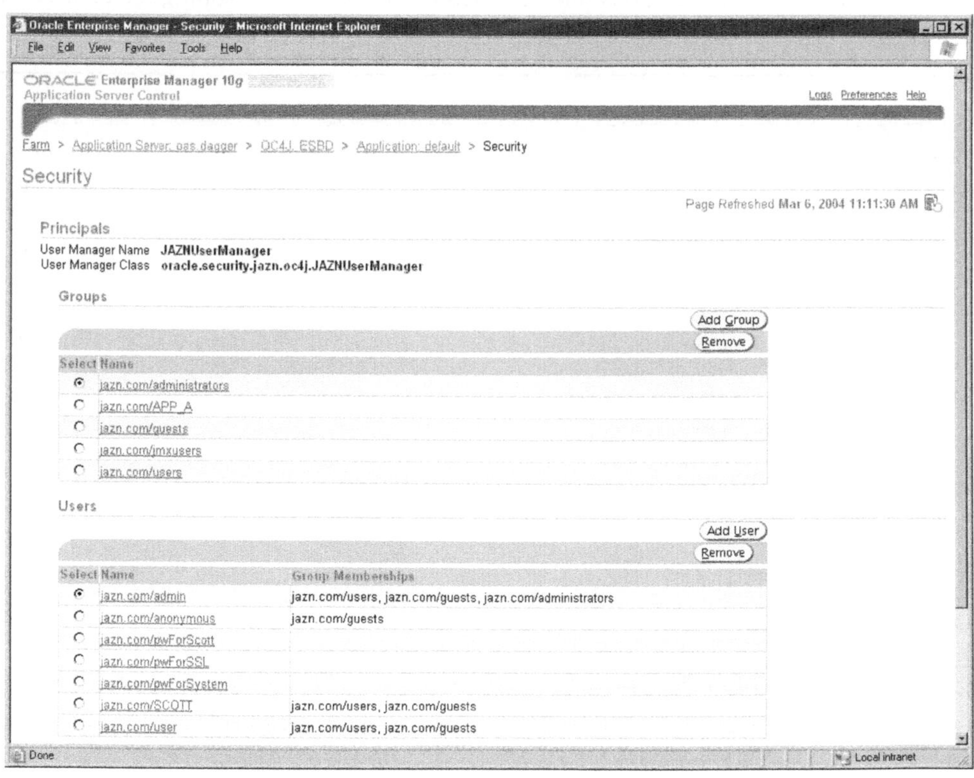

FIGURE 6-2. *Oracle Enterprise Manager allows you to control access to the application by adding users and groups to the application's security domain.*

Connecting the Application User to the Database

Now that you have the application deployed and your users created, you need to link the application users to the database. You will utilize proxy authentication for this task.

From Chapter 4, you will recall that proxy authentication technology was developed to help solve the challenge of securely passing the user identity to the database, thus allowing the database to employ its security capabilities at a user level. Typically, applications establish a connection pool to the database. The *connection pool,* which is a pool of preestablished database connections, links the application and users to a database schema. Oracle connections involve two steps.

The first step is to establish the physical connection from the client to the database. A network circuit is established; this task can take several hundred milliseconds (not that fast for highly scalable applications). The second step is to create the user's database session. This is when the user identification and authentication occurs. This step is "lightweight," meaning that it doesn't require as many computing resources. The first step is much slower than the second step because proxy authentication with connection pools involves the creation of database sessions (step two) over existing physical connections (step one). The result is high throughput for the applications. The security or the "proxy" part of proxy authentication allows the connections to occur without the application needing the end-user's password.

Configuring the Data Source for Proxy Authentication

J2EE applications use a data source to define database connections. This section describes how to configure a data source to support proxy authentication. The following examples are specific to the Oracle Application Server 10*g*. This process differs from the code examples in Chapter 4 because this example assumes the application has now been deployed to the Oracle Application Server.

There are two necessary steps required here. First, you want to use proxy authentication for secure identity preservation, so you have to configure a data source to use the proper JDBC drivers. Only Oracle's thick JDBC drivers support proxy authentication. Second, you have to configure the data source to connect to the appropriate database schema. This is the schema from which you will issue your proxy authentication.

As shown in Figure 6-3, the data source can be configured using Oracle Enterprise Manager. The data source record contains the necessary connection information required to connect your application, using proxy authentication, to the database.

The JDBC driver field specifies the connection object that will be used. Note that the required JDBC driver is the OracleOCIConnectionPool class because it supports the proxy authentication capability. The database username and password are also set here. While it may appear that the password for the user is "APP_PUBLIC", it isn't. The password was originally set in the Cleartext field and then updated to use the Indirect Password feature. This ensures the password can't be seen from the administration screen.

The data sources are stored in an OS file called data-sources.xml. The file lists all the data sources used within the application. Here is a sample data source record:

```
<data-source
  class="com.evermind.sql.DriverManagerDataSource"
  name="OracleDS"
  location="jdbc/OracleCoreOCIDS"
  xa-location="jdbc/xa/OracleXADS"
  ejb-location ="jdbc/OracleDS"
```

```
connection-driver="oracle.jdbc.pool.OracleOCIConnectionPool"
username="APP_PUBLIC"
password="->APP_PUBLIC"
url="jdbc:oracle:oci:@dagger"
inactivity-timeout="30"
min-connections="3"
max-connections="10"/>
```

FIGURE 6-3. *Oracle Enterprise Manager can be used to configure the data sources required to connect J2EE applications to databases.*

Note that the account password is not stored in cleartext. By selecting Use Indirect Password from the Enterprise Manager Edit Data Source screen, the entry will only be a placeholder for the application server to look up the actual password. The "->" in the preceding data source file indicates that the password is stored indirectly.

Getting the User Identity

The application has been deployed and configured. Users have been given appropriate privileges to execute the application. You can now look at the code the application will use to obtain the user's identity and pass it through to the database.

The most common way to retrieve the user's name is by calling a standard J2EE method getUserPrincipal() available from the HTTPServletRequest object. This will return the authenticated user's name, for example, "Knox":

```
String currentUser = request.getUserPrincipal().getName();
```

There is an alternative method you can use. For applications configured to run with Oracle SSO, you can make a different call. The following code returns not the user's name, but rather their distinguished name (DN). DNs are unique for each user. The DN will not only identify the user, but also allow you to easily make the proxy authentication call to the database.

```
String userDN = request.getHeader("Osso-User-Dn"); // for 10gAS SSO
```

These two examples are important because they show the two common ways to identify the user. More importantly, they provide the information you need for proxy authentication. Recall that proxy authentication can occur four ways. The two most common are proxy by username and proxy by distinguished name. If you have the user's name, you can proxy by username. If you have the user's DN, you can proxy by distinguished name. For this application, you will use the user's DN.

Proxy Authenticating with Connection Pools

You next establish a connection pool that will be used for proxy authentication. The pool's initial connections will be made based on the data source you just created. To obtain a data source connection, you have to use an InitialContext object. This object will return the appropriate data source (database connection) based on the string parameter passed in the lookup method:

```
  InitialContext initial = new InitialContext();
  OracleOCIConnectionPool ds = (OracleOCIConnectionPool)
                              initial.lookup("jdbc/OracleCoreOCIDS");
```

The connection is made by matching the string parameter (bolded) with the location tag located in the data-sources.xml file. As seen in Figure 6-4, this field is also specified in the Enterprise Manager Configuration screen for the J2EE application. The boxed area shows the Location field, which is matched in the context's lookup method.

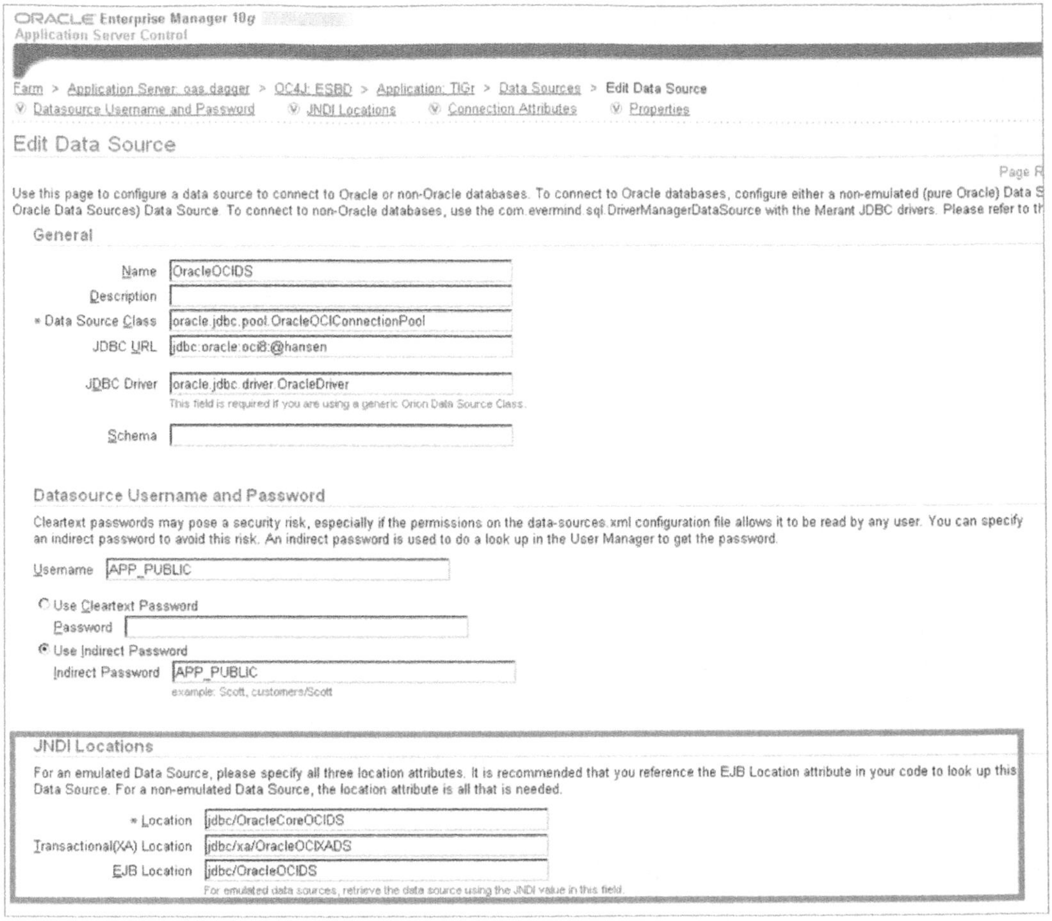

ORACLE Enterprise Manager 10*g*
Application Server Control

Farm > Application Server: oas.dagger > OC4J: ESBD > Application: TIGr > Data Sources > Edit Data Source

Datasource Username and Password | JNDI Locations | Connection Attributes | Properties

Edit Data Source

Page R

Use this page to configure a data source to connect to Oracle or non-Oracle databases. To connect to Oracle databases, configure either a non-emulated (pure Oracle) Data S Oracle Data Sources) Data Source. To connect to non-Oracle databases, use the com.evermind.sql.DriverManagerDataSource with the Merant JDBC drivers. Please refer to th

General

Name: OracleOCIDS
Description:
* Data Source Class: oracle.jdbc.pool.OracleOCIConnectionPool
JDBC URL: jdbc:oracle:oci8:@hansen
JDBC Driver: oracle.jdbc.driver.OracleDriver
This field is required if you are using a generic Orion Data Source Class.
Schema:

Datasource Username and Password

Cleartext passwords may pose a security risk, especially if the permissions on the data-sources.xml configuration file allows it to be read by any user. You can specify an indirect password to avoid this risk. An indirect password is used to do a look up in the User Manager to get the password.

Username: APP_PUBLIC

Use Cleartext Password
Password:
Use Indirect Password
Indirect Password: APP_PUBLIC
example: Scott, customers/Scott

JNDI Locations

For an emulated Data Source, please specify all three location attributes. It is recommended that you reference the EJB Location attribute in your code to look up this Data Source. For a non-emulated Data Source, the location attribute is all that is needed.

* Location: jdbc/OracleCoreOCIDS
Transactional(XA) Location: jdbc/xa/OracleOCIXADS
EJB Location: jdbc/OracleOCIDS
For emulated data sources, retrieve the data source using the JNDI value in this field.

FIGURE 6-4. *The database connection is resolved by matching the location field for the data source defined for the application.*

Proxy by Distinguished Name

At this point, you have the data source but you haven't established the user's proxy session. For the proxy authentication, you'll use the distinguished name value of the user identity. To do this, you'll first need a Properties object, and then you'll seed it with your distinguished name.

To establish the proxy authentication connection, you do not use the standard getConnection method. You must use the getProxyConnection method of your DataSource object. You have to pass the properties to the connection to indicate the identity of the user you wish to become (or become proxy to). The following snippet of Java code shows what's required for looking up the data source and establishing the proxy connection:

```
// retrieve user's distinguished name
String userDN = request.getHeader("Osso-User-Dn");
// retrieve the connection pool for our data source
InitialContext initial = new InitialContext();
OracleOCIConnectionPool ds = (OracleOCIConnectionPool)
                             initial.lookup("jdbc/OracleCoreOCIDS");
// set the user's name to be used in the proxy connection call
Properties prop = new Properties();
prop.put(OracleOCIConnectionPool.PROXY_DISTINGUISHED_NAME ,userDN  );
// make the proxy connection
Connection conn = ds.getProxyConnection(
                  OracleOCIConnectionPool.PROXYTYPE_DISTINGUISHED_NAME,
                  prop);
```

Database Account Setup

For proxy authentication with EUS, the database will have at least two accounts for this single application. One account will be used for establishing the connection pools for the application's initial connection. The other account(s) will be used as the shared schema account for the actual end users.

Connection Pool Database Account—Least Privileges

It's important to understand that the proxy authentication design is fundamentally different than the design used by most applications today. Most applications will connect all end users to the same database schema. That is not necessarily bad. However, in doing so, the application schema is usually granted all privileges required by all users (otherwise the application will not be able to perform the operations required by all users). If this isn't done in a controlled way, your architecture will be in violation of the least-privilege principle. Your goal with any architecture is to maintain the least-privilege principle.

The connection pool will connect to the database and then create a new database session for the end user(s). For the account to which your connection pool will first be established (APP_PUBLIC in the previous code), it's important to ensure least privileges so that if, for some reason, the account is compromised, you have limited the actions that can be performed. Granting only the privilege needed to connect to the database complies with the least privilege principle.

To create a least-privilege account for your proxy-ready connection pool, simply create a database user and give them a single privilege: the privilege to connect to the database. Recall that this is *not* the CONNECT role. The only privilege needed will be the CREATE SESSION privilege. Here is sample code to create a public user and assign them the connection privilege:

```
sec_mgr@DAGGER> CREATE  USER app_public IDENTIFIED BY tiarhpw2r
  2    DEFAULT TABLESPACE users
  3    TEMPORARY TABLESPACE temp;

User created.

sec_mgr@DAGGER> GRANT CREATE SESSION TO app_public;

Grant succeeded.
```

User Database Account(s)

With Oracle EUS, you can have dedicated schemas or shared schemas. This example is only being performed for a single shared schema but there is no reason why you couldn't use more. Remember that the way to create a shared schema is to specify an empty distinguished name. The following code creates the user and also grants the necessary connection privilege:

```
sec_mgr@DAGGER> CREATE  USER user_public_global IDENTIFIED GLOBALLY AS '';

User created.

sec_mgr@DAGGER> GRANT  CREATE SESSION TO user_public_global;

Grant succeeded.
```

You can now grant any other necessary privileges required for your application. Keep in mind that this should be done in a least-privilege manner. Any privileges that are consistent for all application users can be directly granted to the USER_PUBLIC_GLOBAL schema. Any differences in privilege sets should be implemented with Enterprise Roles and database Global Roles (see Chapter 7). This will ensure that two users that require different privileges but are connected to the same shared schema will actually have different privileges.

You are not quite done. You have two accounts: one for the application's connection pool and the other for the shared schema used for the Enterprise Users. You need to bridge these two accounts—you need to allow for proxy authentication.

The connection pool will connect to APP_PUBLIC, and the actual end users will be authenticated. In Chapter 4, you saw the privilege to perform a proxy authentication was given to the end user schema, for example, SCOTT. Because the users are Enterprise Users and have no schema, you have to grant the proxy authentication privileges to the Enterprise User shared schema:

```
sec_mgr@DAGGER> ALTER USER user_public_global
  2      GRANT CONNECT THROUGH app_public
  3      AUTHENTICATED USING DISTINGUISHED NAME;

User altered.
```

The mapping for the end users, which is stored in OiD, places the users in the USER_PUBLIC_GLOBAL schema after database authentication. The preceding DDL allows the connection pool schema to perform its proxy authentication.

Authentication Blueprint

Let's review a blueprint of your connection design. Figure 6-5 illustrates the results of your configuration.

The figure can be described by following the sequential steps listed here parenthetically. The user (Knox, in this example) first attempts to access the application (1). The application server knows the user is unauthenticated and redirects the user to the single sign-on (SSO) server (2). SSO challenges the user for credentials (3) and authenticates the credentials with the LDAP server (4). The SSO server provides the user's authenticated identity to the application (5).

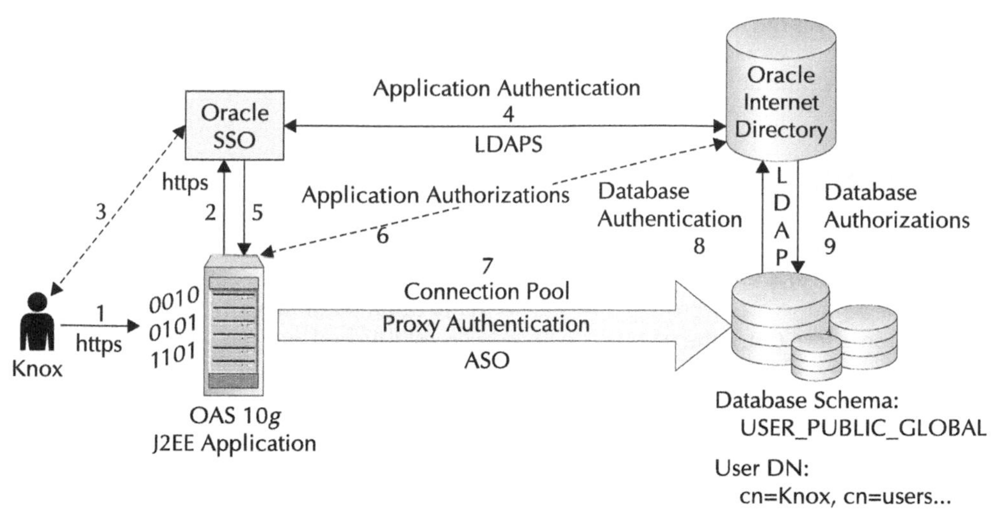

FIGURE 6-5. *User information can be centrally managed in the LDAP directory.*

The application server verifies the user's privilege to execute the application by retrieving their authorizations from the LDAP server. The user's identity is needed to perform this step. Note that the SSO server is not an authorization server; no authorization information about the user is initially provided. The applications have to implement their own authorization mechanism. The Oracle Application Server does this automatically for the J2EE applications by retrieving the user's authorizations from the LDAP server (6).

The application now has an identified, authenticated, and privileged user. A connection is retrieved from the connection pool. The connection pool is connected to the APP_PUBLIC database schema. A proxy authentication is then made based on the user's distinguished name, which was provided by the SSO (7).

The database, upon receiving the proxy authentication request, will first look for the user in its local table of users. Because no schema exists in the database for the end user, the database must refer to the LDAP server to determine in which schema the user should reside (8). If you were authenticating directly to the database using a password, the password would be authenticated in the LDAP server at this point. The LDAP server also provides a list of any database Global Roles the end user has for this specific database (9).

The users are mapped to the USER_PUBLIC_GLOBAL schema. The database verifies the privilege for a proxy connection to occur from the APP_PUBLIC schema to the USER_PUBLIC_GLOBAL schema and the privilege to create a database session. Once the privileges are verified, the user is logged on to the database. The database session is then automatically set up by the database; that is, logon triggers will fire, roles will be enabled, and so on.

Points of Interest

The preceding authentication architecture works easily because the user is created and managed in a central place. Both the SSO server and the database refer to the same place for user authentication (the same place doesn't mean the same physical server but the same entry within the same server).

A client-server application could authenticate the user directly to the database using the same password the user supplied to the web-based application. The user would be placed in the same database schema and would have the same privileges as they did when accessing the database through the web application. The authentication consistency is important for ensuring security consistency.

Performance

The initial application authentication process naturally requires some time. However, for the web applications, the authentication process only happens once. Steps one through four are not performed for the user's subsequent requests. The SSO server and applications both establish a "web session" with the user's browser. This is normally done automatically without requiring any application code. Once the web session has been established, subsequent requests happen without delay.

Connecting to the database is different. Proxy authentication to an Enterprise User is slower than proxy authentication for a user managed within the database. The database has to authenticate the user and look up the schema and roles for the user in the LDAP server. In my tests, this can add a couple hundred milliseconds to the connection time. Your performance goal is to drive the database connection time to zero. The way to do this is to cache the database session for the user.

There are two risks to caching the database session for each user. First, each user session requires memory. Both the application server and the database server will require enough memory to handle open connections to support all concurrent users. Proxy authentication only creates a new database session, so the memory requirements are minimal. Nevertheless, an evaluation has to be done to determine if this task can be accomplished given the expected (concurrent) user load.

The second risk involves the nature of web applications. In the web environment, there is no guarantee the user will make another web request. If the application has opened a database session for a user that will never return, then memory and processing resources are wasted on the application server and the database. The solution to the performance challenge is to use caching. The solution to the wasted resources problem is to ensure that sessions are closed after a period of inactivity.

You can do this by creating a Java helper program. The Java object will automatically close the database sessions at the appropriate time. The object will be invoked not by your application, but by the application server (actually the web container). Web applications can be configured to release resources after a period of inactivity. This session time-out period will be used as the time period to close the database session.

To use this capability, the object has to implement a specific Java interface. By doing so, the application server will automatically call this object's valueUnbound method when the user's web session expires. You simply need to close the database session within this method.

```
package OSBD;
import javax.servlet.http.*;

public class DBHolder implements HttpSessionBindingListener
{
  oracle.jdbc.OracleConnection conn = null;
  public DBHolder() { }
  public void valueBound(HttpSessionBindingEvent event){}
```

```
  public void valueUnbound(HttpSessionBindingEvent event) {
      if (conn != null) {
        try {
          conn.close();
        } catch (java.sql.SQLException ex) {
          System.out.println("can't close SQL conn..."+ex);
        }
      }
  }
  public void setConnection(oracle.jdbc.OracleConnection c) {
    conn = c;
  }
  public oracle.jdbc.OracleConnection getConnection() {
      return conn;
  }
}
```

To use this design from a JSP or Servlet, use the web application server (container) ability to store values in memory. The following represents the complete code for doing this as a JSP:

```
<%@ page contentType="text/html;charset=windows-1252"%>
<%@ page import="javax.naming.*,javax.sql.*,oracle.jdbc.*,java.sql.*"%>
<%@ page import="java.util.*,oracle.jdbc.pool.OracleOCIConnectionPool"%>
<%@ page import="oracle.jdbc.pool.OracleDataSource,OSBD.*"%>
<%@ page import="oracle.jdbc.oci.OracleOCIConnection"%>
<%
OracleConnection conn = null;
    // retrieve user's distinguished name
String userDN = request.getHeader("Osso-User-Dn");
    // Try to obtain database session (connection)
    // from the Web session
DBHolder hold = (DBHolder) session.getAttribute("conn");
    // check to see if connection was cached
if (hold == null) {
      // no connection, create a new one
  InitialContext initial = new InitialContext();
  OracleOCIConnectionPool ds = (OracleOCIConnectionPool)
                              initial.lookup("jdbc/OracleCoreOCIDS");

      // set user's name for proxy connection call

  Properties prop = new Properties();
  prop.put(OracleOCIConnectionPool.PROXY_DISTINGUISHED_NAME,userDN);
      // make the proxy connection
  conn = ds.getProxyConnection(
         OracleOCIConnectionPool.PROXYTYPE_DISTINGUISHED_NAME, prop);
      // save connection in session
  hold = new DBHolder();
  hold.setConnection(conn);
```

```
  session.setAttribute("conn", hold);
} else {
    // Use the saved connection
    conn = hold.getConnection();
  }
  // Can use connection to access database now
  // Note: Do NOT close the connection! DBHolder will do that
%>
```

The process is simple. You first try to get a cached connection from the user's application session. If a connection doesn't exist, create a new one and store it in the application server session cache. Any subsequent requests will use this cached database connection thus ensuring performance is maintained. Subsequent connections will have a zero cost connect time.

It's important that you never issue a direct call to close your database connection. The helper object (DBHolder) will do this for you automatically when the user's web session expires and the application server invokes the valueUnbound method. Using this technique, you can achieve both security and performance.

Proxy Authentication Alternatives

The previous architecture works in many cases, but there are situations when proxy authentication can't be used. From a security perspective, proxy authentication is ideal because database security can be fully exploited with little or no application coding. Login triggers fire, database privileges and roles are automatically enabled, and auditing can be used to track the end user's actions.

If proxy authentication can't be used (both the proxy authentication requests and the EUS authentication introduce latency), the application must include directions for the database so that database security can also be used. This can be done by passing user information to the database prior to performing any database-related work within the application.

There are three popular ways to pass user information to the database: use a PL/SQL package, use the Oracle built-in Client Identifiers, and use an application context. I'll discuss the first two ways here. Application contexts are similar to using a PL/SQL package and are covered in Chapter 9.

Application Directed Security

Recall from Chapter 4 that the Oracle implicit connection cache has a zero time associated with retrieving an already established connection from the connection pool. This is because both the physical connection and database session are already established. This connection pooling mechanism is highly desirable because it has eliminated the database connection and session creation time.

To use these connections securely, the application has to convey the user's information to the database before any procedures or queries are executed. Additionally, the application has to reset the database state between different and subsequent user requests. Database object and system privileges will be stored in roles and selectively enabled and disabled for appropriate users. The application has to manage the process of knowing when to enable and disable roles for the users. Roles are discussed in Chapter 7.

All of this extra work is done to ensure that nothing about the previous user's session will leak into the current user's session. A frequent trick for storing information about a user in the database session is to use PL/SQL package variables with "getter" and "setter" functions. The package variables are private for each database session and can be easily cleared between user requests.

For this to work effectively, the web user must be bound to a database session for the duration of their request. The application will set information about the user by invoking a PL/SQL procedure. The database security functions (views, triggers, VPD, auditing, and so on) can then reference the values in the package.

A simple example shows how easy this technique can be. First, you'll create a PL/SQL package to store the user information:

```
sec_mgr@KNOX10G> CREATE OR REPLACE PACKAGE user_info
AS
  PROCEDURE set_name (p_name IN VARCHAR2);

  FUNCTION get_name
    RETURN VARCHAR2;
END;
/

Package created.

sec_mgr@KNOX10G> CREATE OR REPLACE PACKAGE BODY user_info
AS
  g_name  VARCHAR2 (32767);

  PROCEDURE set_name (p_name IN VARCHAR2)
  AS
  BEGIN
    g_name := UPPER (p_name);
  END;

  FUNCTION get_name
    RETURN VARCHAR2
  AS
  BEGIN
    RETURN g_name;
  END;
END;
/

Package body created.
```

A table is created and populated based on the SCOTT.EMP table. Your application will access the table through a view that will filter the records returned based on the value in the PL/SQL package.

```
sec_mgr@KNOX10G> CREATE TABLE people_tab AS SELECT * FROM scott.emp;

Table created.

sec_mgr@KNOX10G> CREATE OR REPLACE VIEW person_view
AS
  SELECT *
```

```
  4      FROM people_tab
  5     WHERE ename = user_info.get_name;

View created.
```

The application is responsible for setting the user's name prior to querying from the view. I'll show the following examples in SQL*Plus, but the process is identical for Java or any other application.

```
sec_mgr@KNOX10G> -- set the user's identity
sec_mgr@KNOX10G> EXEC user_info.set_name('SCOTT');

PL/SQL procedure successfully completed.

sec_mgr@KNOX10G> -- get all rows for the user
sec_mgr@KNOX10G> SELECT ename, job, sal
  2     FROM person_view;

ENAME      JOB              SAL
---------- --------- ----------
SCOTT      ANALYST         3000
```

The package variables are private to the database session. This is important because you have multiple database sessions connected to the same database schema. When the user request is finished, and prior to returning the connection to the connection pool, the application has to reset the values in the package:

```
sec_mgr@KNOX10G> -- reset all package variables
sec_mgr@KNOX10G> EXEC dbms_session.reset_package;

PL/SQL procedure successfully completed.

sec_mgr@KNOX10G> -- show session state has been reset
sec_mgr@KNOX10G> SELECT * FROM person_view;

no rows selected
```

Object and system privileges are controlled by database roles. The application has to enable the role(s), set the user's identity, do its work, reset the package state, and finally, disable the roles. Securing the privileges and roles is discussed in Chapter 7.

A convenient method for implementing this is to create an object that returns a user connection after calling all the initialization procedures. A complementary method would be used to reset the database state and close the connection (returning it to the connection pool). This is shown in the upcoming "Java Application Setup" section.

Application User Proxy—Client Identifiers

Oracle supports another method for conveying user identifying information to the database. This approach, known as *Application User Proxy,* uses something called Client Identifiers. The *Client Identifier* is string value that is stored in the user's database session. Specifically, the Client Identifier is an attribute in the USERENV namespace that can be set by calling the SET_IDENTIFIER procedure in the publicly accessible DBMS_SESSION package.

The application user proxy capability was built to allow applications using connection pools to easily pass information about the real end user to the database. The Client Identifier can also be used when the user has authenticated to the database (either directly or via proxy authentication). Thus, you can use the Client Identifier for something other than just the user's identity.

The biggest value Client Identifiers bring as opposed to using the PL/SQL package or application contexts is that the value is audited. In Chapter 8, you'll see how to effectively audit user actions for accountability. When connecting users and applications to the database using an application-level connection pool (that is, not using proxy authentication), Client Identifiers allow the database auditing to preserve end user identity.

Using Client Identifiers

Setting and retrieving the Client Identifier is simple: you pass a string to the SET_IDENTIFIER procedure. The string can be anything, but it's usually some useful identifying piece of information about the user, such as their username.

The following example shows how to set and retrieve the Client Identifier. You can optionally replace the view previously defined using the Client Identifier to determine the record returned.

```
sec_mgr@KNOX10G> EXEC dbms_session.set_identifier('SCOTT');

PL/SQL procedure successfully completed.

sec_mgr@KNOX10G> COL username format a15
sec_mgr@KNOX10G> SELECT SYS_CONTEXT ('userenv',
  2                       'client_identifier') username
  3    FROM DUAL;

USERNAME
---------------
SCOTT

sec_mgr@KNOX10G> -- replace view
sec_mgr@KNOX10G> CREATE OR REPLACE VIEW person_view
  2  AS
  3    SELECT *
  4      FROM people_tab
  5     WHERE ename =
  6             SYS_CONTEXT ('userenv',
  7                          'client_identifier');

View created.

sec_mgr@KNOX10G> -- get all rows for the user
sec_mgr@KNOX10G> SELECT ename, job, sal
  2    FROM person_view;

ENAME      JOB              SAL
---------- --------- ----------
SCOTT      ANALYST         3000
```

As with the PL/SQL package implementation, the application is responsible for setting the Client Identifier before any database work as well as resetting the value between requests. To clear the identifier value, invoke the CLEAR_IDENTIFIER procedure in the DBMS_SESSION package:

```
sec_mgr@KNOX10G> -- reset value
sec_mgr@KNOX10G> EXEC dbms_session.clear_identifier;

PL/SQL procedure successfully completed.

sec_mgr@KNOX10G> SELECT * FROM person_view;

no rows selected
```

Securing the Client Identifier

One particular challenge of Client Identifiers is that they can be set by anyone to anything. Recall that setting the Client Identifier is done by invoking a procedure in the DBMS_SESSION PL/SQL package. The privilege to execute the DBMS_SESSION package has been granted directly to PUBLIC, making it accessible to anyone in the database! There are good reasons for this; however, you should never base security on the Client Identifier value alone. It's important to understand that Oracle's decision to grant PUBLIC execute on DBMS_SESSION doesn't create a security vulnerability. It's our specific implementation and reliance on Client Identifiers for security that is risky.

CAUTION
Don't use Client Identifiers for security purposes until you have first secured the ability to set the value.

One approach to solving this problem is to create a wrapper procedure for setting and resetting the Client Identifier. First, revoke the execute privileges on DBMS_SESSION to PUBLIC; this has to be done as the SYS user. Next, grant execute privileges on the DBMS_SESSION to SEC_MGR.

CAUTION
This is done for illustrative purposes; don't run this on your production system(s) until you have finished reading this section and have tested on a test database!

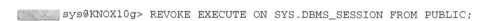

```
sys@KNOX10g> REVOKE EXECUTE ON SYS.DBMS_SESSION FROM PUBLIC;

Revoke succeeded.

sys@KNOX10G> GRANT EXECUTE ON DBMS_SESSION TO sec_mgr;

Grant succeeded.
```

Next, create your wrapper package to set and reset the Client Identifier values. As illustrated here, wrapping is an effective way to implement and ensure that the least-privilege principle is being used.

```
sec_mgr@KNOX10G> CREATE OR REPLACE PACKAGE client_info_mgr
  AS
    PROCEDURE set_info (p_info IN VARCHAR2);

    PROCEDURE clear_info;
  END;
  /

Package created.

sec_mgr@KNOX10G> CREATE OR REPLACE PACKAGE BODY client_info_mgr
  AS
    PROCEDURE set_info (p_info IN VARCHAR2)
    AS
    BEGIN
      -- Optionally perform any validation
      -- or verification prior to setting value
      SYS.DBMS_SESSION.set_identifier (p_info);
    END;

    PROCEDURE clear_info
    AS
    BEGIN
      SYS.DBMS_SESSION.clear_identifier;
    END;
  END;
  /

Package body created.

sec_mgr@KNOX10G> -- grant execute privileges to our connection
sec_mgr@KNOX10G> -- pool schema
sec_mgr@KNOX10G> GRANT EXECUTE ON client_info_mgr TO app_public;

Grant succeeded.
```

Revocation Risk

There is a caveat with this approach. While you may have strengthened the security, you have also introduced an issue with supportability. Three negative things may occur.

- The revocation of the execute privileges on DBMS_SESSION may break existing applications.
- Many applications may depend on other procedures in the DBMS_SESSION package, so you would have to either wrap every procedure needed, or re-create new, smaller packages that are subsets of DBMS_SESSION.

- Altering default grants and privileges is generally considered unsupported because it's considered "tampering" with the Oracle internal mechanisms. Thus, this action may invalidate your support for either Oracle or some other applications.

Note the number of objects that goes invalid immediately upon the privilege revocation:

```
sys@KNOX10G> SELECT COUNT (*)
  2    FROM all_objects
  3   WHERE status = 'INVALID';

  COUNT(*)
----------
         0

sys@KNOX10G> REVOKE EXECUTE ON SYS.DBMS_SESSION FROM PUBLIC;

Revoke succeeded.

sys@KNOX10G> SELECT COUNT (*)
  2    FROM all_objects
  3   WHERE status = 'INVALID';

  COUNT(*)
----------

        24
```

You can view the objects that went invalid and recompile the SYS-owned objects. For objects not owned by SYS, you may need to grant direct execute privileges on DBMS_SESSION to allow them to be recompiled.

NOTE
You should ensure that the direct grants to DBMS_SESSION are really needed. Perhaps some applications can use the CLIENT_INFO_MGR package instead.

I use the following code to dynamically build a script that I execute to recompile the objects. It's good to edit and validate the script prior to executing it.

```
SET pages 999
SET lines 80
SET heading off
SET feedback off
SET termout off
SPOOL recomp.sql
SELECT    'Alter package SYS.'
       || object_name
       || ' compile;'
  FROM all_objects
```

```
 WHERE status = 'INVALID'
   AND owner = 'SYS'
   AND object_type = 'PACKAGE'
UNION ALL
SELECT    'Alter package SYS.'
       || object_name
       || ' compile body;'
  FROM all_objects
 WHERE status = 'INVALID'
   AND owner = 'SYS'
   AND object_type = 'PACKAGE BODY'
UNION ALL

SELECT DISTINCT    'grant execute on dbms_session to '
                || owner
                || ';'
           FROM all_objects
          WHERE status = 'INVALID'
            AND owner != 'SYS'
UNION ALL
SELECT    'Alter package '
       || owner
       || '.'
       || object_name
       || ' compile body;'
  FROM all_objects
 WHERE status = 'INVALID'
   AND owner != 'SYS'
   AND object_type = 'PACKAGE BODY'
UNION ALL
SELECT    'Alter package SYS.'
       || object_name
       || ' compile body;'
  FROM all_objects
 WHERE status = 'INVALID'
   AND owner = 'SYS'
   AND object_type = 'PACKAGE BODY'
/
SPOOL off
SET heading on
SET feedback on
SET termout on
-- EDIT and VALIDATE script recomp.sql
edit recomp.sql
@recomp.sql

SELECT object_name, object_type, owner
  FROM all_objects
 WHERE status = 'INVALID';
```

Client Identifiers Reinforced

If you are reluctant to revoke privileges on DBMS_SESSION, then consider using the PL/SQL security package (for example, USER_INFO) or an application context in conjunction with the Client Identifier. When doing this, you're checking to ensure the user hasn't modified the publicly available Client Identifier. You set the user information in both the Client Identifier and the secure PL/SQL program or application context. The Client Identifier will be audited, and you can trust the program or application context. Validating the values can be done simply. To do this, update the view you created earlier:

```
sec_mgr@KNOX10G> -- set username in both places
sec_mgr@KNOX10G> EXEC user_info.set_name('SCOTT');

PL/SQL procedure successfully completed.

sec_mgr@KNOX10G> EXEC dbms_session.set_identifier('SCOTT');

PL/SQL procedure successfully completed.

sec_mgr@KNOX10G> COL client_id format a15
sec_mgr@KNOX10G> COL program_name format a15
sec_mgr@KNOX10G> -- show values are consistent
sec_mgr@KNOX10G> SELECT SYS_CONTEXT ('userenv',
  2                      'client_identifier')
  3                                          client_id,
  4          user_info.get_name program_name
  5     FROM DUAL;

CLIENT_ID       PROGRAM_NAME
--------------- ---------------
SCOTT           SCOTT

sec_mgr@KNOX10G> -- Ensure Client ID and User info
sec_mgr@KNOX10G> -- are consistent before returning rows
sec_mgr@KNOX10G> CREATE OR REPLACE VIEW person_view
  2  AS
  3     SELECT *
  4       FROM people_tab
  5      WHERE ename = user_info.get_name
  6        AND user_info.get_name =
  7               SYS_CONTEXT ('userenv',
  8                            'client_identifier');

View created.

sec_mgr@KNOX10G> -- test database security
sec_mgr@KNOX10G> SELECT ename, job, sal
  2     FROM person_view;

ENAME      JOB              SAL
---------- --------- ----------
SCOTT      ANALYST         3000
```

```
sec_mgr@KNOX10G> -- change client identifier
sec_mgr@KNOX10G> EXEC dbms_session.set_identifier('KING');

PL/SQL procedure successfully completed.

sec_mgr@KNOX10G> -- Note user cannot change user_info as
sec_mgr@KNOX10G> -- it should be protected
sec_mgr@KNOX10G> SELECT * FROM person_view;

no rows selected
```

The database security is working in concert with the application security. The application has to set the values in the database. The database verifies that the values have been set and are consistent *before* returning any data. This same technique can be used with triggers, VPD, and secure application roles.

Leveraging Database Security with Anonymous Connection Pools

You now have an understanding of all the components needed to use the database security with "anonymous" connections. You'll next see how to link a Java application into this database security.

Database Setup

There are a few steps to do within the database. First, grant access to the view to a password-protected database role and disable the role. This will provide the object-level access control for your view.

```
sec_mgr@KNOX10G> -- create synonym for View
sec_mgr@KNOX10G> CREATE SYNONYM app_public.person_view
  2             FOR sec_mgr.person_view;

Synonym created.

sec_mgr@KNOX10G> -- create a password protected role
sec_mgr@KNOX10G> CREATE ROLE person_view_app_role
  2    IDENTIFIED BY thisistherolepassword;

Role created.

sec_mgr@KNOX10G> -- grant privileges to select on view to role
sec_mgr@KNOX10G> GRANT SELECT ON person_view TO person_view_app_role;

Grant succeeded.

sec_mgr@KNOX10G> -- grant role to connection pool (application) schema
sec_mgr@KNOX10G> GRANT person_view_app_role TO app_public;
```

```
Grant succeeded.

sec_mgr@KNOX10G> -- disable role forcing application to set
sec_mgr@KNOX10G> ALTER USER app_public DEFAULT ROLE NONE;

User altered.
```

The most efficient way to set up the database security is to create a single procedure that performs all the steps—set the Client Identifier, set the username in the PL/SQL package, and enable the role. You are striving for efficiency, and one procedure call from the application will be faster than three.

```
sec_mgr@KNOX10G> CREATE OR REPLACE PROCEDURE enable_person_view (
    p_user      IN  VARCHAR2,
    p_password  IN  VARCHAR2)
  AUTHID CURRENT_USER
  AS
  BEGIN
    -- Set Client Identifier. Value can be audited.
    client_info_mgr.set_info (p_user);
    -- Set PL/SQL Package info for user.
    -- This value can be used for fine grained access control
    user_info.set_name (p_user);
    -- Enable role which allows access to View
    DBMS_SESSION.set_role
           (    'person_view_app_role identified by '
             || p_password);
  END;
  /

Procedure created.
```

Grant execute privileges on the preceding procedure and set up a synonym for the application schema. The synonym is used so the application code doesn't have to directly reference the SCHEMA.PROCEDURE when executing the call:

```
sec_mgr@KNOX10G> -- grant execute privileges to application schema
sec_mgr@KNOX10G> GRANT EXECUTE ON enable_person_view TO app_public;

Grant succeeded.

sec_mgr@KNOX10G> -- create synonym for application
sec_mgr@KNOX10G> CREATE SYNONYM app_public.enable_person_view
                FOR sec_mgr.enable_person_view;

Synonym created.
```

Finally, you need to create a complementary procedure that clears the database session state:

```
sec_mgr@KNOX10G> CREATE OR REPLACE PROCEDURE reset_state
  AUTHID CURRENT_USER
  AS
  BEGIN
    -- Clear the Client Identifier.
    DBMS_SESSION.clear_identifier;
    -- clear the PL/SQL package state
    DBMS_SESSION.reset_package;
    -- Disable roles
    DBMS_SESSION.set_role ('none');
  END;
  /

Procedure created.

sec_mgr@KNOX10G> -- create synonym for application
sec_mgr@KNOX10G> CREATE SYNONYM app_public.reset_state
               FOR sec_mgr.reset_state;

Synonym created.

sec_mgr@KNOX10G> -- grant execute privileges to application role
sec_mgr@KNOX10G> GRANT EXECUTE ON reset_state TO app_public;

Grant succeeded.
```

Java Application Setup

An efficient way to handle the calls to the database for initialization and deinitialization of the database sessions is to create a new Java object. The object's role is to setup and break down the database security for the reusable database sessions. You'll create two methods. The first method returns a connection from that which has already been initialized; that is, the connection will be retrieved from the pool and will have executed the PL/SQL procedure ENABLE_PERSON_VIEW. The method requires the user's name as a parameter.

The second method, the complementary method, clears the database session state and returns the connection to the pool.

```
package OSBD;
import java.sql.*;
import oracle.jdbc.pool.OracleDataSource;

public class ConnMgr
{
  OracleDataSource ods;
  public ConnMgr()
  { // create connection pool
      try {
      ods = new OracleDataSource();
      ods.setURL("jdbc:oracle:thin:@DKNOX:1521:KNOX10G");
      ods.setUser("app_public");
```

```
        ods.setPassword("tiarhpw2r");
        ods.setConnectionCachingEnabled(true); // be sure set to true
        java.util.Properties prop = new java.util.Properties();
        prop.setProperty("InitialLimit", "3");
        prop.setProperty("MinLimit", "10");
        prop.setProperty("MaxLimit", "100");
        ods.setConnectionCacheProperties (prop);
      } catch (Exception e)    { System.out.println(e.toString()); }
    }
    public Connection getConnection(String userInfo)
    { // return an initialized connection
     Connection conn = null;
        try {
        conn = ods.getConnection("app_public", "tiarhpw2r");
        // Initialize the database session.
        // Use bind variables for performance and
        // to guard against SQL Injection attacks
        CallableStatement cstmt =
          conn.prepareCall("{CALL enable_person_view(?,?)}");
        cstmt.setString(1,userInfo);
        cstmt.setString(2,"thisIsTheRolePassword");
        cstmt.executeUpdate();
        cstmt.close();
      } catch (Exception e)    { return conn; }
     return conn;
    }
    public void closeConnection(Connection conn)
    { // reset database session and close connection
      try {
        // Reset the database session
        CallableStatement cstmt = conn.prepareCall("{CALL reset_state}");
        cstmt.close();
        conn.close();
      } catch (Exception e)    { System.out.println(e.toString()); }
    }
}
```

Next, test the setup for security and performance. To do this, use timings to check how long it takes to get an initialized connection. The test code creates an instance of the ConnMgr that defines the connection pool to the APP_PUBLIC user. The getConnection method returns the initialized connection. The first invocation will create your connection pool. Time this as well as a subsequent connection to a different user:

```
package OSBD;
import java.sql.*;
import oracle.jdbc.pool.OracleDataSource;

public class FastConnect
{
```

```
  public static void main(String[] args)
  {
    long connectTime=0, connectionStart=0, connectionStop=0;
    long connectTime2=0, connectionStart2=0, connectionStop2=0;
    ConnMgr cm = new ConnMgr();
    // time first connection. This connection initializes pool.
    connectionStart = System.currentTimeMillis();
    Connection conn = cm.getConnection("SCOTT");
    connectionStop = System.currentTimeMillis();
    String query = "select ename, job, sal from person_view";
    try {
      // show security by querying from View
      Statement stmt = conn.createStatement();
      ResultSet rset = stmt.executeQuery(query);
      while (rset.next()) {
        System.out.println("Name:    " + rset.getString(1));
        System.out.println("Job:     " + rset.getString(2));
        System.out.println("Salary:  " + rset.getString(3));
    }
      stmt.close();
      rset.close();
      // close the connection which resets the database session
      cm.closeConnection(conn);
      // time subsequent connection as different user
      connectionStart2 = System.currentTimeMillis();
      conn = cm.getConnection("KING");
      connectionStop2 = System.currentTimeMillis();
      // ensure database can distinguish this new user
      stmt = conn.createStatement();
      rset = stmt.executeQuery(query);
      while (rset.next()) {
        System.out.println("Name:    " + rset.getString(1));
        System.out.println("Job:     " + rset.getString(2));
        System.out.println("Salary:  " + rset.getString(3));
      }
      stmt.close();
      rset.close();
      cm.closeConnection(conn);
    } catch (Exception e)    { System.out.println(e.toString()); }
    // print timing results
    connectTime = (connectionStop - connectionStart);
    System.out.println("Connection time for Pool: " + connectTime + " ms.");
    connectTime2 = (connectionStop2 - connectionStart2);
    System.out.println("Subsequent connection time: " +
                       connectTime2 + " ms.");
  }
}
```

The results of executing this program show that the anonymous connection pool can maintain both database security and high performance (as measured by the subsequent connections from the pool):

```
Name:    SCOTT

Job:     ANALYST

Salary: 3000

Name:    KING

Job:     PRESIDENT

Salary: 5000

Connection time for Pool: 1071 ms.

Subsequent connection time: 0 ms.
```

Identifying Information

This chapter focused on using the end user's name as the identifying piece of information. This is certainly the most common case, but you don't have to be restricted to only the user's name. The more information you can provide to the database, the more security the database may be able to apply. For example, you can pass the end user's IP address. Because the application is connected to the database, the database has no idea of where the user is connecting from. A security policy may use this information to restrict or allow access to database objects.

User authorizations that are known to the application and not to the database can also prove useful to the database. If the user isn't authenticated to the database, the database may not be able to distinguish between an application administrator and a simple application user.

The application itself can authenticate itself to the database by passing some authorization token, such as a password, to the database. This is useful in ensuring that the users are accessing the database via a specific application. You can concatenate all these items together and place them in either or both the Client Identifier and/or the secure PL/SQL package. The package will allow you to store multiple attributes of multiple data types.

Summary

Defense in depth for database application means the application shouldn't be the only security mechanism. To enable database security, you have to follow the simple principle of identity preservation.

In this chapter, you explored two ways of doing this. The integrated authentication approach uses a common user known to the applications, SSO, and database. The single source of truth for these entities is the LDAP server, which contains the user's authentication and authorization information. This allows an easy way to create and manage users. This design is also natural and intuitive; the users exist and their privileges can be easily validated.

From a security perspective, this design is ideal. The user is known everywhere and changes to the user's privilege set are immediately in effect for all applications and databases that are part of the system. If performance becomes an issue in this environment, you can use web session management to assist in database session caching, which will eliminate subsequent connection times. You looked at a sample application to illustrate how to do this.

The alternative approach uses connection pools bound to a single database schema. Many people are attracted to this design for performance reasons. With a little work, security can also become part of this solution. Using roles, PL/SQL packages, and Client Identifiers, you built a sample Java application that maintained both performance and security.

In Chapter 7, you'll look at privileges and database roles in more detail, which will help you to understand how to effectively implement and verify access controls for the database. The access controls determine who gets access to what and how. Ultimately, the data security relies on proper enforcement of access controls. As illustrated from several examples in this chapter, roles extend security further into the database.

PART III

Authorizations and Auditing

CHAPTER 7

Privileges and Roles

his chapter discusses database privileges and roles. Understanding privileges and how they can be granted is important to employing effective security. Roles allow administrators to grant users the necessary privileges needed to perform their job. Roles are a powerful and manageable way to provide a least-privileged environment, which is important to ensuring a sound and secure database.

The intent of this chapter is not to duplicate the Oracle product documentation, which discusses both privileges and roles. The objective here is to point out some of the important and subtle aspects that are associated with privileges and roles. This is a very important chapter because database access, and to a large extent database security, relies on user privileges.

Access Control, Authorizations, and Privileges

We'll begin by reviewing a few terms: access control, authorizations, and privileges. You will find these terms littered throughout security policies. These terms, while sometimes used interchangeably, are in fact different. A good understanding is helpful and often necessary in discussions about security policies and implementations.

Access Control

Access control is the process of allowing or preventing access to a resource. There are many ways to determine access or implement access control. A simple way to describe access control is to associate it with a commonly understood implementation called access control lists.

Access control lists (*ACLs*) are a common way for people to describe the security policy associated with a given application or database. The list is conceptual in most cases and describes who can access what and how they can do it. The ACLs are derived from the organization's security policies. It's important to understand that the list *is not* the enforcement mechanism. The enforcement mechanism is something inside the application or database engine that refers to the list to determine access.

Enforcing Access Control

Think of access control mechanisms as the sentry standing guard at an entry portal. The guard's job is simply to permit or restrict people from entering the portal. The decision to allow entry may be based on anything, such as a list of approved names, proof of an organizational affiliation, or possession of some kind of permission slip or token. The important thing is that the role of the guard is well defined and narrowly focused. The job is to grant or deny access based on something. As people wish to gain entry, the guard will either allow entry or disallow entry.

The access control mechanisms in the database "stand guard" over database objects, such as tables, views, and procedures. The database decides who gets access to what based on privileges. Privileges, however, can be obtained in multiple ways. Effective security design implies the importance of understanding how privileges can be given, obtained, and managed.

Authorizations

A person is considered *authorized* when they are allowed to perform an action as described by some governing policy. A boarding pass may authorize a person to get on an airplane. A special badge may authorize a person to enter a secure area. That is, the sentry standing guard should allow them access because they are approved and allowed to gain entry. This doesn't mean the guard has to let them pass, only that the guard *should* let them pass.

An authorization translates into one or more privileges, such as the privilege to be in a secure area or the privilege to access a database. The access control mechanisms of the application or database are actually implemented by checking a user's privileges. Authorizations are abstractions. They represent a binding between a security policy and the actual privileges a user has in a specific context.

Privileges

When a user performs any action in or on the database, the database will verify that the user has the rights to successfully execute the action. These rights or permissions are known as privileges.

The access control mechanisms in the database determine access based on user (schema) privileges. The privileges are the permissions or the actual rights needed to perform any and all specific database actions—queries, updates, table creations, establish database connections, and so on.

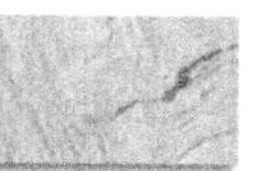

NOTE
Privileges are the permissions or the actual rights needed to perform an action.

Database privileges occur at three levels: system privileges, object privileges, and intra-object privileges. System and object privileges are relevant for an understanding of database roles. Intra-object privileges will be discussed in Part IV, "Fine-Grained Access Controls."

System Privileges

The database supports a number of very useful and convenient *system privileges.* I like to decompose system privileges into two categories. The first types are the privileges that are applicable for all objects across the entire database. That is, these privileges are not specific to any one object in the database, but rather to all objects of a specific type. I call these the "ANY" privileges, of which there are over 100.

Consider the EXECUTE ANY PROCEDURE system privilege. This allows the authorized user to successfully execute any procedure defined in any (non-SYS) schema in the database. It also allows them to view the source code for any (non-SYS) procedure in the database. Note that the ANY privileges don't apply to certain SYS objects that are protected when the O7_DICTIONARY_ACCESSIBILITY initialization parameter is set to FALSE; this fact also expresses why the parameter should be set to false.

The ANY privileges are very powerful, and they are applicable not only to existing database objects but also to any objects created in the future. Be cautious and cognizant of this. It's easy to assume that system privileges are appropriate when there is only one application running in the database. The security flaw occurs when a newly installed application is added or consolidated into the existing database and the administrator of the first application now has privileges on the new application, too.

The other class of system privileges either affects the state of the database or allows processes to occur in or on the database. For example, the ability to issue ALTER DATABASE, ALTER SYSTEM, and ALTER USER are examples of other system privileges. Even the ability to log in to the database, the CREATE SESSION privilege, is a system privilege.

System privileges are important because they are both powerful in what they can do and pervasive in the number of things they can do it to.

Viewing System Privileges

The SYSTEM_PRIVILEGE_MAP view lists many of the data system privileges and can be helpful when you forget the exact name of the privilege. For example, you know there is a privilege to manage application contexts but you can't remember what the privilege is, so you could issue the following query:

```
SELECT NAME
  FROM system_privilege_map
 WHERE NAME LIKE '%CONTEXT%';
```

This view lists the privileges but doesn't tell you who has the privileges or what the privileges allow the user to do. To determine what a privilege does requires research into the Oracle product documentation (start with the Database Security Guide). To determine who has a system privilege, you need to query DBA_SYS_PRIVS. For example, if you want to see who has the SELECT ANY TABLE privilege, you would issue the following query:

```
SELECT grantee
  FROM dba_sys_privs
 WHERE PRIVILEGE = 'SELECT ANY TABLE';
```

The results from this query will show both the users and the database roles that have the privilege. As you will read in the "Roles" section later in the chapter, *roles* act as containers of privileges that can ease the security administration duties. Granting a role to a user effectively grants the user all the privileges that were granted to that role. Unfortunately, there is no easy way to see all the privileges that a user has because the privileges can be granted both directly to the user and indirectly through roles.

There are several solutions to this. In the following example, a view is constructed that will show a user all their system privileges, regardless of whether the privileges were granted directly, granted to PUBLIC, or inherited from a role. The view is based on one created by Thomas Kyte for the "ask Tom" website. The view displays all roles for the current user. This view is a helper object to another view that will display all the users' system privileges. You'll also build one that displays all the users' object privileges.

You'll first need access to some very sensitive tables that reside in the SYS schema. You will have to grant the SELECT privilege with the GRANT OPTION because you'll create views based on these tables and you want the views to be accessible to others. The following privileges were granted in the setup of security manager schema in Appendix A:

```
GRANT SELECT ON sysauth$ TO sec_mgr WITH GRANT OPTION;
GRANT SELECT ON user$ TO sec_mgr WITH GRANT OPTION;
GRANT SELECT ON dba_tab_privs TO sec_mgr WITH GRANT OPTION;
GRANT SELECT ON dba_sys_privs TO sec_mgr WITH GRANT OPTION;
```

The first view displays all possible paths a user can receive a privilege. It lists all the roles, the user's name, and the user group PUBLIC because a grant to any of these will enable the privilege for the user:

```
sec_mgr@KNOX10g> CREATE OR REPLACE VIEW all_user_priv_path
  AS
    SELECT DISTINCT usr.NAME granted_role
               FROM (SELECT     *
                             FROM SYS.sysauth$
                       CONNECT BY PRIOR privilege# = grantee#
                START WITH grantee# = UID OR grantee# = 1) sauth,
                    SYS.user$ usr
              WHERE usr.user# = sauth.privilege#
    UNION ALL
    SELECT USER
      FROM DUAL
    UNION ALL
    SELECT 'PUBLIC'
      FROM DUAL
 /

View created.

sec_mgr@KNOX10g> GRANT SELECT ON all_user_priv_path TO PUBLIC;

Grant succeeded.

sec_mgr@KNOX10g> CREATE PUBLIC SYNONYM all_user_priv_path
    FOR all_user_priv_path;

Synonym created.
```

Note that you can set the values of USER and UID (in bold above) to a specific user to see the privilege path for that user. The USER_ID column of the ALL_USERS view will provide you with the UID for your user.

Logging in as SYSTEM, you can test this view. The first query shows what might typically be issued when checking a user's roles. Unfortunately, this only shows direct role grants. The subsequent query uses the view created above to show all roles that have been granted either directly or indirectly:

```
system@KNOX10g> -- Show all directly granted roles for user
system@KNOX10g> SELECT granted_role
    FROM dba_role_privs
   WHERE grantee = USER;

GRANTED_ROLE
------------------------------
DBA
MGMT_USER
AQ_ADMINISTRATOR_ROLE

system@KNOX10g> -- Show all directly granted roles,
system@KNOX10g> -- indirectly granted roles,
system@KNOX10g> -- USER and PUBLIC. This is the
```

```
system@KNOX10g> -- sum of all ways a user can receive a privilege
system@KNOX10g> SELECT * FROM all_user_priv_path;
GRANTED_ROLE
------------------------------
AQ_ADMINISTRATOR_ROLE
DBA
DELETE_CATALOG_ROLE
EXECUTE_CATALOG_ROLE
EXP_FULL_DATABASE
GATHER_SYSTEM_STATISTICS
HS_ADMIN_ROLE
IMP_FULL_DATABASE
JAVA_ADMIN
JAVA_DEPLOY
MGMT_USER
OLAP_DBA
SCHEDULER_ADMIN
SELECT_CATALOG_ROLE
WM_ADMIN_ROLE
XDBADMIN
SYSTEM
PUBLIC

18 rows selected.
```

By including the static strings for the USER (which resolves to SYSTEM in the preceding example) and PUBLIC, you are sure to include privileges granted directly to the user as well as privileges granted to PUBLIC. You can now create the view that displays all system privileges for a user:

```
sec_mgr@KNOX10g> CREATE OR REPLACE VIEW user_system_privs
  AS
    SELECT DISTINCT PRIVILEGE
               FROM dba_sys_privs
              WHERE grantee IN (SELECT *
                                  FROM all_user_priv_path)
  /

View created.

sec_mgr@KNOX10g> GRANT SELECT ON user_system_privs TO PUBLIC;

Grant succeeded.

sec_mgr@KNOX10g> CREATE PUBLIC SYNONYM user_system_privs
    FOR user_system_privs;

Synonym created.

sec_mgr@KNOX10g> -- Check system privileges for CTXSYS
sec_mgr@KNOX10g> conn ctxsys
```

```
Enter password:
Connected.
ctxsys@KNOX10g> select * FROM user_system_privs;

PRIVILEGE
----------------------------------------
ALTER SESSION
CREATE CLUSTER
CREATE DATABASE LINK
CREATE INDEXTYPE
CREATE OPERATOR
CREATE PROCEDURE
CREATE PUBLIC SYNONYM
CREATE SEQUENCE
CREATE SESSION
CREATE SYNONYM
CREATE TABLE
CREATE TRIGGER
CREATE TYPE
CREATE VIEW
DROP PUBLIC SYNONYM
UNLIMITED TABLESPACE

16 rows selected.
```

NOTE
All system privileges should be considered extremely powerful and should be guarded strongly and granted only when absolutely necessary.

Object Privileges

While system privileges are general, *object privileges,* as the name suggests, are relevant to a specific object. For example, a user requires the SELECT privilege on the SCOTT.EMP table to successfully issue queries against the table (assuming they don't have the SELECT ANY TABLE system privilege). As with system privileges, the object privileges can be granted several ways.

Viewing Object Privileges

You can create the analogous view for displaying a user's object privileges based on the ALL_USER_PRIV_PATH view:

```
sec_mgr@KNOX10g> CREATE OR REPLACE VIEW user_object_privs
  AS
    SELECT DISTINCT PRIVILEGE,
                    owner,
                    table_name object,
                    grantee
               FROM dba_tab_privs
              WHERE grantee IN (
                             SELECT *
```

```
 10                                FROM all_user_priv_path)
 11  /

View created.

sec_mgr@KNOX10g> GRANT SELECT ON user_object_privs TO PUBLIC;

Grant succeeded.

sec_mgr@KNOX10g> CREATE PUBLIC SYNONYM user_object_privs
  2    FOR user_object_privs;

Synonym created.

sec_mgr@KNOX10g> SELECT COUNT (*)
  2    FROM user_object_privs;

  COUNT(*)
----------
     20811
```

There are too many actual object privileges to list due mainly to the number of grants that have been made to the user group PUBLIC. The USER_OBJECT_PRIVS view is helpful in determining if the user has privileges on objects within a specific schema. The following query shows all the object privileges the SEC_MGR user has on SCOTT's objects:

```
sec_mgr@KNOX10g> -- Show all object privileges user has
sec_mgr@KNOX10g> -- for any of SCOTT's objects
sec_mgr@KNOX10g> SELECT privilege, object
  2    FROM user_object_privs
  3   WHERE owner = 'SCOTT';

PRIVILEGE            OBJECT
-------------------- ------------------------------
SELECT               DEPT
SELECT               EMP
```

Both of these views will be referenced below to illustrate other points regarding privileges and roles.

I find it useful to have a script that will allow an administrator to check the object privileges granted to other users. The following script, saved in the file "obj_privs.sql," allows you to check the object privileges granted to a user on objects contained in a specific schema. This differs from the view above because you don't have to be logged on as the user to check the privileges. This script also shows how the above views can be adapted to meet other "customized" security queries. The important part is that this shows not only what privileges are available but also how the privileges were received. This will help you in ensuring the least privilege principle is being followed.

```
/*** File obj_privs.sql ***/
SET verify off
COL privilege format a20
COL "Object Name" format a20
COL "Privilege Granted To" format a20

PROMPT Checking object privileges:
PROMPT The following lists the privileges a user has on an owner's objects
ACCEPT USERNAME prompt  '> Enter user''s name          : '
ACCEPT OWNERNAME prompt '> Enter object owner''s name : '
SELECT PRIVILEGE,
       table_name "Object Name",
       grantee "Privilege Granted To"
  FROM (SELECT DISTINCT PRIVILEGE,
                        owner,
                        table_name,
                        grantee
                   FROM dba_tab_privs
                  WHERE grantee IN (
        SELECT DISTINCT usr.NAME
                          granted_role
                   FROM (SELECT     *
                               FROM SYS.sysauth$
                         CONNECT BY PRIOR privilege# =
                                      grantee#
                         START WITH grantee# =
                                      (SELECT user#
                                         FROM SYS.user$
                                        WHERE NAME =
                                               UPPER
                                                 ('&username'))
                                 OR grantee# =
                                      1) sauth,
                        SYS.user$ usr
                  WHERE usr.user# =
                          sauth.privilege#
        UNION ALL
        SELECT UPPER
                    ('&username')
          FROM DUAL
        UNION ALL
        SELECT 'PUBLIC'
          FROM DUAL))
 WHERE owner = UPPER ('&ownername') order by 2;
```

Running the script on my database, I can check the object privileges SCOTT has on the SEC_MGR schema:

```
sec_mgr@KNOX10g> @obj_privs
Checking object privileges:
```

```
The following lists the privileges a user has on an owner's objects
> Enter user's name          : scott
> Enter object owner's name : sec_mgr

PRIVILEGE            Object Name          Privilege Granted To
-------------------- -------------------- --------------------
SELECT               ALL_USER_PRIV_PATH   PUBLIC
EXECUTE              DEBUG_POLICY         SCOTT
SELECT               ENV                  PUBLIC
EXECUTE              GET_TIMESTAMP        PUBLIC
SELECT               GET_TRACE_FILENAME   PUBLIC
EXECUTE              PEOPLE_CTX_MGR       SCOTT
SELECT               USER_OBJECT_PRIVS    PUBLIC
SELECT               USER_SYSTEM_PRIVS    PUBLIC

8 rows selected.
```

Synonyms

The database allows you to create synonyms for your objects. *Synonyms* allow you to provide convenient and user-friendly names for objects. It's a good method for obscuring the owner and real name of the object. For example, a table called SHARED can be created and a publicly available synonym can be defined to reference the table.

```
sec_mgr@KNOX10g> -- Create a table
sec_mgr@KNOX10g> CREATE TABLE SHARED (x NUMBER);

Table created.

sec_mgr@KNOX10g> -- Create a public synonym on table.
sec_mgr@KNOX10g> -- Change table name.
sec_mgr@KNOX10g> CREATE PUBLIC SYNONYM the_table FOR SHARED;

Synonym created.
```

Authorized and privileged users will be able to access the SHARED table by direct reference to SEC_MGR.SHARED or by synonym reference with the simple name "THE_TABLE." From a security perspective, *the public synonym does not mask the identity of the underlying object*—the synonym is merely an alias for the real object. Notice that SCOTT will know the synonym is referencing the SEC_MGR.SHARED object even though he doesn't have access to the table:

```
scott@KNOX10g> -- Describe synonym THE_TABLE
scott@KNOX10g> DESC the_table
ERROR
ORA-04043: object "SEC_MGR"."SHARED" does not exist
```

Privileges and Synonyms

It's important to understand how privileges are used with synonyms. Privileges granted to synonyms are actually privilege grants to the base objects. It would be logical to assume that grants given by way of a synonym would be revoked when the synonym was dropped. That is not what happens. Dropping the synonym does not remove the privileges that were granted by way of that synonym.

An example proving this also illustrates an important point: mixing object and privilege grants may add confusion to the security management and administration process. First, create a table and populate it with some data. You'll create a public synonym and then grant SELECT privileges on the synonym:

```
sec_mgr@KNOX10g> CREATE  TABLE t AS SELECT * FROM DUAL;

Table created.

sec_mgr@KNOX10g> CREATE PUBLIC SYNONYM t_synonym FOR sec_mgr.t;

Synonym created.

sec_mgr@KNOX10g> -- privilege to access T given to synonym
sec_mgr@KNOX10g> GRANT  SELECT ON t_synonym TO scott;

Grant succeeded.
```

Connect as SCOTT. Note that SCOTT can reference the base table directly.

```
scott@KNOX10g> SELECT * FROM sec_mgr.t;

D
-
X
```

Next, drop the synonym.

```
sec_mgr@KNOX10g> DROP PUBLIC SYNONYM t_synonym;

Synonym dropped.
```

This didn't revoke the privileges on the object. SCOTT can still access the table.

```
scott@KNOX10g> SELECT * FROM SEC_MGR.t;

D
-
X
```

The point to this exercise is that haphazard or random assignment of privileges, via synonyms in some cases and direct objects in others, can lead to confusion.

System and Object Privileges Together

One challenging area associated with access control is determining what privileges a user has and how they received them. Often the privilege can be derived multiple ways. This is convenient but it may also be a security risk, because oversight of this fact could allow an administrator to make a mistake, leaving access to something in the database. For example, the privilege to query the table T just created could occur by direct grant or by possessing the SELECT ANY TABLE system privilege.

The following example shows this. SCOTT gets the system privilege to query any table:

```
system@KNOX10g> GRANT SELECT ANY TABLE TO scott;

Grant succeeded.
```

As the table owner, you decide that you no longer want SCOTT to access your table. You could have also revoked the privilege from a role to which SCOTT belonged. Unfortunately, you may be unaware that SCOTT has been granted the system privilege.

```
sec_mgr@KNOX10g> REVOKE SELECT ON t FROM scott;

Revoke succeeded.

sec_mgr@KNOX10g> -- Ensure no one has table privs
sec_mgr@KNOX10g> SELECT grantee
  2     FROM dba_tab_privs
  3    WHERE owner = 'SEC_MGR' AND table_name = 'T';

no rows selected
```

Revoking one privilege doesn't affect the other. The system privilege is still available to SCOTT. You also should have checked the SELECT ANY TABLE privilege. Consequently, revoking only the object privilege doesn't prevent SCOTT from querying the table.

```
scott@KNOX10g> SELECT * FROM SEC_MGR.t;

D
-
X
```

The solution to this problem is knowledge. Understanding the database privileges and how they can be issued and received is absolutely necessary for ensuring a secure database. Also, there are two system privileges that are extremely powerful: GRANT ANY PRIVILEGE and GRANT ANY OBJECT PRIVILEGE allow the recipient to grant any system privilege and any object privilege to any schema. This is great if the grantor is a security administrator but very bad if the grantor is a hacker.

Privilege Persistence

Another important concept to understanding privileges is in how they persist. If you grant a privilege to a user with administrative rights, then that user can grant the privilege to other users. If the user that had the administrative rights is dropped, all object privileges they granted to other users are also dropped. However, none of the system privileges are dropped.

The following example illustrates this subtle but important point. You'll create three users. The first is the data schema that will hold your objects:

```
system@KNOX10g> -- Create a data schema
system@KNOX10g> CREATE USER data_owner
  2    IDENTIFIED BY VALUES 'no pwd'
  3    DEFAULT TABLESPACE users
  4    TEMPORARY TABLESPACE temp;

User created.

system@KNOX10g> -- Grant quota privileges to data schema
system@KNOX10g> ALTER USER data_owner
  2  QUOTA 10 m ON "USERS";

User altered.

system@KNOX10g> -- Create a table in the data schema.
system@KNOX10g> -- To create a table in another schema, you
system@KNOX10g> -- need the CREATE ANY TABLE system priv.
system@KNOX10g> CREATE TABLE data_owner.t AS SELECT * FROM DUAL;

Table created.

system@KNOX10g> -- Create a procedure in the data schema
system@KNOX10g> -- To create a procedure in another schema, you
system@KNOX10g> -- need the CREATE ANY PROCEDURE system priv.
system@KNOX10g> CREATE PROCEDURE data_owner.foo
  2  AS
  3  BEGIN
  4    NULL;
  5  END;
  6  /

Procedure created.
```

Next create a "security officer" schema. This schema will control privileges on the DATA_OWNER schema's objects. The security officer will subsequently require object privileges on DATA_OWNER's objects and a few system privileges.

```
system@KNOX10g> -- create a junior security officer
system@KNOX10g> CREATE USER sec_mgr_jr IDENTIFIED BY sec_mgr_jr;

User created.

system@KNOX10g> GRANT CREATE ROLE TO sec_mgr_jr;

Grant succeeded.

system@KNOX10g> -- delegate privs to the junior security officer
system@KNOX10g> -- object privs
system@KNOX10g> GRANT ALL ON data_owner.t TO sec_mgr_jr
  2    WITH GRANT OPTION;
```

```
Grant succeeded.

system@KNOX10g> GRANT EXECUTE ON data_owner.foo TO sec_mgr_jr
  2    WITH GRANT OPTION;

Grant succeeded.

system@KNOX10g> -- system privs
system@KNOX10g> GRANT ALTER SESSION TO sec_mgr_jr WITH ADMIN OPTION;

Grant succeeded.

system@KNOX10g> GRANT CREATE SESSION TO sec_mgr_jr WITH ADMIN OPTION;

Grant succeeded.

system@KNOX10g> GRANT CREATE SYNONYM TO sec_mgr_jr WITH ADMIN OPTION;

Grant succeeded.

system@KNOX10g> GRANT CREATE SEQUENCE TO sec_mgr_jr WITH ADMIN OPTION;

Grant succeeded.
```

Next, create a database user, SOME_USER, that represents the user who will be accessing the DATA_OWNER objects. Then log in as the security officer. The security officer will create a role and assign some object and system privileges to the role. The officer will grant the role to the user. Additional object and system privileges are granted directly to the user.

```
system@KNOX10g> -- create a user for this example
system@KNOX10g> CREATE USER some_user IDENTIFIED BY some_user;

User created.

system@KNOX10g> -- junior security officer grants privs to some_user
system@KNOX10g> CONNECT sec_mgr_jr/sec_mgr_jr
Connected.
sec_mgr_jr@KNOX10g> CREATE ROLE data_owner_access;

Role created.

sec_mgr_jr@KNOX10g> -- grant direct object privs
sec_mgr_jr@KNOX10g> GRANT SELECT ON data_owner.t TO some_user;

Grant succeeded.

sec_mgr_jr@KNOX10g> GRANT EXECUTE ON data_owner.foo TO some_user;

Grant succeeded.

sec_mgr_jr@KNOX10g> -- grant role object privs
```

```
sec_mgr_jr@KNOX10g> GRANT INSERT ON data_owner.t TO data_owner_access;

Grant succeeded.

sec_mgr_jr@KNOX10g> GRANT data_owner_access TO some_user;

Grant succeeded.

sec_mgr_jr@KNOX10g> -- grant direct system privs
sec_mgr_jr@KNOX10g> GRANT ALTER SESSION TO some_user;

Grant succeeded.

sec_mgr_jr@KNOX10g> GRANT CREATE SESSION TO some_user;

Grant succeeded.

sec_mgr_jr@KNOX10g> -- grant role system privs
sec_mgr_jr@KNOX10g> GRANT CREATE SYNONYM TO data_owner_access;

Grant succeeded.

sec_mgr_jr@KNOX10g> GRANT CREATE SEQUENCE TO data_owner_access;

Grant succeeded.
```

By connecting as the user, you can verify the user has the role, the object, and the system privileges.

```
sec_mgr_jr@KNOX10g> -- show some user can connect and query table
sec_mgr_jr@KNOX10g> CONNECT some_user/some_user
Connected.
some_user@KNOX10g> SELECT *
  2    FROM session_roles;

ROLE
------------------------------
DATA_OWNER_ACCESS

some_user@KNOX10g> COL PRIVILEGE FORMAT A15
some_user@KNOX10g> COL OWNER FORMAT A15
some_user@KNOX10g> COL TABLE_NAME FORMAT A15
some_user@KNOX10g> SELECT *
  2    FROM user_object_privs
  3   WHERE owner = 'DATA_OWNER';

PRIVILEGE       OWNER           TABLE_NAME
--------------- --------------- ---------------
EXECUTE         DATA_OWNER      FOO
INSERT          DATA_OWNER      T
SELECT          DATA_OWNER      T
```

```
some_user@KNOX10g> SELECT *
  2    FROM user_system_privs;

PRIVILEGE
---------------
ALTER SESSION
CREATE SEQUENCE
CREATE SESSION
CREATE SYNONYM

some_user@KNOX10g> DESC data_owner.t
 Name                                      Null?    Type
 ----------------------------------------- -------- ------------
 DUMMY                                              VARCHAR2(1)
```

This is where it may get confusing. Now drop the security manager.

```
system@KNOX10g> -- drop junior security officer
system@KNOX10g> -- this drops the object privilege
system@KNOX10g> -- but does not drop the system privilege
system@KNOX10g> DROP USER sec_mgr_jr CASCADE;

User dropped.
```

NOTE
You didn't drop the data objects—they still exist. When you reconnect as the database user, you'll notice that all access to the data objects (the object privileges) is gone, yet all of the system privileges remain. The role still exists as well, but object privileges given to the role have also been dropped.

```
some_user@KNOX10g> SELECT *
  2    FROM session_roles;

ROLE
------------------------------
DATA_OWNER_ACCESS

some_user@KNOX10g> DESC data_owner.t
ERROR:
ORA-04043: object data_owner.t does not exist


some_user@KNOX10g> SELECT *
  2    FROM user_object_privs
  3   WHERE owner = 'DATA_OWNER';

no rows selected
```

```
some_user@KNOX10g> SELECT *
  2    FROM user_system_privs;

PRIVILEGE
---------------
ALTER SESSION
CREATE SEQUENCE
CREATE SESSION
CREATE SYNONYM
```

Effective security management requires us to understand these Oracle privilege principles.

Roles

Database roles are a way of indirectly assigning privileges to users, which helps in the overall management aspects of security. In the database, there are many privileges that allow the users to do many things. The privileges can be granted directly to the users or granted to database roles that, in turn, are granted to the database users. By doing the latter, you can simplify security administration. Figure 7-1 shows how privilege maintenance can be simplified.

If you want to add or remove a privilege from a group of users, you can issue a single statement adding or removing the privilege from the role. This adds or removes the privilege from every user that has been granted that role. If you directly grant privileges to users and you have 100 users, you would have to issue 100 separate statements to add or remove a privilege for those users.

Role Hierarchies

Utilizing roles, the task of granting or revoking privileges to multiple users can be accomplished with a single statement. I am all for efficiency; however, a tricky part to managing privileges via roles is that roles can be granted to other roles. This nesting adds wonderful flexibility in capturing real-world security policies. Unfortunately, the flexibility can also lead to complexity and confusion when trying to unravel what privileges are granted to what or whom.

The previous scripts will help you in determining specific privileges a user has regardless of how the privileges were obtained. You should nonetheless consider the management aspect when creating the role structure in your database; limiting the number of nested roles will help simplify the complexity of your privilege structures and make overall security management easier.

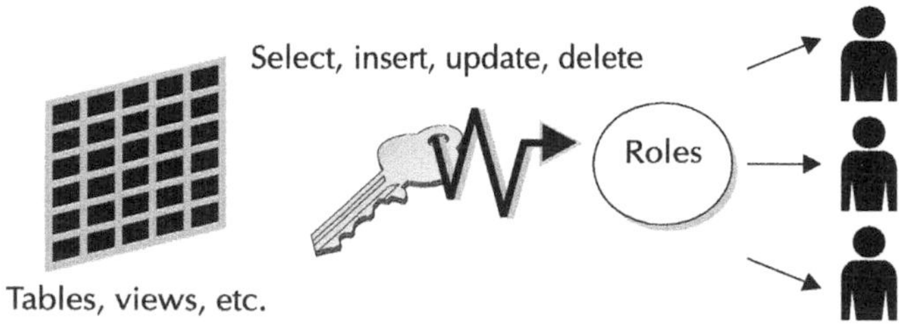

FIGURE 7-1. *Database roles simplify privilege maintenance tasks.*

To help in this endeavor, the following package will display all roles for a user as well as how the user received that role. This role hierarchy depiction is helpful when combined with the *obj_privs.sql* script, previously shown, in determining how a privilege granted to a role finally ended in a user's set of available privileges (or privilege domain). First, to illustrate the complexity associated with nested role grants, several roles are created and granted to other roles with one role finally being directly granted to the user SCOTT:

```
sec_mgr@KNOX10g> CREATE ROLE a;

Role created.

sec_mgr@KNOX10g> CREATE ROLE b;

Role created.

sec_mgr@KNOX10g> CREATE ROLE c;

Role created.

sec_mgr@KNOX10g> CREATE ROLE d;

Role created.

sec_mgr@KNOX10g> CREATE ROLE e;

Role created.

sec_mgr@KNOX10g> GRANT a TO b;

Grant succeeded.

sec_mgr@KNOX10g> GRANT b TO c;

Grant succeeded.

sec_mgr@KNOX10g> GRANT c TO d;

Grant succeeded.

sec_mgr@KNOX10g> GRANT e TO c;

Grant succeeded.

sec_mgr@KNOX10g> -- Granting D to SCOTT will give SCOTT all roles
sec_mgr@KNOX10g> GRANT d TO scott;

Grant succeeded.
```

The following package uses recursion to display the roles granted for a user in the hierarchy they were granted:

```
sec_mgr@KNOX10g> CREATE OR REPLACE PACKAGE show_role_hierarchy
AS
  PROCEDURE display (p_username IN VARCHAR2);
END;
/

Package created.

sec_mgr@KNOX10g> CREATE OR REPLACE PACKAGE BODY show_role_hierarchy
AS
--------------------------------------------------------
  FUNCTION convert_level (p_level IN NUMBER)
    RETURN VARCHAR2
  AS
    l_str  VARCHAR2 (32767);
  BEGIN
    FOR i IN 1 .. p_level
    LOOP
      l_str := l_str || '..';
    END LOOP;

    RETURN l_str;
  END;
--------------------------------------------------------
  PROCEDURE recursive_role_getter (
    p_role    IN  VARCHAR2,
    p_level   IN  NUMBER)
  AS
  BEGIN
    FOR irec IN (SELECT   granted_role
                     FROM dba_role_privs
                    WHERE grantee = UPPER (p_role)
                 ORDER BY 1)
    LOOP
      DBMS_OUTPUT.put_line (   'Indirect Role: '
                            || convert_level (p_level)
                            || irec.granted_role
                            || ' via '
                            || p_role);
      recursive_role_getter (irec.granted_role,
                             p_level + 1);  -- recurse
    END LOOP;
  EXCEPTION
    WHEN OTHERS
    THEN
      NULL;
  END;
--------------------------------------------------------
  PROCEDURE display (p_username IN VARCHAR2)
  AS
```

```
  BEGIN
    FOR rec IN (SELECT   granted_role
                    FROM dba_role_privs
                   WHERE grantee = UPPER (p_username)
                ORDER BY 1)
    LOOP
      DBMS_OUTPUT.put_line (    'Direct Role:   '
                             || rec.granted_role);
      recursive_role_getter (rec.granted_role, 1);
    END LOOP;
  END;
--------------------------------------------------------
END;
/

Package body created.
```

Tracing the Privilege

By combining the previous procedure with the USER_OBJECT_PRIVS view, you can identify precisely how a user received a privilege. To illustrate this, a table is created and select privileges are granted on the table to role A.

```
sec_mgr@KNOX10g> -- Create a table and grant privileges to role A
sec_mgr@KNOX10g> CREATE TABLE obj_of_interest AS SELECT * FROM DUAL;

Table created.

sec_mgr@KNOX10g> GRANT SELECT ON obj_of_interest TO a;

Grant succeeded.
```

You can use the obj_privs.sql script or log on as SCOTT and query the USER_OBJ_PRIVS view to determine what privileges SCOTT has on the table as well as how he received the privilege:

```
sec_mgr@KNOX10g> -- See if SCOTT has access to table OBJ_OF_INTEREST.
sec_mgr@KNOX10g> -- This query can be run as SCOTT or you can
sec_mgr@KNOX10g> -- execute the obj_privs.sql script
sec_mgr@KNOX10g> conn scott/tiger
Connected.
scott@KNOX10g> COL privilege format a20
scott@KNOX10g> COL object format a20
scott@KNOX10g> COL grantee format a20
scott@KNOX10g> SELECT privilege, object, grantee
  2    FROM user_object_privs
  3   WHERE owner = 'SEC_MGR' AND OBJECT = 'OBJ_OF_INTEREST';

PRIVILEGE            OBJECT               GRANTEE
-------------------- -------------------- --------------------
SELECT               OBJ_OF_INTEREST      A
```

You now see how the role hierarchy can be useful. The privilege was granted to A. How did the user get role A? A direct query on the DBA_ROLE_PRIVS view and using the Oracle Enterprise Manager will only tell you that SCOTT has role D. You know the user must have role A, but it's not obvious how he got it. Running the role hierarchy display program, you can see the role relationships:

```
scott@KNOX10g> conn sec_mgr/oracle10g
Connected.
sec_mgr@KNOX10g> EXEC show_role_hierarchy.display('scott')
Direct Role:    CONNECT
Direct Role:    D
Indirect Role: ..C via D
Indirect Role: ....B via C
Indirect Role: ......A via B
Indirect Role: ....E via C
Direct Role:    RESOURCE

PL/SQL procedure successfully completed.
```

The USER_OBJ_PRIVS view told you SCOTT received the SELECT privilege from role A. This output shows you that A was granted to B, B was granted to C, C granted to D, and finally D was directly granted to SCOTT.

Designing for Definer and Invoker Rights

There exists an often overlooked dependency on roles and PL/SQL named programs. Oracle allows two modes of operation for executing named PL/SQL: definer rights and invoker rights.

Definer rights is the default mode for PL/SQL programs and is the mode that has been in place for years. As such, many people are familiar with how to design and implement effective and secure PL/SQL applications using the definer rights mode. There is a relationship to roles with definer rights in that roles are disabled.

NOTE
All database roles are disabled while compiling, and more importantly, while executing named PL/SQL programs created with definer rights.

Not only are roles disabled, but you also can't make a SET ROLE call to enable them from inside a definer rights program. This isn't a severe limitation, but knowledge of this is important in designing applications and determining how users and roles will be used by your applications. It's also helpful in preventing misfiled bugs or technical assistance requests.

The following example shows how one might accidentally fall into this role-based predicament. In the previous section, you established that SCOTT has the SELECT privilege on SEC_MGR.OBJ_OF_INTEREST table by way of a role grant. SCOTT can query the table directly and therefore he can write an anonymous block of PL/SQL that queries the table without problems. But notice when he takes the PL/SQL block that just successfully executed and places it in a procedure, the table access is prohibited:

```
scott@KNOX10g> -- User can query table.
scott@KNOX10g> SELECT *
      FROM sec_mgr.obj_of_interest;

D
-
X

scott@KNOX10g> -- User can query table within
scott@KNOX10g> -- an anonymous PL/SQL block.
scott@KNOX10g> DECLARE
      l_dummy  VARCHAR2 (1);
    BEGIN
      SELECT dummy
        INTO l_dummy
        FROM sec_mgr.obj_of_interest;
      DBMS_OUTPUT.put_line ('Value: ' || l_dummy);
    END;
    /
Value: X

PL/SQL procedure successfully completed.

scott@KNOX10g> -- User cannot create a procedure.
scott@KNOX10g> CREATE OR REPLACE PROCEDURE show_obj
    AS
      l_dummy  VARCHAR2 (1);
    BEGIN
      SELECT dummy
        INTO l_dummy
        FROM sec_mgr.obj_of_interest;
      DBMS_OUTPUT.put_line ('Value: ' || l_dummy);
    END;
    /

Warning: Procedure created with compilation errors.

scott@KNOX10g> show error
Errors for PROCEDURE SHOW_OBJ:

LINE/COL ERROR
-------- -------------------------------------------------
4/14     PL/SQL: SQL Statement ignored
5/30     PL/SQL: ORA-00942: table or view does not exist
```

SCOTT has the select privilege by default. However, the role that contains the privilege is disabled during the program's compilation. The role is also disabled during program execution so using dynamic SQL to get the program to compile will not solve the problem either. Note the script ran as an anonymous PL/SQL block; anonymous blocks and straight SQL queries allow roles to remain enabled.

Invoker rights is the alternate model for program execution in the Oracle database. To use the SELECT privilege granted to the role requires SCOTT to compile the program with invoker rights. The syntax in the previous procedure also will have to be modified because the database roles are *only enabled for invoker rights during execution,* not during compilation. Therefore, dynamic SQL will have to be used to get the procedure to compile. The following code does this. The procedure is converted from the default definer rights to an invoker rights by adding the AUTHID CURRENT_USER directive as seen in line 2:

```
scott@KNOX10g> -- Use dynamic SQL and invoker rights
scott@KNOX10g> CREATE OR REPLACE PROCEDURE show_obj
  2  AUTHID CURRENT_USER
  3  AS
  4     l_dummy   VARCHAR2 (1);
  5  BEGIN
  6     EXECUTE IMMEDIATE     'SELECT dummy '
  7                        || 'FROM sec_mgr.obj_of_interest'
  8                   INTO l_dummy;
  9     DBMS_OUTPUT.put_line ('Value: ' || l_dummy);
 10  END;
 11  /

Procedure created.

scott@KNOX10g> EXEC show_obj
Value: X
```

Often the most practical solution for the roles and named PL/SQL dilemma is to simply remove the role dependency and make the direct privilege grants to the user creating the procedure. Granting select privilege on OBJ_OF_INTEREST directly to SCOTT would allow the original definer rights program to compile and execute.

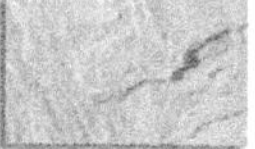

NOTE

The point to this is that all privileges needed to compile and execute the PL/SQL have to be directly granted to the user or granted to PUBLIC (although I would discourage grants to PUBLIC). Privileges received via roles aren't available. Understanding this relationship is critical to ensuring the successful and effective implementation of your PL/SQL programs.

Selective Privilege Enablement

One of the greatest advantages to using roles is that roles provide the ability to selectively enable and disable privileges for the user. Unlike directly granted system and object privileges, which are enabled (and thus "on") all the time, roles can be granted to a user but not enabled. The privileges for the user are not "on" until the role is enabled.

I've seen people try to mimic selective privileges by having their application, at execution time, dynamically grant and revoke object privileges. For example, they might create a procedure that the application will call to enable the privileges. Likewise, there will be a procedure to undo the user's privileges.

In the following example, privileges to control access to DATA_OWNER's objects have been granted to the SEC_MGR schema.

```
system@KNOX10g> -- delegate privs to the security administrator
system@KNOX10g> GRANT ALL ON data_owner.t TO sec_mgr
    WITH GRANT OPTION;

Grant succeeded.

system@KNOX10g> GRANT EXECUTE ON data_owner.foo TO sec_mgr
    WITH GRANT OPTION;

Grant succeeded.
```

If you were to implement dynamic privilege enablement, you might create a program similar to the following:

```
sec_mgr@KNOX10g> CREATE OR REPLACE PROCEDURE set_privs
  AS
  BEGIN
    EXECUTE IMMEDIATE    'grant select on DATA_OWNER.T to '
                      || USER;
  END;
  /

Procedure created.

sec_mgr@KNOX10g> CREATE OR REPLACE PROCEDURE unset_privs
  AS
  BEGIN
    EXECUTE IMMEDIATE    'revoke select on DATA_OWNER.T from '
                      || USER;
  END;
  /

Procedure created.

sec_mgr@KNOX10g> GRANT EXECUTE ON set_privs TO scott;

Grant succeeded.

sec_mgr@KNOX10g> GRANT EXECUTE ON unset_privs TO scott;

Grant succeeded.
```

For the user to selectively enable their privileges, the application simply calls the SET_PRIVS procedure while logged in as the appropriate user.

```
scott@KNOX10g> select * from data_owner.t;
select * from data_owner.t
                         *
ERROR at line 1:
ORA-00942: table or view does not exist


scott@KNOX10g> exec sec_mgr.set_privs;

PL/SQL procedure successfully completed.

scott@KNOX10g> select * from data_owner.t;

D
-
X
```

This is a *bad* design. The major flaw exists because the privileges aren't restricted to the user for just that application. A user may log in to the database and gain access to the object without having to do anything. This is because they query after the SET_PRIVS has been executed and before the UNSET_PRIVS. *Do not use this design.*

An alternate design for supporting selective privileges is based on assigning the roles to a user but not enabling the role by default. For example, to prevent a user from accessing a particular application's data, you might force the users to possess the APP_USER role. An application user is granted the role, *but the role is not enabled by default.* When the user accesses the database via the application, the application knows it has to enable the role and does so transparently for the user:

```
sec_mgr@KNOX10g> CREATE ROLE app_user_role;

Role created.

sec_mgr@KNOX10g> -- Grant privileges to role
sec_mgr@KNOX10g> GRANT ALL ON data_owner.t TO app_user_role;

Grant succeeded.

sec_mgr@KNOX10g> -- Grant role to user(s)
sec_mgr@KNOX10g> GRANT app_user_role TO scott;

Grant succeeded.

sec_mgr@KNOX10g> -- Disable this role by default.
sec_mgr@KNOX10g> -- Privileges are not available
sec_mgr@KNOX10g> -- until role is enabled
sec_mgr@KNOX10g> ALTER USER scott DEFAULT ROLE ALL
```

```
  2    EXCEPT app_user_role;

User altered.
```

If the user logs in via SQL*Plus and tries to query the application's tables, they will fail because the privileges to do so aren't available until the role is enabled:

```
scott@KNOX10g> SELECT * FROM data_owner.t;
SELECT * FROM data_owner.t
                         *
ERROR at line 1:
ORA-00942: table or view does not exist


scott@KNOX10g> SET ROLE app_user_role;

Role set.

scott@KNOX10g> SELECT * FROM data_owner.t;

D
-
X
```

As you may conclude, this solution doesn't appear to be much better than the procedural-based method. The only difference is the set role implementation only enables the privileges for the database session, whereas the SET_PRIVS procedure will enable the privileges for all database sessions.

In the preceding examples, knowing or not knowing the existence of a procedure or role that has to be executed or enabled provides no security. Basing security on the simple knowledge of things that can be easily guessed or derived is called "security through obscurity," and it's not considered a best practice when used alone.

CAUTION
Forcing applications and users to explicitly enable roles or privileges does not provide adequate security, and believing it does only fosters a false sense of security.

Selective Privilege Use Cases

The real power of selective privileges implemented via roles is exploited when using roles that require something other than just knowing the role's name. You will look at two ways to secure roles soon. Before you do that, you'll look at several important use cases that frame the complexities and requirements for selective privileges through roles.

Privileges Only When Accessed via an Application

One frequent requirement is to only allow user database access when the access is via an application. This is very popular with web applications. You might wonder why this is so hard. The answer: standards and interoperability.

Normally, standards and interoperability are good things. In the security world, standards and interoperability for establishing database connections can be a challenge, because they may facilitate unwanted access into the database. The Oracle database supports numerous applications and protocols—ODBC, JDBC, Oracle Net clients, Web Services, HTTP, FTP, and so on. These protocols and capabilities are important to ensuring interoperability with commercial applications as well as facilitating emerging ways to access data.

From a security standpoint, each one represents an additional window into the database that needs to be secured. The best mechanism for securing them is to shut them off. That may not be a practical choice if other applications need access to the protocols.

What you typically see are users accessing the database via a known application and protocol. The security requirement then is to ensure that this is the only way the users can get to the database. The applications may very well be providing extra layers of security to prevent the users from poking around in the database. Ensuring the users aren't in the database running ad hoc queries is a good thing. It doesn't take much for a user to intentionally or inadvertently launch a denial of service attack via some poorly formed SQL.

The net, as seen in Figure 7-2, is that you want to restrict access to your application tables to the application and the users such that the users are only accessing the tables via the application.

Privileges Based on User and Application

Refining the problem a bit, there is a more complex problem in which the security privileges are based not only on the user, but also on the application. As seen in Figure 7-3, the user may have several applications accessing the same database. The difference between this and the one just described is you're assuming the user has access to the same database through multiple applications. This is a popular model for two application types. The first is a web-based application. The second is an ad hoc reporting tool.

The figure depicts the security concern: the user will point the ad hoc query tool at the web application data or the financial application data. Because the application data may not rely on database security alone (if at all), the user may have full access, or more access, than you'd like. This application data wasn't intended to be accessed in an ad hoc manner. To maintain least privilege, privileges should be based on the user *and the* application, not the user *and all* the applications.

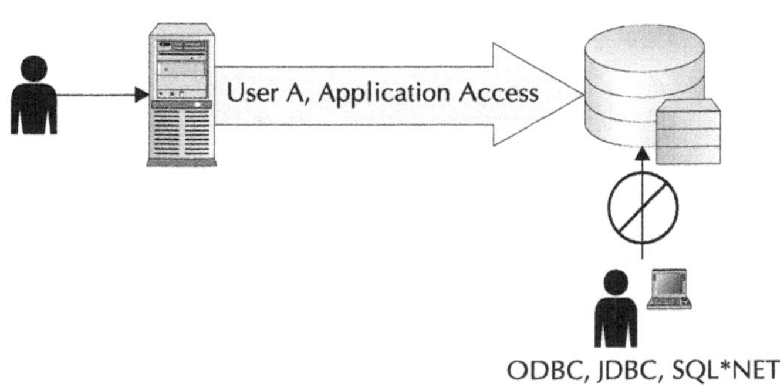

FIGURE 7-2. *Frequent privilege requirement constrains user access to the database only when accessed via an application.*

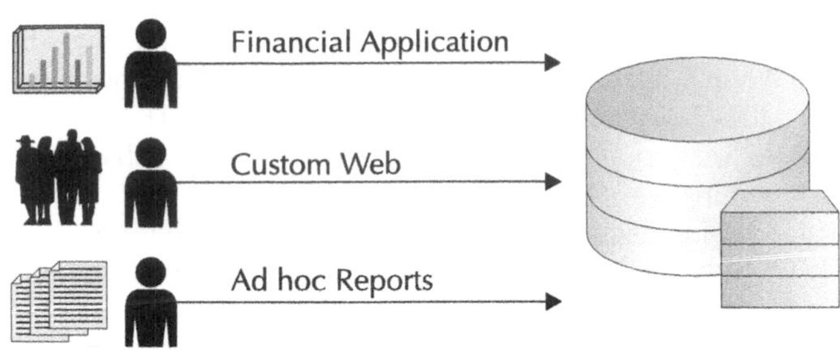

FIGURE 7-3. *Privileges for a user accessing the database via multiple applications should vary depending on which application the user is using.*

Privileges Based on User, Application, Location, and Time

Another variation on privileges can be seen when the same user, using the same application, accesses a database in different ways, from different places, at different times. The point is that arbitrarily complex security policies may be required.

As seen in Figure 7-4, the user may be accessing the application from within her office. Access to the office is physically controlled by the security guard at the entrance of the building and a lock on the office door. Because of the physical security controls, a user accessing the application from within their office provides some sense of assurance that it's really the user. Therefore, the user is allowed all privileges necessary. When the user travels to a field office, the location may still be controlled, but there is less assurance that it's really the user. Therefore, they only get read and insert privileges. Finally, access via a wireless device is trusted the least. Wireless devices are lost and stolen frequently. As such, the user has the ability only to read data. No data manipulation would be allowed. All of these could be constrained to certain hours of the day. If the user tries to gain access on Sunday morning at 3 A.M., they are not allowed.

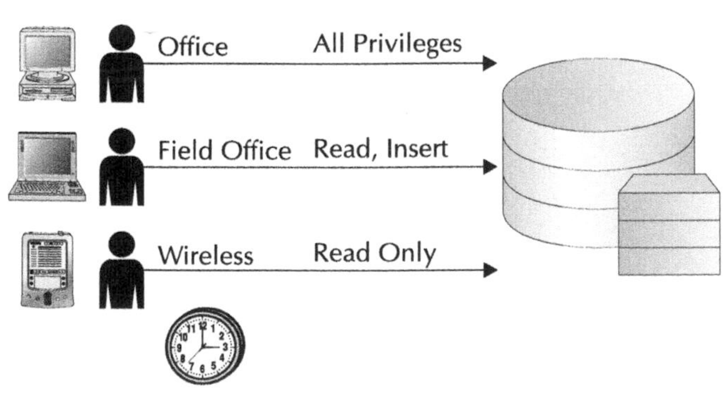

FIGURE 7-4. *User privileges may vary based on access method, location, and time of day.*

The common thread among all these use cases is that the privileges aren't based on the user's identity alone. Privileges should be based on everything you know—the application, how the user authenticated, where they are, the time of day, and of course, the user's identity. The trick to making this work is *selective privilege* support. Roles and their ability to be enabled and disabled are critical to making this work. Just as important is the ability to secure the selective enablement of these roles and privileges.

There's also a philosophical reason why securing the roles is important. If the roles are simply enabled whenever the application makes the SET ROLE call, then the application is in fact controlling the database privileges. That is, the database has no say in the matter. It's just sheepishly following along with whatever the application tells it. This *is not* defense in depth and therefore is not optimal. Let's see how to secure database roles. It involves two variations on roles: password-protected roles and secure application roles.

Password-Protected Roles

Oracle created password-protected roles to help meet the security challenges just presented. Password-protected roles can't be enabled unless the password is provided. Thus, you can prevent users from enabling roles by protecting the role via the password. The primary use case for password-protected roles is prohibiting users from gaining privileges unless they are accessing the database from a specific application. The application knows the role's password, but the users do not. The password is used as a way to authenticate the application to the database.

Password-Protected Role Example

A quick example shows how easy these roles are to use. To create a password-protected role, simply add "identified by <password>" to the CREATE ROLE command. For example, to create a role with a password of "secpass":

```
sec_mgr@KNOX10g> CREATE ROLE pass_protected_role_a
  2     IDENTIFIED BY secpass;

Role created.
```

The syntax is similar to that of creating a user in that the password is followed by the phrase "identified by." The next step is to grant the role to a user. Note that you want to explicitly disable the role; otherwise, it defeats the purpose of having a password-protected role:

```
sec_mgr@KNOX10g> GRANT pass_protected_role_a TO scott;

Grant succeeded.

sec_mgr@KNOX10g> ALTER USER scott DEFAULT ROLE ALL
  2     EXCEPT pass_protected_role_a;

User altered.
```

To enable the role, the user or application has to supply the password via the SET ROLE command or by calling the DBMS_SESSION.SET_ROLE procedure. To enable the preceding role, the user or application could issue either of the following two statements:

```
scott@KNOX10g> -- Set role by command line. This method
scott@KNOX10g> -- is usually done when running SQL*Plus
scott@KNOX10g> SET ROLE pass_protected_role_a
  2    IDENTIFIED BY secpass;

Role set.

scott@KNOX10g> -- Set role by procedure call. This method
scott@KNOX10g> -- is typically done by applications.
scott@KNOX10g> BEGIN
  2    DBMS_SESSION.set_role
  3                  (   'pass_protected_role_A'
  4                   || ' identified by secPass');
  5   END;
  6   /

PL/SQL procedure successfully completed.
```

Note the (unusual) syntax in the procedure call. One might expect the role name as one parameter and the password as a second parameter. This syntax is used because the procedure appends the parameter into the SET ROLE call.

Password-Protected Roles and Proxy Authentication

One limitation with password-protected roles is that they can't be restricted in the proxy authentication DDL statements. You can't control (that is, prevent or allow users from enabling) password-authenticated roles when connected via proxy authentication. For example, you can't prevent the user SCOTT, who performs a proxy authentication via the APP_PUBLIC schema, from enabling the password-protected role PASS_PROTECTED_ROLE_A:

```
sec_mgr@KNOX10g> CREATE USER app_public IDENTIFIED BY oa8sfd8;

User created.

sec_mgr@KNOX10g> ALTER USER scott
  2      GRANT CONNECT THROUGH app_public
  3    WITH ROLE ALL EXCEPT pass_protected_role_a;
  WITH ROLE ALL EXCEPT pass_protected_role_a
                       *
ERROR at line 3:
ORA-28168: attempted to grant password-protected role
```

Not only can you *not* prevent a user from setting the roles, you can't allow the role to be enabled via the connection, either. The gist is that, unlike standard roles, you can't control enabling password-protected roles when using proxy authentication:

```
sec_mgr@KNOX10g> -- Allow role to be enabled when
sec_mgr@KNOX10g> -- proxy authenticated.
sec_mgr@KNOX10g> ALTER USER scott
  2     GRANT CONNECT THROUGH app_public
  3   WITH ROLE pass_protected_role_a;
 WITH ROLE pass_protected_role_a
           *
ERROR at line 3:
ORA-28168: attempted to grant password-protected role
```

Challenges to Securing the Password

The fundamental problem with password-protected roles is in keeping the password a secret. Keep in mind that passwords are considered by some to be "weak" authentication. Choosing a strong password is just as critical for roles as it is for users.

The real challenge with role passwords comes down to four fundamental issues. First, it's difficult to secure the passwords in code. If the passwords are stored in the application code, they may be easily viewed by anyone who can access that code. If the application is a script, then the code is never compiled and the password can be easily seen. The compilation process tends to obfuscate the code, but even doing this may not be adequate protection from programs, such as the common "strings" application found on many UNIX systems.

Having users supply the password may defeat the purpose of having a password-protected role. Recall the requirement that restricts or limits database privileges to users accessing the database only through the application. If the user knows the password, then they can enable it not only from the application, but also from outside the application. One solution to this is to obtain the password via some other method, such as reading it from an encrypted file or from a secure LDAP account.

Second, unlike user passwords that are encrypted or hashed prior to sending them over the network, role passwords may travel in the clear. This will occur if the network traffic isn't being encrypted. Network packet readers come embedded into many applications and can be easily downloaded from the Internet. Also, setting the trace level to ADMIN (16) in the SQLNET.ORA file will capture all SQL*Net network packets. The user can then obtain the role password that has been carefully hidden in the application by simply looking in the SQL*Net trace files. Sending any sensitive traffic over the network is a bad idea and may defeat the successful enforcement of password-protected roles. The solution to this is to use network encryption. The encryption capabilities of the Oracle Networking software provide this protection.

Third, for applications that need to enable the same role, the password would have to be shared. Sharing a password among many applications can be difficult, if not impossible. The password loses its ability to remain a secret when the entire development staff knows the password. Sharing passwords among applications is not easy, practical, or secure.

Fourth, the database still has no say as to whether the privileges are enabled or disabled. The application asks the database to enable the role and the database complies. Consequently, the security resides only in the application.

TIP
Password-protected roles are a valuable tool, but there is a better way: secure application roles.

Secure Application Roles

Secure application roles were introduced in Oracle9*i* Database. They were designed to meet the same requirements of password-protected roles, but they can actually do more.

You need to prevent users or rogue applications from enabling certain roles. To do this, Oracle ensures that the secure application role can only be enabled from within a PL/SQL program. There are two security aspects to this. First, the user or application has to have EXECUTE rights on the PL/SQL program if it ever stands a chance of enabling the role. Second, the PL/SQL program itself will perform a series of verifications and validations to ensure that everything is as it should be *before* setting the role(s). In this way, the PL/SQL program acts as a sentry guarding the role.

This is invaluable, and it solves the problem not resolved in the previous example—the database now has a say in whether or not the roles should be enabled. The application will execute the procedure. In essence, this can be considered a request to turn on the privileges. It's ultimately up to the database and the code you write to determine whether or not the role will be enabled.

For example, if a request to enable a role occurs at 3 A.M. on Sunday morning, the database may decide that this isn't a normal time to be working and that the request might therefore be from a hacker. The database can then elect to not enable the role.

Secure Application Role Example

To create a secure application role, specify the PL/SQL program you want to be used to act as the sentry for your role. The following creates a role appropriately named sec_app_role that will be enabled by the PRIV_MGR program in the SEC_MGR schema:

```
sec_mgr@KNOX10g> CREATE ROLE sec_app_role
  2    IDENTIFIED USING sec_mgr.priv_mgr;

Role created.

sec_mgr@KNOX10g> -- Grant role to scott;
sec_mgr@KNOX10g> GRANT sec_app_role TO scott;

Grant succeeded.

sec_mgr@KNOX10g> -- Disable role.
sec_mgr@KNOX10g> -- User has to enable to get the privileges.
sec_mgr@KNOX10g> ALTER USER scott DEFAULT ROLE CONNECT, RESOURCE;

User altered.
```

There are a couple of things worth noting. First, notice the similar yet one-word different syntax from the password-protected roles—IDENTIFIED *BY* for passwords and IDENTIFIED *USING* for secure application roles. Also, the secure application role program (PRIV_MGR in the preceding example) doesn't have to exist before the role is created. In fact, the schema doesn't even have to exist. The syntax doesn't specify whether the program is a PL/SQL package, procedure, or function. That's because it can be any one of the three. After you create the role, you have to grant the role to appropriate users.

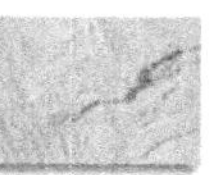

TIP

As mentioned before, if you don't disable the role, it defeats the purpose of having it secured.

In creating the program that enables the secure application role, you have to use invoker rights. In the section discussing definer and invoker rights, you noticed that roles were disabled in definer rights and enabled in invoker. For consistency reasons among others, roles can only be enabled from within invoker rights procedures. This includes standard roles and password protected roles.

To illustrate the effectiveness of secure application roles, remove the previous grant on the DATA_OWNER.T table from the standard APP_USER_ROLE and grant the privilege to the secure application role:

```
sec_mgr@KNOX10g> -- Revoke privilege from standard role
sec_mgr@KNOX10g> REVOKE ALL ON data_owner.t FROM app_user_role;

Revoke succeeded.

sec_mgr@KNOX10g> -- Grant select privilege on T
sec_mgr@KNOX10g> -- to secure application role
sec_mgr@KNOX10g> GRANT SELECT ON data_owner.t
     TO sec_app_role;

Grant succeeded.
```

To protect access to this table, you want to check that the user is accessing the database from the database server machine. Do this by checking for the localhost IP address of 127.0.0.1; this simulates allowing user's privileges only when they have successfully logged into the database server. Note that IP addresses can be spoofed, but it's difficult to spoof the localhost IP address from a foreign machine.

The first security check actually happens before the code executes. The database will verify the user has rights to execute your PL/SQL program. Therefore, you have to grant EXECUTE on the procedure that will enable the secure application role. This procedure, named PRIV_MGR, will need to be accessible to the SCOTT user:

```
sec_mgr@KNOX10g> -- Create secure application role procedure.
sec_mgr@KNOX10g> -- Name of procedure has to match name defined
sec_mgr@KNOX10g> -- to enable the role as given
sec_mgr@KNOX10g> -- in the CREATE ROLE DDL
sec_mgr@KNOX10g> CREATE OR REPLACE PROCEDURE priv_mgr
  AUTHID CURRENT_USER
  AS
  BEGIN
    IF (SYS_CONTEXT ('userenv', 'ip_address') =
                                         '127.0.0.1')
    THEN
      DBMS_SESSION.set_role ('sec_app_role');
    END IF;
  END;
  /
```

```
Procedure created.

sec_mgr@KNOX10g> -- Grant execute privileges
sec_mgr@KNOX10g> GRANT EXECUTE ON priv_mgr TO scott;

Grant succeeded.
```

Logging in as SCOTT using SQL*Plus from a remote server, you'll see that the role will not be enabled, even though the procedure executes successfully. First, view your IP address; then check to see which default roles have been enabled.

```
scott@KNOX10g> -- Show current IP Address
scott@KNOX10g> SELECT SYS_CONTEXT('userenv', 'ip_address') FROM DUAL;

SYS_CONTEXT('USERENV','IP_ADDRESS')
----------------------------------------------------------------------
192.168.0.100

scott@KNOX10g> -- Show enabled roles
scott@KNOX10g> SELECT ROLE FROM session_roles;

ROLE
------------------------------
CONNECT
RESOURCE
```

Even if SCOTT knows he has to enable the SEC_APP_ROLE, he can't:

```
scott@KNOX10g> -- Show role cannot be enabled
scott@KNOX10g> EXEC dbms_session.set_role('sec_app_role');
BEGIN dbms_session.set_role('sec_app_role'); END;

*
ERROR at line 1:
ORA-28201: Not enough privileges to enable application role
 'SEC_APP_ROLE'
ORA-06512: at "SYS.DBMS_SESSION", line 124
ORA-06512: at line 1
```

SCOTT then executes the procedure to enable the role. The procedure will execute successfully. He tries to query the table with no success. Querying the SESSION_ROLES indicates that the role wasn't set by the procedure:

```
scott@KNOX10g> -- Try to enable the secure application role
scott@KNOX10g> EXEC sec_mgr.priv_mgr

PL/SQL procedure successfully completed.

scott@KNOX10g> -- Access object
scott@KNOX10g> SELECT * FROM data_owner.t;
SELECT * FROM data_owner.t
```

```
                              *
ERROR at line 1:
ORA-00942: table or view does not exist


scott@KNOX10g> -- Show enabled roles
scott@KNOX10g> SELECT ROLE FROM session_roles;

ROLE
------------------------------
CONNECT
RESOURCE
```

Performing the same set of operations when directly logged in to the server, you'll see the expected results. The role is set as illustrated in the following code:

```
scott@KNOX10g> SELECT SYS_CONTEXT ('userenv', 'ip_address') FROM DUAL;

SYS_CONTEXT('USERENV','IP_ADDRESS')
----------------------------------------------------------------------
127.0.0.1

scott@KNOX10g> EXEC sec_mgr.priv_mgr

PL/SQL procedure successfully completed.

scott@KNOX10g> SELECT * FROM data_owner.t;

D
-
X

scott@KNOX10g> SELECT ROLE FROM session_roles;

ROLE
------------------------------
SEC_APP_ROLE
```

The benefit of a secure application role is that the database ultimately decides whether the role is enabled or not. This is advantageous because it will allow you to modify your security policy without needing to change your deployed applications. For example, if your policy now says the user can only enable the privileges during business hours, you simply modify your PL/SQL code that guards your role:

```
sec_mgr@KNOX10g> -- Modify security policy to only allow privs
sec_mgr@KNOX10g> -- during 8 a.m. to 5 p.m.
sec_mgr@KNOX10g> CREATE OR REPLACE PROCEDURE priv_mgr
    AUTHID CURRENT_USER
    AS
    BEGIN
      IF (    SYS_CONTEXT ('userenv', 'ip_address') =
```

```
  6                                                   '127.0.0.1'
  7        AND TO_CHAR (SYSDATE, 'HH24') BETWEEN 8 AND 17)
  8     THEN
  9       DBMS_SESSION.set_role ('sec_app_role');
 10     END IF;
 11   END;
 12   /

Procedure created.

sec_mgr@KNOX10g> CONN scott/tiger
Connected.
scott@KNOX10g> COL ip format a16
scott@KNOX10g> COL hour format a5
scott@KNOX10g> SELECT SYS_CONTEXT ('userenv', 'ip_address') ip,
  2         TO_CHAR (SYSDATE, 'HH24') HOUR
  3     FROM DUAL;

IP               HOUR
---------------- -----
127.0.0.1        21

scott@KNOX10g> EXEC sec_mgr.priv_mgr

PL/SQL procedure successfully completed.

scott@KNOX10g> SELECT * FROM data_owner.t;
SELECT * FROM data_owner.t
                         *
ERROR at line 1:
ORA-00942: table or view does not exist
```

Restrictions

As with password-protected roles, secure application roles cannot be constrained by the proxy authentication DDL. Recall the DDL allows you to restrict roles that can be enabled or can't be enabled via a proxy connection. Unfortunately, secure application roles are also not supported.

```
sec_mgr@KNOX10g> ALTER USER scott
  2      GRANT CONNECT THROUGH app_public
  3      WITH ROLE sec_app_role;
    WITH ROLE sec_app_role
              *
ERROR at line 3:
ORA-28168: attempted to grant password-protected role
```

Practical Uses

Secure application roles are a great solution when your architecture depends on the selective nature of enabling roles and privileges. For example, if your application connects to the same schema and you want to maintain separate privileges for separate end users, you can use secure application roles to decide when to enable the privileges.

Secure application roles are the preferred way to meet the requirements listed previously in which privileges are to be granted only after some validation and verification process occurs. They are an excellent tool because the code can not only check environmental attributes, such as the IP address, but the code also can take parameters, which it can use to help make its security decisions.

The best method for implementation is to use a combination of parameters and nonparameter checks. This is because the parameters can be faked or manipulated; the nonparameter information (time, IP address, authentication mode, and so on) is much more controlled and harder for the user or application to alter.

Also, note that this security model is only as good as the code that is written. In the example, you check the IP address. While this is certainly better than nothing, it still represents a single check. Secure application roles are most effective when they check a combination of things. Each check in itself may not be too secure, but generally the combination of all checks provides the necessary security desired and provides defense in depth.

Global Roles and Enterprise Roles

With the introduction of Enterprise User Security (EUS), Oracle added another role type to the database. Global roles were created to allow the users defined in the LDAP server to have not only centralized authentication, but also centralized authorization. Global roles are the name given when talking about this from the database's perspective. That is, the database will create roles that are called global roles.

The roles, when viewed from the LDAP server, are known as enterprise roles. The *enterprise roles* act as a container for the named global roles for each and every database. In the LDAP server, there is a mapping between the enterprise roles and the global roles for each database within the domain.

When an Enterprise User logs in, either directly or via proxy authentication, the database will check the mapping in the LDAP server for its global roles. If the user's enterprise role(s) have global roles for the database, then the database will automatically enable the global roles.

This allows users utilizing the shared schema design to maintain different object and system privileges. Normally, since the schema is shared, any privileges granted directly to the schema would be available to all users that are mapped to that schema. This includes all database roles except for global roles. With this new capability, two users with different enterprise roles, which contain different global roles for the same database, will actually have the different global roles when they log in, even though they are in the same schema.

Creating and Assigning Global and Enterprise Roles

While the global role is created in the database and privileges are assigned to the role, the role cannot be granted to any database users or any other database roles. To create the role, add the clause "identified globally" after the role name:

```
sec_mgr@KNOX10g> -- Create a global role
sec_mgr@KNOX10g> CREATE ROLE app_a_global IDENTIFIED GLOBALLY;

Role created.

sec_mgr@KNOX10g> -- Grant privileges to role as normally done
sec_mgr@KNOX10g> GRANT SELECT ON data_owner.t TO app_a_global;

Grant succeeded.
```

Note that you can't assign the role to any users or any other database roles:

```
sec_mgr@KNOX10g> -- Cannot grant role to users
sec_mgr@KNOX10g> GRANT app_a_global TO scott;
GRANT app_a_global TO scott
*
ERROR at line 1:
ORA-28021: cannot grant global roles


sec_mgr@KNOX10g> -- Cannot grant global role to other roles
sec_mgr@KNOX10g> GRANT app_a_global TO DBA;
GRANT app_a_global TO DBA
*
ERROR at line 1:
ORA-28021: cannot grant global roles
```

To add the role to the user, you have to use the Enterprise Security Manager. To assign the roles to a user, you have to first create an enterprise role. The enterprise role can be any unique name within the enterprise domain. Next, add the global roles for all your databases to the enterprise role. In Figure 7-5, the enterprise role APPA_EROLE is mapped to several global roles in several databases. The APP_A_GLOBAL role is highlighted for the knox10g database.

Next, grant the enterprise role to the user. Clicking on the Users tab in the Enterprise Security Manager brings up the screen that allows the administrator to assign the enterprise role to users. Figure 7-6 shows the Enterprise User Knox has been granted the APPA_EROLE. Underneath the covers, the Enterprise Security Manager has created the role mappings for the databases and the user.

In the following example, the user Knox logs on. This user maps to a shared schema KNOX_DB. The enterprise role APPA_EROLE was granted to Knox. When Knox logs on, the database reads the enterprise role/global role mapping and automatically enables the global role for the user.

```
sec_mgr@KNOX10g> conn knox/oracle10g
Connected.
knox_db@KNOX10g> COL name FORMAT a40
knox_db@KNOX10g> -- Show identity for enterprise user
knox_db@KNOX10g> SELECT SYS_CONTEXT ('userenv', 'external_name') name
  2    FROM DUAL;

NAME
----------------------------------------
cn=Knox,cn=users,dc=iac,dc=oracle,dc=com

knox_db@KNOX10g> -- Show roles.
knox_db@KNOX10g> SELECT ROLE FROM session_roles;

ROLE
------------------------------
APP_A_GLOBAL
```

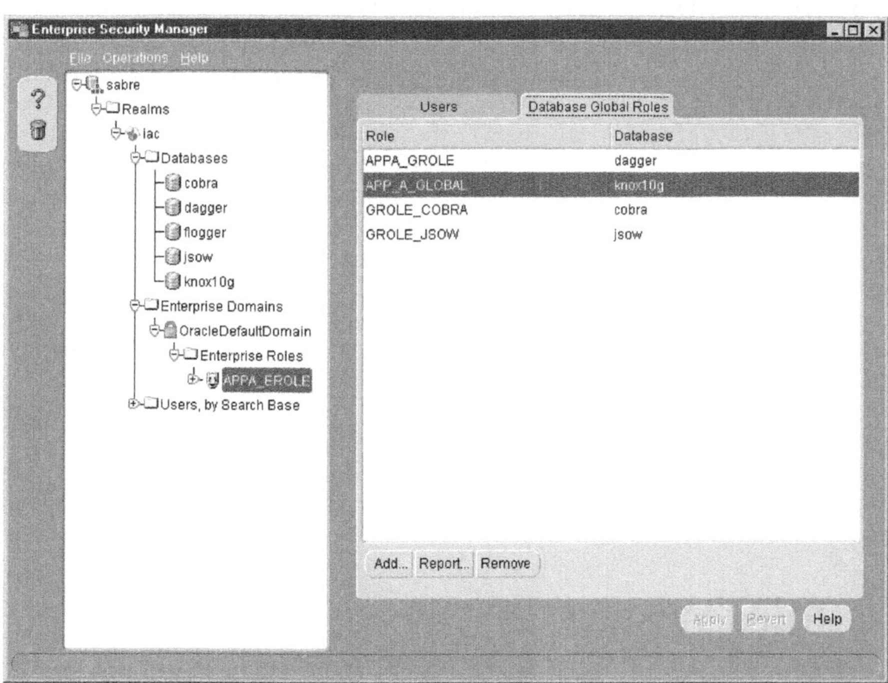

FIGURE 7-5. *The Enterprise Security Manager is the tool that allows for the management of enterprise role, global roles, and their mappings to Enterprise Users.*

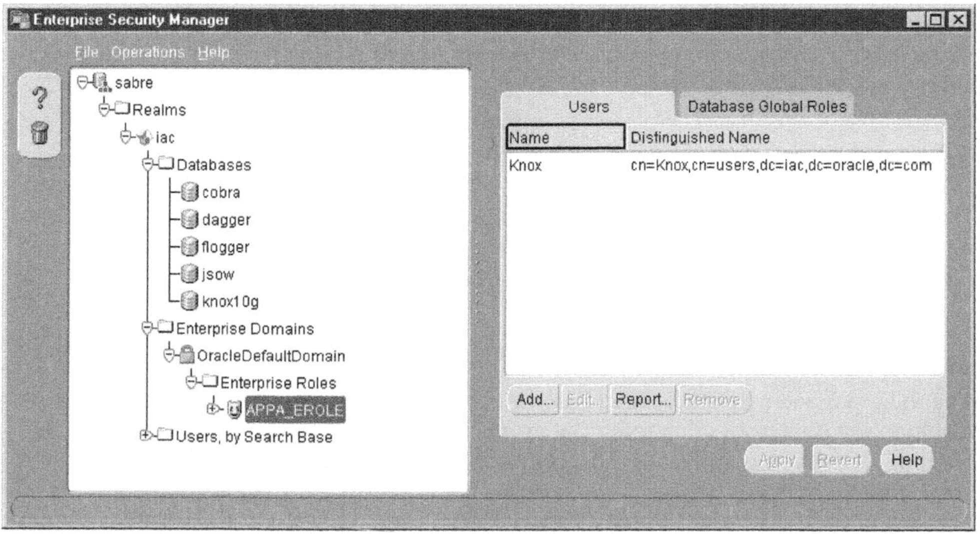

FIGURE 7-6. *Role authorizations are assigned by the Enterprise Security Manager.*

Combining Standard and Global/Enterprise Roles

One of the difficulties with enterprise and global roles is reconciling which users have which privileges when the privileges are granted to global roles. Database privileges granted to global roles cannot be seen from the LDAP server (or the Enterprise Security Manager tool). Likewise, the database only knows of the shared schemas; the actual end users are not known to the database because they are centrally managed in the LDAP server. You have to perform a two-step process. First, determine the privileges that have been granted to the global roles. Next, consult with the LDAP server, which will list all the enterprise roles for the user. The administrator has to then look up each enterprise role to determine which global roles are applicable. It's even hard to describe!

Normally, a code snippet would be provided that would query the LDAP server for the specific user and list all their global roles. Unfortunately, the implementation of enterprise roles is Oracle proprietary and subject to change.

When using the shared schema design, it's a good idea to also use the global and enterprise roles. However, not all privileges have to be granted to global roles. For privileges that are required for all users of a shared schema, the privileges can be granted to the shared schema itself, either directly or via a standard database role. This will make the task of figuring out who has access to what a little easier.

Using Roles Wisely

Standard roles are very powerful. There are a few important things that can affect your design with respect to roles, privileges, and the subsequent assignments to users.

Too Many Roles

The ability to create and assign roles to other roles repeatedly, coupled with the ability to grant privileges to both users and roles in a redundant way, can make absolute security management confusing and difficult. An almost endless hierarchy of roles can be created. The confusion is not from Oracle for allowing roles to be granted to roles or redundant privileges, but rather from administrators' behavior in actually doing this.

TIP

Keep in mind that every role enabled for a user takes up a small percentage of memory. Recall that the MAX_ENABLED_ROLES init.ora parameter restricts the number of roles for this very reason. Take this into consideration when creating and assigning roles.

Naming

Naming roles may seem trivial, but there are (at least) two things to consider. First, role names have to be unique not only from other roles, but also from other usernames. This may seem obvious, but often people develop applications forgetting that the role name is global. If two applications require different privileges granted through roles, but both use applications depending on the same poorly chosen role name—such as "Developer"—then it may not be possible or desirable to install both applications on the same database.

Second, there are often semantics associated with the name. A role named "Administrator" implies powerful privileges. Unfortunately, the name is too vague. If one were conducting a security audit, the role name could be either helpful or a hindrance depending on how carefully the name is chosen. A user with this role is an Administrator of what?

A solution to both of these problems simply requires a bit of thought at the design stage. For example, inserting a prefix for the specific application name in front of the role name may prove to be descriptive as well as helpful in ensuring global uniqueness. You may wish to create the APP_X_DEVELOPER and APP_Y_ADMINISTRATOR roles instead of the plain Developer and Administrator roles given previously.

Dependencies

Roles are not contained in schemas. If user X creates role A, then dropping user X still leaves the role A and all system privileges associated with the role. This is probably desired behavior, but as in the case with synonyms, it's important to understand that a DROP USER X CASCADE doesn't delete the roles or all the subsequent privileges given to the roles.

Finally, it's important to have an understanding of the enabling and disabling behavior as it relates to roles granted to roles. Any roles that are default enabled for a user will also default enable all other roles granted to it; this includes not only the standard roles, but also the password-protected roles and the secure application roles. Consider the following example in which a password-protected role is created. The DBA role is granted to this protected role. Enabling the protected role bypasses the password-protection feature and also default enables the DBA role and all roles granted to it.

```
sec_mgr@KNOX10g> -- Create a user for role example
sec_mgr@KNOX10g> CREATE USER foo IDENTIFIED BY bar;

User created.

sec_mgr@KNOX10g> GRANT CREATE SESSION TO foo;

Grant succeeded.

sec_mgr@KNOX10g> -- Create a password protected role.
sec_mgr@KNOX10g> CREATE ROLE app_1 IDENTIFIED BY secretpassword;

Role created.

sec_mgr@KNOX10g> -- Grant DBA role to protected role.
sec_mgr@KNOX10g> -- Normally this would also protect the DBA role.
sec_mgr@KNOX10g> GRANT DBA TO app_1;

Grant succeeded.

sec_mgr@KNOX10g> -- Make protected role an eligible role for user.
sec_mgr@KNOX10g> GRANT app_1 TO foo;

Grant succeeded.

sec_mgr@KNOX10g> -- CRITICAL MISTAKE: forgot to disable role app_1
```

```
sec_mgr@KNOX10g> CONN foo/bar
Connected.
foo@KNOX10g> -- DBA role and all roles granted to DBA are enabled
foo@KNOX10g> SELECT role FROM session_roles;

ROLE
------------------------------
APP_1
DBA
SELECT_CATALOG_ROLE
HS_ADMIN_ROLE
EXECUTE_CATALOG_ROLE
DELETE_CATALOG_ROLE
EXP_FULL_DATABASE
IMP_FULL_DATABASE
GATHER_SYSTEM_STATISTICS
SCHEDULER_ADMIN
WM_ADMIN_ROLE
JAVA_ADMIN
JAVA_DEPLOY
XDBADMIN
OLAP_DBA

15 rows selected.
```

Example—Putting the Pieces Together

It's often helpful to show an example that uses several technology components together in a complementary way. That is the objective of this example. The context is based on a J2EE application connecting to the database from an application server. The application uses proxy authentication for identity preservation, connection pools for performance, Enterprise Users for manageability, and secure application roles for strict privilege management.

The discussion focuses on the last part—establishing privileges using the secure application role. You'll base your security policy on four separate checks. This design is based on a limited trust model between the database and the application. In this particular example, the application is being trusted to correctly identify itself along with the acting end user.

Application Authentication

The first step in establishing privileges is to ensure the user is accessing the data objects via the application. To do this, first check the static IP address of the application server. The connection to the database will be from the application server, so you can use the USERENV application context to retrieve this. Assuming your application server has an IP address of 138.2.2.20, your check would simply be as follows. Note the code shown here is the function that will be encapsulated in your PL/SQL package that is registered as the guardian for your secure application role.

```
FUNCTION is_authorized_ip
  RETURN BOOLEAN
```

```
AS
BEGIN
  RETURN (sys_context ('userenv', 'ip_address') = '138.2.2.20');
END;
```

Next, check the user authentication path. The connection to the database is supposed to happen through a connection pool that establishes its first connection to the APP_PUBLIC schema. Your check simply verifies that this connection was made with the proxy authenticated user. Note that the APP_PUBLIC schema should require strong authentication, so it would be difficult for someone to fake this.

```
FUNCTION is_proxied_through_app_account
  RETURN BOOLEAN

BEGIN
  RETURN (sys_context ('userenv', 'proxy_user') = 'APP_PUBLIC');
END;
```

For your third check, use the little trick that is the basis of password-protected roles—a password. Use it because it helps to enforce that the application is really your application and not some other application running from the same application server. That is, someone could deploy an application to your application server that is able to use the same connections and would have the same IP address. Force the application to pass a secure token (a password) for this very scenario. Your database procedure will take the token presented from the application and then verify it. Your function ensures they are identical:

```
FUNCTION is_valid_password (p_pass1 IN VARCHAR2,
                            p_pass2 IN VARCHAR2)
  RETURN BOOLEAN
AS
BEGIN
  RETURN (p_pass1 = p_pass2);
END;
```

Note that the problems presented in the password-protected roles section may also be resident here. That's okay, because this is only one in a series of checks. Also, the Java and PL/SQL code can be obfuscated to mitigate the risk of someone viewing the source code potentially figuring out the secure token. An alternate implementation would be for both the application and the database program to obtain the password from an encrypted file on the file system.

Verifying the User

In environments where single sign-on is prevalent, there is often a concern that users will be able to access applications that they aren't supposed to *because* of the single sign-on. This concern is grounded in the belief that as part of the single sign-on infrastructure, an application may not be able to control, at a user level, who is accessing the application. While this is not necessarily true at the application server, within the database, this may be a legitimate concern.

Therefore, you could keep a list of authorized users for your application. The belief is that as owner and administrator of an application and database, you want to maintain ultimate control over who is getting or not getting access. If you suspect someone is either up to no good, or perhaps just issues bad SQL constantly, and you want to prevent them from hitting your database application, you will screen them out using this check. Note that you may not be able to get the person removed from the single sign-on application environment—or maybe not even removed as a database user. As such, you need something at the application level within the database that authorizes the user.

For this task, you have a table of authorized users. You could easily have a table of unauthorized users instead. The table acts as an access control list for our application. Take the user's name and compare it to the list of users in your table. Because your user is an Enterprise User acting within a shared schema, you have to first build a helper function. This function will return the user's nickname by parsing the external name (distinguished name), which is available from the USERENV.

You'll create this as a standalone function because it also has utility in other places within the database. The function takes a parameter, defaulted to the external name, which allows us to test the parsing capability. This is shown below the function. Our nickname is defined as the common name. Because the string for the external name always starts with "cn=<username>, ...", you can parse based on the following code:

```
sec_mgr@KNOX10g> CREATE OR REPLACE FUNCTION eus_username (
    p_ext_name   IN   VARCHAR2
        DEFAULT SYS_CONTEXT ('userenv',
                             'external_name'))
    RETURN VARCHAR2
  AS
  BEGIN
    RETURN UPPER (SUBSTR (p_ext_name,
                          4,
                          INSTR (p_ext_name, ',')
                          - 4));
  END;
  /

Function created.

sec_mgr@KNOX10g> -- Test function
sec_mgr@KNOX10g> VAR eus_id varchar2(40)
sec_mgr@KNOX10g> BEGIN
    :eus_id :=
         'cn=Knox,cn=users,dc=iac,dc=oracle,dc=com';
  END;
  /

PL/SQL procedure successfully completed.

sec_mgr@KNOX10g> COL name FORMAT a10
sec_mgr@KNOX10g> SELECT eus_username (:eus_id) name
    FROM DUAL;

NAME
```

```
----------
KNOX
```

Now that you know the user's name, you can verify that against your lookup table of authorized users. First, create your table:

```
sec_mgr@KNOX10g> CREATE TABLE auth_users
  2     (username VARCHAR2(30));

Table created.
```

Your function will check to see if the user exists in this table. If so, the function returns TRUE. The function is

```
FUNCTION is_authorized_user
  RETURN BOOLEAN
AS
  l_return_val  BOOLEAN := FALSE;
BEGIN
  FOR rec IN (SELECT username
                FROM auth_users
               WHERE username = eus_username)
  LOOP
    l_return_val := TRUE;
  END LOOP;
  RETURN l_return_val;
END;
```

For inserting records into the AUTH_USERS table, use a trigger to ensure the username is stored in uppercase.

Setting the Secure Application Role

You need to create a master procedure for your application to call. The only parameter you need from your application is the secure token (password). Once you verify that everything is as it should be, set the secure application role. Note that this procedure resides in a package that has to be created with invoker rights.

```
  PROCEDURE set_role (p_key IN VARCHAR2 DEFAULT NULL)
  AS
    l_password   VARCHAR2(20) := 'HideTheRolePassword';
  BEGIN
    IF (is_valid_password (p_key, l_password)
         AND is_authorized_user
         AND is_proxied_through_app_account
         AND is_authorized_ip
         )
      THEN
         DBMS_SESSION.set_role ('sec_app_role');
```

```
    END IF;
END;
```

Securing the Source

As with many security-based PL/SQL programs, it's a good idea to obscure the source code for the programs that guard the secure application roles. In the preceding example, wrapping is absolutely necessary to prevent someone in the database (with the requisite privileges) from obtaining the password used in the first verification routine. Hiding the overall verification process also helps to ensure that the implementation remains secure. For example, if an attacker can determine that you are checking for a specific IP address, then they know they have to spoof that IP address.

The WRAP program in Oracle Database 10*g* has been enhanced to obfuscate all code, including strings. Prior to this release, strings were left in the clear. You would then have to derive the string by using functions that would construct the strings utilizing various tricks, such as referring to letters by their CHR values. Assuming you placed the preceding code in a file named Priv_Mgr.sql, you would wrap it by issuing the following:

```
wrap iname=Priv_Mgr.sql
```

The program generates an output file named Priv_Mgr.plb. Searching the .plb file for the password key, note that there are no signs of this. Listing the contents of the file also shows that the source is now secure:

```
C:\> grep -i password Priv_Mgr.plb

C:\> cat Priv_Mgr.plb
CREATE OR REPLACE PACKAGE priv_mgr wrapped
a000000
b2
abcd
abcd
abcd
abcd
abcd
abcd
abcd
abcd
abcd
abcd
abcd
abcd
abcd
abcd
abcd
9
66 9e
y9VKcTgEdb2qWsTj0Oeg5Vw3jNEwg7KXf8tqyi82Z7E04NkaLh78Nv39iAuguKcJCLUP2
AzC0YCFDEkETpk4twUZ90x51GSZwAKZyvma3bX12Xuqoh3kc5KjqaOhTEyJa5OycN/xjN
7DxDKKlsqy0=
/
```

```
CREATE OR REPLACE PACKAGE BODY priv_mgr wrapped
a000000
b2
abcd
abcd
abcd
abcd
bcd
abcd
abcd
abcd
abcd
abcd
abcd
abcd
abcd
abcd
abcd
b
4d9 2b9
dPKBxn1Rob61kqiwWncuQP6yGdgwg/BeLiCMfC9Vxz+VaKY+GPHYoINi/K83qFRsYUPQo
lHnIoyaDog5zkv72HWPIGyetyqUwGTT+yWDIXUrY8yt6VTfI9fZ49q2oJ+HIiKcRl4hpA
DiaUoiYS0V7n6U7tppdwDJHxtr5urNm++aCI2ThgXdMUJ+9Y1
```

This wrapped code is then compiled in the database. The resulting stored PL/SQL source is obfuscated even from the privileged database users who can access the stored source in DBA_SOURCE.

Summary

Database access control is the fundamental mechanism for data security. Oracle provides two different types of privileges: system privileges, which apply across the database, and object privileges, which apply to specific database objects. Effective security implies a good understanding of the different types of privileges and their relationships and dependencies as well as the ability to verify privileges for specific users.

Roles have many advantages. When used carefully and correctly, database roles provide a flexible, secure, and easy way of ensuring least privileges and ultimate database security. Oracle supports different role types for different situations. Standard roles allow users' privileges to be easily aggregated and managed. Global and enterprise roles support Oracle's EUS strategy by allowing different end users to maintain different roles even while mapped to the same database schema.

Another advantage to using roles can also be seen with the ability to support selective privilege enablement. Roles can be enabled or disabled by default. This can facilitate many real-world security policies. To do this effectively, enabling the roles must be done in a secure manner. Password-protected roles provide security for enabling roles. While password-protected roles are good in many situations, they are vulnerable to several password management–related issues.

Extending the ability to protect roles are secure application roles. Secure application roles allow the database to ultimately decide whether a role and its related privileges should be enabled. Security is often not based on the user's identity alone. Access must be controlled based on many things, such as how and when the users authenticated, the application they are using, and the location of the user when accessing the database. Secure application roles provide a way to meet this complex and varying set of requirements.

CHAPTER 8

Effective Auditing for Accountability

uditing is one of those not-so-exciting areas of security that everyone knows they should do but rarely ever does. There are many reasons for this. Some don't know what to audit; some don't know how to audit; some don't know what to do with the audit records once they have audited; and some believe the audit performance overhead is a penalty that doesn't justify the process.

This chapter explores each of these issues. You'll see why auditing is not only possible, but also invaluable. Manual ways to audit will be examined as well as looking at database standard auditing and the improved fine-grained auditing technology. You'll see how the audit records will show you who, what, where, when, and how. You have to determine why and may be able to based on the captured SQL. You'll also explore how auditing can be used as a tool to show how popular an application is, what features are used, and who is using them, and you can establish usage patterns over time. In fine-grained auditing, you'll learn how to control the audit fidelity as well as how to invoke an event handler.

Now a bit of philosophy on how auditing fits and why it's important. Later extensive code examples show various methods and aspects to auditing. You'll see that auditing is a complementary process of the security cycle, and when done effectively it can act as an invaluable tool in your security toolbox.

The Security Cycle

Before discussing *how* and *what* to audit, you need to understand *why* to audit. There is a natural cycle associated with security that begins with prevention, moves to detection, and finishes with response. This cycle is described very well in *Secrets and Lies: Digital Security in a Networked World* by Bruce Schneier (John Wiley & Sons, 2000). What is important about understanding this cycle is that it helps you understand that security isn't exclusively about access control.

Prevention, which includes access control, is the first process in the cycle. It describes all of the measures put in place to control who can do what and how they can do it. In the nondigital world, you see examples of this everywhere, such as locks on doors, electric fences, and security guards restricting access to buildings and building corridors. Many people refer to a system's security to mean only the preventative security measures. While this may seem intuitive, it is incorrect.

Let's look at a bank as a reference. The bank has security designed in from the beginning. The walls are reinforced brick and concrete. This prevents people from mounting a successful Exacto knife attack in which a burglar walks up to a building, usually a residential home, and slices through the siding and insulation, thus creating an instant portal into the structure. Inside the bank you see many other prevention measures such as a security guard, bulletproof glass, and a physical separation from customers, tellers, and money. The vault itself is constructed to prevent robbers from breaking the lock, the door, or slicing through the sides with a torch. The interesting part is that the vaults are not guaranteed to prevent access. They only slow access in attempts to prolong the robbery until the authorities arrive.

This brings us to the next step: detection. Detection can easily occur when the attack happens at a time when people are watching. A bank robbery during the midmorning will be detected by the people being robbed. If the robbery happens at night, on Sunday, or any of the numerous bank holidays, the detection may be more subtle. Enter motion detectors. These are excellent detection devices. It's clear that the motion detectors cannot prevent the robbery. They can only detect it.

Once a security breach is detected, a response is usually desired. In the case of a bank robbery, the police will respond by rushing quickly to the bank. In the case of a residential home burglary, the home's alarm system will notify the alarm company, who will then notify the police. They may first notify the homeowner; in the event that the detection is a false alarm, the homeowner will cancel the call to the police. False alarms happen more than actual break-ins. This is also true for computer systems.

Security begins with a clear and concise security policy. The policy is enforced through proper design and implementation complemented with varying access control capabilities. The lessons from security in the real world translate directly to the computer world. Invariably, something bad will happen. There is no way to build a computer application that is 100 percent secure. You have to rely on auditing for the detection mechanisms to support the overall database security. The response relies on the detection—the audit trail. The section, "Fine-Grained Auditing," shows that the responses can be expedited by an alerting capability.

Auditing for Accountability

Many people use auditing to provide the detection capabilities just described to support their overall database security efforts. Others audit to satisfy compliance with mandatory regulations, corporate or organizational policies, or contractual agreements. Generally, the common thread among all of these is user accountability. You want to ensure users are doing only what they are supposed to. You want to capture privilege abuse and misuse. Auditing allows you to hold your users responsible for their actions by tracking their behavior.

When a person commits a crime, a picture that has captured them in the act can serve as very compelling evidence. An important aspect to auditing is that it can also serve as a deterrent for would-be bad guys. If you know that someone is watching, you are less likely to do something bad. Database auditing can be thought of as the security cameras that capture the actions and diabolical deeds as they unfold. Note that the cameras and auditing may capture both good or expected actions as well as the bad and unexpected actions.

Auditing Provides the Feedback Loop

One thing worse than being robbed is not even knowing that you've been robbed. Auditing can help. The audit records are the means of capturing the robbery. If you're viewing the records and you see something has happened, then you can properly respond. Response may result in readjusting your access control mechanisms and expelling the user.

Two important things have to happen for effective auditing. First, you have to be auditing and auditing on the correct thing. This is analogous to saying you have to have security cameras turned on and facing the right direction. Second, you have to read and interpret the audit records.

The audit records act as a feedback mechanism into the prevention and access control mechanisms you've already established. They also play an important role in any investigative activities that occur either as a result of a breach or in anticipation of one. Without auditing, you may have no way of knowing whether your security is sound or whether your data has been read or modified by an unauthorized user.

Auditing Is Not Overhead

Some people feel that auditing introduces overhead which, when compared to the little value they derive from the audit records, is not worth it. This philosophy is flawed for several reasons.

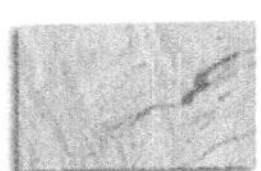

NOTE
Auditing is not overhead.

Auditing all actions by all users on all data is not useful and *will* make a system perform miserably. Auditing must be selective and, when done correctly, it targets the correct data, processes, and users. This means the audit records are, by definition, very useful. The audit records also have to be reviewed and acted on when necessary. This means there is a regular process of reviewing, archiving, and deleting the unneeded records as appropriate. Chances are good that this isn't happening if the performance overhead issue is raised.

Auditing is an art that carefully balances capturing the needed audit records in a way that doesn't introduce detrimental effects on performance. People who are unfamiliar with how and when to audit may in fact end up with a slower performing system with so many audit records that an administrator can't distinguish the people doing legitimate work from the people with malevolent intentions.

The truth about auditing is that it is not overhead. If auditing is done for compliance reasons, or if it's just being done to complete the security cycle, it's necessary and a nonoptional aspect that must be incorporated into the system.

The same is true with other aspects of security. One could argue that access controls add overhead. Checks have to be performed to determine what users can see and do. All of this "overhead" is necessary to ensure the privacy and security of the data. Access controls are not blatantly discarded because there is some overhead associated with them. You accept the overhead associated with access controls, and the users accept it too. Auditing is simply the last phase in your security cycle, and it should not be discarded. You should accept auditing as the complementary security function that it is.

Audit Methods

Auditing takes many forms in today's applications; this section explores popular ways and the benefits and drawbacks of each. It'll discuss application server logs, application auditing, and trigger auditing, and then will conclude with Oracle's standard auditing and fine-grained auditing.

Note that these auditing techniques aren't mutually exclusive. They can and should, as necessary, be combined to build complementary layers of defense within the auditing realm. You will see that each possesses certain advantages and disadvantages. A composite of several auditing techniques will almost surely be the configuration you'll need.

Application Server Logs

Application server access logs and all associated log files for the application server and web server are often considered a basic form of auditing. These files vary in the amount of information they contain. In the general sense, they will list the resources that have been accessed, when and how the access occurred, and the result by way of a status code—for example, success, failure, and unknown.

The logs are very useful. The records contained in the log files are often direct indicators of the actions the user performed. For example, an update posted from a web page would have a distinct URL signature. As such, the user (or rather the user's IP address) can be audited as having invoked some program.

Application server logs are very useful in determining suspicious behavior. Denial of service (DoS) attacks may be evident. Many administrators actually use the logs to track a user's behavior as they navigate a website. This is similar to studying the shopping patterns of customers in department stores.

The challenge with using the application log files is that the information is indirect. It's only useful when combined with other data that links IP addresses to users and the URLs with actual programs. For this reason, application auditing is usually performed in addition to gathering server log files because it can directly audit who is acting on what.

Application Auditing

One of the most frequently used auditing techniques is application auditing, which is the built-in auditing services that are sometimes an actual part of a larger application. Regardless of the implementation language, application auditing is a natural to use, because it can meet most auditing requirements. It can achieve this lofty goal because the auditing is *manually programmed* into the application. As such, it's considered as extensible as the application and the developer's ability will allow.

Many people are quite familiar with application auditing. This technique is often seen when the developers don't understand or can't take advantage of the database auditing. Application auditing may also be the choice when the application wishes to remain database agnostic.

As users perform actions, the application code selectively audits. Various aspects of auditing are generally seen. User logins, data manipulations, and administration tasks can be easily audited. In mature applications, the auditing has been implemented as a service. The business objects within the application call different auditing services and different times to record different actions.

Application Audit Example

Consider an example procedure implemented in PL/SQL. The program could be invoked from an application running either within or outside the database. It may even be called from an application written in another language running outside the database.

This program will be explicitly called by the application at the appropriate time, which will vary from application to application. The example will invoke this auditing when the user performs an update to the SAL column of our table. First, create a copy of the SCOTT.EMP table:

```
scott@KNOX10g> CREATE TABLE emp_copy AS SELECT * FROM emp;

Table created.
```

Next, create the audit table, which is intended to serve as the audit table for all data manipulation on the EMP_COPY table:

```
scott@KNOX10g> CREATE TABLE aud_emp (
       username    VARCHAR2(30),
       action      VARCHAR2(6),
       empno       NUMBER(4),
       column_name VARCHAR2(255),
       call_stack  VARCHAR2(4000),
       client_id   VARCHAR2(255),
```

```
    old_value    VARCHAR2(10),
    new_value    VARCHAR2(10),
    action_date DATE DEFAULT SYSDATE
  )
  /

Table created.
```

The table will capture identifying information about the user performing the action, the action being performed (insert, update, or delete), new and old values, and what, if any, column is referenced. In the case of a delete, just say "ALL" for the column name.

Next, a procedure is created to perform the updates. This code could be embedded into an existing application's code or called from an existing application's code. You can also create a procedure that displays the formatted output of the data in the audit table as follows:

```
scott@KNOX10g> CREATE OR REPLACE PROCEDURE audit_emp (
    p_username      IN  VARCHAR2,
    p_action        IN  VARCHAR2,
    p_empno         IN  NUMBER,
    p_column_name   IN  VARCHAR2,
    p_old_value     IN  VARCHAR2,
    p_new_value     IN  VARCHAR2)
  AS
  BEGIN
  -- check data format and length
  -- not shown here
    INSERT INTO aud_emp
                (username,
                 action,
                 empno,
                 column_name,
                 call_stack,
                 client_id,
                 old_value,
                 new_value,
                 action_date)
         VALUES (p_username,
                 p_action,
                 p_empno,
                 p_column_name,
                 DBMS_UTILITY.format_call_stack,
                 SYS_CONTEXT ('userenv',
                              'client_identifier'),
                 p_old_value,
                 p_new_value,
                 SYSDATE);
  END;
  /

Procedure created.
```

```
scott@KNOX10g> -- create procedure to display audit trail records
scott@KNOX10g> CREATE OR REPLACE PROCEDURE show_aud_emp
AS
BEGIN
  FOR rec IN (SELECT    *
                  FROM aud_emp
              ORDER BY action_date DESC)
  LOOP
    DBMS_OUTPUT.put_line (    'User:         '
                           || rec.username);
    DBMS_OUTPUT.put_line (    'Client ID:   '
                           || rec.client_id);
    DBMS_OUTPUT.put_line (    'Action:       '
                           || rec.action);
    DBMS_OUTPUT.put_line (    'Empno:        '
                           || rec.empno);
    DBMS_OUTPUT.put_line (    'Column:       '
                           || rec.column_name);
    DBMS_OUTPUT.put_line (    'Old Value:   '
                           || rec.old_value);
    DBMS_OUTPUT.put_line (    'New Value:   '
                           || rec.new_value);
    DBMS_OUTPUT.put_line (    'Date:         '
                           || TO_CHAR
                                (rec.action_date,
                                 'Mon-DD-YY HH24:MI'));
    DBMS_OUTPUT.put_line
                 ('-----------------------------');
  END LOOP;
END;
/

Procedure created.
```

The code is simple as written. It's a good idea, however, to check the data types and data lengths prior to inserting (not done here, for brevity).

In this example, the auditing occurs by invoking the AUDIT_EMP procedure from another program when the user performs the actual update.

This popular design uses definer rights to help restrict access to actual database tables. Instead of allowing users to directly manipulate data, they have to invoke a procedure that performs the data manipulation task on the user's behalf. Inside the procedure, there may be some auditing code that captures various aspects of the operation. Perhaps the old and new values are captured, the user, and the time.

```
scott@KNOX10g> CREATE OR REPLACE PROCEDURE update_sal (
  p_empno   IN  NUMBER,
  p_salary  IN  NUMBER)
AS
  l_old_sal  VARCHAR2 (10);
BEGIN
  SELECT     sal
```

```
           INTO l_old_sal
           FROM emp_copy
          WHERE empno = p_empno
     FOR UPDATE;
     UPDATE emp_copy
        SET sal = p_salary
      WHERE empno = p_empno;
     audit_emp
       (p_username       => USER,
        p_action         => 'UPDATE',
        p_empno          => p_empno,
        p_column_name    => 'SAL',
        p_old_value      => l_old_sal,
        p_new_value      => p_salary);
   END;
   /

Procedure created.
```

For example, you want the user BLAKE to perform updates, but you don't need to grant him update on the table directly. Simply grant him execute on the preceding UPDATE_SAL procedure. Do this in addition to granting him the ability to query the EMP_COPY table:

```
scott@KNOX10g> GRANT EXECUTE ON update_sal TO blake;

Grant succeeded.

scott@KNOX10g> GRANT SELECT ON emp_copy TO blake;

Grant succeeded.
```

Now, as user BLAKE, you'll execute the procedure. Note that BLAKE has no idea the procedure is auditing the update. Our audit table has a column for the Client Identifier, which can be set to any meaningful value. By capturing this or any other application context in the audit table, you can obtain more information about the end user's context. Note the security caveats of using the Client Identifier described in Chapter 6.

The application could be setting the value explicitly. As an alternative shown next, a database logon trigger could have set the Client Identifier value transparently. Here's an example trigger that sets the Client Identifier to the user's connected IP Address:

```
sec_mgr@KNOX10g> CREATE OR REPLACE TRIGGER set_ip_in_id
     AFTER LOGON ON DATABASE
   BEGIN
     DBMS_SESSION.set_identifier
                           (SYS_CONTEXT ('userenv',
                                         'ip_address'));
   END;
   /

Trigger created.
```

To test your audit, connect as BLAKE, query to check the original data values, and then execute your update procedure:

```
blake@KNOX10g> SELECT empno, sal
  2    FROM scott.emp_copy
  3   WHERE ename = 'BLAKE';

     EMPNO        SAL
---------- ----------
      7698       2850

blake@KNOX10g> EXEC scott.update_sal(p_empno=>7698, p_salary=>3000);

PL/SQL procedure successfully completed.

blake@KNOX10g> COMMIT ;

Commit complete.

blake@KNOX10g> SELECT empno, sal
  2    FROM scott.emp_copy
  3   WHERE ename = 'BLAKE';

     EMPNO        SAL
---------- ----------
      7698       3000
```

Connecting back as SCOTT, you see the audit data:

```
scott@KNOX10g> EXEC show_aud_emp
User:         BLAKE
Client ID:    192.168.0.100
Action:       UPDATE
Empno:        7698
Column:       SAL
Old Value:    2850
New Value:    3000
Date:         Mar-24-04 13:34
------------------------------
```

The call stack was also preserved for you. The call stack shows (reading from the bottom up) an anonymous PL/SQL block called the SCOTT.UPDATE_SAL procedure, which then called the SCOTT.AUDIT_EMP procedure:

```
scott@KNOX10g> COL call_stack format a50
scott@KNOX10g> COL username format a10
scott@KNOX10g> SELECT username, call_stack
  2    FROM aud_emp;
```

```
USERNAME   CALL_STACK
---------- ---------------------------------------------------
BLAKE      ----- PL/SQL Call Stack -----
             object      line  object
             handle    number  name
           692097F4         1  anonymous block
           694CAF18        12  procedure SCOTT.AUDIT_EMP
           6945FAEC        15  procedure SCOTT.UPDATE_SAL
           693CEA5C         1  anonymous block
```

Benefits

One of the greatest benefits of application auditing is that it's inherently extensible. As security and auditing requirements evolve, application auditing can often be modified to meet these new and ever-changing requirements.

Not only can application auditing support many requirements, but also it controls *how* the auditing is done. This has benefits because applications in the application server may elect to audit to a file on the midtier or audit to a separate database, which would protect the audit records from the administrators of the production database. The auditing implementation can be based on anything. The previous example is only one possible method. Database tables are excellent for auditing because they provide the structure that facilitates the reporting that makes auditing useful. It's generally simple to create SQL reports on the audit data. Many questions such as, "What has the user SCOTT accessed in the last three days?" can be easily answered when the audit records are stored in database tables.

Another major motivator for application auditing is that all aspects of the application can be audited, not only the data access. If the application interfaces with multiple databases, a few flat files, and a web service, all of that can be audited in a consistent way.

Application auditing may also be done to help ensure database independence. To do this effectively, a service layer would be implemented that would separate the auditing interface calls from the actual audit implementation. While this may seem noble at first, the reality is that to get the most use of your investment, your applications should be exploiting as much database technology as possible. Why reinvent the wheel?

Finally, application auditing requires no knowledge of database auditing. Even if knowledge isn't the issue, the database auditing may provide little value if the application architecture doesn't support it. Consider an application that doesn't propagate the user's identity to the database. Database auditing wouldn't add much value, at least not for user-level auditing.

Drawbacks

After all those benefits, you might be tempted to rush right out and build in application auditing. Before you do, consider some of the following issues.

First, the programmatic nature of application auditing can be a drawback as well as a benefit. The audit code is just that—code. It's therefore subject to all the challenges that plague code, such as logic errors, bugs, and the tremendous cost of maintaining the code over time.

From the security angle, the real drawback occurs if the application is bypassed. If a user conducts a direct update on the table, the application auditing will not be done because the application has been circumvented. Applications, especially applications facing large communities of users, will be targeted and possibly hacked. As such, all the security, including the auditing, may be overthrown or at the very least, be in jeopardy.

This hints at another challenge in application auditing. The application has to know that it's supposed to call the auditing programs. One possible way to enforce this is to have the audit program set a signal value in a user-defined application context. You could then create a row-level security policy using views or Virtual Private Database (VPD) that checks for this signal. If you don't understand this now, don't worry—we'll revisit row-level security implemented by views and VPD in Chapters 10 and 11. The point is, without a way to enforce the auditing, the auditing may not occur.

Trigger Auditing

Within the database, a very popular technique for auditing is to utilize database triggers. DML triggers will be explored: Oracle supports triggers for inserts, updates, and deletes. Oracle doesn't support SELECT triggers, but similar functionality can be achieved using fine-grained auditing—details on how to do this are in the "Fine-Grained Auditing" section. Trigger auditing provides transparency, allowing you to enable auditing without requiring application modifications. Applications don't have to be aware of the trigger auditing.

Trigger Audit Example

Auditing via triggers usually consists of writing to an auxiliary auditing table. Generally, the new and old data, along with some other useful information, is captured. Create the trigger to call the AUDIT_EMP procedure defined previously:

```
scott@KNOX10g> CREATE OR REPLACE TRIGGER update_emp_sal_trig
    BEFORE UPDATE OF sal
    ON emp_copy
    FOR EACH ROW
  DECLARE
  BEGIN
    audit_emp (p_username        => USER,
               p_action          => 'UPDATE',
               p_empno           => :OLD.empno,
               p_column_name     => 'SAL',
               p_old_value       => TO_CHAR (:OLD.sal),
               p_new_value       => TO_CHAR (:NEW.sal));
  END;
  /

Trigger created.
```

To test, perform an update on the table as the user BLAKE. For the update, BLAKE requires the update privileges on the table.

```
scott@KNOX10g> GRANT UPDATE(sal) ON emp_copy TO blake;

Grant succeeded.
```

BLAKE now performs a direct update giving everyone in department 20 a 10 percent raise.

```
blake@KNOX10g> UPDATE scott.emp_copy
     SET sal = sal * 1.1
   WHERE deptno = 20;
```

```
5 rows updated.

blake@KNOX10g> COMMIT ;

Commit complete.
```

Returning to SCOTT to view the audit data, you see the updates that occurred for each record:

```
scott@KNOX10g> EXEC show_aud_emp;
User:        BLAKE
Client ID:   192.168.0.100
Action:      UPDATE
Empno:       7369
Column:      SAL
Old Value:   800
New Value:   880
Date:        Mar-24-04 14:23
------------------------------
User:        BLAKE
Client ID:   192.168.0.100
Action:      UPDATE
Empno:       7566
Column:      SAL
Old Value:   2975
New Value:   3272.5
Date:        Mar-24-04 14:23
------------------------------
User:        BLAKE
Client ID:   192.168.0.100
Action:      UPDATE
Empno:       7788
Column:      SAL
Old Value:   3000
New Value:   3300
Date:        Mar-24-04 14:23
------------------------------
User:        BLAKE
Client ID:   192.168.0.100
Action:      UPDATE
Empno:       7902
Column:      SAL
Old Value:   3000
New Value:   3300
Date:        Mar-24-04 14:23
------------------------------
User:        BLAKE
Client ID:   192.168.0.100
Action:      UPDATE
Empno:       7876
Column:      SAL
```

```
Old Value:  1100
New Value:  1210
Date:       Mar-24-04 14:23
------------------------------
User:       BLAKE
Client ID:  192.168.0.100
Action:     UPDATE
Empno:      7698
Column:     SAL
Old Value:  2850
New Value:  3000
Date:       Mar-24-04 13:34
------------------------------

PL/SQL procedure successfully completed.
```

The last record is the original record that was generated in the previous section. The trigger fires five times—once for each row because the trigger fires for each row; you could easily audit at the statement level by making the trigger fire once per statement.

Finally, you can see that the preceding audit records were initiated by the trigger by viewing the call stack:

```
scott@KNOX10g> SELECT DISTINCT call_stack
  2              FROM aud_emp;

CALL_STACK
--------------------------------------------------
----- PL/SQL Call Stack -----
  object      line  object
  handle    number  name
692097F4         1  anonymous block
694CAF18        12  procedure SCOTT.AUDIT_EMP
691DECC0         3  SCOTT.UPDATE_EMP_SAL_TRIG

----- PL/SQL Call Stack -----
  object      line  object
  handle    number  name
692097F4         1  anonymous block
694CAF18        12  procedure SCOTT.AUDIT_EMP
6945FAEC        15  procedure SCOTT.UPDATE_SAL
693CEA5C         1  anonymous block
```

Benefits

One major benefit to trigger auditing is that the auditing can be transparent to the application. If you have purchased an application in which the code can't be modified, then trigger auditing may provide a robust mechanism for adding or augmenting what is already provided. The triggers also can be enabled only when specific columns are being manipulated, as seen in the previous example. The trigger can operate for each row or for each statement. This allows selectivity in auditing and reduces the number of unnecessary audit records. The trigger auditing will also be invoked for all applications regardless of language; that is, no matter how the user interacts with the data, the trigger will audit. This consistency is important.

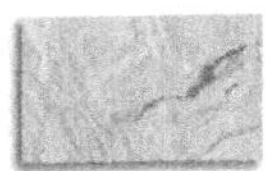

NOTE
As with the application auditing, trigger auditing is programmed. From the benefits angle, this gives you many of the extensibility virtues that were discussed earlier.

Drawbacks

Triggers, while effective, aren't guaranteed. They don't fire for certain actions, such as TRUNCATE statements.

Triggers don't allow applications to pass additional parameters. They are constrained to the table columns. Outside of the new and old values of the data, the only other information the trigger can use are application contexts and environmental data, such as the user's name and connecting IP address.

Also, just like application auditing, triggers have to be created and defined for every object. Calling procedures from within triggers can help if the procedures can be shared across several triggers.

Autonomous Transactions and Auditing

As you may have noticed in the AUDIT_EMP procedure, the transaction wasn't committed. Note what happens then if the user doesn't commit the transaction. First, the audit trail is truncated:

```
scott@KNOX10g> TRUNCATE TABLE aud_emp;

Table truncated.
```

Now, the BLAKE user will check the SAL values, issue an update, and write down the results. Once he has the information he wants, he issues a rollback:

```
blake@KNOX10g> SELECT SUM (sal)
  2     FROM scott.emp_copy
  3    WHERE deptno = 20;

  SUM(SAL)
----------
   11962.5

blake@KNOX10g> UPDATE scott.emp_copy
  2      SET sal = sal * 1.1
  3    WHERE deptno = 20;

5 rows updated.

blake@KNOX10g> SELECT SUM (sal)
  2     FROM scott.emp_copy
  3    WHERE deptno = 20;

  SUM(SAL)
----------
  13158.75
```

```
blake@KNOX10g> ROLLBACK ;

Rollback complete.
```

When the audit trail is queried, there is no audit data! Its as if the update never happened or the audit data has been erased:

```
scott@KNOX10g> EXEC show_aud_emp;

PL/SQL procedure successfully completed.
```

That's because the updates never did happen. At least, the updates never happened from a database transactional perspective. The audit was part of the same transaction, so the rollback removed the audit entries. You know the updates did happen and not only that, but the user was able to see the results of the updates. The rollback performed as it was supposed to.

You may try to solve this issue by immediately placing a commit statement in the procedure, but you can't place a commit in the trigger or you'll receive a runtime "ORA-04092: can't COMMIT in a trigger" error.

Ensuring the audit data isn't erased on rollback is important for auditing in cases where you wish to capture actions being performed even if the actions are later "unperformed." In fact, the Oracle database auditing works precisely on this principle. Rollbacks don't erase the entries from the audit trails. To do this within the database, you can simply utilize autonomous transactions. These transactions are independent of the other transaction that the user session has created.

You can modify both your database trigger and your stored procedure to run as autonomous transactions. Once done, the updates will be audited even if the user issues a rollback. For the procedure, add a PRAGMA in the variables section and add a commit. This commit affects only our autonomous transaction:

```
scott@KNOX10g> CREATE OR REPLACE PROCEDURE audit_emp (
    p_username      IN  VARCHAR2,
    p_action        IN  VARCHAR2,
    p_empno         IN  NUMBER,
    p_column_name   IN  VARCHAR2,
    p_old_value     IN  VARCHAR2,
    p_new_value     IN  VARCHAR2)
  AS
    PRAGMA AUTONOMOUS_TRANSACTION;
  BEGIN
    INSERT INTO aud_emp
                (username,
                 action,
                 empno,
                 column_name,
                 call_stack,
                 client_id,
                 old_value,
                 new_value,
                 action_date)
         VALUES (p_username,
```

```
                    p_action,
                    p_empno,
                    p_column_name,
                    DBMS_UTILITY.format_call_stack,
                    SYS_CONTEXT ('userenv',
                                 'client_identifier'),
                    p_old_value,
                    p_new_value,
                    SYSDATE);
   COMMIT;
 END;
 /

Procedure created.
```

Because both the trigger and the UPDATE_SAL procedure call this procedure, all updates will be audited, regardless of whether there is a commit or rollback issued. To test this, Blake issues the same update:

```
blake@KNOX10g> UPDATE scott.emp_copy
     SET sal = sal * 1.1
   WHERE deptno = 20;

5 rows updated.

blake@KNOX10g> ROLLBACK ;

Rollback complete.
```

User SCOTT can count the audits, and he'll see all five records even though the rollback removed the actual updates. The autonomous transaction-enabled AUDIT_EMP procedure preserved the audit records:

```
scott@KNOX10g> SELECT COUNT (*)
    FROM aud_emp;

  COUNT(*)
----------
         5
```

Data Versioning

New to the Oracle Database 10*g* are expanded Flashback capabilities. See Chapter 10 of the *Oracle High Availability Architectures and Best Practices* product documentation for details. The Flashback Versioning feature allows the user to view data as it has evolved over time. Depending on your auditing requirements, this may be precisely what you need.

Flashback Version Query

To illustrate this capability, refresh the data table and issue a 10 percent raise for everyone in the table:

```
scott@KNOX10g> -- Refresh data
scott@KNOX10g> TRUNCATE TABLE emp_copy;

Table truncated.

scott@KNOX10g> INSERT INTO emp_copy
  2    SELECT * FROM emp;

14 rows created.

scott@KNOX10g> COMMIT ;

Commit complete.

scott@KNOX10g> -- Give everyone a 10% raise
scott@KNOX10g> UPDATE emp_copy
  2     SET sal = sal * 1.1;

14 rows updated.

scott@KNOX10g> COMMIT ;
```

Behind the scenes, it appears the database has logged the updates. To access the data, you can use the following:

```
scott@KNOX10g> -- Show database record of values
scott@KNOX10g> COL ename format a6
scott@KNOX10g> COL sal format a8
scott@KNOX10g> COL "Start" format a12
scott@KNOX10g> COL "End"   format a12
scott@KNOX10g> COL "XID" format a17
scott@KNOX10g> COL operation format a9
scott@KNOX10g> SELECT   ename,
  2           TO_CHAR (sal) sal,
  3           DECODE (versions_operation,
  4                   'I', 'Insert',
  5                   'U', 'Update',
  6                   'D', 'Delete') operation,
  7           versions_xid "XID",
  8           TO_CHAR (versions_starttime,
  9                    'MM/DD HH24:MI') "Start",
 10           TO_CHAR (versions_endtime,
 11                    'MM/DD HH24:MI') "End"
 12      FROM emp_copy
 13     VERSIONS BETWEEN TIMESTAMP MINVALUE AND MAXVALUE
 14     WHERE deptno = 20
```

```
 15  ORDER BY 1, 2;

ENAME  SAL      OPERATION XID              Start        End
------ -------- --------- ---------------- ------------ ------------
ADAMS  1100                                              04/20 16:16
ADAMS  1210     Update    04000F00390B0000 04/20 16:16
FORD   3000                                              04/20 16:16
FORD   3300     Update    04000F00390B0000 04/20 16:16
JONES  2975                                              04/20 16:16
JONES  3272.5   Update    04000F00390B0000 04/20 16:16
SCOTT  3000                                              04/20 16:16
SCOTT  3300     Update    04000F00390B0000 04/20 16:16
SMITH  800                                               04/20 16:16
SMITH  880      Update    04000F00390B0000 04/20 16:16

10 rows selected.
```

The pseudocolumns and syntax that asks the database for the versioned data are in bold. This shows the old data, the new data, the type or operation, when the operation occurred, and that the update was part of the same transaction. Alternatively, the start and end values can be based on SCN.

Flashback Transaction Query

You can now use another feature called Flashback Transaction Query. The transaction ID returned in the preceding query can be used to get additional information stored in the FLASHBACK_TRANSACTION_QUERY view:

```
system@KNOX10g> COL table_owner format a11
system@KNOX10g> COL table_name format a10
system@KNOX10g> COL operation format a10
system@KNOX10g> COL logon_user format a10
system@KNOX10g> SELECT DISTINCT table_owner,
  2                  table_name,
  3                  operation,
  4                  logon_user
  5             FROM flashback_transaction_query
  6            WHERE xid =
  7                       HEXTORAW ('04000C00340B0000')
  8              AND table_name IS NOT NULL;

TABLE_OWNER TABLE_NAME OPERATION  LOGON_USER
----------- ---------- ---------- ----------
SCOTT       EMP_COPY   UPDATE     SCOTT
```

The Flashback capabilities, which allow you to restore data very efficiently, are discussed in the *Oracle High Availability* document. The view stores the SQL statements needed to recover the data to its original state, as you can see:

```
system@KNOX10g> SELECT undo_sql
  2    FROM flashback_transaction_query
```

```
  WHERE xid = HEXTORAW ('0400150012010000')
    AND table_name IS NOT NULL
    AND ROWNUM <= 1;

UNDO_SQL
----------------------------------------------------------------
update "SCOTT"."EMP_COPY" set "SAL" = '1300' where ROWID =
AAAMa1AAEAAACQUAAN';
```

If you wanted to recover the original salary values, you could run the following:

```
system@KNOX10g> -- current data
system@KNOX10g> SELECT ename, sal FROM scott.emp_copy
  WHERE deptno = 20;

ENAME             SAL
---------- ----------
SMITH             880
JONES          3272.5
SCOTT            3300
ADAMS            1210
FORD             3300

system@KNOX10g> -- recover data
system@KNOX10g> DECLARE
   l_undo_sql  VARCHAR2 (32767);
 BEGIN
   FOR rec IN
     (SELECT undo_sql
        FROM flashback_transaction_query
       WHERE xid = HEXTORAW ('0400150012010000')
         AND table_name IS NOT NULL)
   LOOP
     l_undo_sql := REPLACE (rec.undo_sql, ';', '');
     EXECUTE IMMEDIATE l_undo_sql;
   END LOOP;

   COMMIT;
 END;
 /

PL/SQL procedure successfully completed.

system@KNOX10g> SELECT ename, sal FROM scott.emp_copy
  WHERE deptno = 20;

ENAME             SAL
---------- ----------
SMITH             800
JONES            2975
```

```
SCOTT                3000
ADAMS                1100
FORD                 3000
```

The ability to recover the data isn't limited to the transactions. The database supports additional flashback modes: Flashback Table, which allows you to recover an entire table to a point in time; Flashback Drop, which allows you to restore tables that were dropped; and Flashback Database, which recovers the entire database to a point in time. All of these may prove beneficial if a hacker attacks your database and starts corrupting or destroying data.

All of the flashback technology, except Flashback Database, is built on Oracle's multiversion read consistency implementation. This means there is no auditing performance penalty. Oracle is always "logging" the changes. The flashback operations are a new way of exploiting an implementation design that has been available for several years.

NOTE
The flashback features use the undo management system for data access. The data is therefore not permanent. Its lifetime is dependent on the UNDO_RETENTION value and the UNDO_MANAGEMENT initialization variables. To persist the data, you will have to copy it from the Flashback areas.

Standard Database Auditing

From a native database perspective, auditing comes in four flavors: mandatory, standard, Fine-Grained, and administrator (SYS) auditing.

Mandatory Auditing

The database always records three important things: database startup, database shutdown, and users authenticated with the SYSDBA or SYSOPER roles. For the database startup, the audit record also indicates whether standard auditing has been enabled. This allows one to determine if an administrator has disabled auditing (setting the AUDIT_TRAIL value to none or FALSE) and is now restarting the database.

These audit records have to be stored on the operating system because the database isn't available (it's being started or stopped). The actual location varies depending on OS platform—for example, on Windows, the records are written to the Event Logs; on Linux, the audits are generally found in the $ORACLE_HOME/rdbms/audit directory.

Auditing SYS

As of Oracle9*i* Database Release 2, auditing actions performed by users authenticated as SYSDBA or SYSOPER are also supported. The audit records are again written to OS files. This is important for two reasons. First, these users have the most significant privileges in the database, such as the ability to see and modify all data, change passwords, log in to any schema, and drop schemas. As such, it's generally advisable to monitor their actions.

Second, they control the database auditing. If they want to disable it, they have the privileges to do so. They also have the privileges to delete the audit records. Therefore, auditing to the database is useless since the user would be able to modify or delete the audit records. When auditing on SYS, it's important to remember that you shouldn't allow the database user access to the operating system directories where the audits will be written, or else you will suffer from the same challenge as auditing to the database. To enable audits for the SYS user, you have to set the AUDIT_SYS_OPERATIONS initialization parameter to TRUE:

```
system@KNOX10g> ALTER SYSTEM SET audit_sys_operations=TRUE
  2     SCOPE=SPFILE;

System altered.
```

This change is written to the initialization file (init.ora), and the database has to be rebooted for the change to take effect. Trying to change this parameter at runtime results in the error: "ORA-02095: specified initialization parameter cannot be modified". This is a security feature. If the database could be modified at runtime without booting, the SYS user could turn off auditing, do something bad, and then re-enable auditing. By forcing a reboot, you know that you'll have captured both the disabling of the auditing as well as the reboot.

After restarting the database, all successful actions performed by the SYS user will be audited. To illustrate this point, set the parameter to TRUE. Then authenticate as SYSDBA and change the SYS user's password. In Figure 8-1, the Microsoft Event Viewer shows how the event has been audited.

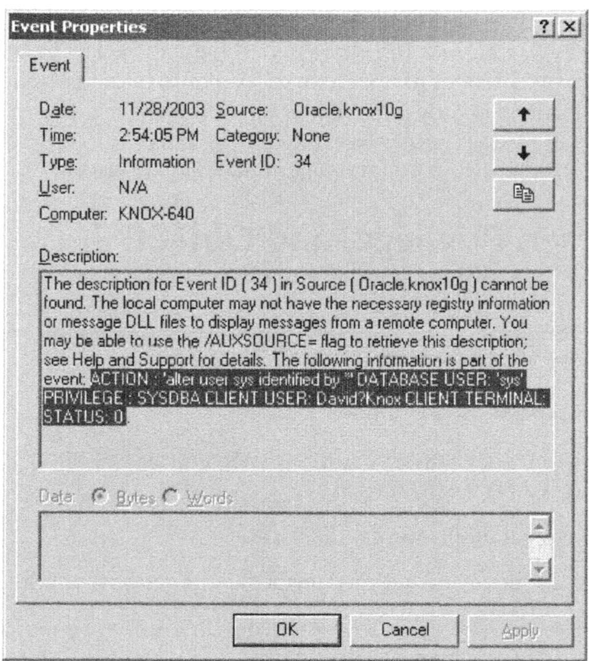

FIGURE 8-1. *Auditing SYS actions ensures accountability for the most privileged database users.*

Enabling Standard Auditing

When most people think of database auditing, they think of standard auditing. Before you can successfully utilize the database standard auditing, you have to enable it by setting the AUDIT_TRAIL initialization parmeter. Note this is a distinctly separate parameter from AUDIT_SYS_OPERATIONS, which just audits the actions of SYS. The AUDIT_TRAIL parameter allows standard database auditing to occur. By default, this parameter is also set to FALSE.

To enable auditing, you can set the AUDIT_TRAIL parameter to several values. Setting the value to "OS" will enable the database audit records to be written to the operating system (OS). As with auditing on SYS, this is a good idea if you're concerned with someone modifying or deleting the audit records that might otherwise be contained within the database. However, auditing to the OS can make it difficult to run reports because the data is in a text file.

To enable auditing for records stored in the database (records are stored in the SYS.AUD$ table), you have to set the AUDIT_TRAIL parameter to either "DB" or to "TRUE". New in Oracle Database 10*g* is the ability to set auditing to "DB_EXTENDED". DB_EXTENDED also enables database auditing but captures additional information in the audit record. The SQL text and any potential bind variables that actually caused the audit to occur, as well as some other useful information, will be captured. You see this in the following example:

```
system@KNOX10g> ALTER SYSTEM SET audit_trail=db_extended SCOPE=SPFILE;

System altered.
```

For the same security precautions just discussed, the database has to be rebooted before the changes will take effect. As a reboot of the database is required, it's best to set the AUDIT_TRAIL parameter and reboot so once you decide what you really want to audit, you'll be able to do it without needing to restart the database. A security best practice is to set the AUDIT_TRAIL value to DB_EXTENDED on database creation. By default the value is not set.

Auditing By User, Privilege, and Object

The database allows for a very robust auditing environment:

- You can audit on objects such as tables and views. For example, every time someone accesses the APP.USER_DATA table an audit will be recorded.
- You can audit procedure executions.
- You can audit when someone exercises a system privilege, such as disabling a trigger or using the SELECT ANY TABLE privilege.
- You can restrict your audits to specific users.
- You can audit for successful actions, unsuccessful actions, or both.
- With all of the preceding, you can audit every time someone performs the action, or audit only once per session regardless of the number of times they perform the action within the session.

The point is that this extensive capability allows you to focus your auditing to precisely the things that are of interest. This fidelity is what makes the auditing a real asset.

Targeted Auditing

As mentioned previously, auditing can only be done successfully once you have a clear idea of why you are auditing and what you are auditing. If you audit too much, you could suffer performance hits, and more importantly, generate excessive and potentially useless records. Culling through thousands of audit records is generally ineffective, especially when most of the audits were done for users that were performing the tasks they were assigned. The greater the fidelity in the auditing capability, the better your chances are of focusing the auditing to just the right level on just the right things.

Auditing can help you identify gaps in your security policies. From the audit records, you may notice that authorized users don't have the necessary privileges, or on the other extreme that they are over privileged. You may even identify contradictions within your security policy. For example, it's typical to have one requirement to support database backups that allows a user to gain access to the entire database. Another requirement based on "need to know" may say that users are only allowed access to certain records based on their affiliation. These two requirements may conflict.

This highlights an important point to auditing. In cases where administrators require super privileges, *auditing may be the only thing you can do to ensure privileges are not abused and misused.* This is exactly why the database supports audits for SYS.

Auditing Best Practices

In addition to targeted auditing, there are a couple of occasions worth constant consideration.

Audit Connections

Auditing when users log on and log off of the database is a good thing to do. It's a matter of common sense. You should also know who has been in your database(s). If something bad happens to the database and you know about when the bad thing happened, it's invaluable to be able to find out who was working in the database when the incident happened. Acknowledging the fact that most database outages are human induced and not a software or hardware failure, auditing connections will help narrow the field of possible suspects.

However, there are two things that have to be done to ensure this type of auditing is effective. Most importantly, you have to be able to distinguish between users. Auditing on applications that conceal the user's identity may be pointless—after all, you really can't distinguish the "who," only that it was a person running the application. For applications with connection pools, this type of auditing may be ineffective.

Second, and this applies to all auditing, you have to do something with the records. With connections, this point is particularly acute. Because the users will be connecting all the time, unless you have a tremendous amount of disk space, you'll have to archive and delete the old records.

To enable auditing for logons and logoffs, simply audit the user's connection. Again, you can do this at a user level or for all users. First, check to ensure that auditing is enabled, and then audit all connections for all users:

```
system@KNOX10g> show parameter audit_trail

NAME                                 TYPE        VALUE
------------------------------------ ----------- ------------
audit_trail                          string      DB_EXTENDED
```

```
system@KNOX10g> AUDIT SESSION;

Audit succeeded.
```

The check for the value of the AUDIT_TRAIL parameter is a good habit. This is because the "audit session;" statement will succeed even if the database auditing is disabled (AUDIT_TRAIL = FALSE). You might think you are auditing, but in reality you aren't.

To complete our example, log on and log off as the user SCOTT (not shown). Upon logon, the database writes an entry to the audit trail:

```
system@KNOX10g> BEGIN
     FOR rec IN
       (SELECT username,
               action_name,
               TO_CHAR (TIMESTAMP, 'Mon-DD HH24:MI')
                                                 LOGON,
               TO_CHAR (logoff_time,
                        'Mon-DD HH24:MI') LOGOFF,
               priv_used,
               comment_text
          FROM dba_audit_trail)
     LOOP
       DBMS_OUTPUT.put_line (    'User:        '
                              || rec.username);
       DBMS_OUTPUT.put_line (    'Action:      '
                              || rec.action_name);
       DBMS_OUTPUT.put_line (    'Logon:       '
                              || rec.LOGON);
       DBMS_OUTPUT.put_line (    'Logoff:      '
                              || rec.LOGOFF);
       DBMS_OUTPUT.put_line (    'Priv Used:  '
                              || rec.priv_used);
       DBMS_OUTPUT.put_line (    'Comments:   '
                              || rec.comment_text);
       DBMS_OUTPUT.put_line
         ('--------------- End of Record ---------------');
     END LOOP;
   END;
   /
User:       SCOTT
Action:     LOGON
Logon:      Mar-24 15:50
Logoff:
Priv Used: CREATE SESSION
Comments:  Authenticated by: DATABASE; Client address:
(ADDRESS=(PROTOCOL=tcp)(HOST=192.168.0.100)(PORT=3445))
--------------- End of Record ---------------

PL/SQL procedure successfully completed.
```

Note the useful information the database automatically places in the COMMENT_TEXT field. The logoff time is NULL because the user in this example is still logged in. Once the user has disconnected, the database updates the audit entry. The ACTION is changed to LOGOFF, and the actual logoff time is indicated as well:

```
system@KNOX10g> /
User:       SCOTT
Action:     LOGOFF
Logon:      Mar-24 15:50
Logoff:     Mar-24 15:53
Priv Used: CREATE SESSION
Comments:  Authenticated by: DATABASE; Client address:
(ADDRESS=(PROTOCOL=tcp)(HOST=192.168.0.100)(PORT=3445))
--------------- End of Record ---------------

PL/SQL procedure successfully completed.
```

This simple ability to track who was connected and when is valuable and may be the only records you have prior to something happening.

Audit Whenever Unsuccessful

Auditing unsuccessful actions represents the database's ability to detect the burglar rattling the windows and checking the doors. You should know when someone is banging on a locked door. This is especially important with truly sensitive data or with data that can be used to derive sensitive information, such as privacy-related data, encryption keys, passwords, and user preferences.

Let's show this in action. You'll enable auditing on a table, but your auditing policy will only audit when users try to access the object but don't have the proper privileges. This may be an indication that the user is trying to gain unauthorized access to our sensitive data.

This will audit by access and not by session. This means for every SQL statement that touches the table (or rather, tries to touch the table), an audit record will be generated. If you audited by session, there would be only one record for each session regardless of the number of actual SQL statements that accessed the table.

```
sec_mgr@KNOX10g> CREATE TABLE t AS SELECT * FROM DUAL;

Table created.

sec_mgr@KNOX10g> -- audit selects on T for failures
sec_mgr@KNOX10g> AUDIT SELECT ON t
  2     BY ACCESS WHENEVER NOT SUCCESSFUL;

Audit succeeded.
```

When an unauthorized user tries to access this table the action will be audited.

```
scott@KNOX10g> SELECT *
  2     FROM sec_mgr.t;
  FROM sec_mgr.t
```

```
                  *
ERROR at line 2:
ORA-00942: table or view does not exist
```

Checking the audit trail, you see this failed attempt to access the table:

```
sec_mgr@KNOX10g> BEGIN
    FOR rec IN (SELECT audit_type,
                       db_user,
                       object_schema,
                       object_name,
                       extended_timestamp,
                       sql_text
                  FROM dba_common_audit_trail)
    LOOP
      DBMS_OUTPUT.put_line (   'Audit Type: '
                            || rec.audit_type);
      DBMS_OUTPUT.put_line (   'Who:        '
                            || rec.db_user);
      DBMS_OUTPUT.put_line (   'What:       '
                            || rec.object_schema
                            || '.'
                            || rec.object_name);
      DBMS_OUTPUT.put_line (   'When:       '
                            || rec.extended_timestamp);
      DBMS_OUTPUT.put_line (   'How:        '
                            || rec.sql_text);
      DBMS_OUTPUT.put_line
        ('--------------- End of Record ---------------');
    END LOOP;
  END;
  /
Audit Type: Standard Audit
Who:        SCOTT
What:       SEC_MGR.T
When:       24-MAR-04 04.11.10.350000 PM -05:00
How:        SELECT * FROM sec_mgr.t
--------------- End of Record ---------------
```

The audit type of "Standard Audit" is used because this new view integrates both the standard audit records and fine-grained audit records.

Tracking Database Use

You can also use auditing to check or verify how the database is being used. For example, you may wonder whether a table, schema, or procedures are still being used. Enabling auditing will indicate if the object(s) is still in use.

Also recall that removing unused schemas is a security best practice. Before you drop the schema, it's best to audit access to objects or connections to the schema to determine if the schema really is unused.

Determining the Audit Status

Evaluating the current audit status is important especially when performance becomes questionable. It can also be useful for proving compliance with a security policy. When you want to inspect the audit status on your objects, you can query the DBA_OBJ_AUDIT_OPTS or the USER_OBJ_AUDIT_OPTS view. The views show the audit status of every object even if auditing isn't enabled. You should therefore form your query to target the specific object or a specific statement of interest:

```
sec_mgr@KNOX10g> COL "select option" format a13
sec_mgr@KNOX10g> SELECT sel "select option"
  2     FROM user_obj_audit_opts
  3    WHERE object_name = 'T';

select option
-------------
-/A
```

The format is a bit cryptic, but it's easy to use once you know the code. The USER_OBJ_AUDIT_OPTS view lists all the options that can be performed on an object. In this query, you're just looking at the select option. There are two values represented for each option. The first field, represented by a hyphen in the above output, indicates if auditing should occur when the user is successful in performing the action. The second field, an "A" in the output above, indicates whether auditing will occur for unsuccessful actions. A hyphen or a blank means no auditing will occur. An "A" means auditing will occur for every access, and an "S" means auditing will occur once for each session.

If you enable auditing by session on the table, you can verify the previous rules:

```
sec_mgr@KNOX10g> AUDIT SELECT ON t BY SESSION WHENEVER SUCCESSFUL;

Audit succeeded.

sec_mgr@KNOX10g> SELECT sel "select option"
  2     FROM user_obj_audit_opts
  3    WHERE object_name = 'T';

select option
-------------
S/A
```

The DBA_STMT_AUDIT_OPTS view shows system wide auditing. The auditing that was enabled to track user logons can be viewed by this query:

```
sec_mgr@KNOX10g> COL user_name format a10
sec_mgr@KNOX10g> COL proxy_name format a10
sec_mgr@KNOX10g> COL audit_option format a20
sec_mgr@KNOX10g> SELECT * FROM dba_stmt_audit_opts;
```

```
USER_NAME  PROXY_NAME AUDIT_OPTION         SUCCESS    FAILURE
---------- ---------- -------------------- ---------- ----------
                      CREATE SESSION       BY ACCESS  BY ACCESS
```

The last essential view is DBA_PRIV_AUDIT_OPTS, which allows you to check the auditing status of system privileges. For example, if you enable auditing for users exercising the SELECT ANY TABLE privilege, you can check the status as follows:

```
sec_mgr@KNOX10g> -- Audit the SELECT ANY TABLE privilege
sec_mgr@KNOX10g> AUDIT SELECT ANY TABLE;

Audit succeeded.

sec_mgr@KNOX10g> COL privilege format a20
sec_mgr@KNOX10g> -- Show privilege auditing
sec_mgr@KNOX10g> SELECT * FROM dba_priv_audit_opts;

USER_NAME  PROXY_NAME PRIVILEGE            SUCCESS    FAILURE
---------- ---------- -------------------- ---------- ----------
                      SELECT ANY TABLE     BY SESSION BY SESSION
```

Extending the Audit Data with Client Identifiers

A similar statement made earlier regarding preventive security measures also holds true with auditing: The more information the database has, the better the security. With auditing, you can augment the audit trails using Client Identifiers. If the user's identity is already known to the database, the Client Identifier should be seeded with other useful information such as the user's IP address, the application they are running, how they authenticated, and anything and everything that can be used to describe the user's operating context. Please see the section "Securing the Client Identifier" in Chapter 6.

As illustrated previously, logon triggers can be used to effectively set meaningful information about the user in the Client Identifier.

The code presented earlier can be modified to set the user's IP address and the program they are using and storing the result in the Client Identifier. The module name can be spoofed by the user but it does often indicate correctly the name of the application being used such as SQL*Plus, MS Excel, or T.O.A.D. Note that changing the program's executable name changes the program and not the module:

```
sec_mgr@KNOX10g> CREATE OR REPLACE TRIGGER set_default_client_info
    AFTER LOGON ON DATABASE
  DECLARE
    l_module  v$session.module%TYPE;
  BEGIN
    SELECT UPPER (module)
      INTO l_module
      FROM v$process a, v$session b
     WHERE a.addr = b.paddr
       AND b.audsid = USERENV ('sessionid');
    DBMS_SESSION.set_identifier
                        (    SYS_CONTEXT
                                           ('userenv',
                                            'ip_address')
```

```
                                || ':'
                                || l_module);
     END;
     /

Trigger created.
```

This code could be extended to capture the authentication mode, the network protocol, or any other valuable piece of information you want to extract from the user session environment.

Now enable auditing on the SCOTT.EMP object. By not specifying when you want to audit, you'll be auditing for both successful and unsuccessful actions as well as auditing by access so you can capture a record for every SQL statement:

```
sec_mgr@KNOX10g> AUDIT SELECT ON scott.emp BY ACCESS;

Audit succeeded.
```

For testing, delete the existing records from the audit table:

```
sys@KNOX10g> DELETE FROM aud$;
```

Next log on as SYSTEM and issue a query on the table:

```
system@KNOX10g> SELECT ename, sal
      FROM scott.emp
     WHERE sal < (SELECT sal
                    FROM scott.emp
                   WHERE ename = 'SCOTT')
       AND deptno = (SELECT deptno
                       FROM scott.emp
                      WHERE ename = 'SCOTT');

ENAME             SAL
---------- ----------
SMITH             800
JONES            2975
ADAMS            1100
```

Now, as SCOTT, issue two more queries:

```
scott@KNOX10g> SELECT SUM (sal) FROM scott.emp;

  SUM(SAL)
----------
     29025

scott@KNOX10g> SELECT ename FROM scott.emp
     WHERE 1 = 2;

no rows selected
```

Checking the audit records, you see there are five records in the audit trail: the two from SCOTT and three that were generated from the single statement issued by SYSTEM. You'll create a procedure to group the records together so you actually see only three results. This ability to correlate records is also a new capability enabled by the DB_EXTENDED value of the AUDIT_TRAIL parameter.

```
sec_mgr@KNOX10g> SELECT COUNT (*)
      FROM dba_common_audit_trail;

  COUNT(*)
----------
         5

sec_mgr@KNOX10g> CREATE OR REPLACE PROCEDURE show_aud
    AS
    BEGIN
      FOR rec IN (SELECT   db_user,
                           client_id,
                           object_schema,
                           object_name,
                           extended_timestamp,
                           sql_text,
                           statementid
                      FROM dba_common_audit_trail
                  GROUP BY db_user,
                           statementid,
                           sql_text,
                           object_schema,
                           object_name,
                           client_id,
                           extended_timestamp
                  ORDER BY extended_timestamp ASC)
      LOOP
        DBMS_OUTPUT.put_line ('Who:   ' || rec.db_user);
        DBMS_OUTPUT.put_line (    'What: '
                              || rec.object_schema
                              || '.'
                              || rec.object_name);
        DBMS_OUTPUT.put_line (    'Where: '
                              || rec.client_id);
        DBMS_OUTPUT.put_line
                     (    'When:  '
                      || TO_CHAR
                              (rec.extended_timestamp,
                               'Mon-DD HH24:MI'));
        DBMS_OUTPUT.put_line ('How:    '
                              || rec.sql_text);
        DBMS_OUTPUT.put_line
          ('-------------- End of Record --------------');
      END LOOP;
```

```
 38  END;
 39  /

Procedure created.

sec_mgr@KNOX10g> EXEC show_aud
Who:   SCOTT
What:  SCOTT.EMP
Where: 192.168.0.100:SQLPLUS.EXE
When:  Mar-24 16:28
How:   SELECT ename FROM scott.emp
 WHERE 1 = 2
-------------- End of Record --------------
Who:   SCOTT
What:  SCOTT.EMP
Where: 192.168.0.100
When:  Mar-24 16:28
How:   SELECT SUM (sal) FROM scott.emp
-------------- End of Record --------------
Who:   SYSTEM
What:  SCOTT.EMP
Where: 192.168.0.100:SQLPLUS.EXE
When:  Mar-24 16:28
How:   SELECT ename, sal
  FROM scott.emp
 WHERE sal < (SELECT sal
                FROM scott.emp
WHERE ename = 'SCOTT')
   AND deptno = (SELECT deptno
                   FROM scott.emp
WHERE ename = 'SCOTT')
-------------- End of Record --------------

PL/SQL procedure successfully completed.
```

The correlation of records was done by the grouping by statementIDs. For other DML types, you also can correlate by transactionID. This will link together all the inserts, updates, and deletes that were part of the same transaction, which allows us to support transaction level auditing in addition to the statement (task) level auditing.

TIP
To disable auditing (useful if you are following along), you have to issue the NOAUDIT command: NOAUDIT SELECT ON scott.emp;.

Peformance Test

No matter what you read, auditing has to be (at least theoretically) slower than not auditing because you are doing more work. A quick test should always be performed in coordination with your auditing policy. In the preceding example, you can run a loop of queries on the table with and without auditing enabled to determine how much the auditing operations will add to your execution time.

Here are the results—your mileage may vary. First, without auditing, query a table 100,000 times in just over six seconds:

```
scott@KNOX10g> BEGIN
    FOR rec IN 1 .. 100000
    LOOP
      FOR irec IN (SELECT ename
                     FROM scott.emp)
      LOOP
        NULL;
      END LOOP;
    END LOOP;
  END;
  /

PL/SQL procedure successfully completed.

Elapsed: 00:00:06.33
```

Auditing can be disabled at the system level via the AUDIT_TRAIL parameter and at the object level via audit policies. The time to execute the preceding was approximately the same, regardless of how the auditing was disabled.

Next, the same 100,000 queries are executed. When auditing by access, this will insert 100,000 records into the audit table. This naturally is where the slow-down occurs:

```
scott@KNOX10g> /

PL/SQL procedure successfully completed.

Elapsed: 00:23:06.22
```

You might expect something like this. There are a lot of records being inserted into a table. The point is that there is no magic with auditing. That insert process is going to take time.

There are a couple of important conclusions that should be obvious from this. First, this test is contrived and doesn't represent any real-world application. It was done intentionally to get the drastic results seen. *You have to test based on your true expected load and access methods.* Querying in the loop shows how fast the database can process serial requests from the same user. It doesn't indicate how it will work concurrently with mulitple users.

Second, this shows how careful consideration has to be given to auditing. One hundred thousand audit records are a lot of records. This might not be the right level of auditing for our specific data usage. You might decide to change the audit from "access" to "sesssion," or you might want to audit only on failed access attempts. Both would limit the number of records and increase performance. The answer is dependent on why you are auditing and what you hope to get from the audit records. One thing the preceding example illustrates is that SCOTT is querying this table many times in a short period of time using the same SQL. Perhaps he is executing a program that is (accidentally) continuously looping.

Caveats

Standard auditing has a few drawbacks. The auditing fidelity, while very good to a point, may not be adequate for some requirements. For example, if you want to capture audits on specific columns or when specific conditions arise, then standard auditing would be ineffective.

Another issue is one that is arguably not part of the auditing domain but nonetheless still frequently brought up. The audits don't indicate what the user actually saw as a result of the query. None of the implementations of auditing in this chapter have that ability by themselves. However, Oracle is aware of this, and the audit records do capture the time of the audit and the SCN (system change number). Either of these values allows an administrator to execute the Flashback ability of the database. Once the Flashback has occurred, you can rerun the query the user ran logged in as the user and see what the user saw when they issued the query. Note if you issue an ALTER SESSION SET CURRENT_SCHEMA=<AuditedUser> you will only be resolving objects as the user; their privileges and context values aren't included, so the results from the Flashback query are very likely to be erroneous.

There are limitations to the longevity of the Flashback data. An alternative for those that are concerned with this issue is to use an Oracle solution called Selective Audit. *Selective Audit* is an Oracle Consulting supported solution that puts Oracle's Standard Auditing on steroids. Search on the term "Selective Audit" on www.oracle.com for more information.

Fine-Grained Auditing

With Oracle9*i* Database Release 9.0.1, Oracle introduced another level of auditing in fine-grained auditing (FGA). Originally, FGA was only possible for SELECT statements. Other DML wasn't supported (the alternative was to use database triggers on insert, update, and delete statements). FGA has been significantly enhanced in Oracle Database 10*g* by allowing audits to extend to all DML statements.

FGA's extension to the standard auditing was actually borne out of the Oracle Consulting work done in the government division. FGA is designed to solve some of the issues illuminated in the previous "Caveats" section. Audit policies sometime require another level of fidelity not currently supported in the standard auditing. The auditing can be more selectively enabled to occur only when certain conditions arise and specific columns are queried. One of the practical aspects of FGA is that it makes the auditing functions behave more like intrusion detection systems. That is, you can set up your preventive security controls as normal. Then you can use the FGA as a safety net to catch things that fall through. You'll see this come to life in the upcoming examples.

In security practice, there is no such thing as perfect security. It's not *whether* you will be compromised, but rather *when* you will be. You can only hope to have the auditing enabled.

Audit Conditions

When FGA was originally introduced, it offered four major advantages over standard auditing: a Boolean condition check, the SQL capture ability, a column-sensitivity feature, and an event handler. The first advantage allowed the auditing to occur only when a specific condition was met. That is, at execution time, the audit policy would test a Boolean condition. If the condition was met, then and only then would the audit occur.

This has enormous advantages. It's very flexible because the Boolean conditions can be anything specified in SQL, including a comparison of the results of function calls. Another advantage is that the conditional auditing helps to eliminate unnecessary audits.

In standard auditing, you could audit anytime someone queried a table. However, you couldn't specify any exemptions to this based on specific conditions. Perhaps you are concerned with privacy issues, and you set up your access control to prevent users from seeing other users' records. In standard auditing, there is no inherent way to validate this policy is being accurately enforced. You could set up auditing for selects on your table. However, the problem is that the audit records would only indicate a user selected from the table and would not indicate whether they were able to access another user's records. You might be able to derive the result set of the query by looking at the SQL captured, but this would prove cumbersome and unreliable. Assuming users are supposed to access the table to see their records, auditing SELECT statements to meet this requirement is ineffective.

With FGA, you can complement the security policy by auditing only when a user is accessing someone else's records. The database allows you to specify a condition that when met will audit.

NOTE
You don't care why or how they circumvented our security policy; auditing is not prevention—it is detection.

Enabling FGA

Enabling FGA is completely different from enabling standard auditing. FGA doesn't rely on any initialization parameters. Instead, you control FGA via the DBMS_FGA package. Consider the following in which you want to audit SCOTT.EMP. Assume you want to audit only when a user is accessing another user's records. This is done by calling the ADD-POLICY procedure and specifying the condition as seen next. If you leave the condition NULL, then the audit will always occur. This is a new feature; in Oracle9*i* Database, to ensure auditing would always occur, you had to define a condition that was always true such as '1=1'.

```
sec_mgr@KNOX10g> BEGIN
    DBMS_FGA.add_policy
                 (object_schema      => 'SCOTT',
                  object_name        => 'EMP',
                  policy_name        => 'Example',
                  audit_condition    => 'ENAME != USER');
  END;
  /

PL/SQL procedure successfully completed.
```

To illustrate FGA at work, you can simply connect as SCOTT and issue queries. Before you do, it's a good practice to ensure the cost-based analyzer is being used (especially for Oracle9*i* Databases). Strange results from FGA can occur if you don't first issue an ANALYZE on the table. Prior to running this, the current audit records were deleted and the standard auditing on the EMP table was disabled:

```
scott@KNOX10g> ANALYZE TABLE emp COMPUTE STATISTICS;

Table analyzed.
```

```
scott@KNOX10g> SELECT sal, comm FROM emp
    WHERE ename = 'SCOTT';

       SAL       COMM
---------- ----------
      3000

scott@KNOX10g> SELECT sal, comm FROM emp
    WHERE deptno = 20;

       SAL       COMM
---------- ----------
       800
      2975
      3000
      1100
      3000
```

Going to the audit trail, you'll notice that only the second query was recorded. This is good because the first query was, by our security policy, an allowable query:

```
sec_mgr@KNOX10g> EXEC show_aud

PL/SQL procedure successfully completed.

sec_mgr@KNOX10g> EXEC show_aud
Who:   SCOTT
What:  SCOTT.EMP
Where: 192.168.0.100:SQLPLUS.EXE
When:  Mar-24 18:34
How:   SELECT sal, comm FROM emp
 WHERE deptno = 20
-------------- End of Record --------------
```

The condition capability of FGA allows you a higher degree of fidelity in the auditing. The trick to making this most effective is to implement the Boolean checks within a separate PL/SQL function. Allowing the complexity to reside inside an external program allows for simplicity in adding and validating the audit policy.

For example, you might want your audit policy to audit only on weekends and off hours. You can create a program that returns true (represented by the number 1) if it is currently outside of normal operating hours (Monday through Friday, 8 A.M.–6 P.M.).

```
sec_mgr@KNOX10g> CREATE OR REPLACE FUNCTION is_off_hours
      RETURN BINARY_INTEGER
    AS
      l_return_val  BINARY_INTEGER;
      l_day_number  VARCHAR2 (1)
                            := TO_CHAR (SYSDATE, 'D');
      l_hour        VARCHAR2 (2)
```

```
                      := TO_CHAR (SYSDATE, 'HH24');
BEGIN
  IF (    l_day_number IN ('1', '7')
      OR l_hour < 8
      OR l_hour > 18)
  THEN
    l_return_val := 1;
  ELSE
    l_return_val := 0;
  END IF;

  RETURN l_return_val;
END;
/

Function created.
```

You can simply update the current policy and add the function as the audit condition. To do this, first drop the policy, and then add it again:

```
sec_mgr@KNOX10g> BEGIN
  DBMS_FGA.drop_policy (object_schema     => 'SCOTT',
                        object_name       => 'EMP',
                        policy_name       => 'Example');
  DBMS_FGA.add_policy
    (object_schema      => 'SCOTT',
     object_name        => 'EMP',
     policy_name        => 'Example',
     audit_condition    => 'SEC_MGR.IS_OFF_HOURS = 1');
END;
/

PL/SQL procedure successfully completed.
```

The result is that your audit condition will then audit all selects on the EMP table after normal operating hours. You have time-sensitive auditing. Unfortunately, when you execute a query as SCOTT, it fails as follows:

```
scott@KNOX10g> select * from emp;
select * from emp
              *
ERROR at line 1:
ORA-28112: failed to execute policy function
```

SCOTT doesn't have execute privileges on the IS_OFF_HOURS function. To resolve this, grant execute on the function to SCOTT. Note that you specified the schema.function name when you registered the policy. This is also critical because the policy would fail to execute if the function couldn't be resolved by the invoking user. (This could provide a useful and additional tool to protecting your database tables.)

```
sec_mgr@KNOX10g> GRANT EXECUTE ON is_off_hours TO scott;

Grant succeeded.
```

The privilege to execute the audit event handler function is of significance mostly because this behavior isn't consistent with the policy functions used in Oracle's DBMS_RLS feature, which provides row-level security (discussed in detail in Chapter 10).

Column Sensitivity

A second advantage FGA introduced was the notion of column sensitivity. Assume now that users are allowed to access other users' records, just not the salary field within those records. In this case, your sensitive column is the SAL column. If the user's query doesn't touch this column, then you don't audit.

The actual auditing will occur when both the sensitive column(s) is queried and the Boolean condition is met. In the case that no condition is specified, the auditing will occur only when the sensitive column is queried or manipulated.

As an example, the previous audit policy can be modified to audit when users query other users' salaries. Therefore, you'll have to specify both a condition *and* a sensitivity column:

```
sec_mgr@KNOX10g> BEGIN
    DBMS_FGA.drop_policy (object_schema    => 'SCOTT',
                          object_name      => 'EMP',
                          policy_name      => 'Example');
    DBMS_FGA.add_policy
               (object_schema      => 'SCOTT',
                object_name        => 'EMP',
                policy_name        => 'Example',
                audit_condition    => 'ENAME != USER',
                audit_column       => 'SAL');
  END;
  /

PL/SQL procedure successfully completed.
```

Now, test the auditing by executing several queries. Again the current audit records were deleted prior to running the queries shown here. The comments indicate what should happen with respect to auditing:

```
scott@KNOX10g> -- Aggregate value on sensitive column causes audit
scott@KNOX10g> SELECT SUM (sal) FROM scott.emp;

  SUM(SAL)
----------
     29025

scott@KNOX10g> -- This will not audit since ename = user

scott@KNOX10g> SELECT sal FROM emp
    WHERE ename = 'SCOTT';
```

```
       SAL
----------
      3000

scott@KNOX10g> -- Direct query on column will audit
scott@KNOX10g> SELECT empno, job, sal
  2    FROM emp
  3   WHERE deptno = 10;

     EMPNO JOB              SAL
---------- --------- ----------
      7782 MANAGER         2450
      7839 PRESIDENT       5000
      7934 CLERK           1300

scott@KNOX10g> -- No Audit since SAL column is not queried
scott@KNOX10g> SELECT empno, job
  2    FROM emp
  3   WHERE deptno = 10;

     EMPNO JOB
---------- ---------
      7782 MANAGER
      7839 PRESIDENT
      7934 CLERK

scott@KNOX10g> -- No audit since no records are returned
scott@KNOX10g> SELECT ename FROM emp
  2   WHERE ename = 'KNOX';

no rows selected
```

Viewing the audit records, you see that the first two queries were audited as expected:

```
sec_mgr@KNOX10g> EXEC show_aud

PL/SQL procedure successfully completed.

sec_mgr@KNOX10g> EXEC show_aud
Who:   SCOTT
What:  SCOTT.EMP
Where: 192.168.0.100:SQLPLUS.EXE
When:  Mar-24 19:11
How:   SELECT SUM (sal) FROM scott.emp
-------------- End of Record --------------
Who:   SCOTT
What:  SCOTT.EMP
Where: 192.168.0.100:SQLPLUS.EXE
When:  Mar-24 19:11
How:   SELECT empno, job, sal
```

```
  FROM emp
 WHERE deptno = 10
------------- End of Record -------------

PL/SQL procedure successfully completed.
```

The value provided by the SQL capture shows that the first query really wasn't harmful. There was no direct way for the user to determine the employee's salary.

The lack of audit on the last query verifies that your auditing is selective to your condition and column. There is an important and the often overlooked reason for this: *fine-grained audits occur only when at least one record is returned.* There is no "WHENEVER NOT SUCCESSFUL" in FGA. At first this might seem like a bad idea. After all, there is no way to capture the equivalent of someone banging on a locked door. Unlike standard auditing, a user's failed access doesn't create an FGA audit record. However, this fact is very desirable when you consider that the audits only occur when something of interest has happened. In the preceding example, if there is a record in the audit trail, then the user did access another user's salary.

Capturing SQL

The third jewel brought by FGA was the introduction of a concept called SQL capture. This concept has been extended to standard auditing in Oracle Database 10*g* when you have the AUDIT_TRAIL set to DB_EXTENEDED as was seen in the previous examples. It includes capturing the SQL text as well as the values for any bind variables.

The SQL capture capability is enormous in auditing. It clearly shows what statement caused the audit record to be written. That has an important translation to the real world. First, the queries often indicate the user's intentions. If the query ends with "where ename = 'KING'" then you know the user was targeting KING's records.

The audited SQL can help the security administrator better conclude the actual method the user used when the audit was triggered. Ad hoc queries tend to look much different than packaged application queries, which in turn look different than queries issued by database tools. Administrators can sometimes identify the source by simply looking at the SQL construction.

This is also an invaluable tool because FGA and standard auditing can be used to validate that applications are issuing proper queries. Many times a user's access, while originally believed to be malicious, may in fact have occurred because of a poorly written application. The SQL can show that the user's query was written by the application. Therefore, the user either compromised the application, or the application has a bug. Either way, the audit has provided some very useful and practical information.

A caveat to the SQL capture is that it doesn't capture the modified SQL that results from an applied Virtual Private Database policy.

Acting on the Audit

FGA adds the ability to invoke an event handler. In standard auditing, the records were written as they occurred, but there is no guarantee that they will be viewed and acted upon in a timely fashion. It's possible that the DBA leaves at 6:00 P.M. Friday night. A hacker begins to poke around the system ten minutes later. Finally, on Sunday afternoon, the hacker has gathered enough information to do something destructive. The audit records were being written. Unfortunately, no one was around to hear the screams coming from the database. This is like having a burglar alarm that no one hears. The DBA returns Monday to a compromised database.

It would have been nice if the DBA could have been alerted that something was happening while that something was happening.

With FGA, you do have the ability to invoke an event handler. In this manner, you can see FGA as analogous to a SELECT trigger. The event handler can do anything you like because you write the code.

One thing the event handler shouldn't do is to write (redundant) audit data to a private audit table. I've seen this countless times as people fail to realize that the audit data is already being written. A variation of the theme is a good idea: you may find it useful to write the audit data to another database or to the file system in hopes of protecting the data from a malicious and privileged database administrator.

Writing the Event Handler

The event handler that is used in FGA accepts three parameters: the schema of the object being audited, the name of the object being audited, and the name of the auditing policy. Within the procedure, you can easily access the SQL that caused the auditing to occur. This is obtained by referencing the USERENV context called CURRENT_SQL.

To illustrate an implementation, the following example shows an event handler that sends an e-mail alerting the receiver of the audit. In the e-mail, the details of the audit record are given. The trick is that you don't have to query the audit logs to get the SQL that caused the audit to occur.

```
sec_mgr@KNOX10g> CREATE OR REPLACE PROCEDURE fga_notify (
     object_schema  VARCHAR2,
     object_name    VARCHAR2,
     policy_name    VARCHAR2)
   AS
     l_message    VARCHAR2 (32767);
     l_mailhost   VARCHAR2 (30)
                     := '<your smtp server>';
     l_mail_conn  UTL_SMTP.connection;
     l_from       VARCHAR2 (30)
                           := 'FGA_ADMIN@<your email domain>';
     l_to         VARCHAR2 (30)
                         := '<administrator email address>';
   BEGIN
     l_message :=
          'User '
       || USER
       || ' successfully accessed '
       || object_schema
       || '.'
       || object_name
       || ' at '
       || TO_CHAR (SYSDATE, 'Month DD HH24:MI:SS')
       || ' with this statement:  "'
       || SYS_CONTEXT ('userenv', 'current_sql')
       || '"';
     l_mail_conn :=
            UTL_SMTP.open_connection (l_mailhost, 25);
```

```
   UTL_SMTP.helo (l_mail_conn, l_mailhost);
   UTL_SMTP.mail (l_mail_conn, l_from);
   UTL_SMTP.rcpt (l_mail_conn, l_to);
   UTL_SMTP.DATA (l_mail_conn,
                     UTL_TCP.crlf
                  || 'Subject: FGA Alert'
                  || UTL_TCP.crlf
                  || 'To: '
                  || l_to
                  || UTL_TCP.crlf
                  || l_message);
   UTL_SMTP.quit (l_mail_conn);
 EXCEPTION
   WHEN OTHERS
   THEN
     UTL_SMTP.quit (l_mail_conn);
     raise_application_error
         (-20000,
             'Failed due to the following error: '
          || SQLERRM);
 END;
 /

Procedure created.
```

Now register this as the event handler for our FGA policy:

```
sec_mgr@KNOX10g> BEGIN
   DBMS_FGA.drop_policy (object_schema    => 'SCOTT',
                         object_name      => 'EMP',
                         policy_name      => 'Example');
   DBMS_FGA.add_policy
              (object_schema      => 'SCOTT',
               object_name        => 'EMP',
               policy_name        => 'Example',
               audit_condition    => 'ENAME != USER',
               audit_column       => 'SAL',
               handler_schema     => 'SEC_MGR',
               handler_module     => 'FGA_NOTIFY');
 END;
 /

PL/SQL procedure successfully completed.
```

As seen in Figure 8-2, when a user queries another user's salary, an e-mail is sent to notify the DBA that this has happened. The DBA should then be able to react to the situation and handle it accordingly. The alerting capability is a critical element to helping administrators respond to incidents as they occur.

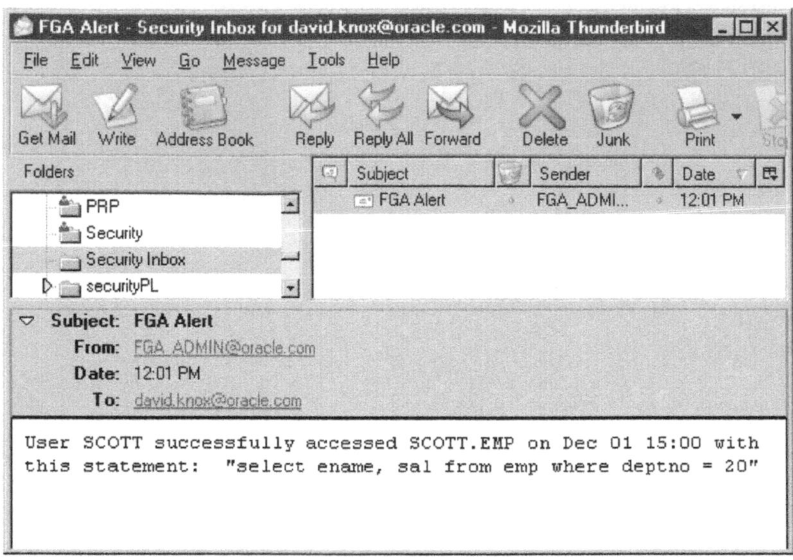

FIGURE 8-2. *Alerts can be sent to administrators to notify them of event occurrences as they happen.*

Invalid Event Handler in Oracle9*i* Database

In Oracle9*i* Database, there is an interesting occurrence that can be witnessed if the event handler throws an exception or is invalid. The database returns a result set that is the opposite of the condition specified. For example, if the condition is "ENAME != USER" meaning you want to audit when a user is accessing another user's records, the database will only return records where "ENAME = USER".

This is known as *failsafe*. The thinking is that the event handler must be doing something critical. Because the event handler can't perform its function, the database will eliminate any potentially harmful records. It does this by reversing the condition.

In Oracle9*i* Database, this was a way to create a column-sensitive, row-level security capability. The following output shows what happens when you apply the same audit policy in an Oracle9*i* Database but have an invalid event handler:

```
system@ORA92> BEGIN
    DBMS_FGA.add_policy
             (object_schema      => 'SCOTT',
              object_name        => 'EMP',
              policy_name        => 'Example',
              audit_condition    => 'ENAME != USER',
              audit_column       => 'SAL',
              handler_schema     => 'NO_SCHEMA',
              handler_module     => 'UNDEFINED');
```

```
END;
/

PL/SQL procedure successfully completed.

system@ORA92> CONN scott/tiger
Connected.
scott@ORA92> SELECT COUNT (ename) FROM emp;

COUNT(ENAME)
------------
          14

scott@ORA92> SELECT ename, sal FROM emp;

ENAME             SAL
---------- ----------
SCOTT            3000
```

You see that the user can access all records when the SAL column (your column-sensitive attribute) is not queried. Once the audit condition and column are specified, the database tries to invoke the event handler. There is no schema in the database or a procedure as defined by the policy. A trace file is generated indicating the error and the database reverses the condition from "ENAME != USER" to "ENAME = USER". Consequently, the user gets only their record.

In Oracle Database 10*g*, there is native support for column-sensitive, row-level security. As such, the behavior in Oracle Database 10*g* is different. The queries aren't modified with the inverse condition. That is, the queries execute as if no event handler were registered, and all rows are returned even when the SAL column is selected.

Caveats

While FGA is powerful, there are some challenges. First, problems with the event handler may not be obvious when the policy is established. In Oracle9*i* Database, the database reversed the condition in the FGA policy. The results might act as a clue that something has gone awry with your event handler. In Oracle Database 10*g*, there is no clue. The event handler is simply not called.

Recall the feature described earlier that prevents users from executing DML if the function in the FGA policy condition can't be resolved or executed. This can be both helpful and hurtful. Assuming that you don't want this to occur, it may be difficult to detect this ahead of time and difficult to rectify it afterwards.

While the audit provides a wealth of information, it doesn't tell you what the user received as a result from the query. You only know that they got at least one record. This leads to another caveat—audits don't occur when no records are returned. This can be good and bad. It's good for indicating that something bad happened, but it's bad in that there is no indication that someone is banging on a locked door. You can, however, combine standard auditing with FGA to accomplish this task.

Summary

Auditing is a complementary part of the security process. Prevention and access control will always be important in security. However, auditing should not be overlooked. Providing the detection and response capabilities can be equally, if not more, important. Auditing effectively is critical to ensuring that performance and the value received from the auditing are congruent.

Oracle standard and fine-grained auditing (FGA) provide a powerful and secure way to ensure user accountability. Standard auditing allows for auditing to occur in many different ways to meet many different requirements. FGA augments this and allows for a higher fidelity in auditing, which reduces the number of extraneous audit records. The event handler can be used to do many powerful things. The auditing acts as both the detection and response system for the database. Similar to motion detectors that are wired to notify the police, the event handlers in FGA can be used to alert administrators of serious incidents the instant that they occur. Instant notification is essential to guarding the data.

Database auditing provides high auditing assurance because the auditing process can't be circumvented or bypassed. The auditing is consistent regardless of application, query, user, and protocols being used to access the data. When done correctly, the auditing can provide valuable information about the users and their interactions with the database. Of most value may be the fact that you do not have to program the auditing. Oracle has already done this for you.

PART IV

Fine-Grained Access Control

CHAPTER 9

Application Contexts for Security and Performance

This chapter looks at a technology that helps you to efficiently implement database security. The technology—called *application context*—was built to increase the performance of fine-grained access control (FGAC) implementations. The material presented here will provide the foundation for using application context as part of your security implementations. The examples are designed to be simple to allow you to focus on how the application context technology can be used.

For the discussions in this chapter, application context will be categorized into the following four different types:

- **Default** The USERENV namespace in which the database populates with environmental data about the user's session
- **Local** The private, application-defined attributes that generally hold user specific data
- **Global** The sharable attributes, accessible by different database sessions, typically used in connection pool implementations
- **External** The private values populated by an external source, such as the Oracle Internet Directory

An application context can be used for many purposes, but their original mission was to support intra-object security (fine-grained access) implementations. The application context capability was created to enhance the performance of Virtual Private Database policies, discussed in Chapter 10.

Application Context

An application context is a set of name-value pairs, held in memory, which can be defined, set, and retrieved by users and applications. Related values can be grouped together. The group is collectively defined and accessed by its name or namespace. Within the namespace, the individual attributes and their associated values are stored in memory and retrieved by calling a PL/SQL function call. By storing the values in either shared or private memory, depending on the context, the access to the values will be very fast.

Typically, application contexts hold several attributes, such as an application or user name, organization, role, and title. Your security policies may reference these attributes in controlling user access. Storing the values in memory saves the time and resources that would be required to repetitively query data tables to retrieve this information. Consequently, you'll often see the application context descriptions in security documentation; however, there is no requirement to use security with an application context or to use an application context with a security implementation.

NOTE
Application context descriptions are often found in security documentation. It's not a requirement to use an application context with a security implementation or to use security with an application context.

Default USERENV Context

The Oracle Database provides a default application context for each database session. It has the namespace of "USERENV". Most of the attributes in USERENV are predefined by the database. This namespace is the replacement for the USERENV function provided in earlier versions of the Oracle Database.

As you have seen by the countless USERENV context examples used in this book, there are many useful USERENV attributes that help provide information about the user's environment. The USERENV attributes give many important details about the database session, such as the client's IP Address, the session identifier, the name of the proxy user if using proxy authentication, the protocol used to connect to the database, and even how the user authenticated. For a complete listing, see the *Oracle Database Security Guide 10g*.

Many of the USERENV attributes are instrumental in enforcing specific database security policies. For example, the user's IP address and authentication mode are available and can be used to govern what a user has access to. The Client Identifier, also an attribute of the default context, can be set by an application and is the only application context value that is audited.

All of the application context attributes are referenced via the SYS_CONTEXT function. The SYS_CONTEXT function takes the namespace as the first parameter and the attribute name as the second parameter and returns the value of the associated attribute. It also takes an optional length value as a third parameter, which truncates the returned value to the number provided.

A useful technique for displaying the attributes you'll use most often is to create a view consisting of the results of the SYS_CONTEXT function. This requires less typing when checking multiple values, and a DESCRIBE conveniently lists all the attributes.

```
sec_mgr@KNOX10g> CREATE OR REPLACE VIEW env
AS
  SELECT SYS_CONTEXT ('userenv', 'session_user')
                                       session_user,
         SYS_CONTEXT ('userenv', 'current_user')
                                       CURRENT_USER,
         SYS_CONTEXT ('userenv', 'current_schema')
                                     current_schema,
         NVL (SYS_CONTEXT ('userenv',
                           'external_name'),
              'NULL') external_name,
         NVL (SYS_CONTEXT ('userenv',
                           'client_identifier'),
              'NULL') client_identifier,
         NVL (SYS_CONTEXT ('userenv',
                           'client_info'),
              'NULL') client_info,
         NVL (SYS_CONTEXT ('userenv',
                           'proxy_user'),
              'NULL') proxy_user,
         SYS_CONTEXT ('userenv',
                      'audited_cursorid')
                                   audited_cursorid,
         SYS_CONTEXT ('userenv', 'entryid')
                                           entryid,
```

```
           NVL (SYS_CONTEXT ('userenv', 'sessionid'),
                'NULL') sessionid,
           SYS_CONTEXT ('userenv', 'isdba') isdba,
           NVL (SYS_CONTEXT ('userenv',
                             'ip_address'),
                'NULL') ip_address,
           SYS_CONTEXT ('userenv', 'db_name')
                                              db_name,
           SYS_CONTEXT ('userenv', 'host') HOST,
           NVL (SYS_CONTEXT ('userenv',
                             'network_protocol'),
                'NULL') network_protocol,
           NVL (SYS_CONTEXT ('userenv',
                             'authentication_type'),
                'NULL') authentication_type,
           SYS_CONTEXT ('userenv', 'policy_invoker')
                                       policy_invoker,
           NVL (SYS_CONTEXT ('userenv',
                             'current_sql'),
                'NULL') current_sql
      FROM DUAL;

View created.

sec_mgr@KNOX10g> GRANT SELECT ON env TO PUBLIC;

Grant succeeded.

sec_mgr@KNOX10g> CREATE PUBLIC SYNONYM env FOR env;

Synonym created.
```

A DESCRIBE on the view also has the benefit of allowing you to see what attributes are available:

```
sec_mgr@KNOX10g> DESC env
 Name                                Null?    Type
 ----------------------------------- -------- -------------
 SESSION_USER                                 VARCHAR2(256)
 CURRENT_USER                                 VARCHAR2(256)
 CURRENT_SCHEMA                               VARCHAR2(256)
 EXTERNAL_NAME                                VARCHAR2(256)
 CLIENT_IDENTIFIER                            VARCHAR2(256)
 CLIENT_INFO                                  VARCHAR2(256)
 PROXY_USER                                   VARCHAR2(256)
 AUDITED_CURSORID                             VARCHAR2(256)
 ENTRYID                                      VARCHAR2(256)
 SESSIONID                                    VARCHAR2(256)
 ISDBA                                        VARCHAR2(256)
 IP_ADDRESS                                   VARCHAR2(256)
```

```
 DB_NAME                                   VARCHAR2(256)
 HOST                                      VARCHAR2(256)
 NETWORK_PROTOCOL                          VARCHAR2(256)
 AUTHENTICATION_TYPE                       VARCHAR2(256)
 POLICY_INVOKER                            VARCHAR2(256)
 CURRENT_SQL                               VARCHAR2(256)

sec_mgr@KNOX10g> COL session_user format a10
sec_mgr@KNOX10g> COL network_protocol format a10
sec_mgr@KNOX10g> COL authentication_type format a20
sec_mgr@KNOX10g> SELECT session_user, authentication_type, ip_address
  2    FROM env;

SESSION_US AUTHENTICATION_TYPE  IP_ADDRESS
---------- -------------------- ---------------
SEC_MGR    DATABASE             192.168.0.100
```

You should view the above attributes and the values they return on your database when connected through various applications. You'll see the USERENV application context provides useful information that can be used in implementing your security policies.

Local Context

Within the USERENV namespace, both the Client Identifier and Client Info attributes can be set by the user or application. Because it's not sufficient to capture all possible information in either or both of these, the database also supports the ability to define separate namespaces with additional attributes. These locally defined application contexts can then be used within any application for any reason.

While the values in the USERENV are automatically set by the database (except for the Client Identifier and Client Info values), the values in a local application context have to be set via a single PL/SQL program unit that is specified when you create the application context.

Creating an Application Context

To create an application context, the user needs the CREATE ANY CONTEXT system privilege. Issue the following SQL to create a context called "CTX_EX".

```
sec_mgr@KNOX10g> CREATE CONTEXT ctx_ex USING sec_mgr.ctx_ex_mgr;

Context created.
```

This creates an application context with a namespace of "CTX_EX". The only program authorized to set and clear values within this application context is the "trusted" program CTX_EX_MGR, which resides in the SEC_MGR schema. Other than calling it a trusted program, Oracle assigns no special name to the program that manages the values for an application context (CTX_EX_MGR, in the previous example). Because it's convenient to have a name, it'll be referred to as the "namespace manager."

Execute privileges on the CTX_EX_MGR program are required to set or clear—perform write operations on—the attributes in the CTX_EX namespace. However, reading the values is done through the publicly accessible SYS_CONTEXT function.

You probably don't want all database users to have the ability to invoke the namespace manager, so you shouldn't grant execute privileges to the namespace manager to PUBLIC. Restricting execute ability on the namespace manager provides an initial layer of security. Without the ability to manipulate the values, the values are considered secure.

A second layer of security comes from the implementation code itself. Often, the namespace manager performs the critical checks and validations *prior* to setting any values within the application context.

Setting Context Attributes and Values

The values in the application context are set by invoking the DBMS_SESSION.SET_CONTEXT procedure from within the namespace manager. Within an application context, you can create the name-value pairs relevant to your application(s). The most popular approach to exploiting application contexts is to store values that were derived as the result of a function, internal database query, or external query (for example, a query to an LDAP server). By executing the function or query once and storing the result in the application context, subsequent references by your database security implementations will be much faster than if they had to invoke a function or perform an internal or external query. This proves extremely valuable when the value is referenced in the SQL predicate or the where clause of a query. In this situation, the context values will be executed once for each row in the table—fast execution is critical to query performance.

To illustrate this, create a simple table that holds user information. Suppose you wish to restrict records for a user to those only within their organization or department. You'll use an application context to capture the user's department number. The department number value is set once, and then referenced many times. Each reference will use the context value, thus sparing a SQL query from looking up this information. You should also consider setting the value transparently via a logon trigger. First, create the data table to hold your lookup values:

```
sec_mgr@KNOX10g> CREATE TABLE lookup_dept
  2  AS SELECT ename username, deptno FROM emp;

Table created.
```

To set the values in the context, you have to implement a function, procedure, or package in the SEC_MGR schema that has the name of CTX_EX_MGR. Note you have to name the program CTX_EX_MGR because this was what you defined when you previously created the namespace. It's most common to use a PL/SQL package for managing an application context. The package generally contains all the related procedures and functions that are required to perform verification or validation about the user and set the specific attributes within the namespace.

For this example, only one procedure is required for setting the value. In instances where the values need to be reset or cleared, such as when reusing a shared database session within a connection pool, an additional procedure will also be created. It's good practice to provide one procedure to set and another procedure to clear individual attributes:

```
sec_mgr@KNOX10g> CREATE OR REPLACE PACKAGE ctx_ex_mgr
  2  AS
```

```
  PROCEDURE set_deptno;
  PROCEDURE clear_deptno;
END;
/

Package created.

sec_mgr@KNOX10g> CREATE OR REPLACE PACKAGE BODY ctx_ex_mgr
AS
-----------------------------------------
  PROCEDURE set_deptno
  AS
    l_deptno  NUMBER;
  BEGIN
    SELECT deptno
      INTO l_deptno
      FROM lookup_dept
     WHERE username =
             SYS_CONTEXT ('userenv',
                          'session_user');
    DBMS_SESSION.set_context
                        (namespace    => 'ctx_ex',
                         ATTRIBUTE    => 'deptno',
                         VALUE        => l_deptno);
  END set_deptno;

-----------------------------------------
  PROCEDURE clear_deptno
  AS
  BEGIN
    DBMS_SESSION.clear_context
                        (namespace    => 'ctx_ex',
                         ATTRIBUTE    => 'deptno');
  END clear_deptno;
-----------------------------------------
END ctx_ex_mgr;
/

Package body created.
```

CAUTION
The security for this example is based on the data stored in the LOOKUP_DEPT table. Guarding access and manipulation of this data is therefore critical.

To set an application context automatically, use a database logon trigger:

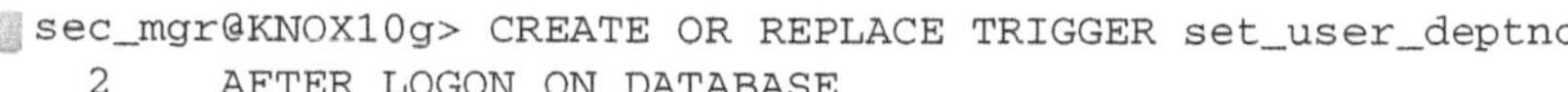

```
sec_mgr@KNOX10g> CREATE OR REPLACE TRIGGER set_user_deptno
  AFTER LOGON ON DATABASE
```

```
BEGIN
  sec_mgr.ctx_ex_mgr.set_deptno;
EXCEPTION
  WHEN NO_DATA_FOUND
  THEN
    -- If no data is found, user is not in the table
    -- so the value will not be set.
    -- If this exception is not handled, then some users
    -- may be unable to logon
    NULL;
END;
/

Trigger created.
```

Note that you do not have to grant execute privileges on the namespace manager for your users to be able to execute the program when it's called from a database logon trigger. The ability to execute the namespace manager comes from the definer rights model used by the logon trigger, which fires automatically after users have authenticated.

Testing the design by logging in as SCOTT, the value is automatically set and can be retrieved by querying the SYS_CONTEXT function:

```
C:\>sqlplus scott/tiger

SQL*Plus: Release 10.1.0.2.0 - Production on Thu Mar 25 13:24:29 2004

Copyright (c) 1982, 2004, Oracle.  All rights reserved.


Connected to:
Oracle Database 10g Enterprise Edition Release 10.1.0.2.0 - Production
With the Partitioning, Oracle Label Security, OLAP and Data Mining
options

scott@KNOX10g> COL deptno format a10
scott@KNOX10g> SELECT SYS_CONTEXT ('ctx_ex', 'deptno') deptno
    FROM DUAL;

DEPTNO
----------
20
```

NOTE
The namespaces and attribute values are case-insensitive. Setting or referencing these can be done in either upper- or lowercase. The names given to the namespaces, however, have to be unique across the database.

Applying the Application Context to Security

You can now use this application context to implement your database security policies. You'll see plenty more examples of how to use application contexts for security within views and for Virtual Private Database (VPD) in Chapters 10 and 11. For a quick example, consider a view that restricts users' queries to records within the department in which they work. Using the application context, create a view that implements this record level security (also known as fine-grained access) with the following:

```
scott@KNOX10g> CREATE OR REPLACE VIEW my_dept_ctx
  AS
    SELECT *
      FROM emp
     WHERE deptno = SYS_CONTEXT ('ctx_ex', 'deptno');

View created.

scott@KNOX10g> -- View restricts records based on value of
scott@KNOX10g> -- application context
scott@KNOX10g> SELECT ename, deptno FROM my_dept_ctx;

ENAME          DEPTNO
---------- ----------
SMITH              20
JONES              20
SCOTT              20
ADAMS              20
FORD               20
```

A different example shows how you might employ the context to do trigger-based security. Say you wish to create a trigger that prevents users from modifying data outside their department. You should consider using the application context for this implementation because the trigger will execute for each row and consequently needs to perform very quickly. The following example illustrates this point:

```
scott@KNOX10g> -- Create a trigger which prevents a user from
scott@KNOX10g> -- modifying data outside their department
scott@KNOX10g> CREATE OR REPLACE TRIGGER restrict_updates
    BEFORE DELETE OR UPDATE
    ON emp
    FOR EACH ROW
  BEGIN
    IF (:OLD.deptno !=
                    SYS_CONTEXT ('ctx_ex', 'deptno'))
    THEN
      raise_application_error
        (-20001,
            CHR (10)
         || '**  You can only update records within your department.'
         || CHR (10)
```

```
             || '**  Your department number is '
             || SYS_CONTEXT ('ctx_ex', 'deptno'));
      END IF;
    END;
    /

Trigger created.
```

Issuing an unqualified update or delete validates the trigger is working:

```
scott@KNOX10g> UPDATE emp
         SET ename = ename
       WHERE deptno = 10;
UPDATE emp
       *
ERROR at line 1:
ORA-20001:
**  You can only update records within your department.
**  Your department number is 20
ORA-06512: at "SCOTT.RESTRICT_UPDATES", line 5
ORA-04088: error during execution of trigger 'SCOTT.RESTRICT_UPDATES'


scott@KNOX10g> DELETE FROM emp;
DELETE FROM emp
            *
ERROR at line 1:
ORA-20001:
**  You can only update records within your department.
**  Your department number is 20
ORA-06512: at "SCOTT.RESTRICT_UPDATES", line 5
ORA-04088: error during execution of trigger 'SCOTT.RESTRICT_UPDATES'
```

You may want to check how this implementation compares with a SQL-based alternative. To illustrate this, you can time how long it takes to issue updates on the table. Each update causes the trigger to fire. You can run two tests—one using the application context and another querying the department number from within the trigger itself:

```
scott@KNOX10g> SET timing on
scott@KNOX10g> -- Issue authorized updates.
scott@KNOX10g> -- Each update will cause trigger to fire
scott@KNOX10g> BEGIN
      FOR i IN 1 .. 100000
      LOOP
        UPDATE emp
           SET ename = ename
         WHERE deptno = 20;
      END LOOP;
    END;
    /
```

```
PL/SQL procedure successfully completed.

Elapsed: 00:00:41.18
```

It took 41 seconds using the application context implementation. Changing the trigger code implementation, you have to fetch the department number from the lookup table. The trigger is based on the value returned from this table:

```
scott@KNOX10g> set timing off
scott@KNOX10g> -- Modify trigger to use select instead of context
scott@KNOX10g> CREATE OR REPLACE TRIGGER restrict_updates
    BEFORE DELETE OR UPDATE
    ON emp
    FOR EACH ROW
  DECLARE
    l_deptno  NUMBER;
  BEGIN
    SELECT deptno
      INTO l_deptno
      FROM lookup_dept
     WHERE ename = USER;

    IF (:OLD.deptno != l_deptno)
    THEN
      raise_application_error
        (-20001,
            CHR (10)
         || '**  You can only update records within your department.'
         || CHR (10)
         || '**  Your department number is '
         || l_deptno);
    END IF;
  END;
  /

Trigger created.

scott@KNOX10g> SET timing on
scott@KNOX10g> -- Time new trigger implementation based on SQL query
scott@KNOX10g> BEGIN
    FOR i IN 1 .. 100000
    LOOP
      UPDATE emp
         SET ename = ename
       WHERE deptno = 20;
    END LOOP;
  END;
  /

PL/SQL procedure successfully completed.

Elapsed: 00:01:01.58
```

The performance increase you see from using an application context is directly proportional to the amount of time you save from not having to fetch the value from a query. In the previous example, querying the table to get a user's department number is not overwhelmingly time consuming. In real applications, the queries typically perform several joins and take more time to execute. It's in these cases that application contexts provide the most benefit.

Secure Use

An important point to using the locally defined application context is that the values are private to the user's session. The values are stored in the database session's User Global Area (UGA). The values can't be viewed by the DBA or anyone else. This allows you to set very sensitive information in the context with the assurance that the values will not be recovered by anyone other than the session user.

The corollary to this is that anytime you're sharing a database session among different users, when using a connection pool for example, then you are responsible for clearing the application context between users. You can use the CLEAR_CONTEXT procedure to clear individual values as is shown in the CTX_EX_MGR, or you can clear all application contexts for the session by invoking DBMS_SESSION.CLEAR_ALL_CONTEXT.

Common Mistakes

While there is tremendous flexibility in using an application context, they can be a little difficult to debug. The following represent some of the popular mistakes encountered by people new to developing applications that use an application context.

Incorrect Namespace or Attribute

Debugging code that references application context values can be frustrating if the program has misspelled either the namespace or the attribute. *Referencing a context namespace that doesn't exist or a value that doesn't exist within a namespace* does not *cause an error—it simply returns a null value.* This is in contrast to accessing an undefined attribute in the USERENV namespace. In this case, the database does throw an error:

```
sec_mgr@KNOX10g> -- Database errors with undefined attribute
sec_mgr@KNOX10g> SELECT SYS_CONTEXT ('userenv', 'foo') FROM DUAL;
SELECT SYS_CONTEXT ('userenv', 'foo') FROM DUAL
                                  *
ERROR at line 1:
ORA-02003: invalid USERENV parameter


sec_mgr@KNOX10g> -- No errors for user's undefined attribute
sec_mgr@KNOX10g> SELECT SYS_CONTEXT ('ctx_ex', 'dptno') FROM DUAL;

SYS_CONTEXT('CTX_EX','DPTNO')
-----------------------------------------------------------------

sec_mgr@KNOX10g>
```

Good coding practices can resolve this. For example, using package variable constants for the attribute names in the namespace manager is one good solution to this problem:

```
sec_mgr@KNOX10g> CREATE OR REPLACE PACKAGE ctx_ex_mgr
AS
  namespace   CONSTANT VARCHAR2 (6) := 'CTX_EX';
  deptno      CONSTANT VARCHAR2 (6) := 'DEPTNO';
  PROCEDURE set_deptno;
  PROCEDURE clear_deptno;
END;
/

Package created.

sec_mgr@KNOX10g> CREATE OR REPLACE PACKAGE BODY ctx_ex_mgr
AS
-----------------------------------------
  PROCEDURE set_deptno
  AS
    v_deptno  NUMBER;
    BEGIN
      SELECT deptno
        INTO v_deptno
        FROM lookup_dept
       WHERE username =
               SYS_CONTEXT ('userenv',
                            'session_user');
      DBMS_SESSION.set_context
               (namespace    => ctx_ex_mgr.namespace,
                ATTRIBUTE    => ctx_ex_mgr.deptno,
                VALUE        => v_deptno);
  END set_deptno;
-----------------------------------------
  PROCEDURE clear_deptno
  AS
  BEGIN
    DBMS_SESSION.clear_context
               (namespace    => ctx_ex_mgr.namespace,
                ATTRIBUTE    => ctx_ex_mgr.deptno);
  END clear_deptno;
-----------------------------------------
END ctx_ex_mgr;
/

Package body created.
```

Incorrect Namespace Manager

Another frequent mistake occurs when misnaming or having an inconsistency with the namespace manager, that is, between the program defined to implement the context and the one you think is implementing the context. The context creation DDL defines what the program is. During compilation of the non-namespace manager program, the database doesn't (and can't) tell you that you're trying to set a context namespace that isn't registered for the program. Upon execution, the error message indicates "insufficient privileges," which isn't particularly helpful.

In this example, the namespace manager is set to be the CTX_MGR program. Since the program isn't qualified with a schema name, the database assumes the current user's schema (SYSTEM in this example):

```
system@KNOX10g> CREATE CONTEXT ctx_ex USING ctx_mgr;

Context created.
```

Implementing the CTX_MGR in a different schema or using a program with a name other than CTX_MGR will cause an error. Notice a correctly named program in the SEC_MGR schema compiles, but fails to execute:

```
system@KNOX10g> CONN sec_mgr/oracle10g
Connected.
sec_mgr@KNOX10g> -- Oops, this is in the wrong schema
sec_mgr@KNOX10g> CREATE OR REPLACE PROCEDURE ctx_mgr
  2  AS
  3  BEGIN
  4    DBMS_SESSION.set_context
  5                     (namespace     => 'CTX_EX',
  6                      ATTRIBUTE     => 'favorite_color',
  7                      VALUE         => 'blue');
  8  END;
  9  /

Procedure created.

sec_mgr@KNOX10g> -- No compile errors, so assume everything is fine
sec_mgr@KNOX10g> EXEC ctx_mgr;
BEGIN ctx_mgr; END;

*
ERROR at line 1:
ORA-01031: insufficient privileges
ORA-06512: at "SYS.DBMS_SESSION", line 82
ORA-06512: at "SEC_MGR.CTX_MGR", line 4
ORA-06512: at line 1
```

It's only upon checking the DBA_CONTEXT view that you see the mistake.

```
sec_mgr@KNOX10g> COL schema format a15
sec_mgr@KNOX10g> SELECT SCHEMA, PACKAGE, TYPE
  2    FROM dba_context
  3   WHERE namespace = 'CTX_EX';

SCHEMA          PACKAGE                        TYPE
--------------- ------------------------------ ----------------------
SYSTEM          CTX_MGR                        ACCESSED LOCALLY
```

Global Context

With Oracle9*i* Database, the application context capability was augmented with the introduction of global contexts. As the name implies, these values are accessible by separate sessions and separate users. Unlike the local contexts, which are stored in the user's private memory space (the UGA), the global contexts are stored in the shared memory area, also known as the SGA.

Uses

Global application context can be used when you want to share values across database sessions, as may be the case in connection pool applications. Note that this implies the values are not user specific or private data. With a global application context, a value can be set once, and each session of the connection pool will have access to the value. If you were to try this with local application contexts, there would have to be a context set in each session. Thus, the global context saves memory on the server machine and is easier to use because you only have to initialize it once.

Another popular application is to use the global context to pass state information about a user that is transitioning between two applications, such as from Oracle Forms to Oracle Reports. The gist is that global application contexts are a great way to pass information between database sessions. A few of the following examples also illuminate some of the possibilities available when using global contexts.

From a security perspective, you may or may not opt to use global contexts. As the name implies, the values are shared. Often the attributes that are set are session specific and sensitive. As such, local application contexts should be used. In this spirit of completeness, the various ways in which global contexts can be set and secured will be covered.

Examples

The global context example presented here is based on a homeland security scenario. In this there is the concept of a threat level. The *threat level* is a global value to which our applications will reference when determining access to data. When the value is set to normal, users can access all the data. When the threat level is elevated, the applications tighten their security. You'll create the global context first and then see how you can use it in a security implementation.

To begin, the syntax for creating the context differs from local application contexts. There are several different uses of a global context, as you will see. As the values for the global context are stored in the SGA, the database provides a way to monitor how much SGA a user session is utilizing. Querying the USERENV for the global_context_memory provides this information:

```
SELECT SYS_CONTEXT ('userenv', 'global_context_memory')
  FROM DUAL;
```

To create a global context, add the "accessed globally" to the end of the create context DDL statement:

```
sec_mgr@KNOX10g> -- Create a global context indicating current
sec_mgr@KNOX10g> -- threat level
sec_mgr@KNOX10g> CREATE CONTEXT global_threat_ctx
  2    USING sec_mgr.global_ctx_mgr ACCESSED GLOBALLY;

Context created.
```

The DBMS_SESSION.SET_CONTEXT procedure accepts five parameters. By varying the values passed, you vary how the resulting context can be used. The procedure specification is as follows:

```
PROCEDURE SET_CONTEXT
 Argument Name                  Type                    In/Out Default?
 ------------------------------ ----------------------- ------ --------
 NAMESPACE                      VARCHAR2                IN
 ATTRIBUTE                      VARCHAR2                IN
 VALUE                          VARCHAR2                IN
 USERNAME                       VARCHAR2                IN     DEFAULT
 CLIENT_ID                      VARCHAR2                IN     DEFAULT
```

The USERNAME and CLIENT_ID parameters are DEFAULT, which means you don't have to pass a value for those parameters.

Values Shared for All Users

The global examples begin with the requirement of sharing a value for all sessions and all users in the database. Start by specifying only the first three parameters of the SET_CONTEXT procedure, which allows the least restrictive use of the context. Any user in the database will be able to access the values. The namespace manager will have two procedures: one for setting the attribute and another that clears all attributes in the namespace:

```
sec_mgr@KNOX10g> CREATE OR REPLACE PACKAGE global_ctx_mgr
  AS
    PROCEDURE set_level (p_threat_level IN VARCHAR2);
    PROCEDURE clear;
  END;
  /

Package created.

sec_mgr@KNOX10g> CREATE OR REPLACE PACKAGE BODY global_ctx_mgr
  AS
    PROCEDURE set_level (p_threat_level IN VARCHAR2)
    AS
    BEGIN
      DBMS_SESSION.set_context
                 (namespace    => 'global_threat_ctx',
                  ATTRIBUTE    => 'threat_level',
                  VALUE        => p_threat_level);
    END;

    PROCEDURE clear
    AS
    BEGIN
      DBMS_SESSION.clear_all_context
                                  ('global_threat_ctx');
    END;
```

```
END;
/

Package body created.
```

Execute the procedure that sets the context and then verify the value:

```
sec_mgr@KNOX10g> EXEC global_ctx_mgr.set_level ('normal');

PL/SQL procedure successfully completed.

sec_mgr@KNOX10g> COL threat_level format a25

sec_mgr@KNOX10g> SELECT SYS_CONTEXT ('global_threat_ctx',
                          'threat_level') threat_level
    FROM DUAL;

THREAT_LEVEL
-------------------------
normal
```

If you're executing this example and you get NULL instead of the output above, your Client Identifier has been set. This is a new use of the Client Identifier. With global application contexts, the session's Client Identifier drives what values are returned from the SYS_CONTEXT function. Refer to the upcoming examples for more information. To clear your Client Identifier, execute the CLEAR_IDENTIFIER procedure in the DBMS_SESSION package:

```
EXEC dbms_session.clear_identifier;
```

There are many uses for global application context. In this example, the global context will be used as the global indicator for the applications. Suppose you're tracking assets for the U.S. Navy. (It really doesn't matter what the data is for this example.) This simple table lists the assets and their status:

```
sec_mgr@KNOX10g> CREATE TABLE asset$
  (
    itemid           VARCHAR2(30),
    item             VARCHAR2(255),
    status           VARCHAR2(16)
  );

Table created.

sec_mgr@KNOX10g> INSERT INTO asset$
                 (itemid, item, status)
          VALUES ('AC1234516',
                  'USS John F. Kennedy  (CV 67) ',
                  'c-1');

1 row created.
```

```
sec_mgr@KNOX10g> COMMIT ;

Commit complete.
```

This example requires only a single record. Our security implementation is based on a view. The view uses the value of the global context to determine whether the records should be returned. If the value is normal, then all records are returned; otherwise, no records are returned. If you don't understand the logic in this view, don't worry; see Chapter 10 for more details on how views can be used to provide data security.

```
sec_mgr@KNOX10g> -- Create a view based on value of context.
sec_mgr@KNOX10g> -- Show all records when value is normal,
sec_mgr@KNOX10g> -- show no records when value is elevated or undefined
sec_mgr@KNOX10g> CREATE OR REPLACE VIEW assets
  2  AS
  3    SELECT itemid, item, status
  4      FROM asset$
  5     WHERE 1 = decode(SYS_CONTEXT ('global_threat_ctx',
  6                        'threat_level'), 'normal',1,'elevated',0,0);

View created.

sec_mgr@KNOX10g> GRANT SELECT ON assets TO scott;

Grant succeeded.
```

To test this policy, first query the view and then change to the SCOTT schema and query the view, which shows the results are consistent:

```
sec_mgr@KNOX10g> -- test View
sec_mgr@KNOX10g> EXEC global_ctx_mgr.set_level ('normal');

PL/SQL procedure successfully completed.

sec_mgr@KNOX10g> COL item format a30
sec_mgr@KNOX10g> COL status format a6
sec_mgr@KNOX10g> SELECT item, status FROM assets;

ITEM                           STATUS
------------------------------ ------
USS John F. Kennedy  (CV 67)   c-1

sec_mgr@KNOX10g> -- value exists for SCOTT too
sec_mgr@KNOX10g> CONN scott/tiger
Connected.
scott@KNOX10g> CREATE SYNONYM assets FOR sec_mgr.assets;

Synonym created.

scott@KNOX10g> SELECT item, status FROM assets;
```

```
ITEM                           STATUS
------------------------------ ------
USS John F. Kennedy  (CV 67)   c-1
```

You can set the value to elevated and verify the security policy is implemented correctly. Note, you don't have to clear the context value first.

```
scott@KNOX10g> CONN sec_mgr/oracle10g
Connected.
sec_mgr@KNOX10g> -- Change in value changes result set
sec_mgr@KNOX10g> EXEC global_ctx_mgr.set_level ('elevated');

PL/SQL procedure successfully completed.

sec_mgr@KNOX10g> -- Will not get any records since value is "elevated"
sec_mgr@KNOX10g> SELECT count(*) FROM assets;

  COUNT(*)
----------
         0

sec_mgr@KNOX10g> CONN scott/tiger
Connected.
scott@KNOX10g> SELECT count(*) FROM assets;

  COUNT(*)
----------
         0
```

Values Shared for All Sessions of Same Schema

In the next example, the username parameter is passed to the SET_CONTEXT procedure. The desired effect is to make the attribute value sharable across all sessions for the same schema. Note the same schema will be used for different end users for both connection pool applications (not using proxy authentication) and for the shared schema implementation of directory authenticated Enterprise Users.

This is a different definition of global: it is global but only for a schema. If you are not part of the schema, you cannot access the value or you get a different value.

```
sec_mgr@KNOX10g> CREATE OR REPLACE PACKAGE global_ctx_mgr
AS
  PROCEDURE set_level (
    p_threat_level  IN  VARCHAR2,
    p_user          IN  VARCHAR2);

  PROCEDURE clear;
END;
/

Package created.
```

```
sec_mgr@KNOX10g> CREATE OR REPLACE PACKAGE BODY global_ctx_mgr
AS
  PROCEDURE set_level (
    p_threat_level  IN  VARCHAR2,
    p_user          IN  VARCHAR2)
  AS
  BEGIN
    DBMS_SESSION.set_context
                (namespace    => 'global_threat_ctx',
                 ATTRIBUTE    => 'threat_level',
                 VALUE        => p_threat_level,
                 username     => p_user);
  END;

  PROCEDURE clear
  AS
  BEGIN
    DBMS_SESSION.clear_all_context
                              ('global_threat_ctx');
  END;
END;
/

Package body created.

sec_mgr@KNOX10g> EXEC global_ctx_mgr.set_level ('normal', 'SEC_MGR');

PL/SQL procedure successfully completed.

sec_mgr@KNOX10g> SELECT item, status FROM assets;

ITEM                           STATUS
------------------------------ ------
USS John F. Kennedy  (CV 67)   c-1

sec_mgr@KNOX10g> -- SCOTT no longer has a value for this
sec_mgr@KNOX10g> CONN scott/tiger
Connected.
scott@KNOX10g> SELECT item, status FROM assets;

no rows selected
```

The security is now more obvious. The global context values are only visible to a specific schema. Because all sessions of the schema will see the value, this is an ideal design for connection pools and shared schemas for directory authenticated users.

Note that you could have specified any username in the SET_CONTEXT call because there is no mechanism restricting the setting of values for users within global contexts. If the SEC_MGR set the value for SCOTT user, then the SEC_MGR could set it but would be unable to access it afterward.

```
scott@KNOX10g> CONN sec_mgr/oracle10g
Connected.
sec_mgr@KNOX10g> -- Set the value for SCOTT.
sec_mgr@KNOX10g> -- This "erases" the value that was stored for SEC_MGR
sec_mgr@KNOX10g> EXEC global_ctx_mgr.set_level ('normal', 'SCOTT');

PL/SQL procedure successfully completed.

sec_mgr@KNOX10g> SELECT item, status FROM assets;

no rows selected

sec_mgr@KNOX10g> -- SCOTT can see the value
sec_mgr@KNOX10g> CONN scott/tiger
Connected.
scott@KNOX10g> SELECT item, status FROM assets;

ITEM                           STATUS
------------------------------ ------
USS John F. Kennedy  (CV 67)   c-1
```

The lesson here is the more information you pass to the SET_CONTEXT procedure, the more restrictive the access becomes.

Using the Client Identifier

As you may have noticed in the first example, the value of the Client Identifier determines the values returned by the global context. In the case that you don't supply a username and do supply the Client Identifier, you have effectively shared the values across all sessions, for all schemas (users) that have the same value set in the Client Identifier. This is consistent with the first example because the value for the Client Identifiers was the same: they were both NULL.

For this example, the view-based security isn't used in efforts to better present how the context values can be set and retrieved:

```
sec_mgr@KNOX10g> CREATE OR REPLACE PACKAGE global_ctx_mgr
AS
  PROCEDURE set_level (
    p_threat_level  IN  VARCHAR2,
    p_client_id     IN  VARCHAR2);
  PROCEDURE clear;
END;
/

Package created.

sec_mgr@KNOX10g> CREATE OR REPLACE PACKAGE BODY global_ctx_mgr
AS
  PROCEDURE set_level (
    p_threat_level  IN  VARCHAR2,
    p_client_id     IN  VARCHAR2)
  AS
```

```
    BEGIN
      DBMS_SESSION.set_context
                   (namespace     => 'global_threat_ctx',
                    ATTRIBUTE     => 'threat_level',
                    VALUE         => p_threat_level,
                    client_id     => p_client_id);
    END;
    PROCEDURE clear
    AS
    BEGIN
      DBMS_SESSION.clear_all_context
                                   ('global_threat_ctx');
    END;
  END;
  /

Package body created.
```

Notice the namespace manager does not specify a USER but does specify the Client Identifier. To illustrate this, call the procedure twice. The first time, set one format associated with the Client Identifier of "Application Alpha". The second call, change the Client Identifier to "Application Beta". But first, reset the values in the namespace:

```
sec_mgr@KNOX10g> -- Clear the namespace
sec_mgr@KNOX10g> EXEC global_ctx_mgr.clear;

PL/SQL procedure successfully completed.
```

Next, set a different value for two different Client Identifiers. The Identifiers represent two separate applications:

```
sec_mgr@KNOX10g> -- Set global context for ID
sec_mgr@KNOX10g> BEGIN
    global_ctx_mgr.set_level ('App A Value',
                              'Application Alpha');
    global_ctx_mgr.set_level ('App B Value',
                              'Application Beta');
  END;
  /

PL/SQL procedure successfully completed.
```

To test, set your Client Identifier to the different values and check the context. Do this for both users to demonstrate that the values are accessible to any database user that has the Client Identifier set appropriately.

```
sec_mgr@KNOX10g> -- set Client ID
sec_mgr@KNOX10g> EXEC dbms_session.set_identifier('Application Alpha')

PL/SQL procedure successfully completed.
```

```
sec_mgr@KNOX10g> COL threat_level format a25
sec_mgr@KNOX10g> SELECT SYS_CONTEXT ('global_threat_ctx',
  2                           'threat_level') threat_level
  3     FROM DUAL;

THREAT_LEVEL
-------------------------
App A Value

sec_mgr@KNOX10g> EXEC dbms_session.set_identifier('Application Beta');

PL/SQL procedure successfully completed.

sec_mgr@KNOX10g> SELECT SYS_CONTEXT ('global_threat_ctx',
  2                           'threat_level') threat_level
  3     FROM DUAL;

THREAT_LEVEL
-------------------------
App B Value

sec_mgr@KNOX10g> CONN scott/tiger
Connected.
scott@KNOX10g> -- Client ID is not set, so no value
scott@KNOX10g> SELECT SYS_CONTEXT ('global_threat_ctx',
  2                           'threat_level') threat_level
  3     FROM DUAL;

THREAT_LEVEL
-------------------------


scott@KNOX10g> -- set ID allows access to value
scott@KNOX10g> EXEC dbms_session.set_identifier('Application Alpha');

PL/SQL procedure successfully completed.
scott@KNOX10g> /

THREAT_LEVEL
-------------------------
App A Value

scott@KNOX10g> EXEC dbms_session.set_identifier('Application Beta');

PL/SQL procedure successfully completed.

scott@KNOX10g> /

THREAT_LEVEL
-------------------------
App B Value
```

There is no inherent security in the Client Identifier by default. Any user can set it to any value; therefore, don't rely on this for any security-specific implementations until you secure the Client Identifier (see Chapter 6 for an example of how to do this).

Sharing Values While Protecting Values

The final permutation sets all the parameters in the SET_CONTEXT call. This call has interesting effects. Just like the preceding example, the global values are different when using different Client Identifiers within the same schema. The difference is that the values are not shared across database schemas. The modified SET_LEVEL procedure is shown here:

```
PROCEDURE set_level (
  p_threat_level  IN  VARCHAR2,
  p_user          IN  VARCHAR2 DEFAULT NULL,
  p_client_id     IN  VARCHAR2)
AS
BEGIN
  DBMS_SESSION.set_context
              (namespace     => 'global_threat_ctx',
               ATTRIBUTE     => 'threat_level',
               VALUE         => p_threat_level,
               username      => p_user,
               client_id     => p_client_id);
END;
```

To illustrate this, set the username and Client Identifier. This makes the context available only to the schema with the appropriate Client Identifier set:

```
sec_mgr@KNOX10g> -- Clear the namespace
sec_mgr@KNOX10g> EXEC global_ctx_mgr.clear;

PL/SQL procedure successfully completed.

sec_mgr@KNOX10g> -- Set values for the SEC_MGR user
sec_mgr@KNOX10g> BEGIN
      global_ctx_mgr.set_level
        (p_threat_level      => 'ClientID Alpha:SEC_MGR value',
         p_user              => 'SEC_MGR',
         p_client_id         => 'Application Alpha');
      global_ctx_mgr.set_level
        (p_threat_level      => 'ClientID Beta:SEC_MGR value',
         p_user              => 'SEC_MGR',
         p_client_id         => 'Application Beta');
    END;
    /

PL/SQL procedure successfully completed.

sec_mgr@KNOX10g> -- show values
sec_mgr@KNOX10g> EXEC dbms_session.set_identifier('Application Alpha')
```

```
PL/SQL procedure successfully completed.

sec_mgr@KNOX10g> COL threat_level format a30
sec_mgr@KNOX10g> SELECT SYS_CONTEXT ('global_threat_ctx',
  2                       'threat_level') threat_level
  3     FROM DUAL;

THREAT_LEVEL
------------------------------
ClientID Alpha:SEC_MGR value

sec_mgr@KNOX10g> EXEC dbms_session.set_identifier('Application Beta')

PL/SQL procedure successfully completed.

sec_mgr@KNOX10g> /

THREAT_LEVEL
------------------------------
ClientID Beta:SEC_MGR value

sec_mgr@KNOX10g> CONN scott/tiger
Connected.
scott@KNOX10g> -- SCOTT cannot see values
scott@KNOX10g> EXEC dbms_session.set_identifier('Application Alpha');

PL/SQL procedure successfully completed.

scott@KNOX10g> SELECT SYS_CONTEXT ('global_threat_ctx',
  2                       'threat_level') threat_level
  3     FROM DUAL;

THREAT_LEVEL
------------------------------
```

Providing a different username with the same Client Identifier does not create an additional (or new) entry for the schema associated with the username. Instead, changing the username value *overwrites* the previous value. In the following example, the second call, which sets the value for SCOTT, overwrites the value just set for SEC_MGR. The SEC_MGR doesn't get this subsequent value (it's secured from the SEC_MGR). Instead, the SEC_MGR value is now null. It's important to understand this for effective implementation, and more importantly, for effective debugging.

```
scott@KNOX10g> CONN sec_mgr/oracle10g
Connected.
sec_mgr@KNOX10g>
sec_mgr@KNOX10g> BEGIN
  2    global_ctx_mgr.set_level
  3      (p_threat_level     => 'ClientID Alpha:SEC_MGR value',
```

```
      p_user             => 'SEC_MGR',
      p_client_id        => 'Application Alpha');
   -- This call erases the one just set
   global_ctx_mgr.set_level
     (p_threat_level     => 'ClientID Alpha:SCOTT value',
      p_user             => 'SCOTT',
      p_client_id        => 'Application Alpha');
 END;
 /

PL/SQL procedure successfully completed.

sec_mgr@KNOX10g>
sec_mgr@KNOX10g> EXEC dbms_session.set_identifier('Application Alpha');

PL/SQL procedure successfully completed.

sec_mgr@KNOX10g> COL threat_level format a30
sec_mgr@KNOX10g> SELECT SYS_CONTEXT ('global_threat_ctx',
                         'threat_level') threat_level
    FROM DUAL;

THREAT_LEVEL
------------------------------


sec_mgr@KNOX10g> EXEC dbms_session.set_identifier('Application Beta');

PL/SQL procedure successfully completed.

sec_mgr@KNOX10g> /

THREAT_LEVEL
------------------------------
ClientID Beta:SEC_MGR value

sec_mgr@KNOX10g> CONN scott/tiger
Connected.
scott@KNOX10g> EXEC dbms_session.set_identifier('Application Alpha');

PL/SQL procedure successfully completed.

scott@KNOX10g> SELECT SYS_CONTEXT ('global_threat_ctx',
                         'threat_level') threat_level
    FROM DUAL;

THREAT_LEVEL
------------------------------
ClientID Alpha:SCOTT value
```

```
scott@KNOX10g> EXEC dbms_session.set_identifier('Application Beta');

PL/SQL procedure successfully completed.

scott@KNOX10g> /

THREAT_LEVEL
------------------------------

scott@KNOX10g>
```

This last example illustrates some of the important aspects of understanding how global application contexts work. If you don't have a complete grasp of this, you could very easily think you're providing a secure security policy when it's actually an insecure solution. The global application context is a powerful and practical tool; just ensure you have tested your SET_CONTEXT calls to validate that the values are appropriately shared *and* protected as desired.

External and Initialized Globally

Oracle Database also supports application contexts that have their values derived from external sources. The motivation for external context is that the values will be automatically populated for the user. The external sources can be a job queue process, a database link, or a program using the OCI interface. The directory server can also be used to automatically set a context. When used in conjunction with Enterprise Users, the database automatically places any attribute values defined in the inetOrgPerson object inside a namespace called the SYS_LDAP_USER_DEFAULT.

To illustrate how easy this is to use, create a view based on the EMP table that restricts users' access to records that fall within their department. The view will use the department number that is stored for the Enterprise User in the directory server:

```
sec_mgr@KNOX10g> CREATE TABLE people$ AS SELECT * FROM scott.emp;

Table created.

sec_mgr@KNOX10g> CREATE VIEW people
  AS
    SELECT *
      FROM people$
     WHERE deptno =
              SYS_CONTEXT ('sys_ldap_user_default',
                           'departmentnumber');

View created.
```

Now, grant access to the shared schema to which the Enterprise Users will connect. Assume the users are mapped to the DB_SUBTREE schema:

```
sec_mgr@KNOX10g> GRANT SELECT ON people TO db_subtree;

Grant succeeded.
```

You can view the Enterprise Users with the Enterprise Security Manager as illustrated in Figure 9-1. Note that the window allows you to view the users' information and includes their department number. The department number attribute is pictured here for the Knox user and has a value of 10. This value can be set with the OiDDAS application or with the Oracle Directory Manager application.

FIGURE 9-1. *Attributes in the inetOrgPerson LDAP object are automatically populated in the SYS_LDAP_USER_DEFAULT namespace.*

To show how the value is automatically populated, log on as the Enterprise User and query the view just created.

```
sec_mgr@KNOX10g> conn knox/oracle10g
Connected.
db_subtree@KNOX10g> SELECT ename, deptno FROM sec_mgr.people;

ENAME          DEPTNO
---------- ----------
CLARK              10
KING               10
MILLER             10
```

The database also supports the ability to create application specific attributes that are also stored in the LDAP directory. On login, the attributes are automatically applied to an application context. This again only works for Enterprise Users. Details on how to configure this can be found in the *Oracle Database Security Guide 10g*.

Summary

Fine-grained access control (FGAC) brings security to the insides of your data tables. The technology enabler for FGAC is application contexts.

Application context are an efficient and flexible mechanism for storing security related information. The Oracle Database provides many default attributes in the USERENV namespace. These attributes are automatically populated and generally provide useful information about the user's environment—IP address, authentication method, and more. The Client Identifier is also part of the USERENV namespace. This attribute can be set by a user or application and has the added benefit of being recorded in the audit trails.

The ability to define your own name-value contexts allows for many creative security solutions. Application context values can be created and managed locally. Each context is held in the user's private memory regions and is therefore secure for each database session. Local application contexts are ideal for performing security functions. They are secure because they are private for the session, and they can only be manipulated by the namespace manager. They are fast because the values are stored in memory. They are flexible because they can be set to any user-defined string.

You can also define global application contexts. This allows the sharing of information, in a secure manner, across database schemas and database sessions. The database provides various ways in which global contexts can be defined and used. Global contexts are a great utility in connection pooled applications and shared schema designs.

The Oracle Database also supports contexts initialized by external sources. When the source is initialized by the directory, the design supports Oracle's centralized user management strategy, which is a critical component to the Identity Management functionality.

Chapters 10 and 11 further investigate ways to use application context to provide fine-grained access control for tables, views, and synonyms.

CHAPTER 10

Implementing Fine-Grained Access Controls with Views

In Chapter 7, you were introduced to database system and object privileges. System privileges allow the user to access data or execute procedures on a global- or system-wide scale. Object privileges, on the contrary, allow the user rights on specific objects. The commonality between the two is that the security privileges are coarse-grained and only regulate actions at the object level.

This chapter reviews various ways of restricting access to data within the most critical database objects: the data tables. You will see how database views can be used as effective security mechanisms for providing security for the individual table rows and columns. There are some limitations and challenges present in the various approaches as well and these will be addressed. You'll also see how views can be effectively designed and implemented to overcome many of the most difficult security challenges that exist today.

This chapter begins with an introduction to the requirements driving row-level security or, as it's called within Oracle, fine-grained access control. Defense in depth is the guiding principle. Oracle has developed many tools that can be used to secure the data to a fine level of granularity. Knowing how to exploit those tools is an invaluable asset in providing complete data security.

Introduction to Fine-Grained Access

Security protections start with good identification and authentication. Once you know the user's identity, you can determine what they are authorized to do and enable the necessary privileges for them to do their work. This can be done successfully by using system and object privileges and database roles in accordance with the least privilege principle. Privileges on database objects is the primary security control governing access to data—even still, it may not be sufficient for your security requirements.

Object Access

You have already seen how object and system privileges allow or disallow access to data objects such as tables, views, and procedures. A user with the select privilege on a table will be able to read all records within that table. The select privilege operates at the object level (where the table is the object in this example). The key distinction here is that the database privileges apply to accessing the object (table or view) but do not specify the security within the object. Limiting access to data within tables is desirable and is often a security requirement.

To understand the requirement better, consider a physical security example that can be used as lesson for digital security: office building security.

For many office buildings, physical security is a concern. As such, a security infrastructure is built and supported. Security guards are employed, security badges are issued to authorized users, and doors and elevators are locked and require some special key to open or activate them.

The first layer of security occurs at the perimeter: gaining access to the facility on which the building resides. This is analogous to the digital first step of identification and authentication. Next, you enter the building and encounter a security checkpoint. In this case, the building is similar to a database table or view: it represents a single object or entity that you wish to protect. Once you get through this security checkpoint, you have access to the building but not necessarily access to every corridor and office within.

Fine-Grained Access

Many of today's office buildings have secured areas such as floors, corridors and rooms. Most offices within the building are kept locked. The office occupant and perhaps the occupant's boss and the cleaning crew are the only people with the keys to enter the office. Everyone accepts the fact that people with access to the building do not need nor have access to everything within the building. In a sense, this is an enforcement of the least privilege principle—people have privileges to access only to what they need to do their job and nothing more.

These physical security principles can be applied to data in your databases. While many users may require access to records stored in the same table, most users do not need access to all records within the table. This is especially true for tables with sensitive information.

Need to Know

There is a security tenet commonly practiced that says users can only access data to which they have a "need to know." It is similar to least privileges in that you are trying to minimize the data to which a user has access. For the organizations that deal with classified data, the need-to-know concept is used extensively to protect information. The reasons are based on the fact that the fewer people who know a piece of information, the easier it is to manage and secure it. While you may trust many people with knowledge of certain critical information, such as the DBA passwords to your databases, need to know dictates that only the people that have a *requirement* for the information will get access to it. Think of the risks created if everyone knew the administrator passwords—anyone would be able to gain access to the critical data, and you wouldn't know who accessed what.

For applications in many industries, the need-to-know concept provides a guiding principle in the development of security policies. For example, doctors need to know the diagnosis of the patients they are treating. For privacy reasons, enforcing this access helps ensure that a nosy doctor doesn't exploit his role as a physician. The doctor should not be looking at the medical records of random patients because they do not need to know that information. Need to know holds true for tax accountants, financial institutions, and many other professions in many industries.

The database must therefore support the ability to provide access to some records while simultaneously restricting access to others. There are several ways to ensure need to know within a database application. The methods can be grossly categorized as security within the application or security within the database. Defense in depth suggests the use of security in the application *and* security in the database whenever practical and possible. The remainder of this chapter will focus on implementing fine-grained access controls through database views to support the need-to-know security requirements.

Secure Views

Oracle has supported database views for many years. Views can be used to solve many challenges, and views can be a tremendous security tool. Views can hide columns. Views can mask data values. Views can aggregate data to remove personally identifiable information for maintaining privacy. The part I like best is that the view is not redundant or duplicated data; it is nothing more than stored SQL.

An effective security design usually involves the judicious use of views for any or all of the reasons just cited. Views are database objects and access to them occurs at the object level. However, privileges on the view are separate and distinct from the privileges on the underlying objects the view accesses. Allowing users access to a view and not to the underlying objects is an effective security technique for insulating your sensitive data.

Consider the example where the user SCOTT wishes to allow certain users to ascertain the number of employees for each department. He does not have to allow access to the EMP and DEPT tables. He can simply create a view that performs the calculation. Granting access to the view then allows users to retrieve this summary data while simultaneously maintaining separate security for the underlying objects:

```
scott@KNOX10g> -- Create a view showing employee
scott@KNOX10g> -- distribution by department.
scott@KNOX10g> CREATE OR REPLACE VIEW emp_dist
     AS
       SELECT    INITCAP (d.dname) "Department",
                 COUNT (e.ename) "Total Employees"
           FROM dept d, emp e
          WHERE e.deptno = d.deptno
       GROUP BY dname;

View created.

scott@KNOX10g> -- Grant privileges to query view to user blake
scott@KNOX10g> GRANT SELECT ON emp_dist TO BLAKE;

Grant succeeded.

scott@KNOX10g> CONN blake/blake
Connected.
blake@KNOX10g> -- BLAKE can query view
blake@KNOX10g> SELECT * FROM scott.emp_dist;

Department     Total Employees
-------------- ---------------
Accounting                   3
Research                     5
Sales                        6

blake@KNOX10g> -- BLAKE cannot query base tables
blake@KNOX10g> SELECT * FROM scott.emp;
SELECT * FROM scott.emp
                    *
ERROR at line 1:
ORA-00942: table or view does not exist
```

This is an excellent technique in cases where privacy needs to be maintained. The view could easily be showing a medical researcher the number of patients that have been diagnosed with a certain illness. Likewise, the view could show a bank manager the number of customers with certain financial status. As the actual names are hidden by the view, any sensitive information that can be derived by correlating the department, diagnosis, or financial status with an individual is prevented.

Views for Column-Level Security

Views are an ideal tool for providing column-level security (CLS). What is CLS? *CLS* has three possible definitions:

- Preventing access to the column
- Masking the column values
- Controlling access to the values within a column

Column Removal

In the first definition of CLS, preventing access to the column means that the column is inaccessible to your users. For example, your security policy for the EMP table may dictate that you want to remove access to the SAL column because it contains sensitive data. The column values should not just be hidden—the column should not exist.

The view solution for CLS simply selects all columns except the SAL column. Then, by granting the users access to the view and not to the underlying table, you have successfully removed user access to your sensitive column data.

This example is largely a security by design solution—the security was done prior to developing and deploying any application code. This example may or may not be a possible solution for existing designs and fielded applications. For many applications, views can replace tables because many applications have no bias for querying directly against tables or directly against views.

However, a challenge may exist if an application can only access tables or if an application is already written and you expect it to go against a specifically defined table. In the last case, you may be able to rename the table and create the view with the name the table originally had. For example, if your application queries the EMP table and you want to provide a view that consists only of the ENAME and JOB columns, you could issue the following SQL to rename the table and create a view in its place:

```
-- rename existing table
ALTER TABLE emp RENAME TO emp$;
-- create view that removes sensitive columns
CREATE VIEW emp
AS
  SELECT ename, job
    FROM emp$;
-- grant access to view
GRANT SELECT ON emp TO user1;
-- revoke access from table
REVOKE SELECT ON emp$ FROM user1;
```

This trick may not work in all cases because some applications may depend on the existence of some or all of the columns you are attempting to remove. Removing access to the column may break an already developed application. Note that this is an indication that the application requires exclusive security rights over your data.

In many cases, views are the best and easiest method for providing CLS when the requirement dictates that users should not have access to a column.

Masking Column Values

The second CLS definition says some but not all of the column values are accessible. For this definition, I am only referring to the user reading or issuing SELECT statements. You will see how to implement CLS for data modification later in this section.

For the values that are not to be seen, you can mask the values returned to the user. For example, you may elect to return the string "NOT AUTHORIZED" or return the value zero when a user queries a column to which you wish to hide its real value. Be careful: a value of zero may imply one meaning (the actual value is zero) versus your intended meaning (the user does not have access).

Another masking option is to return a null value. Returning null values is a good choice because they are a standard value for data that does not exist. However, just as returning a zero value has a caveat, null values may incorrectly indicate the absence of a value when in reality the value exists but the user is not authorized to see it. If the application needs to distinguish between actual null values and masked data, then null values should not be used.

Consider an example where users can access only their salary. Users should be prohibited from accessing other users' salary data. Because the user can access their salary, you cannot simply omit the SAL column from the view definition.

To meet this CLS requirement, a view can be used with a function that masks the values of the salary column. Views with functions are an effective column-level security technique. The functions can return different values for different rows based on a policy decision that is implemented within the function.

Putting this example to life begins by creating a simple table:

```
scott@KNOX10g> CREATE TABLE people
  AS SELECT ename username, job, sal salary, deptno
    FROM emp
    WHERE deptno = 20;

Table created.
```

The view will use the Oracle built-in DECODE function to implement the column masking. If the user accessing the record is the same as the person in the record, then they are allowed to see the salary; otherwise, a null value is returned.

```
scott@KNOX10g> -- create view that only returns the salary
scott@KNOX10g> -- for the user issuing the query
scott@KNOX10g> CREATE OR REPLACE VIEW people_cls
  AS
    SELECT username,
           job,
           deptno,
           DECODE (username,
                   USER, salary,
                   NULL) salary
      FROM people;

View created.
```

When granting privileges on the view, you can allow the user to read all records because the DECODE function provides the CLS to mask other users' salaries. Do not grant privileges on the PEOPLE base table.

The column masking requirement is very popular in applications such as those used by some reporting tools. The reports have a predefined structure that often requires the existence of a column value for all records. A challenge exists in producing the report and maintaining security because you may not want the report users to see the actual values in all the columns for all the records. The view can be used as the source for the report generation:

```
scott@KNOX10g> SELECT * FROM people_cls;

USERNAME        JOB            DEPTNO     SALARY
--------------- --------- ---------- ----------
SMITH           CLERK              20
JONES           MANAGER            20
SCOTT           ANALYST            20       3000
ADAMS           CLERK              20
FORD            ANALYST            20
```

Updates to CLS Views

The previous view provides security for select statements. Note that even aggregate queries are subject to the security:

```
scott@KNOX10g> -- Computing salaries for everyone will only
scott@KNOX10g> -- return user's salary. This is good security.
scott@KNOX10g> SELECT SUM (salary) FROM people_cls;

SUM(SALARY)
-----------
       3000
```

For data updates, a user cannot issue direct updates on the view. This could break your applications:

```
scott@KNOX10g> -- Give everyone a 10% raise.
scott@KNOX10g> -- This will fail on the derived column
scott@KNOX10g> UPDATE people_cls
  2     SET salary = salary * 1.1;
   SET salary = salary * 1.1
       *
ERROR at line 2:
ORA-01733: virtual column not allowed here
```

This is an easy problem to solve. Oracle provides Instead-of triggers for performing DML operations on complex views. You can simply create an Instead-of trigger for this view. When you do this, you want to ensure the trigger's behavior is consistent with the security policy provided by the view. For this example, this translates to having the user update only the records for the salaries they can see:

```
scott@KNOX10g> -- Create "instead of" trigger to perform updates on
scott@KNOX10g> -- base table. Trigger code is based on view security.
scott@KNOX10g> -- If user can see the salary, then update the record.
scott@KNOX10g> CREATE OR REPLACE TRIGGER people_sal_update
      INSTEAD OF UPDATE
      ON people_cls
      FOR EACH ROW
    DECLARE
    BEGIN
      -- If salary is not null, then user has read access
      -- so perform update to base table
      IF :OLD.salary IS NOT NULL
      THEN
        -- Update base table
        UPDATE people
           SET salary = :NEW.salary
         WHERE username = :NEW.username;
      END IF;
    END;
    /

Trigger created.
```

To demonstrate the effectiveness, you can view the current values, issue an update, and then validate the effects of the update. Note that the intention of this view is to transparently provide the CLS for the table. The base table should not be accessible to the application or users:

```
scott@KNOX10g> -- Display current values.
scott@KNOX10g> SELECT username, salary FROM people;

USERNAME       SALARY
---------- ----------
SMITH             800
JONES            2975
SCOTT            3000
ADAMS            1100
FORD             3000

scott@KNOX10g> -- Give everyone a 10% raise by updating view.
scott@KNOX10g> -- This will succeed now the trigger has been created.
scott@KNOX10g> -- Only the invoking user's record will be updated.
scott@KNOX10g> UPDATE people_cls
       SET salary = salary * 1.1;

5 rows updated.

scott@KNOX10g> -- show effects of update
```

```
scott@KNOX10g> SELECT username, salary FROM people;

USERNAME       SALARY
---------- ----------
SMITH             800
JONES            2975
SCOTT            3300
ADAMS            1100
FORD             3000
```

The update statement succeeds for all view records. The actual table update occurred only for the SCOTT user, as bolded in the previous output.

Performance of Views with CLS Functions

Using functions, such as DECODE, in the view definition is a powerful and convenient way to mask column values. However, security often competes with performance. You should always conduct a performance test on your security design before you begin building your applications on it. To test the performance of this design, create a PL/SQL function. Oracle built-in functions such as DECODE generally perform well and always outperform user-created PL/SQL functions, so this test will use the latter.

```
sec_mgr@KNOX10g> -- Creating performance test view
sec_mgr@KNOX10g> CREATE OR REPLACE FUNCTION view_filter (
  2    p_owner  IN  VARCHAR2)
  3    RETURN VARCHAR2
  4  AS
  5  BEGIN
  6    RETURN p_owner;
  7  END;
  8  /

Function created.
```

There is no security in the function because the test should isolate the cost of calling the PL/SQL function for each record. This design is consistent with the previous implementation example because the view uses a function's return value to generate a column.

TIP
Always conduct a performance test on your security design before you begin building your applications on it. It's easier to try alternative approaches before the application is built.

This test will time how long it takes to count records from a base table and compare that result to accessing the function-computed column in the view. To ensure your time quantities are measurable (Oracle queries can be done very quickly), you'll need a large table. The following SQL creates the large table:

```
sec_mgr@KNOX10g> CREATE TABLE big_tab AS
  2  SELECT * FROM all_objects;
```

```
Table created.

sec_mgr@KNOX10g> -- increase table size
sec_mgr@KNOX10g> BEGIN
    FOR i IN 1 .. 5
    LOOP
      INSERT INTO sec_mgr.big_tab
        (SELECT *
           FROM sec_mgr.big_tab);
      COMMIT;
    END LOOP;
  END;
  /

PL/SQL procedure successfully completed.

sec_mgr@KNOX10g> ANALYZE TABLE big_tab COMPUTE STATISTICS;

Table analyzed.
```

Next, two views are created. The first uses the VIEW_FILTER PL/SQL function just created. The second uses the Oracle built-in DECODE function:

```
sec_mgr@KNOX10g> -- Create view calling user-defined PL/SQL function
sec_mgr@KNOX10g> CREATE OR REPLACE VIEW big_ud_view
  AS
    SELECT owner, view_filter (owner) function_owner
      FROM big_tab;

View created.

sec_mgr@KNOX10g> -- Create view calling a built-in PL/SQL function
sec_mgr@KNOX10g> CREATE OR REPLACE VIEW big_bi_view
  AS
    SELECT owner,
           DECODE (owner, owner, owner) function_owner
      FROM big_tab;

View created.
```

The performance test consists of counting all the records from the base table and the two views:

```
sec_mgr@KNOX10g> SET timing on
sec_mgr@KNOX10g> -- time the query on the base table
sec_mgr@KNOX10g> SELECT COUNT (owner) FROM big_tab;

COUNT(OWNER)
------------
     1323520
```

```
Elapsed: 00:00:06.57
sec_mgr@KNOX10g> -- time the query on the PL/SQL function view
sec_mgr@KNOX10g> SELECT COUNT (function_owner) FROM big_ud_view;

COUNT(FUNCTION_OWNER)
---------------------
              1323520

Elapsed: 00:00:14.53
sec_mgr@KNOX10g> -- time the query on the DECODE view
sec_mgr@KNOX10g> SELECT COUNT (function_owner) FROM big_bi_view;

COUNT(FUNCTION_OWNER)
---------------------
              1323520

Elapsed: 00:00:06.81
```

The Oracle built-in DECODE function adds almost no time to the overall query. The user-defined PL/SQL function view processed 1.3 million records in under 15 seconds. You can consider this either acceptable or twice as slow.

Also, note this is in some ways a best-case scenario. Any security code that is implemented in the function will slow the performance. Optimizing that code is important to performance. You should consider using application contexts, and Oracle built-in functions whenever possible to increase performance. Other optimization suggestions can be found in the "Tuning PL/SQL Applications for Performance" chapter of the *Oracle PL/SQL User's Guide and Reference.*

CLS for Controlling Access to All Records within a Column

The database provides a CLS mechanism by default. This is the third definition of CLS. For inserts and updates, you can control at the object level whether a user has the ability to affect the values within the column. For example, to ensure the user can update only their phone number, you can specifically restrict the update privileges to just this column:

```
scott@KNOX10g> ALTER TABLE people ADD (phone_number VARCHAR2(20));

Table altered.

scott@KNOX10g> GRANT UPDATE (phone_number) ON people TO user1;

Grant succeeded.
```

The ability for the database to support column-level privileges allows the user to insert or update specific columns in a table while simultaneously restricting modifications to other columns. In cases where a user is allowed to change the column value for all records, this definition of CLS satisfies the security requirements.

Understand that the column-level privileges allow the user to update the column value for all records in the table. This may or may not be desirable. In the previous example, it may be unlikely that a user should have the ability to update other users' phone numbers.

```
user1@KNOX10g> UPDATE scott.people
  2      SET phone_number = '555-1212';

5 rows updated.
```

The unqualified update just changed everyone's phone number. This is a critical and often overlooked point: the database column privileges do not provide security for the individual rows. You have to provide that yourself.

Views for Row-Level Security

One particularly useful aspect of views is that they provide row-level security. Row-level security, sometimes referred to as fine-grained access control, ensures that security is applied not only to the object (for example, a database table) but also to each row within the object. When combined with a check constraint, views in this manner are simple to understand, implement, and manage.

Let's investigate views as an implementation of row-level security. In this example, a view is used for an application that allows a user to update their personal record. Your requirements dictate that the Edit screen of your application will need to query all sensitive fields of the record. The user is allowed to issue updates but only to their record. Enforcing security at the database requires you to ensure that a user (or hacker) can't update or modify someone else's record.

This example will be based on a view that ensures the only record displayed to the user will be theirs. The view's security will eliminate all other records. This is done by adding a predicate or where clause to the query on the base table.

```
scott@KNOX10g> CREATE OR REPLACE VIEW people_edit
  2  AS
  3    SELECT * FROM emp
  4     WHERE ename =
  5             SYS_CONTEXT ('userenv', 'session_user')
  6           WITH CHECK OPTION;

View created.
```

This example assumes the users will be directly authenticated to the database. Furthermore, each user has an exclusive schema in which the schema name matches the value stored in the ENAME column. However, this view could be easily modified to support a user identity based on the client identifier, the enterprise user's external name, or some identifying value set in an application context.

You can see the queries are restricted to user records by querying from the view. Updates behave in a similar manner. When SCOTT tries to update another record, the update simply doesn't occur:

```
scott@KNOX10g> SELECT empno, ename, sal
  2    FROM people_edit;
```

```
     EMPNO ENAME             SAL
---------- ---------- ----------
      7788 SCOTT            3000

scott@KNOX10g> -- try to update another user's record
scott@KNOX10g> UPDATE people_edit
  2      SET ename = 'Bozo'
  3    WHERE ename = 'KING';

0 rows updated.
```

Just as updating records outside of the view definition has no effect, deletes are also constrained to the view definition. Inserts are allowed as long as the ENAME value matches the user's name:

```
scott@KNOX10g> -- Try to delete all records.
scott@KNOX10g> DELETE FROM people_edit;

1 row deleted.

scott@KNOX10g> -- Inserts work as long as compliant
scott@KNOX10g> -- with view's definition
scott@KNOX10g> INSERT INTO people_edit
  2              (empno, ename, sal)
  3        VALUES (7788, 'SCOTT', '3000');

1 row created.

scott@KNOX10g> INSERT INTO people_edit
  2              (empno, ename, sal)
  3        VALUES (7788, 'SCOTT2', '3000');
INSERT INTO people_edit
            *
ERROR at line 1:
ORA-01402: view WITH CHECK OPTION where-clause violation
```

By introducing the CHECK option with the view (seen in line 6 of the view creation), the database will enforce inserts and updates on the view so that the resulting values don't conflict with the view's definition. While this could be considered a security solution, the database actually enforces the CHECK option for data integrity reasons.

Functions in Views for Row-Level Security

A popular approach to creating security within views is to place a PL/SQL function inside the view definition. When placed in the select list (before the FROM in the SQL) of the view definition, the function performs the role of column-level security. When the function is placed after the WHERE, or SQL predicate, the function acts as a row-level security mechanism. While functions in views for row-level security may be operationally correct and an interesting solution, overall view performance should be evaluated.

To illustrate the effect on performance, consider a view that calls a PL/SQL function in the SQL where clause. The function performs the security. The security policy for this example once again says the user can see only their records. You can determine if the record belongs to a user because your function accepts a record owner parameter. An exemption exists for a user with the SYSDBA role—these users get to see all records. Assume this added condition will require the use of a PL/SQL function:

```
sec_mgr@KNOX10g> -- Create the row security function.
sec_mgr@KNOX10g> -- This function will be called by the view.
sec_mgr@KNOX10g> CREATE OR REPLACE FUNCTION view_filter (
    p_owner  IN  VARCHAR2)
    RETURN NUMBER
  AS
  BEGIN
    IF (   p_owner = USER
        OR SYS_CONTEXT ('userenv', 'isdba') = 'TRUE')
    THEN
      RETURN 1;
    ELSE
      RETURN 0;
    END IF;
  END;
  /

Function created.
```

The view for this example queries BIG_TAB, the approximately1.3 million row table based on an aggregated copy of the ALL_OBJECTS table created previously in the "Performance of Views with CLS Functions" section. The view places the security function in the where clause. By doing so, the function acts as a row-level security enforcement mechanism.

```
sec_mgr@KNOX10g> -- Creating view over table with function to filter rows
sec_mgr@KNOX10g> CREATE OR REPLACE VIEW big_view
  AS
    SELECT *
      FROM big_tab
     WHERE 1 = view_filter (owner);

View created.
```

The point of this exercise is to show that while the results are technically correct, the performance may not be acceptable. For performance comparison, first query by counting all records on the base table. Modify this query adding the security (the security the function ultimately implements) into the where clause. This will return the same number of records as the view, so your performance number shouldn't be influenced by the number or records returned:

```
sec_mgr@KNOX10g> SET timing on
sec_mgr@KNOX10g> SELECT COUNT (*)
    FROM big_tab
   WHERE 1 = DECODE (owner, USER, 1, 0)
      OR SYS_CONTEXT ('userenv', 'isdba') = 'TRUE';
```

```
  COUNT(*)
----------
      1184

Elapsed: 00:00:06.90
```

Run a query against the view for comparison. The where clause is implemented in the view function, so you don't need to specify it in the query:

```
sec_mgr@KNOX10g> SELECT COUNT(*) FROM big_view;

  COUNT(*)
----------
      1184

Elapsed: 00:01:07.60
```

The difference in times is due to the overhead of invoking a PL/SQL function for every record (all 1.3 million rows) in the table. The query results are the same, but the performance certainly isn't. This is because the security implementation isn't an effective performance implementation. You could have modified the view definition to include the security logic there:

```
sec_mgr@KNOX10g> CREATE OR REPLACE VIEW big_view2
  AS
    SELECT * FROM big_tab
     WHERE 1 = DECODE (owner, USER, 1, 0)
        OR SYS_CONTEXT ('userenv', 'isdba') = 'TRUE';

View created.
```

Doing this increases the performance while maintaining the security. Calling the built-in database functions, such as DECODE and CASE statements, is an effective way to implement security while maintaining performance.

There may be a point at which the security logic becomes so complex that a PL/SQL function call is desired or needed. Making the call to a PL/SQL function will reduce the performance, which may or may not make the security implementation an effective solution. Helping to solve this problem is the Virtual Private Database technology discussed in Chapter 11.

Viewing Problems

While views are popular methods for implementing security, mixing security policies for different DML statements adds complexity. Usually multiple views have to be created, one for each policy and statement. For example, the SELECT view may allow users to see all records, INSERT and UPDATE views can be created to allow updates within the user's department, and a DELETE view can ensure users can delete only their records.

Additionally, the object security has to be maintained so that the DML privileges are granted directly to the view objects in congruence with their desired functionality (for example, grant select on SELECT_VIEW, grant delete on DELETE_VIEW, etc.). Instead-of triggers may also need to be developed to support the DML operations on columns in the views.

Finally, to get all this to work correctly, you need to ensure the application knows to issue selects on the SELECT_VIEW, deletes on the DELETE_VIEW, and so on. It would be undesirable to allow the user to issue deletes on the SELECT_VIEW.

The process of creating different views for different users with different policies can create a problem that gets exacerbated as the user roles and policies increase in complexity. For this reason, Oracle created integrated row-level security and branded the functionality as Virtual Private Database.

Summary

Fine-grained access control brings security to the insides of the data tables. Need to know governs the handling of data in both the digital and nondigital information worlds. Within the database, views are an effective technique for implementing fine-grained access control in support of protecting sensitive data on a need-to-know basis.

Views can be used for various definitions of column security. They can remove entire columns from the user's access or mask a column's values. The database also provides column security through object privileges on insert and update operations. Views can be easily defined and managed and often implemented transparently for almost all simple security requirements. Views can be used with both Oracle built-in functions and user-defined functions to provide fine-grained access control and should always be one of the first security solutions to be considered.

However, views aren't always a perfect solution. The performance degradation of views with user-defined PL/SQL functions, especially when used with row-level security, may make them impractical for certain situations. A view-based security solution can be difficult to manage as the number and complexity of the views increases. Many of the benefits can be diminished if the view solution requires copious numbers of Instead-of triggers.

In the next chapter, you'll see another effective technique for providing fine-grained access control: Virtual Private Database provides row-level security in a manner that supports the complex security policies that often inspire the use of views with PL/SQL functions, but does so in a way that maintains better performance characteristics and is easier to manage.

CHAPTER 11

Row-Level Security with Virtual Private Database

or many years, Oracle's customers repeatedly asked for a logical and elegant method for applying security policies to the data within database tables. And for many years, Oracle responded by saying, "Use views with functions." As Chapter 10 illustrates, in many circumstances this is just not a practical solution. Oracle, recognizing their customer's needs, introduced Virtual Private Database (VPD) technology with Oracle Database 8.1.5.

This chapter illustrates how VPD can be used to provide row-level security. The chapter begins with a "Quick Start" section that introduces you to the ease and power that VPD can provide. This section can also serve as a refresher for you later.

Next, the chapter examines the various aspects of VPD including how to enable the row-level security features as well as providing examples of how it works with different DML statements—select, insert, update, and delete. One of the most valuable sections is "Debugging RLS Policies," which offers tips and tricks for troubleshooting the VPD implementation. The transparency that works as your ally for security reasons also works against you when things go wrong. The chapter explores common mistakes to avoid as well as ways to help you track down the source of your errors.

Oracle Database 10*g* introduces a new feature to VPD called Column Sensitive polices, and you will see how to use this. The VPD Performance section suggests how to maintain high-performing security policies and provides examples of the new caching methods introduced in the Oracle Database 10*g* release.

The Need for Virtual Private Databases

When I first began working for Oracle, I was asked to work on a Department of Defense (DoD) project that was using a special version of Oracle called *Trusted Oracle*. Trusted Oracle ran on special "trusted" operating systems. I was familiar with Oracle, and I was familiar with UNIX operating systems, but working with Trusted Oracle was really bizarre. A lot of what I had learned about access controls and security was somehow deficient in this world.

The one behavior that I quickly realized was distinctly different was that Trusted Oracle transparently filtered data records. I found out that the DoD security requirements dictated mandatory separation of records based on a user's authorizations. In this case the users were authorized for access at different sensitivity levels—SECRET, CONFIDENTIAL, and UNCLASSIFIED. The data was intermingled within tables at various sensitivity levels. One user accessing the data would see one set of records, and a different user with different authorizations would see a different set of records.

The interesting part was that the security was implemented so that it was transparent and could not be subverted. The manner in which Trusted Oracle behaved and the requirements from customers in other industries gave Oracle the idea of abstracting the row-level security features from Trusted Oracle into a framework that would support practically any data model and security policy. This was the genesis of the Virtual Private Database technology.

Officially, the phrase "Virtual Private Database (VPD)" refers to the use of row-level security (RLS) *and* the use of application contexts. (Application contexts were discussed in detail in Chapter 9.) However, the term "VPD" is commonly used when discussing the use of the row-level security features irrespective of implementation.

Row-Level Security Quick Start

Many examples you see using VPD involve the use of application contexts and/or several data tables with esoteric column names and complicated referential integrity constraints. I find that these elements, while truthful in their representation of many database schemas, tend to confuse and mislead the reader about how the row-level security technology works and precisely what is needed to enable it. Using RLS is easy, and the purpose of this section is to prove this very point.

VPD's row-level security allows you to restrict access to records based on a security policy implemented in PL/SQL. A *security policy,* as used here, simply describes the rules governing access to the data rows. This process is done by creating a PL/SQL function that returns a string. The function is then registered against the tables, views, or synonyms you want to protect by using the DBMS_RLS PL/SQL package. When a query is issued against the protected object, Oracle effectively appends the string returned from the function to the original SQL statement, thereby filtering the data records.

Quick Start Example

This example will focus on the process required to enable RLS. The intention is to keep the data and security policy simple so as not to distract from how to enable an RLS solution.

The RLS capability in Oracle requires a PL/SQL function. The function accepts two parameters, as shown next. The database will call this function automatically and transparently. The string value returned from the function (called the *predicate*) will be effectively added to the original SQL. This results in an elimination of rows and thus provides the row-level security.

The security policy for this example will exclude Department 10 records from queries on SCOTT.EMP. The PL/SQL function to implement this will look as follows:

```
sec_mgr@KNOX10g> CREATE OR REPLACE FUNCTION no_dept10 (
    p_schema   IN  VARCHAR2,
    p_object   IN  VARCHAR2)
    RETURN VARCHAR2
  AS
  BEGIN
    RETURN 'deptno != 10';
  END;
  /

Function created.
```

To protect the SCOTT.EMP table, simply associate the preceding PL/SQL function to the table using the DBMS_RLS.ADD_POLICY procedure:

```
sec_mgr@KNOX10g> BEGIN
    DBMS_RLS.add_policy
               (object_schema      => 'SCOTT',
                object_name        => 'EMP',
                policy_name        => 'quickstart',
                policy_function    => 'no_dept10');
```

```
END;
/

PL/SQL procedure successfully completed.
```

That's it; you are done! To test this policy, log on as a user with access to the SCOTT.EMP table and issue your DML. The following shows all the department numbers available in the table. Department 10 is no longer seen because the RLS policy transparently filters out those records:

```
scott@KNOX10g> -- Show department numbers.
scott@KNOX10g> -- There should be no department 10.
scott@KNOX10g> SELECT DISTINCT deptno FROM emp;

    DEPTNO
----------
        20
        30
```

The important point is that row-level security can be trivial to implement.

NOTE
RLS has no requirements or dependencies on the use of application contexts, the user's identity, or the predicate referencing the table's columns.

Changing the security implementation is trivial, too. Suppose the security policy is changed so that no records should be returned for the user SYSTEM:

```
sec_mgr@KNOX10g> -- change policy implementation to
sec_mgr@KNOX10g> -- remove all records for the SYSTEM user
sec_mgr@KNOX10g> CREATE OR REPLACE FUNCTION no_dept10 (
    p_schema   IN  VARCHAR2,
    p_object   IN  VARCHAR2)
    RETURN VARCHAR2
  AS
  BEGIN
    RETURN 'USER != ''SYSTEM''';
  END;
  /

Function created.

sec_mgr@KNOX10g> -- Test by counting records as SCOTT
sec_mgr@KNOX10g> -- then by counting records as SYSTEM
sec_mgr@KNOX10g> CONN scott/tiger
Connected.
scott@KNOX10g> SELECT COUNT(*) Total_Records FROM emp;
```

```
TOTAL_RECORDS
-------------
           14

scott@KNOX10g> CONN system/manager
Connected.
system@KNOX10g> SELECT COUNT(*) Total_Records FROM scott.emp;

TOTAL_RECORDS
-------------
            0
```

Notice that the security policy implemented by the function can change without requiring any re-registration with the DBMS_RLS package.

RLS In-Depth

The preceding example can help you get started, but there is much more to RLS than this. The security policies can be much more complex, and the policy functions typically return dramatically different strings based on user authorizations.

There are some similarities between RLS and some of the view examples you read about in Chapter 10. Row-level security is enforced by a PL/SQL function, and the role of the PL/SQL function is the same as it was when used in the view examples. The difference between RLS and views is how the PL/SQL is invoked.

The policy function's job is to return a string (varchar2) that will serve as a predicate or a where clause to the original query. In effect, the original query is modified, the predicate string is attached, and the query is executed. For example, a simple query `select * from EMP` might be augmented by an RLS policy function that returns the predicate `ename = USER`. The effective SQL that is then executed will be `select * from EMP where ename = USER`. You'll see a diagram of this process later in Figure 11-1.

The PL/SQL functions are registered to tables, views, or synonyms by invoking the DBMS_RLS.ADD_POLICY procedure. The DBMS_RLS package is not granted to everyone; administrators will require direct execute privileges on the package. The ADD_POLICY procedure requires, at minimum, the name of the object to which the policy will be applied, a name for the policy, and the name of a PL/SQL function that will implement the security policy.

The policies can be applied to SELECT, INSERT, UPDATE, DELETE, and INDEX statements. The index affects CREATE INDEX and ALTER INDEX DDL commands. Whenever a user directly or indirectly accesses a protected table, view, or synonym, the RLS engine is transparently invoked, the PL/SQL function registered will execute, and the SQL statement will be modified and executed.

Benefits

RLS is very flexible and very granular. By default, the policy applies to all DML statements. The ADD_POLICY procedure accepts a STATEMENT_TYPES parameter that allows the administrator to specify which DML operations the policy is to apply. This granularity also allows the database to apply separate policies based on the DML type. For example, the database can easily support a policy to allow all records for SELECT statements; an INSERT, UPDATE policy to restrict records to a user's department on insert and update operations; and a DELETE policy that restricts DELETE operations to only the user's record.

Multiple policies also can be applied to the same object: the database logically ANDs the policies together. That is, if there is one policy that returns `ename = USER` and another policy (on the same object for the same DML) that returns `sal > 2000`, the database will automatically add both policies, effectively generating `where ename = USER` *and* `sal > 2000`.

The security from VPD derives from the fact that the predicates are used to restrict records returned by the original query, regardless of how the query was issued or who issued the query. This record filtering provides consistent row-level security that is guaranteed to work irrespective of the applications interacting with the data. The entire process is transparent to the application originally issuing the query. One of the strongest arguments for VPD is that the security is tightly fixed to the data it protects—it's consistent, centrally managed, and it can't be bypassed.

To understand why this is desirable, look at an alternative security model in which the application implements the record filtering. A particular challenge arises when the same data is required by multiple applications. In this case, the security about the data has to be replicated to all the applications. Varying programming languages, COTS applications, and design models often make this an arduous job at best.

The database's ability to support security for the data at both an object level and within the object (intra-object) are crucial for ensuring consistent and constant security. Programming languages are born and die within a few years. Applications change in functionality, design, and use even more frequently than that. A well-defined database schema will invariably outlive both. Therefore, a proper security model at the database is paramount to ensuring overall data security. By using features like VPD, the database implements the security policies and thus any application using the data will have the security policies automatically applied.

Setup

You now have the background to understand why VPD is a good tool, now you will see more examples of how to use it. In the next example, you'll solve the challenge posed in the "Viewing Problems" section in Chapter 10: a user is allowed to see all records; to insert and update records only within their department; and to delete only their individual record. You could build this with three views, but your application code would have to switch between views based on the type of operation it wishes to perform, and you would have to write Instead-of triggers. VPD will allow you to enforce two policies. Thus, any currently written SQL doesn't have to be altered as the security policy is created, altered, or deleted.

Setting the Application Context

For this example, the RLS policy will be applied to the PEOPLE table. To enforce the security just described, two policies will be needed: the first will manage the insert and update operations restricting records to the user's department; the second will manage delete operations to ensure the user can only delete their own records.

Restricting insert and updates to the user's department requires knowing what department the user belongs to. To make this as efficient as possible, the user's department number will be stored in an application context. While this is being done for illustrative purposes, application contexts are not required to implement RLS. A lookup table is created to support the population of the context values. The application context setup will involve three steps: creating an application context for the department number, building the namespace manager program to populate the context with the appropriate value, and invoking the namespace manager automatically when the user logs on.

The following code sample for setting up the application context is similar to an example given in Chapter 9. More details about why the code is written as it is are given in that chapter. The code is shown here again as a convenience.

The security manager will set the context values. As such, select privileges are required on the PEOPLE table. The security manager then creates the lookup table.

```
scott@KNOX10g> -- Recreate the people table to include all rows from EMP
scott@KNOX10g> DROP TABLE people;

Table dropped.

scott@KNOX10g> CREATE TABLE people
  AS SELECT ename username, job, sal salary, deptno
    FROM emp;

Table created.

scott@KNOX10g> GRANT SELECT ON people TO sec_mgr;

Grant succeeded.

scott@KNOX10g> CONN sec_mgr/oracle10g
Connected.
sec_mgr@KNOX10g> -- Create table to populate application context values
sec_mgr@KNOX10g> CREATE TABLE lookup_dept
  AS SELECT username, deptno FROM scott.people;

Table created.
```

The namespace manager program will set the context based on the user's department number as stored in the LOOKUP_DEPT table:

```
sec_mgr@KNOX10g> -- Create namespace for application context
sec_mgr@KNOX10g> CREATE CONTEXT people_ctx USING sec_mgr.people_ctx_mgr;

Context created.

sec_mgr@KNOX10g> -- Create namespace manager program for modifying context.
sec_mgr@KNOX10g> CREATE OR REPLACE PACKAGE people_ctx_mgr
  AS
    PROCEDURE set_deptno;
    PROCEDURE clear_deptno;
  END;
  /

Package created.

sec_mgr@KNOX10g> CREATE OR REPLACE PACKAGE BODY people_ctx_mgr
  AS
  ----------------------------------------
```

```
  PROCEDURE set_deptno
  AS
    l_deptno  NUMBER;
  BEGIN
    SELECT deptno
      INTO l_deptno
      FROM lookup_dept
     WHERE username =
             SYS_CONTEXT ('userenv',
                          'session_user');
    DBMS_SESSION.set_context
                        (namespace    => 'people_ctx',
                         ATTRIBUTE    => 'deptno',
                         VALUE        => l_deptno);
  END set_deptno;
-----------------------------------------
  PROCEDURE clear_deptno
  AS
  BEGIN
    DBMS_SESSION.clear_context
                       (namespace    => 'people_ctx',
                        ATTRIBUTE    => 'deptno');
  END clear_deptno;
-----------------------------------------
END people_ctx_mgr;
/

Package body created.

sec_mgr@KNOX10g> -- do NOT have to grant execute on namespace manager
```

To populate the context value automatically, a logon trigger will be used:

```
sec_mgr@KNOX10g> -- do NOT have to grant execute on namespace manager
sec_mgr@KNOX10g> CREATE OR REPLACE TRIGGER set_user_deptno
    AFTER LOGON ON DATABASE
BEGIN
    sec_mgr.people_ctx_mgr.set_deptno;
EXCEPTION
    WHEN NO_DATA_FOUND
    THEN
      -- If user is not in table,
      -- a no_data_found is raised
      -- If exception is not handled, then users not in table
      -- will be unable to log on
      NULL;
END;
/

Trigger created.
```

Test the context by logging in as the SCOTT user:

```
sec_mgr@KNOX10g> CONN scott/tiger
Connected.
scott@KNOX10g> COL deptno format a8
scott@KNOX10g> SELECT SYS_CONTEXT ('people_ctx',
                            'deptno') deptno
       FROM DUAL;

DEPTNO
--------
20
```

Creating the Policy Function

All RLS policy functions are passed two parameters by the database when they are invoked. The first is the name of the schema that owns the object for which the RLS policy is being invoked. The second is the name of the object for which the RLS policy is being invoked. These two parameters are helpful because a single policy function (PL/SQL program) may be applied to multiple objects in multiple schemas. The parameters can then be used to determine specifically which object the policy is being invoked.

A good practice is to create your policy functions with the parameter values defaulted to null. This will allows you to test the function directly:

```
sec_mgr@KNOX10g> -- Create policy function.
sec_mgr@KNOX10g> CREATE OR REPLACE FUNCTION dept_only (
       p_schema   IN  VARCHAR2 DEFAULT NULL,
       p_object   IN  VARCHAR2 DEFAULT NULL)
       RETURN VARCHAR2
     AS
     BEGIN
       RETURN 'deptno = sys_context(''people_ctx'',''deptno'')';
     END;
     /

Function created.
```

Notice that this policy function is created in the security manager's schema. This is important because access to the policy function should be guarded.

NOTE
Your users should not have execute privileges on the policy function, nor should they be able to alter or drop the function.

This last requirement generally implies the function is separated from the data schema to which it will be applied. In some cases, you can see the predicate string that will be used by displaying the return value of the function:

```
sec_mgr@KNOX10g> -- Test policy function.
sec_mgr@KNOX10g> col predicate format a50
```

```
sec_mgr@KNOX10g> SELECT dept_only predicate FROM DUAL;

PREDICATE
--------------------------------------------------
deptno = sys_context('people_ctx','deptno')
```

This policy function is quite simple; in fact, it could just as easily have been implemented in a view. You are using VPD instead of views because this policy is only relevant to inserts and updates.

Applying the Insert/Update Policy

The security requirement implemented by the preceding code is supposed to be in effect on all inserts and updates. After running the following statement, the database will call the DEPT_ONLY function in the SEC_MGR schema whenever someone inserts or updates the SCOTT.PEOPLE table:

```
sec_mgr@KNOX10g> -- apply RLS policy to table
sec_mgr@KNOX10g> BEGIN
      DBMS_RLS.add_policy
                 (object_schema       => 'SCOTT',
                  object_name         => 'PEOPLE',
                  policy_name         => 'PEOPLE_IU',
                  function_schema     => 'SEC_MGR',
                  policy_function     => 'Dept_Only',
                  statement_types     => 'INSERT,UPDATE',
                  update_check        => TRUE);
    END;
    /

PL/SQL procedure successfully completed.
```

The combination of object schema, object name, and policy name has to be unique. A good practice for the policy name is to choose something that describes the intended use of the policy. PEOPLE_IU is my way of indicating a policy on the PEOPLE table for insert and update operations. Likewise, choosing a function name that is descriptive about what the function results are is also good practice. The DEPT_ONLY implies the function restricts records at the department level. As a result of executing the ADD_POLICY procedure, the following SQL

```
update people
  set ename = '<NEW_VALUE>'
```

will be effectively transformed into

```
update people
  set ename = '<NEW_VALUE>'
  where deptno = sys_context('people_ctx','deptno')
```

Figure 11-1 depicts how this occurs.

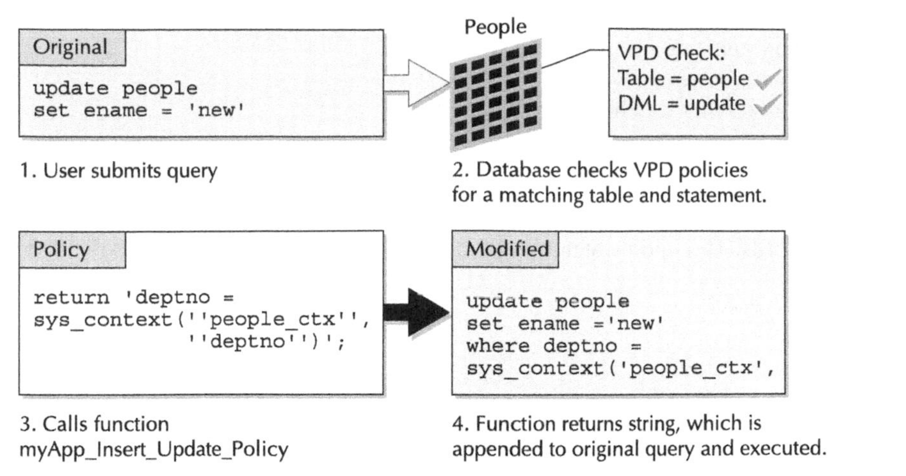

FIGURE 11-1. *Queries are modified transparently by the RLS policy.*

Testing VPD Protected Insert and Updates

A quick test validates that the policy is working. For the test, simply update a record within your department (Department 20 for SCOTT), and update a record outside your department. The following query returns a record from each so you can properly issue your update statements:

```
sec_mgr@KNOX10g> CONN scott/tiger
Connected.
scott@KNOX10g> SELECT username, deptno
  2    FROM people
  3   WHERE username < 'C';

USERNAME        DEPTNO
---------- ----------
ALLEN               30
BLAKE               30
ADAMS               20
```

Testing the updates should show that updates to records in Department 20 will be successful. Updates to records outside Department 20 should not succeed:

```
scott@KNOX10g> -- Update to department 20 user
scott@KNOX10g> -- This should succeed.
scott@KNOX10g> UPDATE people
  2     SET username = 'GRIZZLY'
  3   WHERE username = 'ADAMS';

1 row updated.
```

```
scott@KNOX10g> -- Update to department 30 user
scott@KNOX10g> -- This should not update anything.
scott@KNOX10g> UPDATE people
  2      SET username = 'BOZO'
  3    WHERE username = 'BLAKE';

0 rows updated.
```

Note that zero errors are thrown for the second update. The modified SQL simply excludes all possible records. The update statement was effectively augmented and resolved to the following:

```
UPDATE people
   SET ename   = 'Bozo'
 WHERE ename   = 'BLAKE'
   AND deptno = SYS_CONTEXT ('people_ctx', 'deptno')
```

The SYS_CONTEXT function will resolve to the number 20 for the user SCOTT. Because there is no BLAKE record with a deptno = 20, zero records are updated.

To test the inserts, try to insert a new record for Department 20, then insert a record outside Department 20:

```
scott@KNOX10g> -- This insert should work as deptno = 20
scott@KNOX10g> INSERT INTO people
  2                (username, job, salary, deptno)
  3         VALUES ('KNOX', 'Clerk', '3000', 20);

1 row created.

scott@KNOX10g> -- This insert should not work
scott@KNOX10g> INSERT INTO people
  2                (username, job, salary, deptno)
  3         VALUES ('ELLISON', 'CEO','90000', 30);
INSERT INTO people
            *
ERROR at line 1:
ORA-28115: policy with check option violation
```

Note the insert operation fails with an error. This operation fails because you set the UPDATE_CHECK=TRUE in the ADD_POLICY procedure call. The default value for UPDATE_CHECK is FALSE. If you had not specified TRUE, the insert would have succeeded. This behavior is consistent with that of a view with a check option.

The Delete RLS Policy Example

The delete policy says that the user can only delete their record. This function can be implemented as follows:

```
sec_mgr@KNOX10g> CREATE OR REPLACE FUNCTION user_only (
  2    p_schema   IN   VARCHAR2 DEFAULT NULL,
```

```
    p_object  IN  VARCHAR2 DEFAULT NULL)
    RETURN VARCHAR2
  AS
  BEGIN
    RETURN 'username = sys_context(''userenv'',''session_user'')';
  END;
  /

Function created.
```

To apply the delete policy, specify DELETE statements in the ADD_POLICY procedure and provide the USER_ONLY function for the POLICY_FUNCTION:

```
sec_mgr@KNOX10g> -- apply delete policy to table
sec_mgr@KNOX10g> BEGIN
    DBMS_RLS.add_policy
               (object_schema      => 'SCOTT',
                object_name        => 'PEOPLE',
                policy_name        => 'People_Del',
                function_schema    => 'SEC_MGR',
                policy_function    => 'user_only',
                statement_types    => 'DELETE');
  END;
  /

PL/SQL procedure successfully completed.
```

Testing the delete policy, you'll notice that a delete statement that attempts to delete all records actually results in only one actual deletion—the user's very own record:

```
scott@KNOX10g> DELETE FROM people;

1 row deleted.

scott@KNOX10g> SELECT * FROM people
    WHERE username = 'SCOTT';

no rows selected
```

Again, the database has transparently augmented the SQL statement. The policy function restricts delete operations to the user's record. Therefore, the most users can ever delete is their record.

The RLS Layer of Security

If you want to prevent users from accessing all records (including their own), first use the object privileges to enforce this to ensure the user doesn't have the privileges on the table.

To strengthen the security, you can also use RLS. RLS provides an additional layer of security and will even prevent someone with the DBA role or an ANY system privilege—SELECT ANY TABLE—from accessing your protected table(s). Note this doesn't imply the table is protected from a DBA with malicious intentions. The DBA can alter the policy function, drop the table, disable the RLS policy, and so on. The shear fact of being a DBA doesn't override the RLS capability. In the previous example, a DBA who can read records from your table still can't delete any records because the delete policy restricts access to the records matching USERNAME with the schema name:

```
scott@KNOX10g> CONN system/manager
Connected.
system@KNOX10g> -- user has SELECT ANY TABLE so he can see all records
system@KNOX10g> SELECT COUNT(*) FROM scott.people;

  COUNT(*)
----------
        14

system@KNOX10g> -- user cannot delete records as RLS prevents this
system@KNOX10g> DELETE FROM scott.people;

0 rows deleted.
```

Returning Zero Records

The most effective way to prevent records from being accessed within an RLS policy function is to return a string that consists of something that can never happen. An easy example is the string "1=0". Be aware—returning a null or a zero length string has the opposite effect, and all rows are returned.

CAUTION
Returning null from the policy function allows all records to be accessed.

You might find it useful to create a function that eliminates all records. You can then use it anytime you want to quickly lock down a table:

```
sec_mgr@KNOX10g> -- Create a function to be used with RLS
sec_mgr@KNOX10g> -- that will always eliminate all records.
sec_mgr@KNOX10g> CREATE OR REPLACE FUNCTION no_records (
    p_schema  IN  VARCHAR2 DEFAULT NULL,
    p_object  IN  VARCHAR2 DEFAULT NULL)
    RETURN VARCHAR2
  AS
  BEGIN
    RETURN '1=0';
  END;
  /

Function created.
```

There are several ways to create a READ ONLY table or view; here you can see another. Adding the NO_RECORDS function to an RLS policy for inserts, updates, and deletes effectively makes the table READ ONLY.

```
scott@KNOX10g> CREATE TABLE people_ro AS SELECT * FROM emp;

Table created.

scott@KNOX10g> conn sec_mgr/oracle10g
Connected.
sec_mgr@KNOX10g> BEGIN
    DBMS_RLS.add_policy
        (object_schema      => 'SCOTT',
         object_name        => 'PEOPLE_RO',
         policy_name        => 'PEOPLE_RO_IUD',
         function_schema    => 'SEC_MGR',
         policy_function    => 'No_Records',
         statement_types    => 'INSERT,UPDATE,DELETE',
         update_check       => TRUE);
  END;
  /

PL/SQL procedure successfully completed.
```

As indicated by the tests here, the RLS policy helps to ensure the table maintains its READ ONLY status:

```
sec_mgr@KNOX10G> scott@KNOX10g> -- User can read all records
scott@KNOX10g> SELECT COUNT (*) FROM people_ro;

  COUNT(*)
----------
        14

scott@KNOX10g> -- Cannot update any records
scott@KNOX10g> UPDATE people_ro
      SET ename = NULL;

0 rows updated.

scott@KNOX10g> -- Cannot delete records
scott@KNOX10g> DELETE FROM people_ro;

0 rows deleted.

scott@KNOX10g> -- Cannot insert new records
scott@KNOX10g> INSERT INTO people_ro (ename) VALUES ('KNOX');
INSERT INTO people_ro (ename) VALUES ('KNOX')
            *
```

```
ERROR at line 1:
ORA-28115: policy with check option violation
```

RLS Exemption

While the RLS provides wonderful security, it can be problematic when doing database administration tasks such as performing data backups. As you have seen, even the DBAs and the data owner cannot bypass the RLS policy. If you perform an export as the data owner or another administrator while an RLS policy was enabled, you may very well end up with a dataless backup file.

For this reason (and a few others), there is an EXEMPT ACCESS POLICY privilege. This privilege allows the grantee to be exempted from *all* RLS functions. An administrator who has to perform data backups can use this privilege to ensure backup ability for all the data in the tables. The following example illustrates how this privilege is granted and the affect it has on enabled RLS policies:

```
system@KNOX10g> CONN system/manager
Connected.
system@KNOX10g> -- Show system is affected by RLS policy.
system@KNOX10g> -- No records should be deleted.
system@KNOX10g> DELETE FROM scott.people_ro;

0 rows deleted.

system@KNOX10g> -- grant privilege to bypass RLS policies
system@KNOX10g> GRANT EXEMPT ACCESS POLICY TO SYSTEM;

Grant succeeded.

system@KNOX10g> -- Show system is no longer affected by RLS policy.
system@KNOX10g> -- All records should be deleted.
system@KNOX10g> DELETE FROM scott.people_ro;

14 rows deleted.

system@KNOX10g> ROLLBACK ;
```

EXEMPT ACCESS POLICY is a very powerful privilege. The privilege isn't specific to a schema or policy; it applies to all schemas and all policies. Care should be given to ensure that the privilege is well guarded. By default, users with SYSDBA privileges are exempt from RLS policies. You can determine who has been granted the EXEMPT ACCESS POLICY privilege by checking system privileges, as shown here:

```
sec_mgr@KNOX10g> -- Show users that are exempt from RLS policies
sec_mgr@KNOX10g> SELECT grantee
  2     FROM dba_sys_privs
  3    WHERE PRIVILEGE = 'EXEMPT ACCESS POLICY';

GRANTEE
------------------------------
SYSTEM
```

NOTE
The EXEMPT ACCESS POLICY system privilege allows privileged users to bypass RLS policies. This may be necessary for database backup and recovery, but it can also be a security risk. Guard this privilege tightly.

Audit Exempt Access Policy

You can't prevent privileged users *from* abusing their privileges, you can only catch them doing it. Auditing is an effective way to ensure the RLS exemption privilege is not being abused. The following shows how to enable auditing for this privilege. Once enabled, you should test to ensure that everything is being audited as you think. For this to occur, the system privilege has to be exercised. This too is shown:

```
sec_mgr@KNOX10g> -- Audit the exempt policy system privilege
sec_mgr@KNOX10g> AUDIT EXEMPT ACCESS POLICY BY ACCESS;

Audit succeeded.

sec_mgr@KNOX10g> -- Test audit by exercising the system privilege
sec_mgr@KNOX10g> CONN system/manager
Connected.
system@KNOX10g> DELETE FROM scott.people_ro;

14 rows deleted.

system@KNOX10g> -- Rollback will not erase the audit record
system@KNOX10g> ROLLBACK ;

Rollback complete.

system@KNOX10g> CONN sec_mgr/oracle10g
Connected.
sec_mgr@KNOX10g> -- show audited operation

sec_mgr@KNOX10g> BEGIN
       FOR rec IN (SELECT *
                     FROM dba_audit_trail)
       LOOP
         DBMS_OUTPUT.put_line ('-------------------------');
         DBMS_OUTPUT.put_line ('Who:    ' || rec.username);
         DBMS_OUTPUT.put_line (    'What:   '
                               || rec.action_name
                               || ' on '
                               || rec.owner
                               || '.'
                               || rec.obj_name);
         DBMS_OUTPUT.put_line (    'When:   '
                               || TO_CHAR
                                       (rec.TIMESTAMP,
                                        'MM/DD HH24:MI'));
```

```
      DBMS_OUTPUT.put_line ('How:    "' || rec.sql_text || '"');
      DBMS_OUTPUT.put_line ('Using: ' || rec.priv_used);
    END LOOP;
  END;
  /
-------------------------
Who:   SYSTEM
What:  DELETE on SCOTT.PEOPLE_RO
When:  04/04 14:22
How:   "DELETE FROM scott.people_ro"
Using: DELETE ANY TABLE
-------------------------
Who:   SYSTEM
What:  DELETE on SCOTT.PEOPLE_RO
When:  04/04 14:22
How:   "DELETE FROM scott.people_ro"
Using: EXEMPT ACCESS POLICY

PL/SQL procedure successfully completed.
```

The audit trail shows two records because the SYSTEM user exercised two system privileges when the delete statement was issued. The first privilege, DELETE ANY TABLE, allowed access to the table. The second privilege, EXEMPT ACCESS POLICY, allowed access *within* the table.

Debugging RLS Policies

When an RLS policy fails, the users can no longer access the protected objects. I have found that the chances of this happening are in direct proportion to the complexity of the policy function. When this does happen, having a sound method for troubleshooting the problem is critical to minimizing the down time associated with the error.

There are generally two reasons for a policy error. First, the policy function is invalid and will not recompile or execute. For example, an error will occur if the policy function queries a table that no longer exists. A policy error will also occur if the policy function doesn't exist. This is usually because the function has been dropped or the function has been incorrectly registered in the ADD_POLICY procedure.

The second reason for policy error occurs when the policy function returns a string that, when added to the original SQL, produces an invalid SQL statement. There are many possible reasons why the function can fail. The first step to debugging is to ensure that the function is working.

Broken Policy Functions

Errors caused by an invalid policy function can easily make the VPD transparency disappear. To show this, the following example creates a simple table with a simple policy function. The policy function is dependent on the table.

```
scott@KNOX10g> -- Create a dependency. This table will
scott@KNOX10g> -- be called by the RLS policy function.
scott@KNOX10g> CREATE TABLE t AS SELECT * FROM DUAL;
```

```
Table created.

scott@KNOX10g> -- Create policy function. Function
scott@KNOX10g> -- is dependent on table T.
scott@KNOX10g> CREATE OR REPLACE FUNCTION pred_function (
    p_schema   IN  VARCHAR2 DEFAULT NULL,
    p_object   IN  VARCHAR2 DEFAULT NULL)
    RETURN VARCHAR2
  AS
    l_total_recs  NUMBER;
  BEGIN
    SELECT COUNT (*)
      INTO l_total_recs
      FROM t;
    RETURN '1 <= ' || l_total_recs;
  END;
  /

Function created.
```

The point here is to create and then break a dependency. The policy function is dependent on the table T. Add the policy to your table and check to see that no errors occur on access:

```
scott@KNOX10g> CONN sec_mgr/oracle10g
Connected.
sec_mgr@KNOX10g> -- Add RLS policy to EMP table;
sec_mgr@KNOX10g> BEGIN
    DBMS_RLS.add_policy
                (object_schema       => 'SCOTT',
                 object_name         => 'EMP',
                 policy_name         => 'debug',
                 function_schema     => 'SCOTT',
                 policy_function     => 'pred_function');
  END;
  /

PL/SQL procedure successfully completed.

sec_mgr@KNOX10g> CONN scott/tiger
Connected.
scott@KNOX10g> -- Everything initially works fine
scott@KNOX10g> SELECT COUNT(*) FROM emp;

  COUNT(*)
----------
        14
```

Dropping the table T will invalidate the policy function. The first indication that something is wrong may come when you try to query the EMP table:

```
scott@KNOX10g> -- This drop breaks the policy function
scott@KNOX10g> DROP TABLE t;

Table dropped.

scott@KNOX10g> -- Policy function is invalid and will not recompile;
scott@KNOX10g> SELECT COUNT(*) FROM emp;
SELECT COUNT(*) FROM emp
                     *
ERROR at line 1:
ORA-28110: policy function or package SCOTT.PRED_FUNCTION has error
```

Recovering from this is very easy with Oracle Database 10*g*. You can simply use the Flashback Drop to restore the table T. Once this is done, access to the EMP table is also restored because the policy function will be able to successfully execute:

```
scott@KNOX10g> -- Recover table
scott@KNOX10g> FLASHBACK TABLE t TO BEFORE DROP;

Flashback complete.

scott@KNOX10g> SELECT COUNT(*) FROM emp;

  COUNT(*)
----------
        14
```

Handling Policy Function Exceptions

When the query on EMP was executed after the T table was dropped and before it was recovered, the database threw an error indicating precisely why the query failed. This is very helpful, but it may not be desirable because two potentially sensitive things were revealed. First, it indicated that there is an RLS policy on the table; second, it gave the name of the policy function guarding the table.

You may want to consider suppressing the policy function exceptions to prevent this information from being displayed to the users. The best approach to this requires the use of dynamic SQL that hides the function's database object dependencies. The function still has to return a value. Returning null will allow the user access to all the records. Failing secure means that you should return zero records if an exception is thrown. This example shows how to fail secure:

```
scott@KNOX10g> -- User dynamic SQL and exception handling
scott@KNOX10g> -- to mask policy function errors
scott@KNOX10g> CREATE OR REPLACE FUNCTION pred_function (
  2     p_schema  IN  VARCHAR2 DEFAULT NULL,
  3     p_object  IN  VARCHAR2 DEFAULT NULL)
  4     RETURN VARCHAR2
```

```
AS
  l_total_recs  NUMBER;
BEGIN
  -- Dynamic SQL hides the dependency on table T
  EXECUTE IMMEDIATE 'SELECT COUNT (*) FROM t'
               INTO l_total_recs;
  RETURN '1 <= ' || l_total_recs;
EXCEPTION
  WHEN OTHERS
  THEN
    -- Fail Secure: remove all rows
    RETURN '1=0';
END;
/

Function created.

scott@KNOX10g> SELECT COUNT(*) FROM emp;

  COUNT(*)
----------
        14

scott@KNOX10g> -- This drop breaks the policy function
scott@KNOX10g> DROP TABLE t;

Table dropped.

scott@KNOX10g> -- Policy fails secure. No records are displayed or
scott@KNOX10g> -- exception messages given to user.
scott@KNOX10g> SELECT COUNT(*) FROM emp;

  COUNT(*)
----------
         0
```

The downside to this approach is that it will be more difficult to debug the policy yourself. The solution to this is to comment out or remove the exception handling code, but you should only do this while debugging.

Invalid SQL

A second possible reason a policy may fail is because the SQL returned by the policy function creates an invalid SQL statement. Recall the policy's return value is added to the original SQL. The database will try to parse and execute this final SQL statement. If the SQL is invalid, the policy will throw an error.

Unfortunately, the error message does not indicate how the SQL is malformed. (It's not even clear what the problem is.) For complex policies, or objects that have multiple policies, this can create some frustration.

For this example, the policy function has been modified to support a policy that restricts DML to just the user's record. Unfortunately, the SQL column NAME should really be ENAME. Because the return value is a string, this error does not manifest itself until runtime:

```
scott@KNOX10g> -- Create policy function that returns
scott@KNOX10g> -- records just for the user.
scott@KNOX10g> CREATE OR REPLACE FUNCTION pred_function (
    p_schema  IN  VARCHAR2 DEFAULT NULL,
    p_object  IN  VARCHAR2 DEFAULT NULL)
    RETURN VARCHAR2
  AS
  BEGIN
    -- Restricting records by mapping ENAME
    -- to authenticated database user's name
    RETURN 'name = user';
  END;
  /

Function created.

scott@KNOX10g> SELECT COUNT(*) FROM emp;
SELECT COUNT(*) FROM emp
                     *
ERROR at line 1:
ORA-28113: policy predicate has error
```

An ORA-28113 is the indication that the SQL is bad. It's impossible for the database to know why this is true. Your policy function could have derived the predicate string in an infinite number of ways. The only thing you know is that the resulting SQL is invalid. To debug it, first try to inspect the value returned by the policy function:

```
scott@KNOX10g> SELECT pred_function "Policy Predicate" FROM DUAL;

Policy Predicate
--------------------
name = user
```

Note you can query the DBA_POLICIES view (as shown later in the "Viewing the Original SQL and Predicate" section) to see the PREDICATE but only if the policy doesn't throw an error.

At this point, your best alternative may be to access a trace file. To do this easily, create a simple view (based on another Tom Kyte contribution from asktom.oracle.com) that can determine the trace filename the database will be using:

```
sec_mgr@KNOX10g> -- Create view to display session's current trace file
sec_mgr@KNOX10g> CREATE OR REPLACE VIEW get_trace_filename
  AS
    SELECT    c.VALUE
           || decode(instr(c.value,'\'),0,'/','\')
           || INSTANCE
```

```
                || '_ora_'
                || LTRIM (TO_CHAR (a.spid, 'fm99999'))
                || '.trc' filename
           FROM v$process a,
                v$session b,
                v$parameter c,
                v$thread c
          WHERE a.addr = b.paddr
            AND b.audsid = USERENV ('sessionid')
            AND c.NAME = 'user_dump_dest';

View created.

sec_mgr@KNOX10g> GRANT SELECT ON get_trace_filename TO PUBLIC;

Grant succeeded.

sec_mgr@KNOX10g> CREATE PUBLIC SYNONYM get_trace_filename
                       FOR get_trace_filename;

Synonym created.
```

Connect as a user and reproduce the query that caused the policy error. This is done here as SCOTT:

```
scott@KNOX10g> -- Enable tracing
scott@KNOX10g> ALTER SESSION SET EVENTS
       '10730 trace name context forever, level 12';

Session altered.

scott@KNOX10g> -- Reproduce error.
scott@KNOX10g> -- Issue query; note only selecting ENAME
scott@KNOX10g> SELECT ename FROM emp;
SELECT ename FROM emp
                  *
ERROR at line 1:
ORA-28113: policy predicate has error


scott@KNOX10g> -- view trace file
scott@KNOX10g> COL filename format a50
scott@KNOX10g> SELECT * FROM get_trace_filename;

FILENAME
--------------------------------------------------
C:\ORACLE\ADMIN\KNOX10G\UDUMP\knox10g_ora_3740.trc

scott@KNOX10g> -- fix the policy function
scott@KNOX10g> -- Create policy function that returns
```

```
scott@KNOX10g> -- records just for the user.
scott@KNOX10g> CREATE OR REPLACE FUNCTION pred_function (
    p_schema   IN  VARCHAR2 DEFAULT NULL,
    p_object   IN  VARCHAR2 DEFAULT NULL)
    RETURN VARCHAR2
  AS
  BEGIN
    -- Restricting records by mapping ENAME
    -- to authenticated database user's name
    RETURN 'ename = user';
  END;
  /

Function created.

scott@KNOX10g> -- Re-query to verify policy works
scott@KNOX10g> SELECT ename FROM emp;

ENAME
----------
SCOTT
```

Viewing the contents of the trace file with the name returned from GET_TRACE_FILENAME provides helpful information. The relevant information from the trace file just generated from the previous session is displayed here:

```
-------------------------------------------------------------
Logon user      : SCOTT
Table/View      : SCOTT.EMP
Policy name     : DEBUG
Policy function: SCOTT.PRED_FUNCTION
RLS view :
SELECT  "EMPNO","ENAME","JOB","MGR","HIREDATE","SAL","COMM","DEPTNO" FROM
SCOTT"."EMP"  "EMP" WHERE (name = user)
*** 2004-04-05 13:32:02.874
-------------------------------------------------------------
Error information for ORA-28113:
Logon user      : SCOTT
Table/View      : SCOTT.EMP
Policy name     : DEBUG
Policy function: SCOTT.PRED_FUNCTION
RLS predicate   :
name = user
ORA-00904: "NAME": invalid identifier
-------------------------------------------------------------
Logon user      : SCOTT
Table/View      : SCOTT.EMP
Policy name     : DEBUG
Policy function: SCOTT.PRED_FUNCTION
RLS view :
SELECT  "EMPNO","ENAME","JOB","MGR","HIREDATE","SAL","COMM","DEPTNO" FROM
SCOTT"."EMP"  "EMP" WHERE (ename = user)
```

This file is very useful, especially the section that displays information on the ORA-28113 error. The RLS predicate record (bolded) pinpoints the erroneous SQL.

Be careful, there is a very misleading fact printed, too.

CAUTION
The RLS view is not the actual SQL the database executes.

Many incorrectly believe it is. This should be obvious because the original SQL statement asked only for the ENAME column; the RLS view would have you believe all columns were selected.

Viewing the Original SQL and Predicate

Another view you may find helpful in inspecting your VPD implementations is the V$VPD_POLICY view. This will tell you what policies have been successfully applied to your SQL statements. The PREDICATE column will actually show the SQL string that was appended to the query. You can join this record with V$SQL, which has the original SQL statement as follows:

```
sec_mgr@KNOX10g> -- Nothing in pool - a fresh database
sec_mgr@KNOX10g> SELECT * FROM v$vpd_policy;

no rows selected

sec_mgr@KNOX10g> CONN scott/tiger
Connected.
scott@KNOX10g> -- this will seed the v$vpd_policy view
scott@KNOX10g> SELECT COUNT (*) FROM emp;

  COUNT(*)
----------
         1

scott@KNOX10g> CONN sec_mgr/oracle10g
Connected.
sec_mgr@KNOX10g> -- show VPD Policy results
sec_mgr@KNOX10g> COL object_owner format a12
sec_mgr@KNOX10g> COL object_name format a12
sec_mgr@KNOX10g> COL policy format a6
sec_mgr@KNOX10g> COL sql_fulltext format a26
sec_mgr@KNOX10g> COL predicate format a12
sec_mgr@KNOX10g> SELECT object_owner,
  2          object_name,
  3          policy,
  4          sql_fulltext,
  5          predicate
  6     FROM v$vpd_policy p, v$sql s
  7    WHERE p.sql_id = s.sql_id
  8      AND predicate IS NOT NULL;

OBJECT_OWNER OBJECT_NAME  POLICY SQL_FULLTEXT               PREDICATE
------------ ------------ ------ -------------------------- ------------
SCOTT        EMP          DEBUG  SELECT COUNT (*) FROM emp  ename = user
```

This is a good way of inspecting the policies, but there is one important caveat: *no records are recorded if the policy throws an error.* For policy errors, you will have to use tracing, and even then the *real* SQL is not given.

Null Application Context Values and Recursive Lookups

There are two areas that consistently trap newcomers to VPD. The problem occurs when an RLS policy function references an application context that is null. The reason the application context is null is because the namespace manager is trying to set the context on the table to which the RLS policy is being applied.

This example begins by illustrating the working context. Recall the user's department number is set by a logon trigger. The trigger calls the namespace manager, which sets the value by querying the LOOKUP_DEPT table:

```
sec_mgr@KNOX10g> CONN scott/tiger
Connected.
scott@KNOX10g> -- Context value is set on logon
scott@KNOX10g> COL deptno format a6
scott@KNOX10g> SELECT SYS_CONTEXT ('people_ctx',
                         'deptno') deptno
     FROM DUAL;

DEPTNO
------
20

scott@KNOX10g> CONN sec_mgr/oracle10g
Connected.
sec_mgr@KNOX10g> -- Current view on table
sec_mgr@KNOX10g> SELECT * FROM lookup_dept
    WHERE username = 'SCOTT';

USERNAME       DEPTNO
---------- ----------
SCOTT              20
```

Normally, the lookup table would not exist. It was created specifically to bypass this problem. Nevertheless, the mistake comes next when an RLS policy is added to the LOOKUP_DEPT table. To help with this example, an update policy will be added to the EMP table using the same policy function. Most often the context will be set from the same table the RLS policy will be enforced from which, as you will see, can't be done:

```
sec_mgr@KNOX10g> -- Add Dept level policy to lookup table.
sec_mgr@KNOX10g> -- Policy references people_ctx context.
sec_mgr@KNOX10g> BEGIN
     DBMS_RLS.add_policy
                  (object_schema      => 'SEC_MGR',
                   object_name        => 'lookup_dept',
                   policy_name        => 'lookup_dept_sel',
                   policy_function    => 'dept_only',
                   statement_types    => 'SELECT');
```

```
END;
/

PL/SQL procedure successfully completed.

sec_mgr@KNOX10g> -- Add Dept level policy to EMP table.
sec_mgr@KNOX10g> -- Policy references people_ctx context.
sec_mgr@KNOX10g> BEGIN
   DBMS_RLS.add_policy
              (object_schema      => 'SCOTT',
               object_name        => 'EMP',
               policy_name        => 'EMP_UPD',
               policy_function    => 'dept_only',
               statement_types    => 'UPDATE');
END;
/

PL/SQL procedure successfully completed.
```

Querying from the lookup table shows the expected results. If you are the security administrator, you may feel nothing is wrong:

```
sec_mgr@KNOX10g> -- rows are no longer visible
sec_mgr@KNOX10g> -- since SEC_MGR has not context
sec_mgr@KNOX10g> SELECT * FROM lookup_dept;

no rows selected
```

Connecting as the SCOTT user, you can see the application context wasn't set. The ramifications of this are that any RLS policies that are based on this context will not behave properly:

```
sec_mgr@KNOX10g> CONN scott/tiger
Connected.
scott@KNOX10g> -- Context no longer exists
scott@KNOX10g> COL deptno format A6
scott@KNOX10g> SELECT SYS_CONTEXT ('people_ctx',
                        'deptno') deptno
   FROM DUAL;

DEPTNO
------


scott@KNOX10g> -- Any RLS policies that used the context value will not
cott@KNOX10g> -- behave correctly.
scott@KNOX10g> -- This update would normally succeed for all dept 20 records
scott@KNOX10g> UPDATE emp
    SET ename = ename;

0 rows updated.
```

Recall the policy function being added restricts the user's records to the department in which they work. The department number is stored in the context that is populated from the same table being restricted by the RLS *policy*. This recursive condition prevents the application context from being populated.

The solution to this is to create a different object to be used for populating the application context. The object can be a table or a view. A view is the best because there is no data synchronization that needs to occur. If you create a view, the application context lookup should occur on the table, and the RLS policy should be applied to the view. If you did this the other way, it wouldn't work because the RLS on the base table would still be in effect when the table was accessed by way of the view.

Partitioned Fine-Grained Access Control

Oracle introduced partitioned fine-grained access control in Oracle9*i* Database, which allows you to group together multiple policies and then enable and disable them easily. This is a useful concept when multiple policies exist on the same objects but have conflicting return values.

Recall that Oracle logically ANDs all RLS policies. That is, if there are two policies, A and B, for the same object, then the resulting SQL will be the output of A and B. If policy A returns "deptno = 20" and policy B returns "deptno = 10", then the resulting query will be "deptno = 20 *and* deptno = 10". Because the deptno is either 10 or 20, this query results in zero rows.

Partitioned fine-grained access control allows you to define which RLS policies you want to enable for the user session. This is done by setting the policy name into an application context. The database will then reference this policy name by looking at the value stored in the user's application context and applying that RLS policy.

Normally, I would include an example that illustrates some nuance of the technology. Fortunately, the *Oracle Database Security Guide 10g* has an excellent example of partitioned fine-grained access control. Including a different example here would be redundant.

Column Sensitive VPD

Oracle Database 10g offers a new feature to VPD called Column Sensitive VPD. The objective of this feature is to invoke the security policy when a specific column is referenced.

Let's augment the security on the PEOPLE view to allow users to see only their own salaries. You do still want the user to see other columns of other user records. You can use the same PL/SQL function, USER_ONLY, for this new policy. The added parameter is SEC_RELEVANT_COLS.

```
sec_mgr@KNOX10g> BEGIN
    DBMS_RLS.add_policy
                   (object_schema        => 'SCOTT',
                    object_name          => 'PEOPLE',
                    policy_name          => 'people_sel_sal',
                    function_schema      => 'SEC_MGR',
                    policy_function      => 'user_only',
                    statement_types      => 'SELECT',
                    sec_relevant_cols    => 'SALARY');
  END;
  /

PL/SQL procedure successfully completed.
```

Testing this code, you see a different result than you did with our view. When the SALARY column is queried, the VPD policy is invoked, and only one record is returned; when the SALARY column is not queried, then the policy isn't invoked and all records are returned:

```
sec_mgr@KNOX10g> CONN scott/tiger
Connected.
scott@KNOX10g> -- User can see all records when SALARY column is not
scott@KNOX10g> -- queried. Show first five records only.
scott@KNOX10g> SELECT username FROM people
    WHERE ROWNUM <= 5;

USERNAME
----------
SMITH
ALLEN
WARD
JONES
MARTIN

scott@KNOX10g> -- Adding the salary column causes
scott@KNOX10g> -- the RLS policy to activate
scott@KNOX10g> SELECT username, salary FROM people;

USERNAME       SALARY
---------- ----------
SCOTT            3000
```

To make VPD behave like the column masking view example you saw in Chapter 10 you can use another new parameter to the ADD_POLICY procedure: SEC_RELEVANT_COLS_OPT. Oracle's implementation is consistent with what was done in the view. That is, the values for the sensitive columns are null values. All the other columns and rows are returned:

```
sec_mgr@KNOX10g> BEGIN
     -- Remove current policy
     DBMS_RLS.drop_policy
                    (object_schema    => 'SCOTT',
                     object_name      => 'PEOPLE',
                     policy_name      => 'people_sel_sal');
     -- Add policy again but now add the SEC_RELEVANT_COLS_OPT
     DBMS_RLS.add_policy
          (object_schema            => 'SCOTT',
           object_name              => 'PEOPLE',
           policy_name              => 'people_sel_sal',
           function_schema          => 'SEC_MGR',
           policy_function          => 'user_only',
           statement_types          => 'SELECT',
           sec_relevant_cols        => 'SALARY',
           sec_relevant_cols_opt    => DBMS_RLS.all_rows);
   END;
   /

PL/SQL procedure successfully completed.
```

The final query then results with null salary values for all but the invoking users:

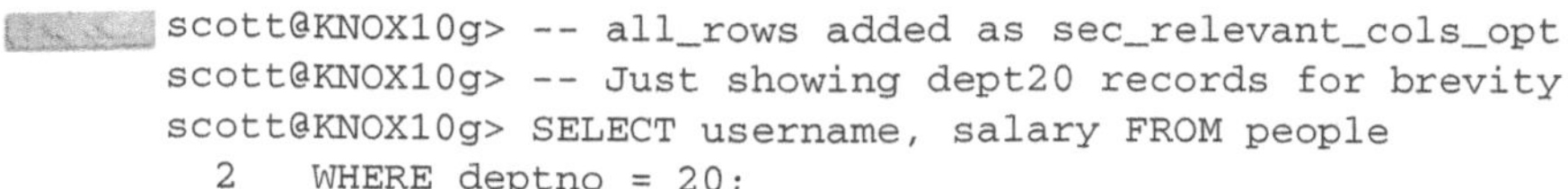

```
scott@KNOX10g> -- all_rows added as sec_relevant_cols_opt
scott@KNOX10g> -- Just showing dept20 records for brevity.
scott@KNOX10g> SELECT username, salary FROM people
  2   WHERE deptno = 20;

USERNAME        SALARY
---------- ----------
SMITH
JONES
SCOTT             3000
ADAMS
FORD
```

NOTE
The SEC_RELEVANT_COLS_OPT is applicable only to select statements.

The column sensitive option is ideal for privacy requirements. The column may be anything sensitive that you want to conceal—salary, a credit card number, patient diagnosis, financial status, and so on. This option allows you to store the sensitive information and the nonsensitive information together with the assurance that anytime someone requests the sensitive data, RLS will remove or mask the values.

VPD Performance

A clear and obvious concern when implementing any type of security is performance. While VPD provides the best security protection—it's consistent and constant—it is not magical. That is, the modified query will be executed and overall performance will be based on this final query string.

One of the easiest ways to ensure high performing VPD is to create indexes on the predicate values. If your policy function returns "username = USER", then an index on the USERNAME column will increase VPD execution.

Bind Variables

Bind variables help to ensure high performance by allowing the database to save valuable computing resources when queries differ only by variable values.

The first area to investigate is the performance of the returned predicate. Because the actual SQL to be executed includes not only the original SQL, but also the SQL returned from the predicate, you have to ensure that this SQL string performs well.

Bind variables are the staple of performance in an Oracle database. Bind variables allow the database to reuse SQL between database sessions; that is, the database can share a single parsed plan for multiple open cursors. The performance is achieved because the database doesn't have to reparse the SQL.

In some of the previous examples, the returned strings consisted of the SYS_CONTEXT function. This is critical because the policy function could have resolved the SYS_CONTEXT function and returned that string. The following will return "deptno = 20" for the SCOTT user:

```
CREATE OR REPLACE FUNCTION dept_only (
  p_schema   IN  VARCHAR2 DEFAULT NULL,
  p_object   IN  VARCHAR2 DEFAULT NULL)
  RETURN VARCHAR2
AS
BEGIN
  -- Return predicate with value resolved.
  RETURN 'deptno = ' || sys_context('people_ctx','deptno');
END;
/
```

This implementation is functionally equivalent to the one implemented before, but it is not equivalent from a performance perspective. Ensuring VPD performance comes from the fact that the SYS_CONTEXT is treated as a bind variable. If you do not use bind variables, but rather return the actual resolved value, for example, "deptno = 20", the database will spend a lot of time reparsing the SQL statements.

Performance as measured here is not based on how the SQL is generated. In the example, the VPD policy is invoked, and the predicate is produced. However, the application could have produced the same or similar SQL. The point is that it doesn't matter how the SQL was generated—if you want to achieve stellar performance, you have to produce good SQL; bind variables are generally a good way to go.

Code Location

Another question on the design revolves around whether the SQL should be modified at the database or at the application. Essentially, from a performance perspective, it does not matter. The same process will have to occur regardless of where it occurs. That is, some procedural logic will fire, check some things, and then determine how to reform the SQL query, thus securing the data for the user.

From a security perspective, the database implementation is much better. It guarantees that the SQL, and thus security, will always be enforced. This has value when the data may be needed by other applications and also helps provide defense in depth in the case that the web application is successfully attacked. In the latter case, the security of the application itself has been compromised, and it is only the database security that will now ensure that an attacker does not gain access to unauthorized data.

Policy Caching

Another question arises on the performance regarding the time required for the database to invoke VPD—a.k.a. "overhead." Because VPD invokes a function each time a statement or cursor is issued, performance can be a concern.

To help ensure things are running extremely fast, the database allows you to cache the VPD policy. In Oracle 9*i* Database, this capability was introduced with a new STATIC_POLICY parameter. When set to TRUE while registering the policy with the DBMS_RLS.ADD_POLICY procedure, the database will cache, on the first execution of the VPD policy, the results from your policy function. This can result in significant performance improvements because the PL/SQL code implementing your VPD policy will not be called in further queries.

You can still create a VPD policy and set the STATIC_POLICY parameter to true; however, that parameter is deprecated in Oracle Database 10*g*. The STATIC_POLICY was a good start, but Oracle realized there are still some enhancements that can be done. In Oracle Database 10*g*, the RLS package supports five new variations of policy caching. The replacement is a parameter called POLICY_TYPE, which allows you to set the caching to one of five different values:

- **STATIC** Equivalent to the STATIC_POLICY=TRUE setting in Oracle9*i* Database. The policy function is executed once, and the resulting string (the predicate) is stored in the Shared Global Area (SGA).
- **SHARED_STATIC** Allows the predicate to be cached across multiple objects that use the same policy function.
- **CONTEXT_SENSITIVE** The server always executes the policy function on statement parsing. The server will only execute the policy function on statement execution if it detects context changes. This makes it ideal for connection pooling solutions that share a database schema and use application contexts to actually perform the user identity switching (see Chapter 6 for an example of how to do this).
- **SHARED_CONTEXT_SENSITIVE** The same as CONTEXT_SENSITIVE except that the policy can be shared across multiple objects that use the same policy function.
- **DYNAMIC** The default, which makes no assumptions about caching. The policy will be invoked every time the SQL statement is parsed or executed.

You will see three examples of the caching: STATIC, SHARED_STATIC, and SHARED_CONTEXT_SENSITIVE. You will not see DYNAMIC because that means no caching, and the CONTEXT_SENSITIVE caching is a subset of the SHARED_CONTEXT_SENSITIVE.

STATIC Caching Example

The first caching example will use the STATIC option, which is equivalent to setting the STATIC_POLICY parameter to TRUE in the Oracle 9*i* Database procedure. To test the caching, the policy function will be modified to incorporate an artificial latency. The DBMS_LOCK.SLEEP procedure simulates a policy function that takes two seconds to execute and will make the caching visible to you. The policy function owner will require execute privileges on the DBMS_LOCK package. Because the RLS will call this function, you can measure the execution time of your query to determine the latency this function causes.

```
sec_mgr@KNOX10g> CREATE OR REPLACE FUNCTION user_only (
    p_schema  IN  VARCHAR2 DEFAULT NULL,
    p_object  IN  VARCHAR2 DEFAULT NULL)
    RETURN VARCHAR2
  AS
  BEGIN
    -- stall for 2 seconds
    DBMS_LOCK.sleep (2);
    RETURN 'username = sys_context(''userenv'',''session_user'')';
```

```
END;
/

Function created.
```

Recall this is the policy function guarding the SALARY column of the PEOPLE table. You can test the caching by querying the salaries from the table. The first query will be done prior to enabling the caching:

```
scott@KNOX10g> SELECT username, salary FROM people
  WHERE deptno = 20;

USERNAME       SALARY
---------- ----------
SMITH
JONES
SCOTT            3000
ADAMS
FORD

Elapsed: 00:00:04.10
```

It took four seconds, not two. The policy is invoked once during the SQL parse phase and once during the statement execution. You can alter the RLS policy to employ the use of the "static" caching for the column-sensitive policy previously defined for the SALARY column of the PEOPLE table:

```
sec_mgr@KNOX10g> BEGIN
   -- Remove current policy
   DBMS_RLS.drop_policy
                  (object_schema    => 'SCOTT',
                   object_name      => 'PEOPLE',
                   policy_name      => 'people_sel_sal');
   -- Add policy again but now with Caching
   DBMS_RLS.add_policy
        (object_schema            => 'SCOTT',
         object_name              => 'PEOPLE',
         policy_name              => 'people_sel_sal',
         function_schema          => 'SEC_MGR',
         policy_function          => 'user_only',
         statement_types          => 'SELECT',
         sec_relevant_cols        => 'SALARY',
         policy_type              => DBMS_RLS.STATIC);
 END;
 /

PL/SQL procedure successfully completed.
```

Enabling the timing feature of SQL*Plus, you can see the benefit to using static caching. The first execution will invoke the policy, and the predicate will be stored in the Shared Global Area:

```
scott@KNOX10g> SELECT username, salary FROM people
  2    WHERE deptno = 20;

USERNAME        SALARY
---------- ----------
SCOTT             3000

Elapsed: 00:00:02.05
```

The two seconds were introduced by PRED_FUNCTION. Any subsequent execution by any user will use the cached policy. To illustrate this, rerun the query. Because the cached predicate is stored in the SGA, the caching can be used for all user sessions across all schemas:

```
scott@KNOX10g> SELECT username, salary FROM people
  2    WHERE deptno = 20;

USERNAME        SALARY
---------- ----------
SCOTT             3000

Elapsed: 00:00:00.01

scott@KNOX10g> -- Reconnect. Establish a different session for same user
scott@KNOX10g> conn scott/tiger
Connected.
scott@KNOX10g> set timing on
scott@KNOX10g> SELECT username, salary FROM people
  2    WHERE deptno = 20;

USERNAME        SALARY
---------- ----------
SCOTT             3000

Elapsed: 00:00:00.01

scott@KNOX10g> -- Connect as a different user
scott@KNOX10g> conn system/manager
Connected.
system@KNOX10g> SET timing on
system@KNOX10g> SELECT username, salary FROM scott.people
  2    WHERE deptno = 20;

no rows selected

Elapsed: 00:00:00.02
```

While the policy will be cached for all users, the returned records are not necessarily the same. In the previous example, the policy always returns the same predicate. When the SYSTEM user executes the query, the policy is cached and different results are returned because the SYS_CONTEXT function returns a different user identity.

SHARED_STATIC Caching

The next cache example uses the SHARED_STATIC setting, which allows the predicate to be cached across multiple objects. This is practical because it's likely that you will be using the same policy function for object references in the same application. This example requires the use of the EMP and DEPT tables and assumes the security policy governing access to these tables is identical. Before you can add the policy, it's important to ensure all other policies have been dropped. The following script will drop all policies governing select statements on the EMP and DEPT tables in the SCOTT schema:

```
-- disable all select policies for EMP and DEPT
DECLARE
  l_str  VARCHAR2 (100);
BEGIN
  FOR rec IN (SELECT *
                FROM dba_policies
               WHERE object_owner = 'SCOTT'
                 AND object_name IN
                        ('EMP', 'DEPT')
                 AND sel = 'YES')
  LOOP
    l_str :=
         'begin DBMS_RLS.drop_policy(''SCOTT'','''
      || rec.object_name
      || ''','''
      || rec.policy_name
      || '''); end;';
    DBMS_OUTPUT.put_line (l_str);
    EXECUTE IMMEDIATE l_str;
  END LOOP;
END;
/
```

To cache across objects, the objects have to be sharing the same policy function. This example will use a function in the security manager schema that again sleeps for two seconds. Because the policy predicate used in the previous example referenced the ENAME column, which is not a column in the DEPT table, the policy function has to be modified to prevent an error. Because in this example you are only interested in cache performance, the policy function will sleep for two seconds and then simply return null:

```
sec_mgr@KNOX10g> -- VPD function, injects 2 second delay
sec_mgr@KNOX10g> CREATE OR REPLACE FUNCTION pred_function (
  2     p_schema  IN  VARCHAR2 DEFAULT NULL,
  3     p_object  IN  VARCHAR2 DEFAULT NULL)
  4     RETURN VARCHAR2
```

```
AS
BEGIN
  DBMS_LOCK.sleep (2);
  -- return all records
  RETURN NULL;
END;
/

Function created.
```

This predicate function is then applied to both the EMP and DEPT tables:

```
sec_mgr@KNOX10g> BEGIN
  -- Add policy on EMP table
  DBMS_RLS.add_policy
           (object_schema      => 'SCOTT',
            object_name        => 'EMP',
            policy_name        => 'EMP_SEL_CACHE',
            function_schema    => 'SEC_MGR',
            policy_function    => 'PRED_FUNCTION',
            statement_types    => 'SELECT',
            policy_type        => DBMS_RLS.shared_static);
  -- Add policy on DEPT table
  DBMS_RLS.add_policy
           (object_schema      => 'SCOTT',
            object_name        => 'DEPT',
            policy_name        => 'DEPT_SEL_CACHE',
            function_schema    => 'SEC_MGR',
            policy_function    => 'PRED_FUNCTION',
            statement_types    => 'SELECT',
            policy_type        => DBMS_RLS.shared_static);
END;
/

PL/SQL procedure successfully completed.
```

Connect as SCOTT and query either of the tables. Notice the first query will cache the predicate for both tables:

```
scott@KNOX10g> SET timing on
scott@KNOX10g> -- Query one of the tables
scott@KNOX10g> SELECT COUNT (*) FROM emp;

  COUNT(*)
----------
        14

Elapsed: 00:00:02.34
scott@KNOX10g> -- run again to see if predicate is cached
scott@KNOX10g> /
```

```
  COUNT(*)
----------
        14

Elapsed: 00:00:00.01
scott@KNOX10g> -- Query a different table that uses same policy function
scott@KNOX10g> -- The database should use the cached predicate
scott@KNOX10g> SELECT COUNT (*) FROM dept;

  COUNT(*)
----------
         4

Elapsed: 00:00:00.01
```

The behavior with this is consistent with the STATIC example in that the caching exists across sessions and schemas:

```
scott@KNOX10g> -- Query as a different session
scott@KNOX10g> -- Cache is shared across sessions
scott@KNOX10g> conn system/manager
Connected.
system@KNOX10g> SELECT COUNT (*) FROM scott.dept;

  COUNT(*)
----------
         4

Elapsed: 00:00:00.01
```

The benefit gained from this caching technique is directly proportional to the number of tables sharing the policy function.

SHARED_CONTEXT_SENSITIVE

The final caching example uses the SHARED_CONTEXT_SENSITIVE setting. This will allow caching for the user's session up until a user-defined application context is changed. To begin, first drop the current policies by running the script given in the beginning of the previous example. The output is shown here:

```
begin DBMS_RLS.drop_policy('SCOTT','DEPT','DEPT_SEL_CACHE'); end;
begin DBMS_RLS.drop_policy('SCOTT','EMP','EMP_SEL_CACHE'); end;
```

Next, add the RLS policy to EMP and DEPT, changing the policy type to SHARED_CONTEXT_SENSITIVE:

```
sec_mgr@KNOX10g> -- add shared_context_sensitive policies
sec_mgr@KNOX10g> BEGIN
  2    -- Add policy on EMP table
  3    DBMS_RLS.add_policy
  4             (object_schema       => 'SCOTT',
```

```
             object_name         => 'EMP',
             policy_name         => 'EMP_SEL_CACHE',
             function_schema     => 'SEC_MGR',
             policy_function     => 'PRED_FUNCTION',
             statement_types     => 'SELECT',
             policy_type         => DBMS_RLS.shared_context_sensitive);
  -- Add policy on DEPT table
  DBMS_RLS.add_policy
            (object_schema       => 'SCOTT',
             object_name         => 'DEPT',
             policy_name         => 'DEPT_SEL_CACHE',
             function_schema     => 'SEC_MGR',
             policy_function     => 'PRED_FUNCTION',
             statement_types     => 'SELECT',
             policy_type         => DBMS_RLS.shared_context_sensitive);
END;
/

PL/SQL procedure successfully completed.
```

The database will cache the policy until a user-defined application context is manipulated. It doesn't have to be a context that has any direct relationship to the tables the policy protects. Therefore, the application context defined earlier will be adopted for this example by the addition of a new SET_DEPTNO procedure. The new package specification and new procedure code are listed:

```
sec_mgr@KNOX10g> CREATE OR REPLACE PACKAGE people_ctx_mgr
AS
  PROCEDURE set_deptno;
  PROCEDURE set_deptno(p_deptno in number);
  PROCEDURE clear_deptno;
END;
/

Package created.
```

The following code is for the new procedure only:

```
  PROCEDURE set_deptno (p_deptno IN NUMBER)
  AS
  BEGIN
    DBMS_SESSION.set_context
                     (namespace    => 'people_ctx',
                      ATTRIBUTE    => 'deptno',
                      VALUE        => p_deptno);
  END set_deptno;

```

Execute privileges are granted to SCOTT to allow him to directly manipulate the application context. This is done to illustrate how the caching works, and you wouldn't grant privileges to execute on this namespace manager to users if the context values it set were to be used for security purposes:

```
sec_mgr@KNOX10g> GRANT EXECUTE ON people_ctx_mgr TO scott;

Grant succeeded.
```

You can see from the following test results that this type of caching is indeed functionally different from the previous two. The test first queries the EMP table, which causes the predicate to be cached for the EMP and DEPT tables.

```
scott@KNOX10g> SET timing on
scott@KNOX10g> -- Query one of the tables. Predicate is not yet cached
scott@KNOX10g> SELECT COUNT (*) FROM emp;

  COUNT(*)
----------
        14

Elapsed: 00:00:02.05
scott@KNOX10g> -- Query a different table that uses same policy function
scott@KNOX10g> -- The database should use the cached predicate
scott@KNOX10g> SELECT COUNT (*) FROM dept;

  COUNT(*)
----------
         4

Elapsed: 00:00:00.01
```

You might think the Client Identifier, which is a type of application context, could be used to trigger a switch in the caching, but it cannot. This is important because you may be relying only on the Client Identifier switch when using a shared schema application pool. If you are, consider securing it using the technique described in Chapter 6.

```
scott@KNOX10g> -- note that changing the Client Identifier has no
scott@KNOX10g> -- effect on cache
scott@KNOX10g> EXEC dbms_session.set_identifier('Some Value');

PL/SQL procedure successfully completed.

Elapsed: 00:00:00.00
scott@KNOX10g> -- Predicate is still cached.
scott@KNOX10g> SELECT COUNT (*) FROM emp;

  COUNT(*)
----------
        14

Elapsed: 00:00:00.01
```

To invalidate the cache, change the value in a user-defined application context. The new SET_DEPTNO procedure does this:

```
scott@KNOX10g> -- Execute the namespace manager procedure.
scott@KNOX10g> -- This changes a context value which tells the database
scott@KNOX10g> -- to invalidate the cached predicate.
scott@KNOX10g> EXEC sec_mgr.people_ctx_mgr.set_deptno(10);

PL/SQL procedure successfully completed.

Elapsed: 00:00:00.01
scott@KNOX10g> SELECT COUNT (*) FROM emp;

  COUNT(*)
----------
        14

Elapsed: 00:00:02.05
```

A difference between this and the previous example is that the caching is session specific. This is because the cache invalidation is based on (local) application contexts, which are always going to be different across sessions. Reconnect to the database and query and you will see the cache is automatically invalidated:

```
scott@KNOX10g> -- Query using a different session.
scott@KNOX10g> -- Cache is not shared across sessions
scott@KNOX10g> conn scott/tiger
Connected.
scott@KNOX10g> SELECT COUNT (*) FROM scott.dept;

  COUNT(*)
----------
         4

Elapsed: 00:00:02.05
```

The policy caching capabilities can increase performance by bypassing the policy invocation. However, there are some situations in which this is not the solution to use.

Caching Caution

A word of caution: cached policies may not prove effective in all situations. The policy function is executed once, and the result is cached. The policy function will never be re-executed, which means any logic used within the function will never be re-executed. There are some situations when this is undesirable. The most obvious is when the predicate changes based on the logic in the policy function. In the previous example, the predicate is constant, while the value returned by the application context changes. This is very desirable and allows for a cached VPD policy.

The implementation of the policy function also influences whether the policy can be cached. For example, the predicate function in the following meets the requirement of restricting access between the hours of 9 A.M. and 5 P.M. However, if this policy is cached, the first access will cause the function to execute, the result will be cached and applied to everyone. If the function first executes at 10 A.M., then the access will be permitted even after 5 P.M.

```
-- Wrong implementation for caching
CREATE OR REPLACE FUNCTION pred_function_9_to_5 (
  p_schema   IN   VARCHAR2 DEFAULT NULL,
  p_object   IN   VARCHAR2 DEFAULT NULL)
  RETURN VARCHAR2
AS
BEGIN
  IF TO_CHAR (SYSDATE, 'HH24') BETWEEN 9 AND 17
  THEN
    RETURN '1=1';
  ELSE
    RETURN '1=0';
  END IF;
END;
```

To correct this, the policy function must either not be cached, or the value must be evaluated each time. The following forces the condition to be evaluated each time:

```
-- Correct implementation for caching.
CREATE OR REPLACE FUNCTION pred_function_9_to_5 (
  p_schema   IN   VARCHAR2 DEFAULT NULL,
  p_object   IN   VARCHAR2 DEFAULT NULL)
  RETURN VARCHAR2
AS
BEGIN
  RETURN 'to_char(sysdate,''HH24'') between 9 and 17';
END;

/
```

The point is that the policy function's implementation cannot be done without regard to the caching strategy. In most cases, caching should be considered and the code should be written to ensure security is always enforced. You should first test without caching to ensure your performance is acceptable. Then enable caching and test the policy with the appropriate use cases to ensure that security is working as desired.

Comparing VPD Performance to View-Based RLS

In the view chapter, you saw a performance test that compared the time required to execute RLS in a view that used a function to filter the records. For even comparisons, you can now build a VPD policy that emulates that security functionality and then test the performance:

```
sec_mgr@KNOX10G> sec_mgr@KNOX10g> CREATE OR REPLACE FUNCTION owner_admin (
  2     p_schema   IN   VARCHAR2 DEFAULT NULL,
  3     p_object   IN   VARCHAR2 DEFAULT NULL)
  4     RETURN VARCHAR2
  5   AS
  6   BEGIN
```

```
    IF (SYS_CONTEXT ('userenv', 'isdba') = 'TRUE')
    THEN
      RETURN NULL;               -- returns all rows
    ELSE
      RETURN 'OWNER = USER';
    END IF;
  END;
  /

Function created.
```

You'll create a new view over your BIG_TAB table. Add your VPD policy to the view you create:

```
sec_mgr@KNOX10g> CREATE OR REPLACE VIEW big_vpd_view
  AS
    SELECT * FROM big_tab;

View created.

sec_mgr@KNOX10g> BEGIN
    DBMS_RLS.add_policy
               (object_name        => 'BIG_VPD_VIEW',
                policy_name        => 'BIG_VPD_VIEW_SIUD',
                policy_function    => 'owner_admin');
  END;
  /

PL/SQL procedure successfully completed.
```

Now for the tests, query once on the base table where you specify the security predicate directly. Query once on the function-based view that was created in the "Functions in Views for Row-Level Security" section in Chapter 10, and finally, query the VPD-based view:

```
sec_mgr@KNOX10g> SET timing on
sec_mgr@KNOX10g> -- time with security built into SQL
sec_mgr@KNOX10g> SELECT COUNT (*)
    FROM big_tab
   WHERE 1 = DECODE (owner, USER, 1, 0)
      OR SYS_CONTEXT ('userenv', 'isdba') = 'TRUE';

  COUNT(*)
----------
      1184

Elapsed: 00:00:07.48
sec_mgr@KNOX10g> -- time with RLS built into view
sec_mgr@KNOX10g> SELECT COUNT (*)
    FROM big_view;
```

```
  COUNT(*)
----------
      1184

Elapsed: 00:01:05.97
sec_mgr@KNOX10g> -- time with VPD
sec_mgr@KNOX10g> SELECT COUNT (*)
  2    FROM big_vpd_view;

  COUNT(*)
----------
      1184

Elapsed: 00:00:06.99
```

The query on the VPD view performs on par with the modified SQL because the SQL is modified by the VPD policy before it is executed.

Summary

Virtual Private Database (VPD) helps resolve some of the challenges associated with views. An RLS policy is defined as a mapping from a PL/SQL implemented security function to a table, view, or synonym. The actual PL/SQL implementation that enforces the VPD can be based on whatever is relevant—IP address, time of day, application context values. The policies also are transparent to queries on the protected objects.

New to Oracle Database 10*g* is the ability to support column-sensitive policies, which allows a more selective invocation of the RLS mechanisms. This is very practical and allows you to more easily store data with different sensitivities within the same table. One of the challenges to implementing VPD is debugging faulty implementations. You saw various best practice techniques for helping to mitigate the debug challenge.

To ensure high performance, the RLS mechanism has been written to modify the SQL before it is parsed and executed. This allows the database to use indexes and optimization plans to ensure fast access to data. Using bind variables and application contexts and enabling policy caching can significantly improve RLS performance.

In Chapter 12, you will explore an implementation (or perhaps an augmentation) of VPD called Oracle Label Security.

CHAPTER 12

Oracle Label Security

his chapter shows how to apply Oracle Label Security (OLS) to your tables to enforce row-level security. OLS has many capabilities that make it an attractive technique for implementing fine-grained access control. OLS is conceptually easy to understand and is based on a proven and well-understood security model. It makes it easy to create, deploy, and maintain your security; and, in contrast to views with functions and VPD, no coding is required to implement row-level security with OLS.

OLS was designed to meet some of the strongest security requirements ever put forth. This chapter offers a brief review of its history, which helps to explain the labeling concept and the behavior of the product. You'll then see an example that illustrates the powerful security that OLS provides and the ease with which it can be provided. After a discussion of tips and tricks, OLS and VPD will be compared.

Classifying Data

OLS is based on the work done for U.S. intelligence agencies and the U.S. Department of Defense (DoD). You don't have to work for an intelligence agency or the DoD to know that they interact with very sensitive information. Not only is the data sensitive, but some of it's more sensitive than others. The data is separated and categorized based on its sensitivity. When the data's sensitivity has been determined, it's marked with a sensitivity designation, also known as a *classification.*

For a simple description, let's assume three levels of classification: top secret, secret, and confidential. *Top secret* data is the most sensitive and requires the highest security. *Secret* is next in sensitivity, and *confidential* data is still sensitive but can be distributed to a wider audience. The security policy says that users with top secret access can see everything; users with secret access can see everything except the top secret data; and the users with confidential access only can see data that is confidential.

Let's consider an example of how to classify information. Assume you're part of the coaching staff for a sports team that will be participating in a big game. You classify the different strategies or game plan you'll be using by the three classifications: confidential, secret, and top secret. The confidential data indicates who will be starting the game and in what position. The starting roster has a "CONFIDENTIAL" label on it. If your opponent knows the starting roster, they'll have some insight into your starting strategy for the game. The secret data is the types of offense and defense patterns you'll use during the game. The list of patterns you plan to execute might be kept in a manila folder labeled "SECRET." This is more sensitive information because knowledge of this may allow your opponent to counter with a pattern that makes your strategy less effective. The top secret information is the details of the play you're about to execute. If your opponent gains access to this, they'll know all the plays you'll make before you make them, which will likely defeat your plans. The play calls are labeled "TOP SECRET."

The data sensitivity is determined based on how devastating the effects would be if the data was accessed by an opponent or someone with bad intentions. Access to data at a specific classification requires the user to have a *clearance*, or be approved for access.

The data classification process may or may not occur within your organization. Whether or not you have consciously categorized your data, it has different levels of sensitivity. For example, any trade secrets or intellectual property that you own may be considered the most sensitive information. You don't have to categorize this as TOP SECRET; you can say this information is CORPORATE PROPRIETARY. It distinguishes the information from the other information within your organization, such as last year's revenue earnings, which is less sensitive and may even be publicly available.

In a healthcare scenario, the patient's information also has different sensitivities and classifications. The patient name isn't as sensitive as their medical diagnosis. Similarly, a company's HR records contain different levels of sensitivity—names and job titles are less sensitive than compensation information. My point is that the concept of data classification and data labeling is applicable to your environment even if you don't work in the intelligence field or for the DoD.

OLS Ancestry

Data classification, labels, and clearances (or user authorizations) are the foundation of OLS. The translation from idea to implementation occurred over several years: the concept of digitally labeling data within the database preceded the OLS product creation by at least six years.

In the early 1990s, the U.S. intelligence agencies and the DoD began asking the computing industry for products that could be used to securely and intuitively manage classified information. The government wanted to use systems that understood the notion of classified data—or data that had been categorized as confidential, secret, top secret, and so on. There was even a strong implication that if the products were built and were proven correct through an established formal process run by the National Security Agency (NSA), the government entities would purchase many of the products.

Consequently, several of the major computer companies, such as Sun, Hewlett-Packard, Digital Equipment Corporation (remember them?), and Oracle, obliged by investing millions of research dollars into implementing these secure products that were able to understand and discriminate between the different levels of classified information.

To handle classified information, these secure systems, sometimes referred to as *trusted* systems, applied classification labels to the information and to the digital processes that operated on the information. This was the digital equivalent of the physical label on the folder holding your game plans.

The label-based security implementations were effective because the users were already familiar with the concepts of data sensitivity and classifications from managing classified data in physical formats, such as documents, folders, and reports. The other part that made it effective was in how the labels were enforced.

Labels and Mandatory Access Control

A common solution was put forth by the vendors building trusted systems. The solution was based on two things: mandatory access controls and data labeling.

Access Controls: Discretionary and Mandatory

In Chapter 7, you read about how the Oracle database will enforce access controls based on privileges. The privileges were either directly associated with an object (called object privileges) or were functionally specific and applied to all objects across the database (called system privileges). This type of access control is called *Discretionary Access Control (DAC).*

The "discretionary" part of DAC refers to the ability of the user to maintain control over the access to the data. As an example, let's assume the user SCOTT has created a document (perhaps it's the plans for the upcoming game). If SCOTT wishes to allow another user, say the user BLAKE, to view the document, he can simply grant access to BLAKE. In the database, this is the equivalent of allowing SCOTT to grant the select privilege on the EMP table to the user BLAKE (assume the document is synonymous with a database table). If SCOTT wants any user to access the EMP data, then SCOTT can, at his discretion, grant access to that user. SCOTT, as owner of the table, has discretionary access control.

There are reasons this access control is simply not sufficient for handling very sensitive data. If the document created by SCOTT contains very sensitive data, allowing SCOTT to release it to anyone he chooses may not be a good idea. SCOTT may intentionally or inadvertently grant access to someone who shouldn't have it. What if BLAKE, without SCOTT's knowledge, had a relationship with someone from the other team and was planning to divulge SCOTT's game plans? Allowing BLAKE to read the document could be disastrous.

If the document is labeled, access to the document can be further restricted. Before users are allowed access, they have to be cleared to the same level as the document. That is, if SCOTT has a top secret document, BLAKE will not be able to access the document unless he also has a top secret clearance, even if SCOTT grants BLAKE access. In the game competition example, the coaching staff would have top secret clearances, the players would have secret clearances, and the support staff would have confidential clearances. Unless BLAKE is a member of the coaching staff, he won't able to access the game plans.

Mandatory Access Control (*MAC*) describes the ability of the trusted computing platform (database, operating system, etc.) to protect classified and labeled data from being inappropriately accessed and disseminated. The MAC enforcements prevent unauthorized users—users with insufficient clearances—from being able to view or disseminate the protected information. The computing platform will not only prevent a user with only secret clearances from accessing top secret data, but it also will prevent a top secret user from passing off the top secret data to a secret user. In the SCOTT-BLAKE relationship, MAC would ensure that BLAKE would be unable to access the game plans unless he were authorized at top secret, which means he is part of the coaching staff. This would be true even if SCOTT granted BLAKE permission to read the plans.

Overall, access is enforced by both DAC and MAC. This defense in depth approach is sometimes confused with what many in the industry refer to as multilevel security. *Multilevel security* actually describes multiple levels of classified data, as opposed to multiple rings of security protecting the data. The DAC allows users to grant and revoke privileges at their discretion. DAC in the database is represented by the privileges (execute, select, delete, etc.) users can grant other users on their (data) objects. MAC restricts access to objects based on the security policies defined in the computing platform. MAC mediates access to data based on matching the user's authorizations to the labels attached to the data. The important point is that DAC can't override MAC—that is, the user can't say, "only give the secret guys the top secret data; I said it's okay." The computing platform will prevent that from occurring.

MAC was introduced not only to prevent malicious users from giving away important classified information but also to prevent users from accidentally releasing sensitive information. For example, the trusted operating systems that implemented MAC prevented users from copying in a top secret window and pasting into a secret window. This ensured the users were making a conscious decision about moving the data between windows, which meant they were moving data between classifications.

Trusted Oracle

Oracle's product for supporting MAC, called Trusted Oracle, was a separate port of the Oracle database and required the use of special (MAC-aware) operating systems. The operating systems were also special versions produced by their respective company.

Trusted Oracle was evaluated by the NSA as meeting B1-level security. *B1 security* defines label-based security protections and defines what a system has to do to be compliant with MAC. The B1 evaluation was an official recognition by an independent authority that Oracle's implementation of MAC was sufficient and complete. This made it suitable for handling classified data.

MAC was strictly enforced by the operating system. The database used the operating system as a guide to enforcing the database MAC security. A security policy was implemented as a set of labels defined and enforced by the operating system. A restriction that later proved to be difficult to handle was that there was only one set of labels available for use by all applications and data.

With Trusted Oracle, every aspect of the database carried a security label—the database processes (SMON, PMON, the listener process, and so on), the database files, database users, and every object within the database had a security label. The database's security labels were directly linked to the operating systems' labels. When processes and users accessed the database, the OS and/or the database compared the security labels to ensure that access was permitted.

Trusted Oracle had many interesting properties. Row-level security was implemented for every table in the database. *Every* row in *every* table contained a label. This included not only user and application data tables but also the database dictionary. What this meant was that an administrator could create an object, such as a table or procedure at the top secret level, and only users connected at top secret would know the object existed!

The database tables contained a pseudocolumn called rowlabel. The *rowlabel,* as the name implies, was the security label for the row. An interesting property of the label was that it was hidden from view. A SELECT * or DESCRIBE on the table wouldn't return the rowlabel. However, the user or application could directly ask for the rowlabel if for some reason they wanted to see it (somewhat analogous to the rowid pseudocolumn still in use today).

While trusted databases and operating systems were readily available for several years, today only a few still exist. Most of the major OS and database vendors abandoned their trusted platforms as they were expensive to maintain, difficult to manage (the administrators had to have special knowledge because the systems didn't behave like their nontrusted siblings) and were frequently a few versions behind in nonsecurity features. Additionally, while MAC security was required or desired for some applications, it wasn't desired for all applications. Unfortunately, MAC couldn't be selectively enabled or disabled. MAC, by definition, was an all-or-nothing technology.

With Trusted Oracle, there were drawbacks as well. The database, like trusted operating systems, required administrators with special MAC knowledge. Operations performed at the wrong security level could have unintended negative consequences. The labeling was inflexible because it was based on the OS labels. The Trusted Oracle database also fell behind functionally because it wasn't released with each new update of the standard Oracle database. As the availability of trusted operating systems diminished, Oracle released its last version of Trusted Oracle, Trusted Oracle version 7.2.3.

Oracle Label Security

Due to the many issues cited in the previous section, customers naturally started asking for the label-based functionality without the strict MAC OS dependence. For databases, this requirement basically meant selective row-level security. Oracle Consulting first responded to this by crafting label-based access control solutions using standard Oracle running on standard operating systems. This could be done because the customer requirements were for row-level security, and their operating environment didn't force them to use Mandatory Access Controls across the entire system.

Oracle Coporation's database security product management team recognized the value to the customers and began to build in native support for labeling and what became known as fine-grained access control, or row-level security. The Virtual Private Database (VPD), released with Oracle 8.1.5, enabled many customers and Oracle consulting, to create row-level security solutions by exploiting native capabilities within the database.

Oracle Label Security entered the market as a product with version 8.1.7 but was initially only released on the Sun Solaris platform. With Oracle9*i* Database, OLS became available on all platforms the database supported. Unlike Trusted Oracle, OLS was developed independent of the operating system on which it ran. This allowed OLS to be supported on all platforms for which Oracle provided a database, as well as all future versions. The version skipping seen with Trusted Oracle wasn't repeated with OLS.

How OLS Works

Oracle Label Security (OLS) allows you to define a security policy that is implemented by marking the data records with security labels. The label markings indicate what rights a person must possess in order to read or write the data. The labels are stored with each record in a special column that is added to the table. The database users are also given labels that indicate their access rights to the data records. When the user accesses the table records, the database's OLS engine compares the user's label with the row's label marking to determine if the user can have access.

This is essentially the same model that Trusted Oracle used in its MAC implementation except that OLS isn't enforced on every database table; it's applied only to the tables that need row-level security.

OLS also supports multiple security policies, or ways to classify the data. You can create a policy with top secret, secret, and confidential classifications, and you can create another policy with proprietary, company sensitive, and public classifications. There is no limit to the number of security policies or the names and semantics of the labels. The following examples will help you better understand how the policy is created, defined, and applied.

Installing OLS

OLS is one of the few options that isn't part of the standard Enterprise Edition installation. To install OLS, you have to choose the Custom Database option with the Oracle Installer and consciously select the Oracle Label Security option. Additionally, you have to choose the tablespace for the OLS option at the appropriate time in the database installation process.

NOTE
OLS is not installed with the default Enterprise Edition installation. You must choose the Custom Database installation to install OLS.

If a database has already been installed, you can use the Oracle Installer (selecting a Custom Database) to add the OLS option. You'll then have to use the Oracle Database Configuration Assistant to install the PL/SQL packages needed to support the OLS functionality. See Appendix C of the *Oracle Label Security Administrator's Guide* for more installation information.

Implementing Label Security

There are five steps necessary to implement OLS; each of these steps is discussed in more detail in the code examples later in this chapter.

1. *Create the OLS policy.* The policy is the container for the labels, user authorizations, and protected database objects.
2. *Define the OLS label components.* Each label consists of a permutation of three components, which are defined in this step.

3. *Create the actual OLS labels you wish to use.* You have to define the valid labels for OLS. Take the components defined in step 2 and create a valid set of labels based on your application's security policy. This step is optional, but it's generally done to ensure label data integrity.

4. *Apply the OLS security policy (labels) to your table(s) or schemas.* This adds a label column to the table and adds the infrastructure required to support the row-level security based on the labels. This step also defines the security enforcement behavior of your policy.

5. *Assign the label authorizations to be used by the users or applications.* This step determines who will ultimately gain access to what. Labels are assigned to "users," which may be a single user or a group of users. OLS mediates access to data by comparing the user's label with the label on the data record(s).

Label Example

Examples are the best tools for illustrating how technology works. I've found that the more complex the technology, the simpler the example needs to be. This allows you to better focus on the technology rather than trying to figure out the semantics of column names and the complicated relationships between data structures. Once the technology principles are understood, you should be able to cast this example onto your specific data structures and applications.

The example application presented here represents a bulletin board for displaying announcements, alerts, and other critical information to employees. The data for this bulletin board will be separated and tailored to individual employees based on their need to know. The users' need to know, or what they are authorized to see, is derived from their seniority, role, and geographical location.

The application table will reside in the SCOTT schema, and the security will be managed from the SEC_MGR schema. This reflects the fact that the data tables often reside in one schema while the security is enforced from a different schema. The data table will contain multiple simple messages. OLS will ultimately ensure only the relevant messages are viewable by the appropriate parties. Therefore, the table requires only the single column to hold the announcement messages:

```
scott@KNOX10g> CREATE TABLE announcements
  2  (MESSAGE      VARCHAR2(4000));

Table created.
```

Creating the Policy

Before you begin to create labels, you need to create a security policy. A policy is the container for everything—the labels, user authorizations, and the protected objects. Unlike Trusted Oracle, which applied one set of security labels across all database objects, OLS allows you to create multiple policies and apply the labels to only selected users and objects. When you create the policy, you have to define the name of the column that will be used to hold your labels. You can optionally provide any default security enforcement options.

The policy for this example will store the labels in a column called ROWLABEL, and OLS will place the security label values in the ROWLABEL column. The choice for your column is important because the column name will be appended to the tables on which you want to enforce your OLS policies. Also, the label column name has to be unique among all the OLS policies in your database. Any additional policies you create will have to use a different column name for the label column.

OLS can be managed two ways. The Oracle Policy Manager provides an easy-to-use graphical interface for administering OLS. Alternatively, OLS provides a set of PL/SQL APIs. This example uses APIs to perform the OLS actions. Snapshots from the Policy Manager will be taken periodically to depict how these actions or the results of the actions are graphically represented. An advantage to the PL/SQL calls is that the PL/SQL code can be saved and replayed at a later time if desired. This is advantageous if you need to rebuild your policies or want to replicate your OLS security across several databases.

Create the OLS policy (ESBD, or Effective Security By Design, for this example) by invoking the SA_SYSDBA.CREATE_POLICY procedure. Privileges to execute this procedure have been granted to the default OLS administrator known as LBACSYS.

```
lbacsys@KNOX10g> BEGIN
    sa_sysdba.create_policy
                          (policy_name     => 'ESBD',
                           column_name     => 'rowlabel');
  END;
  /

PL/SQL procedure successfully completed.
```

Note the default OLS installation leaves the LBACSYS account locked and the password expired. The default password is LBCASYS; the password expiration forces you to change it on the initial logon. Choose a strong password because the account has significant database privileges and a compromise of LBACSYS could be disastrous.

When a policy is created, Oracle automatically creates an administrator database role for the policy. The role name is the policy's name appended with "_DBA". For the ESBD policy created above, the role name is ESBD_DBA. This role and the privileges granted to it will be used for this example. When you grant the ESBD_DBA role to the SEC_MGR schema, you're bestowing administration privileges for the ESBD policy to the SEC_MGR user:

```
lbacsys@KNOX10g> -- Privs and authorization to administer the ESBD policy
lbacsys@KNOX10g> GRANT esbd_dba TO sec_mgr;

Grant succeeded.
```

Viewing the results of the policy creation in Figure 12-1, you see that the policy was created, the column defined to hold the label (ROWLABEL), and the policy default status enabled. The Hide Policy Column check box is grayed out because once the policy is created, this option can't be changed. You'll see a workaround to this in the upcoming "Changing the Hidden Status" section.

Least Privileges for OLS Administrators

The SEC_MGR will also require the execute privileges on several OLS-related programs. The details of what operations the programs perform are discussed throughout the example as they are used. Note that, in spite of the name, OLS doesn't grant all privileges necessary for performing all OLS administration tasks to the <policy_name>_DBA role. This was consciously done to allow for further separation of duties for OLS policy administrators. OLS controls who can manage the

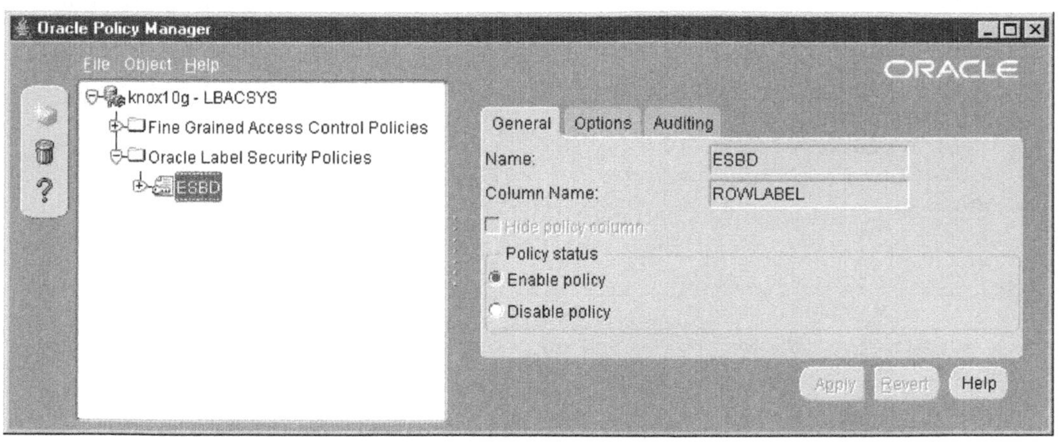

FIGURE 12-1. *A policy can be easily created by executing the PL/SQL package or utilizing the Oracle Policy Manager.*

OLS policy and then further controls what specific actions they can take while managing the policy. In this example, the SEC_MGR will perform all the OLS administration duties. The following privileges are therefore required:

```
lbacsys@KNOX10g> -- Privs to create components that make up valid labels
lbacsys@KNOX10g> GRANT EXECUTE ON sa_components  TO sec_mgr;

Grant succeeded.

lbacsys@KNOX10g> -- Privileges to create the valid labels
lbacsys@KNOX10g> GRANT EXECUTE ON sa_label_admin TO sec_mgr;

Grant succeeded.

lbacsys@KNOX10g> -- Privileges to assign authorization labels to users
lbacsys@KNOX10g> GRANT EXECUTE ON sa_user_admin  TO sec_mgr;

Grant succeeded.

lbacsys@KNOX10g> -- Privileges to convert a character string to
lbacsys@KNOX10g> -- its numeric label representation
lbacsys@KNOX10g> GRANT EXECUTE ON char_to_label  TO sec_mgr;

Grant succeeded.
```

OLS makes many interesting and practical uses of the core security capabilities of the database. For example, the role for the policy, ESBD_DBA, is restricted to operations within the specific policy. If you create a new policy and then try to create label components from the SEC_MGR schema, you'll witness this security control:

```
lbacsys@KNOX10g> -- Create a new OLS Policy, but don't assign privileges
lbacsys@KNOX10g> BEGIN
      sa_sysdba.create_policy
                  (policy_name     => 'Different_Policy');
    END;
    /

PL/SQL procedure successfully completed.

lbacsys@KNOX10g> CONN sec_mgr/oracle10g
Connected.
sec_mgr@KNOX10g> /***
sec_mgr@KNOX10g>   Try to administer the new policy.
sec_mgr@KNOX10g>   This will fail because the user does not have role
sec_mgr@KNOX10g>     authorization.
sec_mgr@KNOX10g> **/
sec_mgr@KNOX10g> BEGIN
      sa_components.create_level
                 (policy_name     => 'Different_Policy',
                  long_name       => 'foo',
                  short_name      => 'bar',
                  level_num       => 9);
    END;
    /
BEGIN
*
ERROR at line 1:
ORA-12407: unauthorized operation for policy Different_Policy
```

Label Components

The second step in the process is to create the label components. The label components are the names and the relationships of the different classifications the policy will contain. The policy administrator requires two things to create components: execute privileges on the SA_COMPONENTS package and the policy's database role. This is why the preceding example did not work: the SEC_MGR was not granted the DIFFERENT_POLICY_DBA role.

When the SA_COMPONENTS program executes, it verifies that the invoker is a member of the role for the respective policy. The role does not even have to be enabled. OLS uses the database role as an authorization. However, the execute privileges aren't granted to the role by default (recall the execute on SA_COMPONENTS was the first privilege granted to the SEC_MGR in the "Creating the Policy" section).

A label is composed of three components: at least one level, zero or more compartments, and zero or more groups. Data access is controlled by combining the values of all three components into a single label and then allowing or disallowing access based on the resulting label values. This example will eventually create a label that uses all three components. For each component, example code will illustrate how the individual component behaves in restricting or allowing access to data. Once combined, the overall access is determined by the combination of all three components.

Levels

The first component to a label is the security level. Levels act as rankings of data and user authorizations. Create the levels by executing the SA_COMPONENTS.CREATE_LEVEL procedure. (SA stands for "Secure Access," which was one of the consulting product names given to OLS before it officially became Oracle Label Security.)

There are three parts describing the level: a short name, a long name, and most importantly, a level number. The level number is most important because it's used to determine the ranking. A higher number indicates a higher level; OLS supports 9,999 levels. This example will use three. The short name is important because it's this value you'll use to refer to your level when referencing it by a character string.

The levels in this scenario represent a simplified hierarchy of an organization. The highest level is reserved for the company's executive members—the CEO, CFO, CIO, and Executive Vice Presidents. Beneath the executive level is the management level. At the lowest level are the employees. The ranking or hierarchy is determined by the number assigned in the LEVEL_NUM parameter. The level names and the level numbers are completely arbitrary except for the relative nature that establishes the ranking. Create the levels as the SEC_MGR:

```
sec_mgr@KNOX10g> BEGIN
    -- Create the highest level for the company executives
    sa_components.create_level
                   (policy_name    => 'ESBD',
                    long_name      => 'Executive Staff',
                    short_name     => 'EXEC',
                    level_num      => 9000);
    -- Create the manager level
    sa_components.create_level
                   (policy_name    => 'ESBD',
                    long_name      => 'Manager',
                    short_name     => 'MGR',
                    level_num      => 8000);
    -- Create the employee level
    sa_components.create_level
                   (policy_name    => 'ESBD',
                    long_name      => 'Employee',
                    short_name     => 'EMP',
                    level_num      => 7000);
  END;
  /

PL/SQL procedure successfully completed.
```

As Figure 12-2 illustrates, the levels can be easily viewed with the Oracle Policy Manager.

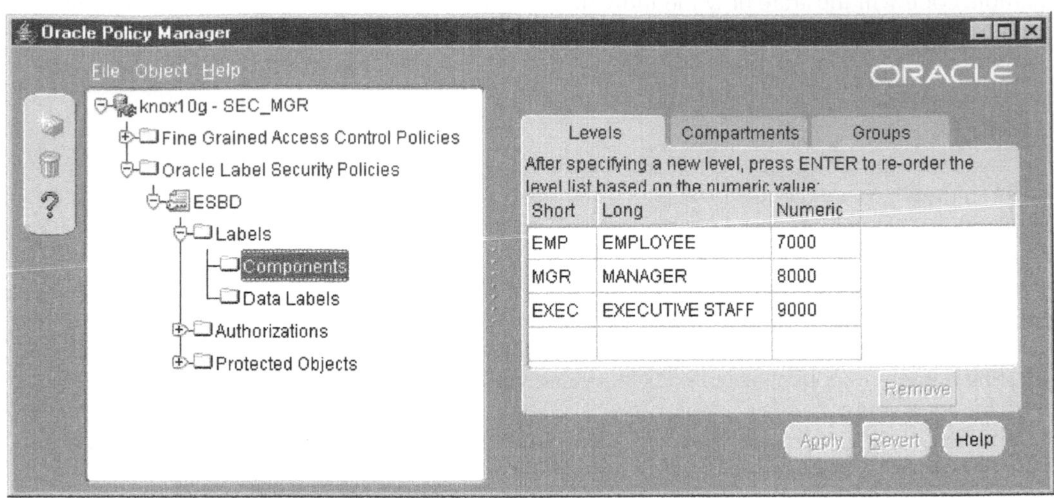

FIGURE 12-2. *Oracle Policy Manager showing the three levels created*

Choosing the Level Numbers

The general principle followed by MAC policies is that users can see their level and below. OLS honors this in its use of levels. The company executives will be able to see everything; the managers will see management and employee information; and the employees will see only employee announcements. Note that the executive staff is at the top of the rankings because their level number is the highest.

For this example, the level numbers could have been {3,2,1} or {100,10,1} with the same ranking effect. A general best practice for level numbers is to leave space between the levels. This allows you to later add levels between existing levels.

It is also a good practice to group related levels. For example, in your organization, you may have several different levels of Vice President (VP). A good implementation would group all the VP titles into the same level range—for example, the 9000–9500 range. Assuming a ranking from highest to lowest, you could assign level numbers as follows:

- **Executive Vice President** Level number 9500
- **Senior Vice President** Level number 9300
- **Group Vice President** Level number 9100

If you later decide to add an Area Vice President title that falls between the Group VP and Senior VP levels, you could assign the new level of 9200 to the Area VP.

Creating Labels

A label consists of three components, and thus far the discussion has only centered on one. To prevent any potential confusion about how OLS works, the level component will now be put to example. The other label components will be added and tested individually for the same reason.

You have to create the valid labels that you want OLS to enforce. You can create the valid labels yourself, as will be done in this example, or you can create the labels dynamically at execution time using the TO_DATA_LABEL function. OLS doesn't automatically create labels just because you created level components. The reason for this will become clear later.

To implement OLS, you have to complete the five-step process; the label creation is step three. The SA_LABEL_ADMIN package allows you to create the labels. The execute privilege was granted directly to the SEC_MGR. To illustrate the ranking effect of the levels, a distinct label will be created for each level:

```
sec_mgr@KNOX10g> -- create labels based on levels
sec_mgr@KNOX10g> BEGIN
    -- Create a label for the executives
    sa_label_admin.create_label
                           (policy_name    => 'ESBD',
                            label_tag      => 1,
                            label_value    => 'EXEC');
    -- Create a label for the management level
    sa_label_admin.create_label
                            (policy_name    => 'ESBD',
                             label_tag      => 2,
                             label_value    => 'MGR');
    -- Create a label for the employees
    sa_label_admin.create_label
                            (policy_name    => 'ESBD',
                             label_tag      => 3,
                             label_value    => 'EMP');
  END;
  /

PL/SQL procedure successfully completed.
```

The labels, like the level component, contain a number as represented by the LABEL_TAG parameter. The label tag, however, is not used for ranking. As you can see, the highest intended level, defined as 'EXEC', has the lowest label tag number. This was done intentionally to demonstrate that the label tag number does not determine the ranking (a common point of confusion).

The label tag is the actual number that is stored in the security column when the policy is eventually applied to the database table(s). One of the benefits to allowing the administrator to choose the label number is that other Oracle database capabilities, such as partitioning and ordering of data based on the label tag values, can be used. Be careful choosing the label tag number because the number has to be unique for all labels in all policies in the database.

NOTE
The label's tag number has to be unique not only for the OLS policy you are working with, but also for all OLS policies in the database.

Figure 12-3 shows how the Oracle Policy Manager employs the label tag number to order the labels when displaying them graphically. Note the tag number *does not* imply the label's security.

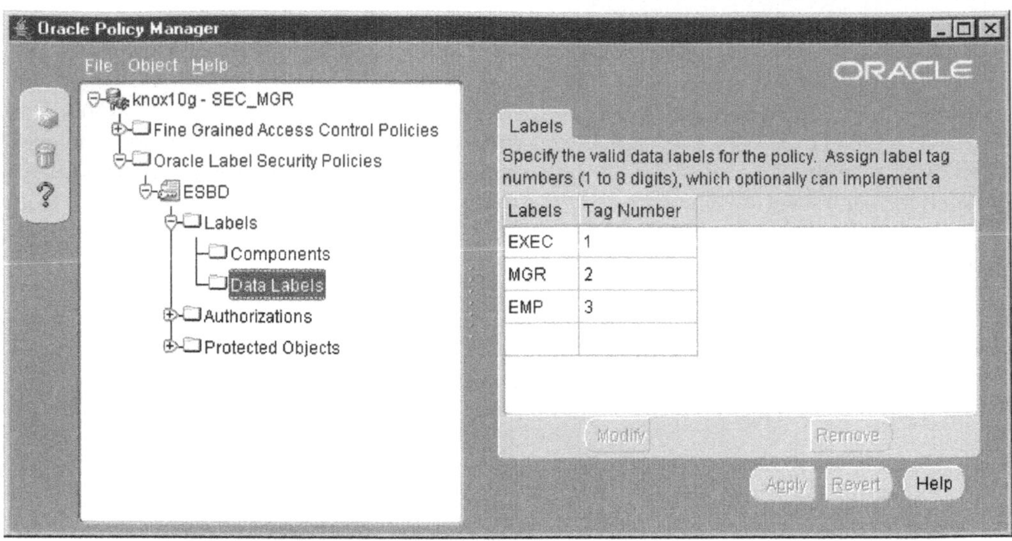

FIGURE 12-3. *The Oracle Policy Manager uses the label tag number to order the display layout of the labels.*

To exercise the OLS policy, you'll need a few data records. The ANNOUNCEMENTS table is populated with three messages, one intended message for each level:

```
scott@KNOX10g> INSERT INTO announcements
  2       VALUES ('This message is only for the Executive Staff.');

scott@KNOX10g> INSERT INTO announcements
  2       VALUES ('All Managers: employee compensation announcement...');

scott@KNOX10g> INSERT INTO announcements
  2       VALUES ('This message is to notify all employees...');


scott@KNOX10g> COMMIT ;
```

Applying the Policy

The policy has been established, the level components defined, and the valid labels created. The next step is to apply the OLS policy (labels) to the table. This is done by executing the APPLY_TABLE_POLICY procedure of the SA_POLICY_ADMIN package. The procedure allows you to override any default options defined when you created the policy so that different tables using the same policy can have different enforcement characteristics.

To begin, choose the 'NO_CONTROL' option indicating that you don't want OLS to enforce any security. Applying a policy to the table alters the table and adds the label column. There is an important reason for not enforcing OLS: until the label column values are populated, you'll not be able to access any of the data. That is, OLS returns no records when the label values are undefined or are null. For pre-existing data, you should first set the appropriate label values and then activate the label enforcement.

```
sec_mgr@KNOX10g> BEGIN
    sa_policy_admin.apply_table_policy
                     (policy_name      => 'ESBD',
                      schema_name      => 'SCOTT',
                      table_name       => 'ANNOUNCEMENTS',
                      table_options    => 'NO_CONTROL');
  END;
  /

PL/SQL procedure successfully completed.
```

You can see the effect of the APPLY_TABLE_POLICY procedure by looking at the table's structure. The table was altered and a column of NUMBER(10) was added. The column name is ROWLABEL as defined when you created the policy.

```
scott@KNOX10g> DESCRIBE announcements
 Name                                          Null?    Type
 --------------------------------------------- -------- --------------
 MESSAGE                                                VARCHAR2(4000)
 ROWLABEL                                               NUMBER(10)
```

The SEC_MGR can now update the OLS labels. Allowing the security administrator to do this ensures you are abiding by the separation of duty policy. However, the SEC_MGR doesn't have the privileges to query or update the ANNOUNCEMENT table. Therefore, SCOTT has to grant the DAC object-level privileges on the table:

```
scott@KNOX10g> GRANT SELECT, INSERT, UPDATE
    ON announcements TO sec_mgr;

Grant succeeded.
```

The table's records are ready to be labeled. To label the existing records, you can simply issue a SQL update statement. The best approach is to first set all the rows to the lowest level (EMP), then gradually and selectively update the records for the remaining levels:

```
scott@KNOX10g> -- Set all records to lowest level
scott@KNOX10g> UPDATE scott.announcements
     SET ROWLABEL = char_to_label ('ESBD', 'EMP');

3 rows updated.

scott@KNOX10g> -- Increase level for manager's records
scott@KNOX10g> UPDATE scott.announcements
     SET ROWLABEL = char_to_label ('ESBD', 'MGR')
   WHERE UPPER (MESSAGE) LIKE '%MANAGE%';

1 row updated.

scott@KNOX10g> -- Increase level for manager's records
scott@KNOX10g> UPDATE scott.announcements
```

```
     SET ROWLABEL = char_to_label ('ESBD', 'EXEC')
   WHERE UPPER (MESSAGE) LIKE '%EXECUTIVE%';

1 row updated.

scott@KNOX10g> COMMIT ;
```

This process of setting the security label based on the content is one of the most common methods for labeling data. Many times the sensitivity is directly derived by the contents of the data. Common data attributes, such as who inserted the record, when it was inserted, and/or how it was inserted, also can help to determine what the label should be.

Authorizing Access

The last step in the OLS creation process is to create the user authorizations. Within OLS, an *authorization* is a named collection consisting of a label, privileges, and auditing directives. The authorization sometimes referred to as a security "profile" is associated with a user or group of users.

The authorization is named by the administrator. If the name given to the authorization is the same as a database user name (schemas), then the database users will automatically receive the authorizations when they log on. OLS builds database log-on triggers automatically to enable user authorizations. However, *the authorizations do not have to be actual database users.* This is one of the most misunderstood capabilities of OLS.

NOTE
OLS user authorizations don't need to be actual database users; the names can represent groups of users, application names, IP domains, or whatever is relevant.

If the authorization name is set to something other than a database user, it's the responsibility of the user or application to map and enable the appropriate authorization to the appropriate database sessions. You will see how to do this in the upcoming "Profile Access" section.

For this scenario, three authorizations are created: one authorization representing the general employees, one authorization for the managers, and one for the executives:

```
sec_mgr@KNOX10g> BEGIN
    sa_user_admin.set_user_labels
                     (policy_name         => 'ESBD',
                      user_name           => 'ALL_EMPLOYEES',
                      max_read_label      => 'EMP');
    sa_user_admin.set_user_labels
                       (policy_name       => 'ESBD',
                        user_name         => 'ALL_MANAGERS',
                        max_read_label    => 'MGR');
    sa_user_admin.set_user_labels
                          (policy_name    => 'ESBD',
                           user_name      => 'ALL_EXECS',
                           max_read_label => 'EXEC');
  END;
  /

PL/SQL procedure successfully completed.
```

As illustrated by the Oracle Policy Manager in Figure 12-4, the three authorizations created are not intended to be directly associated with any one specific database user. Rather, each authorization represents a group of users.

Testing the Labels

You can now activate the OLS enforcement on the table. To change the policy enforcement options, you have to first remove the policy and then re-add it with the enforcement options specified. Start by enforcing OLS for read access, which will restrict all select operations on the table:

```
sec_mgr@KNOX10g> BEGIN
    sa_policy_admin.remove_table_policy
                     (policy_name    => 'ESBD',
                      schema_name    => 'SCOTT',
                      table_name     => 'ANNOUNCEMENTS');
    sa_policy_admin.apply_table_policy
                    (policy_name     => 'ESBD',
                     schema_name     => 'SCOTT',
                     table_name      => 'ANNOUNCEMENTS',
                     table_options   => 'READ_CONTROL');
  END;
  /

PL/SQL procedure successfully completed.
```

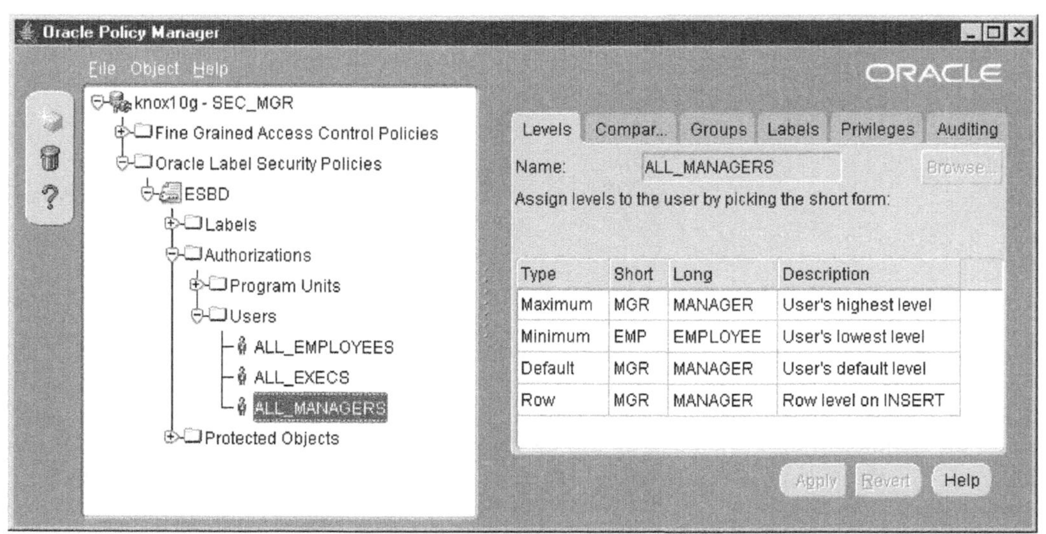

FIGURE 12-4. *User authorizations or profiles don't have to be associated with actual database schemas; they can represent anything, such as applications or groups of users.*

Special OLS Privileges

OLS allows you to assign privileges to override the security enforcement for performing special OLS actions. The privileges aren't standard database system or object privileges. The following list summarizes the privileges that you can assign, thus allowing the authorized user to bypass the specific label security enforcements:

- **PROFILE ACCESS** Allows the user to switch their security profile. This is discussed in the next section.
- **READ** Allows the user to select any data. This is valuable for inspecting labels and performing exports of data.
- **WRITE** Allows the user to override the OLS protections for each of the label components. The OLS ability to restrict write operations is covered in the upcoming "Writing to OLS Protected Tables" section.
- **FULL** This is the shortcut for granting both read and write privileges.

The privileges are unique to OLS and only can be enabled by invoking the SA_USER_ADMIN.SET_USER_PRIVS procedure either directly or via the Oracle Policy Manager. The privileges are set when the authorization profile is set. For database users, this will be done automatically by a database log on trigger.

Profile Access

To test the row-level security, you need to assume the security authorizations for each of the authorizations you have created. The profile access privilege allows a user to set their security authorizations to that of another (user's) profile. *Profile* refers to the specific authorizations defined for a user or group of users. You can enable it for the security manager as follows:

```
sec_mgr@KNOX10g> -- give sec_mgr privs to test levels
sec_mgr@KNOX10g> BEGIN
       sa_user_admin.set_user_privs
                        (policy_name     => 'ESBD',
                         user_name       => 'SEC_MGR',
                         PRIVILEGES      => 'PROFILE_ACCESS');
     END;
     /

PL/SQL procedure successfully completed.
```

In the upcoming Figure 12-5, you can see the Oracle Policy Manager verifying the PROFILE_ACCESS privilege for the SEC_MGR user.

The SEC_MGR can now set the OLS security profile to be any one of the three authorization "users" just defined. To take advantage of this new privilege, the SEC_MGR has to reset his profile. This is done by relogging in to the database. Querying the ANNOUNCEMENTS table shows the results of the OLS security:

```
sec_mgr@KNOX10g> CONN sec_mgr/oracle10g
Connected.
sec_mgr@KNOX10g> COL message format a63
sec_mgr@KNOX10g> -- Set the authorization to the employees
```

```
sec_mgr@KNOX10g> BEGIN
    sa_session.set_access_profile ('ESBD',
                                   'ALL_EMPLOYEES');
  END;
  /

PL/SQL procedure successfully completed.

sec_mgr@KNOX10g> SELECT MESSAGE FROM scott.announcements;

MESSAGE
--------------------------------------------------------------
This message is to notify all employees...

sec_mgr@KNOX10g> -- Set the authorization now to be the managers
sec_mgr@KNOX10g> BEGIN
    sa_session.set_access_profile ('ESBD',
                                   'ALL_MANAGERS');
  END;
  /

PL/SQL procedure successfully completed.

sec_mgr@KNOX10g> SELECT MESSAGE FROM scott.announcements;

MESSAGE
--------------------------------------------------------------
All Managers: employee compensation announcement...
This message is to notify all employees...

sec_mgr@KNOX10g> -- Set the authorization to be the executive staff
sec_mgr@KNOX10g> BEGIN
    sa_session.set_access_profile ('ESBD',
                                   'ALL_EXECS');
  END;
  /

PL/SQL procedure successfully completed.

sec_mgr@KNOX10g> SELECT MESSAGE FROM scott.announcements;

MESSAGE
--------------------------------------------------------------
This message is only for the Executive Staff.
All Managers: employee compensation announcement...
This message is to notify all employees...
```

This example shows how the data is easily separated and secured based on the user's authorizations. The employees will see only the employee message(s). The managers will see the management messages as well as the employee messages, and the executive staff will see all messages.

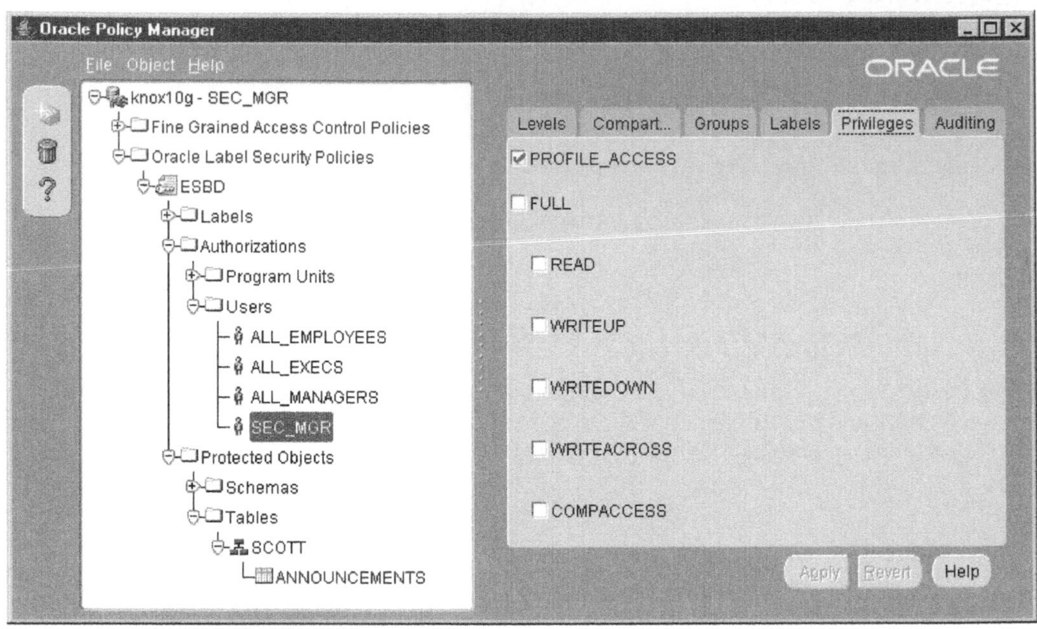

FIGURE 12-5. *Special access privileges can be efficiently inspected, assigned, and removed using the Oracle Policy Manager.*

TIP
Switching the user profile changes the database session's security authorizations and allows you to use OLS in applications that use shared schema designs such as connections pools, Enterprise Users, Oracle Portal, and HTMLDB.

Checking Current Read Authorizations

It's often desirable, especially when debugging, to determine what the current session's authorizations are. The SA_SESSION package provides the useful functions for doing this:

```
sec_mgr@KNOX10g> -- Set the Label to executives
sec_mgr@KNOX10g> BEGIN
    sa_session.set_access_profile ('ESBD',
                                   'ALL_EXECS');
  END;
  /

PL/SQL procedure successfully completed.
```

```
sec_mgr@KNOX10g> -- Verify the label
sec_mgr@KNOX10g> COL "Read Label" format a25
sec_mgr@KNOX10g> SELECT sa_session.read_label ('ESBD') "Read Label"
     FROM DUAL;

Read Label
-------------------------
EXEC
```

Compartments

Now that you have an idea of how to create, apply, and test OLS, the scenario can be augmented to capture the remaining two components. The compartments will be the next component. *Compartments* describe the security process of compartmentalizing information. The compartments are categories of data that require exclusive membership for access to occur—they are not hierarchical.

Compartmentalization is provided to separate information for need to know. For this example, you may wish to post messages to a subgroup of the employees, managers, or executives. To do this, three categories or compartments can be added. There will be one category for sales employees, one for developers, and another for the remaining employees who generally support the internal systems for support and development:

```
sec_mgr@KNOX10g> BEGIN
     sa_components.create_compartment
                       (policy_name    => 'ESBD',
                        long_name      => 'Product Sales',
                        short_name     => 'SALES',
                        comp_num       => 1000);
     sa_components.create_compartment
                       (policy_name    => 'ESBD',
                        long_name      => 'Product Development',
                        short_name     => 'DEV',
                        comp_num       => 100);
     sa_components.create_compartment
                       (policy_name    => 'ESBD',
                        long_name      => 'Internal Support',
                        short_name     => 'IS',
                        comp_num       => 10);
   END;
   /

PL/SQL procedure successfully completed.
```

Figure 12-6 shows the results of executing the preceding PL/SQL. Note the compartment number is also used by the Policy Manager for display order. The short name is the character string used to reference the compartment by a string and should therefore only be as long as needed to distinguish the compartments. You can create up to 9,999 distinct compartments.

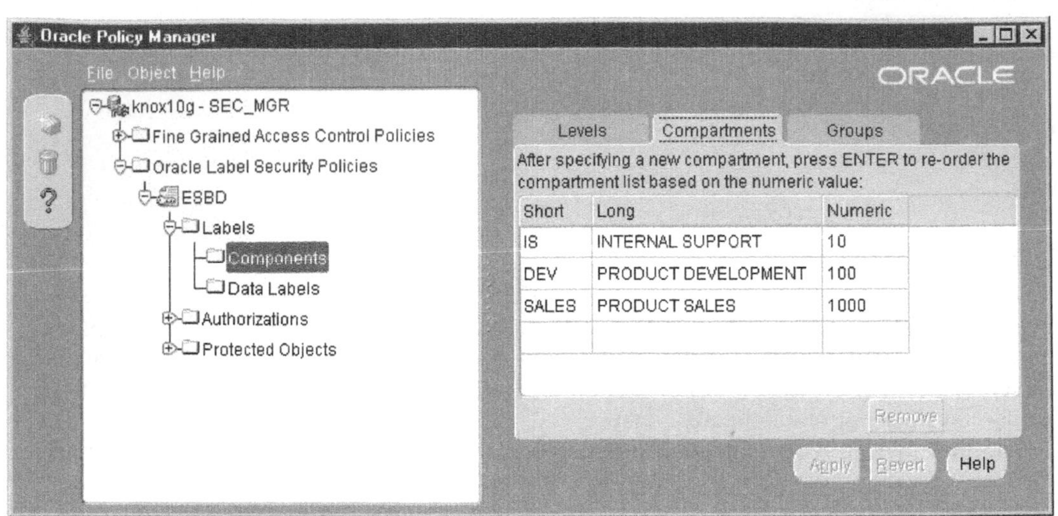

FIGURE 12-6. *Compartments create nonhierarchical categories of data.*

Creating Compartment Labels

You're now ready to create new labels based on the compartment components. The compartments can be combined with the already established levels. It's important to understand that there isn't always a label for every combination of every component. You should only create labels that will be valid within your security policy.

The first label will be for the executive staff. They should be able to view all data regardless of compartment.

Note

This is my contrived policy and there is nothing that forces the highest level to be able to access all of the compartments.

This label must be defined with all compartments. Any compartments not listed will be inaccessible to this label:

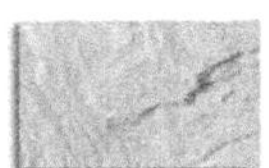

```
sec_mgr@KNOX10g> BEGIN
    sa_label_admin.create_label
                (policy_name    => 'ESBD',
                 label_tag      => 10,
                 label_value    => 'EXEC:SALES,DEV,IS');
  END;
  /

PL/SQL procedure successfully completed.
```

For the managers, assume there are two categories: sales managers and development managers. In this example, there are no internal support managers so you will not create a label to represent that role.

```
sec_mgr@KNOX10g> BEGIN
     sa_label_admin.create_label
                         (policy_name     => 'ESBD',
                          label_tag       => 20,
                          label_value     => 'MGR:SALES');
     sa_label_admin.create_label
                         (policy_name     => 'ESBD',
                          label_tag       => 25,
                          label_value     => 'MGR:DEV');
   END;
   /

PL/SQL procedure successfully completed.
```

The next three labels are used to represent the employees of sales, development, and internal support.

```
sec_mgr@KNOX10g> BEGIN
     sa_label_admin.create_label
                         (policy_name     => 'ESBD',
                          label_tag       => 30,
                          label_value     => 'EMP:SALES');
     sa_label_admin.create_label
                         (policy_name     => 'ESBD',
                          label_tag       => 35,
                          label_value     => 'EMP:DEV');
     sa_label_admin.create_label
                         (policy_name     => 'ESBD',
                          label_tag       => 39,
                          label_value     => 'EMP:IS');
   END;
   /

PL/SQL procedure successfully completed.
```

Figure 12-7 shows the nine distinct labels available in the policy. Again, a good practice is to apply some logic to the label tag numbering. The tag numbers are displayed in ascending order. The numbers for this example were picked to show rankings from highest at the top to lowest at the bottom. Single component labels have one digit. Double component labels have two digits. For the double component labels, executives have been given the range of numbers 10–19; the managers have the range 20–29, and the employees have the range of 30–39.

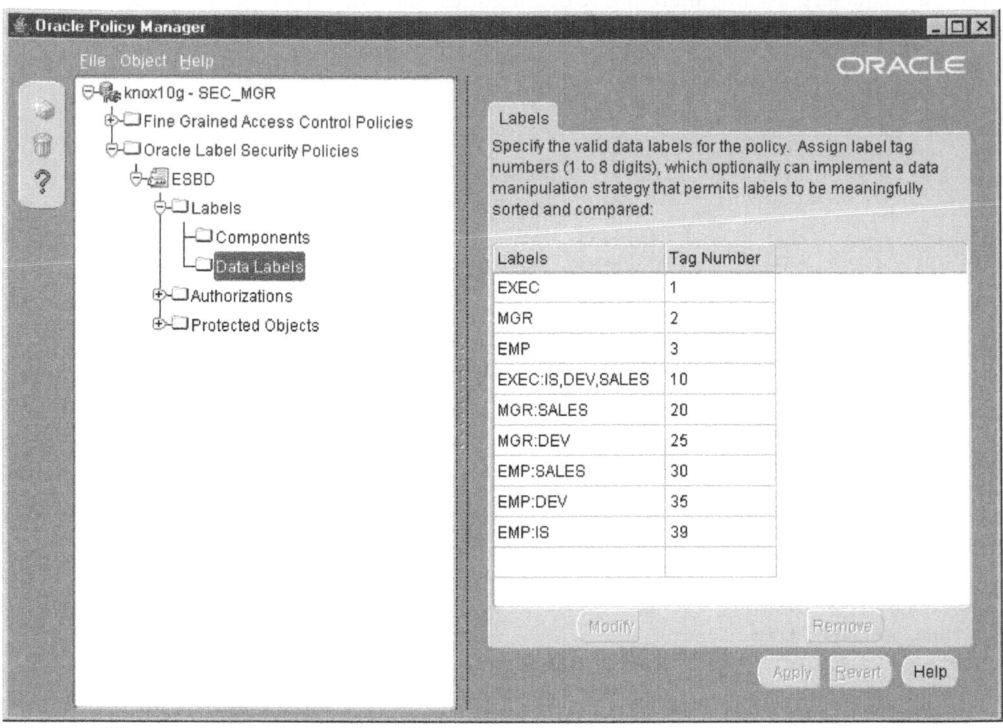

FIGURE 12-7. *Logically chosen label tag numbers can assist in an administrator's ability to easily view and interpret the security associated with the label.*

Authorizations for Compartments

The read control label enforcement has already been applied to the ANNOUNCEMENT table. To test the compartment component, you still have to create the authorizations that will allow access to the new compartment labels. For the executives, modify the current authorization to add the new compartments by executing the ADD_COMPARTMENTS procedure:

```
sec_mgr@KNOX10g> BEGIN
    sa_user_admin.add_compartments
                          (policy_name     => 'ESBD',
                           user_name       => 'ALL_EXECS',
                           comps           => 'SALES,DEV,IS');
  END;
  /

PL/SQL procedure successfully completed.
```

For the managers and employees, create new authorizations with relevant authorization names (user names). This security policy requirement dictates that there are only sales managers and development managers. Therefore, you will create only two new authorizations, one for each.

```
sec_mgr@KNOX10g> BEGIN
   sa_user_admin.set_user_labels
                  (policy_name       => 'ESBD',
                   user_name         => 'SALES_MANAGERS',
                   max_read_label    => 'MGR:SALES');
   sa_user_admin.set_user_labels
                  (policy_name       => 'ESBD',
                   user_name         => 'DEV_MANAGERS',
                   max_read_label    => 'MGR:DEV');
 END;
 /

PL/SQL procedure successfully completed.
```

Finally, create the three new authorizations for the employees, one for each compartment.

```
sec_mgr@KNOX10g> BEGIN
   sa_user_admin.set_user_labels
                  (policy_name    => 'ESBD',
                   user_name      => 'SALES_EMPLOYEES',
                   max_read_label => 'EMP:SALES');
   sa_user_admin.set_user_labels
                  (policy_name    => 'ESBD',
                   user_name      => 'DEV_EMPLOYEES',
                   max_read_label => 'EMP:DEV');
   sa_user_admin.set_user_labels
                  (policy_name    => 'ESBD',
                   user_name      => 'INTERNAL_EMPLOYEES',
                   max_read_label => 'EMP:IS');
 END;
 /

PL/SQL procedure successfully completed.
```

A set of labels is associated with each user authorization or profile created. The read capabilities are being tested now, but the profiles also contain the user's write authorizations. Figure 12-8 shows how the Oracle Policy Manager will allow you to determine access for a user profile by selecting the Labels tab. The sales managers will be authorized to read and write data labeled with the numeric value representing MGR:SALES.

Adding Data to OLS Protected Tables

To test the compartments, a few more messages will be added to the table. These messages are meant for designated subgroups of employees and managers. Thus, the data is secured on a need-to-know basis.

Inserting records now is different than it was previously because the table has the label security column. To show an alternative method for applying labels to data, the insert statements will include the label values. This isn't a requirement, and you'll see in the "Using the Default Session Label" section how the labels can be automatically applied to the records.

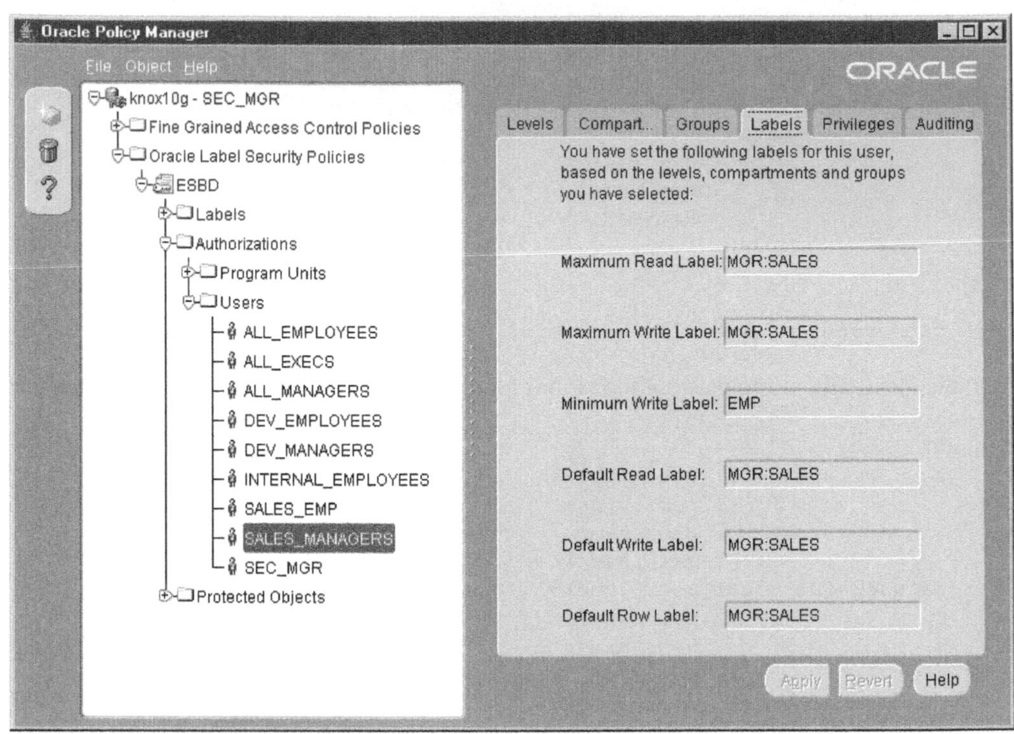

FIGURE 12-8. *User authorizations consist of a set of operation-specific labels that can be viewed by the Policy Manager.*

The labels are populated with the numeric value corresponding to their user-friendly character representation. The CHAR_TO_LABEL function converts the character string to the label's tag number automatically. However, you can alternatively insert the label number if you know what the label number is. For example, according to Figure 12-7, the MGR:SALES label is really stored as the number 20; an insert with the number 20 is equivalent to an insert using the CHAR_TO_LABEL function for MGR:SALES.

```
scott@KNOX10g> INSERT INTO scott.announcements
  2               (MESSAGE, ROWLABEL)
  3        VALUES ('New updates to quotas have been assigned.',
  4                char_to_label ('ESBD', 'MGR:SALES'));

1 row created.

scott@KNOX10g> INSERT INTO scott.announcements
  2               (MESSAGE, ROWLABEL)
  3        VALUES ('New product release date meeting scheduled.',
  4                char_to_label ('ESBD', 'MGR:DEV'));
```

```
1 row created.

scott@KNOX10g> INSERT INTO scott.announcements
  2            (MESSAGE, ROWLABEL)
  3       VALUES ('Quota club trip destined for Hawaii.',
  4             char_to_label ('ESBD', 'EMP:SALES'));

1 row created.

scott@KNOX10g> INSERT INTO scott.announcements
  2            (MESSAGE, ROWLABEL)
  3       VALUES ('Source control software updates distributed next week.',
  4             char_to_label ('ESBD', 'EMP:DEV'));

1 row created.

scott@KNOX10g> INSERT INTO scott.announcements
  2            (MESSAGE, ROWLABEL)
  3       VALUES ('Firewall attacks increasing.',
  4             char_to_label ('ESBD', 'EMP:IS'));

1 row created.

scott@KNOX10g> COMMIT ;
```

To test the compartments, set the authorizations to the different users and query. If you use an authorized user that has no compartments, they'll see no compartmentalized data:

```
sec_mgr@KNOX10g> -- If user authorizations do not include compartments,
sec_mgr@KNOX10g> -- then no data is returned
sec_mgr@KNOX10g> EXEC sa_session.set_access_profile('ESBD','ALL_EMPLOYEES');

PL/SQL procedure successfully completed.

sec_mgr@KNOX10g> SELECT MESSAGE FROM scott.announcements;

MESSAGE
--------------------------------------------------------------
This message is to notify all employees...
```

Employees with compartment authorizations will see all the data within their compartment and the data that has no compartments. This is the subtle detail that is very important to understand.

```
sec_mgr@KNOX10g> -- Users with compartments see their compartments
sec_mgr@KNOX10g> -- and non-compartment labeled data.
sec_mgr@KNOX10g> -- Set authorization profile for sales employees
sec_mgr@KNOX10g> BEGIN
  2    sa_session.set_access_profile
  3                                  ('ESBD',
  4                                   'SALES_EMPLOYEES');
```

```
 END;
 /

PL/SQL procedure successfully completed.

sec_mgr@KNOX10g> SELECT MESSAGE
     FROM scott.announcements;

MESSAGE
--------------------------------------------------------
This message is to notify all employees...
Quota club trip destined for Hawaii.
```

With the managers, you start to see the access controlled by the combination of their levels and compartments. Managers can see all the data employees can, but only within their compartment. Development managers can't see any sales data regardless of the level of that data. To help illustrate this, the message and the security label can be queried:

```
sec_mgr@KNOX10g> -- Managers can still see all employee data within
sec_mgr@KNOX10g> -- the same compartment.
sec_mgr@KNOX10g> COL "OLS Label" format a10
sec_mgr@KNOX10g> BEGIN
     sa_session.set_access_profile ('ESBD',
                                    'DEV_MANAGERS');
 END;
 /

PL/SQL procedure successfully completed.

sec_mgr@KNOX10g> SELECT MESSAGE,
          label_to_char (ROWLABEL) "OLS Label"
     FROM scott.announcements;

MESSAGE                                                  OLS Label
-------------------------------------------------------- ----------
All Managers: employee compensation announcement...      MGR
This message is to notify all employees...               EMP
New product release date meeting scheduled.              MGR:DEV
Source control software updates distributed next week.   EMP:DEV
```

The final query shows the security policy allows the executives access to everything:

```
sec_mgr@KNOX10g> -- Executives have access to all information.
sec_mgr@KNOX10g> BEGIN
     sa_session.set_access_profile ('ESBD',
                                    'ALL_EXECS');
 END;
 /
```

```
PL/SQL procedure successfully completed.

sec_mgr@KNOX10g> SELECT MESSAGE,
          label_to_char (ROWLABEL) "OLS Label"
     FROM scott.announcements;

MESSAGE                                                  OLS Label
-------------------------------------------------------- ----------
This message is only for the Executive Staff.            EXEC
All Managers: employee compensation announcement...      MGR
This message is to notify all employees...               EMP
New updates to quotas have been assigned.                MGR:SALES
New product release date meeting scheduled.              MGR:DEV
Quota club trip destined for Hawaii.                     EMP:SALES
Source control software updates distributed next week.   EMP:DEV
Firewall attacks increasing.                             EMP:IS

8 rows selected.
```

Groups

The last component of an OLS label is the group. Groups are hierarchical; you can create a parent group with children groups underneath. The parent can see the children records, but the siblings can't see each other's records. For this example, a parent group called Corporate is created:

```
sec_mgr@KNOX10g> BEGIN
     sa_components.CREATE_GROUP
                             (policy_name    => 'ESBD',
                              long_name      => 'Corporate',
                              short_name     => 'CORP',
                              group_num      => 1,
                              parent_name    => NULL);
   END;
   /

PL/SQL procedure successfully completed.
```

The next groups are created under the Corporate group and are based on geographical regions. US is a group representing all the company's offices in the United States. To further define the U.S. office locations, two other groups are created to represent the New York (NY) office and the Los Angeles (LA) office.

```
sec_mgr@KNOX10g> -- Create groups based on geographical regions
sec_mgr@KNOX10g> BEGIN
     -- Create group representing offices in the U.S.
     sa_components.CREATE_GROUP
                         (policy_name    => 'ESBD',
                          long_name      => 'United States',
                          short_name     => 'US',
```

```
                      group_num      => 100,
                      parent_name    => 'CORP');
   -- Create group representing the New York office.
   -- This is a child of the US group.
   sa_components.CREATE_GROUP
                     (policy_name    => 'ESBD',
                      long_name      => 'New York',
                      short_name     => 'NY',
                      group_num      => 110,
                      parent_name    => 'US');
   -- Create group representing the Los Angeles office.
   -- This is a child of the US group.
   sa_components.CREATE_GROUP
                     (policy_name    => 'ESBD',
                      long_name      => 'Los Angeles',
                      short_name     => 'LA',
                      group_num      => 120,
                      parent_name    => 'US');
 END;
 /

PL/SQL procedure successfully completed.
```

This hierarchy has NY and LA as children of US, and US as a child of CORP. Two other groups make this example interesting. The first group represents the company facilities for countries in Europe, Middle East, and Africa. The second represents countries in Asia and those located bordering the Pacific Ocean.

```
sec_mgr@KNOX10g> -- International
sec_mgr@KNOX10g> BEGIN
   sa_components.CREATE_GROUP
                     (policy_name    => 'ESBD',
                      long_name      => 'Europe Middle_East Africa',
                      short_name     => 'EMEA',
                      group_num      => 200,
                      parent_name    => 'CORP');
   sa_components.CREATE_GROUP
                     (policy_name    => 'ESBD',
                      long_name      => 'Asia and Pacific',
                      short_name     => 'APAC',
                      group_num      => 300,
                      parent_name    => 'CORP');
 END;
 /

PL/SQL procedure successfully completed.
```

The result of these group creations can be easily viewed with Oracle Policy Manager. Figure 12-9 illustrates the final groups and their heritage.

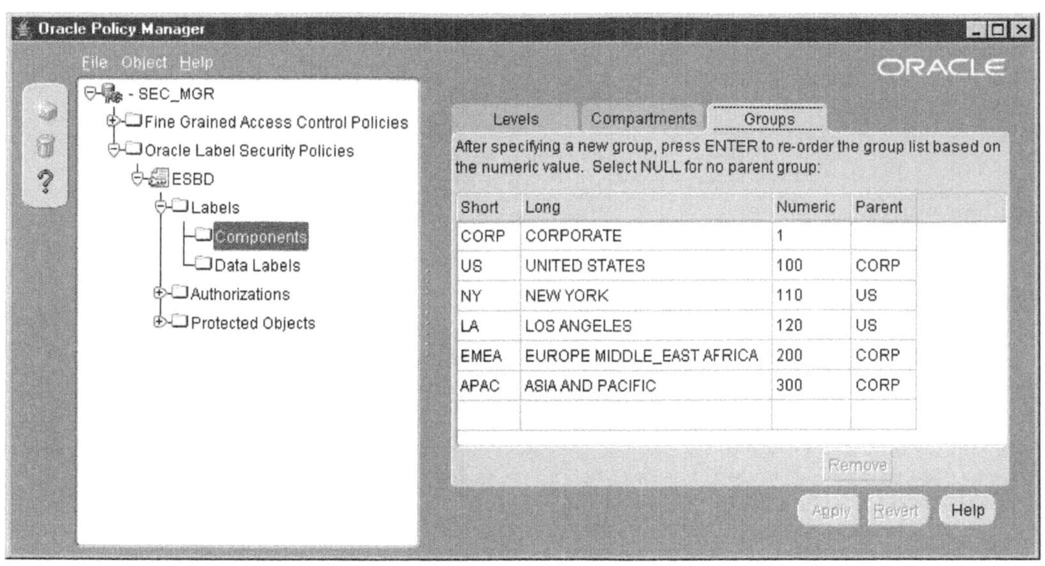

FIGURE 12-9. *OLS groups support hierarchical organizations as seen here, where CORP is the parent or grandparent of all groups.*

Creating Labels with Levels, Compartments, and Groups

You are now ready to create the final labels, which consist of items from all three components. The first group of labels is intended to be for data accessed by the sales force. There will be sales representatives located in New York and Los Angeles. There will be U.S. managers overseeing the representatives. You can also create the EMEA sales manager:

```
sec_mgr@KNOX10g> -- Create labels with levels, compartments and groups
sec_mgr@KNOX10g> -- Sales in US and EMEA.
sec_mgr@KNOX10g> -- Note US is divided into overall US, LA and then NY
sec_mgr@KNOX10g> BEGIN
    -- Sales managers for EMEA
    sa_label_admin.create_label
                     (policy_name     => 'ESBD',
                      label_tag       => 300,
                      label_value     => 'MGR:SALES:EMEA');
    -- Sales manager for all of U.S.
    sa_label_admin.create_label
                     (policy_name     => 'ESBD',
                      label_tag       => 310,
                      label_value     => 'MGR:SALES:US');
    -- New York sales reps
    sa_label_admin.create_label
```

```
                   (policy_name      => 'ESBD',
                    label_tag        => 320,
                    label_value      => 'EMP:SALES:NY');
    -- Los Angeles sales reps
    sa_label_admin.create_label
                   (policy_name      => 'ESBD',
                    label_tag        => 330,
                    label_value      => 'EMP:SALES:LA');
  END;
  /

PL/SQL procedure successfully completed.
```

The final labels are for the development staff. There are U.S. and APAC developers. The development managers all work from the corporate facility.

```
sec_mgr@KNOX10g> -- Develop in US and APAC
sec_mgr@KNOX10g> -- Managers reside in corporate facility only
sec_mgr@KNOX10g> BEGIN
    -- US developers
    sa_label_admin.create_label
                   (policy_name      => 'ESBD',
                    label_tag        => 400,
                    label_value      => 'EMP:DEV:US');
    -- APAC developers
    sa_label_admin.create_label
                   (policy_name      => 'ESBD',
                    label_tag        => 410,
                    label_value      => 'EMP:DEV:APAC');
    -- US developers
    sa_label_admin.create_label
                   (policy_name      => 'ESBD',
                    label_tag        => 450,
                    label_value      => 'MGR:DEV:CORP');
  END;
  /

PL/SQL procedure successfully completed.
```

The final labels can be easily seen in Figure 12-10. This is an important view because it lists the only valid labels available to the policy.

Authorizations for Levels, Compartments, and Groups

The labels are created, but nobody has the authorizations to access any data that will be labeled with the final component mixture. To create the authorizations that'll be used with these final labels, augment the executives' authorization by adding the corporate group. Because the corporate group is the parent or grandparent of all other groups, adding this one group will give all executives access to all data regardless of which groups the data is labeled:

```
sec_mgr@KNOX10g> -- Setup level, compartment and group authorizations
sec_mgr@KNOX10g> -- add groups to executives. Only need to add root group
sec_mgr@KNOX10g> BEGIN
      sa_user_admin.add_groups
                     (policy_name    => 'ESBD',
                      user_name      => 'ALL_EXECS',
                      groups         => 'CORP');
    END;
    /

PL/SQL procedure successfully completed.
```

Next, assign authorizations for the sales managers and sales representatives, as shown in the following code.

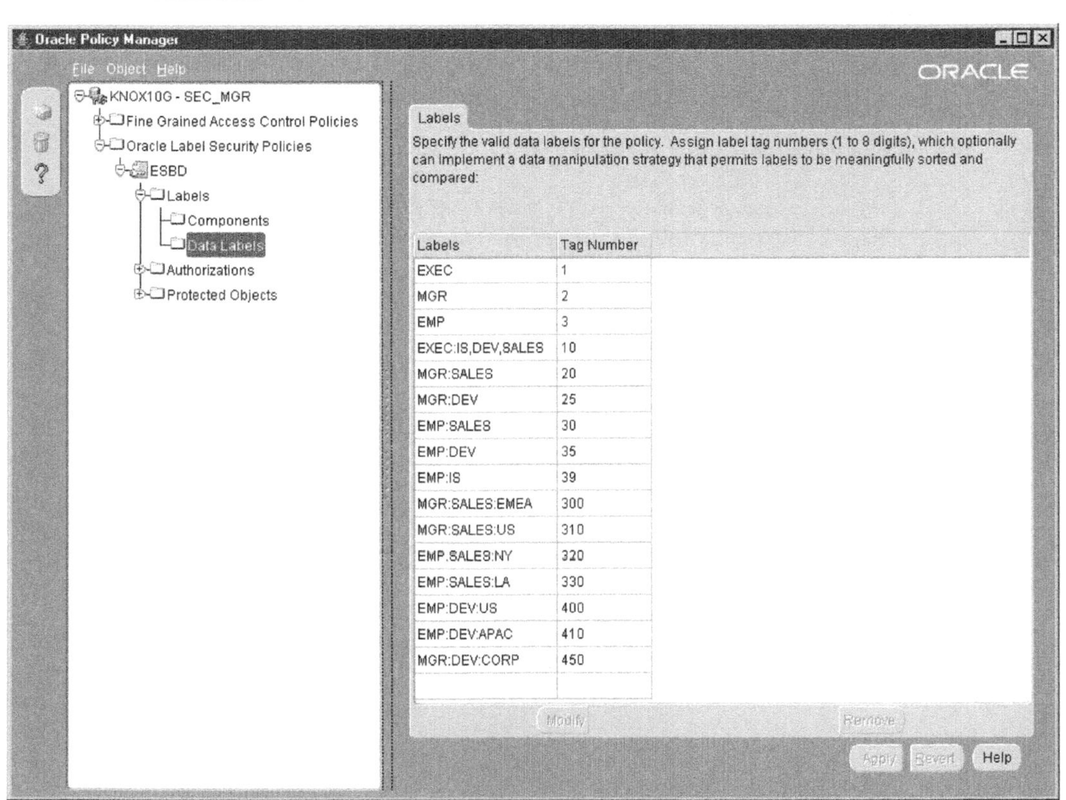

FIGURE 12-10. *Oracle Policy Manager shows all the valid labels available to a policy.*

```
sec_mgr@KNOX10g> -- Create authorizations for US and EMEA sales managers
sec_mgr@KNOX10g> BEGIN
    sa_user_admin.set_user_labels
                  (policy_name        => 'ESBD',
                   user_name          => 'US_SALES_MGR',
                   max_read_label     => 'MGR:SALES:US');
    sa_user_admin.set_user_labels
                  (policy_name        => 'ESBD',
                   user_name          => 'EMEA_SALES_MGR',
                   max_read_label     => 'MGR:SALES:EMEA');
  END;
  /

PL/SQL procedure successfully completed.

sec_mgr@KNOX10g> -- Create authorizations for NY and LA sales reps
sec_mgr@KNOX10g> BEGIN
    sa_user_admin.set_user_labels
                  (policy_name        => 'ESBD',
                   user_name          => 'NY_SALES_REP',
                   max_read_label     => 'EMP:SALES:NY');
    sa_user_admin.set_user_labels
                  (policy_name        => 'ESBD',
                   user_name          => 'LA_SALES_REP',
                   max_read_label     => 'EMP:SALES:LA');
  END;
  /

PL/SQL procedure successfully completed.
```

For the development managers, use the same approach used for the executives—augment the existing DEV_MANAGERS authorization to include the corporate group:

```
sec_mgr@KNOX10g> -- Create authorizations for the development staff.
sec_mgr@KNOX10g> -- Add groups to managers. Only need to add root
sec_mgr@KNOX10g> BEGIN
    sa_user_admin.add_groups
                  (policy_name     => 'ESBD',
                   user_name       => 'DEV_MANAGERS',
                   GROUPS          => 'CORP');
  END;
  /

PL/SQL procedure successfully completed.
```

The final authorizations are for the developers. By simply adding APAC and US, you have defined and categorized the entire development staff:

```
sec_mgr@KNOX10g> -- Add developer profiles
sec_mgr@KNOX10g> BEGIN
    -- Create authorizations for APAC developers
```

```
    sa_user_admin.set_user_labels
                   (policy_name       => 'ESBD',
                    user_name         => 'APAC_DEVELOPER',
                    max_read_label    => 'EMP:DEV:APAC');
    -- Create authorizations for US developers
    sa_user_admin.set_user_labels
                   (policy_name       => 'ESBD',
                    user_name         => 'US_DEVELOPER',
                    max_read_label    => 'EMP:DEV:US');
  END;
  /

PL/SQL procedure successfully completed.
```

It has taken several hundred lines of formatted code, but the security policy is now in place and can be easily reproduced by re-executing the OLS PL/SQL APIs. The Oracle Policy Manager can do everything that was done through the preceding APIs and requires significantly less typing.

Using the Default Session Label

You saw how data can be labeled by issuing an update statement to the table and by including the label in the insert statement. Another interesting technique for labeling data is to use an OLS capability, which will create the label automatically. The option is called LABEL_DEFAULT. When enabled, OLS will use a database trigger to populate the label column based on the user's current (write) authorization label. To do this, you have to change the policy options. This requires you to drop and then re-add the policy:

```
sec_mgr@KNOX10g> -- Use default write session
sec_mgr@KNOX10g> -- authorization for data label. Have to drop
sec_mgr@KNOX10g> -- then re-add policy with label_default option.
sec_mgr@KNOX10g> BEGIN
    sa_policy_admin.remove_table_policy
                  (policy_name     => 'ESBD',
                   schema_name     => 'SCOTT',
                   table_name      => 'ANNOUNCEMENTS');
    sa_policy_admin.apply_table_policy
                  (policy_name     => 'ESBD',
                   schema_name     => 'SCOTT',
                   table_name      => 'ANNOUNCEMENTS',
                   table_options   => 'LABEL_DEFAULT,READ_CONTROL');
  END;
  /

PL/SQL procedure successfully completed.
```

To insert data now, you can omit the ROWLABEL column, and OLS will use the user's current write label to populate the data's label. Recall in Figure 12-8 that the write label is the same as the read label in this example. If you set the session profile (authorization) to the US sales managers and insert data, the data is automatically tagged as MGR:SALES:US.

```
sec_mgr@KNOX10g> -- Insert data as a US sales manager. OLS will
sec_mgr@KNOX10g> -- automatically label data based on user's write label.
sec_mgr@KNOX10g> BEGIN
      sa_session.set_access_profile ('ESBD',
                                     'US_SALES_MGR');
    END;
    /

PL/SQL procedure successfully completed.

sec_mgr@KNOX10g> INSERT INTO scott.announcements
                 (MESSAGE)
          VALUES ('Presidential outlook for economy may affect revenue.');

1 row created.

sec_mgr@KNOX10g> COMMIT ;

Commit complete.

sec_mgr@KNOX10g> -- Check label of inserted message
sec_mgr@KNOX10g> SELECT MESSAGE,
            label_to_char (ROWLABEL) "OLS Label"
      FROM scott.announcements
     WHERE MESSAGE LIKE 'Pres%';

MESSAGE                                                  OLS Label
-------------------------------------------------------- ------------
Presidential outlook for economy may affect revenue.     MGR:SALES:US
```

Follow this same procedure to validate the different authorizations. This is not just a good idea for this example, this is a good practice before fielding your security policy.

```
sec_mgr@KNOX10g> -- Insert sales data using session label.
sec_mgr@KNOX10g> BEGIN
    -- Insert data as NY sales rep
      sa_session.set_access_profile ('ESBD',
                                     'NY_SALES_REP');
      INSERT INTO scott.announcements
                  (MESSAGE)
           VALUES ('Party in Madison Ave. office cancelled');
    -- Insert data as LA sales rep
      sa_session.set_access_profile ('ESBD',
                                     'LA_SALES_REP');
      INSERT INTO scott.announcements
                  (MESSAGE)
           VALUES ('Earthquake preparation team meeting tonight.');
    -- Insert data as APAC developer
      sa_session.set_access_profile ('ESBD',
                                     'APAC_DEVELOPER');
```

```
    INSERT INTO scott.announcements
                (MESSAGE)
         VALUES ('National Language Support API released.');
    COMMIT;
  END;
  /

PL/SQL procedure successfully completed.
```

OLS automatically labels the data based on the user's session label. This is convenient and allows the label security to be transparent to many applications. Now that the data has been labeled, you should validate that the labels are what you expect them to be.

Testing the Labels

The final read tests can be performed by setting the authorizations to the various users and validating the returned data. This is what you should do before going operational with your data. Alternatively, you can query as a user who can see all the data. This will allow you to cross-check the labels to ensure everything is as it should be:

```
sec_mgr@KNOX10g> COL message format a55
sec_mgr@KNOX10g> COL "OLS Label" format a12
sec_mgr@KNOX10g> BEGIN
    sa_session.set_access_profile ('ESBD',
                                   'ALL_EXECS');
  END;
  /

PL/SQL procedure successfully completed.

sec_mgr@KNOX10g> SELECT MESSAGE,
         label_to_char (ROWLABEL) "OLS Label"
    FROM scott.announcements;

MESSAGE                                                 OLS Label
------------------------------------------------------- ------------
This message is only for the Executive Staff.           EXEC
All Managers: employee compensation announcement...     MGR
This message is to notify all employees...              EMP
New updates to quotas have been assigned.               MGR:SALES
New product release date meeting scheduled.             MGR:DEV
Quota club trip destined for Hawaii.                    EMP:SALES
Source control software updates distributed next week.  EMP:DEV
Firewall attacks increasing.                            EMP:IS
Party in Madison Ave. office cancelled                  EMP:SALES:NY
Presidential outlook for economy may affect revenue.    MGR:SALES:US
Earthquake preparation team meeting tonight.            EMP:SALES:LA
National Language Support API released.                 EMP:DEV:APAC

12 rows selected.
```

The preceding output is valuable because it's easy to do the side-by-side comparison of data and its security marking. Once you have a clear understanding of your security policy, you'll be able to issue simple queries that return some relevant piece of data and its security label, which will in turn allow you to validate your row-level security access. If you see anything that looks like it can be accessed by too many people, simply update the security label and the data will no longer be available.

Comparing the Labels

Another valuable verification test takes the current data labels and compares them to the user's authorization labels. OLS determines access by comparing the user's read label with the record's label. OLS first determines what levels the user is authorized for, then determines the groups, and finally, the compartments. When the user's authorizations allow them access to the records, the user's label is said to *dominate* the record's label.

You can quickly test the authorizations and data labels to ensure the labels and authorizations are working to your understanding. The following example tests the authorizations for a U.S. sales manager:

```
sec_mgr@KNOX10g> -- Label dominance check.
sec_mgr@KNOX10g> COL "User's Read Label" format a20
sec_mgr@KNOX10g> COL "Data Record Labels" format a20
sec_mgr@KNOX10g> BREAK on "User's Read Label"
sec_mgr@KNOX10g> BEGIN
  2    sa_session.set_access_profile ('ESBD',
  3                                  'US_SALES_MGR');
  4  END;
  5  /

PL/SQL procedure successfully completed.

sec_mgr@KNOX10g> SELECT   sa_session.read_label ('ESBD')
  2                              "User's Read Label",
  3           label_to_char (ROWLABEL)
  4                              "Data Record Labels"
  5      FROM scott.announcements
  6  GROUP BY ROWLABEL;

User's Read Label    Data Record Labels
-------------------- --------------------
MGR:SALES:US,NY,LA   MGR
                     EMP
                     MGR:SALES
                     EMP:SALES
                     MGR:SALES:US
                     EMP:SALES:NY
                     EMP:SALES:LA

7 rows selected.
```

This is a good exercise because it's important to understand the dominance relationship between the user authorizations and the data that will be accessed. If you're unsure of a user's access, run a query such as the one just shown. The labels don't lie, and OLS will not produce an incorrect result. Mistakes can happen during the component definitions and the user authorizations. You should periodically run a report that validates your security policy. Understanding the dominance relationship is critical to an effective OLS implementation.

Hiding the Label

OLS provides the ability to hide the label column. Hiding the column means that the ROWLABEL column will not appear in a table DESCRIBE or a SELECT * query. Additionally, insert statements that insert data into all columns (for example, insert into <table> values ...) don't need to specify the label column. You may recall that this column hiding was the behavior that Trusted Oracle exhibited.

Hiding the column can be desirable when you want to obscure the row-level security mechanism from users or applications. However, the user or application can always ask for the label column assuming they know the column name. OLS allows the column to be hidden, but not because it makes the data more secure. If your security is based on the users not knowing the column name, or *security through obscurity*, you have big challenges ahead of you! Hiding the column allows OLS to be transparently applied to tables with minimal impact on existing applications—those that issue SELECT * queries and insert all column statements. There also are many tools that model database tables. Hiding the label column is desirable for these tools because the label column shouldn't appear in the table models.

OLS will hide the column when the HIDE directive is passed to either the DEFAULT_OPTIONS parameter of the SA_SYSDBA.CREATE_POLICY procedure, or the TABLE_OPTIONS parameter of the APPLY_TABLE_POLICY procedure. Note that while the label column name is constant for the policy, the HIDE option is enforced on a table-by-table basis.

Changing the Hidden Status

Once an OLS policy has been applied to a table, you can't change the hidden status of the label column without losing your labels. The effect is illustrated here. Assume you now want to hide the ROWLABEL column on the ANNOUNCEMENTS table. Because you are changing a policy option, you'll have to remove the policy and then re-apply with the HIDE directive. Unfortunately, OLS will not let you hide the existing label column:

```
sec_mgr@KNOX10g> -- Drop OLS policy.
sec_mgr@KNOX10g> BEGIN
    sa_policy_admin.remove_table_policy
                     (policy_name     => 'ESBD',
                      schema_name     => 'SCOTT',
                      table_name      => 'ANNOUNCEMENTS');
  END;
  /

PL/SQL procedure successfully completed.

sec_mgr@KNOX10g> -- Add Policy with Hide option.
```

```
sec_mgr@KNOX10g> BEGIN
     sa_policy_admin.apply_table_policy
       (policy_name       => 'ESBD',
        schema_name       => 'SCOTT',
        table_name        => 'ANNOUNCEMENTS',
        table_options     => 'HIDE,LABEL_DEFAULT,READ_CONTROL');
   END;
   /
BEGIN
*
ERROR at line 1:
ORA-12445: cannot change HIDDEN property of column
ORA-12432: LBAC error: cannot HIDE column
```

The only way to change the hidden status is to remove the policy with the DROP_COLUMN parameter (of the REMOVE_TABLE_POLICY procedure) set to TRUE. The problem with this is that when the column is dropped, all the labels in the column are also dropped. This is a problem if you don't want to *remove* the labels and only want to *hide* them. Note in the previous code that the column wasn't dropped. The policy has been removed, but the labels still reside with the data. A simple fact motivating why this is so important: it recently took me eight hours to label the data in a single table!

A solution to this is to copy the label values to another column before you drop the column. To do this, alter the table and add a new column:

```
scott@KNOX10g> -- Add temporary column to table
scott@KNOX10g> ALTER TABLE announcements ADD (temp_label NUMBER(10));

Table altered.
```

Next, copy the label values from the OLS label column to your temporary column. Be sure you can access all rows before you try to copy. For this operation, you can either set your authorization to a profile that can access all the records or execute as a user that has the special OLS READ privilege. Refer back to "Special OLS Privileges" for more details on how to do this. To simplify this example, the ALL_EXECS profile is set as follows:

```
sec_mgr@KNOX10g> -- Set access to all rows
sec_mgr@KNOX10g> BEGIN
     sa_session.set_access_profile ('ESBD',
                                    'ALL_EXECS');
   END;
   /

PL/SQL procedure successfully completed.

sec_mgr@KNOX10g> -- Copy labels to temporary column
sec_mgr@KNOX10g> UPDATE scott.announcements
      SET temp_label = ROWLABEL;

12 rows updated.

sec_mgr@KNOX10g> COMMIT ;
```

```
Commit complete.

sec_mgr@KNOX10g> -- Verify update
sec_mgr@KNOX10g> COL message format a55
sec_mgr@KNOX10g> COL "OLS Label" format a12
sec_mgr@KNOX10g> SELECT rownum,
          label_to_char (ROWLABEL) "OLS Label",
          rowlabel "Label Value",
          temp_label "Temp Label Value"
     FROM scott.announcements;

    ROWNUM OLS Label    Label Value Temp Label Value
---------- ------------ ----------- ----------------
         1 MGR:SALES             20               20
         2 MGR:DEV               25               25
         3 EMP:SALES             30               30
         4 EMP:DEV               35               35
         5 EMP:IS                39               39
         6 EMP:SALES:NY         320              320
         7 EMP:SALES:LA         330              330
         8 EMP:DEV:APAC         410              410
         9 MGR:SALES:US         310              310
        10 EXEC                   1                1
        11 MGR                    2                2
        12 EMP                    3                3

12 rows selected.
```

Now remove the policy with the DROP_COLUMN set to TRUE. This will drop the ROWLABEL column from the table. Next, re-apply the policy with the HIDE option:

```
sec_mgr@KNOX10g> -- Remove policy and re-apply with HIDE option
sec_mgr@KNOX10g> BEGIN
     sa_policy_admin.remove_table_policy
       (policy_name     => 'ESBD',
        schema_name     => 'SCOTT',
        table_name      => 'announcements',
        DROP_COLUMN     => TRUE);
     sa_policy_admin.apply_table_policy
       (policy_name       => 'ESBD',
        schema_name       => 'SCOTT',
        table_name        => 'ANNOUNCEMENTS',
        table_options     => 'HIDE,LABEL_DEFAULT,READ_CONTROL');

   END;
   /

PL/SQL procedure successfully completed.
```

The last step is to copy the values back to the OLS-enforced label column and drop the temporary column:

```
sec_mgr@KNOX10g> -- Copy values back to rowlabel column
sec_mgr@KNOX10g> UPDATE scott.announcements
  2      SET ROWLABEL = temp_label;

12 rows updated.

sec_mgr@KNOX10g> COMMIT ;

Commit complete.

sec_mgr@KNOX10g> -- Verify update
sec_mgr@KNOX10g> SELECT ROWNUM,
  2          label_to_char (ROWLABEL) "OLS Label",
  3          ROWLABEL "Label Value",
  4          temp_label "Temp Label Value"
  5     FROM scott.announcements;

    ROWNUM OLS Label    Label Value Temp Label Value
---------- ------------ ----------- ----------------
         1 MGR:SALES             20               20
         2 MGR:DEV               25               25
         3 EMP:SALES             30               30
         4 EMP:DEV               35               35
         5 EMP:IS                39               39
         6 EMP:SALES:NY         320              320
         7 EMP:SALES:LA         330              330
         8 EMP:DEV:APAC         410              410
         9 MGR:SALES:US         310              310
        10 EXEC                   1                1
        11 MGR                    2                2
        12 EMP                    3                3

12 rows selected.

sec_mgr@KNOX10g> -- Drop temporary column
sec_mgr@KNOX10g> conn scott/tiger
Connected.
scott@KNOX10g> ALTER TABLE announcements DROP COLUMN temp_label;

Table altered.

scott@KNOX10g> DESC announcements
 Name                                      Null?    Type
 ----------------------------------------- -------- ---------------
 MESSAGE                                            VARCHAR2(4000)
```

Writing to OLS Protected Tables

While the preceding examples performed a few insert operations, the major emphasis until now has been on read protection of the data. The READ_CONTROL option placed on tables uses Oracle's VPD technology to limit the records returned by queries. Inserts, updates, and deletes of data, collectively known in the OLS world as *write control*, use VPD and after-row database triggers to enforce the security policies.

User authorizations are defined by combinations of levels, compartments, and groups. There are specific algorithms followed by OLS to control how data is accessed for SELECT, INSERT, UPDATE, and DELETE operations. The *Oracle Label Security Administrator's Guide* produces an excellent explanation with flow diagrams for these algorithms; search for "Label Evaluation Process" in Chapter 3 of the guide for more information.

Understanding Write Authorizations

When OLS applies security for reading or writing data, it can be thought of as a set filtering process. The first access mediation is based on the user's level. There is a valid set of data that falls into the user's authorization level. This set is then further filtered based on the user's compartment authorizations. Lastly, the resulting set is filtered by the user's group authorizations.

This set filtering description is useful in understanding how OLS implements write access controls. A user's write authorizations are a subset of their read authorizations. Put another way, a user can never write data that they can't read. This basic principle will help you in understanding and assigning OLS privileges to the user because there *is* a read-write access control relationship.

For each label component, the OLS administrator can define three access lists that determine the user's read and write authorizations. The first list is a set of all possible values the user can possess within their session for that component. That is, a user can never set their label to anything outside of this list. For levels, this is the range between and including the minimum and maximum level. For compartments and groups, this is the Write access control list. The Write lists are the set to which the user can perform insert, update, or delete operations.

The next access list is called Default. Entries in the Default list are automatically set for the user when their profile is set either during logon or when the SET_ACCESS_PROFILE procedure is executed.

Lastly, there is a Row list. This list becomes part of the label for any data that is inserted or updated when the LABEL_DEFAULT option is enabled. You witnessed this for inserted data with the examples in the "Using the Default Session Label" section.

Figure 12-11 illustrates the three lists for the Compartments component as seen from the Oracle Policy Manager for the US_SALES_MGR profile. The figure shows the user has the SALES compartment for WRITE, DEFAULT, and ROW. WRITE specifies the user can perform insert, update, or delete operations on data labeled with the SALES compartment; DEFAULT indicates the SALES compartment is set in the user's label when the profile is enabled; and ROW indicates the SALES compartment automatically will be written to the data label if using the LABEL_DEFAULT option.

Level Insertion

The best way to ensure your understanding of write operations is to study an example. The following example uses the level component to show how the write controls are enforced with OLS. The other label components behave similarly, and you can add them once you are comfortable with access controls based on a single component.

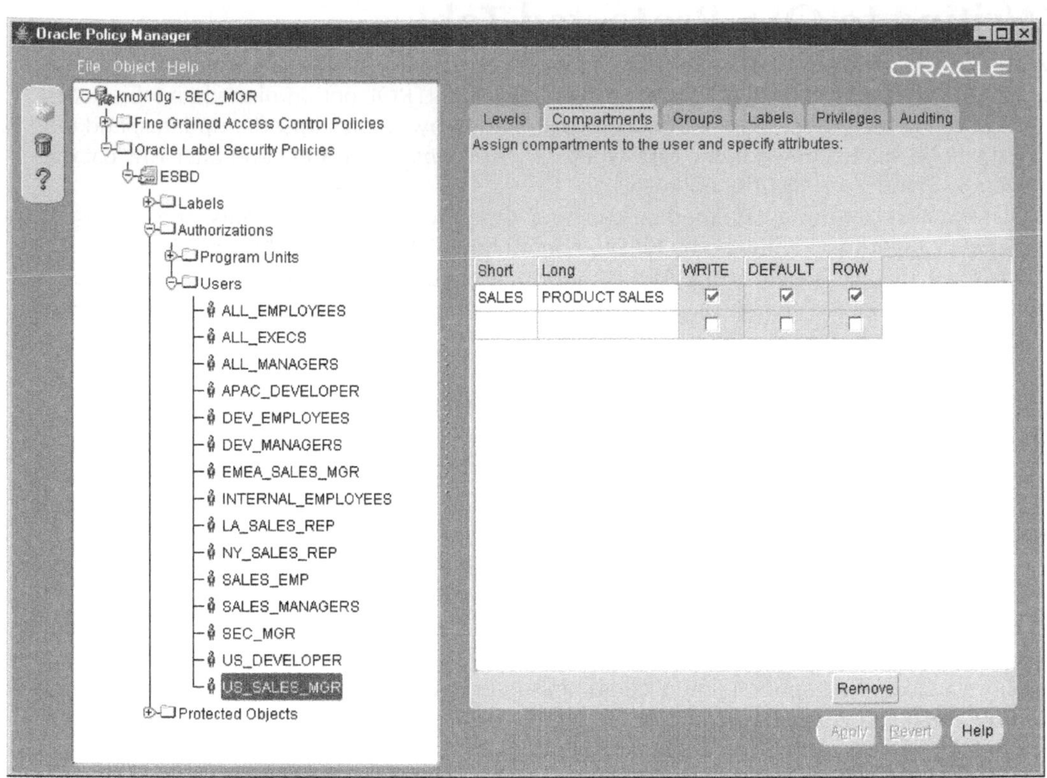

FIGURE 12-11. *User authorization labels are set and row access is determined by the WRITE, DEFAULT, and ROW attributes.*

When the user authorizations were created earlier, the level values were automatically set using the value passed in the MAX_READ_LABEL parameter. However, you can further control the different attributes (access lists) of the level component by invoking the SET_LEVELS procedure in the SA_USER_ADMIN package. The procedure accepts four parameters for defining the user's level characteristics: a maximum level (max_level), a minimum level (min_level), a default level (def_level), and a row level (row_level).

In this test, the user SCOTT will be authorized with specific level values. Assume your security policy says SCOTT is a manager and he should also be allowed to write data as an employee. Furthermore, when he logs in, he should automatically be allowed to access management-level information. However, if he is adding new records or updating existing data, you want the data to be labeled at the employee level:

```
sec_mgr@KNOX10g> -- Create scott's authorizations.
sec_mgr@KNOX10g> -- Give a different read level and insert level
sec_mgr@KNOX10g> BEGIN
       sa_user_admin.set_levels
                    (policy_name    => 'ESBD',
```

```
                        user_name      => 'SCOTT',
                        max_level      => 'MGR',
                        min_level      => 'EMP',
                        def_level      => 'MGR',
                        row_level      => 'EMP');
END;
/

PL/SQL procedure successfully completed.
```

At no time will the user's label contain a level value greater than the maximum level defined by the user's maximum level. Also, at no time will the user's label contain a level below the user's minimum level. The user's label can fluctuate between the maximum and minimum values.

The user's default level is set to the value assigned by their default setting. The row level is the level to which the data will be labeled when the user performs an insert or update and the LABEL_DEFAULT option is in effect. When SCOTT logs in, his authorizations are automatically set. SCOTT can query his session label to see that it has been automatically set to manager:

```
sec_mgr@KNOX10g> CONN scott/tiger
Connected.
scott@KNOX10g> COL "Select Label" format a15
scott@KNOX10g> COL "Insert Label" format a15
scott@KNOX10g> SELECT sa_session.read_label ('ESBD') "Select Label",
            sa_session.row_label ('ESBD') "Insert Label"
       FROM DUAL;

Select Label    Insert Label
--------------- ---------------
MGR             EMP
```

When SCOTT performs an insert, the data will be automatically labeled at the employee level since the ROW_LEVEL parameter was set to EMP.

```
scott@KNOX10g> INSERT INTO announcements
          VALUES ('Scott will be out of the office.');

1 row created.

scott@KNOX10g> COL "OLS Label" format a12
scott@KNOX10g> COL message     format a50
scott@KNOX10g> SELECT MESSAGE, label_to_char (ROWLABEL) "OLS Label"
       FROM announcements
     WHERE MESSAGE LIKE 'Scott%';

MESSAGE                                            OLS Label
-------------------------------------------------- ------------
Scott will be out of the office.                   EMP
```

OLS allows the user to change their session's label for levels, compartments, and groups. You can change the label by executing the SA_SESSION.SET_LABEL procedure. In the following example, SCOTT's label is changed setting the read value to EMP. Any subsequent queries for the session will be restricted to EMP level data.

```
scott@KNOX10g> -- Show default labels user can access
scott@KNOX10g> COL "User Read Label" format a20
scott@KNOX10g> COL "Data Record Labels" format a20
scott@KNOX10g> BREAK on "User's Read Label"
scott@KNOX10g> SELECT sa_session.read_label('ESBD') "User Read Label"
  2          label_to_char (ROWLABEL) "Data Record Labels"
  3       FROM scott.announcements
  4   GROUP BY ROWLABEL;

User Read Label      Data Record Labels
-------------------- --------------------
MGR                  MGR
MGR                  EMP

scott@KNOX10g> -- Change the user's default read label
scott@KNOX10g> EXEC sa_session.set_label('ESBD','EMP');

PL/SQL procedure successfully completed.

scott@KNOX10g> /

User Read Label      Data Record Labels
-------------------- --------------------
EMP                  EMP
```

Note that this change is only temporary. When the user logs in later, they will assume the original default label. To change the default row label (which affects insert and update statements), execute the SET_ROW_LABEL procedure. However, you can't set the default row label to a value outside the user's current session (read) label. Recall the principle in the beginning of the section—a user can never write data that they can't read:

```
scott@KNOX10g> -- This fails if session label is set to EMP
scott@KNOX10g> EXEC sa_session.set_row_label('ESBD','MGR');
BEGIN sa_session.set_row_label('ESBD','MGR'); END;

*
ERROR at line 1:
ORA-12470: NULL or invalid user label: session row label
(other error messages deleted)

scott@KNOX10g> -- Reset session and try again
scott@KNOX10g> EXEC sa_session.set_label('ESBD','MGR');

PL/SQL procedure successfully completed.

scott@KNOX10g> EXEC sa_session.set_row_label('ESBD','MGR');
```

```
PL/SQL procedure successfully completed.

scott@KNOX10g> INSERT INTO announcements
       VALUES ('Scott's management meeting is cancelled.');

1 row created.

scott@KNOX10g> SELECT MESSAGE, label_to_char (ROWLABEL) "OLS Label"
    FROM announcements;

MESSAGE                                              OLS Label
---------------------------------------------------- ------------
Scott will be out of the office.                     EMP
Scott's management meeting is cancelled.            MGR
All Managers: employee compensation announcement... MGR
This message is to notify all employees...           EMP
```

For compartments and groups, the administrator can set three lists: Write, Default, and Row. The Write enforcement option is analogous to the minimum and maximum levels within the level components. The Default and Row enforcement options are analogous to the corresponding Default and Row options set in the level component.

Groups and Compartments Dependency

Most of the OLS access control algorithms are obvious and easy to understand, but a nuance of the OLS write controls behavior needs to be explained.. *Write* controls are governed by considering not only the individual compartment or group write authorizations but also the combination of *read and write* privileges for compartments and groups. The point of interest is the condition when data has been labeled with both compartments and groups. The user has the ability to write to the data as long as they have write access to one of the groups and read access to all of the compartments. *Write access to the compartments isn't needed.* To show this dependency in action, the write controls are enabled on the ANNOUNCEMENTS table:

```
sec_mgr@KNOX10g> DECLARE
    l_options  VARCHAR2 (50)
      := 'HIDE,LABEL_DEFAULT,WRITE_CONTROL,READ_CONTROL';
  BEGIN
    sa_policy_admin.remove_table_policy
                     (policy_name     => 'ESBD',
                      schema_name     => 'SCOTT',
                      table_name      => 'ANNOUNCEMENTS');
    sa_policy_admin.apply_table_policy
                     (policy_name       => 'ESBD',
                      schema_name       => 'SCOTT',
                      table_name        => 'ANNOUNCEMENTS',
                      table_options     => l_options);
  END;
  /

PL/SQL procedure successfully completed.
```

Two compartments are added for SCOTT. Since SCOTT carries no commission (as determined by a NULL value in the EMP table), you can conclude that SCOTT works in development and will therefore have read and write access to data labeled with the DEV compartment:

```
sec_mgr@KNOX10g> -- Add DEV compartment to SCOTT
sec_mgr@KNOX10g> -- for read/write operations
sec_mgr@KNOX10g> BEGIN
     sa_user_admin.add_compartments
                  (policy_name     => 'ESBD',
                   user_name       => 'SCOTT',
                   comps           => 'DEV',
                   access_mode     => sa_utl.read_write,
                   in_def          => 'Y',
                   in_row          => 'Y');
   END;
   /

PL/SQL procedure successfully completed.
```

The SALES compartment will also be granted to SCOTT but with *read only access*. You'll see in the following code that this can be overridden based on the existence of groups. The SALES compartment will be set in SCOTT's default label but not as his default row label since SCOTT, who works in development, shouldn't write data labeled with the SALES compartment.

```
sec_mgr@KNOX10g> -- Add SALES compartment for SCOTT as read only.
sec_mgr@KNOX10g> BEGIN
     sa_user_admin.add_compartments
                  (policy_name     => 'ESBD',
                   user_name       => 'SCOTT',
                   comps           => 'SALES',
                   access_mode     => sa_utl.read_only,
                   in_def          => 'Y',
                   in_row          => 'N');
   END;
   /

PL/SQL procedure successfully completed.
```

Figure 12-12 illustrates the results of these two additions.

Lastly, SCOTT is added to the US group. Recall this is a parent group of the LA and NY groups, so SCOTT will be able to access records labeled with those groups too.

```
sec_mgr@KNOX10g> -- Add US group to Scott for read/write operations
sec_mgr@KNOX10g> -- both as a default label and as insert/update label
sec_mgr@KNOX10g> BEGIN
     sa_user_admin.add_groups
```

```
                    (policy_name      => 'ESBD',
                     user_name        => 'SCOTT',
                     GROUPS           => 'US',
                     access_mode      => sa_utl.read_write,
                     in_def           => 'Y',
                     in_row           => 'Y');
 END;
 /

PL/SQL procedure successfully completed.
```

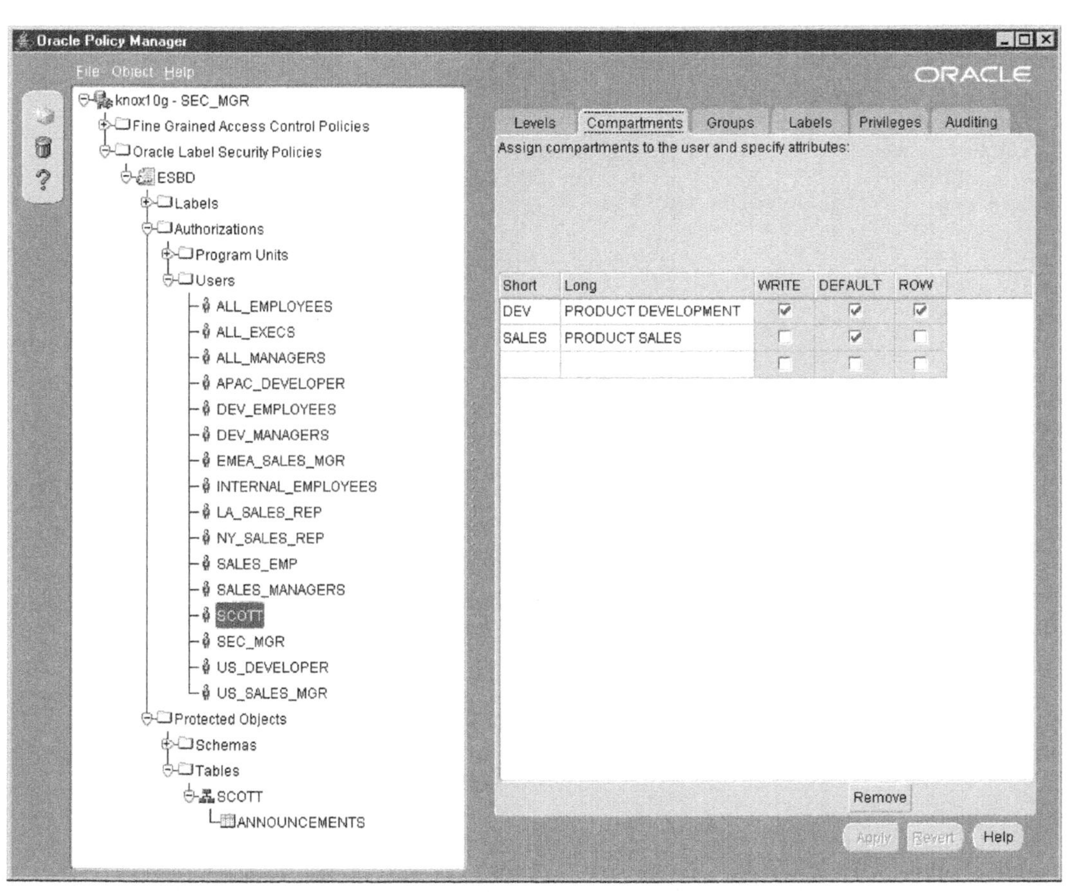

FIGURE 12-12. *Write authorizations can be easily verified using Oracle Policy Manager.*

SCOTT's final label authorizations can now be tested. In the following code, the first query shows SCOTT's read and write label authorizations. Note that the SALES compartment isn't in his write label. The subsequent query shows the label distribution in the table. Also note that there are four records that have a SALES compartment as part of the label:

```
scott@KNOX10g> -- Show user's read and write labels
scott@KNOX10g> SELECT sa_session.read_label ('ESBD') "Read Label",
  2          sa_session.write_label ('ESBD') "Write Label"
  3     FROM DUAL;

Read Label                     Write Label
------------------------------ ------------------------------
MGR:DEV,SALES:US,NY,LA         MGR:DEV:US,NY,LA

scott@KNOX10g> -- Show how labels are spread across data in table
scott@KNOX10g> SELECT label_to_char (ROWLABEL) "OLS Label",
  2          COUNT (ROWLABEL) "Total Records Labeled"
  3       FROM announcements
  4   GROUP BY ROWLABEL;

OLS Label    Total Records Labeled
------------ ---------------------
MGR                              2
EMP                              2
MGR:SALES                        1
MGR:DEV                          1
EMP:SALES                        1
EMP:DEV                          1
MGR:SALES:US                     1
EMP:SALES:NY                     1
EMP:SALES:LA                     1

9 rows selected.
```

The importance of the bolded records is shown next. SCOTT issues a delete, which targets all data labeled with the SALES compartment, but SCOTT doesn't have write access to this compartment. How many records will get deleted?

```
scott@KNOX10g> -- Delete data labeled with SALES compartment.
scott@KNOX10g> DELETE FROM announcements
  2         WHERE label_to_char (ROWLABEL) LIKE '%:SALES:%';

3 rows deleted.

scott@KNOX10g> SELECT label_to_char (ROWLABEL) "OLS Label",
  2          COUNT (ROWLABEL) "Total Records Labeled"
  3       FROM announcements
  4   GROUP BY ROWLABEL;

OLS Label    Total Records Labeled
```

```
------------ ---------------------
MGR                             2
EMP                             2
MGR:SALES                       1
MGR:DEV                         1
EMP:SALES                       1
EMP:DEV                         1

6 rows selected.
```

SCOTT successfully deleted records labeled with the SALES compartment even though he doesn't have write access to the SALES compartment. This is not a bug. The dependency is best summarized in the *Oracle Label Security Administrator's Guide*, which has been slightly altered to fit the example, but otherwise states the following: If the data label has groups, and the user has write access to one of the groups, the user only needs read access to (all) the compartments to write the data. If the data label has no groups, then the user must have write access on all the compartments in the label to write the data.

The deleted records contained group components to which SCOTT had write access (the US group of which NY and LA are children). Those bolded records are shown in the query prior to the delete statement. The preceding bolded record wasn't deleted because it has no group component in its data label. SCOTT doesn't have write access to the SALES compartment, so that record wasn't deleted.

Tips and Tricks

The following section discusses a few of the most interesting and useful features in OLS that are worth highlighting.

Restricted Updates to the Labels

A wonderful capability provided by OLS is to protect updates to the label itself. This helps to ensure that a user doesn't accidentally or willingly reclassify data by changing its label from a more secure label to a less secure label.

Protecting the label requires the LABEL_UPDATE option to be specified when the policy is applied to the table. When LABEL_UPDATE is enforced, OLS will not allow users to change the value of the security label. To illustrate this, the table must have the LABEL_UPDATE option enforced:

```
sec_mgr@KNOX10g> -- Enable label_update enforcement
sec_mgr@KNOX10g> BEGIN
       sa_policy_admin.remove_table_policy
                        (policy_name     => 'ESBD',
                         schema_name     => 'SCOTT',
                         table_name      => 'ANNOUNCEMENTS');
       sa_policy_admin.apply_table_policy
         (policy_name       => 'ESBD',
          schema_name       => 'SCOTT',
          table_name        => 'ANNOUNCEMENTS',
          table_options     =>     'HIDE,LABEL_DEFAULT,LABEL_UPDATE,'
```

```
                               || 'WRITE_CONTROL,READ_CONTROL');
   END;
   /

PL/SQL procedure successfully completed.
```

To demonstrate the new enforcement, two updates are issued: one to the MESSAGE column and one to the ROWLABEL column. Since the ROWLABEL column is the label column, OLS will prevent this update from occurring:

```
scott@KNOX10g> -- User can update certain standard columns
scott@KNOX10g> UPDATE announcements
       SET MESSAGE = INITCAP (MESSAGE)
     WHERE label_to_char (ROWLABEL) like '%DEV%';

2 rows updated.

scott@KNOX10g> -- User is not authorized to change the security label
scott@KNOX10g> UPDATE announcements
       SET ROWLABEL = char_to_label ('ESBD', 'EMP')
     WHERE label_to_char (ROWLABEL) like '%DEV%';
UPDATE announcements
       *
ERROR at line 1:
ORA-12406: unauthorized SQL statement for policy ESBD
```

To change the label, the user requires a special OLS privilege. The user can be authorized to change the label with the WRITEUP or WRITEDOWN privileges. WRITEUP allows the user to increase the level component of the label. WRITEDOWN allows the user to decrease the level component. Independent of this is the ability to change the compartment or group for a label that is authorized with the WRITEACROSS privilege. These privileges are part of the write control OLS special privileges referred to in the "Special OLS Privileges" section.

To allow SCOTT to reclassify management data as employee data, you have to grant the WRITEDOWN privilege:

```
sec_mgr@KNOX10g> -- Grant the writedown privilege to SCOTT
sec_mgr@KNOX10g> BEGIN
      sa_user_admin.set_user_privs
                     (policy_name    => 'ESBD',
                      user_name      => 'SCOTT',
                      PRIVILEGES     => 'WRITEDOWN');
   END;
   /

PL/SQL procedure successfully completed.

sec_mgr@KNOX10g> -- Have to reset the authorizations be re-enabling
sec_mgr@KNOX10g> -- the profile. This is done automatically on logon.
sec_mgr@KNOX10g> CONN scott/tiger
Connected.
```

```
scott@KNOX10g> -- Reclassify data making it available to all
scott@KNOX10g> -- developers
scott@KNOX10g> UPDATE announcements
      SET ROWLABEL = char_to_label ('ESBD', 'EMP:DEV')
    WHERE label_to_char (ROWLABEL) = 'MGR:DEV'
  /

1 row updated.
```

Protecting the label is a good safety feature and allows for separation of duty. You can prevent the content users from manipulating the security labels. The security manipulation can then be handled by the security administrator.

Trusted Procedures

OLS authorizations can be given to PL/SQL programs as well as to users or applications. This is a powerful way to ensure least privileges are maintained without sacrificing the ability to view and manipulate OLS protected data.

A typical use is to create a procedure that performs security label manipulation. That is, in the preceding example, instead of granting the WRITEDOWN privilege to SCOTT, you could create a PL/SQL program to perform the date relabeling. You would grant the WRITEDOWN privilege to the program and then grant execute privileges on the program to SCOTT. This adds finer levels of security because SCOTT can't reclassify just any data, and it ensures the data labels are manipulated in a secure and meaningful way.

Trusted procedures can also help solve the challenge associated with the fact that OLS session authorizations do not transfer from object owner to object invoker the way definer rights procedures do. Assume you create a function that allows users to check the number of messages that contain a value. This would be applicable in an inventory application in which you're trying to determine how many items of a specific type are left in inventory. You don't want to grant direct access to the table. Normally, you would create a function that returns the number of messages based on the parameter string and then grant execute privileges on the function to the users:

```
scott@KNOX10g> -- Create function to return number of messages.
scott@KNOX10g> CREATE OR REPLACE FUNCTION get_quantity (
    p_message  IN  VARCHAR2)
    RETURN PLS_INTEGER
  AS
    l_total  PLS_INTEGER;
  BEGIN
    SELECT COUNT (*)
      INTO l_total
      FROM announcements
     WHERE UPPER (MESSAGE) LIKE
                       '%' || UPPER (p_message)
                       || '%';
    RETURN l_total;
  END;
  /

Function created.
```

```
scott@KNOX10g> SELECT get_quantity ('scott') FROM DUAL;

GET_QUANTITY('SCOTT')
---------------------
                    2

scott@KNOX10g> GRANT EXECUTE ON get_quantity TO blake;
```

When BLAKE logs on, you can see that he has no authorizations. Even though he can execute the function, the label authorizations used in the procedure creation are not transferred to him. Consequently, when he executes the function, he gets no data:

```
blake@KNOX10g> -- Blake has no authorizations
blake@KNOX10g> SELECT sa_session.read_label ('ESBD') "Read Label",
  2         sa_session.write_label ('ESBD') "Write Label"
  3    FROM DUAL;

Read Label                     Write Label
------------------------------ ------------------------------


blake@KNOX10g> SELECT scott.get_quantity ('scott') FROM DUAL;

SCOTT.GET_QUANTITY('SCOTT')
---------------------------
                          0
```

Assume that you want the user BLAKE to know the number of records. You can authorize the function with the special OLS privileges that are required. In this example, the function requires the READ privilege. The READ privilege allows the authorized program full access to all records, regardless of the user's current read label:

```
sec_mgr@KNOX10g> -- Authorize the procedure
sec_mgr@KNOX10g> BEGIN
  2    sa_user_admin.set_prog_privs
  3               (policy_name          => 'ESBD',
  4                schema_name          => 'SCOTT',
  5                program_unit_name    => 'get_quantity',
  6                PRIVILEGES           => 'READ');
  7  END;
  8  /

PL/SQL procedure successfully completed.
```

When BLAKE executes the function again, the results are securely and accurately returned:

```
blake@KNOX10g> SELECT scott.get_quantity ('scott') FROM DUAL;

SCOTT.GET_QUANTITY('SCOTT')
---------------------------
                          2
```

NOTE
Trusted procedures should be used any time you want to further restrict the operations a user has to perform. The trusted procedures allow you to maintain a true least-privilege environment.

Label Functions

Data can be labeled in three ways: directly, indirectly using the LABEL_DEFAULT option, or by using a labeling function. The labeling function will override the LABEL_DEFAULT and LABEL_UPDATE enforcement options. The function's logic can be anything creative needed to fulfill the security policy. The function is called with a before-row trigger. As such, you can pass both new and old values to the function.

Label functions are an excellent method for creating the labels. Many times the labels are derived from information contained in the record or from information in other tables that is referenced by fields in the record. The label also can be based on information about the user's environment.

Complex logic can be implemented within the function. For example, the contents of certain fields may determine the sensitivity level of the data, and the user's IP address may determine the group component to the data. Taken together, the label can be easily constructed and inserted.

Label Function Example

Consider the following example where the label function will determine the level based on the content of the message. This is contrived here, but in practice it's very common to set the label based on the values in other columns of the data record. The label's compartment will be based on the active OLS user profile. For SCOTT, there is a 1:1 mapping from the user SCOTT to the profile SCOTT. Since SCOTT works in development, the compartment will be labeled as DEV for him. Otherwise, the compartment is set to SALES:

```
sec_mgr@KNOX10g> -- Create a label function.
sec_mgr@KNOX10g> CREATE OR REPLACE FUNCTION gen_label (
    p_message  VARCHAR2)
    RETURN lbacsys.lbac_label
  AS
    l_label  VARCHAR (80);
  BEGIN
    -- If message contains "manage" (assuming structured format)
    -- then label as MGR. If message contains "employee"
    -- then must be EMP data. Otherwise label with EXEC
    CASE
      WHEN UPPER (p_message) LIKE '%MANAGE%'
      THEN
        l_label := 'MGR';
      WHEN UPPER (p_message) LIKE '%EMPLOYEE%'
      THEN
        l_label := 'EMP';
      ELSE
        l_label := 'EXEC';
    END CASE;
    -- If authorization profile is SCOTT, then
```

```
    -- add compartment DEV. Otherwise label as sales.
    CASE
      WHEN sa_session.sa_user_name('ESBD') = 'SCOTT'
      THEN
        l_label := l_label || ':DEV';
      ELSE
        l_label := l_label || ':SALES';
    END CASE;

    RETURN to_lbac_data_label ('ESBD', l_label);
  END;
  /

Function created.
```

To apply the label function, you have to remove the other label checks and specify the label function in a separate parameter. Notice the message parameter will be passed to the label function from a row trigger:

```
sec_mgr@KNOX10g> -- Apply label function
sec_mgr@KNOX10g> BEGIN
    sa_policy_admin.remove_table_policy
                     (policy_name    => 'ESBD',
                      schema_name    => 'SCOTT',
                      table_name     => 'ANNOUNCEMENTS');
    sa_policy_admin.apply_table_policy
      (policy_name       => 'ESBD',
       schema_name       => 'SCOTT',
       table_name        => 'ANNOUNCEMENTS',
       label_function    => 'SEC_MGR.GEN_LABEL(:new.message)',
       table_options     =>    'HIDE,READ_CONTROL,WRITE_CONTROL');
  END;
  /

PL/SQL procedure successfully completed.
```

Testing simply requires you to insert a couple of records and then verify the label. SCOTT will insert two records; the first record should be labeled at the EMP level, and the second record at the MGR level. Both should have DEV as the compartment:

```
scott@KNOX10g> -- Insert an employee record
scott@KNOX10g> INSERT INTO announcements
              (MESSAGE)
       VALUES ('All employees should call in sick tomorrow.');

1 row created.

scott@KNOX10g> -- Insert a manager record
```

```
scott@KNOX10g> INSERT INTO announcements
  2              (MESSAGE)
  3        VALUES ('All managers are required to work late.');

1 row created.

scott@KNOX10g> COMMIT;
```

You can then insert records as another user. The SET_ACCESS_PROFILE sets the user's identity for OLS. The following insert will then be done as the ALL_EXECS user.

```
sec_mgr@KNOX10g> BEGIN
  2    sa_session.set_access_profile ('ESBD',
  3                                   'ALL_EXECS');
  4  END;
  5  /

PL/SQL procedure successfully completed.

sec_mgr@KNOX10g> -- Insert record as executive.
sec_mgr@KNOX10g> INSERT INTO scott.announcements
  2              (MESSAGE)
  3        VALUES ('Stock split announcement tonight');

1 row created.
```

The last message did not contain "manage" or "employee," so it'll have the EXEC level. Since the insert wasn't done as SCOTT, the compartment will be SALES. You can verify this:

```
sec_mgr@KNOX10g> -- Verify labels
sec_mgr@KNOX10g> COL "OLS Label" format a12
sec_mgr@KNOX10g> COL message format a51
sec_mgr@KNOX10g> SELECT MESSAGE,
  2         label_to_char (ROWLABEL) "OLS Label"
  3    FROM scott.announcements
  4   WHERE MESSAGE LIKE 'All%'
  5         OR MESSAGE LIKE 'Stock%';

MESSAGE                                             OLS Label
--------------------------------------------------- -----------
Stock split announcement tonight                    EXEC:SALES
All Managers: employee compensation announcement... MGR
All employees should call in sick tomorrow.         EMP:DEV
All managers are required to work late.             MGR:DEV
```

The second record in the result set was from an earlier insert. The other records were labeled as they were supposed to be. The label function is widely used and helps to guarantee that the label created, and thus the security enforced is congruent with the data sensitivity.

Storing the Labels in OID

New to Oracle Database 10*g* is the ability to centralize the OLS policies. The policies can now be stored in the Oracle Internet Directory (OiD). This architecture is desirable when using the Enterprise User Security (EUS) option. The enterprise users' passwords, enterprise roles, and OLS authorizations can all be centrally managed. This OLS policy centralization also is advantageous when you want to ensure that multiple databases have a consistent OLS policy.

Once centralized, the policies can't be manipulated from within the database. This can be beneficial in ensuring not only label integrity across the organization's databases, but also that the labels and authorizations aren't accidentally or intentionally corrupted.

One restriction to using centralized policies is that it's in all-or-nothing design. You can't have some policies stored in OiD and others stored in the database. You will also be unable to use the Policy Manager for administering the OLS policies. See Chapter 5 of the *Oracle Label Security Administrator's Guide* for more details on using OLS in this manner.

Using Labels with Connection Pools and Shared Schemas

There are several popular shared schema designs. Regardless of whether you're using Oracle's EUS shared schema approach or a connection pool that connects to the database as a single database user, OLS can still be used.

The secret is in the use of the SET_ACCESS_PROFILE procedure. The end user's authorization can be created as an OLS user authorization even though the user isn't known to the database. When the user makes a request, or authenticates, the application or a logon trigger can make the call to set the user's authorizations to that of the real end user.

There is no reason why the authorizations can't also be representations of groups of users. You saw this in the examples throughout this chapter. Another scenario is to create authorizations that are IP addresses or server domains of the incoming clients. The IP addresses can represent an application from an application server or an individual server.

OLS provides the ability to combine labels via the MERGE_LABEL function. The result is that a user's authorization can be combined with an application to create a restricted authorization for the user's session based on how they are connected.

The last trick to using shared schemas is to set the authorization to a value that returns no data. This is a good resting place for the database session between user actions. You don't need an actual label, only a valid level. Create a level with the value of zero:

```
sec_mgr@KNOX10G> begin
    sa_components.create_level(policy_name => 'ESBD',
                               long_name   => 'System Low',
                               short_name  => 'SYSLOW',
                               level_num   => 0);
  end;
  /

PL/SQL procedure successfully completed.
```

Next, assign the level to the authorization you want to use. You have to create the level because the SET_USER_LABELS procedure requires one for the MAX_READ_LABEL:

```
sec_mgr@KNOX10G> begin
    sa_user_admin.set_user_labels(
      policy_name    => 'ESBD',
```

```
  4      user_name      => 'NOBODY',
  5      max_read_label => 'SYSLOW');
  6  end;
  7  /

PL/SQL procedure successfully completed.
```

Testing with this authorization validates the desired result—no data is returned:

```
sec_mgr@KNOX10G> exec sa_session.set_access_profile('ESBD','NOBODY');

PL/SQL procedure successfully completed.

sec_mgr@KNOX10G> select count(*)
  2    from scott.announcements;

  COUNT(*)
----------
         0
```

It's clearly important to ensure that no data is labeled at SYSLOW. As it exists now, data can't be labeled at SYSLOW because there is no valid label containing the SYSLOW level. SYSLOW only exists as a level component.

```
sec_mgr@KNOX10G> insert into scott.announcements
  2   values ('Too low to insert');

1 row created.
```

Don't let the "1 row created" fool you; the data isn't there.

```
sec_mgr@KNOX10G> select message,
  2          label_to_char(rowlabel) "OLS Label"
  3    from scott.announcements;

no rows selected
```

OLS Consideration Factors

OLS is a very powerful security tool; however, there are a few situations of which you should be aware. The frequently asked question is, "Will OLS work with my existing applications?" The answer is definitely maybe.

There are two determining factors. The first involves the addition of the column to existing tables. Adding this column, even if hidden, could render your applications unsupported. In some cases, it may not be technically possible to alter the table and add the column without breaking something.

The second factor, which also resides with VPD, is that in providing row-level security, OLS may fool the application into thinking the data is corrupted. For an application that expects to see all the data, the transparent filtering of data records could be misinterpreted as a data integrity problem. There is no easy answer as to whether OLS will break or not break an existing application.

The other major impediment to implementing labels lies in the limits of the labels themselves. The limits on the components and labels make OLS unsuitable for certain security policies, especially when the labels are to be matched to a user community (i.e., a distinct label for each user) and the user community far exceeds 10,000. Additionally, while you can have up to 10,000 levels, compartments, and groups, the label's character representation—for example, MGR:SALES:US—is constrained to 4,000 characters. In some cases, this limitation is reached long before the levels, compartments, or groups are exhausted.

VPD Versus Label Security

Another common question that arises is, "When should I use VPD, and when should I use OLS?" Personally, I always try OLS first. In many ways, OLS is an easier tool for creating and managing row-level security. After all, it implements the security code for you.

The answer, however, is dependent on the security policy and how well the data lends itself to labeling. If you can create a labeling policy that is congruent with your security policy, then OLS is definitely the way to proceed. If you work for an intelligence agency, or the Department of Defense, then you should clearly be using OLS because the product was specifically designed for you. Chapter 2 of the *Oracle Label Security Administrator's Guide* gives five sample labeling policies that can help serve as a template for creating your very own policy.

Advantages of OLS

Why not let the facts determine the choice for you? OLS provides a GUI (Oracle Policy Manager) to administer and maintain the security. This greatly simplifies the deployment and maintenance of the security solution. The Policy Manager can help non-DBAs understand or possibly audit the security implementation. This supports the separation of duty concept.

OLS also requires zero security code. Coding refers to the implementation of the security policy. The previous examples were not code, rather they were calls to administer the code that implements the labels. No coding required is desirable. Mistakes in security code can be difficult to find and fix.

OLS has been evaluated by independent testing. Oracle spent nearly one million dollars testing OLS under the Common Criteria (ISO 15408) evaluations. The tests were performed by security experts. The conclusion, as given by the EAL4 evaluation, is that OLS sufficiently meets the rigorous security requirements it was designed to meet. Chances are pretty significant that the code you write will not be evaluated with the same amount of rigor.

OLS is an out-of-the-box, no coding required, row-level security solution. Unfortunately, all the world's security policies can't be implemented via label based access controls.

Advantages of VPD

One certain fact exists: there is nothing that OLS can do that VPD can't do. The opposite is not true. There are quite a few things VPD can do that OLS can't. For example, OLS doesn't work on views or synonyms. OLS needs a real column of type number to store the labels. (However, OLS can be placed on the underlying tables from which the views will query.)

VPD or views are appropriate when access is user oriented. That is, if the policy restricts access based on who is executing the query and there is a column in the record that maps to this user.

VPD supports partitioned access to tables in which different policies can be dynamically enabled and disabled based on a driving application context. For OLS to emulate this, it would have to enforce multiple policies on the same table, each one adding a policy-specific label column to the table. It's quite possible the OLS policies would exclude each other, thus rendering the solution ineffective.

New to Oracle 10*g* VPD is support for column-sensitive row-level security. OLS hasn't yet inherited this capability.

VPD and OLS

You don't have to choose OLS or VPD; you can use both. In fact, OLS makes it very easy to add a VPD predicate. The APPLY_TABLE_POLICY procedure accepts a VPD predicate as a parameter. For this example, if you want to restrict message reading to business hours, add a VPD predicate to the existing OLS policy:

```
sec_mgr@KNOX10G> begin
      sa_policy_admin.remove_table_policy (
        policy_name => 'ESBD',
        schema_name => 'SCOTT',
        table_name  => 'ANNOUNCEMENTS');
      sa_policy_admin.apply_table_policy (
        policy_name    => 'ESBD',
        schema_name    => 'SCOTT',
        table_name     => 'ANNOUNCEMENTS',
        table_options  => 'HIDE,LABEL_DEFAULT,LABEL_UPDATE,' ||
                          'WRITE_CONTROL,READ_CONTROL',
        predicate      => 'to_char(sysdate,''D'') not in (1,7)');
    end;
    /

PL/SQL procedure successfully completed.

sec_mgr@KNOX10G>
sec_mgr@KNOX10G> conn scott/tiger
Connected.
scott@KNOX10G> select to_char(sysdate,'D') from dual;

T
-
6

scott@KNOX10G> select * from total_announcements;

TOTAL_MESSAGES
--------------
            14
```

Setting the date to Saturday, you can re-execute the query to validate that VPD is working, too:

```
scott@KNOX10G> select to_char(sysdate,'D') from dual;

T
-
```

```
scott@KNOX10G> select * from announcements;

no rows selected
```

This is an excellent solution for security policies that require user-level restrictions. Generally, user-level access isn't given with OLS, because it would imply that there is a label created for every user. You could do this for up to 10,000 users, at which time you would run out of compartments or groups.

The VPD predicate added to OLS can use application context capabilities, any functions, and anything that VPD can use. Many times the security policy has a part that can be easily done with labels, and a part that isn't so easy to do with labels. Combining OLS and VPD gives you the best of both worlds.

Policy Predicate Tip

Another great use of the policy predicate is to allow it to function as an easy way to grant access to data for users without specific authorizations. For example, if you wanted all employees to get access to data labeled as EMP, which has a label tag value of three, you could add a predicate as follows:

```
sec_mgr@KNOX10g> begin
    sa_policy_admin.remove_table_policy (
      policy_name => 'ESBD',
      schema_name => 'SCOTT',
      table_name  => 'ANNOUNCEMENTS');
    sa_policy_admin.apply_table_policy (
      policy_name    => 'ESBD',
      schema_name    => 'SCOTT',
      table_name     => 'ANNOUNCEMENTS',
      table_options  => 'HIDE,LABEL_DEFAULT,LABEL_UPDATE,' ||
                        'WRITE_CONTROL,READ_CONTROL',
      predicate      => 'OR ROWLABEL = 3');=
  end;
  /

PL/SQL procedure successfully completed.
```

This will allow any database user, even ones without any OLS authorizations, to access the EMP data. Using the value of the ROWLABEL instead of the CHAR_TO_LABEL function ensures that this query will execute quickly.

Using this technique, you don't have to create authorization tags for every user. You could also have specified, OR ROWLABEL is NULL for data that has yet to be labeled for an existing table to which you have just applied an OLS policy and haven't yet labeled any data.

Note the use of the OR in the predicate above. This tells OLS to apply its policy, *or* apply your predicate condition. If you do not include an OR, then the predicate is automatically added to the OLS policy enforcement by way of a logical AND. You will find this a very useful feature to augmenting standard OLS capabilities.

Summary

One of the beneficial outcomes to the explorations into MAC security was that the solutions became repeatable and well understood. The concept of providing fine-grained access control based on labels was validated and proven secure. Independent tests were conducted by the NSA. OLS uses the lessons learned from over ten years of building MAC solutions based on labels and applies them to today's Oracle database. The result is a secure, easy-to-manage capability that has a proven track record and heritage.

The intention of OLS is to provide a technical implementation that reflects a defined security policy. Creating an accurate labeling scheme may be the most important step in the entire process, and it's certainly the most challenging. However, unlike most security implementations, once the security policy has been translated into labels, the hard part is done.

There are many benefits to using OLS. The security can easily be made transparent. The security code writing is not only done for you, but it has also been evaluated. OLS is flexible, allowing you to change your policy enforcements on the fly. Most importantly, the system security is maintainable. One of the greatest challenges of any application implementation is supportability and maintenance of the code into the future. The Policy Manager provides an easy way to inspect, audit, review, and change the security policies.

What OLS can't solve alone can be easily augmented with VPD. These two tools are complementary and not exclusionary. Together, these two technologies fight the evil forces of full-table access, bringing row-level security to all.

Chapter 13 delves even deeper into data protection with element-level protections provided by a new database encryption tool. Hint: this one is a lot easier to pronounce than its predecessor.

CHAPTER 13

Database Encryption

any people think security is encryption and encryption is security. Encrypt it and it is secure, where "it" applies to anything and everything. This is a fallacy. Encryption is a critical element to security, but it plays different roles in different situations. For networks, encryption is a major part of the overall security. With databases, encryption is another layer of security defense, and you have to use it wisely; otherwise, you risk a zero increase in overall security and possibly a decrease in performance, usability, and accessibility; worst of all, you create a false sense of security.

This chapter evaluates the use of database encryption with Oracle's new DBMS_CRYPTO package. This package, which replaces the DBMS_OBFUSCATION_TOOLKIT, provides significantly enhanced capabilities for encrypting, hashing, and keyed hashing (message authentication codes) of database data, all without leaving the confines of the secure database environment. Overall, encryption will be analyzed to determine when it's an appropriate tool and when it's not. You'll look at examples of how to invoke encryption, explore the challenges and issues associated with it, and review how to really use the encryption capabilities with some database encryption best practices.

Encryption 101

Encryption has an interesting history. It dates back thousands of years and can even be traced to the Roman Empire. At that time, it was common for Julius Caesar, who was acting President and CEO of the Roman Empire, to send messages to his generals in the field. The messages were very sensitive because they gave orders on how to proceed on new military objectives.

The messages were sent by way of a messenger and there was a great risk that the messenger would be captured before the message was delivered. This seriously jeopardized the military strategy. As such, a simple encryption algorithm was devised and used to encrypt the messages. Only the generals and Julius Caesar knew how to encrypt and decrypt the messages. If the messenger was captured, bribery, persuasive arguments, or torturing techniques were ineffective in uncovering the content of the encrypted messages.

This helps to put the use of encryption into proper perspective. It's important to understand the basic problem that encryption was designed to solve. Encryption provides protection of sensitive data for an *unprotected* medium. The messages represented sensitive data, and the messengers had to cross unprotected mediums (land, mountains, water, and so on).

NOTE
Encryption protects sensitive data for an unprotected medium.

In today's internetworked world, encryption is widely used because it clearly meets the criteria for which it was designed: encryption protects sensitive data passing through the unprotected Internet. Many security professionals have extensive experience in the network security realm and have a strong understanding of cryptography. This is one reason encryption is so popular today.

Databases and database security are significantly different from networks and network security. This is a very important principle because the value encryption provides differs when applied to problems outside its original problem definition. This will be your guiding principle for understanding when to use and when not to use encryption within the database.

The Basics

Encryption is the process of taking plaintext data and converting it into an undecipherable form. The result is encrypted data, which is formally known as ciphertext. Once the data has been encrypted, it generally needs to be decrypted. The decryption (the act of unencrypting) of data returns the ciphertext to its original plaintext form. The study of these two processes is called *cryptography*.

A plethora of books are available on the market discussing cryptography (my personal favorite is Bruce Schneier's *Applied Cryptography: Protocols, Algorithms, and Source Code in C*, John Wiley & Sons). The mathematics involved and the issues and nuances of cryptography are staggering in number and complexity and well beyond the scope of this book. Fortunately, you don't need to understand all aspects of encryption. This chapter defines only what you need to know to make the critical decisions about how and when to use encryption within the database.

Encryption Choices

There are many ways to encrypt data, but there are fewer ways to do it effectively. Many people are inclined to write their own encryption, just as Julius Caesar did. However, unless they are geniuses or very lucky, chances are their encryption will be poor. Today, effective encryption implies the use of standard and proven encryption algorithms. The proven part is important because it ensures that the encryption doesn't have some fatal flaw that would allow an unauthorized person to determine the contents of the sensitive data.

Given that you wish to use standard encryption algorithms, there are quite a few from which to choose. Before you start picking algorithms to use in the database, you need to understand a little more about how encryption works.

The Algorithm and the Key

To encrypt data, two things are required: an encryption algorithm and an encryption key. The high level description of encrypting data is quite simple: plaintext data is fed into the encryption algorithm. An encryption key is also provided. Together, the algorithm uses the key and very sophisticated logic to encrypt the data. The process of decryption is analogous. It also requires a key and an algorithm.

Figure 13-1 illustrates how basic symmetric key encryption works. A plaintext message "Meet at Robert's" is encrypted using an algorithm and a key. To recover the original message, the same key and algorithm must be used.

The overall strength of the encryption isn't determined by just the algorithm or the key size. The strength is in the combination of the two. A common misconception is that larger keys for one algorithm mean that algorithm is stronger than another algorithm that uses a smaller key size. Some algorithms demand larger keys to make them as strong as other algorithms that use smaller key sizes. However, in some cases larger keys used within the same algorithm do make the encryption stronger.

By studying Figure 13-1, it may become clear that there remains a challenge to effective encryption. If Julius is sending General Suchnsuch an encrypted message, the general needs to know both the algorithm and the key that was used to encrypt the message. Studies of cryptography have shown that with today's algorithms, the only thing that needs to remain a secret is the key. Public knowledge of the algorithm doesn't aid the attacker in recovering the sensitive data. Obscuring the algorithm may seem like good security, but it's only a nuisance to a determined attacker.

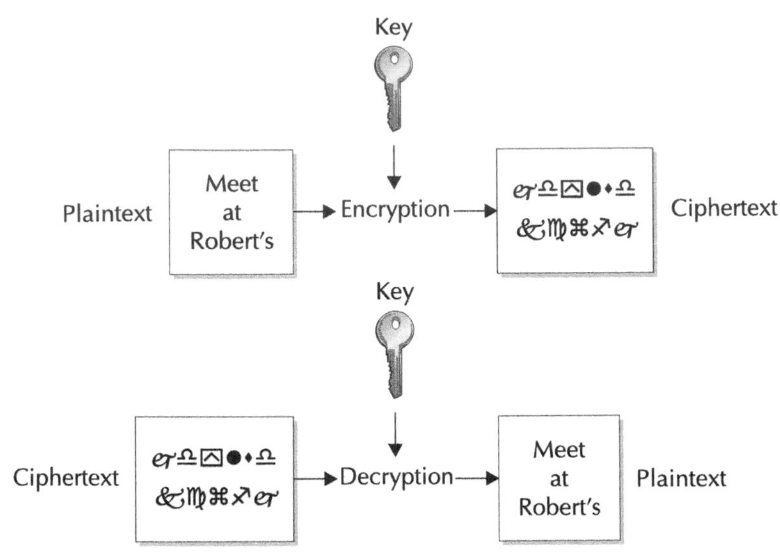

FIGURE 13-1. *Symmetric key encryption requires the use of the same key for both the encryption and decryption process.*

NOTE
This point can't be over-emphasized: many cycles are wasted on "protecting the algorithm" in the real world. If knowledge of the algorithm is sufficient to break your code, then your algorithm isn't an encryption scheme at all.

Symmetric Key Encryption

There are two categories of encryption used today. The first is called *symmetric key encryption.* The algorithms for symmetric key encryption use the same key for both the encryption and decryption process; they are symmetric! A message encrypted with one key can only be decrypted with that exact same key.

Symmetric key algorithms are very secure and very efficient at encrypting and decrypting data. Some popular examples are RC4, RC5, DES, triple-DES (3DES), and the new Advanced Encryption Standard (AES). Because of their strength and efficiency, these are the algorithms used for "bulk encryption"—they encrypt large amounts of data.

When two people want to use symmetric key encryption, they need to have either a pre-established key or a secure way to transport the key. When two parties already know each other, it's possible that they will both already know the encryption key. For two parties that have never met and now wish to share data securely, the problem of getting the key between the two parties becomes the major challenge. You can't leave the key in plaintext because an attacker could see it. If you encrypt the key, you have to do so with another key, which only moves the problem elsewhere. This motivated the development of the second flavor of encryption, called *asymmetric key encryption* or *public key encryption (PKE).*

Public Key Encryption

With PKE, two keys act in a complementary manner. The PKE algorithms are mathematical inverses. Whatever one key does, the other key undoes. Furthermore, knowing the algorithm and having one of the keys doesn't give the attacker an advantage in determining the other key or in recovering the encrypted data.

With PKE, the two keys are usually called the *private key* and the *public key.*

NOTE
Data encrypted with the private key can only be decrypted with the public key, and vice versa.

"Private" and "public" are used to describe the keys because it's typical for the public key to be accessible to many people. The private key remains a secret known only to the owner. As long as the private key remains private, this scenario works beautifully.

PKE therefore solves the key distribution problem. For two parties to communicate, they need access only to each other's public keys. Figure 13-2 illustrates how PKE can be used to send a secret message between two parties. To ensure that the recipient (the server in the figure) is the only one that should receive the message, the message is encrypted with the recipient's public key. As such, only the recipient will be able to decrypt the message because the only key that can be used is their private key (which only they have). Trying to decrypt the message with an incorrect key yields gibberish. An interloper will be unsuccessful in decrypting the message because they will not have the private key. Note the public key can't be used to decrypt the message that was also encrypted with the public key.

There is another complementary capability that PKE provides. The private key can be used as an authentication method from the sender. As Figure 13-3 illustrates, a sender can encrypt a message with their private key. The recipient can use the client's public key to decrypt the message. If the message decrypts, then the client's identity is authenticated because only the sender has access to their private key and so only they could have encrypted the message.

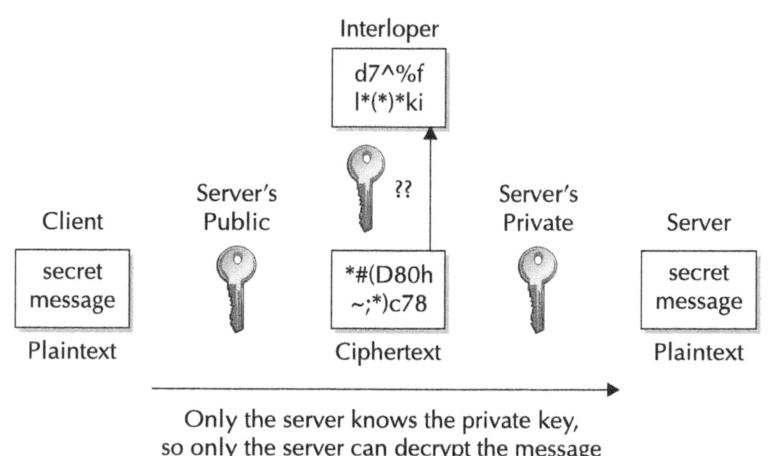

FIGURE 13-2. *Public key encryption uses two complementary keys to securely pass sensitive data.*

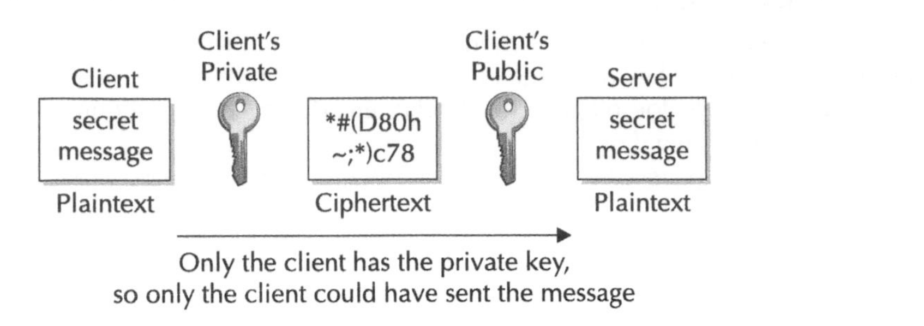

FIGURE 13-3. *Public key encryption can be used to authenticate parties to one another.*

Symmetric Key and Public Key

Unfortunately, the public key algorithms require larger keys to achieve the same strength received from their symmetric key counter parts. Consequently, the public key algorithms perform more slowly and are more computationally expensive.

Today, public key and symmetric key encryption are used together as a part of the standard SSL network protocol. SSL is the de facto standard encryption mechanism for data on the Internet. Due to its superior performance characteristics, symmetric key encryption is used within SSL for bulk data encryption. To transport the symmetric keys securely between the two parties, public key encryption is used to encrypt the symmetric keys. In Figures 13-2 and 13-3, the secret message is actually the symmetric encryption key.

Public key technology gets more than its fair share of the attention considering that proportionately it actually encrypts a lot less data than symmetric key encryption. This is because the administrators and users have to interface directly with the public key technology. The symmetric key algorithms are neatly concealed and hidden from view.

Understanding and acknowledging the use of public key and symmetric key encryption is important to the Oracle Database because the database only supports symmetric key algorithms. The performance and efficiency of symmetric key algorithms make them a natural choice for the database. Unfortunately, this leaves open the issue of key management, which is addressed in the "Key Management" section later in this chapter.

When to Use Database Encryption

Often this section is found further toward the end of the chapter, but I felt it's important to address this area first in hopes of ensuring that the example code isn't put into place without an essential understanding of how effective or ineffective the database encryption solution may be.

The controversy surrounds the definition of the problem encryption is meant to solve: protection of data in an *unprotected* medium. This is worth consideration because the database is *not* an unprotected medium! This is only one chapter of an entire book dedicated to proving this very point.

When people ask me how to do database encryption, I usually respond with the question, "Why do you want to do database encryption?" It is important to answer this correctly and honestly. Doing so will help you determine how and when to encrypt your database.

Reasons Not to Encrypt

Encrypting data destined for the unprotected Internet is obviously a wise decision. Within the database, the choice to do encryption isn't always as obvious. Your security decisions should be made by asking yourself, "Why am I trying to protect this, and who am I trying to protect it from?"

Let's analyze the reasons to encrypt data in more detail. Consider an initial request to encrypt all the data in the EMP table. The request is issued in an attempt to abide by the following security policy:

- *The data in the EMP table is sensitive.* The data should only be viewed by people who are authorized to access the data. Authorized users are the DBAs and the users whose names appear in the ENAME column.
- *All access should be controlled at the user level.* That is, the identification and authorizations should be unique for each user.
- *Release of data should be on a need-to-know basis only.* Users can only see records within their department.

This policy could be applied to practically every data table. The good news is the database can satisfy all of these requirements without ever requiring the data be encrypted. Strong authentication of the users is the first step to providing requirements one and two. System privileges, object privileges, and fine-grained access controls will satisfy all three requirements if you have a good identification and authentication process. Auditing can also be used to ensure the requirements are being met.

Encrypting the data provides no additional benefits to the requirements. For this request, answering why you want to encrypt illustrates an important point: *a user is either authorized to see data, or they are not.* If the data is encrypted, then you'll have to decrypt it for the authorized personnel. If they are not authorized, then they should not and will not get access to the data in either its plaintext or encrypted form. It's a bad industry practice to allow users access to encrypted sensitive data even if the data is protected by the encryption.

By encrypting the data unnecessarily, you may create unintended consequences. First, as just discussed, the encryption adds no measurable addition to the security. It may create a false sense of security if you believe that the encryption process determines user authorizations differently or better than the standard access controls. It does not, and it should not.

Encryption and decryption require computational resources. Consequently, you could be putting an extra load on a database server or stressing it to the point that response times become unsatisfactory. Also, consider the fact that the data is unusable in its encrypted state. The database can't make effective comparisons of values, computations can't be performed, and basic database operations will be ineffective on encrypted data. The encryption conceals the data not only from the users but also from the database.

With encryption comes a responsibility to manage the encryption keys. Failure to properly manage the keys can be disastrous on two accounts. First, if the keys are compromised, the data will be decrypted, thus defeating the entire process. Second, if the keys are lost, the data can never be decrypted.

The biggest example of misapplying database encryption is when it's used to encrypt passwords that are stored in a database table. The section "Hashing," later in the chapter, discusses why encryption is inappropriate and then shows you how to effectively secure passwords and allow them to be used for authentication.

Reasons to Encrypt

The preceding policy does not cite any strong reasons to encrypt data, but that does not mean that there aren't any reasons. The two most common reasons people say they need to encrypt are to comply with a "regulation" (legal, industry, or organizational mandate) or to hide the data from the DBAs.

Encrypting data "just in case someone steals my server, raw database files, or backups" is also a valid request. However, you should consider the statements I just made regarding performance and usability of the encrypted data. Selectively encrypting the data generally provides the best solution. The performance impact is minimized, and security on the extra-sensitive data can be achieved.

Let's now analyze how effective encryption is at hiding data from the DBAs.

Hiding Data from the DBA

Probably the strongest reason cited by people wanting to encrypt database data is to hide the data from the DBAs. Depending on your interpretation, this either makes perfect sense or represents a conflicting requirement. On the sensible side, if you want to ensure that the employees' salaries or health status are kept private, you should encrypt the data to prevent the DBAs from seeing it. When it comes to privacy-related data, hiding data from the DBAs is a perfectly valid requirement.

The conflict is the requirement to allow DBAs access to data for administrative tasks, but to prevent access when the data is not being used for administrative tasks. This statement is clearly in conflict with itself. Table and database backups, rebuilds of indexes, etc., all require the DBAs to have access to all the data. However, you don't want DBAs to access your data and see its value. The solution is in the phrase "see its value." Encryption will allow you to restate the requirement as "full access to data for administrative tasks, but no access to the contents of the private data." This is a valid requirement, but nevertheless a difficult if not impossible one to fulfill.

Encrypting the data to hide it from the DBAs is a valid request. The challenge remains in doing this successfully. If you are to encrypt the data in the database, then you will have to execute a program to perform the encryption and decryption operations. DBAs can execute any and all programs in the database. The problem now isn't preventing the DBA from reading the data, but preventing them from executing the program that decrypts the data. In addition, unless the source code has been secured, the DBA can view the program's source to determine how it works. No matter what you encrypt, the DBA can always destroy or change your data. This fact is important to acknowledge: if you don't trust your DBAs, get new ones.

Recall that encryption and decryption require an algorithm and a key. If you can prevent the DBA from obtaining the encryption key (remember, the database only performs symmetric key encryption), then the data will be hidden. Hiding data from the DBAs turns into a problem of hiding the keys from the DBAs. Let's talk more about the encryption keys in the "Key Management" section later in this chapter.

DBMS_CRYPTO

The DBMS_CRYPTO package is new to Oracle Database 10*g*. This package replaces the DBMS_OBFUSCATION_TOOLKIT which, while still available, has been deprecated. DBMS_CRYPTO adds several new encryption algorithms, hashing algorithms, and a key-hashed capability. It shouldn't be overlooked that the package name is both easier to type and easier to pronounce.

There are two additional places to find information on the new package. Chapter 22 of the *PL/SQL Packages and Type Reference 10*g *Release 1* is a good starting resource that explains the organization of the package. As a reference source, however, it lacks code examples. In addition to the code in this chapter, actual code examples can be found in Chapter 16 of *Developing Applications Using Data Encryption of the Oracle Database Security Guide 10*g *Release 1*.

The default privileges on DBMS_CRYPTO are secure. That is, the package has no explicit grants given to the DBA group or to PUBLIC. Before you can begin, you have to grant execute privileges on the package to your security manager. The *Oracle Database Security Guide 10*g also strongly recommends that you revoke the PUBLIC execute privileges from the DBMS_OBFUSCATION_TOOLKIT. If an attacker can't execute the program to decrypt the data, then recovering the original text becomes even more difficult.

The DBMS_CRYPTO package is very robust. The application developer can choose from a potpourri of encryption algorithms, padding techniques, initialization vectors, and block cipher modifiers. Padding techniques are the methods used to ensure the data sizes are congruent with the algorithm being used. Many of the encryption algorithms require the data to be padded to an 8-byte boundary. An *initialization vector (IV)* is random data that is prepended to the actual data you want to encrypt. It adds security for data values that are of low cardinality (that is, they don't have many differences) because the resulting ciphertext for two identical values that use different IVs will be different. This makes breaking the encryption more difficult. Block cipher modifiers allow you to specify how a block cipher algorithm is implemented. There are four block cipher modifiers: Electronic Code Book (ECB) will encrypt each block of data independently of the previous and subsequent blocks; Cipher Block Chaining (CBC) uses an exclusive-OR (XOR) of the previous data block with the current block before it is encrypted; Cipher Feedback (CFB) allows the data to be smaller than the block size (no padding is required); and Output Feedback (OFB) uses data from the previous block to fill the rightmost slots of the current block.

Don't worry if you don't understand the differences in algorithms, padding, or modifiers. You can strongly and securely encrypt the data using the recommended settings you see in the examples. For those die-hard cryptographers who understand the differences and have specific preferences, the DBMS_CRYPTO package will allow you to exploit the different padding, initialization vectors, and cipher modifiers.

Encryption Routines

DBMS_CRYPTO provides one encryption function and two encryption procedures. The function is based on the RAW data type. It accepts a key, data, and optional IV parameter of type RAW, and it also returns a RAW data type. The two encryption procedures are LOB oriented. One procedure accepts a BLOB as the data parameter; the other procedure accepts a CLOB as the data parameter. Both procedures expect a key and an optional IV of type RAW, and both procedures write the encrypted data to a BLOB data type.

At first, there seems to be something missing. What happened to support for VARCHAR2? It's not an oversight. The VARCHAR2 data type is not directly supported. The encryption function can be easily used by translating the VARCHAR2 data types using the UTL_RAW package. The VARCHAR2 encrypted data can be corrupted if updated by two users or databases that are using different character sets—this is discussed in more detail in the "Storing Encrypted Data" section, later in the chapter. To encrypt any data type that is not a RAW, CLOB, or BLOB, you'll have to perform data type translation.

DBMS_CRYPTO solves many of the challenges that existed with its predecessor. The encryption procedures are designed to handle all large objects. LOB support was missing from the DBMS_OBFUSCATION_TOOLKIT. In addition, DBMS_CRYPTO automatically pads all data when using the block encryption algorithms (or block ciphers). The block ciphers operate on 8-byte boundaries and require that the data fall evenly on the byte boundaries. For the data that does not fall on the boundary, padding has to be used to increase the data size. For example, the character string "123456789" has to be padded with an additional 7 characters to make its total length 16 characters, which is evenly divisible by 8. Prior to DBMS_CRYPTO, the developer had to manually pad the data.

DBMS_CRYPTO Simple Example

This first example illustrates how to invoke the encryption function for the DBMS_CRYPTO package:

```
sec_mgr@KNOX10g> -- DBMS_CRYPTO simple example
sec_mgr@KNOX10g> DECLARE
    -- Variable for the encryption algorithm that will be used.
    -- Using AES with 128-bit key size on a CBC modifier
    -- and padded using the PKCS#5 padding standard
    l_algorithm  PLS_INTEGER
      :=   dbms_crypto.encrypt_aes128
         + dbms_crypto.chain_cbc
         + dbms_crypto.pad_pkcs5;
    -- Variable for the data that will be encrypted.
    l_data       VARCHAR2 (4)   := 'DATA';
    -- Variable for the key that will be used for the encryption.
    -- Key has to be 16 bytes for AES128 algorithm
    l_key        VARCHAR2 (16) := 'TheEncryptionKey';
    -- Initialization vector. Vector has to be
    -- 16 bytes for AES128 algorithm.
    l_iv         VARCHAR2 (16) := '0123456789012345';
  BEGIN
    DBMS_OUTPUT.put_line
      (    'Encrypted DATA: '
       || UTL_RAW.cast_to_varchar2
           (dbms_crypto.encrypt
                      (UTL_RAW.cast_to_raw (l_data),
                       l_algorithm,
                       UTL_RAW.cast_to_raw (l_key),
                       UTL_RAW.cast_to_raw (l_iv))));
  END;
  /
Encrypted DATA: ε^≡ ∞⊗ ≤ T^¯óRí

PL/SQL procedure successfully completed.
```

The output from the encryption function was converted back to a string to illustrate that 'DATA' no longer looks like a valid string—it's encrypted.

The encryption algorithm was set by defining a local variable that is the resulting summation of the algorithm, the block modifier, and the padding. This is discussed in more detail in the "Encryption Algorithms" section, later in the chapter.

The DBMS_CRYPTO package is complete in the sense that you can use it to encrypt practically all of the standard data types after you convert them to a RAW, CLOB, or BLOB.

While working with the procedures and functions, you may find that you have to repetitively perform data type conversions. You'll notice in the preceding example that the data, the key, and the IV have to be converted to the RAW data type. This may or may not be a problem with your data. I find that it is easier to produce examples when the data, keys, and IVs are strings.

The encryption key size and the IV size can be 8, 16, 24, or 32 bytes and are dependent on the encryption algorithm that will be used. This example artificially creates the exact size key and IV. A key that is too short or too long will cause an error. An IV that is too short will cause an error, and only the first 8, 16, 24, or 32 bytes of the IV will be used based on the algorithm. Depending on how you generate your IV and key, you may have to truncate or pad those values in addition to converting them.

DATA_CRYPTO Package

For many of your practical uses, you may find it easier to create a package that can be used to cast your data types for you. To help illustrate how encryption can be used, the DATA_CRYPTO package presented here will act as a wrapper for the database's DBMS_CRYPTO. The DATA_CRYPTO package will make data encryption easier when performing SQL-based updates, and it will also simplify the example code. The complete package specifications and the implementation of the package body are given in Appendix B.

Based on the complexity of the example just shown, encryption and decryption functions for the character, date, and number data types will be provided. The DATA_CRYPTO functions will perform the data type casting. All functions accept the key as a character string. The package will ensure the key is the appropriate size for the given algorithm.

The functions are named ENCRYPT_<data type> and DECRYPT_<data type>; for example, ENCRYPT_CHAR is used for encrypting character data. The returning values for the encryption function and the input data type for the decryption function are RAW data types. You will see later in the "Storing Encrypted Data" section that storing encrypted data as a RAW is important for ensuring that you will be able to decrypt it later. There is an additional ENCRYPT and DECRYPT function that accepts character data and returns encrypted character data. These two complementary functions are used for illustrative purposes.

As mentioned, DBMS_CRYPTO provides encryption and decryption procedures for BLOBs and CLOBs. However, both procedures return BLOBs, and both are procedures as opposed to functions. The DATA_CRYPTO package will provide BLOB functions. There is also a function to return encrypted CLOB data, which is helpful in illustrating examples.

The IV isn't used in efforts to help simplify the code examples. You'll be able to understand how the encryption works without their use. You should note that IVs can make encrypting data with repeating values, which use repeating keys, more secure.

Encryption Algorithms

The DBMS_CRYPTO supports DES, triple-DES with two keys, triple-DES with three keys, AES with three different key sizes, and the RC4 algorithms. DBMS_CRYPTO determines the proper algorithm by its numeric value as opposed to a string value. The algorithm parameter is therefore a numeric data type. The base algorithm (for example, DES, 3DES, and AES) has a numeric value that is added to the numeric value for the block modifier (for example, CBC, CFB, ECB, and OFB) and the padding algorithms (for example, PKCS5, Zeros, ORCL, or None). The DATA_CRYPTO package will support the various algorithms but will be defaulted to the Oracle-recommended CBC block modifier and the Oracle-recommended PKCS5 data padding. The DATA_CRYPTO package uses global package variables and stores the computed numerical value for the algorithms:

```
  -- Strongest AES at 256-bit key length (32-bytes)
  g_aes256     CONSTANT PLS_INTEGER
    :=    dbms_crypto.encrypt_aes256
        + dbms_crypto.chain_cbc
        + dbms_crypto.pad_pkcs5;
```

These algorithms can be easily modified to accommodate a different block chaining algorithm or different padding algorithms by modifying this definition. To make it easy to pass these algorithms to procedures, a DATA_CRYPTO function is provided for each algorithm that returns the algorithms numeric value:

```
FUNCTION aes256
  RETURN PLS_INTEGER
AS
BEGIN
  RETURN g_aes256;
END;
```

This allows you to easily pass the algorithm as a parameter to the DATA_CRYPTO.ENCRYPT functions from SQL statements:

```
sec_mgr@KNOX10g> COL Encrypted format a32
sec_mgr@KNOX10g> SELECT
  2     data_crypto.encrypt ('Data', 'Key', data_crypto.aes256) encrypted
  3     FROM DUAL;

ENCRYPTED
------------------------------
¦lé+=&n-ç0?Ç+f±ß
```

GET and SET functions

The DATA_CRYPTO package allows the user to set and modify the default encryption algorithm by calling getter and setter procedures. Recall the DBMS_CRYPTO package resolves the encryption algorithm by evaluating its numerical value. This user-friendly version translates the number to text, making testing and debugging easier:

```
  -- Set encryption algorithm
  -- Stores value in global package variable
  PROCEDURE set_algorithm (p_enc_algorithm IN PLS_INTEGER);

  -- return character representation of currently set algorithm
  FUNCTION get_algorithm
    RETURN VARCHAR2;
```

Similarly, if you want to set the encryption key to be used in successive encryption and decryption operations, a set key procedure is provided. The key is stored in a package variable:

```
-- Stores key as a RAW in a global package variable
-- Key is sized based on algorithm passed or the globally
-- defined algorithm
PROCEDURE setkey (
  p_key             IN   VARCHAR2,
  p_enc_algorithm   IN   PLS_INTEGER DEFAULT NULL
);
```

Key Sizing

The DBMS_CRYPTO function and its procedures accept RAW keys. The keys have to be the correct size for the algorithm being used. The key size varies from 8 bytes for DES to 32 bytes for AES256. The RC4 algorithm will take a key of any size. As you will soon see, one popular approach to key management is not storing the keys but rather (securely) computing the encryption keys. Therefore, it's desirable to have a routine that ensures the key size is appropriate for the algorithm being used.

The examples used in this chapter will use string-based keys for the encryption and decryption parameter. The DBMS_CRYPTO requires the key to be a RAW, so a function is provided to convert the key to a RAW and adjust it to the appropriate size:

```
-- Return RAW key of appropriate size based on algorithm
-- If algorithm is null, the global algorithm will be used.
FUNCTION getkey (
  p_key             IN   VARCHAR2 DEFAULT NULL,
  p_enc_algorithm   IN   PLS_INTEGER DEFAULT NULL
)
  RETURN RAW;
```

This function will also provide utility if you want to directly invoke the DBMS_CRYPTO and ensure the key is sized appropriately as shown here:

```
sec_mgr@KNOX10g> SELECT dbms_crypto.encrypt
                          (UTL_RAW.cast_to_raw ('data'),
                           data_crypto.aes,
                           data_crypto.getkey (   'my encryption key'
                                               || ' of some random length',
                                               data_crypto.aes
                                              )
                          ) encrypted
     FROM DUAL;

ENCRYPTED
--------------------------------
CF7723ECBFCFF059B2A62BC2DB9BA56F
```

The DATA_CRYPTO.GETKEY function will use the left-most bytes of the key passed. Keys that are too large for the algorithm will be truncated. Keys that are too small will be right padded with binary zeros.

NOTE
Two identical values encrypted with the same key result in the same ciphertext; therefore, careful attention to the encryption keys and their lengths is important to ensuring the data encryption is effectively implemented.

Keys that are too small or too large can result in a less secure implementation. (This is probably why Oracle does not automatically size the keys for you.) You'll see an example of this in the "Weak Keys" section.

Weak Keys

The DBMS_CRYPTO package does not truncate or pad encryption keys in any way. This leaves the responsibility for creating the appropriately sized keys to the developer. There are a few important things to consider.

The DATA_CRYPTO.GETKEY is a convenience function. It pads or truncates keys for the relevant encryption algorithm. It uses the left-most bits for the truncation. It is therefore possible to provide two different keys that get truncated to the same encryption key. That is, if the key is too long for the algorithm, then its truncation may remove the uniqueness:

```
sec_mgr@KNOX10g> COL encrypted1 format a16
sec_mgr@KNOX10g> COL encrypted2 format a16
sec_mgr@KNOX10g> EXEC data_crypto.set_Algorithm(data_crypto.DES);

PL/SQL procedure successfully completed.

sec_mgr@KNOX10g> SELECT data_crypto.encrypt_char ('Data',
  2                                  'ThisKeyIsOver8bytes')
  3                                                    encrypted1,
  4         data_crypto.encrypt_char ('Data',
  5                                  'ThisKeyIsAlsoOver8bytes')
  6                                                    encrypted2
  7     FROM DUAL;

ENCRYPTED1       ENCRYPTED2
---------------- ----------------
0DCA01D7A8E26AAF 0DCA01D7A8E26AAF
```

The DES algorithm requires an 8-byte key. The DATA_CRYPTO.GETKEY function truncates the key to the first 8 bytes. The two preceding keys result in the same key, which subsequently produces the same ciphertext.

The DATA_CRYPTO.GETKEY will also pad the encryption key to make it the appropriate length. The overall strength of the algorithm is influenced by the uniqueness and variations in all elements of the key. If you elect to use AES256, the key size is 32 bytes. If you use a key with one character (a key size of 1 byte), then the remaining key bytes (characters) will be the same—you will have 1 byte that you provided and 31 bytes of binary zeros. This could make it much easier for an attacker to guess your encryption key.

The DATA_CRYPTO.GETKEY is provided for convenience and as a reference. Understanding the implications of key size and thus overall strength is important to ensuring the encryption process will be effective.

Encryption Examples

The purpose of this section is to give an overview of how encryption can be performed with different data. You'll see a few examples of encrypting data with various algorithms. To start, a simple encryption of character data is presented. The output will be viewed both as a string and as a RAW. The decryption is done to verify that you can successfully recover the original data:

```
sec_mgr@KNOX10g> DECLARE
    l_plaintext       VARCHAR2 (12) := 'This is data';
    l_key             VARCHAR2 (20) := 'This is the Key';
    l_encrypted_text  VARCHAR2 (24);
    l_encrypted_raw   RAW (24);
    l_decrypted_text  VARCHAR2 (20);
  BEGIN
    l_encrypted_raw  := data_crypto.encrypt_char (l_plaintext, l_key);
    l_encrypted_text := data_crypto.encrypt (l_plaintext, l_key);
    l_decrypted_text := data_crypto.decrypt (l_encrypted_text, l_key);
    DBMS_OUTPUT.put_line ('PlainText:         ' || l_plaintext);
    DBMS_OUTPUT.put_line ('Key:               ' || l_key);
    DBMS_OUTPUT.put_line ('Encrypted RAW:     ' || l_encrypted_raw);
    DBMS_OUTPUT.put_line ('Encrypted string:  ' || l_encrypted_text);
    DBMS_OUTPUT.put_line ('Decrypted:         ' || l_decrypted_text);
  END;
  /
PlainText:        This is data
Key:              This is the Key
Encrypted RAW:    A84513EC540BF7E87BCA3AF29A0CAD34
Encrypted string: ε^≡ ∝⊗ ≤ T^¯óRí
Decrypted:        This is data
```

Invoking encryption is done very easily. The challenge remains as to how to store encrypted data and how to mange the encryption keys. All of these issues will be addressed after a few more preliminary points are made.

Encrypting Character, Numbers, and Dates

Three of the basic data types you may be encrypting and storing are character, number, and dates. As seen in the next example, this can be accomplished fairly easy using the DATA_CRYPTO package. A simple table is created and populated with an encrypted string, number, and date:

```
sec_mgr@KNOX10g> CREATE TABLE enc_val_tab
  (charval RAW(32),
  dateval RAW(64),
  numval  RAW(32));

Table created.

sec_mgr@KNOX10g> EXEC data_crypto.setkey('EncryptionKey');

PL/SQL procedure successfully completed.
```

```
sec_mgr@KNOX10g> INSERT INTO enc_val_tab
  2       VALUES (data_crypto.encrypt_char (USER),
  3               data_crypto.encrypt_date (SYSDATE),
  4               data_crypto.encrypt_number (10));

1 row created.

sec_mgr@KNOX10g> COMMIT ;
```

You can see the data is stored encrypted and can be reconstructed through the decryption process:

```
sec_mgr@KNOX10g> COL "Character Data" format a20
sec_mgr@KNOX10g> COL "Number Data" format a20
sec_mgr@KNOX10g> COL "Date Data" format a20
sec_mgr@KNOX10g> -- Show stored data is encrypted. Have to convert
sec_mgr@KNOX10g> -- data from RAW to view.
sec_mgr@KNOX10g> SELECT UTL_RAW.cast_to_varchar2 (charval)
  2                                      "Character Data",
  3        UTL_RAW.cast_to_varchar2 (numval)
  4                                         "Number Data",
  5        UTL_RAW.cast_to_varchar2 (dateval)
  6                                           "Date Data"
  7    FROM enc_val_tab;

Character Data       Number Data          Date Data
-------------------- -------------------- --------------------
_6-?é?¤+P÷Q¥¯ ÷$     px b?¦$+êUâÿ¦ñ¦ä     ¡ùµ¿ò-¦º'>+" ¦-¦

sec_mgr@KNOX10g> -- Show decrypted values
sec_mgr@KNOX10g> SELECT data_crypto.decrypt_char (charval)
  2                                      "Character Data",
  3        TO_CHAR(data_crypto.decrypt_number (numval))
  4                                         "Number Data",
  5        TO_CHAR
  6               (data_crypto.decrypt_date (dateval),
  7                'DD-MON-RRRR HH24:MI:SS')
  8                                           "Date Data"
  9    FROM enc_val_tab;

Character Data       Number Data Date Data
-------------------- ----------- --------------------
SEC_MGR              10          10-APR-2004 00:00:00
```

Everything in the preceding looks functional unless you wanted to preserve the time when you stored the date value.

Encrypting Dates and the NLS_DATE_FORMAT

Encrypting dates is a particularly onerous task. The date has to first be converted to a character string, then to a RAW (RAW data is the preferred way to store data). The decryption process must undergo the same steps in reverse order—RAW data is converted to character, then character is converted back to date.

To do this successfully, you have to ensure your NLS_DATE_FORMAT is set to capture all of the DATE attributes. For example, if the format is DD-MON-RR, then you will lose the time aspect of your date in the data casting operations. The DATA_CRYPTO package will perform the data casting, but you are responsible for ensuring the NLS_DATE_FORMAT is set appropriately.

This can be a bit more challenging than it might first appear. Notice that the user logged in through SQL*Plus does not get the database's default NLS_DATE_FORMAT setting:

```
sec_mgr@KNOX10g> -- ** Show that current format only shows date not time **
sec_mgr@KNOX10g> COL date_format format a25
sec_mgr@KNOX10g> SELECT SYS_CONTEXT ('userenv', 'nls_date_format')
                                               DATE_FORMAT,
         SYSDATE
    FROM DUAL;

DATE_FORMAT               SYSDATE
------------------------- ---------
DD-MON-RR                 10-APR-04

sec_mgr@KNOX10g> -- The current format was not set by the init.ora parameter
sec_mgr@KNOX10g> SHOW parameter nls_date_format

NAME                                 TYPE        VALUE
------------------------------------ ----------- ------------------------------
nls_date_format                      string      DD-MON-RRRR HH24:MI:SS
```

You can reset the date format by issuing an ALTER SESSION, but you will have to remember to do this every time prior to encrypting data. An alternative is to create a database logon trigger. Note that the trigger does not have to set everyone's date format. The following trigger just alters the date format for the SEC_MGR and SCOTT users:

```
sec_mgr@KNOX10g> -- Create logon trigger to set date format to capture time.
sec_mgr@KNOX10g> -- Consider only setting format for specific users.
sec_mgr@KNOX10g> CREATE OR REPLACE TRIGGER nls_date_logon
    AFTER LOGON ON DATABASE
  BEGIN
    IF USER IN ('SEC_MGR', 'SCOTT')
    THEN
      EXECUTE IMMEDIATE
        'alter session set nls_date_format=''DD-MON-RRRR HH24:MI:SS''';
    END IF;
  END;
  /

Trigger created.

sec_mgr@KNOX10g> -- Show new format
sec_mgr@KNOX10g> CONN sec_mgr/oracle10g
```

```
Connected.
sec_mgr@KNOX10g> SELECT SYS_CONTEXT ('userenv', 'nls_date_format')
  2                                               DATE_FORMAT,
  3          SYSDATE
  4     FROM DUAL;

DATE_FORMAT                 SYSDATE
-------------------------   --------------------
DD-MON-RRRR HH24:MI:SS      10-APR-2004 11:20:07

sec_mgr@KNOX10g> -- NOTE the format is not set for all users
sec_mgr@KNOX10g> CONN system/manager
Connected.
system@KNOX10g> -- show new format
system@KNOX10g> SELECT SYS_CONTEXT ('userenv', 'nls_date_format')
  2                                               DATE_FORMAT,
  3          SYSDATE
  4     FROM DUAL;

DATE_FORMAT                 SYSDATE
-------------------------   ---------
DD-MON-RR                   10-APR-04
```

Once the NLS_DATE_FORMAT has been set appropriately, you'll be able to preserve the time aspects of your date:

```
sec_mgr@KNOX10g> -- Remove previous records.
sec_mgr@KNOX10g> TRUNCATE TABLE enc_val_tab;

Table truncated.

sec_mgr@KNOX10g> -- Set encryption key
sec_mgr@KNOX10g> EXEC data_crypto.setkey('EncryptionKey');

PL/SQL procedure successfully completed.

sec_mgr@KNOX10g> -- Insert values. NLS_DATE_FORMAT will preserve time.
sec_mgr@KNOX10g> INSERT INTO enc_val_tab
  2       VALUES (data_crypto.encrypt_char (USER),
  3               data_crypto.encrypt_date (SYSDATE),
  4               data_crypto.encrypt_number (10));

1 row created.

sec_mgr@KNOX10g> COMMIT ;

Commit complete.

sec_mgr@KNOX10g> -- Show decrypted values
sec_mgr@KNOX10g> COL "Character Data" format a20
```

```
sec_mgr@KNOX10g> COL "Date Data" format a20
sec_mgr@KNOX10g> SELECT data_crypto.decrypt_char (charval)
  2                                    "Character Data",
  3         TO_CHAR(data_crypto.decrypt_number (numval))
  4                                          "Number Data",
  5         TO_CHAR
  6                (data_crypto.decrypt_date (dateval),
  7                 'DD-MON-RRRR HH24:MI:SS')
  8                                              "Date Data"
  9    FROM enc_val_tab;

Character Data       Number Data Date Data
-------------------- ----------- --------------------
SEC_MGR              10          10-APR-2004 11:56:47
```

Encrypting CLOBs and BLOBs

The DBMS_CRYPTO package supports the encryption of CLOBs and BLOBs. However, this support is only manifested through the use of procedures. The DATA_CRYPTO package will convert these procedures to functions. For the CLOB data, the ciphertext is also returned as a CLOB.

In the following example, a table is created that holds CLOBs. This simulates a table that might hold large documents. A CLOB is inserted and then encrypted using a simple SQL update statement.

```
sec_mgr@KNOX10g> CREATE TABLE docs
  2  (doc_id NUMBER(4),
  3  doc     CLOB)
  4  /

Table created.

sec_mgr@KNOX10g> INSERT INTO docs
  2       VALUES (1, 'This is CLOB data');

1 row created.

sec_mgr@KNOX10g> COMMIT ;

Commit complete.

sec_mgr@KNOX10g> EXEC data_crypto.setkey('This is the Key');

PL/SQL procedure successfully completed.

sec_mgr@KNOX10g> UPDATE docs
  2     SET doc = data_crypto.encrypt (doc);

1 row updated.

sec_mgr@KNOX10g> COL Encrypted format a32
sec_mgr@KNOX10g> COL Decrypted format a32
```

```
sec_mgr@KNOX10g> SELECT doc encrypted, data_crypto.decrypt (doc) decrypted
    FROM docs;

ENCRYPTED                        DECRYPTED
-------------------------------- --------------------------------

??N??¦ôa+2IDJ°?-#?_-4o_ÉÖx+| æ{ This is CLOB data
```

To test the BLOB encryption, a file is loaded from the file system and stored as a BLOB in the table. The BLOB is then encrypted using a SQL update statement. To verify this process, the BLOB is converted to a CLOB and the value is printed. To begin, a file directory is created and access to the directory is granted to SEC_MGR:

```
system@KNOX10g> CREATE OR REPLACE DIRECTORY doc_dir AS
                                  'C:\tmp\esbd';

Directory created.

system@KNOX10g> GRANT ALL ON DIRECTORY doc_dir TO sec_mgr;

Grant succeeded.
```

The DOCS table is modified to hold the BLOB files. The file can be loaded into the table using the DBMS_LOB package. Once loaded, the BLOB can be easily encrypted.

```
sec_mgr@KNOX10g> DROP TABLE docs;

Table dropped.

sec_mgr@KNOX10g> CREATE TABLE docs
  (doc_id NUMBER(4),
  doc      BLOB)
  /

Table created.

sec_mgr@KNOX10g>
sec_mgr@KNOX10g> DECLARE
    l_blob   BLOB;
    l_bfile  BFILE;
  BEGIN
    INSERT INTO docs
         VALUES (1, EMPTY_BLOB ())
      RETURNING doc
           INTO l_blob;

    l_bfile := BFILENAME ('DOC_DIR', 'sample.xml');
    DBMS_LOB.fileopen (l_bfile);
    DBMS_LOB.loadfromfile (l_blob,
                           l_bfile,
```

```
                                DBMS_LOB.getlength (l_bfile));
     DBMS_LOB.fileclose (l_bfile);
   END;
   /

PL/SQL procedure successfully completed.

sec_mgr@KNOX10g> EXEC data_crypto.setkey('This is the Key');

PL/SQL procedure successfully completed.

sec_mgr@KNOX10g> UPDATE docs
         SET doc = data_crypto.encrypt (doc);

1 row updated.

sec_mgr@KNOX10g> COMMIT ;

Commit complete.
```

Verifying the contents requires a BLOB to CLOB conversion. The BLOB is decrypted, then converted to a CLOB that is printed. The resulting decryption can be compared to the original by using the SQL*Plus Host command:

```
sec_mgr@KNOX10g> DECLARE
       l_encrypted_blob  BLOB;
       l_decrypted_blob  BLOB;
       l_decrypted_clob  CLOB;
       l_lang            NUMBER := DBMS_LOB.default_lang_ctx;
       l_warning         NUMBER;
       l_t_offset        NUMBER := 1;
       l_src_offset      NUMBER := 1;
     BEGIN
       SELECT doc
         INTO l_encrypted_blob
         FROM docs;

       DBMS_LOB.createtemporary (l_decrypted_blob, TRUE);
       DBMS_LOB.createtemporary (l_decrypted_clob, TRUE);
       -- decrypt BLOB
       l_decrypted_blob := data_crypto.decrypt (l_encrypted_blob);
       -- convert to CLOB for display
       DBMS_LOB.converttoclob (l_decrypted_clob,
                               l_decrypted_blob,
                               DBMS_LOB.lobmaxsize,
                               l_t_offset,
                               l_src_offset,
                               DBMS_LOB.default_csid,
                               l_lang,
                               l_warning
```

```
                               );
      DBMS_OUTPUT.put_line (l_decrypted_clob);
    END;
    /
<?xml version="1.0"?>
  <document>
    <value>security rawks</value>
  </document>


PL/SQL procedure successfully completed.
```

You can see this data corresponds with the data in your file:

```
sec_mgr@KNOX10g> HOST cat C:\tmp\esbd\sample.xml
<?xml version="1.0"?>
  <document>
    <value>security rawks</value>
  </document>
```

This example used an XML file, which would probably be stored in a CLOB or as an XMLType. You cannot encrypt an XMLType because the database interprets and validates the XML automatically; trying to store encrypted data in this type will fail. BLOBs are ideal for storing true binary data, such as images and audio data. Encrypting this data provides added security.

Encryption In-Depth

This section discusses many of the issues you need to understand for practicing effective data encryption.

Keys, Data, and IVs

It should be obvious that using a different encryption algorithm will yield different ciphertext. There is also a strong relationship between the encryption key, the data, and the IVs used within the same algorithm. As you go through the next examples, you will see this relationship. This is important because the relationship dictates how to effectively use the encryption keys based on the data and algorithms.

The following examples show the encrypted data as RAWs because it is easier to distinguish differences in the hexadecimal RAW output than the mangled character representation illustrated previously.

The first important principle is that changing the keys on the same data results in different ciphertext. If you encrypt the data with a key that changes for each record, then two records with the same values will result in different ciphertext:

```
sec_mgr@KNOX10g> COL data format a6
sec_mgr@KNOX10g> COL "Encrypted with Key1" format a34
sec_mgr@KNOX10g> COL "Encrypted with Key2" format a34
sec_mgr@KNOX10g> SELECT 'Data' DATA,
            data_crypto.encrypt_char ('Data', 'Key1')
```

```
                                "Encrypted with Key1",
          data_crypto.encrypt_char ('Data', 'Key2')
                                "Encrypted with Key2"
     FROM DUAL;

DATA   Encrypted with Key1                 Encrypted with Key2
------ ----------------------------------- -----------------------------------
Data   6F0FA69188F00D8DEE30F38783FA2BDF    11C843B0AF268E10F5C8B65071D2AEF4
```

Notice the encrypted output (ciphertext) changed when the key changed. The ciphertext will also change if the data changes but the key stays the same:

```
sec_mgr@KNOX10g> -- changing data
sec_mgr@KNOX10g> COL "'Data1' key: 'TheSecretKey'" format a36
sec_mgr@KNOX10g> COL "'Data2' key: 'TheSecretKey'" format a36
sec_mgr@KNOX10g> SELECT data_crypto.encrypt_char ('Data1',
                                   'TheSecretKey')
                        "'Data1' key: 'TheSecretKey'",
          data_crypto.encrypt_char ('Data2',
                                   'TheSecretKey')
                        "'Data2' key: 'TheSecretKey'"
     FROM DUAL;

'Data1' key: 'TheSecretKey'          'Data2' key: 'TheSecretKey'
------------------------------------ ------------------------------------
0F938AA8EE43E237403CB99D1DC546E6     4FD06CE09FFE899697B0DF47A8E1BBF7
```

If you want to use the same key to encrypt the same data values, an initialization vector has to be added to the encryption call to ensure duplicate ciphertext is not produced:

```
sec_mgr@KNOX10g> -- Changing IVs allows different ciphertext for
sec_mgr@KNOX10g> -- the same data and the same key.
sec_mgr@KNOX10g> DECLARE
     -- The encryption algorithm that will be used.
     l_algorithm  PLS_INTEGER
       :=   dbms_crypto.encrypt_aes
          + dbms_crypto.chain_cbc
          + dbms_crypto.pad_pkcs5;
     -- First initialization vector. Vector has to be
     -- 16 bytes.
     l_iv1         RAW (16)
          := UTL_RAW.cast_to_raw ('0123456789012345');
     -- Second initialization vector. Vector has to be
     -- 16 bytes.
     l_iv2         RAW (16)
          := UTL_RAW.cast_to_raw ('1123456789012345');
     -- The data that will be encrypted
     l_data        VARCHAR2 (4)   := 'DATA';
     -- The key that will be used for the encryption.
     -- Key has to be 16 bytes
```

```
   l_key         VARCHAR2 (16) := 'TheEncryptionKey';
BEGIN
  DBMS_OUTPUT.put_line
    (   'Encrypted with IV1: '
     || dbms_crypto.encrypt
                   (UTL_RAW.cast_to_raw (l_data),
                    l_algorithm,
                    UTL_RAW.cast_to_raw (l_key),
                    l_iv1));
  DBMS_OUTPUT.put_line
    (   'Encrypted with IV2: '
     || dbms_crypto.encrypt
                   (UTL_RAW.cast_to_raw (l_data),
                    l_algorithm,
                    UTL_RAW.cast_to_raw (l_key),
                    l_iv2));
END;
/
Encrypted with IV1: C8EE5EDFB8A252F0A171E93C642754C6
Encrypted with IV2: 764E9898B28CA68D621096989D772694
PL/SQL procedure successfully completed.
```

The bolded values in the IVs show that a 1-byte difference in the IV will completely change the resulting ciphertext. The most important point in this section is that you generally know the uniqueness of the data you wish to encrypt. If all the encryption inputs are the same—key, data, algorithm, and IV—then *the ciphertext will also be the same*. This may be undesirable. Consider the following example:

```
sec_mgr@KNOX10g> CREATE TABLE people
  (ename VARCHAR2(12),
  deptno VARCHAR2(16));

Table created.

sec_mgr@KNOX10g> INSERT INTO people
    SELECT ename, deptno
      FROM scott.emp;

14 rows created.

sec_mgr@KNOX10g> break on deptno
sec_mgr@KNOX10g> SELECT ename, deptno
              FROM people
              order by deptno, ename;

ENAME        DEPTNO
------------ ----------------
CLARK        10
KING
MILLER
ADAMS        20
```

```
FORD
JONES
SCOTT
SMITH
ALLEN          30
BLAKE
JAMES
MARTIN
TURNER
WARD
```

If you wish to encrypt the DEPTNO column in this table, you might issue the following:

```
sec_mgr@KNOX10g> EXEC data_crypto.setkey('Deptno Key');

PL/SQL procedure successfully completed.

sec_mgr@KNOX10g> UPDATE people
  2     SET deptno = data_crypto.encrypt (deptno);

14 rows updated.
```

First set the encryption key to "Deptno Key." This will maintain the same key for all encrypted updates. While the data was encrypted, the relationship and association of person to DEPTNO is still maintained. This is due to the fact that the same key was used for all records.

```
sec_mgr@KNOX10g> COL "Encrypted Deptno" format a32
sec_mgr@KNOX10g> BREAK on "Encrypted Deptno"
sec_mgr@KNOX10g> SELECT ename, UTL_RAW.cast_to_raw (deptno) "Encrypted Deptno"
  2      FROM people
  3  ORDER BY deptno, ename;

ENAME        Encrypted Deptno
------------ --------------------------------
CLARK        2C2209E50EBA89F28E78E3DADF247E3D
KING
MILLER
ALLEN        2F044687D0D897871586A7ED400DD599
BLAKE
JAMES
MARTIN
TURNER
WARD
ADAMS        C580432E9DAC481E575A0ACB396A8B3A
FORD
JONES
SCOTT
SMITH

14 rows selected.
```

If you wish to obscure the relationship, you have to use a different key for each row. In the following example, the records are encrypted using a unique key for each record:

```
sec_mgr@KNOX10g> TRUNCATE TABLE people;

Table truncated.

sec_mgr@KNOX10g> INSERT INTO people
  2    SELECT ename, deptno
  3      FROM scott.emp;

14 rows created.

sec_mgr@KNOX10g> UPDATE people
  2     SET deptno = data_crypto.encrypt (deptno, ename);

14 rows updated.
```

Since the ENAME is different for each row, two rows with the same DEPTNO will result in different encrypted values:

```
sec_mgr@KNOX10g> SELECT   ename,
  2            UTL_RAW.cast_to_raw (deptno) "Encrypted Deptno"
  3      FROM people
  4  ORDER BY deptno, ename;

ENAME        Encrypted Deptno
------------ --------------------------------
JAMES        023C3C40FDECF587CFE9D51300EA66B8
TURNER       17A3A806CB7C9314CA83957FF0DAD5B7
KING         458DABDAFAB4235C402200435100E614
CLARK        67583C666C4C06DB78088998942D21EB
WARD         7CF35398CD84BFE22D12F9560653C920
FORD         82CA438DB5491AE23B9D46CD08149958
MILLER       9FADCF5BDEF03C926281FB02EEFEDC61
MARTIN       A14FF7184C9C2304596E40A7BE91C00A
SMITH        AC4A6BB34AC7EE7136108D6661CD5452
ADAMS        C01ED18F64343111A666017B53AD3C3D
JONES        C5BFFFFE0CC7CC936F958F9FB931BAB3
ALLEN        CB04A624191CB5EBF5F028C05A46E540
BLAKE        D6948B6A87B00F816C14E5DD071B4431
SCOTT        FD42777AAD3A82292304C97B94933DD8

14 rows selected.
```

Storing Encrypted Data

There are a few important issues concerning the storage of encrypted data as character data (either VARCHAR2 or CLOB).

The practical use of storing the character data is in question. The encryption process completely mangles the data. Any letters or numbers no longer look like letters or numbers. Much of the data has become nonprintable. Some applications, publishing software, or terminals expecting printable characters may not enjoy the encrypted version.

When using the block encryption algorithms (all algorithms except RC4), storing the encrypted data as a VARCHAR2 or CLOB can create problems with translations between different character sets. VARCHAR2 and CLOB data is interpreted and translated between character sets when moving the data between databases. When doing this with encrypted data, the conversion process will rearrange the data. If this is done, the decryption process will not return the original data.

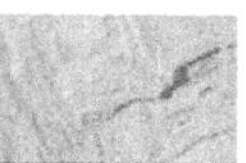

CAUTION
Encrypted data stored as character data will not be successfully decrypted unless the encryption and decryption sessions have the same NLS character set.

The solution to this is to store the data either as a RAW or a BLOB. RAW and BLOB data types will not undergo character set translation. To support this, the DATA_CRYPTO package returns RAW data for encryption of character, number, and date data.

To illustrate the importance of this, consider the following example. A table is created that holds names and salaries. The salary will be encrypted and stored both as a VARCHAR2 and as a RAW.

```
sec_mgr@DAGGER> CONN sec_mgr/oracle10g@dagger
Connected.
sec_mgr@DAGGER> DROP TABLE people;

Table dropped.

sec_mgr@DAGGER> CREATE TABLE people
  2  (NAME VARCHAR2(30),
  3  salary VARCHAR2(16),
  4  raw_salary RAW (32));

Table created.

sec_mgr@DAGGER> -- populate table
sec_mgr@DAGGER> INSERT INTO people
  2              (NAME, salary)
  3     SELECT ename, sal
  4       FROM scott.emp
  5      WHERE ROWNUM <= 3;

3 rows created.

sec_mgr@DAGGER> -- Encrypt salaries, use name as key
sec_mgr@DAGGER> -- Encrypt salary as RAW
sec_mgr@DAGGER> UPDATE people
  2      SET raw_salary =
```

```
  3                data_crypto.encrypt_char (salary, NAME);

3 rows updated.

sec_mgr@DAGGER> -- encrypt salary as VARCHAR2
sec_mgr@DAGGER> UPDATE people
  2      SET salary = data_crypto.encrypt (salary, NAME);

3 rows updated.

sec_mgr@DAGGER> COMMIT ;

Commit complete.

sec_mgr@DAGGER> COL decrypted_salary format a16
sec_mgr@DAGGER> COL decrypted_raw_salary format a13
sec_mgr@DAGGER> -- Can decrypt both RAW and varchar2
sec_mgr@DAGGER> SELECT NAME,
  2         data_crypto.decrypt_char (raw_salary, NAME)
  3                                   decrypted_raw_salary,
  4         data_crypto.decrypt (salary, NAME)
  5                                       decrypted_salary
  6     FROM people;

NAME                           DECRYPTED_RAW DECRYPTED_SALARY
------------------------------ ------------- ----------------
SMITH                          800           800
ALLEN                          1600          1600
WARD                           1250          1250
```

Everything appears to be working until…a client connects to the database and their character set is different than that of the user who initially saved the VARCHAR2 data. When this occurs, the VARCHAR2 data will not decrypt. The other client in this example will be another database server accessing the data over a database link:

```
sec_mgr@KNOX10g> CREATE DATABASE LINK dagger USING 'dagger';

Database link created.

sec_mgr@KNOX10g> -- Can still decrypt RAW
sec_mgr@KNOX10g> COL decrypted_raw_salary format a13
sec_mgr@KNOX10g> SELECT NAME,
  2         data_crypto.decrypt_char (raw_salary, NAME)
  3                                   decrypted_raw_salary
  4     FROM people@dagger;

NAME                           DECRYPTED_RAW
------------------------------ -------------
SMITH                          800
ALLEN                          1600
```

```
WARD                            1250

sec_mgr@KNOX10g> -- Cannot decrypt VARCHAR2
sec_mgr@KNOX10g> SELECT NAME,
  2          data_crypto.decrypt (salary, NAME)
  3                                         decrypted_salary
  4     FROM people@dagger;
       data_crypto.decrypt (salary, NAME)
       *
ERROR at line 2:
ORA-28817: PL/SQL function returned an error.
ORA-06512: at "SYS.DBMS_CRYPTO_FFI", line 67
ORA-06512: at "SYS.DBMS_CRYPTO", line 41
ORA-06512: at "SEC_MGR.DATA_CRYPTO", line 318
ORA-06512: at "SEC_MGR.DATA_CRYPTO", line 354
ORA-06512: at line 1
```

You can compare the character sets and see they are different:

```
sec_mgr@KNOX10g> -- Show character sets are different
sec_mgr@KNOX10g> col "Remote Character Set" format a30
sec_mgr@KNOX10g> col "Local Character Set" format a30
sec_mgr@KNOX10g> SELECT a.VALUE "Remote Character Set",
  2          b.VALUE "Local Character Set"
  3     FROM v$nls_parameters@dagger a,
  4          v$nls_parameters b
  5    WHERE a.parameter = 'NLS_CHARACTERSET'
  6      AND b.parameter = 'NLS_CHARACTERSET';

Remote Character Set           Local Character Set
------------------------------ ---------------------------
WE8ISO8859P1                   WE8MSWIN1252
```

You would see the same results if you used CLOBs and BLOBs instead of VARCHAR2 and RAW. The DBMS_CRYPTO package returns RAWs and BLOBs for this reason and the DATA_CRYPTO provides these functions to support these uses as well.

Note that the translation problem will occur for any insert or updates to encrypted data when the encrypting and decrypting character sets are not identical. Importing data that was exported in a different character set will also cause problems. The safest and best method for handling encrypted data is to store it as a RAW or BLOB. The only exception is when you can guarantee that the character sets will never differ.

Encrypted Data Sizes

Encrypting data with block ciphers does change the data size. Recall the DBMS_CRYPTO will automatically pad data for block ciphers. For the DES-based algorithms, the padding will be to the next highest 8-byte boundary. For the AES-based algorithms, the padding will be to the next highest 16-byte boundary.

The following example illustrates this fact. A table is created and populated. A helper procedure is also created to assist in populating the table. The table is populated by taking data records of six different sizes—1, 7, 8, 15, 16, and 32 bytes, respectively—and encrypting them with each of the algorithms. The data is specifically sized around the block boundaries. This will illustrate how a data element that is originally 8 bytes in length may have to be stored in a 16-byte column.

```
sec_mgr@KNOX10g> CREATE TABLE enc_data_sizes
     (algorithm VARCHAR2(6),
     dataval VARCHAR2(256),
     enc_dataval VARCHAR2(256),
     raw_enc_dataval RAW(256));

Table created.

sec_mgr@KNOX10g> -- Create a procedure which will be called
sec_mgr@KNOX10g> -- iteratively to perform the insert operation
sec_mgr@KNOX10g> CREATE OR REPLACE PROCEDURE insert_enc_record (
     p_dataval  IN  VARCHAR2)
   AS
   BEGIN
     INSERT INTO enc_data_sizes
                 (algorithm,
                  dataval,
                  enc_dataval,
                  raw_enc_dataval)
          VALUES (data_crypto.get_algorithm,
                  p_dataval,
                  data_crypto.encrypt (p_dataval),
                  data_crypto.encrypt_char (p_dataval));
   END;
   /
Procedure created.
sec_mgr@KNOX10g> -- Populate table
sec_mgr@KNOX10g> DECLARE
     l_dataval  VARCHAR2 (32);
   BEGIN
     data_crypto.setkey ('thisIsTheEncryptKey');

     FOR i IN 1 .. 32
     LOOP
       -- checking padding around block boundaries
       IF (i IN (1, 7, 8, 15, 16, 32))
       THEN
         l_dataval := RPAD ('x', i, i);
         data_crypto.set_algorithm (data_crypto.des);
         insert_enc_record (l_dataval);
         data_crypto.set_algorithm (data_crypto.des3);
         insert_enc_record (l_dataval);
         data_crypto.set_algorithm (data_crypto.aes);
         insert_enc_record (l_dataval);
         data_crypto.set_algorithm
```

```
                                   (data_crypto.aes192);
        insert_enc_record (l_dataval);
        data_crypto.set_algorithm
                                   (data_crypto.aes256);
        insert_enc_record (l_dataval);
        data_crypto.set_algorithm (data_crypto.rc4);
        insert_enc_record (l_dataval);
      END IF;
    END LOOP;
  END;
  /

PL/SQL procedure successfully completed.
sec_mgr@KNOX10g> commit;
```

You can now view the effect of the encryption on the original data sizes. The results are consistent regardless of the encrypting data's type (VARCHAR2, RAW, CLOB or BLOB):

```
sec_mgr@KNOX10g> BREAK on algorithm
sec_mgr@KNOX10g> COL algorithm format a9
sec_mgr@KNOX10g> SELECT   algorithm,
           LENGTH (dataval) "Original Size",
           LENGTH (enc_dataval) "Encrypted Size",
           LENGTH (enc_dataval) - LENGTH (dataval) "Padded Bytes"
      FROM enc_data_sizes
  ORDER BY algorithm, "Original Size";

ALGORITHM Original Size Encrypted Size Padded Bytes
--------- ------------- -------------- -----------
AES                   1             16          15
                      7             16           9
                      8             16           8
                     15             16           1
                     16             32          16
                     32             48          16
AES192                1             16          15
                      7             16           9
                      8             16           8
                     15             16           1
                     16             32          16
                     32             48          16
AES256                1             16          15
                      7             16           9
                      8             16           8
                     15             16           1
                     16             32          16
                     32             48          16
DES                   1              8           7
                      7              8           1
                      8             16           8
```

```
                    15                 16              1
                    16                 24              8
                    32                 40              8
DES3                 1                  8              7
                     7                  8              1
                     8                 16              8
                    15                 16              1
                    16                 24              8
                    32                 40              8
RC4                  1                  1              0
                     7                  7              0
                     8                  8              0
                    15                 15              0
                    16                 16              0
                    32                 32              0
```

The output shows for the AES algorithm, data up to 15 bytes will be padded to 16 bytes. The 1-byte string was padded with 15 bytes, and the 15-byte string was padded with 1 byte. This is consistent with each 16-byte block size—a 32-byte string is padded to 48 bytes.

For DES, the same is true except the block size is 8 and not 16. All data smaller than 8 bytes will be padded up to 8 bytes. Data of 8–15 bytes will be padded to 16 bytes, and so on.

The striking exception is the RC4 algorithm. RC4 is not a block cipher, but a stream cipher. This means the data is encrypted for each byte, and the bytes don't have to be collected into blocks of 8 or 16 for the encryption process.

Hashing

Hashing is the process of taking plaintext data and running it through a "hash" function, which converts it to a fixed-length encrypted-like value. Hashing differs from encryption in that it is a unidirectional process. The output is called the hash and it's indistinguishable from its original input form. The hash property is that once the data has been hashed, it can't be returned to its original form. There is no unhash function. Encrypted data, on the contrary, can be decrypted. The other important principle to performing a hash operation is that the resulting hash yields no information about the original data.

When you look at the results of hashing data, it looks very much like encrypted data. It's completely undecipherable:

```
sec_mgr@KNOX10g> COL "Hashed Data" format a30
sec_mgr@KNOX10g> COL "Encrypted Data" format a30
sec_mgr@KNOX10g> SELECT data_crypto.hash ('Data')
  2                                     "Hashed Data",
  3          data_crypto.encrypt ('Data', 'k')
  4                                  "Encrypted Data"
  5     FROM DUAL;

Hashed Data                    Encrypted Data
------------------------------ ------------------------------
ñ?<zMû ;µ-';?                  +¦ÖOY=nçça-§Wz
```

Hashing and encryption are fundamentally different. Like encryption, hashing is popular for storing values that are very sensitive. However, with hashing you can never retrieve the original data. This makes hashing very suitable for some situations and unsuitable for others.

The best example of hashing is in securing passwords. Passwords, in almost all cases, are hashed and not encrypted. To authenticate a person, the password provided by the user is hashed, and the result is compared to the resulting hash that is stored for the user. In this manner, an attacker who acquires the table storing the passwords has practically no chance at recovering the original passwords. If the passwords were encrypted, the attacker would only have to figure out the encryption key and algorithm used to encrypt the passwords to recover the passwords. With a hash-based password algorithm, the only way to get the password is to guess passwords, hash them, and then compare the resulting hash.

DBMS_CRYPTO Hashing

The DBMS_CRYTPO package provides support for MD4, MD5, and SHA-1 hash algorithms. Each hashing algorithm is supported by a PL/SQL function. There is one function that accepts a RAW, one that accepts CLOBs, and one that accepts BLOBs. All three return a RAW data type. The RAW is returned because the hashed output is of fixed size. The hashing algorithms take any arbitrary input size and return a fixed output size (128 bits for MD4 and MD5 and 160 bits for SHA).

The DBMS_CRYPTO hashing functions are also wrapped by functions in the DATA_CRYPTO package. The default algorithm is set to SHA. The return types are RAW for the HASH2RAW function and VARCHAR2 for the HASH function. It doesn't make sense to store the hashed CLOB data in a CLOB column, nor to store the hashed BLOBs in a BLOB column because the hashed values are extremely small (20 bytes at most).

Hashing Algorithms

The DATA_CRYPTO package supports all three algorithms the DBMS_CRYPTO supports. Functions are provided so the algorithm may be called within a SQL statement:

```
  g_md4         CONSTANT PLS_INTEGER       := dbms_crypto.hash_md4;
  g_md5         CONSTANT PLS_INTEGER       := dbms_crypto.hash_md5;
  g_sha         CONSTANT PLS_INTEGER       := dbms_crypto.hash_sh1;

  FUNCTION md4
    RETURN PLS_INTEGER
  AS
  BEGIN
    RETURN g_md4;
  END;
...
```

To test the hashing, a table is created that contains a user and their password. The initial password is the InitCap of the user's name (this is a bad practice and is done here for illustrative purposes only). For user SCOTT, the password will be "Scott."

```
sec_mgr@KNOX10g> DROP TABLE people;

Table dropped.
```

```
sec_mgr@KNOX10g> CREATE TABLE people
    (ename VARCHAR2(12),
     password VARCHAR2(30));

Table created.

sec_mgr@KNOX10g> INSERT INTO people
      SELECT ename, INITCAP (ename)
        FROM scott.emp;

14 rows created.

sec_mgr@KNOX10g> UPDATE people
       SET PASSWORD = data_crypto.HASH (PASSWORD);

14 rows updated.

sec_mgr@KNOX10g> COL password format a40
sec_mgr@KNOX10g> SELECT ename, utl_raw.cast_to_raw(PASSWORD) password
      FROM people
     WHERE ROWNUM <= 3;

ENAME        PASSWORD
------------ ----------------------------------------
SMITH        96BCF8C98F94B6ACE4A4B716CF0E3B32743A08B1
ALLEN        CEF92E8D1C84BBAA35CE6FB2942B26BC98D92C2C
WARD         31D20079CB16C9DF490A8337CD142C5D095EEAA5
```

The passwords as stored are unrecoverable; you can't uncompute the values or derive the original value by simply looking at the hash result.

To authenticate a user, you can write a function that computes the hash of the password provided and verifies it with the one stored:

```
CREATE OR REPLACE FUNCTION is_user_auth (
  p_username   IN   VARCHAR2,
  p_password   IN   VARCHAR2
)
  RETURN BOOLEAN
AS
  l_hashed_password   VARCHAR2 (20);
  l_user_is_authed    BOOLEAN       := FALSE;
BEGIN
  FOR rec IN (SELECT PASSWORD
                FROM people
               WHERE UPPER (ename) = UPPER (p_username))
  LOOP
    l_hashed_password := data_crypto.HASH (p_password);

    IF l_hashed_password = rec.PASSWORD
    THEN
```

```
      l_user_is_authed := TRUE;
    END IF;
  END LOOP;

  RETURN l_user_is_authed;
END;
/
```

Testing this function shows how password authentication should be performed. Note that this example assumes a case-sensitive password:

```
sec_mgr@KNOX10g> BEGIN
    IF (is_user_auth ('scott', 'scott'))
    THEN
      DBMS_OUTPUT.put_line ('Scott authenticated with "scott"');
    ELSE
      DBMS_OUTPUT.put_line ('Scott could not authenticate with "scott"');
    END IF;

    IF (is_user_auth ('scott', 'Scott'))
    THEN
      DBMS_OUTPUT.put_line ('Scott authenticated with "Scott"');
    ELSE
      DBMS_OUTPUT.put_line ('Scott could not authenticate with "Scott"');
    END IF;
  END;
  /
Scott could not authenticate with "scott"
Scott authenticated with "Scott"

PL/SQL procedure successfully completed.
```

Message Authentication Codes

Message Authentication Codes (MAC—not to be confused with the Mandatory Access Control (MAC) discussed in the last chapter) expand on hashing algorithms by adding a secret key. The key is used in computing the hash, and the same key is required to verify the hash. Often this process is referred to as hashed message authentication codes or HMAC.

DBMS_CRYPTO supports the RFC 2104 standard for HMAC. The two algorithms supported for this are based on the MD5 and SHA algorithms. These are distinguished from the base hash functions with a "hmac" prefix. You can see this in the assignment of the DATA_CRYPTO HMAC package variables:

```
  g_hmac_md5  CONSTANT PLS_INTEGER      := dbms_crypto.hmac_md5;
  g_hmac_sha  CONSTANT PLS_INTEGER      := dbms_crypto.hmac_sh1;
```

The problem with the standard hashing is that an attacker could predict, guess, or assume the basic hashing algorithm used to compute the hash. In the preceding, an attacker could perform an offline attack on the password fields by simply doing what you did—calculate the hash given the standard data input.

If you use a MAC, the attacker would also have to know the key used to compute the HMAC. In this manner, the hash is secured by the key the same way encrypted data is:

```
sec_mgr@KNOX10g> UPDATE people
       SET PASSWORD = INITCAP (ename);

14 rows updated.

sec_mgr@KNOX10g> -- compute HMAC using key
sec_mgr@KNOX10g> UPDATE people
       SET PASSWORD =
                   data_crypto.mac (PASSWORD, 'MAC Password Key');

14 rows updated.

sec_mgr@KNOX10g> SELECT ename, UTL_RAW.cast_to_raw (PASSWORD) PASSWORD
      FROM people
     WHERE ROWNUM <= 3;

ENAME        PASSWORD
------------ ----------------------------------------
SMITH        88E02617F4999A033AE332E5062B198AEF7D7ECC
ALLEN        377B8B51C15D57216C5A57945F86D5009F9E22DA
WARD         A838B3ABAFF605FD1B6CCCF71325DC7F9CBE4898
```

If you try to authenticate SCOTT now using your old function, you get a false reading:

```
sec_mgr@KNOX10g> BEGIN
      IF (is_user_auth ('scott', 'Scott'))
      THEN
        DBMS_OUTPUT.put_line ('Scott authenticated with "Scott"');
      ELSE
        DBMS_OUTPUT.put_line ('Scott could not authenticate with "Scott"');
      END IF;
    END;
    /
Scott could not authenticate with "Scott"
```

To authenticate now, the authentication function has to be modified to include the key to the HMAC function:

```
sec_mgr@KNOX10g> CREATE OR REPLACE FUNCTION is_user_auth (
      p_username  IN  VARCHAR2,
      p_password  IN  VARCHAR2
    )
      RETURN BOOLEAN
    AS
      l_hashed_password  VARCHAR2 (20);
      l_user_is_authed   BOOLEAN       := FALSE;
    BEGIN
```

```
    FOR rec IN (SELECT PASSWORD
                  FROM people
                 WHERE UPPER (ename) = UPPER (p_username))
    LOOP
      l_hashed_password := data_crypto.mac (p_password,
                                            'MAC Password Key');

      IF l_hashed_password = rec.PASSWORD
      THEN
        l_user_is_authed := TRUE;
      END IF;
    END LOOP;

    RETURN l_user_is_authed;
  END;
  /

Function created.

sec_mgr@KNOX10g> BEGIN
    IF (is_user_auth ('scott', 'Scott'))
    THEN
      DBMS_OUTPUT.put_line ('Scott authenticated with "Scott"');
    ELSE
      DBMS_OUTPUT.put_line ('Scott could not authenticate with "Scott"');
    END IF;
  END;
  /
Scott authenticated with "Scott"

PL/SQL procedure successfully completed.
```

As with encryption, the success in implementing HMAC is in keeping the key a secret. Exposing the key reduces the HMAC to a simple hashing function. This does not imply that hashing by itself is not sufficient or secure. This merely points out that HMAC can provide more security if an attacker can determine the hashing algorithm and has access to the hashed results because the attacker must then also obtain the key.

Performance

Encryption is a classic security versus performance dual. Encrypting and decrypting within software can be particularly challenging because the crypto processes are very CPU intensive. Most implementations that require high volumes of encryption and decryption use specialized hardware to achieve the acceptable performance.

Within the database, you can look at encryption performance overall, but every situation will be different in the real world. My personal experiences have shown that the Oracle Database encryption performance characteristics make it a suitable and effective solution.

The following example represents the summarization of a few performance tests run with the DBMS_CRYPTO package. The tests try to isolate the actual encryption and decryption processes. Admittedly, the results were different and better than I predicted. Undoubtedly, your results will vary.

Two basic test types were run. The first was a loop test that encrypted (or decrypted) 20 bytes of data. The loop size was 1,000,000. This test measured how fast the database could encrypt or decrypt 20 bytes of data 1,000,000 times. To try and isolate the encryption process from the PL/SQL looping time, I first timed how long a basic PL/SQL loop would take. The following code illustrates how I captured the clock time and CPU time for this process:

```
sec_mgr@KNOX10g> SET feedback off
sec_mgr@KNOX10g> SET verify off
sec_mgr@KNOX10g> SET timing off
sec_mgr@KNOX10g> SET sqlprompt 'sql> '
sql> COL "CPU Start Value" new_val cpu_start
sql> COL name format a25
sql>
sql> -- Define a variable to hold size of for loop
sql> VAR loop_size number;
sql> -- Set loop size to one million
sql> BEGIN
  2    :loop_size := 1000000;
  3  END;
  4  /
sql> /*****  PL/SQL function in loop  *******/
sql> @pl_loop.sql
sql> --- Create sample PL/SQL function
sql> CREATE OR REPLACE FUNCTION do_nothing
  2    RETURN RAW
  3  AS
  4  BEGIN
  5    RETURN NULL;
  6  END;
  7  /
sql>
sql> -- Test time to loop calling a PL/SQL function
sql> @cpu_start
sql> SELECT b.VALUE "CPU Start Value"
  2    FROM v$statname a, v$mystat b
  3   WHERE a.statistic# = b.statistic#
  4     AND a.NAME = 'CPU used by this session';

CPU Start Value
---------------
              3
sql> DECLARE
  2    l_data  RAW (40);
  3    l_start_time     NUMBER;
  4    l_end_time       NUMBER;
  5  BEGIN
  6    l_start_time := DBMS_UTILITY.get_time;
  7    FOR i IN 1 .. :loop_size
  8    LOOP
  9      l_data := do_nothing;
```

```
     END LOOP;
     l_end_time := DBMS_UTILITY.get_time;
     DBMS_OUTPUT.put_line (    'PL/SQL Loop Time: '
                          || (l_end_time - l_start_time) / 100
                          || ' seconds');
   END;
   /
PL/SQL Loop Time: 1.52 seconds
sql> @cpu_stop
sql> SELECT b.VALUE "CPU End Value",
            (b.VALUE - &cpu_start) / 100
                                 "hsecs of CPU Units used"
      FROM v$statname a, v$mystat b
     WHERE a.statistic# = b.statistic#
       AND a.NAME = 'CPU used by this session';

CPU End Value hsecs of CPU Units used
------------- -----------------------
          143                     1.4
sql> /****************  eor  ****************/
```

The PL/SQL loop required 1.52 seconds and consumed 1.4 units of CPU. The code illustrates the basic approach to how all the algorithms were tested. The first encryption test is for the AES encryption with the CBC block chaining and the PKCS5 padding (the Oracle recommended settings and the DATA_CRYPTO default). Note this code also shows how to invoke the DBMS_CRYPTO package directly:

```
sql> /***********  AES encryption  **********/
sql> @aes
sql> @cpu_start
CPU Start Value
---------------
            143
sql> DECLARE
     l_algo       PLS_INTEGER
       :=    dbms_crypto.encrypt_aes
          + dbms_crypto.chain_cbc
          + dbms_crypto.pad_pkcs5;
     l_key        RAW (16)
          := UTL_RAW.cast_to_raw ('0123456789012345');
     l_data       RAW (20)
       := UTL_RAW.cast_to_raw ('01234567890123456789');
     l_enc_data  RAW (40);
     l_start_time     NUMBER;
     l_end_time       NUMBER;
   BEGIN
     l_start_time := DBMS_UTILITY.get_time;
     FOR i IN 1 .. :loop_size
     LOOP
       l_enc_data :=
```

```
          dbms_crypto.encrypt (l_data, l_algo, l_key);
      END LOOP;
      l_end_time := DBMS_UTILITY.get_time;
      DBMS_OUTPUT.put_line (    'AES Encryption Time: '
                             || (l_end_time - l_start_time) / 100
                             || ' seconds');
    END;
    /
AES Encryption Time: 18 seconds
sql> @cpu_stop
CPU End Value hsecs of CPU Units used
------------- -----------------------
         1793                    16.5
sql> /**************** eor ****************/
```

If you subtract the PL/SQL loop time, the database is encrypting 20 bytes of data 1,000,000 times in 16.5 seconds. I ran an AES decryption process, too. The following summarizes the results for the remaining algorithms, with block modifiers and padding:

```
AES Decryption Time: 18.68 seconds
17.21 hsecs of CPU Units used

DES Encryption Time: 19.04 seconds
17.18 hsecs of CPU Units used

Triple DES, 2 Key Encryption Time: 22.01 seconds
20.11 hsecs of CPU Units used

Triple DES, 3 keys Encryption Time: 22.6 seconds
20.72 hsecs of CPU Units used

AES 192-bit key Encryption Time: 18.33 seconds
16.56 hsecs of CPU Units used

AES 256-bit key Encryption Time: 19.76 seconds
17.43 hsecs of CPU Units used

RC4 Encryption Time: 23.02 seconds
21.11 hsecs of CPU Units used

AES with CFB modifier Encryption Time: 18.01 seconds
16.44 hsecs of CPU Units used

AES with CFB modifier Encryption Time: 17.47 seconds
15.96 hsecs of CPU Units used

AES with OFB modifier Encryption Time: 17.63 seconds
16.13 hsecs of CPU Units used

AES Encrypt: Pad Zeros
Time: 17.89 seconds
```

```
16.4 hsecs of CPU Units used

AES Encrypt: Pad ORCL
Time: 18.13 seconds
16.49 hsecs of CPU Units used

AES Encrypt: Pad None
Time: 16.96 seconds
15.56 hsecs of CPU Units used
```

The SQL details and full unaltered results are located in Appendix C.

Key Management

Encryption, as it is traditionally done, possesses a few operating characteristics that do not convey to databases. This is one reason database encryption is difficult—it is unlike most traditional uses of encryption.

Encryption generally has two participants: the sender of the data and the receiver of the data, which means that the challenge to key management (the creation, propagation, and destruction of encryption keys) is a two-person, point-to-point problem. (An implicit third person acts as the attacker, but this is immaterial for the discussion.)

For example, if the emperor wants to send his general a message, he has to securely create and deliver the key to the general. This is a person-to-person or point-to-point activity. If the emperor wants to send the same message to ten generals, he will have to create ten separate keys—one for each general. If ten generals want to send messages to each other, there will be a lot of keys being created and passed about.

A database generally allows many users to share and access data with many other users. The notion of personal or private keys is therefore not applicable (or at least not without some added work). For example, it is rare that a user will input data in the database and encrypt it so only they can get access. Instead, they usually want to encrypt the data so that only the authorized recipients can decrypt it. This implies that the data will be encrypted once for each recipient. Many times the recipients are not known to the user when the data is entered.

Another major difference in encryption can be seen by comparing database and network encryption. In network encryption, you have a point-to-point strategy. But the difference goes further. For each network session, a new set of keys is generated. When the session is closed, the keys are destroyed because they are no longer needed. The keys are needed only long enough to pass the data from one point to the other. Saving the keys for future access is not required.

When you encrypt data in the database, the data may have an indeterminate lifetime. This means that you not only have to create and pass the keys to authorized users, but you also need some way to preserve the keys for access into the future.

Don't forget about those DBAs, who have the ability to peer into everything that occurs within the database. Access to the database log files may also provide valuable information to the DBAs. This significantly differs from standard encryption uses in which the administrators may only see and access at most half of the conversation, either the sender or receiver (unless both are within the domain of the administrator).

Ultimately, the success or failure of the encryption for providing added defense lies in the ability to protect the encryption key. Oracle's policy on key management is simple: there are no restrictions in how you want to manage the keys. The decision is completely up to you.

Key Management Options

Oracle recommends several options for key management. I will start off with one that seems the most intuitive: storing the keys in the database.

Storing Keys in the Database

There are several effective ways to store keys in the database. A major benefit to doing this is that the keys are maintained with the data. This may be important from a backup and recovery perspective because the keys and the data need to be maintained to a consistent point in time.

The approach I prefer is not to simply store the keys in a table; this is not adequate. You have to protect this table with multiple techniques. Access should be limited and potentially protected with a secure application role. The rows should be protected by VPD and OLS. Auditing access to the key table will help to ensure that unauthorized yet privileged users are not querying the table. Encrypting the encryption keys with a master key is also an effective way to protect the table in the event someone does gain access to the table.

Here is an example of how to store the keys in an auxiliary table. You'll need a table to hold the keys and the relationship of the key to the record which it was used. The table name (KM for key management) and column names are somewhat obscure. This is done intentionally to prevent data dictionary snooping from divulging the use of the table (`SELECT owner, table_name, column_name FROM dba_tab_cols WHERE column_name LIKE '%KEY%'`). Obscuring this relationship is also helpful in protecting the data.

```
CREATE TABLE km
(pk VARCHAR2(30),
ek  RAW(48));
```

For the sample data table, encrypt the salaries from the PEOPLE table by re-creating the PEOPLE table based on the EMP table.

```
sec_mgr@KNOX10g> CREATE TABLE people
  2  (NAME VARCHAR2(30),
  3  salary VARCHAR2(16));

Table created.

sec_mgr@KNOX10g> INSERT INTO people
  2     SELECT ename, sal
  3       FROM scott.emp;

14 rows created.
```

Next, create a PL/SQL encryption handler for this table. Its job is to encrypt the data with a secret key. It creates the key, stores the key, and fetches the key automatically. A parameter has to be passed to unlock the encryption and decryption functions, which prevents someone with the EXECUTE ANY PROCEDURE privilege from decrypting the values.

```
CREATE OR REPLACE PACKAGE enc_people
AS
  FUNCTION enc_salary (
```

```
    p_salary       IN   VARCHAR2,
    p_name         IN   VARCHAR2,
    p_unlock_code  IN   VARCHAR2 DEFAULT NULL)
    RETURN VARCHAR2;

  FUNCTION dec_salary (
    p_salary       IN   VARCHAR2,
    p_name         IN   VARCHAR2,
    p_unlock_code  IN   VARCHAR2 DEFAULT NULL)
    RETURN VARCHAR2;
END;
/

CREATE OR REPLACE PACKAGE BODY enc_people
AS
  -- master encryption key. This package has to be wrapped
  -- with the 10g wrap. Otherwise key will be visisble.
  g_master_key    VARCHAR2 (32)
                          := 'ThisIsTheSuperSecretMasterKey';
  -- code provided to unlock the encrypt and decrypt operations
  g_unlock_code  VARCHAR2 (10) := 'OpenSesame';
```

To create the key, develop a function that generates a pseudorandom string. Due to a bug in the initial release of the DBMS_CRYPTO, the random key generation has to rely on the old DBMS_OBFUSCATION_TOOLKIT. You'll need to execute on DBMS_OBFUSCATION_TOOLKIT for this implementation.

```
  FUNCTION create_key (p_seed IN VARCHAR2 DEFAULT NULL)
    RETURN VARCHAR2
  -- return a  pseudo-random 32-byte string
  AS
    l_key    VARCHAR2 (32);
    l_seed   VARCHAR2 (80)
               := NVL (p_seed, DBMS_RANDOM.STRING ('p', 80));
  BEGIN
    l_key :=
         DBMS_OBFUSCATION_TOOLKIT.des3getkey
                                       (which           => 1,
                                        seed_string     => l_seed)
      || DBMS_OBFUSCATION_TOOLKIT.desgetkey
                                        (seed_string     => l_seed);
    RETURN l_key;
  END;
```

The encryption keys will be different for each record, and they will be stored in an encrypted form using a master key. This prevents someone from successfully decrypting the data even if they obtain the keys from our stored table (for example, someone with the SELECT ANY TABLE privilege might try this).

```
FUNCTION enc_salary (
  p_salary       IN  VARCHAR2,
  p_name         IN  VARCHAR2,
  p_unlock_code  IN  VARCHAR2 DEFAULT NULL)
  RETURN VARCHAR2
AS
  l_key         RAW (32);
  l_stored_key  RAW (48);
BEGIN
  IF (   p_unlock_code IS NULL
      OR p_unlock_code != g_unlock_code)
  THEN
    RETURN NULL;
  END IF;

  data_crypto.set_algorithm (data_crypto.aes);
  -- create a key and size it for algorithm
  l_key := data_crypto.getkey (create_key);
  -- encrypt key with master
  l_stored_key :=
    data_crypto.encryptraw (l_key,
                            g_master_key,
                            data_crypto.aes256);
  -- store relationship between key and primary key
  INSERT INTO km
       VALUES (p_name, l_stored_key);
  -- return resulting encrypted data
  RETURN data_crypto.encrypt (p_salary, l_key);
END;
```

To decrypt the data, the user or application must provide the unlock code.

```
FUNCTION dec_salary (
  p_salary       IN  VARCHAR2,
  p_name         IN  VARCHAR2,
  p_unlock_code  IN  VARCHAR2 DEFAULT NULL)
  RETURN VARCHAR2
AS
  l_key  RAW (48);
BEGIN
  IF (   p_unlock_code IS NULL
      OR p_unlock_code != g_unlock_code)
  THEN
    RETURN NULL;
  END IF;

  SELECT data_crypto.decryptraw (ek,
                                 g_master_key,
                                 data_crypto.aes256)
    INTO l_key
    FROM km
   WHERE pk = p_name;
```

```
      RETURN data_crypto.decrypt (p_salary,
                                  l_key,
                                  data_crypto.aes);
    END;
  END;
  /
```

To test this, issue a SQL update statement to encrypt all the salaries. The unlock code has to be provided to ensure an authorized user or application is calling the function.

```
sec_mgr@KNOX10g> UPDATE people
  2       SET salary =
  3              enc_people.enc_salary (salary, NAME, 'OpenSesame');

14 rows updated.

sec_mgr@KNOX10g> COMMIT ;

Commit complete.

sec_mgr@KNOX10g> COL salary format a16
sec_mgr@KNOX10g> SELECT NAME, salary
  2     FROM people
  3    WHERE ROWNUM <= 3;

NAME                           SALARY
------------------------------ ----------------
SMITH                          ¯3++9?+|íá¡¦)
ALLEN                          W¦8?'j¦¦±$?+¦Qû
WARD                           &¦¦¿@ÿxNg¦d¶O
```

You can decrypt by executing the decrypt function in the package. Note the unlock code has to be provided here. Also, a user simply trying to decrypt the records using the key stored in the KM table is unsuccessful since these keys have also been encrypted. Notice the encryption keys also were encrypted with a different and stronger algorithm (AES256) than was the data (AES128).

```
sec_mgr@KNOX10g> -- data has to be decrypted this way.
sec_mgr@KNOX10g> SELECT NAME,
  2          enc_people.dec_salary (salary, NAME, 'OpenSesame')
  3                                                            salary
  4     FROM people
  5    WHERE ROWNUM <= 3;

NAME                           SALARY
------------------------------ ----------------
SMITH                          800
ALLEN                          1600
WARD                           1250
```

```
sec_mgr@KNOX10g> -- cannot decrypt without code. code is also case-sensitive
sec_mgr@KNOX10g> SELECT NAME,
             enc_people.dec_salary (salary, NAME, 'OPENSESAME')
                                                           salary
        FROM people
       WHERE ROWNUM <= 3;

NAME                           SALARY
------------------------------ ----------------
SMITH
ALLEN
WARD

sec_mgr@KNOX10g> -- p_unlock_code is default NULL'ed
sec_mgr@KNOX10g> SELECT NAME, enc_people.dec_salary (salary, NAME) salary
        FROM people
       WHERE ROWNUM <= 3;

NAME                           SALARY
------------------------------ ----------------
SMITH
ALLEN
WARD

sec_mgr@KNOX10g> -- note we cannot decrypt without this function
sec_mgr@KNOX10g> DECLARE
        l_key  RAW (48);
      BEGIN
        SELECT ek
          INTO l_key
          FROM km
         WHERE pk = 'SCOTT';

        FOR rec IN (SELECT *
                      FROM people
                     WHERE NAME = 'SCOTT')
        LOOP
          DBMS_OUTPUT.put_line (   'Scott''s Salary: '
                                || data_crypto.decrypt
                                                  (rec.salary,
                                                   l_key));
        END LOOP;
      END;
      /
DECLARE
*
ERROR at line 1:
ORA-28817: PL/SQL function returned an error.
ORA-06512: at "SYS.DBMS_CRYPTO_FFI", line 67
ORA-06512: at "SYS.DBMS_CRYPTO", line 41
```

```
ORA-06512: at "SEC_MGR.DATA_CRYPTO", line 319
ORA-06512: at "SEC_MGR.DATA_CRYPTO", line 355
ORA-06512: at line 13
```

This last line shows the error that is thrown when an incorrect key is supplied to the decryption algorithm. This example should be used to help motivate ideas for you to employ in storing the encryption keys in the database. This approach doesn't guarantee that the keys are absolutely secured from the DBAs.

Application Managed Keys

The challenge of database stored keys is there is a substantial risk that the data can be discovered by a skilled and determined DBA. An alternate solution to this is to have the application manage the keys. With this, the key is only passed to the encryption and decryption programs. Anyone with full access to the database will be unable to recover the keys.

A similar approach to that used with the database stored keys can be taken. The application can store the keys in a file on the application server. This file should be encrypted with a master application key.

An important part to key management is ensuring the keys are always available to unlock the data. Therefore, a strategy should be developed to ensure the application managed keys are securely stored and backed up. If the keys are lost, the data is lost.

Computed Keys

You saw in many of the examples that an effective way to manage the keys is to *not* actually store the keys. The keys can be deterministically computed. That is, a function can return the key for the record based on a secure algorithm.

This approach is analogous to using a combination lock versus a keyed lock. The secret to a combination lock is in knowing the combination. If the algorithm is protected, then the keys are protected. Therefore, any procedures in the database should be wrapped to prevent privileged users from uncovering the secure algorithm.

This technique is attractive because it may involve the least amount of auxiliary work. For example, you could BIT_XOR the primary key with the schema name and instance name of the database server. This would encrypt the data and ensure that it is protected for this database instance and schema; thus, exporting to a different database or schema would not be allowed. Looking at the encryption procedure signature, it would not be obvious how the key is computed, only that the primary key was one of the components:

```
CREATE OR REPLACE FUNCTION enc_some_data (
  p_data   IN   VARCHAR2 DEFAULT NULL,
  p_key     IN   VARCHAR2 DEFAULT NULL)
  RETURN VARCHAR2
AS
  l_key         RAW (64);
  l_other_val   RAW (64);
BEGIN
  l_other_val :=
    UTL_RAW.cast_to_raw (    SYS_CONTEXT ('userenv',
                                          'instance_name')
                          || SYS_CONTEXT ('userenv',
```

```
                                                    'current_schema'));
  l_key :=
    UTL_RAW.bit_xor (UTL_RAW.cast_to_raw (p_key),
                     l_other_val);
  RETURN data_crypto.encrypt
                              (p_data,
                               UTL_RAW.cast_to_varchar2 (l_key));
END;
/

CREATE OR REPLACE FUNCTION dec_some_data (
  p_data   IN  VARCHAR2 DEFAULT NULL,
  p_key     IN  VARCHAR2 DEFAULT NULL)
  RETURN VARCHAR2
AS
  l_key          RAW (64);
  l_other_val   RAW (64);
BEGIN
  l_other_val :=
    UTL_RAW.cast_to_raw (    SYS_CONTEXT ('userenv',
                                          'instance_name')
                          || SYS_CONTEXT ('userenv',
                                          'current_schema'));
  l_key :=
    UTL_RAW.bit_xor (UTL_RAW.cast_to_raw (p_key),
                     l_other_val);
  RETURN data_crypto.decrypt
                              (p_data,
                               UTL_RAW.cast_to_varchar2 (l_key));
END;
/
```

You could even use the application's IP address as a component to the key. This would make the encrypted data only available to the application coming from the same IP address.

Protecting the Key Procedures

The secret to the database stored keys and computationally derived keys is in protecting the source. Wrapping the PL/SQL code is mandatory. If this isn't done, there is a risk that the code will be analyzed, the algorithm will be figured out, and hidden keys will be discovered.

You can wrap the ENC_SALARY and DEC_SALARY functions by saving the code to a file called enc_some_data.sql. Then you execute the wrap program and load the resulting .PLB file:

```
C:\tmp>wrap iname=enc_salary.sql

PL/SQL Wrapper: Release 10.1.0.2.0- Production on Thu Feb 26 17:42:26 2004

Copyright (c) 1993, 2004, Oracle.  All rights reserved.

Processing enc_some_data.sql to enc_some_data.plb
```

In SQL*Plus, you can load the PLB file. Querying the source shows that your algorithm is secure from prying eyes:

```
sec_mgr@KNOX10g> @enc_some_data.plb

Function created.

Function created.

sec_mgr@KNOX10g> SELECT   text
  2       FROM user_source
  3      WHERE NAME = 'ENC_SOME_DATA'
  4   ORDER BY line;

TEXT
---------------------------------------------------------------------------
FUNCTION enc_some_data wrapped
a000000
b2
abcd
abcd
abcd
abcd
abcd
abcd
abcd
abcd
abcd
abcd
abcd
abcd
abcd
abcd
abcd
8
287 185
/UgrsuAFkDp50zTPJiyOpAhbxm0wgzsJLUgVfC/NbmRTYkpGBOXlhMxbhnXTPQ33EGuRe+nM
Gp/KHTfcz895hPMYFvVNsOvt/s/+uUgrJzcCs8oNyhcZFEN2rUs2cFLna1CmDEiVbgUShUNf
nJ41nPLwZilcK6bqVFgXk/RjPUl67v9JPdAhetmaNwAikbfnBG4MDAzi/zcmzz7Spj8j3KxF
oulBV29oqGtrFptC6q3TYIxxqEv1scQTYfjygL3kgWNPTJ07mOhj4ofE3jOYwJ21ByfXSIYq
uvwT0J9MsDFSdjjcHbDr4d4BVkttPIYrwtmNctQfnSS5G4rsRjtvEdT5b+a4DVKfV9D9uUBV
kNFG6eqvDnc6Xbn9viT32A==
```

To maintain security, you should encrypt all package bodies, procedures, and functions that perform your key management. Because views and trigger code cannot be wrapped, they should be modified to call the wrapped code procedures passing any parameters (for example, :NEW and :OLD) as needed.

The Best Key Management Strategy

To answer the question on how to manage keys, one has to first ask what you are using encryption to protect against. For example, if you are using encryption to hide data from the DBAs (which is probably not even possible), then storing the keys in the database is *not* the safest approach. If you are encrypting to reduce risks associated with physical server theft, storing the keys on the server's file system is not a good idea.

The most secure technique uses a combination of methods. For example, an application could set a value in an application context. The encryption and decryption procedures could use this value in combination with a stored key (perhaps XORed as in the preceding code) to derive the key. Using sophisticated key management makes the solution more secure, but it can also be difficult to manage and maintain. There is no single best solution for key management. The pros and cons of the approach should be evaluated. Performance, maintainability, and recoverability are all important to consider along with the security.

Summary

Database encryption differs from most other uses of encryption due to the nature of databases and database applications. Understanding why you are encrypting the data is important to ensuring that you are doing it properly. There are several important issues with database encryption. Understanding how to store the data is important for recovery and for making the data accessible to different databases. The encryption and decryption process can be made relatively transparent using a combination of views and table triggers.

Performance is the competing factor with encryption. This is especially true for software-based encryption. Selectively encrypting the data helps to ensure performance is maintained while still providing element-level protection for the most sensitive data. Data in its encrypted state is unusable. Careful attention has to be paid to understand how to design the data structures to allow for successful and high performing queries while also maintaining encryption.

Ultimately, the security of the encryption relies on how effectively the keys are managed. There are several options to key management. You saw how to securely store the keys in the database. Deriving the keys or having the application manage the keys are also very practical solutions. Combining several techniques will provide the safest key management implementation. In practically every case, wrapping the PL/SQL code provides added security that the key, algorithm, or both will not be discovered.

In many cases, the requirement for encrypting database data is to hide the data from the DBAs. This will be difficult—if not impossible—for the very skilled and determined DBAs. However, it is possible to make the job extremely challenging. As pointed out in the beginning of the book, effective security is about risk management, not risk avoidance. Database encryption can be effective in providing another layer of security for the database data.

PART V

Appendixes

APPENDIX A

Setting Up the Security Manager

Separation of duty is an important security principle. It means that different users will perform different actions. The objective is to create and manage users and assign privileges in a way that maximizes security. The least privilege principle serves as a guide. For this book, the SEC_MGR user performs most of the security-related administration tasks. This appendix lists the privileges given to the SEC_MGR user to fulfill the mission of security manager for the examples given herein.

The privileges are granted directly to the user. This is done to allow the user to create procedures using the default definer rights model. In the definer rights model, roles are disabled. The SEC_MGR was created originally with only the CREATE SESSION privilege. Privileges were added as needed on a case-by-case basis. No default roles—DBA, RESOURCE, and CONNECT—were ever granted. This ensures that the only privileges granted were the ones needed to perform a specific action. This is the least privilege principle and it should serve as a guide for you in creating administrators for your databases.

This schema isn't meant to serve as the template for your database security administrators. These privileges are shown here to allow you to follow along with the examples. The privileges for the examples used throughout the book could have been granted when the examples were presented, which would have ensured that any example could be run as is (autonomously). However, doing so was both a distraction to the example and redundant because many of the same privileges were needed for many different examples.

Many of the grants have to be made from SYS since the objects are dictionary protected objects. Comments are provided whenever possible to explain when and where the privileges are referenced.

```
-- connect as SYS to run this script
CONN sys/oracle as sysdba

/***  Create the Security Manager ***/
-- Create the security manager. Password is simple.
-- CHANGE this password for a production environment.
CREATE USER sec_mgr IDENTIFIED BY oracle10g
  DEFAULT TABLESPACE users
  TEMPORARY TABLESPACE temp;
-- Grant privileges to place data in the tablespace.
-- This is necessary for creating tables.
ALTER USER sec_mgr
    QUOTA UNLIMITED
    ON "USERS";
-- Privilege to log on to the database.
-- ADMIN given to allow sec_mgr to grant priv to others.
GRANT CREATE SESSION TO sec_mgr WITH ADMIN OPTION;
-- Privilege to change database session
GRANT ALTER SESSION TO sec_mgr;

/***        Base Privileges        ***/
-- The following grants form the basis of the privileges
-- needed for performing many of the examples.
GRANT CREATE PROCEDURE TO sec_mgr;
```

```
GRANT CREATE TABLE TO sec_mgr;
GRANT CREATE VIEW TO sec_mgr;
GRANT CREATE TYPE TO sec_mgr;
GRANT CREATE TRIGGER TO sec_mgr;
GRANT CREATE OPERATOR TO sec_mgr;
GRANT CREATE SEQUENCE TO sec_mgr;

/***        User Management        ***/
-- Privileges to create and manage users.
GRANT CREATE USER TO sec_mgr;
GRANT ALTER USER TO sec_mgr;
GRANT DROP USER TO sec_mgr;
-- Privilege to inspect user passwords
GRANT SELECT ON dba_users TO sec_mgr;
-- Privilege to inspect proxy users
GRANT SELECT ON proxy_users TO sec_mgr;

/***        Role Privileges        ***/
-- Role administration privileges
GRANT CREATE ROLE TO sec_mgr;
GRANT ALTER ANY ROLE TO sec_mgr;
GRANT GRANT ANY ROLE TO sec_mgr;
GRANT DROP ANY ROLE TO sec_mgr;
-- Privileges to inspect and validate role privileges.
GRANT SELECT ON SYS.dba_role_privs TO sec_mgr;
GRANT SELECT ON SYS.role_role_privs TO sec_mgr;

/*** Privileges for misc examples ***/
-- Privileges to manage synonyms
GRANT CREATE SYNONYM TO sec_mgr;
GRANT CREATE PUBLIC SYNONYM TO sec_mgr;
GRANT DROP PUBLIC SYNONYM TO sec_mgr;
GRANT CREATE DATABASE LINK TO sec_mgr;
-- Privilege to create a database logon trigger
GRANT ADMINISTER DATABASE TRIGGER TO sec_mgr;
GRANT CREATE ANY TRIGGER TO sec_mgr;
-- Privileges to create security profiles
GRANT CREATE PROFILE TO sec_mgr;
GRANT DROP PROFILE TO sec_mgr;
-- Privilege to query database initialization parameters
GRANT SELECT ON v_$parameter TO sec_mgr;

/***    Chapter specific examples ***/
-- Used to create all_user_Priv_path in Chapter 7
GRANT SELECT ON sysauth$ TO sec_mgr WITH GRANT OPTION;
GRANT SELECT ON user$ TO sec_mgr WITH GRANT OPTION;
GRANT SELECT ON dba_tab_privs TO sec_mgr WITH GRANT OPTION;
GRANT SELECT ON dba_sys_privs TO sec_mgr WITH GRANT OPTION;
GRANT SELECT ON v_$process TO sec_mgr WITH GRANT OPTION;
GRANT SELECT ON v_$session TO sec_mgr WITH GRANT OPTION;
```

```
GRANT SELECT ON v_$parameter TO sec_mgr WITH GRANT OPTION;
GRANT SELECT ON v_$thread TO sec_mgr WITH GRANT OPTION;
GRANT SELECT ON v_$mystat TO sec_mgr WITH GRANT OPTION;
GRANT SELECT ON v_$statname TO sec_mgr;

/***       Audit Privileges       ***/
GRANT AUDIT ANY TO sec_mgr;
GRANT AUDIT SYSTEM TO sec_mgr;
GRANT SELECT ON dba_common_audit_trail TO sec_mgr;
GRANT SELECT ON dba_obj_audit_opts TO sec_mgr;
GRANT SELECT ON dba_priv_audit_opts TO sec_mgr;
GRANT SELECT ON dba_stmt_audit_opts TO sec_mgr;
-- Privilege to establish Fine-Grained Auditing
GRANT EXECUTE ON DBMS_FGA TO sec_mgr;
-- Flashback privileges used in auditing chapter.
GRANT SELECT ON flashback_transaction_query TO sec_mgr;
GRANT FLASHBACK ANY TABLE to sec_mgr;

/***       FGAC Privileges        ***/
-- Privileges to create and delete application context
GRANT CREATE ANY CONTEXT TO sec_mgr;
GRANT DROP ANY CONTEXT TO sec_mgr;
GRANT SELECT ON dba_context TO sec_mgr;
-- Privilege to establish VPD policies
GRANT EXECUTE ON DBMS_RLS TO sec_mgr;
-- Inspect VPD policies
GRANT SELECT ON dba_policies TO sec_mgr;
-- Use SLEEP procedure in a VPD caching example
GRANT EXECUTE ON DBMS_LOCK TO sec_mgr;

/***   Encryption Privileges      ***/
-- Execute privileges for the encryption package: Ch. 13
GRANT EXECUTE ON dbms_crypto TO sec_mgr;
```

APPENDIX B

DATA_CRYPTO Package

The DBMS_CRYPTO package provides a comprehensive set of procedures and functions that will allow you to encrypt and decrypt data in the confines of the database. For most of the basic data types, such as VARCHAR2, dates, and numbers, you'll have to convert the data to a RAW prior to invoking the DBMS_CRYPTO package. CLOB and BLOB encryption is natively supported but only through procedures. Also, the encryption key used must be a RAW and has to be the appropriate size for the encryption algorithm you'll be using.

These are facts and not criticisms. The DBMS_CRYPTO package is implemented effectively and these requirements are, at most, inconvenient. Chapter 13 discusses relevant issues, such as storing encrypted data and the importance of the encryption key, and gives many examples of how to encrypt and decrypt data.

The DATA_CRYPTO package provided here is meant to serve two purposes. First, it simplifies the encryption and decryption calls by performing the data-type castings and algorithmic-based key sizing. The encryption and decryption programs are administered as functions so they can be called within SQL statements. See Chapter 13 for examples.

The second purpose of DATA_CRYPTO is to serve as a template for implementing your specific encryption/decryption code. The code illustrates how to invoke DBMS_CRYPTO, and it implicitly offers suggestions for helper functions that you might administer. This should allow you to more easily encrypt and decrypt data that is important in supporting the wide-scale use of stored database encryption.

```
CREATE OR REPLACE PACKAGE data_crypto
AS
/* DATA_CRYPTO
 *
 * This package is a utility that invokes procedures and functions in
 * the default DBMS_CRYPTO package. This
 * package provides functions for strings, numbers,
 * dates, CLOB, and BLOBs. Helper functions are also
 * provided. Default encryption is AES 128-bit. Default
 * hash is SHA.
 *
 */

---------------------------------------------------------
--                  Encryption                         --
---------------------------------------------------------

  -- Returns integer value for encryption algorithm
  -- The DES algorithm. Requires 8-byte key.
  FUNCTION des
    RETURN PLS_INTEGER;

  -- Triple DES using 3 distinct keys
  FUNCTION des3
    RETURN PLS_INTEGER;

  -- Triple DES using 2 keys
```

```
FUNCTION des32
  RETURN PLS_INTEGER;

-- AES at 128-bit. Requires 16-byte key
FUNCTION aes
  RETURN PLS_INTEGER;

-- Stronger AES with at 192-bit key length (24-bytes)
FUNCTION aes192
  RETURN PLS_INTEGER;

-- Strongest AES at 256-bit key length (32-bytes)
FUNCTION aes256
  RETURN PLS_INTEGER;

-- Stream Cipher Algorithms
-- Key size is variable.
FUNCTION rc4
  RETURN PLS_INTEGER;

-- Set encryption algorithm
-- Stores value in global package variable
PROCEDURE set_algorithm (p_enc_algorithm IN PLS_INTEGER);

-- return character representation of currently set algorithm
FUNCTION get_algorithm
  RETURN VARCHAR2;

-- Stores key as a global package variable
-- Key is sized based on algorithm passed or globally
-- defined algorithm
PROCEDURE setkey (
  p_key             IN  VARCHAR2,
  p_enc_algorithm   IN  PLS_INTEGER DEFAULT NULL);

-- return RAW key of appropriate size based on algorithm
-- if algorithm is null, the global algorithm will be used.
FUNCTION getkey (
  p_key             IN  VARCHAR2 DEFAULT NULL,
  p_enc_algorithm   IN  PLS_INTEGER DEFAULT NULL)
  RETURN RAW;

-- encrypts VARCHAR2 and return VARCHAR2 data
-- calls encrypt with utl_raw casting
FUNCTION encrypt (
  p_data            IN  VARCHAR2,
  p_key             IN  VARCHAR2 DEFAULT NULL,
  p_enc_algorithm   IN  PLS_INTEGER DEFAULT NULL)
  RETURN VARCHAR2;

-- decrypts VARCHAR2 and return VARCHAR2 data
```

```
FUNCTION decrypt (
  p_data           IN  VARCHAR2,
  p_key            IN  VARCHAR2 DEFAULT NULL,
  p_enc_algorithm  IN  PLS_INTEGER DEFAULT NULL)
  RETURN VARCHAR2;

-- Accept string data and return RAW output
-- RAW output is not interpreted by database
-- and is therefore more suitable for storage
FUNCTION encrypt_char (
  p_data           IN  VARCHAR2,
  p_key            IN  VARCHAR2 DEFAULT NULL,
  p_enc_algorithm  IN  PLS_INTEGER DEFAULT NULL)
  RETURN RAW;

-- Accept RAW data and return as VARCHAR2
-- This is the complimentary function for encrypt_char
FUNCTION decrypt_char (
  p_data           IN  RAW,
  p_key            IN  VARCHAR2 DEFAULT NULL,
  p_enc_algorithm  IN  PLS_INTEGER DEFAULT NULL)
  RETURN VARCHAR2;

-- encrypts number and return raw data
FUNCTION encrypt_number (
  p_data           IN  NUMBER,
  p_key            IN  VARCHAR2 DEFAULT NULL,
  p_enc_algorithm  IN  PLS_INTEGER DEFAULT NULL)
  RETURN RAW;

-- decrypts raw and returns number data
FUNCTION decrypt_number (
  p_data           IN  RAW,
  p_key            IN  VARCHAR2 DEFAULT NULL,
  p_enc_algorithm  IN  PLS_INTEGER DEFAULT NULL)
  RETURN NUMBER;

-- encrypts date and return raw data
FUNCTION encrypt_date (
  p_data           IN  DATE,
  p_key            IN  VARCHAR2 DEFAULT NULL,
  p_enc_algorithm  IN  PLS_INTEGER DEFAULT NULL)
  RETURN RAW;

-- decrypts raw and returns data as date
FUNCTION decrypt_date (
  p_data           IN  RAW,
  p_key            IN  VARCHAR2 DEFAULT NULL,
  p_enc_algorithm  IN  PLS_INTEGER DEFAULT NULL)
  RETURN DATE;

-- encrypts a CLOB and return value as CLOB
```

```
  -- done as function for performing SQL updates
  FUNCTION encrypt (
    p_data            IN  CLOB,
    p_key             IN  VARCHAR2 DEFAULT NULL,
    p_enc_algorithm   IN  PLS_INTEGER DEFAULT NULL)
    RETURN CLOB;

  -- decrypts a CLOB and return value as CLOB
  -- done as function for performing SQL updates
  FUNCTION decrypt (
    p_data            IN  CLOB,
    p_key             IN  VARCHAR2 DEFAULT NULL,
    p_enc_algorithm   IN  PLS_INTEGER DEFAULT NULL)
    RETURN CLOB;

  -- encrypts a BLOB and return value as BLOB
  -- done as function for performing SQL updates
  FUNCTION encrypt (
    p_data            IN  BLOB,
    p_key             IN  VARCHAR2 DEFAULT NULL,
    p_enc_algorithm   IN  PLS_INTEGER DEFAULT NULL)
    RETURN BLOB;

  -- decrypts a BLOB and return value as BLOB
  -- done as function for performing SQL updates
  FUNCTION decrypt (
    p_data            IN  BLOB,
    p_key             IN  VARCHAR2 DEFAULT NULL,
    p_enc_algorithm   IN  PLS_INTEGER DEFAULT NULL)
    RETURN BLOB;

----------------------------------------------------------
--                      HASHING                         --
----------------------------------------------------------

  -- returns integer value for hashing algorithm
  FUNCTION md4
    RETURN PLS_INTEGER;

  FUNCTION md5
    RETURN PLS_INTEGER;

  FUNCTION sha
    RETURN PLS_INTEGER;

  -- sets global hashing algorithm
  PROCEDURE set_hash_algorithm (
    p_hash_algorithm  IN  PLS_INTEGER);

  -- return global hashing algorithm as string
```

```
  FUNCTION get_hash_algorithm
    RETURN VARCHAR2;

  -- Computes hash and return value as RAW
  -- Uses p_hash_algorithm if passed, else
  -- uses the global variable
  FUNCTION hash2raw (
    p_data             IN  VARCHAR2,
    p_hash_algorithm   IN  PLS_INTEGER DEFAULT NULL)
    RETURN RAW;

  -- Computes hash and return value as VARCHAR2
  -- Uses p_hash_algorithm if passed, else
  -- uses the global variable
  FUNCTION HASH (
    p_data             IN  VARCHAR2,
    p_hash_algorithm   IN  PLS_INTEGER DEFAULT NULL)
    RETURN VARCHAR2;

---------------------------------------------------------
--       Hashed Message Authentication Codes           --
---------------------------------------------------------
  -- returns integer value for hashing algorithm
  FUNCTION hmac_md5
    RETURN PLS_INTEGER;

  FUNCTION hmac_sha
    RETURN PLS_INTEGER;

  -- returns string value for current HMAC algorithm
  FUNCTION get_hmac_algorithm
    RETURN VARCHAR2;

  -- Sets global HMAC algorithm to p_hash_algorithm
  PROCEDURE set_hmac_algorithm (
    p_hash_algorithm   IN  PLS_INTEGER);

  -- Computes hashed message authentication code.
  -- Returns value as RAW
  -- Uses p_hash_algorithm if passed, else
  -- uses the global hmac variable
  FUNCTION mac2raw (
    p_data             IN  VARCHAR2,
    p_key              IN  VARCHAR2 DEFAULT NULL,
    p_hash_algorithm   IN  PLS_INTEGER DEFAULT NULL)
    RETURN RAW;

  -- Computes hashed message authentication code.
  -- Returns value as VARCHAR2
  -- Uses p_hash_algorithm if passed, else
```

```
  -- uses the global hmac variable
  FUNCTION mac (
    p_data              IN  VARCHAR2,
    p_key               IN  VARCHAR2 DEFAULT NULL,
    p_hash_algorithm    IN  PLS_INTEGER DEFAULT NULL)
    RETURN VARCHAR2;
END;
/
```

```
CREATE OR REPLACE PACKAGE BODY data_crypto
AS
-----------------------------------------------------------
--   Integer values for encryption algorithms
--   Values are sum of base encryption algorithm,
--   the block modifier, and the padding scheme
-----------------------------------------------------------

  -- 56-bit DES
  g_des        CONSTANT PLS_INTEGER
    :=    dbms_crypto.encrypt_des
       + dbms_crypto.chain_cbc
       + dbms_crypto.pad_pkcs5;
  -- Triple DES using 3 distinct keys
  g_des3       CONSTANT PLS_INTEGER
    :=    dbms_crypto.encrypt_3des_2key
       + dbms_crypto.chain_cbc
       + dbms_crypto.pad_pkcs5;
  -- Triple DES using 2 keys
  g_des32      CONSTANT PLS_INTEGER
    :=    dbms_crypto.encrypt_3des
       + dbms_crypto.chain_cbc
       + dbms_crypto.pad_pkcs5;
  -- AES at 128-bit. Requires 16-byte key
  g_aes        CONSTANT PLS_INTEGER
    :=    dbms_crypto.encrypt_aes
       + dbms_crypto.chain_cbc
       + dbms_crypto.pad_pkcs5;
  -- Stronger AES with at 192-bit key length (24-bytes)
  g_aes192     CONSTANT PLS_INTEGER
    :=    dbms_crypto.encrypt_aes192
       + dbms_crypto.chain_cbc
       + dbms_crypto.pad_pkcs5;
  -- Strongest AES at 256-bit key length (32-bytes)
  g_aes256     CONSTANT PLS_INTEGER
    :=    dbms_crypto.encrypt_aes256
       + dbms_crypto.chain_cbc
       + dbms_crypto.pad_pkcs5;
  -- Stream Cipher Algorithms
```

```
  -- Key size is variable.
  g_rc4        CONSTANT PLS_INTEGER
                                   := dbms_crypto.encrypt_rc4;
  -- define the default encryption algorithm
  -- modify this value to change your defaults
  g_enc_algorithm      PLS_INTEGER      := g_aes;
  -- create a global variable for holding key
  -- RC4 has no key size limit
  g_key                VARCHAR2 (32767);
---------------------------------------------------------
--                 HASHING
--   Integer values for hashing and HMAC algorithms
---------------------------------------------------------
  -- Hash Algorithms
  g_md4        CONSTANT PLS_INTEGER   := dbms_crypto.hash_md4;
  g_md5        CONSTANT PLS_INTEGER   := dbms_crypto.hash_md5;
  g_sha        CONSTANT PLS_INTEGER   := dbms_crypto.hash_sh1;
  -- globally defined (default) hashing algorithm
  g_hash_algorithm     PLS_INTEGER      := g_sha;
  -- MAC Functions
  g_hmac_md5  CONSTANT PLS_INTEGER   := dbms_crypto.hmac_md5;
  g_hmac_sha  CONSTANT PLS_INTEGER   := dbms_crypto.hmac_sh1;
  -- globally defined (default) hashing algorithm
  g_hmac_algorithm     PLS_INTEGER      := g_hmac_sha;

---------------------------------------------------------
--   Functions for returning the integer value
--   of respective algorithms
---------------------------------------------------------
  FUNCTION des
    RETURN PLS_INTEGER
  AS
  BEGIN
    RETURN g_des;
  END;

---------------------------------------------------------
  FUNCTION des3
    RETURN PLS_INTEGER
  AS
  BEGIN
    RETURN g_des3;
  END;

---------------------------------------------------------
  FUNCTION des32
    RETURN PLS_INTEGER
  AS
  BEGIN
    RETURN g_des32;
```

```
  END;

-----------------------------------------------------------
  FUNCTION aes
    RETURN PLS_INTEGER
  AS
  BEGIN
    RETURN g_aes;
  END;

-----------------------------------------------------------
  FUNCTION aes192
    RETURN PLS_INTEGER
  AS
  BEGIN
    RETURN g_aes192;
  END;

-----------------------------------------------------------
  FUNCTION aes256
    RETURN PLS_INTEGER
  AS
  BEGIN
    RETURN g_aes256;
  END;

-----------------------------------------------------------
  FUNCTION rc4
    RETURN PLS_INTEGER
  AS
  BEGIN
    RETURN g_rc4;
  END;

-----------------------------------------------------------
  FUNCTION get_algorithm
    RETURN VARCHAR2
  -- returns string value for current encryption algorithm
  AS
    l_enc_algorithm  VARCHAR2 (6);
  BEGIN
    CASE
      WHEN g_enc_algorithm = g_des
      THEN
        l_enc_algorithm := 'DES';
      WHEN g_enc_algorithm = g_des32
      THEN
        l_enc_algorithm := 'DES32';
      WHEN g_enc_algorithm = g_des3
      THEN
```

```
      l_enc_algorithm := 'DES3';
    WHEN g_enc_algorithm = g_aes
    THEN
      l_enc_algorithm := 'AES';
    WHEN g_enc_algorithm = g_aes192
    THEN
      l_enc_algorithm := 'AES192';
    WHEN g_enc_algorithm = g_aes256
    THEN
      l_enc_algorithm := 'AES256';
    WHEN g_enc_algorithm = g_rc4
    THEN
      l_enc_algorithm := 'RC4';
  END CASE;

  RETURN l_enc_algorithm;
END;

---------------------------------------------------------
PROCEDURE set_algorithm (p_enc_algorithm IN PLS_INTEGER)
-- sets global encryption algorithm to p_enc_algorithm
-- check to ensure algorithm is valid
AS
  l_err_msg  VARCHAR2 (200);
BEGIN
  IF (p_enc_algorithm IN
        (g_des,
         g_des3,
         g_des32,
         g_aes,
         g_aes192,
         g_aes256,
         g_rc4))
  THEN
    g_enc_algorithm := p_enc_algorithm;
  ELSE
    l_err_msg :=
         'Unsupported encryption algorithm: '
      || 'Use one of the following DATA_CRYPTO variables: '
      || 'DES, DES3, DES32, AES, AES192, AES256, RC4';
    raise_application_error (-20001, l_err_msg);
  END IF;
END;

---------------------------------------------------------
PROCEDURE setkey (
  p_key             IN  VARCHAR2,
  p_enc_algorithm   IN  PLS_INTEGER DEFAULT NULL)
```

```
  -- sets global encryption key to p_key. Key is sized
  -- according to p_enc_algorithm or global algorithm
  AS
  BEGIN
    -- check pad key and store
    g_key := getkey (p_key, p_enc_algorithm);
  END;

--------------------------------------------------------
  FUNCTION get_key_size (p_enc_algorithm IN PLS_INTEGER)
    RETURN PLS_INTEGER
  -- return key size in bytes based on algorithm used
  AS
    l_blocks  PLS_INTEGER := 2;
  BEGIN
    -- need case statement
    CASE
      WHEN NVL (p_enc_algorithm, g_enc_algorithm) = g_des
      THEN
        l_blocks := 1;
      WHEN NVL (p_enc_algorithm, g_enc_algorithm) = g_des32
      THEN
        l_blocks := 3;
      WHEN NVL (p_enc_algorithm, g_enc_algorithm) = g_des3
      THEN
        l_blocks := 3;
      WHEN NVL (p_enc_algorithm, g_enc_algorithm) = g_aes
      THEN
        l_blocks := 2;
      WHEN NVL (p_enc_algorithm, g_enc_algorithm) = g_aes192
      THEN
        l_blocks := 3;
      WHEN NVL (p_enc_algorithm, g_enc_algorithm) = g_aes256
      THEN
        l_blocks := 4;
    -- RC4 does not require key padding
    END CASE;

    RETURN l_blocks * 8;
  END;

--------------------------------------------------------
  FUNCTION padkey (p_key IN VARCHAR2)
    RETURN VARCHAR2
  -- Pads p_key out 8-bytes. Used to increase Key size
  -- Padding to the right to preserve any uniqueness
  -- presented with the key
  AS
  BEGIN
    RETURN RPAD (p_key,
```

```
                  (TRUNC (LENGTHB (p_key) / 8) + 1) * 8,
                  CHR (0));
  END;

------------------------------------------------------------
  FUNCTION getkey (
    p_key             IN  VARCHAR2 DEFAULT NULL,
    p_enc_algorithm   IN  PLS_INTEGER DEFAULT NULL)
    RETURN RAW
  -- return raw key of size congruent with algorithm
  -- only work on key if p_key is not null
  AS
    -- Key size changes based on algorithm
    -- Need to compute key size based on the algorithm being used
    -- Key size only restricted to block ciphers
    l_key_size        PLS_INTEGER;
    l_key             VARCHAR2 (32767) := NVL (p_key, g_key);
    -- algorithm is passed. Actual determination done in getKeySize.
    l_enc_algorithm   PLS_INTEGER;
  BEGIN
    -- if using RC4, no padding is required
    IF (NVL (p_enc_algorithm, g_enc_algorithm) = rc4)
    THEN
      RETURN NVL (UTL_RAW.cast_to_raw (p_key), g_key);
    END IF;

    -- need to contract or expand key based on algorithm
    l_key_size := get_key_size (p_enc_algorithm);
    -- key may be too long. Truncate using first bytes
    l_key := SUBSTR (l_key, 1, l_key_size);

    -- if key is too short, we have to pad
    WHILE LENGTH (l_key) < l_key_size
    LOOP
      l_key := padkey (l_key);
    END LOOP;

    -- last loop iteration may have made key too large
    -- need to ensure key size is not too large.
    -- also convert result to RAW
    RETURN UTL_RAW.cast_to_raw (SUBSTR (l_key, 1,
                                        l_key_size));
  END;

------------------------------------------------------------
  FUNCTION encrypt_char (
    p_data            IN  VARCHAR2,
    p_key             IN  VARCHAR2 DEFAULT NULL,
    p_enc_algorithm   IN  PLS_INTEGER DEFAULT NULL)
    RETURN RAW
```

```
-- takes data and key in varchar2 and returns varchar2 encrytped data
-- Key and algorithm are passed, or default global value is used.
AS
  -- convert data to RAW for crytpo algorithm
  l_input       RAW (32767)
                 := UTL_RAW.cast_to_raw (p_data);
  l_algorithm  PLS_INTEGER
      := NVL (p_enc_algorithm, g_enc_algorithm);
BEGIN
  RETURN dbms_crypto.encrypt
                   (src     => l_input,
                    typ     => l_algorithm,
                    KEY     => getkey
                                  (p_key,
                                   l_algorithm));
END;

----------------------------------------------------------
  FUNCTION decrypt_char (
    p_data           IN  RAW,
    p_key            IN  VARCHAR2 DEFAULT NULL,
    p_enc_algorithm  IN  PLS_INTEGER DEFAULT NULL)
    RETURN VARCHAR2
  -- takes encrypted varchar2 data and plaintext varchar2 key
  -- and returns decrypted varchar2 data.
  -- Key and algorithm are passed, or default global value is used.
  AS
    -- convert data to RAW for crytpo algorithm
    l_algorithm  PLS_INTEGER
        := NVL (p_enc_algorithm, g_enc_algorithm);
  BEGIN
    RETURN UTL_RAW.cast_to_varchar2
          (dbms_crypto.decrypt
                     (src     => p_data,
                      typ     => l_algorithm,
                      KEY     => getkey
                                   (p_key,
                                    l_algorithm)));
  END;

----------------------------------------------------------
  FUNCTION encrypt (
    p_data           IN  VARCHAR2,
    p_key            IN  VARCHAR2 DEFAULT NULL,
    p_enc_algorithm  IN  PLS_INTEGER DEFAULT NULL)
    RETURN VARCHAR2
  -- Takes plaintext data and returns encrypted data as varchar2
  -- Key and algorithm are passed, or default global value is used.
  AS
  BEGIN
```

```
    RETURN UTL_RAW.cast_to_varchar2
                    (encrypt_char (p_data,
                                   p_key,
                                   p_enc_algorithm));
  END;

------------------------------------------------------------
  FUNCTION decrypt (
    p_data           IN  VARCHAR2,
    p_key            IN  VARCHAR2 DEFAULT NULL,
    p_enc_algorithm  IN  PLS_INTEGER DEFAULT NULL)
    RETURN VARCHAR2
  -- takes encrypted varchar2 data
  -- and returns decrypted varchar2 data.
  -- Key and algorithm are passed, or default global value is used.
  AS
  -- convert data to RAW for crytpo algorithm
  BEGIN
    RETURN (decrypt_char
                    (UTL_RAW.cast_to_raw (p_data),
                     p_key,
                     p_enc_algorithm));
  END;

------------------------------------------------------------
  FUNCTION encrypt_number (
    p_data           IN  NUMBER,
    p_key            IN  VARCHAR2 DEFAULT NULL,
    p_enc_algorithm  IN  PLS_INTEGER DEFAULT NULL)
    RETURN RAW
  -- takes data and key in number format and returns raw encrytped data
  -- Key and algorithm are passed, or default global value is used.
  AS
    -- convert data to RAW for crytpo algorithm
    l_input      RAW (32767)
             := UTL_RAW.cast_from_number (p_data);
    l_algorithm  PLS_INTEGER
         := NVL (p_enc_algorithm, g_enc_algorithm);
  BEGIN
    RETURN dbms_crypto.encrypt
                     (src    => l_input,
                      typ    => l_algorithm,
                      KEY    => getkey
                                    (p_key,
                                     l_algorithm));
  END;

------------------------------------------------------------
  FUNCTION decrypt_number (
    p_data           IN  RAW,
```

```
    p_key             IN  VARCHAR2 DEFAULT NULL,
    p_enc_algorithm   IN  PLS_INTEGER DEFAULT NULL)
    RETURN NUMBER
  -- takes encrypted raw data and plaintext varchar2 key
  -- and returns decrypted number data.
  -- Key and algorithm are passed, or default global value is used.
  AS
    -- convert data to RAW for crytpo algorithm
    l_algorithm  PLS_INTEGER
        := NVL (p_enc_algorithm, g_enc_algorithm);
  BEGIN
    RETURN UTL_RAW.cast_to_number
            (dbms_crypto.decrypt
                       (src    => p_data,
                        typ    => l_algorithm,
                        KEY    => getkey
                                     (p_key,
                                      l_algorithm)));
  END;

-----------------------------------------------------------
  FUNCTION encrypt_date (
    p_data            IN  DATE,
    p_key             IN  VARCHAR2 DEFAULT NULL,
    p_enc_algorithm   IN  PLS_INTEGER DEFAULT NULL)
    RETURN RAW
  -- takes date and key and returns raw encrytped data
  -- Key and algorithm are passed, or default global value is used.
  AS
    -- convert data to RAW for crytpo algorithm
    l_input      RAW (32767)
        := UTL_RAW.cast_to_raw (TO_CHAR (p_data));
    l_algorithm  PLS_INTEGER
        := NVL (p_enc_algorithm, g_enc_algorithm);
  BEGIN
    RETURN dbms_crypto.encrypt
                      (src    => l_input,
                       typ    => l_algorithm,
                       KEY    => getkey
                                    (p_key,
                                     l_algorithm));
  END;

-----------------------------------------------------------
  FUNCTION decrypt_date (
    p_data            IN  RAW,
    p_key             IN  VARCHAR2 DEFAULT NULL,
    p_enc_algorithm   IN  PLS_INTEGER DEFAULT NULL)
    RETURN DATE
  -- takes encrypted raw data and plaintext varchar2 key
```

```
-- and returns decrypted date.
-- Key and algorithm are passed, or default global value is used.
AS
  -- convert data to RAW for crytpo algorithm
  l_algorithm  PLS_INTEGER
      := NVL (p_enc_algorithm, g_enc_algorithm);
BEGIN
  RETURN TO_DATE
          (UTL_RAW.cast_to_varchar2
             (dbms_crypto.decrypt
                     (src    => p_data,
                      typ    => l_algorithm,
                      KEY    => getkey
                                  (p_key,
                                   l_algorithm))));
END;

---------------------------------------------------------
FUNCTION encrypt (
  p_data           IN  CLOB,
  p_key            IN  VARCHAR2 DEFAULT NULL,
  p_enc_algorithm  IN  PLS_INTEGER DEFAULT NULL)
  RETURN CLOB
-- encrypts a CLOB and return value as CLOB
-- done as function for performing SQL updates
AS
  l_encrypted_blob  BLOB;
  l_encrypted_clob  CLOB;
  l_lang            NUMBER := DBMS_LOB.default_lang_ctx;
  l_warning         NUMBER;
  l_t_offset        NUMBER := 1;
  l_src_offset      NUMBER := 1;
BEGIN
  DBMS_LOB.createtemporary (l_encrypted_blob, TRUE);
  DBMS_LOB.createtemporary (l_encrypted_clob, TRUE);
  dbms_crypto.encrypt (dst    => l_encrypted_blob,
                       src    => p_data,
                       typ    => NVL (p_enc_algorithm,
                                      g_enc_algorithm),
                       KEY    => getkey (p_key,
                                         p_enc_algorithm));
  DBMS_LOB.converttoclob (l_encrypted_clob,
                          l_encrypted_blob,
                          DBMS_LOB.lobmaxsize,
                          l_t_offset,
                          l_src_offset,
                          DBMS_LOB.default_csid,
                          l_lang,
                          l_warning);
```

```
    RETURN l_encrypted_clob;
  END;

---------------------------------------------------------
  FUNCTION decrypt (
    p_data           IN  CLOB,
    p_key            IN  VARCHAR2 DEFAULT NULL,
    p_enc_algorithm  IN  PLS_INTEGER DEFAULT NULL)
    RETURN CLOB
  -- decrypts a CLOB and return value as CLOB
  -- done as function for performing SQL updates
  AS
    l_encrypted_blob  BLOB;
    l_decrypted_blob  BLOB;
    l_decrypted_clob  CLOB;
    l_lang            NUMBER := DBMS_LOB.default_lang_ctx;
    l_warning         NUMBER;
    l_t_offset        NUMBER := 1;
    l_src_offset      NUMBER := 1;
  BEGIN
    DBMS_LOB.createtemporary (l_encrypted_blob, TRUE);
    DBMS_LOB.createtemporary (l_decrypted_blob, TRUE);
    DBMS_LOB.createtemporary (l_decrypted_clob, TRUE);
    DBMS_LOB.converttoblob (l_encrypted_blob,
                            p_data,
                            DBMS_LOB.lobmaxsize,
                            l_t_offset,
                            l_src_offset,
                            DBMS_LOB.default_csid,
                            l_lang,
                            l_warning);
    dbms_crypto.decrypt (dst    => l_decrypted_blob,
                         src    => l_encrypted_blob,
                         typ    => NVL (p_enc_algorithm,
                                        g_enc_algorithm),
                         KEY    => getkey (p_key,
                                           p_enc_algorithm));
    l_t_offset := 1;
    l_src_offset := 1;
    DBMS_LOB.converttoclob (l_decrypted_clob,
                            l_decrypted_blob,
                            DBMS_LOB.lobmaxsize,
                            l_t_offset,
                            l_src_offset,
                            DBMS_LOB.default_csid,
                            l_lang,
                            l_warning);
    RETURN l_decrypted_clob;
  END;
```

```
---------------------------------------------------------
  FUNCTION encrypt (
    p_data           IN  BLOB,
    p_key            IN  VARCHAR2 DEFAULT NULL,
    p_enc_algorithm  IN  PLS_INTEGER DEFAULT NULL)
    RETURN BLOB
  -- encrypts a BLOB and return value as BLOB
  -- done as function for performing SQL updates
  AS
    l_encrypted_blob  BLOB;
  BEGIN
    DBMS_LOB.createtemporary (l_encrypted_blob, TRUE);
    dbms_crypto.encrypt (dst    => l_encrypted_blob,
                         src    => p_data,
                         typ    => NVL (p_enc_algorithm,
                                        g_enc_algorithm),
                         KEY    => getkey (p_key,
                                           p_enc_algorithm));
    RETURN l_encrypted_blob;
  END;

---------------------------------------------------------
  FUNCTION decrypt (
    p_data           IN  BLOB,
    p_key            IN  VARCHAR2 DEFAULT NULL,
    p_enc_algorithm  IN  PLS_INTEGER DEFAULT NULL)
    RETURN BLOB
  -- decrypts a BLOB and return value as BLOB
  -- done as function for performing SQL updates
  AS
    l_decrypted_blob  BLOB;
  BEGIN
    DBMS_LOB.createtemporary (l_decrypted_blob, TRUE);
    dbms_crypto.decrypt (dst    => l_decrypted_blob,
                         src    => p_data,
                         typ    => NVL (p_enc_algorithm,
                                        g_enc_algorithm),
                         KEY    => getkey (p_key,
                                           p_enc_algorithm));
    RETURN l_decrypted_blob;
  END;

---------------------------------------------------------
--                      HASHING                        --
---------------------------------------------------------

  -- Following functions return integer value of associated
  -- hashing algorithm
---------------------------------------------------------
  FUNCTION md4
```

```
    RETURN PLS_INTEGER
  AS
  BEGIN
    RETURN g_md4;
  END;

-----------------------------------------------------------
  FUNCTION md5
    RETURN PLS_INTEGER
  AS
  BEGIN
    RETURN g_md5;
  END;

-----------------------------------------------------------
  FUNCTION sha
    RETURN PLS_INTEGER
  AS
  BEGIN
    RETURN g_sha;
  END;

-----------------------------------------------------------
  FUNCTION get_hash_algorithm
    RETURN VARCHAR2
  -- return string representation of current hash algorithm
  AS
    l_hash_algorithm  VARCHAR2 (3);
  BEGIN
    CASE
      WHEN g_hash_algorithm = g_md4
      THEN
        l_hash_algorithm := 'MD4';
      WHEN g_hash_algorithm = g_md5
      THEN
        l_hash_algorithm := 'MD5';
      WHEN g_hash_algorithm = g_sha
      THEN
        l_hash_algorithm := 'SHA';
    END CASE;

    RETURN l_hash_algorithm;
  END;

-----------------------------------------------------------
  PROCEDURE set_hash_algorithm (
    p_hash_algorithm  IN  PLS_INTEGER)
  -- sets global hashing algorithm to p_hash_algorithm
  AS
    l_err_msg  VARCHAR2 (50);
```

```
  BEGIN
    -- check to ensure algorithm is valid
    IF (p_hash_algorithm IN (g_md4, g_md5, g_sha))
    THEN
      g_hash_algorithm := p_hash_algorithm;
    ELSE
      l_err_msg :=
           'Unsupported Hash algorithm: '
        || 'Use one of the following DATA_CRYPTO variables: '
        || 'MD4, MD5, SHA';
      raise_application_error (-20002, l_err_msg);
    END IF;
  END;

-----------------------------------------------------------
  FUNCTION hash2raw (
    p_data            IN  VARCHAR2,
    p_hash_algorithm  IN  PLS_INTEGER DEFAULT NULL)
    RETURN RAW
  -- Computes hash and return value as RAW
  -- Uses p_hash_algorithm if passed, else
  -- uses the global variable
  AS
    l_input  RAW (32767) := UTL_RAW.cast_to_raw (p_data);
  BEGIN
    RETURN dbms_crypto.HASH (src    => l_input,
                             typ    => NVL
                                         (p_hash_algorithm,
                                          g_hash_algorithm));
  END;

-----------------------------------------------------------
  FUNCTION HASH (
    p_data            IN  VARCHAR2,
    p_hash_algorithm  IN  PLS_INTEGER DEFAULT NULL)
    RETURN VARCHAR2
  -- Computes hash and return value as VARCHAR2
  -- Delegates call to hash2raw function
  AS
  BEGIN
    RETURN UTL_RAW.cast_to_varchar2
                               (hash2raw (p_data,
                                          p_hash_algorithm));
  END;

-----------------------------------------------------------
--            Hashed Message Authentication Codes        --
-----------------------------------------------------------

  -- Following functions return integer value of associated
```

```
  -- hmac algorithms
---------------------------------------------------------
  FUNCTION hmac_sha
    RETURN PLS_INTEGER
  AS
  BEGIN
    RETURN g_hmac_sha;
  END;

---------------------------------------------------------
  FUNCTION hmac_md5
    RETURN PLS_INTEGER
  AS
  BEGIN
    RETURN g_hmac_md5;
  END;

---------------------------------------------------------
  FUNCTION get_hmac_algorithm
    RETURN VARCHAR2
  -- return string representation of current HMAC algorithm
  AS
    l_hash_algorithm  VARCHAR2 (3);
  BEGIN
    CASE
      WHEN g_hash_algorithm = g_hmac_md5
      THEN
        l_hash_algorithm := 'HMAC_MD5';
      WHEN g_hash_algorithm = g_hmac_sha
      THEN
        l_hash_algorithm := 'HMAC_SHA';
    END CASE;

    RETURN l_hash_algorithm;
  END;

---------------------------------------------------------
  PROCEDURE set_hmac_algorithm (
    p_hash_algorithm  IN  PLS_INTEGER)
  -- sets global hashing algorithm to p_hash_algorithm
  AS
    l_err_msg  VARCHAR2 (50);
  BEGIN
    -- check to ensure algorithm is valid
    IF (p_hash_algorithm IN (g_hmac_md5, g_hmac_sha))
    THEN
      g_hmac_algorithm := p_hash_algorithm;
    ELSE
      l_err_msg :=
           'Unsupported HMAC algorithm: '
        || 'Use one of the following DATA_CRYPTO variables: '
```

```
        || 'HMAC_MD5, HMAC_SHA';
      raise_application_error (-20002, l_err_msg);
    END IF;
  END;

---------------------------------------------------------
  FUNCTION mac2raw (
    p_data            IN  VARCHAR2,
    p_key             IN  VARCHAR2 DEFAULT NULL,
    p_hash_algorithm  IN  PLS_INTEGER DEFAULT NULL)
    RETURN RAW
  -- Computes hash message authentication code.
  -- Returns value as RAW
  -- Uses p_hash_algorithm if passed, else
  -- uses the global hmac variable
  AS
    l_input      RAW (32767)
                         := UTL_RAW.cast_to_raw (p_data);
    l_algorithm  PLS_INTEGER
               := NVL (p_hash_algorithm, g_hmac_algorithm);
  BEGIN
    IF (l_algorithm NOT IN (g_hmac_sha, g_hmac_md5))
    THEN
      raise_application_error
                          (-20003,
                           'Unsupported HMAC algorithm.');
    END IF;

    RETURN dbms_crypto.mac (src    => l_input,
                          typ    => l_algorithm,
                          KEY    => getkey (p_key));
  END;

---------------------------------------------------------
  FUNCTION mac (
    p_data            IN  VARCHAR2,
    p_key             IN  VARCHAR2 DEFAULT NULL,
    p_hash_algorithm  IN  PLS_INTEGER DEFAULT NULL)
    RETURN VARCHAR2
  -- Computes MAC and returns value as VARCHAR2
  -- Delegates call to mac2raw function
  AS
  BEGIN
    RETURN UTL_RAW.cast_to_varchar2
                               (mac2raw (p_data,
                                         p_key,
                                         p_hash_algorithm));
  END;
---------------------------------------------------------
END;
/
```

APPENDIX C

DBMS_CRYPTO Performance Test Results

Tests performed on WinXP running on Dell laptop with a Pentium M processor 1600MHz and 1GB of RAM. The tests were done to show relative performance times and the database and operating system were not optimized for the tests. The following represents timings for 20 bytes of data encrypted 1,000,000 times with various algorithms, block modifiers, and padding schemes. The SQL to generate the timings is displayed at first to allow you to understand how the numbers were calculated. The output of the SQL script files is then turned off to abbreviate this listing.

Clock times and CPU times are bolded.

```
sec_mgr@KNOX10g> SET linesize 70
sec_mgr@KNOX10g> SET pagesize 9999
sec_mgr@KNOX10g> SET feedback off
sec_mgr@KNOX10g> SET verify off
sec_mgr@KNOX10g> SET timing off
sec_mgr@KNOX10g> SET sqlprompt 'sql> '
sql> COL "CPU Start Value" new_val cpu_start
sql> COL name format a25
sql>
sql> -- Define a variable to hold size of for loop
sql> VAR loop_size number;
sql> -- Set loop size to one million
sql> BEGIN
       :loop_size := 1000000;
     END;
     /
sql> /*****  PL/SQL function in loop  *******/
sql> @pl_loop.sql
sql> --- Create sample PL/SQL function
sql> CREATE OR REPLACE FUNCTION do_nothing
       RETURN RAW
     AS
     BEGIN
       RETURN NULL;
     END;
     /
sql>
sql> -- Test time to loop calling a PL/SQL function
sql> @cpu_start
sql> SELECT b.VALUE "CPU Start Value"
       FROM v$statname a, v$mystat b
      WHERE a.statistic# = b.statistic#
      AND a.NAME = 'CPU used by this session';

CPU Start Value
---------------
              5
sql> DECLARE
       l_data  RAW (40);
       l_start_time  NUMBER;
       l_end_time    NUMBER;
     BEGIN
```

```
    l_start_time := DBMS_UTILITY.get_time;
    FOR i IN 1 .. :loop_size
    LOOP
     l_data := do_nothing;
    END LOOP;
    l_end_time := DBMS_UTILITY.get_time;
    DBMS_OUTPUT.put_line (      'PL/SQL Loop Time: '
                          || (l_end_time - l_start_time) / 100
                          || ' seconds');
  END;
  /
PL/SQL Loop Time: 1.53 seconds
sql> @cpu_stop
sql> SELECT b.VALUE "CPU End Value",
           (b.VALUE - &cpu_start) / 100
                          "hsecs of CPU Units used"
    FROM v$statname a, v$mystat b
   WHERE a.statistic# = b.statistic#
   AND a.NAME = 'CPU used by this session';

CPU End Value hsecs of CPU Units used
------------- -----------------------
          146                    1.41
sql> /****************  eor  ****************/
sql>
sql> /***********  AES encryption  **********/
sql> @aes
sql> @cpu_start
sql> SELECT b.VALUE "CPU Start Value"
    FROM v$statname a, v$mystat b
   WHERE a.statistic# = b.statistic#
   AND a.NAME = 'CPU used by this session';

CPU Start Value
---------------
            147
sql> DECLARE
    l_algo    PLS_INTEGER
     :=   dbms_crypto.encrypt_aes
        + dbms_crypto.chain_cbc
        + dbms_crypto.pad_pkcs5;
    l_key     RAW (16)
        := UTL_RAW.cast_to_raw ('0123456789012345');
    l_data    RAW (20)
     := UTL_RAW.cast_to_raw ('01234567890123456789');
    l_enc_data  RAW (40);
    l_start_time  NUMBER;
    l_end_time    NUMBER;
  BEGIN
    l_start_time := DBMS_UTILITY.get_time;
    FOR i IN 1 .. :loop_size
```

```
     LOOP
     l_enc_data :=
        dbms_crypto.encrypt (l_data, l_algo, l_key);
     END LOOP;
     l_end_time := DBMS_UTILITY.get_time;
     DBMS_OUTPUT.put_line (       'AES Encryption Time: '
                          || (l_end_time - l_start_time) / 100
                          || ' seconds');
   END;
   /
AES Encryption Time: 17.82 seconds
sql> @cpu_stop
sql> SELECT b.VALUE "CPU End Value",
           (b.VALUE - &cpu_start) / 100
                        "hsecs of CPU Units used"
      FROM v$statname a, v$mystat b
     WHERE a.statistic# = b.statistic#
     AND a.NAME = 'CPU used by this session';

CPU End Value hsecs of CPU Units used
------------- -----------------------
         1790                   16.43
sql> /****************  eor  ****************/
sql>
sql> /*******  AES decryption process  ******/
sql> @aes_d
sql> @cpu_start
sql> SELECT b.VALUE "CPU Start Value"
      FROM v$statname a, v$mystat b
     WHERE a.statistic# = b.statistic#
     AND a.NAME = 'CPU used by this session';

CPU Start Value
---------------
           1790
sql> DECLARE
     l_algo    PLS_INTEGER
     :=   dbms_crypto.encrypt_aes
        + dbms_crypto.chain_cbc
        + dbms_crypto.pad_pkcs5;
     l_key          RAW (16)
                 := UTL_RAW.cast_to_raw ('0123456789012345');
     l_data         RAW (20)
             := UTL_RAW.cast_to_raw ('01234567890123456789');
     l_enc_data  RAW (40);
     l_dec_data  RAW (40);
     l_start_time  NUMBER;
     l_end_time    NUMBER;
   BEGIN
     -- Encrypt data
```

```
      SELECT dbms_crypto.encrypt (l_data, l_algo, l_key)
        INTO l_enc_data
        FROM DUAL;
     l_start_time := DBMS_UTILITY.get_time;
     FOR i IN 1 .. :loop_size
     LOOP
     l_dec_data := dbms_crypto.decrypt (l_enc_data, l_algo, l_key);
     END LOOP;
     l_end_time := DBMS_UTILITY.get_time;
     DBMS_OUTPUT.put_line (      'AES Decryption Time: '
                          || (l_end_time - l_start_time) / 100
                          || ' seconds');
   END;
   /
AES Decryption Time: 18.68 seconds
sql> @cpu_stop
sql> SELECT b.VALUE "CPU End Value",
          (b.VALUE - &cpu_start) / 100
                           "hsecs of CPU Units used"
     FROM v$statname a, v$mystat b
    WHERE a.statistic# = b.statistic#
     AND a.NAME = 'CPU used by this session';

CPU End Value hsecs of CPU Units used
------------- -----------------------
         3503                   17.13
sql>
sql> /****************  eor  ****************/
sql>
sql> ---- Change algorithm being executed ----
sql> SET echo off
sql> /****************  DES  ****************/
sql> @des

CPU Start Value
---------------
           3504
DES Encryption Time: 18.4 seconds

CPU End Value hsecs of CPU Units used
------------- -----------------------
         5200                   16.96
sql> /****************  eor  ****************/
sql>
sql> /*********  Triple DES, 2 key  *********/
sql> @des32

CPU Start Value
---------------
           5200
```

```
Triple DES, 2 Key Encryption Time: 21.72 seconds

CPU End Value hsecs of CPU Units used
------------- ----------------------
         7186                  19.86
sql> /****************  eor  ****************/
sql>
sql> /*********  Triple DES, 3 key  *********/
sql> @des3

CPU Start Value
---------------
           7186
Triple DES, 3 keys Encryption Time: 22.3 seconds

CPU End Value hsecs of CPU Units used
------------- ----------------------
         9237                  20.51
sql> /****************  eor  ****************/
sql>
sql> /*******  AES with 192-bit key  ********/
sql> @aes192

CPU Start Value
---------------
           9238
AES 192-bit key Encryption Time: 18.06 seconds

CPU End Value hsecs of CPU Units used
------------- ----------------------
        10902                  16.64
sql> /****************  eor  ****************/
sql>
sql> /*******  AES with 256-bit key  ********/
sql> @aes256

CPU Start Value
---------------
          10903
AES 256-bit key Encryption Time: 18.9 seconds

CPU End Value hsecs of CPU Units used
------------- ----------------------
        12624                  17.21
sql> /****************  eor  ****************/
sql>
sql> /****************  RC4  ****************/
sql> ---- RC4 ----
sql> @rc4_p

CPU Start Value
```

```
---------------
         12624
RC4 Encryption Time: 22.89 seconds

CPU End Value hsecs of CPU Units used
------------- -----------------------
        14733                   21.09
sql> /****************  eor  ***************/
sql>
sql> ---- Block Chaining Modifiers -----------
sql> SET echo on
sql> /*******  AES with CFB modifier  *******/
sql> @aes_cfb
sql> @cpu_start
sql> SELECT b.VALUE "CPU Start Value"
       FROM v$statname a, v$mystat b
      WHERE a.statistic# = b.statistic#
      AND a.NAME = 'CPU used by this session';

CPU Start Value
---------------
         14733
sql> DECLARE
       l_algo      PLS_INTEGER
       :=   dbms_crypto.encrypt_aes
          + dbms_crypto.chain_cfb
          + dbms_crypto.pad_none;
       l_key           RAW (16)
                 := UTL_RAW.cast_to_raw ('0123456789012345');
       l_data          RAW (20)
             := UTL_RAW.cast_to_raw ('01234567890123456789');
       l_enc_data      RAW (40);
       l_start_time    NUMBER;
       l_end_time      NUMBER;
     BEGIN
       l_start_time := DBMS_UTILITY.get_time;

       FOR i IN 1 .. :loop_size
       LOOP
       l_enc_data :=
          dbms_crypto.encrypt (l_data, l_algo, l_key);
       END LOOP;

       l_end_time := DBMS_UTILITY.get_time;
       DBMS_OUTPUT.put_line ('AES with CFB modifier Encryption Time: '
                        || (l_end_time - l_start_time) / 100
                        || ' seconds');
     END;
     /
AES with CFB modifier Encryption Time: 17.54 seconds
```

```
sql> @cpu_stop
sql> SELECT b.VALUE "CPU End Value",
  2        (b.VALUE - &cpu_start) / 100
  3                          "hsecs of CPU Units used"
  4    FROM v$statname a, v$mystat b
  5   WHERE a.statistic# = b.statistic#
  6   AND a.NAME = 'CPU used by this session';

CPU End Value hsecs of CPU Units used
------------- -----------------------
        16342                   16.09
sql> /****************  eor  ****************/
sql> SET echo off
sql> /*******  AES with ECB modifier  *******/
sql> @aes_ecb

CPU Start Value
---------------
          16342
AES with ECB modifier Encryption Time: 17.25 seconds

CPU End Value hsecs of CPU Units used
------------- -----------------------
        17933                   15.91
sql> /****************  eor  ****************/
sql>
sql> /*******  AES with OFB modifier  *******/
sql> @aes_ofb.sql

CPU Start Value
---------------
          17933
AES with OFB modifier Encryption Time: 17.62 seconds

CPU End Value hsecs of CPU Units used
------------- -----------------------
        19544                   16.11
sql> /****************  eor  ****************/
sql>
sql> ---------------- Padding ----------------
sql> SET echo on
sql> /*****  padding with BINARY ZEROS ******/
sql> ---- padding with binary zeros ----
sql> @pad0.sql
sql> @cpu_start
sql> SELECT b.VALUE "CPU Start Value"
  2    FROM v$statname a, v$mystat b
  3   WHERE a.statistic# = b.statistic#
  4   AND a.NAME = 'CPU used by this session';

CPU Start Value
```

```
---------------
         19545
sql> DECLARE
    l_algo       PLS_INTEGER
    :=   dbms_crypto.encrypt_aes
       + dbms_crypto.chain_cbc
       + dbms_crypto.pad_zero;
    l_key            RAW (16)
                := UTL_RAW.cast_to_raw ('0123456789012345');
    l_data           RAW (20)
            := UTL_RAW.cast_to_raw ('01234567890123456789');
    l_enc_data    RAW (40);
    l_start_time  NUMBER;
    l_end_time    NUMBER;
  BEGIN
    l_start_time := DBMS_UTILITY.get_time;

    FOR i IN 1 .. :loop_size
    LOOP
    l_enc_data :=
      dbms_crypto.encrypt (l_data, l_algo, l_key);
    END LOOP;

    l_end_time := DBMS_UTILITY.get_time;
    DBMS_OUTPUT.put_line ('AES Encrypt: Pad Zeros');
    DBMS_OUTPUT.put_line ('Time: '
                      || (l_end_time - l_start_time) / 100
                      || ' seconds');
  END;
  /
AES Encrypt: Pad Zeros
Time: 17.68 seconds
sql> @cpu_stop
sql> SELECT b.VALUE "CPU End Value",
         (b.VALUE - &cpu_start) / 100
                       "hsecs of CPU Units used"
    FROM v$statname a, v$mystat b
   WHERE a.statistic# = b.statistic#
   AND a.NAME = 'CPU used by this session';

CPU End Value hsecs of CPU Units used
------------- -----------------------
        21174                   16.29
sql> /****************  eor  ***************/
sql> SET echo off
sql> /*****  padding with ORACLE PAD ********/
sql> ---- padding with oracle       ----
sql> @padorcl.sql

CPU Start Value
```

```
---------------
          21174
AES Encrypt: Pad ORCL
Time: 17.89 seconds

CPU End Value hsecs of CPU Units used
------------- -----------------------
        22818                  16.44
sql> /****************  eor  ****************/
sql>
sql> /************  NO PADDING **************/
sql> @padnone.sql

CPU Start Value
---------------
          22819
AES Encrypt: Pad None
Time: 16.83 seconds

CPU End Value hsecs of CPU Units used
------------- -----------------------
        24371                  15.52
sql> /****************  eor  ****************/
```

Index

B

C

D

E

H

I

L

M

N

O

P

R

S

T

U

W

X

Z

INTERNATIONAL CONTACT INFORMATION

AUSTRALIA
McGraw-Hill Book Company
Australia Pty. Ltd.
TEL +61-2-9900-1800
FAX +61-2-9878-8881
http://www.mcgraw-hill.com.au
books-it_sydney@mcgraw-hill.com

CANADA
McGraw-Hill Ryerson Ltd.
TEL +905-430-5000
FAX +905-430-5020
http://www.mcgraw-hill.ca

GREECE, MIDDLE EAST, & AFRICA (Excluding South Africa)
McGraw-Hill Hellas
TEL +30-210-6560-990
TEL +30-210-6560-993
TEL +30-210-6560-994
FAX +30-210-6545-525

MEXICO (Also serving Latin America)
McGraw-Hill Interamericana Editores
S.A. de C.V.
TEL +525-1500-5108
FAX +525-117-1589
http://www.mcgraw-hill.com.mx
carlos_ruiz@mcgraw-hill.com

SINGAPORE (Serving Asia)
McGraw-Hill Book Company
TEL +65-6863-1580
FAX +65-6862-3354
http://www.mcgraw-hill.com.sg
mghasia@mcgraw-hill.com

SOUTH AFRICA
McGraw-Hill South Africa
TEL +27-11-622-7512
FAX +27-11-622-9045
robyn_swanepoel@mcgraw-hill.com

SPAIN
McGraw-Hill/
Interamericana de España, S.A.U.
TEL +34-91-180-3000
FAX +34-91-372-8513
http://www.mcgraw-hill.es
professional@mcgraw-hill.es

UNITED KINGDOM, NORTHERN, EASTERN, & CENTRAL EUROPE
McGraw-Hill Education Europe
TEL +44-1-628-502500
FAX +44-1-628-770224
http://www.mcgraw-hill.co.uk
emea_queries@mcgraw-hill.com

ALL OTHER INQUIRIES Contact:
McGraw-Hill/Osborne
TEL +1-510-420-7700
FAX +1-510-420-7703
http://www.osborne.com
omg_international@mcgraw-hill.com

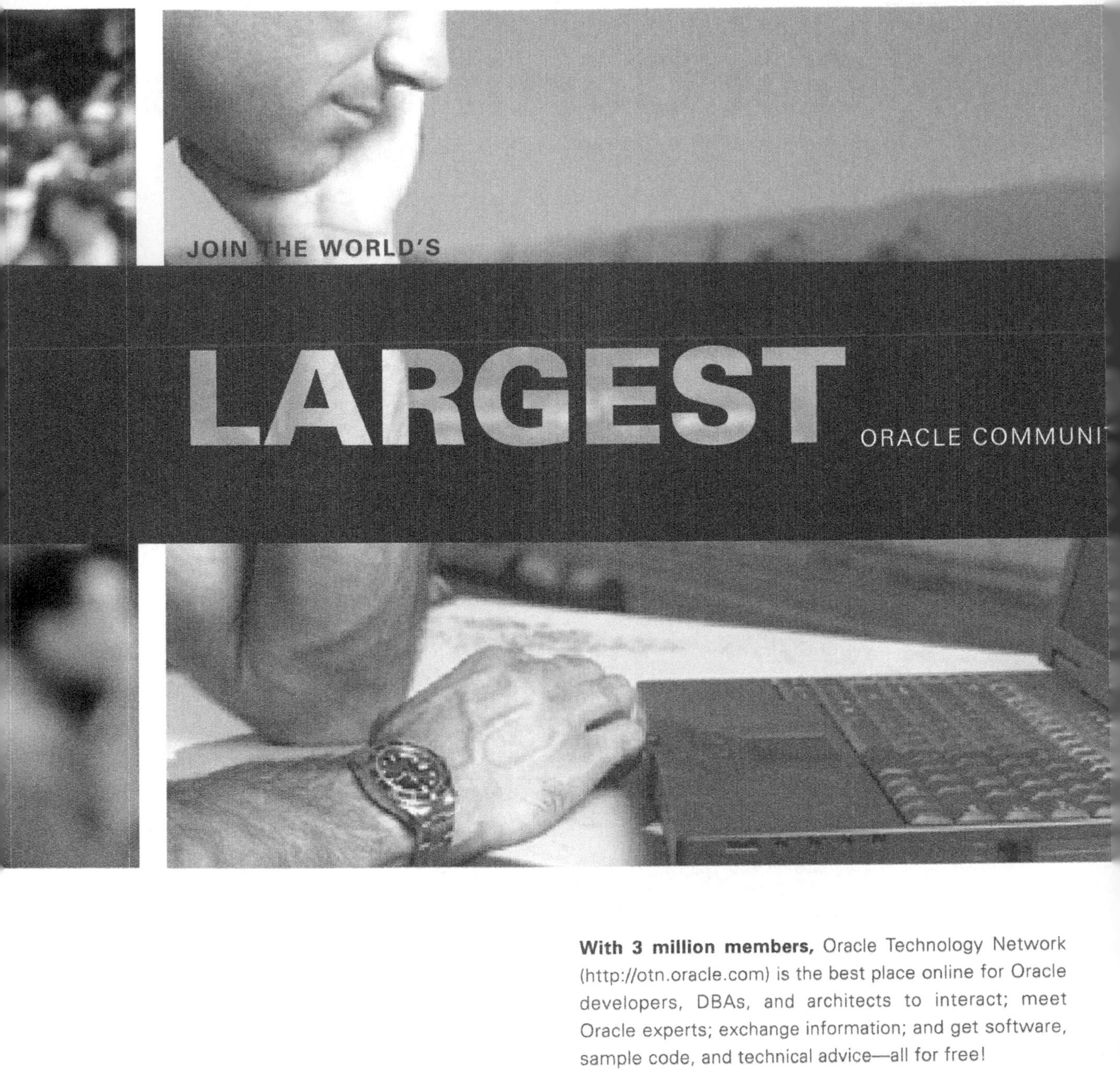
JOIN THE WORLD'S
LARGEST
ORACLE COMMUNI

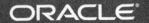

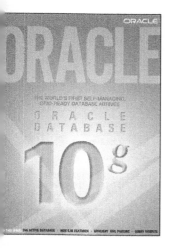